P9-CZV-878

Encyclopedia of Holocaust Literature

Edited by
David Patterson, Alan L. Berger,
and Sarita Cargas

Oryx Holocaust Series

Oryx Press
Westport, Connecticut • London

*The rare Arabian Oryx is believed to have inspired the myth of the unicorn. This desert
antelope became virtually extinct in the early 1960s. At that time, several groups of
international conservationists arranged to have nine animals sent to the Phoenix Zoo
to be the nucleus of a captive breeding herd. Today, the Oryx population
is over 1,000, and over 500 have been returned to the Middle East.*

Library of Congress Cataloging-in-Publication Data

Encyclopedia of Holocaust literature / edited by David Patterson, Alan L. Berger and Sarita Cargas.
  p. cm.—(Oryx Holocaust series)
  Includes bibliographical references and index.
  ISBN 1–57356–257–2 (alk. paper)
  1. Holocaust, Jewish (1939–1945), in literature—Encyclopedias. 2. Holocaust, Jewish
(1939–1945)—Personal narratives—Encyclopedias. 3. Holocaust, Jewish
(1939–1945)—Biography. I. Patterson, David. II. Berger, Alan L., 1939– III. Cargas,
Sarita. IV. Series.

PN56.H55 E53 2002
809'.93358—dc21   2001036639

British Library Cataloguing in Publication Data is available.

Library of Congress Catalog Card Number: 2001036639
ISBN: 1–57356–257–2

First published in 2002

Oryx Press, 88 Post Road West, Westport, CT 06881
An imprint of Greenwood Publishing Group, Inc.
www.oryxpress.com

Printed in the United States of America

The paper used in this book complies with the Permanent
Paper Standard issued by the National Information
Standards Organization (Z39.48–1984).

10 9 8 7 6 5 4 3 2 1

Dedicated, with deepest gratitude, to the memory of one of the world's most revered scholars of Holocaust literature, Harry James Cargas, whose inspiration led to the creation of this volume.

Contents

Preface

Organization and Aim of the *Encyclopedia of Holocaust Literature*

The thread running through the distinctive characteristics of the genres of Holocaust literature (which are outlined in the Introduction to this volume) is a motif of personal testimony to the dearness of humanity. Invariably underlying the novels, diaries, and dramas is an individual's struggle to return to life, meaning, and identity. Because the lives of the authors in this volume are so central to Holocaust literature, the encyclopedia is organized by authors. The entries are not organized according to topics; rather, they are organized according to lives lived in a testimony to life.

The body of primary and secondary texts in Holocaust literature is vast and steadily growing. While this encyclopedia is generally intended for an English-speaking audience, Holocaust literature is written in all the languages of European Jewry, and many outstanding works have yet to be translated into English. To simplify the selection of authors for inclusion in the limited space available here, second-generation authors are excluded. A second-generation literature is emerging in its own right—a literature with its own defining features which are fundamentally different from those in this encyclopedia of Holocaust literature. All the authors selected for this volume survived the Holocaust, perished in the Holocaust, or were otherwise closely connected to the Holocaust; nearly all of them—some notable exceptions are Tadeusz Borowski and Charlotte Delbo—are Jewish. Authors who have merely incorporated the Holocaust theme into a work—such as William Styron, Thomas Keneally, and Sylvia Plath—and who have no other direct link to the Holocaust are not included. Furthermore, all 128 authors included in this volume have had their works examined in one or more critical editions dealing with Holocaust literature. Finally, an asterisk following a name denotes a cross-reference. (A list of book-length studies of Holocaust literature can be found in the Bibliography of Critical Studies of Holocaust Literature at the end of this volume.)

Using these guidelines, we consulted several Holocaust scholars for their advice on entries for the encyclopedia. Even with such guidelines, however, the selection of authors for inclusion in an encyclopedia of Holocaust literature poses a number of difficulties. While the aim of the encyclopedia is to include works on the basis of their excellence and influence, arguments concerning which are the best or most influential are unavoidable. One may ask, for example, why Abel Jacob Herzberg and not Stanislaw Adler? Or why Kitty Hart and not Eugene Kogon? Once all the factors have been weighed, the answers to such questions lie as much in the interests and expertise of the contributors as in the quality of the literature; such is the reality constituting any encyclopedia. This reality limits the scope of the encyclopedia, but it does not preclude the pursuit of the project. To provide readers with information both on texts included in this volume and on other works of Holocaust literature, we have included a comprehensive list of primary works in the Bibliography of Primary Works of Holocaust Literature at the end of the encyclopedia.

While variations in the lives and works of the Holocaust authors listed in this volume have led to some variation in the organization of specific entries, all the entries answer the same basic questions about the author and his or her work: What is the nature of the author's literary response to the Holocaust? What is his or her place in Holocaust literature? What does the author's work contribute to an understanding of the Holocaust? What is distinctive about the author's work? What are some key moments in the author's life? What issues does the author's work pose for the reader? To address these questions in a coherent manner, the entries are generally organized into three primary divisions: (1) an opening section on why the author's work has a significant or distinctive place in Holocaust literature, (2) a second section containing information on the author's biography, and (3) a critical examination of the highlights of the author's work. In most cases, the third section of the entry will be the longest, since the focus of the encyclopedia is the literature, not the author; of course, these categories overlap somewhat.

The encyclopedia also includes three appendixes. Appendix 1 lists authors by date of birth to allow readers to acquire quickly a chronological sense of the people and works discussed in this volume. Appendix 2 lists authors by country of birth. Due to the collapse of the Austro-Hungarian and Russian empires after World War I and the breakup of the Soviet Union in 1991, the birthplaces of many authors are today in a different country, but this appendix will give readers a sense of the geographic and cultural background of the people included in this book. Finally, for authors listed under their more well-known pen names, Appendix 3 provides users with birth names.

The differences that distinguish Holocaust literature, however, call for a different critical approach to its study. As the work of witnesses, Holocaust literature transforms its reader into a witness—one cannot engage it without being implicated by it. If Holocaust literature transforms any reader into a witness, such a transformation is no less powerful for the scholars who have written these entries. In exploring a literature that responds to the slaughter of a people, the contributors do not always maintain the cold detachment that is characteristic of other reference works. We believe this sense of urgency on the part of the contributors is a distinctive feature of the volume, one that conveys something of what Holocaust literature is all about. In encountering a literary text that emerges from the Holocaust, one encounters the cry of a human soul; such a text is never merely a text. The contributors, therefore, have done more than engage in an academic exercise—they have met a responsibility. With the variations that one would expect, the contributors' writing styles may at times reflect a certain passion, but those styles are always guided by the care demanded by any encyclopedia.

The *Encyclopedia of Holocaust Literature* is intended for all students and teachers of the Holocaust, regardless of their levels of learning. Its aim is to provide brief information about Holocaust authors and their works, to convey a sense of what distinguishes Holocaust literature, and to open up avenues for further research. Although the witnesses who have undertaken a literary response to the Holocaust grow fewer and fewer with the passing of each year, the critical response to their work has just begun. This encyclopedia is part of that beginning.

A Word of Acknowledgement and Remembrance

This encyclopedia would never have taken form had it not been for the preliminary work of the late Harry James Cargas. Well known for his courageous questions and insight in Holocaust studies, the loss of Professor Cargas has been sorely felt by the students, teachers, and colleagues who knew him both personally and professionally. We would also like to acknowledge, with sorrow, the passing of one of this volume's contributors: David Hirsch. Professor Hirsch added a great deal to the study and understanding of Holocaust literature; his was a voice of clarity that guided many of us through the confusion of struggling to come to terms with this event that has changed humanity forever. Finally, the editors would like to acknowledge, with gratitude, the research efforts of Bonnie Lander of Florida Atlantic University.

Introduction

"A novel about Treblinka," Elie Wiesel has said, "is either not a novel or not about Treblinka."[1] If he is right, the very phrase "Holocaust literature" appears to be a contradiction in terms because the flames of Treblinka are the antithesis of the affirming flame that characterizes literature as an expression of the soul. As an expression of the soul, literature explores the depths of substance in life and dearness in humanity; as an assault on the soul, Treblinka exploits the emptiness of life and the wretchedness of humanity. Literature takes ordinary words and struggles to impart to them extraordinary meaning; Treblinka drains words of their meaning and the soul of its significance. Literature is in constant pursuit of a higher truth and a deeper insight; Treblinka insists that there is no truth or insight to be sought but only the devouring of one people by another. Treblinka means that power is the sole reality. And when power is the sole reality, literature is nothing more than propaganda—a novel about Treblinka is either not a novel or not about Treblinka. *And yet . . . .*

These words—*and yet*—make life and literature possible even after Treblinka. Indeed, if life is to have a possibility in the aftermath of that suffocating darkness, it is Holocaust literature that will breathe possibility into life. What, then, is Holocaust literature? It is the testimony that gropes toward community in the wake of a radical assault on the very substance of community. This literature attests that a human being, even and especially after the Shoah, is *homo narrans,* struggling to tell a tale that defies telling even as it compels the writer to bear witness.

The Phenomenon of Holocaust Literature

Holocaust literature arises in response to an event that would render the capacity both for response and for literary expression impossible. *And yet* it is there. It is there because the soul is there, if only as a remnant. Holocaust literature transcends the particulars of the event defined by death to affirm a movement of return to life. If a novel about Treblinka is not a novel, it is because the literary fiction that deals with the concentrationary universe addresses a world—or an anti-world—that no other novel has ever addressed. It does not follow the adventures of a hero like Don Quixote or David Copperfield because there is no hero in any conventional sense of the word. It is not a tale of coming of age because it is rooted in a realm in which aging was rendered "unnatural," even criminal. It takes up no critique of society because here the very bulwarks of civilized society have cracked.

Thus, if a novel about Treblinka is not a novel, it is because such a novel contains more than its pages can hold. If it is not about Treblinka, it is because such a work is about more than Treblinka; indeed, it is about something antithetical to Treblinka. Its very existence attests to the existence of something that Treblinka would negate. The literary response to the Holocaust is a human being's endeavor to restore to life a relationship to humanity that harbors the affirmation of life. It entails a movement of memory—for memory is its defining feature—by which a soul undertakes a movement of return. Contrary to everything represented by National Socialism—contrary to the indifference that enabled genocidal murderers to thrive—Holocaust literature is a testimony to the absolute dearness of every human being. It teems with a sense of urgency which disturbs our comfort and complacency to put to us the question put to the first human being: Where are you? Thus it transforms death into life by transforming its reader into a witness.

While the genres of Holocaust literature represented in this volume are the same as the genres of literature in general, certain features distinguish them from traditional generic distinctions. Some of the characteristics of the Holocaust novel that set it apart from the traditional genre have already been mentioned. Here it may be added that when authors of Holocaust fiction create characters they undertake the task of recreating their own souls in the light of a radical assault on everything that would define the soul. Ordinarily a novel may be constructed on a question about what there is to hold dear, about the way of life that characterizes a culture, or about finding one's way in the world. The Holocaust novel, by contrast, seeks to recover a capacity for questioning. It seeks to reconstruct a world that can be questioned. It seeks a voice not in response to an existing discourse but in response to what Alvin Rosenfeld calls "the emptiness and silence of an Imposed Absence"[2] which would render all questioning, all discourse, mute.

Similarly, the Holocaust memoir is not a reflection on a life in the twilight of one's years. It is not the memory of a life called to mind in the tranquility of an armchair; rather, it is the memory of one's own death, as when Moshe the Beadle in Elie Wiesel's *Night* returns from a mass grave and cries out to the people of Sighet, "I wanted to come back to Sighet to tell you the story of my death!"[3] It is a memory that contains the voices of the millions who can no longer speak, uttered in an effort not to recall a life but to recover it. Memory in the Holocaust memoir would summon a past for the sake of opening up a future. Henri Bergson has said that "there is no recollection which is not linked by contiguity with the totality of events which precede and also with those which follow it."[4] Memory in the Holocaust memoir, however, is situated not within a contiguity; rather, it emerges from the core of a rupture. Contiguity itself has been undone because the events that transpire in the concentrationary universe do not belong to the coordinate system of other events.

The Holocaust memoir does not so much undertake a movement in the midst of a contiguity as it seeks a recovery from the midst of a rupture. "The rupture," says Edmond Jabès, "is primarily due to God who wanted to be absent, who fell silent. To rediscover the divine word means to pass through this rupture."[5] Unlike other memoirs, the Holocaust memoir sets out to recover a divine word—that is, a word that is tied to meaning in life—if only to call it into question. The essence of memory in the Holocaust memoir, therefore, entails not just a recovery of time but a recovery of the eternal *in* time. To the extent that the Holocaust memoir would recover a trace of the divine word, it bears the marks of prayer. If the Holocaust memoir is against silence, it is against the silence of God; if it is about the recovery of human life, it is also about the recovery of the life of the divine—or at least a life of meaning. In the memory of God's silence, that silence takes on a voice heard in the memory's act of response. God speaks despite Himself. He speaks because the Jew remembers and thus refuses to remain silent—despite himself.

Alan Mintz points out that "when the survivor writes about the Holocaust it has the effect of an evasion interrupted or curtailed rather than an experience encountered or investigated; and when he writes of other things, the Holocaust seems to hover as an ontological condition."[6] Thus cast in an ontological category of its own, the Holocaust memoir is the soul's memory of itself and, through memory, the soul's struggle to recover itself. Many survivors, moreover, speak as though it were the soul's memory of God and God's memory of Himself in a struggle to recover Himself. As in the recitation of the Eighteen Benedictions, the survivor asks God to open the survivor's lips—not, however, to sing God's praise but to confront God with what has become of His divine image once imprinted on the human soul. "What man did at Auschwitz," says Wiesel, "could not have been done outside of God; in some way He too was at work—was He questioning man? Was He showing His face? What a face! In a sense, at Auschwitz God was afraid—afraid of Himself."[7] That fear is the wound that will not heal; in the Holocaust memoir, memory has no closure.

Memoirs by hidden children constitute a special angle of vision on the Holocaust, Jewish identity, and a stolen childhood. Nazism's youngest victims, in Nechama Tec's phrase, lived "between two worlds." Some were in hiding and hidden from view. Anne Frank is the best-known example. Other hidden children were, however, visible. These children passed as Christians. Hidden children had to live in silence and guard against spontaneity, a hallmark of childhood. Frequently, their Christian identity was far better informed than their Jewish self-understanding. After the war, these children remained silent about their experience for many years. Their memoirs only began appearing after nearly forty years. In May 1991 the first Hidden Child Conference, held in New York City, provided the impetus for several important developments. First and foremost, it validated the now adult children's sense of themselves as survivors. Second, the gathering brought with it recognition that others had been in the same situation during the Kingdom of Night. Finally, the gathering generated widespread recognition that the experience of hidden children immeasurably adds to our knowledge of the Holocaust and its aftermath.

Like the Holocaust memoir, the Holocaust diary bears certain features that distinguish it from other diaries. In contrast to the generic aspects of other diaries, the Holocaust diary harbors a consciousness of accountability that is explicit and pronounced, not merely implied, and that situates the diarist before his or her community; this consciousness imparts to the Holocaust diary a spirit of testimony. To be sure, the time measured by the Holocaust diary's daily entry is made of this responsibility. If the Holocaust diary is a record of the day's events, it is that those events are awash in Jewish blood; in the Holocaust diary, time is made of blood. That is why Avraham Tory, for example, writes on April 6, 1943, "Blood trickles into the huge cup of Jewish suffering."[8] Not "my" suffering but *Jewish* suffering—the life time of the diarist is inextricably tied to communal time, and Jewish blood is an essential element of Jewish community. The Holocaust diary characteristically includes not only the consciousness of personal experience but also the consciousness of communal ordeal.

The diarist who maintains an account of the ordeal does so in a realm where keeping such accounts is a capital crime. Furthermore, he or she writes not just in the midst of suffering but along the edge of annihilation. Thus distinguished from other diaries, "the extremity of experience recorded in the Holocaust diary," Barbara Foley points out, "entails a profound readjustment of accustomed patterns of literary communication. Ordinarily serving to mediate between two aspects of the self—the one that performs, the other that records the performance in peace at the end of the day—the diary projects a self whose principal performance is the act of testimony."[9] The act of testimony is an act of responsibility that situates the diarist and the diary within a relation to the community and its tradition, covenant, and mission. God, for example, invariably finds His way into the Holocaust diary in its concern for prayer, holy days, and the sanctification of life; like Jews themselves, this Jewish diary cannot do without the relation to the God of Abraham, whether it manifests itself in Anne Frank's observance of the Sabbath or in Moshe Flinker's vision of a messianic age. The context for the diary is more than the historical moment—it is the Jewish tradition, which, more than an accumulation of customs, is a history of the sacred.

For the Holocaust diarist, however, both the past as tradition and the future it makes possible are *elsewhere*. Far from being a flight from the world or from life, the "escape" of these diarists into their diaries is a flight *to* the world from the anti-world, a flight *to* life from the kingdom of death. Their clinging to an ideal is not a clinging to some fantasy but to the reality of such things as home and family in the face of a radical unreality. Thus, while other diaries seek to record and preserve the experience of the world, Holocaust diaries seek to recover the world itself. While other diaries offer an account of life upon the day's completion, Holocaust diaries struggle to recover a life despite the day's destruction. While other diaries are projected toward a future that is yet to be realized, Holocaust diaries are written in the shadow of a doom that is certain to come. While other diaries contain the individual's interrogation of himself or herself in the pursuit of meaning, the Holocaust diary includes an interrogation of God and humanity after the loss of meaning. While other diaries are written for the diarist, the Holocaust diary is written for others—living, dead, and yet to be born.

Similar distinctions can be made with respect to Holocaust poetry and Holocaust drama. Whereas the poets of the past have been viewed as language makers, Holocaust poets must do their work in the wake of an assault on language. Whereas poets of the past struggled to take words to greater depths of meaning, Holocaust poets struggle to return meaning to words. The meanings of such words as *left, right, flames, chimneys, cold, hunger, ghetto, resettlement, oven, dog, man, God, good,* and *evil* have been twisted and torn. Following this perversion and mutilation of words, the images invoked by Holocaust poets in their poetry have also been transformed. In an effort to mend word and meaning, Holocaust poets often draw upon the language and images of sacred texts; indeed, the word *Holocaust* itself comes from a discourse concerning sacred things. Drawing that language into its own text, Holocaust poetry constitutes a text that has never appeared before.

As for Holocaust drama, it too has its difficulties. Holocaust dramatists must stage human encounters from within the ruins of the undoing of the human image. They must compose dialogues in contexts where all dialogical relation has been undone. The framework within which Holocaust dramatists stage their drama also has its problems. Drawing upon scenery not of this world, they must nevertheless situate it within the world. To do a "scene" is to enact a segment of life from the space and time of the world; but when the world is Auschwitz—a realm that revolves along different orbits of space and time—the very notion of a "scene" becomes problematic.

These features that *distinguish* Holocaust literature from the rest of literature, however, do not *exclude* it from the corpus of literary accomplishment. Therefore, Holocaust literature is subject to treatment in literary reference works such as this encyclopedia, which is itself an effort to draw a response to the anti-world into the contexts of a world in which there are libraries, bookstores, readers, and scholars. Indeed, Holocaust literature's distinguishing features, as well as its proliferation, call for a comprehensive guide such as this one.

Endnotes

1. Elie Wiesel, et al., *Dimensions of the Holocaust* (Evanston, Ill.: Northwestern University Press, 1977), 7.

2. Alvin Rosenfeld, *A Double Dying: Reflections on Holocaust Literature* (Bloomington: Indiana University Press, 1980), 15.

3. Elie Wiesel, *Night*, trans. Stella Rodway (New York: Bantam, 1982), 5.

4. Henri Bergson, *Matter and Memory*, trans. N.M. Paul and M.E. Dowson (New York: Macmillan, 1929), 222.

5. Edmond Jabès, *From the Desert to the Book*, trans. Pierre Joris (Barrytown, N.Y.: Station Hill, 1990), 59.

6. Alan Mintz, *Hurban: Response to Catastrophe in Hebrew Literature* (New York: Columbia University Press, 1984), 259.

7. Elie Wiesel, *Against Silence: The Voice and Vision of Elie Wiesel*, ed. Irving Abrahamson, vol. 3 (New York: Holocaust Library, 1985), 309.

8. Avraham Tory, *Surviving the Holocaust: The Kovno Ghetto Diary*, trans. Jerzy Michalowicz, ed. Martin Gilbert (Cambridge, Mass.: Harvard University Press, 1990), 280.

9. Barbara Foley, "Fact, Fiction, Fascism: Testimony and Mimesis in Holocaust Narratives," *Comparative Literature* 34 (Fall 1982): 337.

Encyclopedia of Holocaust Literature

A

Abse, Dannie (1923–)

Dannie Abse's Welsh origin forms a major subject in his autobiographical writing, his fiction, and his poetry. His first volume of poetry, *After Every Green Thing* (1949), was followed by *Walking Under Water* (1952) and such other volumes as *Poems, Golders Green* (1962). His novels include *Ash on a Young Man's Sleeve* (1954) and *Some Corner of a Foreign Field* (1956). He also wrote plays: *O. Jones, O. Jones* (1970) and *The View from Row G: Three Plays* (1990). In addition, he has published collections of occasional writing and pieces of journalism, indicating the degree to which his everyday life impinges on his writing.

Dannie Abse was born in 1923 in Cardiff, Wales. He studied medicine at the Welsh National School of Medicine and continued his medical training at King's College and Westminster Hospital when he moved to London in 1943. He qualified as a doctor in 1950. After serving a stint in the Royal Air Force he practiced medicine in London and pursued his literary endeavors.

Abse's principal genre is poetry, of which he has produced nearly a dozen volumes. His Jewish background forms a major part of his consciousness, both that which he has personally experienced, and that to which he feels historically connected. He is unusual in combining a sense of Welshness and Jewishness, both principal elements in his feeling of life. His own life indeed touches closely on that of his fictional and poetic personae. His early poetry is well shaped, produced in measured tones in studied metrical form, with strong traces of T.S. Eliot.

Walking Under Water is learned and carefully crafted. With *A Small Desperation* (1968), he turns more to personal experience, and he attempts to recall the past, both his own individual past, and the larger past of collective history. With *Ask the Bloody Horse* (1986), Abse's work takes on a more demotic and colloquial character. One of the poems, written in the 1980s, entitled "Joke," intentionally recalls the title of one of Sigmund Freud's books. The whole poem is a small nugget consisting of a joke about a man riding on a horse; Freud comes along and asks the man where he is going, to which the man answers, "Ask the horse." In the poem one sees not only the development of an introduced and natural argot, the punch line appropriate to a "joke" as Freud understood it, but also the characteristically Jewish turn of the response. One also witnesses something of the tragic stance of the respondent, the sense that he was not in control of his own fate. His apparently majestic stance as a horse rider was misleading, and he was in fact at the mercy of other, external forces.

The sense of Fate is modified in his work by the appreciation of a playing out of a rivalry that in fact incorporates two Fates. This is metaphorized in a poem of a later collection, dealing with the rivalry between Yiddish and

Hebrew for possession of the Jewish soul. In the poem "Of Two Languages" (from *Remembrance of Crimes Past*, 1990), he relates a meeting between one Dov and the great Hebrew author S.Y. Agnon on Mount Carmel. Dov overheard Agnon speaking Yiddish to his companion, and he voiced his disapproval that a great Hebrew author should so demean himself. But Agnon's answer is that this is an appropriate tongue when going downhill, whereas uphill, he would pronounce in Hebrew. The Jew speaks two languages; Yiddish to men, and Hebrew to God. This is a succinct summary of a view of Jewish history.

When Jewish history comes to include the Holocaust, Abse sees the terrible tensions that arise. Jewish history aspires to the divine, as it is the divine source that has selected the Jew and given him that contact. But history has also reduced the status of the individual, dragging him in the dust, reducing him to the level of suffering being, able to share his painful stories with cosufferers. Appropriately, the medium for this specific communication is an argot, derived from other sources and sharing with these others, such as German, so much.

Abse's work, written in English, is both Welsh and Jewish. It is not written in the Welsh or the Jewish languages, but it bears traces of the history of the two and absorbs the consciousness of both. Abse has written fiction and autobiography, and each partakes of the elements of the other. *Ash on a Young Man's Sleeve*, described as a novel, foreshadows his autobiography, *A Poet in the Family* (1974). The title echoes the Eliot line from "Little Gidding," asserting that ashes on an older man's sleeve "Is all the ash burnt roses leave." That dust indicates "[w]here a story ended."

But this novel places the events at the beginning of a story. If this is a novel in the traditional sense, it is a novel told in the first person, from the point of view of someone very like the author himself. In order to capture the atmosphere of the times invoked, it is told idiosyncratically, with the equivalent of a Welsh lilt and with the typically Welsh inversion of noun and adjective. The household was Jewish as well as Welsh, and the mother could speak Welsh and Yiddish as well as English. The narrator early

became a revolutionary, or, at least, a keen Labour supporter.

If Abse's poetry bears traces of Eliot, his prose bears the unmistakable marks of Dylan Thomas. The author opens his account with a recall of the year 1934. But it is most important that this recall is effected through the eyes of an eleven-year-old child. The scene is replete with fleeting memories, random events—some private, some to do with his family or friends, and some sparks of the public concern. One becomes acquainted with the prevalent and growing hostility to foreigners, the darkening war clouds that finally lead to the Holocaust, and the local scene, including the rise of Oswald Mosley who leads his blackshirts on the march in England. One thus enters the mind of an adolescent, which, as filtered by a now adult memory, records all without discrimination or intervention. This is all part of the basic material which has served the writer throughout his later, prolific production.

SELECTED WORKS BY THE AUTHOR
Ash on a Young Man's Sleeve. London: Vallentine, Mitchell, 1973; *Ask the Bloody Horse*. London: Hutchinson, 1986; *Remembrance of Crimes Past: Poems*. New York: Persea, 1993; *Small Desperation: Poems*. London: Hutchinson, 1968; *White Coat, Purple Coat: Collected Poems 1948–1988*. New York: George Braziller, 1992.

Leon I. Yudkin

Aichinger, Ilse (1921–)

Ilse Aichinger, an early writer of Holocaust literature, published her only novel, *Herod's Children* (Die groëssere hoffnung or the greater hope) in 1948. Aichinger regarded the end of the war as a liberation from fascism and the beginning of the restoration of a sensitive, spiritual society. Through her writing, she protests the Nazi use of language as an instrument of destruction. Her language—dreamlike, ambiguous, spiritual, paradoxical, surreal—is punctuated by quiet and even by silences. She most closely resembles Franz Kafka in her evocation of an atmosphere of absurdity and impotence in the face of authority and Virginia Woolf in her lyricism and fluidity of language. Like Kafka, she writes from the victim's perspective: the helpless but hopeful innocent, the isolated human for whom relationships are transient, frustrating, or impossible. Aichinger's recognition of the truth of paradox places her in the category of highly serious, philosophical, and provocative writers whose works are haunting, if not disturbing, and whose language is poetic, full of graceful motion.

Born on November 1, 1921, in Vienna to a Jewish mother, a physician, and a Gentile father, a teacher who became a policeman under the Nazis, she was labeled a half-Jew or *Mischlinge.* Aichinger was educated at Catholic convent schools and graduated from high school in 1939, but, as a *Mischlinge,* she was prohibited from attending the university. Aichinger's twin sister, artist Helga Michie, emigrated to England, but Ilse stayed in Vienna with her mother, who was unable to obtain a visa. Although her parents divorced when she was five, her father sheltered his ex-wife and daughter during the war. Nevertheless, Aichinger spent the war years as an antifascist activist and as a forced laborer in both a factory and in a pharmacy, living in fear of her own and her mother's deportation. Her mother disappeared during the war, and Aichinger was never able to trace her. Many more of her Jewish relatives died, presumably in concentration camps, including her grandmother, who was the inspiration for the depiction of the grandmother in *Herod's Children.*

A visit to her sister immediately after the war endeared her to British culture, an influence frequently reflected in her choice of her characters' names. In 1946 Aichinger enrolled in the medical school at the University of Vienna but left after five semesters and the publication of *Herod's Children,* which is based on her observations and experiences and which she apparently wrote while she was a student. In 1949 she, Inge Scholl, the sister of resistance fighters Hans and Sophie Scholl, and others established the Academy for Arts and Designs in West Germany. Her activism led to an invitation to join Gruppe 47, an antifascist group of writers and artists. She received its coveted literary prize in 1952 for her story "The Mirror-Tale" and much attention for another of her stories, "The Bound

Man." In 1953 she married poet Guenter Eich (d. 1972) and bore two children, Clemens, who died in 1998, and Mirjam. The recipient of many distinguished prizes, Aichinger has been recognized with the Austrian State Prize for the Encouragement of Literature (1952), the Literary Prize of the City of Bremen (1955), the Immermann Prize of the City of Düsseldorf (1955), the Bavarian Literature Prize (1961), the Nelly Sachs Prize (1971), the Trakl Prize (1979), the Petrarca Prize (1982), the Kafka Prize (1983), and the Grosser Literaturpreis der bayerischen Akademic (1991). She continues to give readings in both English and German.

Herod's Children, written in the voice of a youthful girl who seeks understanding and escape, established Aichinger as a powerful writer. The child narrator, Ellen, is imbued with the hope of the future. She restlessly appeals to officials to secure the visa that would provide safe transit from Nazi-occupied Austria. Ellen's experiences are set in a surrealistic bureaucracy— an endless labyrinth—which offers false promise and irrational excuses. The adult world that impedes her is devoid of spirituality, heavy with irrational prohibitions, and doomed to murder its young and, with it, hope. Ellen's father, a Nazi policeman, becomes a function of the state, hidden by the helmet designed to inhibit emotion. In this fascist society, the child enables her grandmother to die, understands the need to transform language into a medium that bridges separations, values laughter and narrative, and threatens the inauthenticity imposed by a regime that devalues life disconnected from spirituality: "You mustn't die before you've been born" (p. 188). The death of the child signals the necessity of a greater hope, one that represents acceptance and moves from Darkness to Light. Laced with Christian and Jewish biblical references, *Herod's Children* is simultaneously a religious and secular work; above all, it is a relentless but never shrill condemnation of totalitarianism.

In a stunning short story, "The Bound Man" (1954), Aichinger quietly confronts us with a prisoner bound by physical ropes who learns to manipulate his body within its confining ties. He uses his ropes to maneuver his body and free his spirit without disturbing his ties, suggesting that the source of salvation lies first in oneself. Aichinger has tightened her writing even more in subsequent works, moving from the expansiveness of the novel to the increasing confines of the short story, the dialogue or radio play, and finally to the poem. Her works reflect terseness and an incremental mastery of diction. She cherishes the flexibility of the word, prefers everyday language, observes and records behavior by choosing words that impart both denotative and connotative meaning, and simultaneously understands the limitation of words to evoke the dimensions and texture of reality. In the words of her major critic, James C. Allridge, she is a "privilege to read" (p. 7).

SELECTED WORKS BY THE AUTHOR
Herod's Children. Trans. Cornelia Schaeffer. New York: Atheneum, 1964.

FOR FURTHER READING
Allridge, James C. *Ilse Aichinger.* Modern German Authors: Texts and Contexts, vol. 2. Chester Springs, Pa.: Dufour Editions, 1969.

Myrna Goldenberg

Améry, Jean (1912–1978)

Jean Améry is the author of one of the classic works of Holocaust literature, a collection of literary essays titled *Jenseits von Schuld und Sühne*, 1977 (*At the Mind's Limits*, 1980). After his ordeal of Gestapo torture and the German death camps, the inner condition of the Nazi victim was Améry's most acute concern. After years of silence, all demanded telling, not only Auschwitz but also the calamitous events in his life that preceded it. In 1964, therefore, he was persuaded to read a radio essay in Stuttgart on the intellectual's experience of Auschwitz, where he himself had been imprisoned in January 1944.

Thus the Austrian-born essayist and novelist Jean Améry entered the German literary scene in 1964, as a hopeful beginner of fifty-two, as he put it in a television interview a few months before his death. For twenty years after being liberated from the Bergen-Belsen concentration camp in 1945, he refused to visit Germany and

to write for or personally address a German audience. No other subject, he stressed, could have moved him to end his self-imposed ban. In 1966 he delivered this first radio address; the result was the book *Jenseits von Schuld und Sühne*. This work immediately established Améry's reputation in Germany as a critical essayist of piercing intellect and unbending integrity, and as a moral spokesman for the victims of the Shoah.

The name Jean Améry itself was a pen name, which the author had adopted in Belgium in 1955, as a symbol of his exile-in-permanence from his Austrian-German past. He was born Hans Maier in 1912, the son of a Jewish father, who died in 1916 as an Austrian rifleman in World War I, and a Catholic mother of partly Jewish origins. After his boyhood and youth in the Austrian provinces and a brief interlude in Berlin, he enrolled at the University of Vienna in 1931, but he never completed his studies there. In 1937, over his mother's objections, he married Regine Berger-Baumgarten, an Austrian-born daughter of Polish-Jewish parents. With her he fled from the Nazis to Belgium in 1938, only to be interred two years later in the Gurs concentration camp in southern France. After his escape from Gurs in 1941 he rejoined his wife in Brussels, where he was apprehended by the Gestapo in 1943 while distributing resistance leaflets; when they learned that he was a Jew, they sent him straight to Auschwitz. Upon his release and return to Belgium in 1945, he discovered that his wife had died of a heart ailment while in hiding. From then on he lived in Brussels as a freelance writer and journalist.

Although the largest part of Améry's work is decidedly personal in character, little of the purely factual data of his life became known, even as successive books, radio talks, and prolific journalistic writings increasingly gained him recognition in Germany as a cultural and political essayist and critic of the highest rank. To his publishers and interested editors, he typically sent a brief sketch with the sparsest of personal information: he had been born in 1912 in Vienna, where he later studied philosophy and literature; he had fled from the Nazis to Belgium in 1938, had worked in the Resistance there, had been imprisoned by the Gestapo in

1943 and deported to various concentration camps, among them Auschwitz, Buchenwald, and Bergen-Belsen; and since 1945 he had been living in Brussels as a freelance writer and journalist. To be sure, he had dealt with his fate during the Third Reich in *At the Mind's Limits,* but in a manner that was as philosophically detached as it was morally passionate. Rather than focusing on the individual aspects of his experience, he had been intent on revealing its exemplary qualities for his disastrous epoch. It was only later, through occasional essays (for example, "Being a Jew" in *Radical Humanism,* 1984), interviews, and the posthumously published book . . . *rtlichkeiten* (1980)—that he revealed more.

In his later years, Améry grew increasingly despondent. His health had been ruined as a result of his time in the camps, and he also feared the decline of his intellectual powers. He was dismayed, too, by right-wing restorative tendencies in what was then West Germany, and after Israel's Six-Day War in June 1967 by a resurgence of anti-Semitism—now under the guise of anti-Zionism—among the German New Left, whom he had always regarded as his allies in the democratic struggle (See "Anti-Semitism on the Left" in *Radical Humanism*). On October 16, 1978, he interrupted a reading tour in Germany and drove to Salzburg, where he took his life in a hotel room that night.

In the first of the five chapters of *At the Mind's Limits,* Améry deals with the capitulation of the intellect when faced with the overwhelmingly stark realities of the death camp; in the next, he examines the phenomenon of torture, which, in transgressing the victim's physical boundaries, robs him irreversibly of "trust in the world" (p. 28); in the middle chapter, he describes the permanent and existential loss of home when one is rejected and betrayed by one's own countrymen; in chapter 4, he examines the victim's resentments as the driving force of his demand that the perpetrator turn back the historical clock by recognizing the moral atrocity of his crime; and in the final chapter, the Catholic-reared Améry explains how he embraced his negatively determined Jewish identity and then secured his personal authenticity through constant revolt against anti-Semitism and the death

threat it aims against the Jew. Meanwhile, in Germany and the United States, scholarly efforts to equate the Nazi Final Solution with other genocides have confirmed Améry's fear that, with the passage of time, the Holocaust would be "submerged in a general 'Century of Barbarism'" (p. 80).

After publishing *At the Mind's Limits,* Améry turned to other subjects. Painfully aware that his career had begun late, in 1968 he published *Über das Altern* (On Aging, 1996), a disconsolate, searching literary portrait of the aging person. In 1971 there followed *Unmeisterliche Wanderjahre* (Botched journeyman years), a deeply introspective account of the author's intellectual odyssey, from the poetic irrationalism of his provincial youth to decisive stations in the Vienna school of neopositivism and, after the war, Jean-Paul Sartre's existentialism, and finally to a radical humanism inspired by the European Enlightenment, in the cause of practical democracy and human dignity. Along with *Über den Freitod,* 1976 (*On Suicide,* 1999), these works were entirely essayistic and constituted what Améry himself called an "autobiographical essay-novel," whereby the term *novel* would refer to their narrative texture and flow rather than to any fictionalizing tendencies in them.

Although *At the Mind's Limits* was Améry's only book dealing with the Holocaust, he took up this topic repeatedly in individual essays, newspaper and journal commentaries, and public addresses. In his reflections on the Warsaw ghetto uprising ("In the Waiting Room of Death" in *Radical Humanism*), he viewed any reconciliation with the murderers alive or dead as "the highest moral commandment," and he extolled the uprising as "the beginning of the end of Jewish history as the story of the sufferer" (p. 35). "Possibly," he declared, "it will be said someday that the history of a more humane humanity began amidst the inhumanity of the ghetto" (p. 36).

Améry's 1974 "novelistic essay" *Lefeu oder der Abbruch* (Lefeu or the demolition) is strongly autobiographical. Its protagonist, Lefeu, is a German-Jewish painter (originally named Feuermann) who is living dismally in a cluttered Paris hotel room after his liberation from the death camp. Tortured by the knowledge that he survived while countless others, including his parents, perished, he attempts intellectually to come to grips with his past and, at the same time, oppose what he calls the *Glanz-Verfall*, the decay in material splendor, of his time. Thematically multilayered and structurally intricate, the novel ends ironically: Lefeu dies of a heart attack while he tries, suicidally, to immolate his paintings and himself before the hotel can be demolished by real estate speculators. Although the novel powerfully reflects Améry's inner state as an Auschwitz survivor, it resists clear designation as a Holocaust work.

Given the short time Améry was granted to accomplish his literary work, his legacy, ten essay volumes (five of them published after his death) and two novels, is all the more remarkable. Although *On Suicide*, in the original German edition, has sold most, *At the Mind's Limits* must be regarded as Améry's most significant and influential work. Along with Primo Levi's* *Survival in Auschwitz*, as a victim's attempt to analyze the experience of the Holocaust, which Améry insisted was singular and irreducible, the book is unsurpassed.

SELECTED WORKS BY THE AUTHOR

At the Mind's Limits: Contemplations by a Survivor on Auschwitz and Its Realities. Trans. Sidney Rosenfeld and Stella P. Rosenfeld. Bloomington: Indiana University Press, 1980; Lefeu oder der Abbruch: Roman-Essay. Stuttgart: Ernst Klett Verlag, 1971; *Radical Humanism: Selected Essays*. Ed. and trans. Sidney Rosenfeld and Stella P. Rosenfeld. Bloomington: Indiana University Press, 1984; . . . *rtlichkeiten*. Stuttgart: Klett-Cotta, 1980; *Widersprüche*. Stuttgart: Ernst Klett Verlag, 1971.

Sidney Rosenfeld

Anatoli, A. (Anatoli Kuznetsov) (1929–1979)

Anatoli Kuznetsov earned his worldwide reputation as a result of the controversy set off by the publication of his heavily censored documentary novel *Babi Yar: A Document in the Form of a Novel* in 1966; the first and most extensive literary treatment of the Holocaust by a Soviet writer allowed to be printed. The novel, a chronicle of the nearly 800-day occupation of Kiev by the Nazis, reflects the methodical nature of the Jewish massacres in Babi Yar, a ravine on the outskirts of the city where 33,771 Jews, separated by the Germans from the general population, were slaughtered in just two days, September 29 and 30, 1941. The killing of Jews continued throughout the occupation. Toward the end of the war, the Germans tried to conceal their crime by digging up and burning the corpses. After the war, the Soviet government refused to acknowledge the Jewish character of the site and commemorate its victims. Defying the calls of Russian and Ukrainian intellectuals to erect a monument at the site, the government built a soccer field and a housing project on the bones and ashes of martyrs. The actions of the Communists reflected the official Soviet policy to treat the Holocaust as just one chapter in the history of World War II. The few positive initial reviews of the book were followed by officially sanctioned, vicious attacks criticizing Kuznetsov's emphasis on the particularity of the Jewish fate.

Until the publication of *Babi Yar*, Anatoli Kuznetsov's career had resembled that of many other Soviet writers. Born in Kiev in 1929, Kuznetsov came from a working-class family; his mother was Ukrainian and his father Russian. He started to write at the age of twenty as a contributor to factory newspapers. In 1955 he joined the Communist Party, often a prerequisite to being able to publish, and in 1957, when *Sequel to a Legend* was issued to positive acclaim, his reputation as a writer of good standing was firmly established. Although not overtly didactic, the novel adheres to the dicta of socialist realism, as it deals with the relationship between a young protagonist and the collective he tries to be part of. The other novels that followed his earlier publications—*The Life of a Young Man, Selenga, At Home,* and *Fire*—dealt with young people and were informed by Kuznetsov's own experiences at construction sites or industrial projects. A. Anatoli died in exile in 1979.

Although Kuznetsov was well aware that writing about the Jewish tragedy could be dangerous, he was compelled to tell the story. As a teenage boy living in the vicinity of the ravine, he had seen his neighbors disappear and witnessed the complicity of the local population. He based *Babi Yar* on notes he had kept, and he incorporated into the text documents he had collected that pertained to the murders. He complemented what he knew of the massacres with other eyewitness accounts, especially that of Dina Pronicheva, one of the very few Jewish survivors. Without ever denying that among the 100,000 bodies buried in the ravine were people of other nationalities, Kuznetsov was determined to underscore the Jewish nature of the Babi Yar slaughter. Kuznetsov saw as the main purpose of his novel a protest against revisionist history. As he maintained in the concluding chapter of the novel, "History cannot be deceived, and it is impossible to conceal something from it forever" (p. 477).

In 1969, angered by the criticism and censorship to which the novel was subjected, Kuznetsov escaped from his KGB handler during a visit to London; with the help of David Floyd of the *Daily Telegraph* and Anatoli Goldberg of the BBC, he asked for political asylum. The Soviet reaction to his defection was swift—he was condemned as a traitor and stripped of his citizenship. Kuznetsov changed his name to A. Anatoli and set out to restore *Babi Yar* to its original form.

The revised manuscript, translated by Floyd, was published in 1970. It contained three overlapping sections: the material published in the Soviet Union set in ordinary type, the material excised by the censor set in heavy type, and between square brackets material the author added to his manuscript. The restored and added sections reflected the writer's desire to recreate historical events as they really happened rather than the officially sanctioned narratives of the government. He accused the Russians rather than the Germans of destroying part of Kiev upon the Red Army's hasty retreat, and he did not shy away from asserting that local collaborators and the Ukrainian *politzei* helped the Germans in implementing the Final Solution. Kuznetsov's extensive comments implied an equation between Joseph Stalin's totalitarianism and German fascism, making it clear that only an honest assessment of history would al-

low the Soviet Union to come to terms with its past and to join world democracies. The mutilation of Kuznetsov's book by censors and the typographical fault lines of the restored manuscript parallel the scars inflicted upon the victims of the Holocaust and the Stalinist repression.

SELECTED WORKS BY THE AUTHOR
Babi Yar: A Document in the Form of a Novel. Trans. David Floyd. New York: Farrar, Straus, and Giroux, 1970.

FOR FURTHER READING
Korey, William, *The Soviet Cage: Anti-Semitism in Russia.* New York: Viking Press, 1973; Young, James E., "Holocaust Documentary Fiction: The Novelist as Eyewitness." In *Writing and the Holocaust,* ed. Berel Lang. New York: Holmes & Meier, 1988.

Asher Z. Milbauer

Anissimov, Myriam (1943–)

Author of seven novels, two fictionalized memoirs, and biographer of the first study of Primo Levi,* Myriam Anissimov has assumed the scars of Holocaust memory in her literary universe. Her books reveal what it means to be a young Jew growing up in France after the genocide. The act of writing allows her to project herself back into a reality she did not know and to explore her own fears and fantasies in light of that reality. Anissimov agonizes from the pain she has inherited, struggling to understand "how the tragic events of the Holocaust that I did not endure, have been able to shape my own conscience as a Jew" ["Une litterature juive pourquoi?" *La Tribune Juive* 300 (1974): 15].

Myriam Frydman (Anissimov is a pen name) was born in 1943 in a refugee camp in Sierre, Switzerland. In 1942, at the time of the roundups of Jews in Vichy, France, her Polish-born father and her mother, of Polish nationality, born in Metz, France, fled to Switzerland from Lyon, France. Her parents had been urged to escape by her politically aware maternal grandfather, an old Communist agitator, who had gone to Germany from Poland. He left Germany in 1934 when the Nazis came into his town and started vandalizing his hat store. He became involved in and even imprisoned for political activities in France. When the war broke out, he was interned in a French camp because he was foreign Jew. Anissimov's parents, who were members of the branch of the Communist Party for foreigners in France, took part in their resistance movement before escaping to Switzerland.

Conditions were harsh in the Swiss camp for refugees. Due to poor heating and lack of warm clothes, the infant Myriam contracted pleurisy and was placed in a Lausanne hospital. Her life was saved by Sister Blanche Sterki, a deaconess working in the hospital, who devoted herself to saving Jewish children placed in her care. For a year and a half, this woman became a surrogate mother to Myriam, even teaching her how to talk. Long after the war, Anissimov found the Protestant nun whose memory she revered throughout her life. She relates her emotional visit to Mademoiselle Sterki in the early 1970s, and her attendance at the nun's funeral in 1992 in her memoirs, *Dans la plus stricte intimité*, 1992 (In the strictest privacy) and *Sa Majesté la Mort*, 1999 (Her majesty, death).

Myriam Anissimov is a journalist as well as a writer. She applies her investigative skills to probing into her family's Holocaust history. In both books, Anissimov relives her parents' wartime experience, reproducing letters they sent to each other from their separate camps in Switzerland. She also cites letters written to her father from Bergen-Belsen after the war from his surviving brother who was obliged to stay there with his wife until 1947 because they were unable to obtain papers. Her father's two other brothers and parents all perished. In *Sa Majesté la Mort,* Anissimov recounts how she went to the southwestern region of France to gain information about her mother's brother, Samuel Frocht, who vanished during the war without a trace. Anissimov also returned to the Swiss refugee camps and actually followed the escape route taken by her parents as the war was drawing to a close.

With their two-year-old daughter, her parents clandestinely crossed the border in April 1945 and returned to Lyon which had been liberated by the Allied Forces. Her father went to work as a tailor and eventually opened a clothes manufacturing business. Also a writer, he published books of humorous short stories and poems in Yiddish. The figure of the father as writer, and Yiddish writer at that, served as an inspiration for Anissimov, although she had ambivalent feelings with regard to his authoritarian relationship to her. The father's presence and his absence (her father died at an early age in an automobile accident in 1957) are recurring motifs in her fiction.

Incorporating autobiographical elements into her novels, Anissimov blends the real with the imaginary. Holocaust imagery resonates throughout her work. A network of themes revolve around death and abandonment, solitude, loss and separation, fear and humiliation. These are evident in works such as *Comment va Rachel?*, 1973 (How is Rachel?) and *Le Resquise*, 1975 (untranslatable), which depict the lonely inner world of a Jewish girl coming of age after the Holocaust.

Anissimov's characters are often portrayed as alienated, uprooted, marginal, adrift in a world without meaning, unable to anchor themselves in tradition or family, emotionally rejected by their parents, in search of their identity, and, above all, looking to belong. Condemned by forces without knowing why, and prey to the injustices of society, they are resigned to the despair and emptiness of lives without meaning. Like the author, Anissimov's protagonists are haunted by collective memories of the past which punctuate their lives in the present. They have been wounded by stories and images impossible to forget.

In *Le Resquise* the main character, Anna, bears the burden of memory. (The title possibly refers to a child's mispronunciation of *l'heure exquise* (the exquisite hour) from Paul Verlaine's poem "La lune blanche.") At an early age, Anna found lying around the house newspapers and magazines containing photos of corpses piled on top of each other. Her father tried to explain to her what had occurred. The child relives the agony of the tormented sights and sounds of victims assassinated in pogroms, death camps, and crematory ovens: "One can remember what one has not seen. Anna still hears the cries of the victims" (p. 163). By the end of the novel, Anna, now a young woman afflicted by personal anxiety and doubts as well as by the histories of the massacres of her people, looks in the mirror and sees "the face of a victim" (p. 195).

Anissimov clearly identifies with the victims and creates characters who are victims of both external and internal circumstances they do not seem to control. *Rue de nuit,* 1977 (Street of night), related in a Kafkaesque manner, is probably her most terrifying account of totalitarian and bureaucratic intrusion into private lives. It shows how an individual can be broken down when the political structures of a state collapse and its moral values disintegrate. The novel demonstrates how innocent people are made to believe in their own guilt.

Unlike Anissimov's other protagonists, who accept their condition of victimhood, Anna in *Rue de Nuit* is an unwilling victim. The role is thrust upon her by higher authorities who prevent her from leading a normal existence. She and her artist friend, Claude, who live together in a large apartment building in a large city are slowly harassed by being spied upon at home and followed in the street. Tactics of surveillance are employed: men dressed in gray stand in the hallway watching the door to their apartment; the apartment is searched when Anna and Claude go out and the journal in which Anna records her dreams is taken; their door is replaced by a glass door by workers who claim to have signed orders. The process of intimidation accelerates. Anna acutely experiences the anguish of being singled out. Who will help us, what fault have we committed to be unjustly accused, judged, and punished without a trial, Anna asks herself (p. 64).

Similar to the central characters of the other novels, Anna lives in fear, waiting for something more terrible to happen. But she does not wholly internalize the feeling of guilt imposed upon her. She believes in her innocence, and she rejects a passive acceptance of the role of victim: "I am afraid. That does not prevent me from asking for explanations." Like a character out of Kafka, she is never given the reason for her persecution which evolves during the course of the novel. However, the desire to protest injustice, to resist, marks a significant change in the development of Anissimov's protagonists.

In Anissimov's novel *La Soie et les cendres,* 1989 (Silk and ashes), elements of genocide haunt the narrative and the mind of Hannah Kaganowski, the protagonist who feels she has been born from human ashes (p. 309). A writer, Hannah earns her living by recycling and selling antique silk, satin, and lace clothes at the Paris Flea Market. One day, she makes an astonishing discovery about the questionable origins of these goods when she sees German words on the containers. Without knowing it, she had been selling the last relics of deported Jews in the death camps. Past and present thus merge in the life of the protagonist.

One should note that in Anissimov's non-Holocaust novels, including *Le Bal aux puces,* 1985 (The ball of the fleas) and *Le Marida,* 1982 (The marriage), the characters and situations depicted are humorous, at times even burlesque. In the memoirs comic passages are juxtaposed with the sad accounts of family members who have disappeared.

Anissimov's immersion in the subject of the Holocaust has culminated in her writing the first biography of Auschwitz survivor, chemist, and humanitarian Primo Levi (1919–1987). In *Primo Levi ou la tragédie d'un optimiste*, 1966 (*Primo Levi: Tragedy of an Optimist*, 1998), she presents an informative and objective narrative of Levi's life, describing his family background, interviewing people who knew him in the camps, consulting unpublished correspondence and other documentation. This thorough exploration, along with her novels showing how trauma has established its grip on a child growing up in the aftermath, establishes Myriam Anissimov as an important Holocaust writer.

Selected Works by the Author

Le bal aux puces. Paris: Julliard, 1985; *Comment va Rachel?* Paris: Editions Deno'l, 1975; *Dans la plus stricte intimité.* Paris: Editions de l'Olivier, 1992; *L'Homme rouge des Tuileries.* Paris: Julliard, 1979; *Le marida.* Paris: Julliard, 1982; *Primo Levi: Tragedy of an Optimist.* Trans. Steve Cox. New York: Overlook, 1998; *Le resquise.* Paris: Deno'l, 1975; *Rue de Nuit.* Paris: Julliard, 1977; *Sa Majesté la mort.* Paris: Editions du Seuil, 1999; *La soie et les cendres.* Paris: Payot, 1989.

For Further Reading

Fine, Ellen S. "The Search for Identity in Post-Holocaust French Literature: The Works of Myriam Anissimov," *Holocaust and Genocide Studies*, 5 (1990): 205–16.

Ellen S. Fine

Appelfeld, Aharon (1932–)

The author of more than thirty volumes of novels, essays, and plays, Aharon Appelfeld is the foremost Israeli author of Holocaust literature and is among the most accomplished among the world's novelists who have emerged from that event. More powerfully than most other writers of fiction, Appelfeld conveys the horror of the Holocaust not through his graphic descriptions of the concentrationary universe but precisely through his silence about it. In one novel after another Appelfeld sounds the depths of people's lives who are entrenched in the shadows of Auschwitz. Through his art he demonstrates that the scope of the Holocaust, both in time and in space, extends far beyond the confines of the camps.

Appelfeld was born in 1932 in Czernowitz, Bukovina, a cosmopolitan city in what was then the Soviet Ukraine; today it is known as Chernovtsy in the independent Ukraine. With his grandparents speaking Yiddish and his parents speaking German, Appelfeld was brought up in a family that was assimilated into Western culture. When he was eight years old, the Nazis murdered Appelfeld's mother and sent his father off to the camps never to return. The young boy was sent to a camp in Transnistria but managed to escape and hide in the forests for two years. In 1946 he made his way to Israel, where he fought in the War of Independence. Appelfeld, who has lived in Israel since its independence, now resides near Jerusalem and is a professor of literature at Ben Gurion University.

Appelfeld's first novel to appear in English, *Badenheim, ir nofesh*, 1975 (*Badenheim 1939*, 1980), is among his most striking. Set in an Austrian resort town frequented by an assortment of Jews, the novel unfolds in the shadow of a future that will mean the destruction of the Jews. The novel makes no mention of Nazi atrocities but rather casts the enemies of the Jews in the role of representatives of the "Sanitation Department," whose task is to identify the Jews for ultimate deportation. While Dr. Pappenheim, one of the novel's main characters, jokes about the "new Order of Jewish Nobility," it "seemed that some other time, from some other place, had invaded the town and was silently establishing itself" (p. 54). That time of destruction yet to come tears the Jews from their own time even before it comes.

A similar tearing of the Jew from his identity and his reality can be seen in Appelfeld's second novel, *Tor ha-pelaot*, 1978 (*The Age of Wonders*, 1981), where there is a shifting from a first-person narrative in the first half of the book to a third-person point of view in the second half. The main character is a boy named Bruno, whose father is a renowned Austrian author at odds with his Jewish origins. Seeking to be assimilated with Austrian society, he opens his home to a Jewish-Christian society only to be abandoned when danger comes. The second part of the novel begins with the adult Bruno, a Holocaust survivor, returning to his hometown after having been gone for twenty years. He discovers that his father "had died half-mad in Theresienstadt, and that before he died he had tried to convert to Christianity" (p. 209). That his father would embrace the tradition of a culture that murdered him inflicts upon Bruno a wound that will not heal. And Appelfeld offers no easy answers.

Another novel dealing with Jewish identity and set in the mountains of pre-Holocaust Austria is *The Retreat* (1984). The founder of the retreat, a man named Balaban, is bent on cleansing himself and all his guests of their "Jewish traits," primarily by waging a war against the "accursed memories" (p. 101) that constitute one's identity. A resort that specializes in assimilation, the retreat is an unreal place that makes the Jews unreal to themselves. As the time of the catastrophe draws near, the Jews soon have no possibility to assimilate and no place to retreat. One of the guests, a man named Herbert, describes his Jewishness as an illness that he does not want to pass on to his children (p. 103). To be sure, the Nazis themselves would soon regard being Jewish as a disease that afflicts humanity, a disease that must be eradicated. The irony is that Balaban is the one who finally falls ill. In a single blow his illness "destroyed the language he had acquired at school, German, and gave him back his mother tongue" (p. 130).

Appelfeld's interest in the fate of the child is elaborately developed in *Hakutonet v'hapasim*, 1983 (*Tzili: The Story of a Life*, 1984). The novel's title character, a Jewish girl, is torn from her family but otherwise has very little experience of the horrors that typify the Holocaust. A character who is for the most part silent, Tzili endures the hardship of going from one shelter to another with very little complaint. From time to time she imagines that she hears her mother calling out to her. "Of her entire childhood, only this [calling out] was left" (p. 158). She slowly learns to mimic the peasants with whom she lives, until she finally meets a Jewish refugee named Mark, by whom she becomes pregnant. While her baby does not survive, Tzili herself lives to set out for Palestine.

In *Erets ha-gome*, 1985 (*To the Land of the Cattails*, 1986), Appelfeld takes his characters along quite a different path of return. Here a thirty-four-year-old woman named Toni and her adolescent son, Rudi, make their way from Vienna to their native Bukovina (which is also the place of Appelfeld's birth). While one might assume that Toni is fleeing to the east in the wake of Germany's annexation of Austria in 1938, Appelfeld, in his characteristic style, makes no mention of the historical event. What is clear is that a Jewish woman who had a child by a Gentile man is trying to return to the home of her mother and father and to her Jewish identity. Along the way they encounter a number of obstacles, most of which are tied to anti-Semitism; when Toni finally reaches her parents' home, she and her son find it empty. Like other Jews in the area, her parents were taken away and slaughtered. Thus the one who seeks a return has no place to return to.

In *Bartfus ben ha-almavet*, 1983 (*The Immortal Bartfuss*, 1988), Appelfeld creates a portrait of a man who lives in Israel after surviving the Holocaust. Highly reflective and with a deeply moral consciousness, Bartfuss is set

adrift in time as he walks the streets of Jaffa. He encounters other survivors, but he appears to have no friends. He is estranged from his family and resents them for "trapping" him. He accuses his wife of surviving at the price of her moral integrity, and yet the reader knows that Bartfuss himself harbors a guilt for having survived. If Bartfuss is distant from his family, Appelfeld keeps his reader at a distance from Bartfuss: while allowing his character's interior life to remain inviolable, Appelfeld nevertheless conveys a profound sense of interiority about Bartfuss.

A character with an equally fathomless interior is Theo Braun, the main character in the novel *Al kol ha-peshaim*, 1988 (*For Every Sin*, 1989). Braun is a survivor of the Holocaust who undertakes the overwhelmingly difficult movement of return—a return home, a return of his soul, a return to humanity—after his "liberation" from "camp number eight." Exploring the question of what it means to be human, the novel examines the question of the scope of human responsibility. Theo is a man who has lost his mother tongue and with it the ability to respond to the suffering of the survivors. When he tells a woman, for example, that "a person must help others," he realizes that he was speaking "in a voice that wasn't his own" (p. 105). The relation of responsibility was lost to the camps. Thus "that language which his mother had inculcated in him with such love would be lost forever. If he spoke, he would speak only in the language of the camps" (pp. 166–67). The scope of the destruction of the Holocaust is as limitless as language itself.

If the Holocaust infects language, then it infects the soul, a point made in Appelfeld's *B'et uv'onah ahat*, 1985 (*The Healer*, 1989). Here the central figure is Felix, a Viennese business executive whose daughter Helga suffers from some mysterious malady. Because Helga is desperately ill, like "all the sick Jews," Felix's wife, Henrietta, convinces him to take Helga to a nameless, mystical healer in the mountains of the East. Of course, the healer himself, a rabbi, is also ill. It remains ambiguous as to whether Jewish tradition can provide healing to the Jewish soul; Helga and her mother end by setting out for a convent, while Felix and his robust,

Germanic son head back for Vienna. They find a Vienna transformed and very hostile toward Jews. The nightmarish journey that led them home is about to turn into a far greater nightmare. But, characteristically, Appelfeld leaves it at that.

With the novel *Katerinah*, 1989 (*Katerina*, 1992), Appelfeld displays his genius for creating characters who at first glance are utterly different from their creator. It is the story of an eighty-year-old Gentile woman told in her own words. She grew up in Ruthenian, an area near Appelfeld's native Bukovina, where she learned the anti-Semitism that characterizes the attitudes of most peasants. As a teenage runaway, however, she was taken into safety by a Jewish family, only to see the Jewish couple later murdered in a pogrom. She bears a child sired by a Jewish man, only to see her child murdered for being a Jew. After being sent to prison for the murderous revenge she took, she was released at the time of the Holocaust. Still shunned by peasant society, Katerina decides to follow a Jewish path, observing the Sabbath, because, it seems to her, there were no Jews left to observe it. It seems that in a world dominated by anti-Semitism, the only way to remain a human being is to adopt the path of the Jews, even if one is not a Jew.

Appelfeld's next novel, *Unto the Soul* (1994), is also set in Ruthenia. Set in a time between catastrophes—like so many of Appelfeld's other works—it is a tale about the price of abandoning the past. The fragmentary form of the novel reflects the sickness in the soul—the sickness of forgetfulness—that it examines. In the novel a brother and sister, Gad and Amalia, are appointed to act as the guardians of the Cemetery of Martyrs somewhere in the mountains. Although they try to remain faithful to their task, they fall farther and farther away from the rites and rituals, the teachings and traditions, that would give their work meaning. Gad forgets his prayers, and Amalia simply falls silent. Both of them fall ill and die. The novel is deeply allegorical and announces the threat of forgetfulness that faces the Jews, particularly in the wake of the Holocaust. What is at stake in the memory of the Holocaust is not only the prevention of another one, but also the very soul of the Jew.

But perhaps the soul of the Jew was in decay before the onslaught of the Holocaust. That appears to be the theme of Appelfeld's novel *Timyon*, 1993 (*The Conversion*, 1998). In this tale the main character, Karl, is an inhabitant of the declining Austria-Hungarian empire who converts from Judaism to Roman Catholicism to advance his career. As the decay of the empire parallels the decay of Karl's soul, one thing remains constant: anti-Semitism. One by one the Jews of Karl's provincial town fall prey to the Church that would make them disappear by robbing them of their spiritual identity. Ironically, the only character who asserts that Jews should remain Jewish—rather than prostitute their very souls—is the madam of a brothel.

Mesilat barzel, 1991 (*The Iron Tracks*, 1998) is the tale of a Jew named Erwin Siegelbaum who survived the spiritual and physical assault of the Holocaust. Like many of Appelfeld's characters, he was raised in Ruthenia, where his parents were murdered by the Nazis. His business takes him on train trips through various towns from which Jews had vanished at the hands of the murderers. He spends his time buying up the artifacts of the dead and hunting down a man Nachtigel, who had been a Nazi camp commandant, Siegelbaum's story conveys two basic Jewish needs in the post-Holocaust era: the need for memory and the need for justice. Both, however, are forever frustrated. The artifacts he collects are poor vessels of the lives they represent, and Nachtigel is a decrepit old man upon whom it is pointless to take vengeance. Both appear to leave Siegelbaum at a dead end where he has nothing left but the ghosts of the dead.

Like many of his characters, Appelfeld himself wrestles with the ghosts of the dead. Unlike his characters, however, he brings them to life through the insightful Jewish memory borne by his ingenious literary art.

SELECTED WORKS BY THE AUTHOR
The Age of Wonders. Trans. Dalya Bilu. Boston: Godine, 1981; *Badenheim 1939*. Trans. Dalya Bilu. New York: Washington Square, 1980; *The Conversion: A Novel*. Trans. Jeffrey M. Green. New York: Schocken, 1998; *For Every Sin*. Trans. Jeffrey M. Green. New York: Weidenfeld and Nicolson, 1989;

The Healer. Trans. Jeffrey M. Green. New York: Grove Press, 1994; *The Immortal Bartfuss.* Trans. Jeffrey M. Green. New York: Weidenfeld and Nicolson, 1988; *The Iron Tracks.* Trans. Jeffrey M. Green. New York: Schocken, 1998; *Katerina.* Trans. Jeffrey M. Green. New York: Random House, 1992; *The Retreat.* Trans. Dalya Bilu. New York: Dutton, 1984; *To the Land of the Cattails.* Trans. Jeffrey M. Green. New York: Weidenfeld and Nicolson, 1986; *Tzili: The Story of a Life.* Trans. Dalya Bilu. New York: E.P. Dutton, 1983; *Unto the Soul.* Trans. Jeffrey M. Green. New York: Random House, 1994.

FOR FURTHER READING
Ramras-Rauch, Gila, *Aharon Appelfeld: The Holocaust and Beyond.* Bloomington: Indiana University Press, 1994.

David Patterson

Arieti, Silvano (1914–1981)

Silvano Arieti combined his "psychiatrist's insight and the storyteller's skill," as Elie Wiesel* expressed it (on the book jacket), to produce one of the most penetrating novels to be written in response to the Holocaust; indeed, Primo Levi* described it as "a book to read again and again with the same piety with which it has been written" (on the book jacket). Titled *The Parnas* (1979), the novel is based on the true-life experiences of the parnas, or chief elder, of the Jewish community in Arieti's native town of Pisa.

Arieti was born on June 28, 1914, the son of Dr. Elio Arieti. He attended the University of Pisa Medical School, where he specialized in neurology and psychiatry. With the rise of fascism in Italy and the approaching epidemic of anti-Semitism, he and his family left for America in 1939; there he received an appointment as a fellow in the Neuropathology Department of the New York State Psychiatric Institute. He also worked at the Pilgrim State Hospital in Brentwood, New York, and at the William Alanson White Institute. Famous throughout the world as the editor of the *American Handbook of Psychiatry* and the author of more than a dozen books in psychiatry, Arieti was especially known for his work on schizophrenia. In 1975 he received the National Book Award for Sciences for his *Interpretation of Schizophrenia.*

The man whom Arieti most admired in his youth was Giuseppe Pardo Roques, the title character in *The Parnas.* Unlike Arieti and his family, Roques was unable to get out of Italy before the Germans arrived; he was murdered, along with the other Jews of Pisa, in the summer of 1944. A man of higher learning and impeccable character, Roques was well known for his kindness and generosity. He suffered, however, from a mysterious mental illness that ultimately confined him to his house and made it impossible for him to escape the Nazis.

During his years of study in Pisa, Arieti dreamed of finding a cure for his elder and mentor who was devoured by the perpetrators of the Holocaust. He wrote *The Parnas*, then, not only as a tribute to the courage and spirituality of Roques but also as an exploration of the bestial evil that characterized the Holocaust. Arieti's work in psychiatry led him to conclude that mental illness "may hide and express the spirituality of man," and in *The Parnas* he makes that point very powerfully. Here Pardo, as Roques is known in the novel, suffers from a phobia of animals, particularly dogs. Like any phobia, this one appears to be completely irrational, until the end of the tale, when the Nazis come to rob and murder the parnas.

As the Germans try to torture him into praising Adolf Hitler, Pardo persists in his adoration of God. As they beat him to death, Pardo sees the Nazis transformed into creatures that bark and howl, "with a snout, fur, four claws, and a tail" (p. 140)—he sees them, in other words, transformed into what they have already become. At that point he realizes what he had truly feared all his life. It was the fear that haunts all humanity in the wake of the Holocaust: not a fear of animals, but a fear of the human being who has allowed himself to be transformed into an animal. Who is worse off than the Jew murdered at the hands of the Nazi? When a German soldier puts this question to Pardo, he answers, "You." The Nazi who sets out to dehumanize the Jew loses his own human image in the process.

In coming to this conclusion in his novel—and in keeping with his theories on the relation between mental illness and spirituality—Arieti examines the most profound spiritual questions that arise from the Holocaust. Pardo's friend Ernesto, in fact, believes that the mental illness is part of the Shekhinah, of God's Indwelling Presence, which has descended upon the parnas. When asked, then, why God remains silent throughout the slaughter of the Jews, Pardo insists that God is not mute. God's lament echoes in every human outcry, but, Pardo declares, "We must choose to hear Him" (p. 71). Through his profound response to the Holocaust in *The Parnas*, Silvano Arieti uses his skills as a psychiatrist and a writer to help his reader hear the One whom Pardo affirms with his dying breath.

SELECTED WORKS BY THE AUTHOR
Abraham and the Contemporary Mind. New York: Basic Books, 1981; *Creativity*. New York: Basic Books, 1976; *Interpreting Schizophrenia*. Northvale, N.J.: Jason Aronson, 1994; *The Intrapsychic Self*. New York: Basic Books, 1976; *Love Can Be Found*. New York: Harcourt Brace Jovanovich, 1977; *The Parnas*. New York: Basic Books, 1979; *The Will to Be Human*. New York: Quadrangle Books, 1972.

David Patterson

B

Bartov, Hanoch (1926–)

Among the most prominent of the Israeli authors of Holocaust fiction, Hanoch Bartov belongs to the 1948 literary generation and is a prolific writer. Bartov has been writing for half a century, and his realistic style mirrors the changes in Israeli society throughout this period. Among other topics, his fiction relates to the waves of immigration, to Holocaust survivors, and to the changing political landscape.

Hanoch Bartov was born in Petach Tikva, Israel, in 1926, and he currently resides in Tel Aviv. During World War II he served in the British Army's Jewish Brigade, and in 1948 he fought in Israel's War of Independence. Bartov is a novelist, playwright, and journalist. Among the awards he has received is the 1965 Shlonsky Prize for his novel *The Brigade,* the Bialik Prize in 1985 for *Be-Emtza Ha-Roman* (In the middle of it all), and in 1998 the President's Literature Award.

Among his most important books is *The Brigade* (*Pitzay bagrut,* 1965). This first-person narrative touches upon human, cultural, and national issues. The book reads like a confessional novel but it is more in the tradition of the bildungsroman, a novel dedicated to the perils of adolescence and growing up. The transition it portrays from innocence to experience is, as is often the case, a painful one. The novel describes the firsthand encounter of a young Israeli-born Jew with survivors of the Holocaust.

The protagonist is a soldier in the Jewish Brigade; the Brigade was composed of Israelis who, like Bartov, fought in the British Army in World War II. The personal encounter with the survivors is at once the affirmation of hope and its denial. The first meeting with a Jew who came "from there" has almost a mystic quality:

> This stranger, who had come to us from out of the darkness, awesome in his appearance, was actually one of us, speaking our language, coming to us straight from the forest, directing his feet to this spot on the border as though to a star. (p. 139)

This revelation of brotherhood transcending boundaries is coupled with personal horror. Elisha Krook, the young protagonist, realizes that a relative of his has survived Auschwitz by working at the crematorium: "more than anything else, I was filled with revulsion at the thought of being connected with him" (p. 139).

The encounter of the Brigade members with individual Germans is complex as well, leading to new questions: How does one hate? What is the moral price of revenge? Can an individual wage a private war? Is the Brigade an army of liberation or an army of retribution? The abstract notion of the enemy must be translated into terms befitting the often bloody everyday encounter with individual Germans.

The young protagonist, thrown into a situation devoid of precedent, is left with self-questioning that is ultimately doomed by a sense of impotence and ambiguity. The final mystery is survival itself. In light of the horror, what price must any survivor pay? If survival is bought at the expense of one's humanity, must the survivor not embrace life as the ultimate value? Facing the Holocaust continues to be a burning issue in the minds of survivors, witnesses, observers, and collaborators. Bartov's novel addresses these issues.

The Brigade raises issues of ethical guilt versus legal guilt and consequently the issues of punishment. Punishment can be reformative or preventative. What is the meaning of punishment in *The Brigade*? What would the rape of a German woman whose father was a Nazi officer accomplish for the frustrated Jewish soldier? The rape, which is eventually prevented, points to the sense of helplessness experienced in the post-Shoah experience. The conflicts faced by the Jewish soldiers entering a German town include questions about the role of a moral duty: What does one have to do? What must one do? What must one refrain from doing?

The choice of the protagonist to intervene on behalf of the German women leaves him empty, almost impotent. Bartov, an important, realistic writer, reacts to the unfolding reality around him. The past, personal and national, is a constant presence, intermingled and forever striving for a defined sense of Israeli identity.

SELECTED WORKS BY THE AUTHOR

The Brigade. Trans. David S. Segal. New York: Holt, Rinehart and Winston, 1968; *Everyone Had Six Wings*. Jerusalem: World Zionist Organization, 1974; *An Israeli at the Court of St. James*. Trans. Ruth Aronson. London: Vallentine Mitchell, 1971; *Whose Little Boy Are You?* Trans. Hillel Halkin. Philadelphia: Jewish Publication Society of America, 1978.

Gila Ramras-Rauch

Becker, Jurek (1937–1997)

Jurek Becker's novel *Jacob the Liar*, 1990 (*Jakob der lügner*, 1969) is a masterpiece of storytelling which weaves together the chimera of hope and the reality of despair in telling the tale of Jacob Heym and the doomed Jews of the Łódź ghetto. While reporting to the commandant's headquarters for punishment, Jacob overhears a radio announcer relating the Soviet army's advance. When he returns to the ghetto, Jacob shares this news with his friend Mischa. The news lifts the spirits of the Jews. Soon the entire ghetto awaits Jacob's reports. There is, however, one problem. Owning a radio is a capital offence. Consequently, Jacob begins to invent "news" items to keep up the morale of his fellow Jews. Becker is a gifted storyteller much in the manner of Sholem Aleichem and Isaac Bashevis Singer.* The difference is that Becker's world was inhabited by human, not supernatural, demons. One concrete result of Jacob's invented news is that the suicide rate in the ghetto drops to zero. His lies instill hope. A movie based on the novel (with the same title) appeared in 1999.

Becker was born in Łódź, Poland, in 1937. Two years later the Nazis invaded Poland; consequently, the author's early childhood was spent, with his parents, in the Łódź ghetto. Following their deportation in 1943, Becker was sent with his mother first to Ravensbruck and then to Sachsenhausen where she died. His father survived Auschwitz and was reunited with the young boy in 1945. Becker's father raised his son in East Berlin (German Democratic Republic) where the future novelist received little or no instruction about his Jewish identity. Becker obtained his high school diploma in 1955. Two years later he joined the Socialist Unity Party. A prolific writer of screen and television plays, as well as short stories, Becker soon became disillusioned with the GDR's pressure on writers to depict the regime in glowing terms. He was expelled from Humboldt University in 1960 and, later, from the Socialist Party. He left the GDR in 1977 and went to live in West Berlin, where he refrained from political activity. West Berlin remained Becker's primary place of residence until his death.

Becker writes in a distinctive, traditional Jewish style. Like the Yiddish mode of Sholem Aleichem, he makes use of aphorisms such as "a bargain is a bargain, and one man alone can't ruin another man" (p. 28), the wisdom of which seem undercut by the grimness of the Jewish situation. Furthermore, his use of repeated phrases such as "Jacob goes to work with a light heart" (p. 126) in a single paragraph has about it the style of a rabbinic incantation. The Łódź ghetto setting serves as a leveler of the Jewish people; the assimilated Leonard Schmidt, who was brought to the ghetto "because his great-grandfather attended the synagogue and his parents had been stupid enough to have him circumcised, although by now they had forgotten why" (p. 107), works together with the devout Herschel Schtamm who prays regularly to God.

The philosophical heart of Becker's novel centers on the question of the role of hope in a hopeless situation. Unlike Tadeusz Borowski*, whose narrator believes that hope kills, the unnamed narrator of *Jacob the Liar* is convinced that "hope must not be allowed to fade away, otherwise [the Jews] won't survive" (p. 60). The untutored Jacob has an ally in the person of Professor Kirschenbaum, a distinguished physician and a secularist. Kirschenbaum, who understands that Jacob has no radio, nevertheless admonishes him, "Well done Mr. Heym, carry on, there is no medicine people need as much as hope" (p. 164). Indeed Jacob's last name, Heym, may be read as Hayim, the Hebrew word for life. Nevertheless, the pressure of having to invent news for his ghetto colleagues compels Jacob to invent a new story: his radio is broken. The murder of Herschel Schtamm so demoralizes the Jewish people that Jacob views it as the impetus to "repair" his radio.

Becker's novel reveals the existence of deceptions on many levels. There is, for example, the fatal deception of the Jewish people by the Nazis who tell their victims to pack a suitcase for Auschwitz. Lina, the young girl who becomes Jacob's ward after her parents are deported, is deceived by Jacob who—hidden behind a partition—"broadcasts" an interview with Winston Churchill. Mischa also deceives his fiancée, Rosa, by intentionally misleading her about the reason she was told to go home only one hour after reporting to work; he knows that her parents are being deported. In the end, however, the deception cannot succeed. Rosa sees her parents being marched to the deportation center. She is the first in the community to doubt Jacob's story. Furthermore, when Jacob tells his friend Kowalski the truth about the radio, Kowalski commits suicide.

Jacob the Liar raises many disturbing moral questions. For example, the reader is invited to speculate on the use of a situational morality in which lying is preferable to telling the truth. Furthermore, Becker's protagonist, true to his name, chooses life over suicide. While he lacks the nobility of character displayed by Professor Kirschenbaum who took poison rather than treat the Nazi commandant, Jacob's dispensing of the "news" made it possible for the Jews to believe that they had a future.

SELECTED WORKS BY THE AUTHOR
Der Boxer. Rostock: Hinstorff, 1976; *Bronstein's Children*. Trans. Leila Vennewitz. San Diego: Harcourt Brace Jovanovich, 1988; *Jacob the Liar*. Trans. Leila Vennewitz. New York: Plume, 1997; *Five Stories*. Ed. David Rock. New York: St. Martin's Press, 1993; *Sleepless Days*. Trans. Leila Vennewitz. New York, 1979.

Alan L. Berger

Berg, Mary (1924–)

Mary Berg's *Warsaw Ghetto: A Diary* (1945) is the first full eyewitness account of life in the Warsaw ghetto to appear in print and the first memoir to report, though not firsthand, that the Germans were using gas to kill the Jews deported from Warsaw. It was published in Yiddish, in serialized form, in the fall of 1944 by S.L. Shneiderman (1906–1996); an English translation by Norbert Guterman (1900–1984) came out in February of the next year. Thus the diary appeared before the war was over in Europe and before Berg could have known the enormity of the German crimes and full details of the Final Solution.

Her work is a universal testimony of human suffering and a tribute to human dignity and initiative. It is the only extant account by a young girl in the Warsaw ghetto and is also rare as testimony to the effects of trauma on youth *in extremis*. Unlike most Warsaw ghetto diaries, Berg's is a private account, not intended for publication. Since 1945, it has been published in seven languages and a play, *A Bouquet of Violets*, based on the diary, was performed in Warsaw in 1986. Excerpts from the diary have also appeared in documentary films, photo collections, histories, and an anthology of ghetto diaries.

Berg was born Miriam Wattenberg in Łódź, Poland, in 1924. Her mother was a naturalized American citizen, and her father was a Polish citizen and prosperous art dealer in Łódź. Berg began to write on October 10, 1939, recounting her family's flight to Warsaw during the German invasion. When they returned home to Łódź, she continued to record her experiences. In December, she and her sister returned to Warsaw. The entries grew more frequent with the ghetto's closure in 1940. She shared them with friends, while recording her daily life and theirs, along with testimony of the events they witnessed in the ghetto.

On July 17, 1942, the Wattenbergs were interned with other foreign nationals in the Pawiak Prison. Berg witnessed the deportations from the ghetto to the *Umschlagplatz* from the prison windows. She began to rewrite some sections which were in "abridged form." She managed to take her diary along when American citizens were sent to an internment camp in Vittel, France, on January 17, 1943. It accompanied her on the exchange ship when she and her family were repatriated.

Shneiderman, a young reporter for the *Jewish Morning Journal*, was on the dock waiting when the *S.S. Gripsholm* arrived in Jersey City on March 16, 1944. He and his wife, Eileen, were born in Poland and fled the Nazis from occupied France in 1940. He met Berg and learned she had brought along her diary, recorded in twelve small notebooks in Polish. He recalled later,

> In a state of awe I read the tiny letters on the densely written pages of her notebooks. Afraid that the books might some day fall into the hands of the Nazis, Mary wrote her notes in a kind of shorthand, using only initials for the people whose names she mentioned. She never used the word "Nazi." Instead, she wrote "they." (*Dziennik zu Getta*, pp. 8–9)

He worked closely with Berg for the next several months, helping her decipher the notebooks and asking her "to explain certain facts and situations which otherwise would have been puzzling not only for American readers but for readers through the world" and amending some spellings. When Berg knew persons had perished, they added full names.

Of particular interest are her detailed accounts of cultural activities, secret schooling, the Graphic Arts school she attended, and social institutions such as the house committees and youth circles. Her acquaintances included "the golden youth" of the ghetto, young friends from Łódź, ghetto police, Judenrat officials, and the son of a Gestapo informer, one of the infamous "13," for whom she felt a revulsion which she did not totally understand. Other friends were apparently involved in the underground, and she admired the youthful *Halutzim*, but confessed she felt "powerless and cannot help anyone" (p. 92).

She describes, with remarkable vividness and a sensitivity beyond her age, the street scenes of the ghetto, the beggars, smuggling, German cruelty, the mad, and the "dreamers of bread" whose "eyes are veiled with a mist that belongs to another world" (p. 48). Although Berg and her family were spared the worst of the suffering owing to her mother's citizenship and the family's prosperity, she reproached herself and others around her for their privilege. She anguished at the sight of a hungry child, "I was overcome by a feeling of utter shame. I had eaten that day, but I did not have a piece of bread for that child" (p. 69). She also feared the impending separation from friends and relatives and knowingly questioned, "Have I the right to save myself and leave my closest friends to their bitter fate?" (p. 162).

SELECTED WORKS BY THE AUTHOR
Dziennik zu Getta Warszawskieg. Introd. S.L. Shneiderman, trans. Maria Salapska. Warsaw: Czytelnik, 1983. "Pages from a Warsaw Diary." *Contemporary Jewish Record* 7 (October-December, 1944): 497–510, 616–25; *Warsaw Ghetto: A Diary.* Ed. S.L. Shneiderman, trans. Norbert Guterman and Sylvia Glass. New York: L.B.. Fischer, 1945.

FOR FURTHER READING
Bard, Mitchell G., *Forgotten Victims: The Abandonment of Americans in Hitler's Camps.* Boulder, Colo.: Westview Press, 1994; Elbaum, Esther, "She Lived in the Warsaw Ghetto: An Interview with Mary Berg,"

Hadassah Newsletter (March-April, 1945): 20–21; Shulman, Abraham, *The Case of Hotel Polski*. New York: Holocaust Library, 1982.

Susan Lee Pentlin

Bitton-Jackson, Livia E. (1931–)

Livia Bitton-Jackson's memoir *Elli: Coming of Age in the Holocaust* (1980) is an important work of Holocaust literature which focuses attention on the crucial role played by the mother-daughter relationship in surviving Auschwitz. The winner of multiple awards—Christopher Award, Eleanor Roosevelt Humanitarian Award, and Jewish Heritage Award—*Elli* tells the tale of the fate of the Hungarian Jews, who were the last to be deported from their native land. In addition, the author details the stages by which the Jews "disappeared as human beings." Bitton-Jackson's description of the "anti-world" of Auschwitz raises crucial questions about the fate of identity under a genocidal regime. Furthermore, the book makes a distinctive contribution to understanding the fragile yet tenacious claim of Jewish tradition after the Shoah.

The author was born in Bratislava where her parents, Marcus and Laura Freedmann, owned a small grocery store. She and her older brother, Bubi, were raised in a traditional Jewish household. Shortly after she received the honors scroll on the last day of class in 1944, Bitton-Jackson and the Jews of Somorja were deported. The author entered Auschwitz at the age of thirteen. Her mother and brother survived. Mr. Freedmann died in Bergen-Belsen two days before the camp was overrun by the British. Bitton-Jackson immigrated to America in 1951. She received a Ph.D. and was a professor of Hebrew and Judaic Studies at various universities including Lehman College and Tel Aviv University. She also served as dean of students at Hunter College. Livia Bitton-Jackson currently resides in Israel.

The subtitle of Bitton-Jackson's book, *Coming of Age in the Holocaust*, invites the reader to compare his or her own coming of age with that of the author. For example, soon after deportation, the young girl witnessed the burning of Bibles and Torah scrolls. She muses, "Our identity. Our soul. Weightless speckles of ash rising, fleeing the flames into nothingness" (p. 38). Underscoring the existential significance of this experience, David Patterson observes that it is "as though being itself were consumed in those flames" (p. 96). Furthermore, the murder of the books precedes the murder of the Jews themselves; "the name and the essence, the very life of the Jew also ascend on the column of smoke and ash" (Patterson, p. 96). Bitton-Jackson heard the mournful intonation of her town's rabbi who proclaimed, "Woe to the generation which witnesses its Torah burned to ashes!"(pp. 38–39).

Bitton-Jackson, like Elie Wiesel*, reports the naiveté of Europe's Jews when faced with the Nazi decree mandating the wearing of a yellow star. For example, Laura Freedmann—much in the manner of Shlomo Wiesel—observes, "[The yellow star] does not kill or condemn. It does not harm. It only means that you are a Jew" (p. 16). Yet the fate of the Jews had already been sealed. The author writes that as the Jews of Somorja were deported to Nagymagyar, they passed "as nonexistent shadows [moving] on the streets unrecognized, unacknowledged, unseen" (pp. 19–20). Later, upon arrival at Auschwitz, Elli vomits; perhaps this is the only appropriate response to the death factory. She encounters the notorious Dr. Josef Mengele who, taken by the young girl's blond hair, decides to permit her to live and tells the youth to say that she is sixteen.

The process of dehumanization and death compete with the instinct for life and nurture in Bitton-Jackson's work. For example, upon seeing the "sexless," "deranged" inmates with their "blank stares," the young girl at first thought that Auschwitz must be an "asylum for the mentally ill" (p. 58). Called animals and whores by the guards, the women were shaved and dehumanized. Yet, Bitton-Jackson, like Erna F. Rubinstein,* reports that this process resulted in feeling that "a burden was lifted. The burden of individuality. Of associations. Of identity. Of the recent past" (p. 60). Not only the body, but the soul as well is "naked, exposed, abused." The nakedness of the women is a metaphysical nudity. The author describes the primal fear of "decimation," a process whereby the Nazis would murder every tenth person. Inmates never knew where their Nazi tormentors would begin counting.

The instinct for nurture was carefully bound to gender. For instance, the women—much as in Cara DeSilva's (ed.) *In Memory's Kitchen*—would trade recipes describing meals they cooked at home "in prehistoric times" (p. 79). The young girls among the women prisoners would recount stories of their first loves, dates, and boyfriends. One day, a bunk collapses on Livia's mother, paralyzing her. When Elli attempts to help her mother, Mrs. Freedmann says, "Leave that white thing alone and help me" (p. 99). The "white thing" is her mother's leg. Ignoring a physician's statement that her mother will die, Elli takes Mrs. Freedmann to the infirmary. She faithfully speaks to her mother every day through knotholes in the wooden wall near her bed. Slowly and painfully her mother regains her strength. In the interim, Elli is "adopted" by a friend of her mother's who has a daughter Elli's age. "Amid the uncaring madness of Auschwitz," writes Elli, "I had found a pocket of love" (p. 102). Both Elli and Mrs. Freedmann manage to share their meager rations with Bubi.

Following the war, Livia reflects on the psychological and theological legacies of the Shoah. She recalls some moments of human freedom such as the time she was asked to recite her poetry in a cattle car taking Jews to Auschwitz. Yet she knows that Auschwitz remains beyond the understanding of those who were not there. "How," she wonders, "can anyone understand the aching that is Auschwitz? The compulsion to fill the void that is Auschwitz? The loss. The total, irreconcilable loss" (p. 211). While her mother retains her faith in God, telling her children that they "will eat only kosher, once again" (p. 195), for Livia, it is different. She belongs to the "void" that is Auschwitz.

Elli is a memoir that engages the reader in a reflection on the horrors of the Third Reich's kingdom of death. Bitton-Jackson's novel raises its readers' consciousness of what it meant to be a Jew under Nazism, and what it means to be human after Auschwitz.

SELECTED WORKS BY THE AUTHOR
Elli: Coming of Age in the Holocaust. New York: Times Books, 1980; *My Bridges of Hope: Searching for Life and Love After Auschwitz.* New York: Simon and Schuster, 1999.

FOR FURTHER READING
Berger, Alan L. "Holocaust Narratives and Human Freedom," CD ROM, International Society for the Study of European Ideas, 1999; DeSilva, Cara, ed., *In Memory's Kitchen: A Legacy from the Women of Terezin.* Trans. Bianca Steiner Brown. Northvale, N.J.: J. Aronson, 1996; Patterson, David, *Sun Turned to Darkness: Memory and Recovery in the Holocaust Memoir.* Syracuse, N.Y.: Syracuse University Press, 1999.

Alan L. Berger

Bor, Josef (1906–1979)

Josef Bor's name is associated with one of the most talked about, most written about European locales: Terezín (Theresienstadt since the Nazi occupation of Czechoslovakia), a town that symbolizes both the tragic fate of Czech Jewry and the incredible capacity of the human spirit to remain resilient in spite of the degradation, deception, and humiliation to which it was subjected by the Germans. Bor was among the approximately 50,000 Jews of Czechoslovakia's prewar Jewish population of about 300,000 to have survived the Holocaust. An inmate in the concentrationary universe for close to three years, he made it his mission to keep the memory of the Jewish martyrs alive through his fictional and autobiographical writings. To do so took courage, for in the postwar years, the Czech Communist government followed the dictates issued by Soviet Russia to fold the Jewish Holocaust into the general fabric of World War II history, denying the Jews the right to their own history, culture, and identity.

Josef Bor (Bondy) was born on July 2, 1906, in Ostrava, Czechoslovakia, into the family of a well-known jurist and community leader, Dr. Julius Bondy. Following in the footsteps of his father, he studied law in Brno and graduated with a law degree in 1924. While practicing law in Ostrava, he pursued graduate studies in philosophy and earned a Ph.D. in 1929. On June 5, 1942, Bor, along with his entire family, was deported to Theresienstadt, where he was interned for over two years, and then shipped to Buchenwald and Auschwitz-Birkenau from which he was liberated in 1945. None of the members of his immediate family survived. Refusing to give in to despair, Josef Bor set up residence in Prague, remarried, raised two sons, and pursued his legal career, first at the Ministry of Defense and later at the Ministry of Industry. He died in 1979.

Bor's wartime experiences and losses weighed heavily upon him. He recorded them in his autobiography *Opustená Panenka* (The abandoned doll), published to wide acclaim in 1961. Two years later, encouraged by his success and at the urging of fellow Terezín survivors, he published *Terezín Requiem*, a semifictional rendition of true events and characters associated with the flourishing of arts, and music in particular, in the Terezín concentration camp. It recreates the efforts of Raphael Schachter, the gifted founder of the Chamber Music Opera in prewar Prague, to engage in a seemingly paradoxical undertaking of playing Giuseppe Verdi's *Requiem*, a Catholic church service for the dead, in a Jewish ghetto sung and performed by Jewish inmates destined for extinction.

Terezín is as much a character in the novel as its protagonist, Raphael Schachter. In Bor's rendition, the town, with its population constantly in flux, symbolizes the precariousness of Jewish existence. Hope of survival is inevitably followed by despair and death. This existential duality, as Bor makes clear from the very start of the novel, is paralleled by the duality of functions assigned to the ghetto by Reinhard Heydrich, the protector of Bohemia and Moravia, and one of the architects of the Final Solution: on the one hand, a transit place for Jews from Czechoslovakia and other European countries on their way to the death camps; on the other, a place of deception designed to fool the world and the Red Cross into believing that the ghetto was a cultural center under the benevolent care of the Germans. The opposite, of course, was true. Of the 141,000 Jews shipped to the ghetto, close to 34,000 died of starvation,

disease, and brutality, and 88,000 perished in the death camps. Among the latter was Raphael Schachter and the entire choir and orchestra that helped him transform a prayer for the dead into a hymn celebrating life and hope.

Willfully oblivious to the Nazi desire to create a Potemkin village, and possessed by what can only be termed as a supernatural longing to create in the face of destruction, musicians and painters, writers and educators of Terezín, pondered "deeply the fundamental questions of life and death" (p. 8), giving birth to new musical compositions, poetry, and paintings that helped them and their audiences to heal the ruptures caused by the war and undermine the Nazi drive to subjugate their art to totalitarian purposes. Bor's novel is permeated by his awareness of Verdi's passion for justice, his belief in the "nobility of the soul," and his conviction that "the artist must look into the future and must not be frightened by the darkness that is all around." Bor must have cherished the thought that Verdi's *Requiem*, never actually intended to be performed as a church service, was a tribute to Alesandro Manzoni, a noted Italian writer, dedicated, as Verdi was, to the cause of justice.

Bor's protagonist, Raphael Schachter, was repulsed by the injustice and inhumanity he witnessed around him. In spite of frequent doubts and despair, he worked tirelessly for eighteen months to create what he termed a "new" and "different" requiem, one that at its core would be imbued "with a fanatical faith in historical justice here in this world" (p. 14), rather than in the world to come, as promised by the Christian requiem. Sung by Jewish inmates in front of Adolf Eichmann and his cohorts, Verdi's *recordare, confutatis maladictis,* the *dies irae,* and the *libera me* assume a meaning Verdi could not have imagined them to carry. They reflect the pain Schachter felt when he saw his choir decimated several times during the eighteen months of rehearsals and its members sent to death camps. Their call is to remember and record the crimes perpetrated against the seed of Abraham. They condemn the killers and their evil deeds and sentence them to hell. They are a plea for deliverance and a call for protest. In Schachter's rendition, *Libera me!* becomes

Li-be-ra-nos! Li-be-ra-nos! "Three strokes short, one long. Beethoven's strokes of fate!" (p. 111).

Schachter's *Requiem* is a triumph of the human spirit. So is Joseph Bor's *Terezín Requiem*, his only work translated into English.

SELECTED WORKS BY THE AUTHOR
Terezín Requiem. Trans. Edith Pargeter. New York: Knopf, 1963.

FOR FURTHER READING
Karas, Joza. *Music in Terezín*: 1941–1945. New York: Beaufort Books, 1985.

Asher Z. Milbauer

Borowski, Tadeusz (1922–1951)

Tadeusz Borowski was a Polish non-Jewish writer whose searing reflections on his imprisonment in Auschwitz have universal importance. His writings make clear that in addition to destroying human beings, the death camps also obliterated all vestige of prewar moral codes. Borowski adopted an ironic tone in writing about the routinized extermination of human beings in Auschwitz: hope kills. Those who survived the camps, attests Borowski, have an obligation: "The first duty of Auschwitzers is to make clear just what a camp is." This obligation, however, entails a moral judgment as well: "But let them not forget that the reader will unfailingly ask: But how did it happen that you survived?" (Kott, Introduction, p. 22). In *This Way for the Gas, Ladies and Gentlemen*, his posthumously published collection of short stories, the author illustrates what the literary critic Andrzej Wirth terms a "hero deprived of all choice." "The tragedy," continues Wirth, "lies not in the necessity of choosing but in the impossibility of making a choice" (cited by Langer, *Versions*, p. 104).

Borowski was born in Zhitomir (Russian Ukraine) to Polish parents. Imprisoned first in Auschwitz and, subsequently, in Dachau, the author had intimate knowledge of the brutality of both Nazis and Communists. His father was taken to a labor camp above the Arctic Circle to dig the White Sea Canal when the boy was four years old. Four years later, his mother was exiled to Siberia. During this time the boy was raised by an aunt. The family was reunited in Warsaw in 1934. Borowski studied at a Franciscan boarding school because his impoverished parents could not afford to send him elsewhere. When the Germans occupied Poland, they decreed that Poles were forbidden to attend secondary schools and college. Consequently, Borowski studied in underground classes, worked as a night watchman, and began writing poetry; several of his poems were clandestinely published.

Caught in the same German trap that snared his fiancée, Borowski spent two months in a prison cell near the Warsaw ghetto. From this vantage point, he was able to witness the ghetto's liquidation. He and his fiancée were deported to Auschwitz in 1943. In one sense, they were fortunate because several weeks earlier it had been decreed that non-Jews were no longer to be gassed. In the summer of 1944 Borowski was sent first to a camp near Stuttgart, then to Dachau. Freed when the American army overran the camp, Borowski went to Berlin and Paris. Ultimately he returned to Warsaw and eventually married his fiancée who had returned from Sweden. In 1948 he published two volumes, *Pożegnanie z Maria* (Farewell to Maria) and *Kamienny Świat* (World of stone). The author consciously identifies himself as the protagonist in *This Way for the Gas, Ladies and Gentlemen*. Shortly after his wife gave birth to their daughter, and just shy of his thirtieth birthday, Borowski committed suicide by gassing himself.

Borowski, like many survivors, views himself as a messenger of the dead. He writes about the victims being taken to the gas chambers that they "begged the orderlies loading them into the crematorium trucks to remember what they saw. And to tell the truth about mankind to those who do not know it" (p. 175). Of what does this truth consist? The author reports the radical inversion of human relations engendered by the death camps. For example, in the title story, a young woman—knowing that women with small children were sent immediately to be gassed—ignores her pleading child. Andrei, a Russian prisoner, eyes "glassy from vodka and the heat," chokes the woman, lifts her in the air and "heaves her on to the truck like a heavy sack of grain," throwing the child after her (p. 43). An SS man standing nearby exclaims, "Gut gemacht, good work. That's the way to deal with degenerate mothers" (p. 43).

Two responses to this unspeakably cruel scene deserve notice. Andrei, after telling the SS man to shut up, takes more swallows of vodka from a canteen hidden under a pile of rags. He then passes the canteen to the narrator who reports that he feels like throwing up. In Auschwitz it was better if one did not have a conscience. Witnessing suffering on an unprecedented scale makes the narrator neither spiritually strong nor empathic. Rather, it literally sickens him.

Borowski's deft use of irony is especially prominent in the story "Auschwitz, Our Home (A Letter)," written as an epistle to his girlfriend incarcerated in the women's section of the camp. Borowski reports that ten thousand men watched as several trucks full of naked women passed by. The women pleaded, "Save us! We are going to the gas chambers! Save us!" Not one of the ten thousand men either made a move or lifted a hand (p. 116). Later on in the same story the narrator comments on the role of hope in the life of death camp inmates. Hope for a better world, which he now realizes was "naïve and immature," is what

makes people go without murmur to the gas chambers, keeps them from risking a revolt, paralyses them into numb inactivity. It is hope that compels man to hold on to one more day of life, because that day may be the day of liberation. Ah, and not even the hope for a different, better world, but simply for life, a life of peace and rest. Never before in the history of mankind has hope been stronger than man, but never also has it done so much harm as it has in this war, in this concentration camp. We were never taught how to give up hope, and this is why today we perish in gas chambers. (pp. 121–22)

The prisoners do, however, have one strong point, their great number: "the gas chambers cannot accommodate all of us" (p. 113).

Auschwitz was not only the present but also the future. One of Borowski's books of poetry, *Wherever the Earth*, written in Polish, envisioned the extermination of the human race. The author pursues this theme in "The World of Stone." Here the narrator has a surrealistic vision of twisted and mangled corpses, "this gigantic stew concocted out of the human crowd, flows along the street, down the gutter, and seeps into space with a loud gurgle, like water into a sewer" (p. 179). Auschwitz is humanity's destiny. Like the suicides of several other writer/survivors, including Paul Celan* and Jean Améry,* Borowski's suicide reveals that the power of the Shoah to destroy life continued well beyond the event itself.

SELECTED WORKS BY THE AUTHOR
Kamienny Świat. Krakow: Czytelnik, 1948; *Pożegnanie z Maria*. Warsaw: Panstwawy Instytut Wydawniczy, 1961; *This Way for the Gas, Ladies and Gentlemen*. Trans. Barbara Vedder, Introduction by Jan Kott. New York: Viking Press, 1967.

FOR FURTHER READING
Kott, Jan, Introduction to *This Way for the Gas, Ladies and Gentlemen*; Langer, Lawrence, *Art from the Ashes*. New York: Oxford University Press, 1995; Langer, Lawrence, *Versions of Survival*. Albany: SUNY Press, 1982, pp. 103–24; Wirth, Andrzej, "A Discovery of Tragedy: The Incomplete Account of Tadeusz Borowski," trans. Adam Czerniawki, *Polish Review* 12 (Summer 1967): 43–52.

Alan L. Berger

Borzykowski, Tuvia (1911–1959)

Tuvia Borzykowski's memoir, *Tsvishn falndike vent*, 1949 (*Between Tumbling Walls*, 1976) contains one of Holocaust literature's most detailed accounts of the fate of Warsaw and its Jews. It is important not only as a literary work but also for its detailed account of the inside workings of Jewish resistance against the Nazis in Warsaw.

Born in 1911 in the Polish town of Radomsk, Tuvia Borzykowski was a member of the Jewish Fighting Organization in Warsaw and a participant in the Warsaw ghetto uprising, which took place from April 19 to May 8, 1943. One of the last ghetto fighters to get out, he managed to escape through a sewage pipe.

After going into hiding for more than a year, he fought in the Warsaw Polish uprising in the spring and summer of 1944. In 1949 he emigrated to Israel, where he died in 1959.

Borzykowski's memoir covers the period from September 1942 to January 1945. Beginning with the founding of the Jewish Fighting Organization in the Warsaw ghetto and ending with the liberation of the city, the memoir covers three stages of resistance in Warsaw. The first stage runs from January 1943, after hundreds of thousands of Warsaw's Jews had already perished in Treblinka, to May 1943, with the crushing of the uprising. Next Borzykowski offers a detailed account of his involvement in the Polish revolt of April–May 1944, when, as he states it, Jewish heroism was at its height. The final stage of resistance began in August 1944, when the remnants of the Jewish Fighting Organization and other Jews joined in the Polish uprising against the Nazis.

Borzykowski's work as a wartime activist began in 1940, when he was summoned to Warsaw to work with Hehaluts, the organization whose mission was to prepare young Jewish men and women for emigration to Palestine. Borzykowski was also working with Dror, the Zionist-Socialist youth movement, at the time. He joined the Jewish Fighting Organization just after the occurrence of the massive deportations to the murder camps in the summer of 1942. When the war ended, Borzykowski devoted himself to Holocaust education; soon after he joined Kibbutz Lochamey Hagettaot (Ghetto Fighters' Kibbutz) in 1949, he and others founded the Ghetto Fighters' House, an institute devoted to research and documentation on Jewish resistance during the Holocaust.

Published in Yiddish in Poland in 1949, Borzykowski's memoir was one of the first testimonies to emerge from the ashes of Warsaw. It is unusual in that it contains not only detailed accounts of his involvement in Jewish resistance, but also a diary Borzykowski kept while he was in hiding in "Aryan" Warsaw from May 17, 1943, to July 27, 1944. After the uprising, Borzykowski made his way into the forest, where he stayed for about a week. Then he decided to return to Warsaw to continue what resistance activity he could while hiding with a Jewish woman and her son, who were able to pass as non-Jews.

Borzykowski's writing is remarkable for its ability to convey a variety of moods which flooded him as he recorded what he was witnessing. He outlines, for example, the stark contrast between the two worlds separated by the ghetto wall; indeed, he is able to articulate very well the reality that the Nazis have created an anti-world alongside the world of humanity. The horror perpetrated in the ghetto spilled into the rest of Warsaw, where a few "fortunate" Jewish children, hidden while their parents were murdered, try to get used to living with their foster parents. "But still," according to Borzykowski, "they are constantly aware of the fact that they have no right to live" (p. 121).

In the diary contained in his memoir, moreover, Borzykowski reminds his reader that Jews in hiding died every day from the very harsh conditions of their hiding places. "I no longer remember that there are such things as sky, sun, fresh air," he writes. "I cannot tell the difference between day and night" (p. 129). Thus Borzykowski reveals that the Nazis annihilated not only the Jews but also the sun and the sky over the Jew, the world that had a place for the Jew, and any time that the Jews could call *life* time.

SELECTED WORKS BY THE AUTHOR
Between Tumbling Walls. Trans. Mendel Kohansky. Tel Aviv: Ghetto Fighters' House and Hakibbutz Hameuchad, 1972.

David Patterson

C

Celan, Paul (1920–1970)

One of the most important German-language poets of the post-Holocaust world, Paul Celan is also one of the most widely anthologized poets to emerge from the Holocaust. Although the difficulties of translation often hinder readers' access to such literature, the work of scholars and translators have opened Celan's poetry to the English-speaking world. Like many poets, moreover, his life and his poetry are so interwoven, that the two are of a piece.

Paul Celan was born Paul Antschel in 1920 in the multiethnic city of Czernowitz. Part of the Austro-Hungarian Empire at the time Antschel's parents were growing up, Czernowitz became Romanian territory in 1919 and was taken by the Soviet Union after World War II. Its population included Poles, Jews, Germans, Armenians, Hungarians, Romanians, Ukrainians, and Moldavians—each brought specific influences to the region's cultural terrain. Antschel spoke German at home, as did most well-educated Jews in Czernowitz, learned Hebrew in religious school, and studied German, Romanian, and French in secular schools. He also spoke Yiddish and later learned Russian and English as well.

While still in high school, Antschel became interested in literature and started to compose his own poetry. The rising anti-Semitism in Romania and the growing influence of the Third Reich pushed him toward other interests. In 1938, after graduating from high school, Antschel left Czernowitz for Tours, France, to study medicine. In the summer, he went home for a vacation. The outbreak of World War II, on September 1, 1939, thwarted his return to France. He stayed in Czernowitz and enrolled at the local university, taking up the study of Romance languages and literature. In June 1940, when the Romanians ceded the region to the Soviets, Russian troops overran the city. Despite the ensuing upheavals, Antschel remained at the university.

The explosions on June 22, 1941, however, changed his life brutally. The Reich invaded the Soviet Union, and the occupying German troops arrived in Czernowitz a few days later. Setting synagogues afire and killing thousands of people during the first twenty-four hours of the occupation, neither the Germans nor their local sympathizers showed any sign of mercy. Anti-Jewish legislation was swiftly enacted and accompanied by violence of unimaginable savagery. Jews were identified, rounded up, deported, and murdered.

During the first wave of deportations, the poet's parents escaped from the ghetto; Antschel himself was called up for forced labor service and put to work in a camp at the Prut River. Ill-clothed, exhausted, and hungry, he still composed poetry. After a few months of grueling service, he returned to Czernowitz. When, in the summer of 1942, deportations started anew, Antschel went into hiding, but his parents refused to do so. By the time he returned, their apartment was empty: his mother and father had been rounded up and deported to the camps in Transnistria. For as long as he lived, Antschel blamed himself for their demise. Had he gone with them, he told people, he could have saved them. But he was wrong. The fate of the Jews in Transnistria was sealed. Antschel's father died of typhus during the fall of 1942; a few months later, his mother was shot in the back of the neck. Learning their fate from returning relatives, Antschel was shaken to the core. He would never recover.

During the summer of 1942, Antschel was called again to work in a forced labor camp, shoveling dirt, stones, and rocks under inhuman conditions. Yet again, despite hardship, he continued to compose poems. Now, as before, he believed that he might be able to touch others with his poems and that out of this encounter mutual understanding might grow. This belief stayed with him until the end of his life; when he lost it, he could live no more.

Antschel returned to Czernowitz in the winter of 1944. Soon thereafter, the Red Army reoccupied the city. By now, the poet feared both Russian anti-Semitism and life under the Soviets. He left Czernowitz and escaped to Romania. In Bucharest, he found a job as a reader for a publisher, undertook poetry translations, discovered literary counterparts, and composed his own lyrics. While staying in the city, from April 1945 until December 1947, he changed his name first from Antschel to Ancel and then to its anagram, Celan, a name that recalls his multiethnic origins. There was yet another choice the poet felt he had to make: he decided to write in German, the language of his mother; the language he spoke at home in his childhood and youth; the language of his first rhymes, songs, and fairy tales; the language that shaped his life and culture, that affected the cadence of his voice and his lyrical vision, as well as his poetic sensibilities. There was a problem, however. By the late 1940s, German was to Celan no longer just his mother tongue; it was the "murderer's-tongue" as well. He had to overcome this hurdle. "There's nothing in the world for which a poet will give up writing," he said later, "not even

when he is a Jew and the language of his poems is German" (Rosenthal, 402–3).

Over the years, all of Celan's poetry collections were published in Germany: *From Treshhold to Treshhold* (1955); *Speech-Grille* (1959); *The No One's Rose* (1963); *Breath-Turn* (1967); *Threadsuns* (1968); *Light-Force* (1970); *Snow-part* (1971); and *Homestead of Time* (1976). By the end of the 1950s, his poems had penetrated German literary life. He received the Literature Prize of the City of Bremen in 1958 and the greatest German literary award, the Büchner Prize, in 1960. But success did not seem to alleviate the poet's anguish over his loss. Forty-nine-years old, in and out of mental hospitals, watching the breakup of his marriage, and concerned about the future of his poetry, Celan felt he had reached the end of his road. He committed suicide in Paris by drowning himself in the Seine on April 20, 1970.

Celan's poetry emerges from the deepest suffering of his life, going back to the wounds he bore upon the loss of his mother and father. In "Winter," for example, the speaker relives his mother's death, as he recalls the snow-covered countryside of the Ukraine and summons his mother, asking, "What would come, Mother: wakening or wound?" (Felstiner, 17). In the lyrics of "Black Flakes," the same landscape returns, offering an imaginary dialogue between mother and son and revealing the young man's heart-rending grief: "Autumn bled all away, Mother, snow burned me through" (Felstiner, 19). And in "Aspen Tree," penned after the war, the speaker moves the images back and forth, between the world of the Ukraine and that of home. Gesturing toward a gap that remains unredeemably open, he laments, "My gentle mother cannot return" (Hamburger, 39).

In Bucharest, Celan first published in Romanian what has since become the most celebrated anthologized poem of the Holocaust, one of the greatest artistic creations of the twentieth-century: "Death Fugue" (1947). Re-creating this piece in German, he published it in his first collection, *The Sand from the Urns* (1948). Besides its extraordinary poetic qualities, "Death Fugue" has become the source of widespread literary disputes. Initiated by the German social philosopher Theodor Adorno, who said that writing poetry after Auschwitz is barbaric because such work would purify and aestheticize the *tremendum*, numerous critical discussions have arisen over the past fifty years, elaborating on both the truth and fallacy of this statement, analyzing the nature of literary treatments of atrocity, and taking stances for or against a purely moral, purely historical, or a purely aesthetic approach toward the literature of the Shoah. While these ongoing discussions have not yet resolved the issue, "Death Fugue" continues to affect multitudes of readers with its metaphorical power, visionary force, and extraordinary counterpuntal structure. One example is the "black milk of daybreak" that the prisoners drink day and night (Hamburger, 60). Juxtaposing the world of the Jews with that of death, "a master from Germany," the piece ends in a "stretto," with all voices appearing in close succession, interconnected, intertwined, yet irreconcilably divided from one another.

Celan also prepared a manuscript of ninety-three poems for publication in Bucharest, but with Soviet domination threatening anew, the poet saw no future in Romania. As soon as the borders started to close, he fled to Vienna. There he met a number of literati, but he did not find what he had hoped to find. Paris was different. There he did not feel urged to wonder about what people did during the war.

His next collection, *Poppy and Remembrance*, came out in Stuttgart in 1952. That same year he married Gisèle de Lestrange, and his life began to take a positive turn. But this change did not alter his frame of mind. He was burdened with the memory of the past and with an anguished awareness of his parents' deaths, his murdered people in Czernowitz, his own ancient Jewish roots, and his experience of exile. He composed poetry to contain his pain. Based on poets such as Stéphane Mallarmé, Arthur Rimbaud, Paul Éluard, and Rainer Rilke, however, his literary tradition insisted on using words that illuminate one another reciprocally, functioning in relationship to each other rather than representing the things of the world. But how could the war the Germans waged against the Jews be forgotten? How could it not be talked

about? And how could the poet's past, his sense of loss, and the memory of his spiritual-cultural experience be communicated in a poem without "telling the story?"

To answer these questions, Celan invented a new means of communication, a new language, out of his personal experience. Coming from the "outside" to German, he broke words down to their constituent elements, changing their syntax, transforming their cadence, juxtaposing foreign terms against them, and inventing new poetic relationships. Touching directly on his roots and deepest resources, his poems manifest a broad spectrum of allusions and wordplays, but they also offer a concrete basis of communication and understanding.

Throughout his life as a poet, the memory of the Shoah laid heavily on Celan: he could live neither in the present nor for the future. Nor could he convince himself of his poetry's ability to communicate the soul of the past. That was his tragedy. For his lyrics have now overcome the barriers of language and culture, more so than the lyrics of most poets of our age. Translated into a wide variety of tongues, they are regarded as monuments of twentieth-century art by most critics and poets of our time. Just as their author described poems like messages in a bottle which touch the lives of others, so does Celan's lyrical work reach its readers to create new literary, cultural, and human encounters of a large shaping significance.

SELECTED WORKS BY THE AUTHOR

Gesammelte Werke. Ed. Beda Allemann and Stefan Reichert, with Rolf Bücher. Frankfurt: Suhrkamp, 1983; *Last Poems: Paul Celan*. Trans. Katherine Washburn and Margret Guillemin. San Francisco: North Point Press, 1986; *Poems of Paul Celan*. Trans. Michael Hamburger. New York: Persea Books, 1988.

FOR FURTHER READING

Chalfen, Israel, *Paul Celan: A Biography of His Youth*. Trans. Maximilian Bleyleben. New York: Persea Books, 1991; Colin, Amy D., ed., *Argumentum e Silentio: International Paul Celan Symposium, Internationales Paul Celan-Symposium*. Berlin: Walter de Gruyter, 1987; Colin, Amy D., *Paul Celan: Holograms of Darkness*. Bloomington: Indiana University Press, 1991; Felstiner, John, *Paul Celan: Poet, Survi-*

vor, Jew. New Haven, Conn.: Yale University Press, 1995; Rosenthal, Bianca, "Quellen zum frühen Celan," *Monatshefte* 75/4 (1983): 402–3.

Zsuzsanna Ozsváth

Cohen, Arthur A. (1928–1986)

Arthur A. Cohen was a Jewish-American essayist, novelist, and theologian whose work raises crucial questions about the relationship between the Shoah and chosenness, theodicy and the Jewish vocation. At home in a variety of Judaic disciplines, the author wrote on Jewish-Christian relations, Jewish history, and the work of such thinkers as Martin Buber and Mordecai M. Kaplan. Cohen wrote six novels and edited another half-dozen books. In addition, he contributed numerous articles and short stories to many publications. His major Holocaust works are a novel, *In the Days of Simon Stern* (1973), and a theological treatise, *The Tremendum: A Theological Interpretation of the Holocaust* (1981). An original thinker, Cohen combined a thorough knowledge of the Bible with a keen sense of philosophical, philological, and theological nuances.

The author, who was born in New York City, received his B.A. and M.A. degrees from the University of Chicago. He cofounded Noonday Press and was the founder and president of Meridian Books. In addition, Cohen was a rare book dealer and an art historian. He served as chairman of the board at YIVO, as an advisory board member for the Institute for Advanced Judaic Studies at Brandeis University, and on the board of PEN American Center. In 1973 Cohen won the Edward Lewis Wallant Prize for *In the Days of Simon Stern*. In addition, his novel *An Admirable Woman* won a National Jewish Book Award in 1984 and, one year later, he received the William and Janice Epstein Award. The author was also a distinguished lecturer who spoke at many universities including Brown where, in 1975, he delivered the Tisch Lecture in Judaic theology.

In the Days of Simon Stern employs biblical, rabbinic, and mystical elements of Judaism in telling the tale of Simon Stern, a multimillionaire who rescues a remnant of those who survived Buchenwald. The very title of the novel, *In the Days* (*Be Yemei*), suggests biblical language and cadence. Divided into four main books, the novel comprises a series of tales within a tale to highlight crucial issues in the post-Auschwitz world. For example, an Elijah-like figure appears and tells Simon Stern "The Legend of the Last Jew on Earth." Set in Spain, the legend's protagonist, Don Raphael, appears to be Catholic but, in reality, is a descendent of *marranos* (secret Jews) forced by the Inquisition to conceal their Jewish identity. His eventual martyrdom—prior to his execution Don Raphael declares, "I endure and my endurance is an offense"—compels the reader to reflect on the continuities and discontinuities between Christian and Nazi Jew hatred, and on the millennial persistence of anti-Semitism.

The novel raises both philosophical and political issues concerning the implications of the Holocaust. For example, Simon Stern's messianic vocation is foretold by a female seer; she correctly predicts that he will be responsible for the deaths of his parents, and that he will attempt to save the Jewish people. In New York, Simon Stern becomes a multimillionaire, learns of the Jewish fate by attending a Madison Square Garden rally addressed by Chaim Wiezmann, rescues survivors of Buchenwald, and builds a compound for them in the lower East Side. The compound, a replica of King Solomon's Temple, represents an attempt to establish a small Bene Brak, a place of Jewish renewal as occurred after the destruction of the Jerusalem Temple. Borrowing from the Jewish mystical tradition, Cohen utilizes a variant of the seventeenth-century relationship between Shabbati Zvi, the false messiah, and Nathan of Gaza who pronounced Zvi the messiah. Simon Stern is told of his messianic vocation by a blind survivor named Nathan Gaza. Unlike his predecessor, blind Nathan sees with extraordinary clarity. He observes that Simon errs in attempting to "force the end," that is, he seeks to hasten the messianic era by assuming the role of deity.

Cohen also underscores the complex relationship between good and evil. Simon Stern engages in lengthy philosophical discussions with Janos Baltar. Baltar, a half-Jew, embodies evil and is described as a "homicidal maniac . . .

a kind of inverted Christ." The antagonist is responsible for an explosion which destroys the compound Stern had built to shelter the survivors. Afterward, Simon Stern renews his task of seeking to achieve a *tikkun* (repair or restoration) of the world at large. Following kabbalistic teachings, the protagonist understands that this work may last for centuries. Cohen portrays Simon Stern as a *lamed-vov zaddik*, one of the thirty-six hidden righteous men upon whose presence the world depends for its existence. Cohen's novel rigorously indicts American indifference to the Holocaust; only the Yiddish press tells what is happening to Europe's Jews. By its inaction and indifference, American bureaucracy aided and abetted Adolf Hitler's bureaucrats of death. Moreover, neither America nor Israel offers a safe haven to the Jewish people. For example, Simon Stern is a visionary who builds castles in the sky, but David Ben-Gurion "built castles in the sand." Redemption cannot, Cohen argues, occur in history.

Cohen explicitly views all Jews as survivors of the Holocaust. This fact is vitally significant for Jewish novelists. He writes that "every Jew who has endured to this hour is a survivor in fact or an accidental survivor at least" (*Tremendum*, p. 22). Theologically, the Holocaust, which Cohen terms the *tremendum* (abysmal evil), "ended forever one argument of history—whether the Jews are a chosen people. They are chosen, unmistakably, extremely, utterly" (p. 11). Consequently, the Holocaust, attests Cohen, forces Jews "as the first people of the human race (biblically speaking) to rethink the premises as once we thought out and affirmed them in the beginning. The flood then, fire and gas in our time. We begin again" (Notes, p. 32). From this, Cohen adduces a distinctive role for the post-Auschwitz novelist: "The novelist (not unlike the theologian) [is] the person empowered by facultative obligation to engage in the speculation of the ultimate moral questions" (Notes, p. 18).

SELECTED WORKS BY THE AUTHOR
The American Imagination After the War: Notes on the Novel, Jews, and Hope. Syracuse, N.Y.: Syracuse University Press, 1981; *In the Days of Simon Stern.* New York: Random House, 1973; *The Natu-*ral and the Supernatural Jew. New York: Behrman House, 1979; *The Tremendum: A Theological Interpretation of the Holocaust.* New York: Crossroad, 1981.

FOR FURTHER READING
Berger, Alan L., *Crisis and Covenant.* Albany: SUNY Press, 1985; Kremer, S. Lillian, *Witness Through the Imagination.* Detroit: Wayne State University Press, 1989.

Alan L. Berger

Cohen, Elie Aron (1909–1993)

An accomplished physician and psychologist, Dr. Elie A. Cohen wrote a memoir which is as much an exploration of the soul as it is a memory of the past. Titled *De Afgrond: Een Egodocument*, 1971 (*The Abyss: A Confession*, 1973), the memoir is intended to be "an *admonitory monument* which will continue to remind us of the depths of misery, madness, and criminality to which man is capable of descending" (p. 13). Cohen not only lived in those depths but wrote about them as a doctor and a psychologist in his *Het Duitse Concentratiekamp: Een Medische en Psychologische Studie*, 1952 (*Human Behavior in the Concentration Camp*, 1953). His other (untranslated) works dealing with the Holocaust kingdom include *De Negentien Treinen naar Sobibor*, 1979 (The death trains to Sobibor) and *Beelden uit de Nacht: Kampherinneringen*, 1992 (Images of the night: Memories of the camp).

Born in 1909 to a secular Jewish family in the Dutch town of Groningen, Cohen was a practicing physician when the Nazis seized control of the Netherlands on May 14, 1940. The Gestapo arrested him, his wife, and their son on August 13, 1943, while they were attempting to flee to Sweden. After a few months in the concentration camp at Amersfoort, the three of them were sent to Westerbork on December 8, 1942. On September 14, 1943, Cohen and his family were transported to Auschwitz, where his wife and four-year-old son were immediately selected for the gas chamber. Cohen worked as a prisoner-doctor in the Lunatics' Ward at Auschwitz until January 18, 1945, when he was evacuated with hundreds of others on the death march to Mauthausen. From Mauthausen he was taken to Melk and from Melk to Ebensee, which was liberated by American troops on May 6, 1945. Cohen returned to his native Holland where he pursued a career in psychology until his death in 1993.

In his memoir Cohen speaks with brutal honesty about himself and with a penetrating eye about the world around him. On his way to the camp at Amersfoort, for example, he observes people sitting in their homes sipping tea as hundreds of Jews are passing by on their way to unspeakable suffering and death. "What a strange thing it is," he writes, "that everyone should live so much for himself alone, and that you no longer care what's happening to someone else" (p. 45). Once in the camp, he realizes that such indifference is necessary for survival—and that is part of his confession: "You looked on, as though through a peephole, taking no part in things yourself" (p. 46). Other points of self-examination include his surprise at not being surprised by the news that his wife and child had been gassed, the madness of struggling to live when he has nothing to live for, his killing a patient who was a threat to the lives of others, and his refusal to provide a man on the way to the gas chamber with narcotics that may have made his dying easier.

The impact of Cohen's soul-searching and his deep sense of responsibility is to implicate the reader who encounters his text. Sitting comfortably at his tea as he looks on, the reader faces the question of what he stands for—and what he will not stand for—each time Cohen confesses a moral dilemma or a moral breakdown. Cohen goes farther than asking what is right and wrong: he explores the very ground of all right and wrong—and the crumbling of that ground: the *Afgrond*. Thus Cohen's memoir leaves the reader with a question not only of what he or she stands *for* but of what he or she stands *on*.

SELECTED WORKS BY THE AUTHOR
The Abyss: A Confession. Trans. James Brockway. New York: W.W. Norton, 1973; *Beelden uit de Nacht: Kampherinneringen.* Baarn, Netherlands: De Prom, 1992; *Human Behavior in the Concentration Camp.* Trans. M.H. Braaksma. Westport, Conn.: Greenwood Press, 1984; *De Negentien Treinen naar Sobibor.* Amsterdam: Elsevier, 1979.

David Patterson

Czerniaków, Adam (1880–1942)

On September 6, 1939, Adam Czerniaków made his first entry in a remarkable diary he kept for nearly three years. Written less than a week after Nazi Germany's invasion of his native Poland, which began World War II on September 1, 1939, Czerniaków's initial notation said, "I could not sleep from midnight to 5 in the morning" (p. 73). That sentence would be as fateful as it was brief, for this Jewish leader in Warsaw, Poland, found no rest from the Holocaust's devastation until he took his own life on July 23, 1942, shortly after writing in his diary for the last time. "It is 3 o'clock. So far 4,000 are ready to go," Czerniaków's final entry stated. "The orders," it went on to say, "are that there must be 9,000 by 4 o'clock" (p. 385). Recorded in his characteristically terse, matter-of-fact style, those orders signaled the beginning of the end for Warsaw's doomed Jewish ghetto. The destination awaiting most of its inhabitants was the Nazi killing center at Treblinka, which was located about fifty miles northeast of the city, near the Malkinia station on the main railroad line between Warsaw and Białystok.

After a three-week siege that destroyed or damaged 25 percent of Warsaw's buildings and killed or injured about 50,000 people, German troops occupied the city on September 29, 1939. The German persecution of Warsaw's Jews began immediately. Within days, it became Czerniaków's business to follow Nazi orders. On October 4, 1939, German authorities told him to set up a *Judenrat* (Jewish council). Initially, its twenty-four members would be responsible for taking a Jewish census and for helping to ghettoize Warsaw's Jews. The Germans put Czerniaków in charge of these ominous tasks because, on September 23, 1939, Colonel Stefan Starzynski, the city's mayor and civil defense commissar, had named him chairman of the Jewish community. That appointment filled a position left open when the previous chairman,

Maurycy Mayzel, fled Warsaw during the war's first week. Czerniaków's diary entry for this date observed that the city suffered from shortages of bread and meat. In response to his appointment as chairman of the Jewish community, he wrote, "A historic role in a besieged city. I will try to live up to it" (p. 76).

In the autumn of 1939, Czerniaków could scarcely have imagined the full significance of that pledge. Nevertheless, soon after the Germans ordered him to establish the Jewish council, he had premonitions that the burdens of his office would become more than he could bear. Czerniaków told his colleagues where a key to his desk drawer could be found. He explained that the drawer held a bottle containing lethal cyanide tablets. If the need arose, there was one for each of the twenty-four council members.

Before the German invasion changed his life, Czerniaków knew better times. Born in 1880 to a middle-class family in Warsaw, he completed his training as a chemical engineer in 1908. He married, and he and his wife, Niunia, had one child, a son named Jas. Although Czerniaków's background was assimilationist, he vigorously defended the interests of Jewish craftsmen and promoted vocational training for Jewish young people. Jewish artisans were among his key supporters when he served in the Warsaw Municipal Council from 1927 to 1934. They also backed his prewar appointment to the executive council of Warsaw's Jewish community, which eventually positioned him for the dubious distinction of heading the Jewish council in the Warsaw ghetto.

When the Germans invaded Poland in September 1939, Warsaw's Jewish population was the largest of any European city. Numbering 375,000, it constituted 30 percent of the city's total. As Jewish refugees arrived, that number approached 450,000. Within a few weeks of their occupation of Warsaw, the Germans made plans for a ghetto, but not until October 12, 1940–on the Jewish calendar it was Yom Kippur (the Day of Atonement)–did Czerniaków's diary record the order that "a ghetto is to be established." He was given a map that defined its area—about 3.5 square miles, which constituted only 2.4 percent of the city's territory. Czerniaków's October 12 diary entry further noted that "until

October 31 the resettlement will be voluntary, after that compulsory" (p. 206).

On November 16, 1940, the Warsaw ghetto was sealed. An 11.5-foot wall, about eleven miles long and topped with broken glass and barbed wire, surrounded it. Forced to build this wall at their own expense, the Jews, who were now trapped inside, faced rapidly deteriorating conditions–overcrowding (seven persons per room on average), starvation, lack of sanitation, disease, and a mounting death rate. In these dire straits, Czerniaków's multiple responsibilities were ultimately incompatible, because he could not really serve Jewish interests and German demands simultaneously. Repeatedly, Czerniaków confronted what the Holocaust scholar Lawrence L. Langer calls "choiceless choices." Such choices are neither normal nor made in circumstances of one's own choosing; they are "choices" that are forced and between options that are unacceptable or worse.

During the pre-ghetto months, the Germans held Czerniaków and his *Judenrat* colleagues responsible for obtaining Jewish workers for forced labor, for fulfilling demands for jewelry and furniture, and for collecting taxes and fines from the city's Jews. From time to time, his persistent efforts led the Germans to delay or modify their demands, but Czerniaków—sometimes beaten, frequently threatened, always abused by the Germans—was powerless to achieve any lasting victories or even to be relieved of his leadership burden.

The German authorities summoned Czerniaków at their whim, and he had to appear promptly. On January 26, 1940, the police informed him that Warsaw's Jews must pay a large fine, which would further impoverish his community's depleted economy. Severe reprisals—100 Jews would be shot—were the price for failure to meet the next morning's deadline. Czerniaków's diary notes that he unsuccessfully asked the Gestapo to cancel the fine, then to allow installment payments, and finally to release the Jews from snow removal, which would save wages that could be put toward the fine. "Nothing came of it," he wrote, but then Czerniaków's diary went on to say that he had made one more request. He asked the Germans to release him from the chairmanship "since I find it impossible to manage the Community under these abnormal conditions" (p. 111). Czerniaków understood the not-so-veiled threat when he was told that such a change would be "inadvisable."

Once the ghetto was sealed, Czerniaków and the Warsaw *Judenrat* were responsible for its welfare, administration, and infrastructure. Czerniaków oversaw a Jewish bureaucracy of 6,000 persons at its peak, which included offices to deal with housing, health, the ghetto's forced-labor economy, and law enforcement. Meanwhile, German policy systematically deprived the ghetto of the resources needed to sustain itself. While Czerniaków tried to cope with the deteriorating circumstances, opinions about him within the ghetto were mixed. His appointment of Joseph Szerynski, a Jew who had converted to Christianity, as head of the less-than-popular *Ordnungsdienst* (the ghetto police), was especially controversial. Yet, the overall appraisal of Czerniaków remains that he was a decent, well-intentioned man who worked from morning to night, month after month, to alleviate Jewish need.

As events unfolded, however, the ghetto was at best a temporary station between prewar freedom and wartime annihilation. By the spring of 1942, Jews were being deported and gassed at Chelmno and Belzec, Nazi killing centers on Polish soil, and two additional death camps—Sobibor and Treblinka—were under construction. Liquidation of the Warsaw ghetto was coming. Czerniaków might have sensed as much on April 29, 1942, for when his diary recorded that the Germans wanted ten maps and population figures for the Warsaw ghetto, those orders did foreshadow deadly actions. Even though the answers were evasive when he asked the Germans for confirmation, Czerniaków noted rumors about deportations by mid-July. On July 22, he learned the worst. All of Warsaw's Jews, "irrespective of sex and age, with certain exceptions, will be deported to the East" (p. 384). The Germans' stated intention was to hold Czerniaków and the *Judenrat* responsible for a daily deportation quota of 6,000 persons. By the time the first wave of deportations came to an end on September 12 (Rosh Hashanah, the Jewish New Year, in 1942), 254,000 of Warsaw's Jews had been murdered in Treblinka's gas chambers.

Czerniaków had hoped that orphans and other children might be exempted from deportation. When he finally realized that even they would not be spared, he went to his desk on July 23, not long after writing his last diary entry. On the Hebrew calendar, it was the 9th of Av, the anniversary of the destruction of the first and second Temples in Jerusalem in 586 B.C.E. and 70 C.E. Czerniaków reportedly wrote a note lamenting that the Germans were, in effect, demanding him to kill the children of his own people. Then he ended his life by using one of the cyanide tablets he had hidden in his desk drawer. The Germans had expected his signature to be on the deportation decree, but Czerniaków left it unsigned.

Although Czerniaków neither spread an alarm about the imminent deportations nor called for resistance against them, his suicide was widely interpreted as an act of protest. Had he lived, Czerniaków might have seen the heroic ghetto uprising led by Mordecai Anielewicz in April 1943, but it is unlikely that he would have escaped the ghetto's utter destruction. Almost half a million Jews had lived there. By the end of World War II, 99 percent of them were dead.

Adam Czerniaków was correct in September 1939 when he suggested that his role would be historic. The same can be said of his diary, which is a key document in the Warsaw ghetto's catastrophic chapter of Holocaust history. It consisted of nine 4 x 7–inch notebooks. Each could fit into Czerniaków's coat pocket. Relatively few of his associates knew about the diary, but it included more than 1,000 pages of his cramped handwriting.

Until Rosalina Pietkiewicz, a survivor of the Warsaw ghetto, purchased the diary from an unidentified source in 1959, its whereabouts was unknown. Since 1964 the original has been preserved by Yad Vashem, the Israeli Martyrs' and Heroes' Remembrance Authority, in Jerusalem. The fifth of the nine notebooks, covering the period from December 14, 1940, to April 22, 1941, remains missing.

Czerniaków's workdays began early. Many of his diary's entries begin with the phrase, "In the morning . . ." The Warsaw ghetto ran out of mornings, but the survival of Czerniaków's diary, which has been published in English, German, and Hebrew, as well as Polish, helps to ensure that the Holocaust history of Warsaw's Jews will be remembered.

SELECTED WORKS BY THE AUTHOR
The Warsaw Diary of Adam Czerniaków: Prelude to Doom. Ed. Raul Hilberg, Stanislaw Staron, and Josef Kermisz, trans. Stanislaw Staron. New York: Stein and Day, 1979.

FOR FURTHER READING
Berenbaum, Michael, *The World Must Know: The History of the Holocaust as Told in the United States Holocaust Memorial Museum.* Boston: Little, Brown, 1993; Gutman, Yisrael, *The Jews of Warsaw, 1939–1943: Ghetto, Underground, Revolt.* Trans. Ina Friedman. Bloomington: Indiana University Press, 1989; Roth, John K., et al., *The Holocaust Chronicle: A History in Words and Pictures.* Lincolnwood, Ill.: Publications International, 2000; Trunk, Isaiah. *Judenrat: The Jewish Councils in Eastern Europe Under Nazi Occupation.* New York: Stein and Day, 1977; Yahil, Leni. *The Holocaust: The Fate of European Jewry, 1932–1945.* Trans. Ina Friedman and Haya Galai. New York: Oxford University Press, 1990.

John K. Roth

D

Delbo, Charlotte (1913–1985)

The imperative to testify for those who died and the bonding of women who nurture each other are recurring themes in Charlotte Delbo's major work, a trilogy entitled *Auschwitz et Après*, 1995 (*Auschwitz and After*, 1995) comprising three separate volumes: *Aucun de nous ne reviendra*, 1965 (*None of Us Will Return*, 1968; retranslated in 1995); *Une Connaissance inutile*, 1970 (*Useless Knowledge*, 1995); and *Mesure de nos jours*, 1971 (*The Measure of Our Days*, 1995). All three volumes were translated and printed in English in one single volume, *Auschwitz and After*, in 1995. Delbo's last book, *La mémoire et les jours*, 1985 (*Days and Memory*, 1990), published shortly after her death, is an extension of the trilogy. This book, like the preceding ones, is composed of a series of incidents, images, poems, and reflections on the camp experience in which Delbo describes the "deep" and dark memory permanently engraved inside her very being.

Born in 1913 in Vigneux-sur-Seine near Paris, Charlotte Delbo was a student of philosophy at the Sorbonne before she began to work full-time as an assistant to the well-known French theater director Louis Jouvet. In 1940, when France fell to the Germans, she was safe in South America on tour with Jouvet and his theater company. After reading about a friend who was executed because of his work in the Resistance, Delbo chose to return to Paris in 1941. She joined her husband, Georges Dudach, who was active in the French underground and began to work for the French Resistance, editing anti-Nazi articles and leaflets. They were arrested by the French collaborationist police on March 2, 1942, and handed over to the Gestapo. A few months later, in May 1942, her husband was executed at the prison of Mont Valérien at the age of twenty-eight. Delbo was imprisoned in La Santé, then Romainville.

In January 1943 she was deported to Auschwitz-Birkenau with a group of 230 French women political prisoners who had taken an active part in the Resistance. They were the only non-Jewish group of women to be deported to Auschwitz-Birkenau. After six months, they were sent to a smaller camp and finally ended up in the German camp of Ravensbrück. The voyage and life histories of each member of the group are described in detail in Delbo's book *Le convoi de 24 janvier*, 1965 (The convoy of January 24). Of the 230 women who were deported, only 49 survived.

In the camps Charlotte Delbo vowed that if she survived she would bear witness or "carry the word" back to the world of the living. This is the title of one of her plays, *Qui rapportera ces paroles?*, 1974 (*Who Will Carry the Word?*, 1982), which depicts the women's experience in Auschwitz. Although individual women characters are presented, the group of twenty-three political prisoners is collectively portrayed as a mass of people, a kind of Greek chorus sustaining one another in the face of disease, beatings, and death. When Françoise, the main character (the spokesperson for Delbo), contemplates suicide in the beginning of the play, she is told by Claire (who does not survive the atrocities): "There must be one who comes back, one who will tell . . . none of us is alone and each must render an account to all the others" (p. 278).

Delbo wrote down her impressions as soon as she could after coming back from the camps (1946), but she kept them in a drawer for twenty years before she was ready to share them with the world. In 1965 they were published as *Aucun de nous ne reviendra*. She seeks to make one feel, to make one see (*donner voir*), a reality that had never before existed through nightmare-like fragments rendered in an incisive yet lyrical language. Phrases with the subject "we" or "they" and rarely "I," denoting the collective experience of women, are repeated in rhythmical incantation. Stark images of cold, light, and silence are solidified into the barren landscape of Auschwitz. Time and movement are suspended; gestures are abolished; sensations no longer exist. In the anonymity of this vast whiteness, women scream out, but their cries are frozen fast into the ice. Delbo describes the trucks loaded with women headed for the gas chambers: "Their mouths shout, their arms stretched out toward us shout, everything about them is shouting. Each body is a shout. . . . Each one is a materialized cry, a howl—unheard. . . . Their cries remain inscribed upon the blue of the sky" (pp. 33–34).

Bodies become strangers, automatons, moving "outside of us. Possessed, dispossessed. Abstract. We were unfeeling" (p. 35). Parts of the body are detached from their owners and take on a life of their own. The power of Delbo's poetic prose lies in her crystallization of images. For example, Block 25 is where women condemned to die are taken, the living among the dead. Naked corpses are stretched out in the snow of the yard. One of them moves her hand: "The fingers open slowly, the snow blooms like a discolored sea anemone" (p. 23). This vivid image makes us feel the death-in-life reality of a living corpse. In another example, a woman falls into the bottom of a snowbank attempting to grab snow to quench her thirst and futilely

struggles to climb back up. "And her hand writhed toward us in a desperate call for help. Her hand falls back—a faded mauve star on the snow" (p. 25). Delbo's striking images of despair transfigure these gestures into word monuments.

From the time she arrived in Auschwitz, Delbo was afraid of losing her memory. In *Useless Knowledge* (1970), she notes, "To lose one's memory is to lose oneself" (p. 188). She devises methods of keeping her memory active. During the glacial hours of the early morning *Appel* (roll call) she would try to remember phone numbers, subway stations, names of stores on a particular street. Above all, she succeeded with much effort in recollecting fifty-seven poems which she would recite to herself as she stood motionless in the cold. Sometimes it took her days to summon one single verse or even one word which refused to come back. She would often share these poems with her block mates as they dug in the marshes or waded in the mud.

Six months after arriving in Auschwitz-Birkenau, only 57 out of her convoy of 230 were still alive. Delbo and seventeen of her surviving comrades were transferred to the satellite camp of Raisko where conditions were better. There the group was able to put on a complete version of Molière's play *The Imaginary Invalid*, reconstructed entirely from memory through a collective effort (*Useless Knowledge*, pp. 168–71). They rehearsed the play when they could, and improvised with the materials at hand to design costumes, scenery, and makeup. Miraculously, the performance took place as scheduled the Sunday after Christmas. Delbo comments that, for a short time, the women once again believed in the magical world of art. Yet she knew that only a short distance away the chimneys continued to spit forth the smoke of human flesh, and this reality could never for a moment be forgotten.

Before Delbo was deported to Auschwitz, she spent over a year in prison, much of it in solitary confinement. In her essay, "Phantoms, My Companions," 1971, written in the form of a letter addressed to her friend, theater director Louis Jouvet, she describes her isolation: "You are alone in a dark hovel . . . . Nothing sees you or visits you, you are abandoned, forgotten" (p.

19). Despite total seclusion, Delbo imagines she is visited by famous literary characters from novels and plays such as Stendhal's hero Fabrice del Dongo of *The Charterhouse of Parma* and Jean Giraudoux's Ondine. The energy and intensity of their companionship sustains her.

When Delbo finally leaves the prison for her journey in the cattle car, her companions abandon her. She realizes that a literary presence can no longer offer solace in a camp such as Auschwitz. However, one evening in Ravensbrück, she encountered a gypsy woman selling all kinds of objects hidden under her dress. Unable to believe her eyes, Delbo spotted the Petits Classiques Larousse edition of Molière's *Le Misanthrope*. Without hesitation, she exchanged her ration of bread for the slim volume, and clutched it to her breast, even though giving up one's bread was one step closer to death. She ran to her barracks to show her comrades the precious acquisition, and each friend cut a piece from her own crust of bread to compensate Delbo for her sacrifice. Every night, Delbo learned a fragment of the play by heart and repeated it the next morning during the *Appel*. For the rest of her stay in the camp, she kept the book under her dress, next to her heart; it literally kept her warm during the winter. The play was left behind when she was liberated at the end of the war.

If in the camps Delbo took refuge in literature as a means of keeping her memory alive, in *The Measure of Our Days* (1971), she describes the gulf that existed between herself and the world of the imaginary, between herself and others. Upon returning to Paris, she felt absent, in a void, floating in a present without reality. Friends came to her room, bringing flowers and books, but the unopened books piled up on her night table, "within reach, out of my grasp," (p. 237). They were useless objects that had nothing to do with life; she felt that everything inside of them was false, empty. Auschwitz had killed her belief in the illusionary universe created by a literary work. The faculty of memory that had enabled her to survive the death camps was now working against her. Memory of the atrocities deadened her ability both to live life in the present and to read books. "This is the part of me that died in Auschwitz," she admits (p. 239).

However, one morning, a strangely familiar voice awakened her. It is Alceste, the main character of *The Misanthrope*. "Why did you wait so long to come back to me?" Delbo asked him. Alceste replied that he had never left her. "I've come back only because you've come back." Sitting by her, he handed her one book, thereby handing her back all books ("Phantoms, My Faithful Ones," p. 314). She understands that Alceste has led her back to herself; a part of her can return to the world of the living.

Yet in much of her writing, Charlotte Delbo testifies to the inability to return from her encounter with death. While her poems reveal her innermost despair, Delbo's sense of loss endows her with the mission to bear witness to women, those who died and those who struggled to survive in the aftermath. Through her visual, musical, and intensely original use of language, she chisels the agony of the victims into a poetics of pain, bringing the reader inside the death camp horror.

SELECTED WORKS BY THE AUTHOR
Auschwitz and After (*Trilogy: None of Us Will Return; Useless Knowledge; The Measure of Our Days*). Trans. Rosette C. Lamont. New Haven, Conn.: Yale University Press, 1995; *Days and Memory*. Trans. Rosette C. Lamont. Marlboro, Vt.: Marlboro, 1990; "Phantoms, My Companions." Trans. Rosette C. Lamont. Massachusetts Review 12 (1971): 10–30; "Phantoms, My Faithful Ones." Trans. Rosette C. Lamont. *Massachusetts Review* 14 (1973): 310–15; *Who Will Carry the Word*? Trans. Cynthia Haft. In *The Theater of the Holocaust: Four Plays*, ed. Robert Skloot. Madison: University of Wisconsin Press, 1982.

FOR FURTHER READING
Lamont, Rosette C., "Charlotte Delbo's Frozen Friezes." *L'Esprit Créateur* 19, no. 2 (1979): 65–74; Langer, Lawrence, "Charlotte Delbo and a Heart of Ashes." In *The Age of Atrocity: Death in Modern Literature*. Boston: Beacon Press, 1978: 201–44.

Ellen S. Fine

Demetz, Hanna (1929–)

Raised Catholic and designated by Nazi law as a *Mischlinge*, a half-caste, Hanna Demetz brings a distinctive perspective to her Holocaust novel *The House on Prague Street* (1970). Demetz wrote the novel to celebrate her family and record their tragedy, making the work both a memorial and a remembrance of the victims of the Holocaust.

Born in northern Bohemia (Sudetenland) in 1929, the child of a Czech-Jewish mother and a German-Catholic father, Hanna Demetz lived through World War II in Czechoslovakia, but was spared the fate of full Jews in Nazi-occupied Europe. Living openly in Czech society, she witnessed her Jewish relatives being deprived of their rights and property and being "transferred" to Theresienstadt, a grim fortress town whose exit was deportation to the death camps.

The House on Prague Street is structured as the recollection of the autobiographical protagonist. Helene Richter's tale, set entirely within a family context, alternates between reports of hardship borne by her maternal Jewish relatives and her own comparative ease as the daughter of a German. The primary importance of this Holocaust text is its struggle with the ethical complexity of the divided self confronted with an unfolding tragedy. By continually shifting from first- to third-person perception, from youthful perspective to superimposed adult retrospective, Demetz balances a young girl's Holocaust era ambivalence with the mature author's psychological and moral reflection. The progressive stages in Helene's understanding of Nazi violation of her Jewish family and neighbors, their transformation from valued citizens to disenfranchised pariahs, parallel her metamorphosis from assimilated Czech to despised half-caste. Ordinary generational conflict, romantic fantasies, and teenage identity crises coexist in Helene's world with expropriations of property, deportations, torture, and murder.

As a *Mischlinge*, located hierarchically between the disenfranchised "full Jew" and the valued German *Volk*, Helene is exempt from full discrimination. Although she is affected by the shrinking sphere of Jewish educational options, as the child of a German she remains relatively safe and is spared the injustices her mother and other family members endure. Illustrative of Helene's divided loyalty to her Jewish mother

and racially mixed friends and to her German associates are juxtaposed scenes of her accommodation to both groups. In one scene she is surreptitiously garbed in a borrowed dirndl dress and white knee socks looking "very Aryan" (p. 100) and feeling very self-satisfied while singing sentimental songs about the homeland to hospitalized soldiers. In another scene she feels guilty for her privileged position and intimate relationship with a German soldier. Helene is plagued by ambivalence—torn between the wish to enjoy security as a German and occasional pangs of guilt for the suffering of her Jewish relatives. She is pained by her family's losses under the Aryanization program, particularly when the grandparents' ancestral home is requisitioned and later confiscated, and pained by observing Jewish powerlessness while awaiting each new restrictive ordinance. She quickly discovers that a Jewish family is a liability, a hindrance to life's pleasures and good fortune. She shares with some other Holocaust chroniclers, such as the unincarcerated Anne Frank,* an overwhelming desire to lead a normal life despite the dire times. Her adolescent response to increasingly severe Jewish deprivations is a resolve to resist entrapment in the dreariness of her Jewish connections, and to participate instead in the German world. In the company of her German father, the soldier who has become her lover, and a maiden aunt, the sole paternal relative who acknowledges her, she enjoys privileges her mother is denied; she rides on public transportation, eats in restaurants, and attends public entertainments. Although the occupation was relatively comfortable for Helene, she is drawn more deeply into the war near its end for, like Demetz, she is conscripted into a labor unit manufacturing hand grenades and there experiences the tension and fear of victims working in close proximity to Nazi masters, albeit on a limited scale.

Demetz, who wanted to counter the failure of German schools to teach Holocaust history adequately, is among the ranks of those who contend that forgetting the Holocaust would compound the tragedy. She addresses the theme of Holocaust memory explicitly in Marie Richter's dialogue and implicitly in Helene's character. To ensure that future generations know what the Nazis did to their victims and that the atrocities be seen from the victims' point of view, Marie insists that her daughter accompany her to Gestapo headquarters to deliver a change of clothes for a family member beaten beyond recognition. She asserts, "Let her see it all. . . . Just let her see everything. Someone will have to know about it later on" (p. 91). After years of alternating between Holocaust evasion and confrontation, Helene encounters Holocaust reality, the quintessential Shoah image—a cattle car filled with skeletal Jewish prisoners. She refrains from commentary; however, it is clear that Helene is finally at the threshold of full comprehension. When she realizes that she is her family's sole survivor, that no one will return, her innocence is shattered and she must go forth in the world because she cannot return to the house on Prague Street, now, in its final metamorphosis, a refuge for camp survivors.

SELECTED WORKS BY THE AUTHOR
The House on Prague Street. Trans. Hanna Demetz. New York: St. Martin's Press, 1980; *The Journey from Prague Street*. New York: St. Martin's Press, 1990.

FOR FURTHER READING
Kremer, S. Lillian, "Hanna Demetz." In *Women's Holocaust Writing: Memory and Imagination*. Lincoln: University of Nebraska Press, 1999.

S. Lillian Kremer

Donat, Alexander (1905–1983)

The memoir *The Holocaust Kingdom* (1978) was written by a man whose name was conferred upon him from the depths of the event he remembers. Originally named Michal Berg, the memoir author exchanged his name with a certain Alexander Donat, so that he, Berg, could be placed on a transport leaving the concentration camp at Vaihingen. Soon after he left with his new name, the one who remained behind as Michal Berg was sent to Kochendorf, where the Nazis murdered him. Thus Donat bears the memory of the one who died bearing his name. With that memory he bears the question that haunts many survivors, "Why was *I* permitted to live?" (p. 293).

Born in 1905, Donat/Berg was a young, accomplished journalist living in Warsaw with his wife, Lena, and their two-year-old son, Wlodek, when the Germans invaded Poland in September 1939. All three survived the war. After entrusting their son to some Polish Catholics, Donat and his wife lived through the uprising in the Warsaw ghetto only to be sent to Majdanek. From there he was sent to a labor camp in Radom; from Radom, he was sent to Vaihingen and other camps, including Auschwitz. Donat's wife was also sent to Auschwitz and from there was transported to Oskar Schindler's factory in Czechoslovakia. He was liberated on April 29, 1945, by the Americans while being transported from Dachau to yet another camp. When Donat and his wife were reunited with their son after the war, he told them that he wanted nothing to do with them because they were Jews who had killed his Lord Jesus Christ. As was often the case, the Catholics who took in the Jewish child took the opportunity to brainwash him. Nevertheless Donat, his wife, and their son immigrated to the United States in 1946, where he went into the printing business. Donat died in 1983.

Written with the eloquence and insight of a skilled journalist, Donat's memoir contains several accounts of incidents that have become well known in Holocaust studies. Commenting, for example, on the transport of the children from Doctor Janusz Korczak's* orphanage in the Warsaw ghetto, he recalls the striking image of Doctor Korczak, who insisted upon accompanying them all the way to Treblinka, as he led their orderly procession to the trains. They marched, says Donat, "without a single tear, in such a terrifying silence that it thundered with indictment and defiance" (p. 71). Perhaps because Donat was himself a young father in his thirties, he was especially sensitive to the plight of the children, beginning with his own child. He saw his little one go from an active, playful toddler to a boy paralyzed with fear; whenever Donat left the room, he relates, his son would "tighten his grip on me, uttering only the single word: 'Daddy'" (p. 94). Here the memoir reveals a definitive dimension of the assault that characterizes the Holocaust: it is the assault on the father *as* a father by rendering him powerless to respond to his little one's cry of "Daddy!"

Donat recalls another commonly related incident, which is also included in Emmanuel Ringelblum's* *Notes from the Warsaw Ghetto*. It illustrates the animalistic image assumed by the Nazis in their treatment of the Jews like animals. According to the story, a German came into the ghetto and was about to take away a mother's child, when he turned and answered her pleas by saying, "If you can guess which of my eyes is a glass eye, I shall spare your child." When she correctly identified the artificial eye, he asked her how she could tell it was the one. She answered: "It looks more human than the other one" (pp. 102–3). Donat recalls that he did not hate the Germans, explaining, "You don't hate a beast of prey, you feel loathing and terror" (p. 102). Thus Donat shows that in their assault on the human image the Nazis are bereft of their own humanity.

As the memory of one who underwent a permanent change of name, much of Donat's memoir is a remembrance of the unraveling of his world and of his identity. "A new kind of life began to take shape over the mass grave of the past," he states (p. 94). What sort of life? This sort: "The very bases of our faith had crumbled: the Polish fatherland whose children we had always considered ourselves; two thousand years of Christianity, silent in the face of Nazism; our own lie-ridden civilization. We were despairingly alone, stripped of all we had held sacred" (pp. 100–101). Here one realizes that sustaining a relation with another human being requires sustaining a certain teaching or idea about humanity. During the Holocaust both the relation and the idea—both the basis of the world and the core of human identity—were under attack.

One of the few to survive the Warsaw ghetto uprising, Donat insightfully points out that, unlike any other uprising, this one was carried out not with the aim of overthrowing a tyrant or of any other victory; rather, he says, "It was undertaken solely for death with dignity" (p. 104). In a world in which it was impossible to live as a human being, the one option remaining was to die like one. Because Donat did not die, his

humanity was still in question. Pursuing that theme, Donat recalls the moment when he was inducted into Majdanek, "I looked at my number: 7,115. From that moment I ceased to be a man, a human being" (p. 168). Hence the sage advice he received from another inmate was to "forget who and what you were" (p. 168). That forgetting, however, is precisely what Donat seeks to overcome in the writing of his memoir.

How does the memoir overcome the forgetting of one's humanity? By remembering how such a forgetting was overcome in the midst of the assault. Donat recalls, for example, the importance of washing one's face, even with snow or dirty water, just to affirm the value of the face and therefore of the person. "Those who failed to wash every day," he observes, "soon died" (p. 173). Donat also recalls the profoundly life-saving significance of the smallest act of kindness in that realm where kindness was all but unknown. Recalling a family that he met in Radom, for instance, he writes, "What brought me back to life, pulled me up out of the depths of despair was warmth, compassion, kind words the Melcers gave me" (p. 237). Thus Donat's human identity was awakened by the humanity of others.

And yet for Donat, as for many other survivors, the return to the world of humanity at the end of the war posed immense difficulties. "I was afraid of my new freedom," he explains. "I was afraid of returning to normal life and its activities because they seemed like desecration of the memory of those who had perished. . . . But most of all I feared going home" (p. 292). Why the fear of home? Because the foundations of the home—the *idea* of the home—had been reduced to ashes along with the mothers, fathers, and children who constitute the home. With this memory Donat reveals a difficulty confronted not only by him but by all humanity: both have emerged from the Holocaust in a state of exile. One task facing both in their remembrance of the event, then, is to labor to reconstitute the world—not just economically or politically but as a dwelling place for one's fellow human being.

SELECTED WORKS BY THE AUTHOR
The Death Camp Treblinka: A Documentary. New York: Holocaust Library, 1979; *The Holocaust Kingdom.* New York: Holocaust Library, 1978.

David Patterson

Dorian, Emil (1893–1956)

Emil Dorian's diary *Jurnal din vremur de prigoanæa*, 1996 (*The Quality of Witness: A Romanian Diary 1937–1944*, 1982) is an eloquent text written by one of Romania's major Jewish literary figures. It is the work of a mature man who had devoted his life to the cause of peace and tolerance but lived to see the atrocities of the Holocaust.

Born in Bucharest in 1893, Dorian served as a physician in World War I. By the mid-1920s Dorian was a poet whose work was widely known for its pacifism and expression of love for humankind. Among his works are five volumes of poetry, four novels, essays on popular topics in medicine, and numerous articles on Romanian and Jewish life. Two of his novels—*Prophets and Clowns* (1930) and *The Poison* (1939)—have specifically Jewish themes; the former is a critique of the Jewish and Gentile bourgeoisie, and the latter deals with the anti-Semitism of the pro-Nazi Antonescu regime. Dorian also published translations of works by Heinrich Heine and Eliezer Steinberg's Yiddish fables. Although the Jews of Bucharest endured pogroms and several hundred were sent to Transnistria, they were not sent *en masse* to the murder camps. As a noted public figure, Dorian avoided deportation to Transnistria; he survived the Holocaust and died in 1956.

During the years when he kept his Holocaust diary he completed a three-volume anthology of Yiddish poetry in translation, even as a Yiddish way of life was being extinguished. On October 20, 1941, he comments on his progress with the anthology, saying, "The harder the blows rained on Jews, the more passionately I plunged into work reaffirming the permanence of Jewish contributions to art" (p. 170). Over the years following the war he served as the director of the libraries and archives for the Federation of Jewish Communities of Romania.

Due to the Romanian Communist government's censorship policies, Dorian's Holocaust diary was published in English translation before it appeared in Romanian; it was thanks only to the devotion of a close friend to whom he entrusted them that Dorian's diaries were preserved. The English edition was prepared by his daughter, Marguerite Dorian, who excerpted selected entries from the first seven notebooks of diaries that Dorian kept from 1937 to 1956, the year of his death. Beginning on December 30, 1937, the diary presents the reader with rare insights into prewar Romania and the rise of anti-Semitic legislation and other measures taken against the Jews before the outbreak of hostilities. The diary ends on August 24, 1944, with Dorian's hopeful yet foreboding reflections on Romania's surrender to the allies. In it unfolds the drama not only of torn allegiances among Romania's Jewish intelligentsia but of the tearing of the soul of a sensitive, insightful, and creative man.

More than most other Holocaust diarists, Dorian had the maturity and the intelligence to recognize the profound nature of the historical upheaval taking place all around him. On February 11, 1938, for example, he wrote, "One could feel every human being shiver at the intimate contact with the essence of historical events" (p. 21). And yet, the more intense his collision with history, the more radical his experience of the collapse of time. On October 22, 1943, for instance, he declared that he had lost all interest in the future; three years later, to the very day, he lost his sense of the present, wondering, "What does it matter that I jot down dates?" (p. 295). This obliteration of a present and a future comes in the wake of a radical assault on memory and therefore on the past. Thus measuring time in increments of days, Dorian's diary contains a record of the assault on time.

Since time alone is omnipresent, its collapse has implications both for the world and for the individual. For the Jew, Dorian pointed out on May 22, 1944, the world has become a place where death itself—that is, the natural death that befalls a normal humanity—no longer exists. On February 5, 1941, he noted the world's reaction to such a condition, lamenting that Jews "have been expelled, tortured, massacred—

while people, or rather countries, looked on with total indifference" (p. 142). At a time when a Jew's crime was being alive, the world's crime was being indifferent. One can see what this means to the individual Jew when, on August 13, 1941, Dorian cried, "I try to tear myself out of the vortex that is pulling me down" (p. 167). On August 15, 1941, [It is] "getting worse: I'm plunged in silence" (p. 167). Revealing the tension between the need to speak and the oppressive silence, Dorian's diary brings out the serious mental, emotional, and spiritual difficulties for the individual who tries to live in a world that is either hostile or indifferent. In doing so, his diary demonstrates how the scope of the Holocaust extends both inward and outward.

Because Dorian is a writer, his diary contains numerous reflections on the literary craft and spiritual dimensions of writing. "All is not lost," he declared, for instance, on July 12, 1938, "while the hope of writing a poem is still alive" (p. 33). On April 6, 1942, he noted, "The spirit must be kept alive if you are to write, and you must write if the spirit is to be kept alive" (p. 203). His reflections on writing, moreover, extend to the question of writing the diary itself. Writing in a time when Jewish writing was forbidden, Dorian sees a certain redemptive significance to his diary. In an entry dated June 2, 1943, he comments on the difference between "writing literature" and keeping the diary. The former he regards almost as indulging in a luxury, the latter as engaging in a testimony; the former he sees as something that stimulates the mind, the latter as something that redeems the soul.

What is remarkable about Dorian's diary, then, is that it opens up the nature of the Holocaust diary as such. It is not a tranquil reflection on the day's events or on one's personal life for the sake of oneself. Rather, it examines a world, a truth, a horror, and a meaning for the sake of a community. Dorian shows us that the Holocaust diary rests on a fundamental accountability; its cry of "Why?" is not a "Why me?" but "Why my neighbor? Why the children and the old ones?" On January 25, 1942, for example, Dorian wrote, "The thought of what is happening to these human beings [the Jews] poisons every moment of my life" (p. 194).

While other diaries offer an account of a life at the end of a day, the Holocaust diary tries to recover a life that is destroyed each day.

SELECTED WORKS BY THE AUTHOR
The Quality of Witness: A Romanian Diary 1937 – 1944. Trans. Mara Soceanu Vamos, ed. Marguerite Dorian. Philadelphia: Jewish Publication Society, 1982.

David Patterson

Dribben, Judith (1924–)

In her powerful memoir *And Some Shall Live* (1969; reprinted in 1970 as *A Girl Called Judith Strick*), Judith Dribben relates the dramatic tale of her work in a partisan underground group during the German occupation of Lvov, Ukraine. The memoir provides rare insights into clandestine partisan activities that range from blowing up bridges to seducing German officers.

Born Judith Strick in 1924 in the Ukrainian town of Rovno, Judith Dribben was living with her mother and father in Lvov when the Germans invaded Russia on June 22, 1941. Because she was adept at several languages, she was able to fool the Germans into thinking that she was a French Christian refugee; later she pretended to be a Russian parachutist. She even obtained work as a maid in the homes of high-ranking Germans and spied on them until she was arrested by the Gestapo. Ultimately, Dribben was sent to Auschwitz; from there she was transferred to a satellite camp near Mauthausen. She escaped shortly before the end of the war, in March 1945, and made her way east to the Red Army. Although she was initially hopeful that she could find a place with the Soviets, she quickly became disillusioned and set out for Palestine. After arriving in Palestine in 1947, she served in the Jewish underground and then in the Israeli army. Later she became one of the founding members of Kibbutz Sde Boker.

One remarkable feature of Dribben's memoir is its examination of the problem of Jewish identity in the midst of the assault on that identity. Articulating the problem in the contexts of Jewish resistance, she makes use of various literary devices to explore it. Able to pass as a non-

Jew, for example, Dribben uses the motif of mirrors to convey her inner conflict over living as a Jew while passing for a non-Jew, even when it was for the sake of the resistance movement. Also connected to the identity issue is the matter of losing her name to a number when she is sent to Auschwitz: "Once the number was there," "there was no chance to escape" (p. 185). The number itself became part of her identity and thus bound her to the Nazi anti-world "more strongly than any chains." For Dribben, writing the memoir became a means of breaking that chain.

Closely connected to the assault on the name is the assault on the One who is known as "the Name" (*HaShem*). Dribben brings out this dimension of the slaughter by relating Nazi comments such as "The Jewish God is burnt to ashes" in connection with the burning of a synagogue (p. 24). When she was in Auschwitz and saw women lighting Sabbath candles, moreover, she found herself longing for the candles that her mother had lit every Friday evening. In this memory of the Sabbath, Dribben articulates how the issue of identity and the assault on the holy intersect in the family. For the family is where she first took on an identity and learned to recognize the holy. That is why she is so careful to note the windowpanes in the camp near Mauthausen which had so many names scratched into them. "Family names, first names, sweethearts' names," she says, "just names. We added our names on the windows" (p. 229).

Indeed, writing her memoir is a way of adding her name to the names of others after her name was nearly lost. When she was liberated she found herself "among strangers," a condition that tempted her to kill herself. Instead, however, she went to Palestine, declaring, "I didn't want to be a homeless Jew any more" (p. 275). For Dribben, her participation in the rebirth of Israel was a kind of rebirth for herself, an ultimate resistance against the ones who tried to murder the holy image of humanity in the murder of the Jews. And writing her memoir in the Holy Land was a way of recovering a definitive link between identity and the holy.

SELECTED WORKS BY THE AUTHOR
And Some Shall Live. Jerusalem: Keter Books, 1969; *A Girl Called Judith Strick.* New York: Cowles Book, 1970.

David Patterson

E

Ettinger, Elżbieta (1925–)

Distinctive for its refutation of the myth of Jewish passivity in the face of Nazi aggression, Elżbieta Ettinger's novel *Kindergarten* (1970) is an important contribution to the corpus of Holocaust literature. A resister herself, Ettinger repudiates the conventional underrepresentation of Jewish organized resistance, and dramatizes resistance inside and outside the ghetto among men, women, and children of all circumstances, linking the themes of resistance and Holocaust-wrought character transformation.

Born in Poland in 1925, Elżbieta Ettinger spent the Holocaust in and out of the Warsaw ghetto, four months in Majdanek, in hiding in Aryan settings, and serving as a partisan engaging in sabotage. Her contribution to Holocaust testimony began with the reports she filed for Emmanuel Ringelblum's* clandestine ghetto history while imprisoned in the Warsaw ghetto. On the Aryan side, Ettinger fought in a resistance unit that blew up bridges and murdered a number of German officials. Escalating Polish anti-Semitism in the late 1960s convinced her to immigrate to America where she wrote *Kindergarten* to counter prevalent American misperceptions of the genocide, Polish anti-Semitism, and Jewish passivity.

In *Kindergarten* the third-person narrative is presented from the consciousness of Elli Rostow who comes of age during the Holocaust under an assumed Christian identity. Entrée to Elli's thoughts and emotions, to her metamorphosis from free citizen to ghettoized pariah, from innocent girl to skeptical adult, is realized through blending dramatic presentation and diary entries. Resistance of the teenage protagonists is initially limited to surviving as Aryans in plain view of people who could denounce them and taking on the responsibility of caring for a precocious four-year-old girl; the child "is always ready for the road" (p. 129), knows how to behave in a way that will not endanger her fellow fugitives, and knows how to conceal her identity in the presence of a German soldier. For "Aryan Jews" the challenge is surviving outside the law, moving from place to place, obtaining false papers, and "passing" as Christians. They must blend with their surroundings; adopt Polish customs, habits, and mannerisms; be convincing Christians in and out of church. They must watch every word, every gesture, lest they betray nervousness or unfamiliarity with the adopted routine. Drawing on her own experience, Ettinger depicts the stress associated with eluding blackmailers, the constant need to alter identity and relocate, the incessant fear of discovery, and the need to be faithful to the assumed character which make the life of the Jew on the Aryan side a harrowing experience.

The novel's active resistance theme is centered in Elli's mother, Maria, a partisan operating from the Aryan side. She is representative of the Jewish women who relied on their "Aryan" looks, forged papers identifying themselves as Poles, and traveled through the cities and towns of Poland as couriers. The second half of the novel shifts the resistance theme from reports of Maria's activities to a dramatic presentation of active resistance by Elli and her associates. In the privileged position of a German office worker, Elli garners information useful to the resistance forces and keeps abreast of developments in the ghettos. She learns of the liquidation of the "Jewish Quarter" of Chelm and the murder of those who tried to evade deportation, much as Ettinger herself did when she worked in a German office. When she learns of the Warsaw ghetto uprising while overhearing a German officer objecting to the official designation of Jews as "the enemy," elevating their status to battlefield opponent, Elli leaves her job without permission and returns to the ghetto where she is a witness to the battle and its many dead.

Madness and suicide loom throughout the novel. Madness is Ettinger's central metaphor and objective correlative for the Nazi world. She injects cameo portraits which brilliantly foreshadow or echo the principal characters' loss of sanity. Elli's madness is triggered not by Gestapo torture, as was her sister's, but by witnessing and participating in ever-increasing violence. Heightening her stress is fear that Adam, her ethnic German lover, a reformed anti-Semite and fellow partisan, whose loyalty she doubts and from whom she keeps secret her Jewish iden-

tity, will lead her into captivity through his resistance work or will betray her to the Nazis. Ettinger concludes *Kindergarten* with Elli's surrender to madness unleashed by her belief that Adam has betrayed her upon her decision to leave him. The novel ends abruptly, as blood drips from Elli's slashed wrist.

The *Times Literary Supplement* reviewer described *Kindergarten* as "a highly self-conscious work, written with exceptional insight into the suffering of the individual in hiding." Ettinger's fictional representation of the dynamics of fugitive status parallels social and psychological insights of respected social scientists. She writes autobiographically and authoritatively on the horrors of hiding in Nazi Europe and effectively depicts the role of Jewish resistance to the Nazi world.

SELECTED WORKS BY THE AUTHOR
Hannah Arendt/Martin Heidegger. New Haven, Conn.: Yale University Press, 1995; *Kindergarten.* Boston: Houghton Mifflin, 1970; *Quicksand.* London: Pandora, 1989; *Rosa Luxemburg: A Life.* Boston: Beacon Press, 1986.

FOR FURTHER READING
Kremer, S. Lillian, "Elżbieta Ettinger." In *Women's Holocaust Writing: Memory and Imagination.* Lincoln: University of Nebraska Press, 1999; *Times Literary Supplement*, February 10, 1989, p. 148.

S. Lillian Kremer

Fénelon, Fania (1918–1983)

Fania Fénelon's memoir *Sursis pour l'orchestre*, 1976 (*Playing for Time*, 1977) became famous with the production of the film version of her book in 1980; the film bore the same English title, and the screenplay was written by Arthur Miller.* Fénelon's book is remarkable not only for its astute and vivid description of the concentrationary universe but also for its insightful portrayal of the women's orchestra in Auschwitz. Each morning as the women went out to work, their footsteps leading to their death were measured by the rhythmic strains of the melodies produced by the Auschwitz orchestra. Fénelon's torment over the incongruity between the beauty of the music and the horrors of the murder camp manifests itself in a theme of identity crisis that runs throughout the memoir; it is a theme that brings out a characteristic assault on the identity of every Jew during the Holocaust.

Born in France in 1918, Fania Fénelon's family name was Goldstein; she took the name Fénelon when she became a singer on the Parisian cabaret circuit. Fénelon had already acquired some renown as a singer by the time she was arrested in late 1943. She was sent to the Drancy concentration camp outside of Paris; from there, in January 1944, she was transported to Auschwitz-Birkenau, where her musical talents became the key to her survival. As one of the forty-one women who belonged to the or-

chestra, Fénelon performed not only when workers left and returned to the camp but also at any other time the SS wanted to listen to their music. The women even played special concerts for Josef Mengele and Heinrich Himmler. Their orchestra was disbanded, however, the following November; and Fénelon was sent to Bergen-Belsen; there she managed to survive until the camp was liberated on April 15, 1945. After the war she resumed her career as a singer in France.

In the preface to her memoir Fénelon makes a remark that underscores the essence of the identity crisis that continually emerges throughout her tale. Commenting on her reflections and memory of the event, she wrote, "It's not me who's doing the thinking, 'it' thinks *for* me . . . . I spend every night there—every night!" (p. ix). The "it" that invades her thoughts and her soul to think *for* her eclipses her sense of who she is and thus holds her in a realm from which she cannot be liberated. The loss of a sense of who she is, both as an individual and as a human being, began the moment she entered the camp. Here she relates that as the SS men leered at her, she "felt considerably less than human: a peculiar, grubby object upsetting the natural order" (p. 19). Alien to the natural order, she falls out of any order of values that might define who she is: "I was no longer anything, not even a slave. For me there was no longer either code or law" (p. 20). To have an identity as a human being is to be part of an order of life and an order of law. Bereft of any place within the law, the Jew is exiled from the order of life; she has no identity because she has no place.

Such is Fénelon's position within the universe of the camp; in that realm the self and soul of her humanity crumble, as though afflicted with a leprosy of the soul. "In Birkenau," she attested, "bits of oneself rotted and fell off without one's knowing they'd gone" (p. 106). And with the bits of oneself goes one's identity. One way in which the women lost a bit of themselves was in the loss of their menstrual cycles. Some of them prayed, Fénelon remembers, in an effort to "exorcise this curse the Germans were holding over [them]: sterility" (p. 89). No longer part of life, they could no longer bear life; there would be no new life to bear their memory or their names.

Adding to the loss of her identity was the loss of her appearance, not only when the Germans shaved her head but when her hair grew back: at the age of twenty-five her hair had turned completely white overnight. In the memoir this incongruity parallels the pervasive incongruity that goes into the unraveling of reality in the concentrationary anti-world. Indeed, it is as if Fénelon were on another planet, on "Planet Auschwitz," as many survivors call it. "It's odd," she wrote, recalling her arrival in the camp. "You can't see the sky; it's as if there weren't one" (p. 18). To be sure, something else has replaced the sky, as one discovers when Fénelon reports a fellow inmate's comment on the magnificent sunset, adding, "But the distant red glow wasn't the sun" (p. 194)—it was the trench filled with the flaming bodies of the Jews from the Hungarian transport. In a world turned upside down the sky had become a cemetery.

In losing the sky, Fénelon loses a dimension of height and a source of light that would enable her to make sense of the world around her. Hence her world turns to madness. "Death, life, tears, laughter," she wrote, "everything was multiplied, disproportionate, beyond the limits of the credible. All was madness" (p. 70). Offering an example of the madness that characterized this anti-world, Fénelon notes that in all the orchestra's performances they were never applauded except one Sunday when they played in the block for the insane (p. 126). Furthermore, what was most rational for her in the world of humanity—the effort to make sense of her surroundings— Fénelon describes as a "mania" in the anti-world. "I continued to believe that there was something to understand," she related, as though confessing to some mental disorder, "that this desire for extermination was motivated by reasons which simply escaped me" (p. 91). What escaped her was the terrible truth that the extermination camp was not a by-product of Nazi ideology—it was its very essence.

Perhaps most disturbing about Fénelon's memoir is the question that it raises about the relation between the Nazis and "high" European culture. Their insistence on having an orchestra in Auschwitz to play the classical works of the great composers while they gas and burn people suggests that an appreciation for great music does not preclude murder. Fénelon's memoir, then, is among the most disconcerting of memoirs because it questions the value that Western culture places on the performing arts and implicates the culture itself.

SELECTED WORK BY THE AUTHOR:
Playing for Time. Trans. Judith Landry. New York: Atheneum, 1977.

David Patterson

Fink, Ida (1921–)

Ida Fink is perhaps best known for *A Scrap of Time*, which was published in 1987. The book, which includes sketches, short stories, and a short play, was greeted with widespread acclaim. One did not have to read much beyond the first selection, "A Scrap of Time," to see that the author of this collection of "scraps" was clearly a master storyteller. Between the time of the actual events that were being portrayed in these highly condensed short works of fiction and the date of publication of the representations there had been an interval of more than forty years. Fink told an interviewer for the *New York Times Book Review* that "she had waited more than ten years before beginning her first stories. 'Subconsciously I needed distance,' she said. 'I was afraid to touch these things with the word'" (July 12, 1987).

"These things" refers to the realities of the Holocaust: the cruelty, destruction, and indifference to human suffering on the part of the perpetrators and their accomplices; the psychological terror and helplessness of the victims. Fink told the *Times* interviewer that the characters in her stories were drawn from real-life originals. More than most writers, Fink succeeds in encompassing the psychological desperation of the Jewish victims in Poland, as well as the complex feelings of greed and malice, fellowship and compassion, courage and fear, that motivated the Polish victims, perpetrators, and rescuers. Fink conveys exquisitely a sense of what it was like, for Poles, as well as Jews, to be living in Poland under the Nazi occupation.

Ida Fink was born in 1921, in the town of Zbaraz, Galicia—Eastern Poland at the time, now Ukraine. Germany invaded Poland from the west in September 1939, and the Soviet Union invaded from the east a few weeks later. From October 1939 until June 1941, she lived under Soviet occupation; after that, under the Nazi regime. The daughter of a physician, Fink was studying to become a concert pianist, but her studies were cut short by the German invasion. When the Germans marched into Soviet-occupied eastern Poland in June 1941, the Nazi killing machine was running in high gear; all Jews were under a death sentence. The Fink family was shut in a ghetto, preliminary to extermination. Fink's father managed to obtain forged documents for Ida and her sister; the two of them escaped from the ghetto and mingled in with a group of gentile Polish women who were being transported to Germany to do forced labor. Fink describes this episode in an autobiographical novel, *The Journey,* 1992; (*Podroz*, 1990). In the same novel, she describes her life of prolonged anxiety in a German labor camp, where she lived in constant fear of being betrayed by some of the Polish women who suspected that Ida and her sister were Jewish.

Having survived this ordeal, Fink returned to Poland and lived there until 1957, when she immigrated to Israel, where she has lived ever since. She has worked for the Yad Vashem Holocaust Memorial in Jerusalem, recording witness accounts of other survivors. *A Scrap of Time* was given the Anne Frank Prize for Literature,

and Fink was awarded the Yad Vashem Prize in 1995, in tribute for her Holocaust writings.

The situations and places in her stories, she has affirmed, are derived from "real"situations and places, that is, from places that once existed in time, and from situations that once actually happened in the physical world. An interviewer from the Polish journal *Gazeta Wyborcza* (July 12, 1994) quoted Fink as saying, "In the story 'The Garden That Floated Away,' the garden is our garden, the neighbors our neighbors. I was really sitting with my sister on the stairs, squinting in the sun, while in the house our father was negotiating Aryan papers for us." Fink wants her readers to know that the events described in the story really happened, but she also wants her readers to know that the actual historical events have been transformed into a work of fiction.

For ten years, she says, she "was afraid to touch these things with the word," and even after ten years, one might say that her portraits of people and events are so delicate that she does just barely "touch [them] with the word." Fink told her *Times* interviewer that she waited ten years before starting to write, but she must have written and revised and refined incessantly, because there is a forty-year gap between the first publication of Fink's literary representations in *Skrawek Czasu* and the historical events themselves.

Although Fink is a survivor who writes as, and is, an authentic firsthand witness, it may be useful to think of her stories as second-generation Holocaust fiction. She waited patiently in relative silence while the number of survivor testimonies, diaries, and memoirs presented to the public proliferated. Thanks to her patience, Fink was able to construct her exquisite artistic gems on the platform of factual information established by witness testimonies and earlier, more direct narratives. Fink's narrators often confront the reader with a deeper inner truth, but at the same time, her fragmentary, nonchronological presentation of events that actually happened in place and time forces the reader to reconstitute the narrative to recover those surface events. But to reconstitute this world meaningfully, the reader is forced to fill in gaps, and therefore must be familiar, at least to some extent, with the historical context of the Holocaust. It is as if Fink assumes that her readers will know something about actual brutal events that have been more graphically described in prior historical, autobiographical, journalistic, and even fictional Holocaust accounts.

The story "A Scrap of Time" is a miracle of art and compression. In this brief tale, Fink exposes the existential abyss that separates normal existence from life as it was lived at the time of the Holocaust, and she does so by means of a brilliant exploration of the intertwining of time, memory, and language. "I want to talk about a certain time not measured in months and years," the narrator announces in the opening sentence of the story. The "time" she wants to talk about is not defined in terms of measured units, but in existential clusters that have been created by the Nazi murderers. "This time" the narrator advises, "was measured not in months but in a word—we no longer said 'in the beautiful month of May,' but 'after the first *"aktzia"*, or the second, or right before the third.' The narrator explains that 'round-up' [*lapanka*, from Polish *lapach*, to grab] was distinguished from 'action' by the borderline of race." Better than any historian, Fink has captured the rupture in time that constitutes the Holocaust.

SELECTED WORKS BY THE AUTHOR
The Journey. Trans. Joanna Wechsler and Francine Prose. New York: Farrar Straus Giroux, 1992; *A Scrap of Time and Other Stories.* Trans. Madeline Levine and Francine Prose. New York: Schocken, 1987; *Traces: Stories.* Trans. Philip Boehm and Francine Prose. New York: Metropolitan Books, 1997.

FOR FURTHER READING
Wilczynski, Marek, "Trusting the Words: Paradoxes of Ida Fink." *Modern Language Studies* 24, no. 4 (Fall 1994): 25–38.

David H. Hirsch

Flinker, Moshe (1926–1944)

Originally written in Hebrew, Moshe Flinker's Holocaust diary, *Hana'ar Moshe*, 1958 (*Young Moshe's Diary*, 1971) reveals traces of greatness in a young soul engaged in a struggle between hope and despair. The depth of this teenager's ordeal lies not only in his insight into history but also in his compassion to the point of guilt over the suffering of his fellow Jews. "I see myself as if I were a traitor," he confesses, "who fled from his people at the time of their anguish" (p. 65). Very much aware of the ramifications of the historical events of his time, Moshe was even more aware of what those events meant for the people of Israel and their relation to the God of Israel. As a devout Zionist, he was determined to be part of his people's return to their homeland, but he could see that their return was becoming more and more impossible. While he says he could see his homeland in his prayers (pp. 81–82), around him his eyes see nothing but ruin.

Born in The Hague on October 9, 1926, Moshe Flinker was educated both in the general studies of public school and in the biblical studies of Hebrew school. In 1940 his father, Eliezer Flinker, a Polish-born businessman living in the Netherlands, moved the family from German-occupied Holland to German-occupied Belgium. A wealthy man, Flinker was able to obtain an "Aryan" permit to live in Brussels, where he and his family remained relatively safe until April 7, 1944, the Eve of Passover; on that date, the Germans began their roundup of the Jews of Brussels. Since the Flinker family was orthodox in their lifestyle, they were unable to hide from the Germans the fact that they were Jews. The entire family was arrested that Passover and sent to Auschwitz. Although Moshe's five sisters and younger brother managed to survive, he and his parents perished.

While writing his diary, from November 1942 to September 1943, Moshe struggled to understand the Holocaust not only in terms of human history but also in terms of sacred history. Indeed, as a religious Jew, he believed that God is involved in the design of history, the aim of which is the messianic era. "It seems to me," he wrote on November 26, 1942, "that the time has come for our redemption" (p. 26). Moshe sees the world war as the "birthpang of the Messiah" (p. 55), which meant that "not from the English nor the Americans nor the Russians but from the Lord Himself will our redemption come" (p. 73). Whereas some diary writers see the absence of God in this event, Moshe tries to see the hand of God. He turns to the prayers and to the Scriptures and incorporates those texts into his own text, making his diary itself into a kind of prayer.

As the night of the Holocaust grew darker, however, Moshe felt himself slipping ever deeper into a spiritual void. On February 2, 1943 he wrote, "When I pray I feel as if I am praying to the wall and am not heard at all. . . . I think that the holy spark which I always felt with me has been taken from me" (p. 77). Before long the Scriptures too are lost on him, as he indicated in an entry dated July 4, 1943: "Formerly, when I took up my Bible and read it, it was as if I had returned to life, as if the Lord had taken pity on me; even in my darkest moments I found consolation in Him. Now even this is denied me" (p. 99). In Moshe's movement from prayer to emptiness, from Holy Word to empty void, one sees a very important feature of this Holocaust diary: the diary begins as a vehicle for God's utterance reverberating in voice of the diarist and ends as a lamentation over the cessation of that utterance.

Thus Moshe sees the content of his diary as a "reflection of [his] spiritual life" (p. 109). If that spiritual life revolves around God's presence and absence, then perhaps Moshe's outcry over the silence of God might bear a trace of God's own outcry. Reading Moshe Flinker's diary, one wonders whether the absent God might be hiding in the question concerning His absence. In any case, this diary written under singular conditions has universal implications for humanity's ongoing inquiry into the meaning of history.

SELECTED WORKS BY THE AUTHOR

Hana'ar Moshe: Yoman shel Moshe Flinker. Jerusalem: Yad Vashem, 1958; *Young Moshe's Diary*. Trans. Shaul Esh and Geoffrey Wigoder. Jerusalem: Yad Vashem, 1971.

David Patterson

Frank, Anne (1929–1945)

The diary written by Anne Frank is probably the single most widely read book to come out of the Holocaust (*Anne Frank: The Diary of a Young Girl*, 1952; first published as *Het Achterhuis*, 1947). Millions of readers have read the story of the teenage girl's two years in hiding. It has been translated into more than thirty-five languages and published in as many countries. Her diary was also the foundation for a successful drama performed worldwide (*The Diary of Anne Frank*, 1956) and a film of the same title (1959; and video, 1984). Especially in the last twenty years, many schoolchildren and adults alike have had their first exposure to the effects of Adolf Hitler's war through Anne's writing. Anne's diary so captured the attention of the world that her name has become symbolic of the six million Jewish victims of the Shoah.

Anneleis Marie Frank was born on June 12, 1929, in Frankfurt, Germany, to her parents, Otto and Edith Frank. She had an older sister, Margot. The Frank family moved to Amsterdam in 1933 both because of the anti-Jewish policies being promulgated in Germany and because of a business opportunity for Otto in the Netherlands. Anne seems to have enjoyed a happy childhood there, although she was nicknamed the fragile one because of her frequent bouts of ill health. In 1941 Anne and her sister were transferred into a school for Jewish children and saw many of their remaining rights withdrawn that year; as Jews they were barred from all facilities open to the general public: libraries, theaters, museums, restaurants, and so on. On July 5, 1942, Margot was the first member of the family to be summoned by the Nazis for labor service. Within the next twenty-four hours, Otto Frank took his family to the hiding place he had been slowly preparing for them. They hid in the upper floors of the warehouse of his business. One week later, as planned, the van Pels, a family of three, joined the Franks in the secret annex, as it has now become known. In November a dentist of one of the non-Jewish people helping them also joined them to make a total of eight residents.

Anne, along with the others, lived in the annex for just over two years, until August 4, 1944, the day they were all betrayed. Two of their five non-Jewish helpers were arrested with them. The eight Jewish victims were first sent to Westerbork, a transit camp, in Holland. In September all eight were transferred to

Auschwitz. Probably in October Anne and Margot were separated from their parents forever when the girls were sent on to Bergen-Belsen. The infamous conditions at Bergen-Belsen that winter proved too much for Anne and Margot. Both most likely succumbed to typhus. First Margot and then Anne a few days later died in late February or early March of 1945, shortly before the British liberated Bergen-Belsen on April 15, 1945. Of the eight people in hiding together only Anne's father, Otto Frank, survived the concentration camps.

Anne began her diary on her thirteenth birthday, June 12, 1942, just a few weeks before they were forced into hiding. (She had been doing some writing prior to this but little is known about it.) Anne's diary is both a fine piece of literature and the testament of a vivacious, lively, and insightful adolescent during very troubled times. Anne bears witness to the struggles and the terrors of the historical circumstances forced upon her, as well as to the more common difficulties of a thirteen- and fourteen-year-old, including menstruation, difficulties with her mother, lack of privacy and conflicting emotions and needs. Her psychological perspicuity shines through in the insightful descriptions of her existential dilemmas, however. For example, when she compares the effects of hiding on the emotional and moral health of the adults and the adolescents she concludes, "Older people have an opinion about everything and are sure of themselves and their actions. It's twice as hard for us young people to hold on to our opinions at a time when ideals are being shattered and destroyed, when the worst side of human nature predominates." (p. 332). Another example is her awareness sometimes of an acute loneliness despite being cooped up in an overcrowded space.

Above all, Anne is exceptionally self-aware, and she does not shy away from self-criticism. She can admit that she behaves stubbornly and sometimes less than charitably toward her mother or the others with whom she is confined. As the youngest in the annex, she hurts when she feels she is not understood or when she is treated like a young child. To read Anne's diary is to get a wonderfully sensitive description of the emotional life of an adolescent. However, it would be a grave injustice to treat the diary as merely representative of average adolescent concerns. Part of its power and hold on us is that it is a tragedy. Anne does not get to finish school, return to her friends she misses so terribly, or become the writer she dreamed of becoming.

Although Anne did not get a chance to enjoy it, her wish to become famous did come true. "I want to go on living even after death" (April 5, 1944, p. 250). Anne had hoped to get her diary published, and she even revised some of her entries with that end in mind. On March 28, 1944, she heard a radio broadcast aired by the Dutch minister of education and culture who was in exile in London calling for "ordinary documents" such as letters and diaries as records of what the occupied Dutch had to endure. The sheets of paper on which she did her rewriting were found and a list of name changes was also found. She planned on keeping the identity of those in hiding, as well as the helpers, concealed. In fact, the first published version of her diary gives the alternate names to many of the people involved. One of the helpers, Miep Gies, who sometimes gave Anne paper for her diary and therefore was well aware of its existence, retrieved all of Anne's writings the afternoon of their arrest. She knew Anne had been so far very private about her diaries, so she did not read them nor allow anyone else to read them. Eventually she returned them to Otto Frank. Gies admitted years later that if she had read them she would have destroyed them because they put too many people's lives in danger.

To many, Anne Frank has become a symbol of the strength and optimism of the human spirit in the midst of tragedy. In July 1944 Anne wrote what was to become the most famous line of her diary and the one most often used to symbolize her spirit. "In spite of everything, I still believe that people are really good at heart" (p. 332). However, as Alex Sagan points out, these lines are actually written in an "overwhelming mood of desolation." In this same passage Anne also wrote, "I see the world being turned into a wilderness, I hear the approaching thunder, which will destroy us too, I can feel the sufferings of millions." (July 15, 1944, p. 332). Scholars caution us to keep Anne's writing in perspective. Some have called her the symbol of the six million Jewish victims of the Holocaust. If we are to give her this status, then we must also attribute to Anne a much greater experience than one of simple optimism. As Cynthia Ozick* reminds us, Anne endured horrendous suffering and a lonely death at the hands of the Nazis after her diary entries ended. Anne Frank would no doubt have had much more to say to us from these experiences.

It should be noted here that the first version of Anne's diary was approved by Otto Frank, and he chose to leave out certain entries or lines which he felt were too private (mentions of her bodily changes), too mundane, or could prove hurtful to the memory of his wife. In 1989 the Netherlands State Institute for War Documentation produced a critical version of the diary (*The Diary of Anne Frank: The Critical Edition*). This large book includes all the versions of Anne's diary as well as several scholarly articles, including one on the authenticity of the diary, which had been repeatedly challenged by right-wing extremists.

In 1955 a dramatic version of the diary was first produced in the United States, and in 1957 the film was made. The play, entitled *The Diary of Anne Frank,* premiered in New York City and won the Pulitzer Prize for drama. It was then performed throughout Europe including the Netherlands and Germany. The stage and film productions made the diary available to many more thousands of people. Both versions of the diary accentuate Anne's optimism. They each end with the above-mentioned oft-quoted line of Anne's basic belief in the goodness of people. An emphasis in both scripts was clearly and intentionally made to present the forgiving side of Anne. With these dramatizations of Anne's diary, however, scholars of the Holocaust once again caution us to remember that the voice of Anne Frank was not one of blithe sanguinity. Her suffering increased one hundred fold outside the secret annex, and this experience, which did not make the stage, was far more representative of the six million victims of the Holocaust. We cannot say that her diary or the scripts that were based on it represent the totality of Anne and her experiences as a victim of the Shoah. Yet there is no denying that Anne's writing put a human face to the unfathomable statistics of the millions of individuals who suffered and died.

SELECTED WORK BY THE AUTHOR:
Anne Frank: The Diary of a Young Girl. New York: Doubleday, 1991.

FOR FURTHER READING
Barnouw, David, and van der Stroom, Gerrold. *The Diary of Anne Frank: The Critical Edition*. Prepared by the Netherlands State Institute for War Documentation. New York: Doubleday, 1989; Ozick, Cynthia, "Who Owns Anne Frank?" *New Yorker*, October 6, 1997, 76–87; Sagan, Alex, "Examining Optimism: Anne Frank's Place in Postwar Culture." In *Anne Frank in Historical Perspective: A Teaching Guide for Secondary Schools*. Los Angeles: Martyrs Memorial and Museum of the Holocaust, 1995.

Sarita Cargas

Frankl, Viktor Emil (1905–1997)

Holocaust survivor Viktor Frankl was the founder of the third Viennese school of psychotherapy (after Sigmund Freud and Alfred Adler). Frankl became an internationally acclaimed psychiatrist as the founder of existential analysis known as logotherapy. His most famous work, *Man's Search for Meaning*, has been translated into twenty-six languages, which makes him one of the most widely read authors to emerge from the Holocaust. This book has two parts: the first describes his experiences in the concentration camps and how they confirmed his belief in the essential role of meaning in our lives. The second section of the book lays out his theory of logotherapy explained below. Though all Frankl's works were published after the war, and indeed molded by his experiences of the war, he was publishing articles on logotherapy in 1937, a year before the Nazis invaded Austria. In all, Frankl wrote about ten books on the subject of logotherapy.

Viktor Frankl was born in Vienna on March 26, 1905, to his parents, Elsa and Gabriel. He attended the same secondary school that Freud had and in fact was drawn to psychology at an early age. Frankl corresponded with Freud as a teenager and at nineteen he published an article in Freud's prestigious psychoanalytic journal. In 1930 he graduated from the University of Vienna Medical School. While involved in counseling for depression at low-cost treatment centers during Austria's economic depression, Frankl was struck by the fact that losing one's job often meant losing one's sense of purpose in life. Thus far psychoanalysis reduced all unhappiness to unresolved past inner conflicts. This explanation did not address the realities Frankl was witnessing when working with the disaffected and suicidal patients of the pre–World War II Vienna. They were suffering from the immediate issues of job and financial losses, not issues left over from childhood.

During the war Frankl was granted an immigration visa to the United States. Because it was only for himself and did not include his parents, he decided to reject it. He married his first wife, and in 1942 Frankl, his new wife, parents, and brother were deported to Auschwitz. Viktor was the only one of them to survive. (A sister survived in Australia.) After the war Frankl returned to the University of Vienna where he taught until he was eighty-five years old. He was also the director of the neurology department at Vienna Polyclinic until 1970. During his career he lectured throughout the world and taught at several American universities including Harvard, Southern Methodist, Stanford, and Duquesne.

Man's Search for Meaning, originally published as *From Death Camp to Existentialism* (1959) (*Ein Psycholog erlebt das Kozentrationslager*, 1946), is Frankl's most explicit account and explanation of life in the concentration camps. It is not just a strictly autobiographical description of his own life in the camps. He set out to discover and explain the effects of the concentration camp on the average prisoner. Based on his own experience and on the mass of published material of others, Frankl concluded that there are three phases of mental reactions for a prisoner. They are the initial period following admission to the camp, the period when one is well entrenched in camp routine, and for survivors, the period following release and liberation.

A main characteristic of the first phase is shock. Frankl describes his own experience of arriving at Auschwitz—his first camp. The trainload of people assumed they were going to perform forced labor at a munitions factory, but when someone saw the sign for Auschwitz and cried out the name, "Everyone's heart missed a beat at that moment. Auschwitz—the name that stood for everything that was horrible" (p. 12). For a moment the truth is incomprehensible. Even when the nightmare is comprehended they might experience another common reaction: the "delusion of reprieve." It is the belief in the midst of horror that maybe it will not be so bad for me. One notices the privileged prisoner who still looks healthy and thinks, "Of course, I will fare as well." But most are not granted such luck, and they all soon discover that the body and psyche in fact can endure that which in normal life they never would have imagined possible—sleep deprivation, severe vitamin deficiency, sores and abrasions which could not be treated, filth, living with the constant threat of death, and so much more that words can barely explain. Understandably, then, followed thoughts of suicide contemplated by almost every person during this first phase especially.

The second phase, on the other hand, is characterized by apathy. At first, prisoners suffered many painful emotions such as disgust, horror, and an excruciating longing for home and family. After a while, they were not able to sustain feelings of intense anguish. Apathy is a psychic survival mechanism which deadens the pain. In the second stage, prisoners no longer felt the need to turn their eyes away when others were being beaten or otherwise tortured. The sick and the dying were everywhere, and one became inured. Frankl wrote, "By means of this insensibility the prisoner soon surrounded himself with a very necessary protective shell" (p. 35). For those who were released from the camps there was a final stage. It was their reaction upon immediate liberation. For many the first response was not one of ecstatic joy. Their emotional life had been thwarted and even the ability to feel pleasure took time to return to them. Also, a prisoner's experience of reality was so radically altered in the concentration camps that the so-called normal experience of freedom felt very unreal. It took time to get used to freedom again. Frankl calls this sense of irreality depersonalization.

For many, of course, bitterness and disillusionment also threatened to alter their personalities permanently. When they got out, others could not understand what the prisoners had endured. Worse, many in the outside world were indifferent to their experiences. Also gone was what the prisoner imagined going home to. There was no old life to return to. One's home and community were gone. How utterly disrupting to the human psyche to survive the destruction of both one's immediate family—parents, siblings, spouses, and children—and extended family—grandparents, aunts, uncles, cousins, nieces, and nephews.

How exactly did the victims of concentration camps resist succumbing to mental breakdowns? Here lies Frankl's main thesis: the will to meaning. Men and women did not commit suicide or give up hope if they felt there was someone or something worth living for. This is what gave meaning to their suffering, or at least gave them motivation to endure it. Fellow prisoners encouraged the prisoner who was losing hope that he or she had a future. They had to be reminded that there was something to look forward to. Frankl believes this need for a reason to exist is fundamental to all people in all situations. Psychological health is predicated on finding meaning to existence.

Frankl explains this thesis in the second part of the book *Man's Search for Meaning*: the need for meaning as the prime motivational force in our lives. Frankl's theory of logotherapy, as it is called, is opposed to Freudian psychoanalysis, which assumes the will to pleasure is our primary motivation, and in contrast to Adlerian psychology which stresses the will to power.

Also, while Freudian therapy focuses on a person's past, logotherapy places the emphasis on the future. Logotherapy presupposes that life is meaningful and that the future for each individual is therefore specific and unique. However, it is often in the light of suffering that people begin to question the meaning of their existence. Here Frankl makes the most radical claim: in suffering we can fulfill life's deepest meaning. "For what matters above all is the attitude we take towards suffering, the attitude in which we take our suffering upon ourselves" (p. 178). Suffering is an unavoidable fact of life; however, we can find meaning in it and make it a meaningful experience. Just as any kind of work can be given value by the integrity with which it is done, so too can we decide to accept suffering and in that take control of the unalterable destiny it may impose on our lives. This is logotherapy's most profound claim about suffering. Though it often comes from the outside in the sense that it comes not by choice, we can still choose to have control over it by the attitude we take toward it. We can suffer nobly.

Frankl's work helped the world understand the mental conditions of the concentration camps, and he also gave a kind of dignity to the experience. Indeed, prisoners and sufferers from the world over wrote to Frankl and credited him with their sanity after reading his work.

SELECTED WORKS BY THE AUTHOR

The Doctor and the Soul: From Psychotherapy to Logotherapy. Trans. Richard Winston and Clara Winston. New York: Vintage Books, 1986; *Man's Search for Meaning: An Introduction to Logotherapy. Part One.* Trans. Ilse Lasch. New York: Pocket Books, 1977. *Viktor Frankl Recollections: An Autobiography.* Trans. Joseph Fabry and Judith Fabry. New York: Insight Books, 1997.

Sarita Cargas

G

Gary, Romain (1914–1980)

Well aware of the problems that mankind had to confront just after World War II and convinced that everyone must take his or her responsibilities, Romain Gary is a clear-headed cosmopolitan and witness of his era. In his writing he fights for the defense of the most fundamental humanist and Jewish values: respect of life, of the individual's rights, and of liberty. He condemns violence in all its forms and dreams of a world of "feminity," of love among men. Pursuing that dream, he makes much use of social and political satire in his first works, such as *Le Grand vestiaire*, 1948 (*The Company of Men*, 1950). In this novel the idealistic protagonist realizes with stupefaction that neither the war nor the suffering has changed anything and that injustice and crime continue to prevail even after the Nazis' departure. The personality that he gives to his heroes, always projections of himself, combines the singular nature of a conscience and the universal quality of a destiny. All his life Gary kept the promise that he made to his humble neighbor in Vilna: to remind the important persons he will meet of the existence of the obscure man in the street.

Romain Gary was born in Lithuania on May 8, 1914. Fleeing Russia and Poland, Gary's Jewish mother took her son with her to Nice, where they lived under financial hardship. She educated her son, instilling him with a pious devotion to France, and predicted he would have a great destiny. In *La Promesse de l'aube*, 1960 (*Promise at Dawn*, 1961), a mixture of autobiography and fiction, Gary idealizes his mother who influenced so deeply his personality. After the defeat of 1940, Gary joined Charles de Gaulle and served as a pilot in the Free French Forces. In 1945 he began a diplomatic career that included his post as secretary to the ambassador in Sofia and in Bern and as consul general in Los Angeles.

The difficulty of his sense of identity is reflected in what he calls his "exil intérieur": he goes by the name of his mother's divorced husband "Kacew," while his real father is supposed to be the actor Yvan Mosjoukine. Gary defines himself as "Asian-Russian, Jewish, a non-practicing Catholic, French, a born… a sort of Gengis Cohn." Like the first picaresque authors, the *conversos* (Christians of Jewish origins), Gary is unable to claim affiliation with any particular religious community. As a child, he became familiar with xenophobia and racial hatred, humiliation, and loneliness—experiences which are those of his preferred character, the Picaro, the bastard with whom he identifies in his picaresque novels. The uncertainty as to his father's identity and the complexity of his own can explain the desire for self-creation he hoped but failed to realize in the mystification of the pen name he took: Emile Ajar.

From *Education européenne*, 1945 (European education) to *La Vie devant soi*, 1975 (*The Life Before Us*, 1986, published under the pseudonym of Emile Ajar) and in the interim the novels *Les Racines du ciel*, 1956 (*The Roots of Heaven*, 1958, Prix Goncourt, 1956), *La Promesse de l'aube*, *L'Angoisse du Roi*

Salomon, 1979 (*King Solomon*, 1983, under the pseudonym Emile Ajar, 1979), and *Les Cerfs-volants,* 1980 (The kite) the war, the concentration camps, and the Shoah are either evoked or are the subject of Gary's work.

La Danse de Gengis Cohn, 1967 (*The Dance of Genghis Cohn*, 1968) is one of the most daring and powerful novels written on the Shoah. It is a *conte philosophique,* comparable to Voltaire's *Candide*, describing the mad epic of humanity bent on his own destruction. Here irreverent metaphors convey the author's love of and anger toward mankind. Beauty, Humanity, and Death conduct the dance that leads the novel's heroes to an ecstatic death which is immediately ridiculed since they are found with their trousers removed. The first part of the tale takes place in 1966 Germany, which, while having proclaimed itself free of Nazis, is on the verge of making a dangerous return to its Nazi roots. An inexplicable wave of killings shocks the people in the city of Licht. The narrator, Moshe Cohn, alias Gengis Cohn, is a comic by trade; he embodies love of life and men, joy, and Jewish consciousness, which the author opposes to Western consciousness. He was exterminated in 1944 in a Polish forest by the Nazi Schatz, whom he has been haunting ever since. The presence of this "Dybbuk," whose philosophical and historical reflections make up the bulk of the narrative, leads to a permanent confrontation between the present and the Shoah. Since he is the only character of the novel who has some depth, the reader identifies with the "dead-living" narrator.

In *The Dance of Genghis Cohn,* Gary gives free rein to his imagination; no reader caught up in the game will require authenticity in a dream which starts out as an absurd imaginary story, continues as an allegory, and ends up as a nightmare. Aware of the historical dimension from the very first line of the story, the reader understands the necessity of a multilayered reading of this parodic police mystery. Rather than attenuating the horror, it is the satire, humor, derision, and burlesque qualities that underscore the inadmissibility of the extermination and condemn the perversion of the mentalities and the language of Nazism. The innumerable literary allusions, the parodic names and chapter titles, the pastiches and citations that make up the narrative accuse literature of betraying humanity. A multitude of ironic references admonish mu-

sic, painting, and sculpture of feeding on human suffering and of transforming them into an aesthetic pleasure.

Gary criticizes the worship of suffering and death in Western culture. He also accuses Christianity of betraying its own values. Convinced that the Shoah owes its genesis to strictly human causes, Gary does not attribute any transcendental significance to it. Neither does he emphasize the uniqueness of the event. With a style that seeks to uncover an empty language strewn with clichés, the novels signed "Ajar" take up Gary's favorite themes. Madame Rosa, the heroine of *La Vie devant soi,* lives haunted by her memory of the persecution. This novel is a sort of parody of *La Promesse de l'aube* but in no way expresses derision. Through Momo's character, the author here makes good on his promise to his own mother never to abandon her, a promise that the war had prevented him from keeping.

In *L'Angoisse du Roi Salomon* we come across once more the author's preferred pair: an older person who knows life and has experienced war, persecution, and Shoah and a younger character without any experience. The older character will teach the younger one true values and how to fight against evil and its various manifestations, particularly those caused by men. Like Elie Wiesel*, Romain Gary believes that the Jew's mission is to give a moral conscience to men and to serve as witness to the Shoah. This is the role of Gengis Cohn. This is also the meaning of the Berlin episode recounted in *La Nuit sera calme*, 1974 (The night will be calm): a survivor comes every day to read a newspaper in Yiddish at a stand in Berlin without buying it, and every day the owner of the stand turns the pages for the Jew without giving him the newspaper.

Romain Gary wrote more than thirty novels, plays, and a significant essay, "Pour Sganarelle," 1980 (For Sganarelle), in which he elaborates his theory of the novel. He has given important interviews which are precious tools for understanding his works. He is also the writer and producer of two films.

SELECTED WORKS BY THE AUTHOR
Les Cerfs-volants. Paris: Gallimard, 1980; *The Company of Men*. Trans. Joseph Barnes. New York: Simon and Schuster, 1950; *The Dance of Genghis Cohn*. Trans. Camilla Sykes. New York: World Publishing, 1968;

Education européene. Paris: Calmann-Lévy, 1945; *King Solomon.* Trans. Barbara Wright. New York: Harper and Row, 1983; *The Life Before Us.* Trans. Ralph Manheim. New York: New Directions, 1986; *La Nuit sera calme.* Paris: Gallimard, 1974; *Promise at Dawn.* Trans. John Markham Beach. New York: Harper, 1961; *The Roots of Heaven.* Trans. Jonathan Griffin. New York: Simon and Schuster, 1958.

FOR FURTHER READING

Bayard, Pierre, *Il était deux fois Romain Gary.* Paris: Presses Universitaires de France, 1990; Bona, Dominique, *Romain Gary.* Paris: Mercure de France, 1987; Cantonnée, Jean-Marie. *Romain Gary/Emile Ajar.* Paris: P. Belford, 1990; Wardi, Charlotte. *Le Génocide dans la fiction romanesque.* Paris: Presses Universitaires de France, 1986.

Charlotte Wardi

Gershon, Karen (1923–1993)

Karen Gershon is one of the most significant contemporary poets in the English language, who relates the experience of exile in the shadow of the Holocaust. Not only did she and her sister Lise go to England with the Kindertransport of 1938, she also wrote about it, as in the volume, *We Came as Children* (1966), which she edited. This is a collection of memoirs of those who had been refugee children and were evacuated to England.

Karen Gershon was born Kaethe Lowenthal in 1923 in the German town of Bielefeld. A year after she and her sister reached England in 1938, Lise went to Palestine; after 1939, Gershon was left to fend for herself because her parents had been murdered by the Nazis. Gershon married Val Tripp in 1948 and immigrated to Israel in 1968 with her husband and four children. In 1973 she and her husband returned to England. Gershon died in 1993 after undergoing heart-bypass surgery.

Gershon was not a prolific writer, and her work is dominated thematically by her experience of exile and the terror of Nazism, which, fortunately, she did not suffer to the full. Her writing, both in its autobiographical and its poetic form, is transparent and direct, relating squarely to its subject. Her subject is not only the fate that she actually endured, but the fate that she might have experienced, had she been

that little bit less fortunate. This is a fate that she feels that she has to project, in constant dread, onto her children. In the poem "Stella's Hair," from *Legacies and Encounters*, she writes of how, looking at her daughter's hair, her imagination leads her to the thought that her children are children whom the Germans would surely have murdered.

Although her immigration to Israel came later, she was already preoccupied by the notion of what the new Jewish State represented and symbolized some years earlier. In her "Israel Notebook 1966," she almost prosaically, although in poetic form, speculates on whether the Israeli revolution will be able to reconstitute the Jewish memory, as well as Jewish fate. She concludes the first poem of the series, in the seventh section, with a verse that also constitutes a polemical assertion, juxtaposing images of victims against images of triumphant prosperity. The poem accepts the dichotomy—exile/home, which in turn carries with it the notion of the pairing—sickness/health, and even further—death/life. There is no ambiguity in the stark contrasting of options. The imagined protagonist, "the Jew," asserts that the Jews come from the desert. Although the death experienced was the product of an aberration resulting from being away from home, the reader finally comes back to the beginning, and can begin to recoup the losses: "This is the country of the resurrection" (p. 68). It is also the land of remembrance. The whole of Jewish existence is built of memory, and the matter remembered is bleak because there is a constant danger that it might haunt the present and snuff out its rather weak flame.

Gershon's poetry is essentially the story of her own life and thought. In the poem "I Set Out for Jerusalem," she asserts that she has always belonged to Jerusalem, even at an earlier stage (*Legacies*, p. 69). This step of coming to Jerusalem is part of the effort of reunification, a rejoining with the ancient people. Indeed, the theme of renewal, supported by the image of fresh water fed by a fountain, is a constant in Gershon's poetry. The hard rock can be fructified, as in the poem, "Nightfall in Jerusalem," where the stones of Jerusalem are compared to a "Messianic rock with people in its veins" (*Legacies,* p. 70). With the "Messianic rock" not only is the generation restored and renewed, but the landscape too is reinvigorated in reaction. The Jerusalem poems are immediately self-referential, without any element of disguise or self-protective metaphorization. The guarantee of a future within a stabilized external framework is sufficient to restore the pleasure conveyed by a sense of generations; the generations of the past now, it seems, have their assured echo in those of the future. The break in continuity was threatened by the events of the Holocaust, and, in most cases, achieved. But ultimate destruction has now been thwarted, and that is what offers the satisfaction expressed in the poetry here.

Gershon's poetry borders on prose. Its subject is the author's life, and, stemming from that, that of the progenitors and the successors. But all life is inevitably problematic, and, even beyond the terrible events of her early years, cannot be taken for granted. The volume ends by telling about her young son, Tony, who tried to kill himself. Senselessly? Who knows?

SELECTED WORKS BY THE AUTHOR
The Bread of Exile: A Novel. London: V. Gollancz, 1985; *Burn Helen: A Novel.* Brighton, England.: Harvester Press, 1980; *The Fifth Generation: A Novel.* London: V. Gollancz, 1987; *Legacies and Encounters: Poems 1966–1971.* London: V. Gollancz, 1972; *A Lesser Child: An Autobiography.* London: Dufour, 1994; *Selected Poems.* New York: Harcourt, Brace and World, 1966; *We Came as Children: A Collective Autobiography.* London: V. Gollancz, 1966.

Leon I. Yudkin

Geve, Thomas (1929–)

Published in Israel in 1958, Thomas Geve's *Youth in Chains* is among the first Holocaust memoirs to appear in print (reprinted under the title *Guns and Barbed Wire: A Child Survives the Holocaust*, 1987). It is a young adult's reflection on a childhood drained away first by Nazi society and then by a Nazi camp. His reflections originally took the form of colored drawings he made while he was recuperating in Buchenwald after his liberation. What began as visual images traced upon Nazi Labor Organization registration forms came to fruition in Geve's remarkable memoir.

Born in the fall of 1929, Thomas Geve spent his earliest years in the Upper Silesian mining town of Beuthen, Germany, where the Nazi regime quickly became the fashion. He attended a Jewish school and was a member of the Bar Kokhba Zionist sports club. In the summer of 1939, his father left for England, and he went with his mother to Berlin, where they hoped to make arrangements for emigration. Then the war broke out.

When the Germans closed all the Jewish schools of Berlin in 1942, Geve found work in the Jewish cemetery at Weisensee. In June 1943 he and his mother were sent to Auschwitz, where they were separated forever. Geve presents a boy's description—but a detailed description—of the camp, its routine, its operators, and its inmates. He writes with a strong sense of community, nearly always using the pronoun *we* rather than *I*. This *we*, moreover, includes Poles, Russians, Ukrainians, Gypsies, and other nationalities; indeed, Gypsies have a relatively prominent role in Geve's memoir. Selected to work as a bricklayer, Geve was able to find ways to survive in Auschwitz; after a time, he was a camp veteran, despite his youth. The death march of January 1945 took him from Auschwitz to Gross-Rosen; from there he was sent to Buchenwald. After the war, he rejoined his father in England and later settled on the Mediterranean, where he took up work as a technical advisor.

Geve's memoir is divided into more than 200 short sections of a page or two in length, each of which relates a facet of the concentrationary universe in a simple style. Drawing on the reader's knowledge and the character's (his own) ignorance, Geve makes effective use of irony, as when he sees a sign that reads *Vernichtungslager* (annihilation camp) at Birkenau and wonders whether they are destroying secret documents or vermin. While at first the memoir may seem to lack the depth and the sophistication of those written by older survivors, it does have numerous moments of insight. One notices, for example, that Geve's memory of his burial of the dead in Berlin is a kind of resurrection of the dead through the memory itself. Similarly, he recalls the activity of burying Torah scrolls in Berlin, and in that very recollection he recovers a truth signified by the scrolls. Geve was not particularly religious, but he does remember that he and other inmates "respected the devotees of the Bible mainly because they helped us. . . . 'Only our own conduct can be our savior,' they acknowledged bravely and stubbornly. 'Through it He reveals Himself'" (pp. 143–44). For Geve, conduct includes the act of remembrance.

Although Geve was only fifteen when the war ended, he sensed the collapse of civilization enough to read it in the eyes of those who visited Buchenwald soon after its liberation. Noting the shock experienced by men and women in the visiting delegations, he points out how their whole concept of Western civilization was being challenged; he also wonders where these eager humanitarians had been in 1937, when Buchenwald was inaugurated. Thus Geve's memoir is more than a personal memory or a slice of history—it is an indictment of history and humanity. The memoir ends, however, not by looking back but with the anticipation of a future filled with hope.

SELECTED WORKS BY THE AUTHOR
Es gibt hier keine Kinder: Auschwitz, Gross-Rosen, Buchenwald: Zeichnungen eines kindlichen Historiker. Göttingen: Wallstein Verlag, 1997; *Guns and Barbed Wire: A Child Survives the Holocaust.* Chicago: Academy Chicago, 1987; *Youth in Chains.* Jerusalem: Rubin Mass, 1958.

David Patterson

Gouri, Haim (1923–)

Haim Gouri became the archetypal representative of so-called Palmach literature (named for the Palmach, the elite commando units of the Haganah); in other words, the new Hebrew literature quintessentially characteristic of the infant Hebrew state. Gouri matured with the foundation of independent Israel; he wrote of it and to it. He was its spokesman, and he became an icon of the times. He was young, male, Sabra (Israeli born), strong, and committed to a powerful, independent Israel, the very antithesis, as it was seen, of the Diaspora existence.

The town of Tel Aviv was only fourteen years old when Gouri was born there in 1923. The son of Russian immigrants, Gouri matriculated at the renowned agricultural school Kaduri. From 1941 to 1949, Gouri served in the Palmach; after being sent to Europe to help Holocaust survivors in the aftermath of the war, Gouri returned to fight in the War of Independence. In the 1950s he studied Hebrew literature, philosophy, and French culture at the Hebrew University in Jerusalem and went on to advanced studies at the Sorbonne in Paris. In addition to writing poetry, fiction, and essays, in the 1970s and 1980s Gouri made a trilogy of documentary films on the Holocaust. Among his most prestigious awards are the Bialik Prize (1975), the Israel Prize (1988), and the Uri Zvi Greenberg Award (1998). Gouri and his wife, Aliza, now live in Jerusalem.

Gouri's first poem was published in *Mishmar* (edited by poet Abraham Shlonsky), in 1945, "Masa yam" (Sea voyage), and his first complete volume of poetry, *Pirhe esh*, 1949 (Flowers of fire, 1949) appeared immediately in the wake of the War of Independence and became its most representative expression. Possibly his best-known poem, "Hineh mutalot gufotenu" (See our corpses are laid out) appeared in that volume. It opens with a statement that all of "our" corpses are laid out, row by row. For these people, life has ceased. But the final stanza introduces another possibility. Opening with the identical phrase, it voices the hope that "we shall flower when the last shout of the shot is silenced." In this poem the narrator identifies with the dead, but he also envisions a possible resurrection when the terrible war ends.

A later poem takes up the theme of the Binding of Isaac. In the poem, "Yerushah" (Heritage), from *Shoshanat haruhot*, 1960 (Lily of the winds), he writes more prosaically about both Abraham and Isaac. But Isaac, the apparently minor figure of the biblical story, is the key. He lived for many days and prospered, but that moment when the imminent sacrifice was thwarted was transmitted to the descendants: "They are born with a knife in their hearts." This Jewish fate, recognized in the Holocaust and in the struggle for the Israeli state, is a perpetual presence.

Because Gouri worked with Jewish survivors in the wake of World War II, he at least indirectly experienced the terror of Nazism for himself. This became one of the themes of his writing and, particularly, of his prose. For Israel the greatest trauma in the postwar years was the Eichmann trial, which brought home the full extent of what happened at the time. Many had been too close to the event and had only their own contact with it, not the overall perspective. The trial presented a larger, more awesome context, albeit some fifteen years later. Gouri wrote an account of that trial in his work *Mul ta hazkhukhit*, 1962 (The glass cage) and followed it with a novel, *Isqat hashokolad*, 1965 (*The Chocolate Deal*, 1968; reprinted 1999), a fictional presentation of an episode under the Nazis.

His most important work of Holocaust literature, *The Chocolate Deal* enters into the minds of two Holocaust survivors, Mordi and Rubi, to explore the condition of radical homelessness that arises in the wake of the catastrophe. Gouri examines the problem of silence, which is a problem of meaning or "the inauguration of the critical period" (p. 9). He opens up the issue of lost identity, as Rubi laments, "I don't want to keep searching for my own name on the list of the missing" (p. 41). And he sounds the depths of a madness peculiar to the survivor, as when Mordi declares, "Already madness is creeping over me. I feel it. Creeping upward" (p. 57). Throughout the novel one detects a profound sense of connection between the author and his characters. Indeed, Gouri has said that in order to understand the Jews, one must understand two things: the Holocaust and the State of Israel.

For the spokesman of Israelism, the Jews at the mercy of the Nazis offered not just an episode within the panorama of Jewish history, but the episode that became the climax and the summary of Jewish non-independence, the situation for which the State of Israel existed to counteract. These two prongs of Jewish existence have become Gouri's themes: the Jews in the Diaspora, which is tragic exile, and the Jews in Israel. The latter stance is neither easy nor comfortable, but it is presented as necessary and unavoidable. A later piece of confessional prose fiction, *Hahaqirah*, 1980 (The investigation) consists of an imaginary questioning of one Reuel, whose biography bears considerable resemblance to the author's own, but who has recently died (according to the book). This work is an attempt to lay bare the sense of guilt at the coverup by the Israeli-born primary figure of his recent past, and the biographical details of his antecedents. Here we have a portrait of the relationship between Israel and real/imagined Diaspora.

Writers often become fixated on the one formative period or episode in their lives, to which they keep returning, and which retains the power of a magnet. For Gouri, that formative period was clearly the post-Holocaust period and the War of Independence, or, more specifically, his association with the Palmach. In his volume of poems *Ad alot hashahar*, 1950 (Until dawn arises), he says in a preface that his ambition is to relate the events of a Palmach squadron. He is already removed from the scene, but he is one with those who fought, and he recognizes that together they form a unit that will always hold together: "For out of one pit have we been scraped out, and one heart has borne us in its beat." The Palmach was a small circle of young, fit, independent Hebrews committed to the cause of Israeli independence, whose fates and lives were to become entwined until the end. Now, only a few months after the awesome events of the fighting, all seems so distant and yet significant, as though enshrined in mythical terms.

There is no more central figure in what is now known as Palmach literature than Gouri. For this group the Palmach indeed became a kind of substitute parent, as it reared a radically different generation. It was a new land, a new cohort, a new language, a new situation, and a new culture. Although this State of Israel was created for the Jewish people, it also represented a radical breach with the recent past, and a shift from the Diaspora, even a reversal of its values. Gouri writes about their move into the Southern Negev, "We moved a great deal in this land. The Palmach, our father, taught us the work" (p. 112). And so the myth was created. The foundation archetype of modern Israel is the figure of the Palmachnik, which Gouri helped to create, and of which he was also the incarnation.

Gouri's *Hasefer hamshuga*, 1971 (The crazy book), a picaresque novel, is a later invocation of that period, a revisitation of the myth twenty years later. Its objective is to perpetuate the memory of the figures involved, and to recall those times. This the author achieves by means of a collage in words, re-creating the atmosphere of the time and place in which the Palmach discovered its function and flourished. This "mad book" further confirmed Gouri as an experimental author, as one who was prepared to mix techniques and media in order to produce a varied scale of effects. Prose is succeeded by poetry, or it is interspersed by verses. Pieces of reportage intervene, and sometimes it is hard to determine whether we are dealing with a matter of fact or invention. The romantic verse has constant overtones of the tragic and mythical. The author is taken by the Israeli slang of the period, which we must remember is the primal Israeli argot, the very first of the new spoken Hebrew, reveling in its newness and in its authenticity, the first Hebrew to be a mother tongue itself, not derived from European sources. But, as ever, Gouri is also constantly in search of the classic form and statement.

SELECTED WORKS BY THE AUTHOR
The Chocolate Deal. Trans. Deymour Simckes. Detroit: Wayne State University Press, 1999; *Words in My Lovesick Blood: Poems*. Trans. Stanley F. Chyet. Detroit: Wayne State University Press, 1996.

Leon I. Yudkin

Gradowski, Salmen (ca. 1908–1944)

The diary of Salmen Gradowski is one of several extraordinary documents written by crematoria workers (the *Sonderkommando*), who existed under horrendous conditions at Birkenau. On March 5, 1945, while excavating the site near Crematorium II, the Soviets discovered Gradowski's diary hidden in a German canteen. Some of the lines written along the top edge of the diary's pages were illegible, but nearly all of the text was preserved intact. It is written in clear, modern, emotional Yiddish. A Polish edition was published in 1973 as part of a collection of documents from Auschwitz; the diary appears in an English edition titled *Amidst a Nightmare of Crime: Manuscripts of Members of Sonderkommando*, published also in 1973 by the State Museum at Auschwitz.

Gradowski was born in 1908 or 1909 in Suwałki, Poland, where he had a religious upbringing. As he grew up, he became a highly educated man who had mastered several languages and studied much of European literature. In November 1942 he and his family were deported from their home in Łuna (near Grodno) to Kiełbasin; from there they were sent to Auschwitz in January 1943. Upon their arrival

in the camp, his entire family—wife Sonya, mother Sara, sisters Esther and Liba, father-in-law Rafael, and brother-in-law Wolf—went from the train to the gas chambers. Although Gradowski does not date his entries, he seems to have begun writing shortly after his arrival in the camp. Buried with his notebook was a letter dated September 6, 1944, which is apparently the day when Gradowski ceased writing down his testimony and decided to bury it.

Gradowski's diary is written in the form of "a letter to a friend." The first twenty of its eighty-one pages deal with events that took place during his deportation to Kiełbasin and then from Kiełbasin to Auschwitz; after that, the diary contains an account of events in Auschwitz, most of which focuses on the suffering of others. In that account two events particularly stand out: the liquidation of the family camp of Czechoslovakian Jews on March 8, 1944 (Purim) and the execution of 200 members of the *Sonderkommando* in September of the same year. Judging from the evidence of other diaries uncovered in Birkenau, Gradowski was one of the active conspirators in the *Sonderkommando* uprising of October 7, 1944, during which he was probably killed.

Although the diary has little information about the anti-world inside the crematoria, several pages, which are devoted to the journey to the camp, provide the reader with a rare look inside the sealed trains. With great care and profound sensitivity Gradowski exposes the Nazis' assault not only on mothers, fathers, and children but on the very idea of a mother, father, and child—especially mother and child—as he describes the agony of thirsty, terrified children and of mothers unable to help them. He shows how the initiation into the camp is characterized by an undoing of the human image and essence, noting, for example, that, once inside the camp, "you are no longer what you were before" (p. 99).

Thus from the very depths of the Nazis' assault on the human image, Gradowski's diary raises the question of what a human being is. If responding to that question is the task of Holocaust literature, his diary holds a prominent place in the effort to respond.

SELECTED WORK BY THE AUTHOR:
"Manuscript of Sonderkommando Member." Trans. Krystyna Michalik. In *Amidst a Nightmare of Crime: Manuscripts of Members of Sonderkommando*, ed. Jadwiga Bezwinska. Oswiecim: State Museum, 1973, pp. 75–108.

David Patterson

Grinberg, Uri Zvi (1894–1981)

Writing under the pseudonym of Tur Malka, Uri Zvi Grinberg was already a major Jewish poet by the time World War II broke out. He went on to become one of the major poets of the Holocaust.

Uri Zvi Grinberg was born to a Hassidic family in Bialykamien, Galicia, in 1894 and received a traditional Jewish education. When he was an infant, the family relocated to Lvov (Lemberg), Galicia, which at the time was part of the Austro-Hungarian monarchy. During World War I his entire family—his parents, his sisters, their husbands, and their children—perished. In 1957 he was awarded the Israel Prize. He died in 1981.

In 1915 Grinberg was conscripted into the Austrian army and fought on the Serbian front. He deserted in 1917 and returned to Lvov where he witnessed the Polish pogroms against the Jews in 1918. As a newspaper editor in the 1920s he warned Polish Jews against impending disaster, and he immigrated in 1924 to Palestine. Originally a socialist, he became a nationalist and a revisionist who challenged suggestions for territorial compromises in the region and joined the struggle to end the British occupation in Palestine.

His early poems (in Hebrew and Yiddish) were published in 1912. His prophetic voice, polemical writing, and the modernist tone are at the base of his aesthetic conception. He believed in the revival of Hebrew spirit and warned against coming catastrophes (as indeed he had done as a journalist). The Arab riots of 1921 and 1929 evoked memories of the pogroms he had witnessed in Europe. In his poetry he called for the mobilization of all resources and the self-sufficiency of the Jewish population. During the years of World War II, Grinberg did not publish. His silence was tied to the Shoah and with his sense that his prophetic warnings had not been heeded.

Grinberg is among the most important Hebrew poets of the modern era. His rich language, his unique epic style, his deep knowledge of canonic sources, as well as his poetic-prophetic tone, all bring to mind the work of William Blake. His poetry is typified by a clear political/ideological element. In his work he chastises Christianity and Islam for their treatment of Jews.

Grinberg was a master stylist who conquered new territories of expression. He consistently created daring metaphors, images, and fantastic landscapes. His modernist approach broke traditionally accepted forms established by H.N. Bialik and his generation. Grinberg felt deeply that he was a poet with a mission—prophetic, political, and aesthetic. He published numerous poetic manifestos in the tradition of the Futurists and other modernists of the early twentieth century.

From a stylistic point of view, Grinberg was a poet of long, expansive lines reminiscent of Walt Whitman. The voice of the speaker goes beyond the personal. Indeed, for Grinberg, God and history are active present powers. In addition he combines expressionistic, surreal, irrational, and mystical elements in his verse. Ultimately for Grinberg, poetry had a national and historical mission. The poet should be involved, engaged in trying to affect his time and his audience. Grinberg is a monumental writer—an evocative poet with deep sense of seriousness, sincerity, and commitment. In the biblical tradition the speaker in his poems often addresses God directly, almost intimately, as in the tradition of Abraham and the Hassidic rabbis.

Lamentation is a central part of Grinberg's poetic and political voice. His symbols are Jewish symbols—the Burning Bush, Sinai, and so on. His mythical poetry combines visions of redemption and destruction, informed by World Wars I and II. Grinberg is a modern poet, a rebel with a high level of involvement and caring.

Grinberg was influenced by German impressionism and Russian *modern* theories; nevertheless, he is entirely versed in the Bible, Midrash, and Kabbala.

In *Rehovot Ha-Nahar,* 1950 (The streets of the river), Grinberg laments the destruction of European Jewry. This poetry is suffused with deep anger and horror at the cruel loss. Having fought in two world wars and having witnessed the cruelty and pain of the pogroms, Grinberg writes in The Modern Hebrew Poem Itself (1988), "The Jews had no bells to ring and summon their God" (p. 68).

Grinberg wrestled with the Shoah and its enormity. Using his poetic power he carved out new terrain in language and new images to try to encompass the loss. While sitting on the shores of the Mediterranean, he views his saintly parents as icons that dominate the depth of seas and heaven and canonizes them as "Martyrs of Silence" (p. 70). In one of his most moving poems, "Amputation of the Wing," which appeared in 1955, the amputated wing functions as a metaphor for the irreparable loss and the continuity of life. Birds are flying with one wing. Once there was "here" (Israel) and a "There" (Diaspora), but now there is no there. Messianic dreams no longer exist yet life continues in a twisted world that has lost its balance.

Uri Zvi Grinberg is in the forefront of the great modern Hebrew poets; his versatility, depth, and innovation are monumental.

SELECTED WORK BY THE AUTHOR
Rehovot Ha-Nahar. Jerusalem: Schocken, 1978.

FOR FURTHER READING
Bradshaw, Stanley, et al., ed., *The Modern Hebrew Poem Itself*. Cambridge, Mass.: Harvard University Press, 1988.

Gila Ramras-Rauch

Grossman, Vasily (1905–1964)

Russian-Jewish writer Vasily Grossman was the first to treat the Holocaust in fictionalized form. In 1943, while the gas chambers and crematoria were still employing the latest in technological advances to rid the world of Jews, Vasily Grossman published "The Old Schoolteacher." This short story was based on his essay "Ukraine Without Jews," a documentary account of the aftermath of Ukrainian Jewry's annihilation as witnessed by the author in his capacity as a war correspondent for a Russian military paper. Both the story and the essay gave rise to many important issues that form the basis for Holocaust studies, most notably in Western Europe and America, in the postwar years. They mark the beginning of his commitment to commemorate the Holocaust in both fictional and documentary form, often against the wishes of the party-sanctioned dictum to prevent the Holocaust from being seen as a uniquely Jewish experience. His resolve was fueled by the brutal murder of his mother and most of the Berdichev Jews by the Nazi occupiers and their local Soviet collaborators. The loss and the need to remember caused the writer to reexamine his relationship with his beloved Russia as well as his identity as a Jew.

Born in Berdichev in 1905, Vasily Grossman came from a town with deep roots in Hasidic Judaism and the Haskalah, but he had no formal Jewish education. His divorced parents were well-educated citizens of Soviet Russia, and, while never denying their Jewish origins, they lived a highly assimilated life. After his graduation as a chemist from Moscow University in 1929, Grossman joined the ranks of the working class to further the socialist dream. He first moved to Donbass, the center of Russia's coal mining industry, where he worked as an engineer; in 1933 he went to Moscow to assume the position of chief chemist at a pencil factory. In 1934, however, Grossman gave up chemistry for the life of a full-time writer.

By and large, Grossman's initial writing efforts fell in line with party-sanctioned dictates to portray the victorious strides of the fledgling Soviet industry toward communism. His novella *Glyukauf* (1934) glorifies the life of a party member and a coal mine leader who values the interests of the collective over those of an individual. Yet even this novel typical of the times raises some doubts about the price that any social order may eventually pay for subjugating the will of the individual to that of a group. Similar concerns are raised in Grossman's more ambitious novel, *Stepan Kolchugin* (1937–1940). Unlike many other works written according to the precepts of Socialist realism in the 1930s, Grossman's writings introduce a vague sense of ambiguity regarding the means used by the party to implement its ends.

What distinguishes Vasily Grossman from many other Jewish writers of the post-revolutionary period is his lack of animosity toward his Jewish roots or the Jewish masses. In fact, his first published story, "In the Town of Berdichev" (1934), is set in Grossman's birthplace, a revered center of learning for Jews and a reviled "kike capital" of the world for anti-Semites. With the ravages of the civil war in the background, a Jewish couple questions the decision of a Red Army commissar stationed in their house to rejoin her battalion and abandon her newborn baby to their care when the Reds are forced to retreat. They are perplexed by her resolve to place ideology over motherhood. They do not hesitate, however, to provide refuge to the child while endangering their own family. Grossman's preoccupation with issues of providing refuge and practicing altruism in his early fiction foreshadows his bitterness at the abandonment of the Jews during the Holocaust and the paucity of rescue efforts made on behalf of the Jews in the country he genuinely loved.

Although skeptical at times about the Communists' ends-justifying-the-means philosophy and aware that Jewish life in Russia remained more precarious than that of other minorities, Grossman remained a Russian patriot. When called upon to fulfill his duty during World War II, he joined the Red Army as an officer and war correspondent for the *Red Star* newspaper. Along with Ilya Ehrenburg, he became the most read, trusted, and revered chronicler of the war. His accounts of the Russian soldiers' heroism and hardships are accounts of an eyewitness and participant rather than those of a reporter, for Grossman was always where the action happened to be. He saw the front and the rear, Stalingrad and Berlin, and he grieved for the losses sustained by his country. His novel *The People Are Immortal* (1942) and his collections of wartime sketches, *Stalingrad* (1943) and *The Years of War* (1946), reflect his pain.

What he also saw was the terrible tragedy that befell the Russian Jews in occupied territories. He discovered that almost all the Jews of Berdichev, nearly 30,000, including his mother, were destroyed in September 1941. He was horrified by the massacre of the Jews in Babi Yar, the site of which he visited when liberating Kiev. And he cried when he wandered through the ashes of Treblinka, listening to eyewitness accounts of genocide and the whispers of the dead souls. Grossman's essay, "The Hell of Treblinka" (1944), used at the Nuremberg trials as testimony, was, in fact, the first eyewitness account of the workings of an extermination camp.

However, writing and publishing about the Jewish fate were complicated. While Joseph Stalin wanted Jewish artistic talent mobilized in raising the patriotic fervor of his people, he was less willing to publicize the fact that the Russian Jews had been singled out for genocide in the occupied territories. While he craved the financial support of the United States and its Jewish community, he would not acknowledge that helping the Nazis in attaining the Final Solution were former Soviet citizens. Aware of Russia's traditional anti-Semitism, he wanted to avoid the appearance that the Russian soldier was fighting in behalf of the Jews rather than his motherland. As a result, Grossman's essay, "Ukraine Without Jews" (1943), a devastating account of the disappearance of a whole people, was published in *Einikeit*, a Yiddish magazine with a limited readership, rather than in the mainstream press. His story "The Old Schoolteacher" (1943) was published in a major journal, but its ending had to be altered to comply with ideological principles. The story relates the fate of a mathematics teacher who sees the war altering the moral fabric of his town's inhabitants during the Nazi occupation. While some have the courage to help the Jews, many stand by or actively cooperate with the Nazis. He wonders at the ability of some Jews to put up a fight, although aware how futile it might be, and he warns that a social order based on fear and terror can bring out the worst in people. The story's "Band-Aid" ending glorifies the Red Army and promises it will avenge the fate of the Jews.

One means to avenge is to remember the victims and tell the story of the Jewish genocide as it really happened. That was the purpose of *The Black Book*, a collection of testimonies and records to document Holocaust atrocities in Nazi-occupied Soviet territory. Grossman, along with Ilya Ehrenburg, was called to edit the collection in 1943. Initially sanctioned by the party, *The Black Book*, although completed and ready for print, was never published. Its plates were destroyed in 1948, when Stalin was preparing to complete Adolf Hitler's war against the Jews. Publishing *The Black Book* and making the public aware of the Holocaust would have jeopardized Stalin's scheme to murder Jewish artists, prevent the conspiracy against Jewish doctors, and hamper the forced repatriation of Jews to the Far East. *The Black Book* was later published in Russia when glasnost and perestroika took hold. Grossman, however, persisted with his mission.

Toward the end of the war, Grossman started to write *Stalingrad*, the first of a two-volume novel conceived as a tribute to the heroic efforts undertaken by the Russian people and the defenders of Stalingrad, where the battle that turned the tide in favor of the Red Army took place. Following the individual stories of several families, the Shaposhnikovs and Shtrums among them, he reflects on their members' struggle to keep a family unit and a country intact in the face of the harshest test: war. In 1948 Grossman submitted the novel for publication. He was surprised at the criticism leveled against it. He was censured for elevating the role of an individual soldier while underplaying the performance of Stalin during the war; most important, he was accused of making the Jewish character, Viktor Shtrum, central to the narrative and the fate of his people more pronounced than that of the Russians. The Holocaust, according to his critics, was but a chapter in the history of the Patriotic War. Even a farewell letter from a ghetto by a Jewish woman calling on her son to remember the victims is seen as provocative; before the novel could be published in book form six years later, the letter was dropped, a chapter on Stalin was added, and the novel was renamed *For a Just Cause*.

The violence done to his book strengthened Grossman's resolve to remember the Holocaust and stress the idea that genocide is a final manifestation of a social order based on fear, terror, and lack of charity. For the next ten years, he forged ahead with the fictional re-creation of the lives of the two families in the second volume, *Life and Fate*, his major literary achievement. The history of the book's publication reflects the history of a tortured relationship between artist and state in a totalitarian regime. Instead of being published, the novel was literally arrested and banned in 1960. This time Grossman was accused of equating Russia's totalitarianism with Nazi fascism, a charge akin to treason. The centrality of the Holocaust in this novel was willfully ignored for reasons of expediency and politics.

While it is a panoramic sweep of the miseries Soviet totalitarianism brought upon the Russian people, *Life and Fate* is also a Holocaust novel. A mother's letter from the Berdichev ghetto before its destruction, and expunged from *For a Just Cause*, is reintroduced and casts a dark shadow upon the whole texture of the novel. Fashioned upon his own mother, the fictional mother spells out clearly Holocaust-related issues that both artists and historians would explore in decades to come: the particularity of the Jewish fate, abandonment by authorities who promised to protect, the paucity of rescue efforts and collaboration on the part of the local population, the role of anti-Semitism and racism as sources of destruction, the existence of Jewish resistance, the imperative to remember helpers, and the dictum to write and commemorate the Holocaust. Among the first to do so, Grossman has tried to penetrate the minds of perpetrators and bystanders and understand how ordinary people could wreak extraordinary havoc. The only way to oppose the inhuman, Grossman insists, is through acts of human kindness and selfless charity—the archenemies of the ends-justify-the-means political philosophy.

Grossman did not live to see *Life and Fate* published in his own country. He died in 1964. Along with two other books, *Peace Be with You* (1988) and *Forever Flowing* (1989), both testaments to the resiliency of the human spirit, his major opus was published posthumously.

SELECTED WORKS BY THE AUTHOR
The Complete Black Book of Russian Jewry. Ed. with Ilya Ehrenburg, trans. David Patterson. Piscataway, NJ: Transaction Publishers, 2001; *Forever Flowing.* Trans. Thomas P. Whitney. Evanston, Ill.: Northwestern University Press, 1997; *Life and Fate.* Trans. Robert Chandler. New York: Harper and Row, 1986.

FOR FURTHER READING
Ellis, Frank. *The Genesis and Evolution of a Russian Heretic.* Oxford, England: Berg, 1994; Garrard, John, and Carol Garrard, *The Bones of Berdichev: The Life and Fate of Vasily Grossman.* New York: Free Press. 1996; Lipkin, Semyon, *Stalingrad Vasiliya Grossmana.* Ann Arbor, Mich.: Ardis Publishers, 1986; Markish, Shimon, *Na Yevreiskye Temi: Primer Vasiliya Grossmana.* Vols. 1 and 2. Jerusalem: Aliya Press, 1985; Milbauer, Asher Z. "Rescue Missions: Vasily Grossman and the Holocaust." *Literature and Belief* 18, no. 2 (1998): 47–74; Yelina, Nina. *Vasily Grossman.* Jerusalem, 1994.

Asher Z. Milbauer

H

Hart, Kitty (1926–)

Kitty Hart's first memoir of the Holocaust was published in 1962 under the title *I Am Alive.* In 1978 she returned to Auschwitz with her son to film what was to become an internationally acclaimed British documentary made for television. Titled *Kitty: Return to Auschwitz* (1980), the film won numerous awards, including the Commonwealth Film and TV Festival Special Award (1980), The Prix Futura Documentary Award (1981), The Royal Television Society Journalism Award for Best Documentary (1981), and the Tokyo Prize (1985). In 1982 her memoir, based both on *I Am Alive* and the documentary film, was published in the United States: *Return to Auschwitz.*

Kitty Hart was born Kitty Felix in Bielsko, Poland, in 1926 to an affluent family. Her mother was a teacher educated in London, and her father was an attorney. Because Bielsko was near the German and Czech borders—a site that seemed the more precarious as the winds of war mounted—her family moved to Lublin in August 1939, where they thought they would be safer. Within weeks, however, the Germans had taken Lublin and implemented their anti-Semitic decrees. After obtaining forged documents identifying them as Poles, Hart and her mother were separated from her father and sent to Germany to work as slave laborers in an I.G. Farben aluminum factory. Both of them, however, were soon found out and sent to Auschwitz. Although

Hart and her mother survived the horrors of the camp, her father was discovered hiding in Lublin and shot.

After the war Hart and her mother went to England, where Kitty had an uncle living in Birmingham. Her memoir opens with her frustrated efforts to tell her tale, as part of her return to the world of humanity. Neither her uncle nor anyone else wanted to hear her story, and when they did hear it they could not fathom it; when asked about her tattoo, she would attempt to explain, only to meet with "an awkward silence" (p. 13). Thus this tale of Auschwitz begins with the difficulty confronting the one who would tell that tale. She tells the tale nevertheless, and she tells it with insight.

Kitty Hart's memoir reveals that, in the midst of the assault on the relationship to one's fellow human beings, survival required maintaining the very relationship that was under assault. "You had to have somebody helping you," she wrote, "and you had to help somebody else" (p. 166). She related, for example, how she and her fellow inmates would create "little families" (p. 69) for one another, and how the thought that she was helping her friend Simon also helped her (p. 80). Most important of all was her relation to her mother, who remained her one contact with her previous life—with life itself.

In that realm where kindness was madness, madness was a constant threat. Paradoxically, to preserve their sanity, prisoners had to deny the reality of the "red, reeking hell" all around them (p. 115). "We were all mad," stated Hart, illustrating the transformation of the world into an anti-world. "The only sensible thing to be" (p. 121). Hart's memoir demonstrates, moreover, that in Auschwitz the denial of an insane reality was a means of maintaining human identity, which in turn was a form of resisting the Nazis' assault on the soul. According to Hart, the Nazis intended to reduce these human beings "to impersonal, downtrodden, nothingness" (p. 76) before reducing their bodies to ashes. Whenever the Nazis succeeded in their design, the result was an entity that would become emblematic of Nazism: the *Muselmann*, those are alive and yet show no signs of life and are indeed the incarnation of nothingness. The only antidote to becoming a *Muselmann* was to keep despair at bay when one had every reason to despair (p. 105).

Even after she somehow survived that realm, Hart's struggle with despair continued. After she returned to the world, she found one way to oppose the despair that had followed her out of the kingdom of death: "to produce Jewish children" (p. 156)—to bear life despite all the death.

SELECTED WORKS BY THE AUTHOR
I Am Alive. London: Abelard and Schuman, 1962; *Return to Auschwitz*. New York: Atheneum, 1982.

David Patterson

Heimler, Eugene (1922–1993)

"A holocaust had obliterated us," wrote Eugene Heimler near the end of his memoir in one of the earliest uses of the word *holocaust* (p. 191). Translated from the Hungarian, Heimler's *Night of the Mist* was first published in English in 1959 (reprinted in 1978 and in 1997). Its title is based on Adolf Hitler's *Nacht und Nebel*, or Night and Fog, decree issued on December 7, 1941, whereby Jews in occupied Europe were to be secretly deported to Germany. Heimler sees his task as one of unmasking a secret that the dead took with them to their graves—or to the sky transformed into a grave. He writes his memoir with a powerful sense of having to deliver a message "to the living from the dead . . . on behalf of the millions who had seen it also—but could no longer speak" (p. 191).

Born Jancsi Heimler in 1922, Eugene Heimler was an aspiring young poet of twenty-one when the Germans invaded his home in Hungary in the spring of 1944. The Gestapo arrested his father almost immediately; Heimler never saw him again. On July 3, 1944, he, his wife, and 6,000 other Jews were taken from the ghetto in their small Hungarian town for deportation to Auschwitz; there his wife, Eva, and the rest of his family perished. Heimler had been in Auschwitz only a short time when he was taken to Buchenwald. From there he was sent to work as a slave laborer in the I.G. Farben factory at Tröglitz; after a matter of weeks, however, he was taken back to Buchenwald. On December 13, 1944, he was transported from Buchenwald to Berga Elster; during a march from Berga Elster to a destination unknown, he was liberated by Czech gendarmes. He made his way back to Hungary but nothing but ghosts were there; in 1947 he moved to England, where he lived and worked as a psychiatric social worker until his death in 1993.

Heimler's memoir is written with the eloquence of a poet and the insight of an analyst. When recalling the time spent in the "shame and suffering" of the ghetto, he explains how the example set by the Hasidim brought a strength to the entire community, and he links that example to a history of Jewish piety in the midst of Jewish suffering. Heimler also observes a transformation that overcame him while in transit on the sealed train: "I had mounted the train of death wearing European clothes, a European man; I alighted at the other end a dazed creature of Auschwitz" (p. 21). What Heimler demonstrates is that the Holocaust implicates all modern notions of the human being and civilization: Is the dazed creature of Auschwitz not a man? If not, then what is he? If not, then what are we and our civilization? Struggling with humanity, Heimler struggles with God, even struggles to reject God in the face of the cruelty and murder of the annihilation camp. "Yet," he realizes, "faith, like desire, persists in man" (p. 102).

In Heimler's memory and understanding of his condition as an orphan, one perceives the orphaned condition of a world that has lost its sense of God, humanity, and civilization; indeed, one way in which Nazis assaulted him as a Jew was to make him into an orphan. He longs for the direction that his father had provided him and the compassion that his mother had shown him. Deprived of this original care, he realizes that the only way to recover it was to offer it. When thanking a Dutch prisoner for an act of kindness, for instance, he recalls that the man told him to "give in your turn to others" (p. 157). When a child in Buchenwald asked him if he was responsible for the little ones in the children's barracks, he recalls "I answered 'Yes,' without knowing why I did so. But in that moment all feelings seemed to affirm that I was indeed responsible" (p. 165).

Once he was free, Heimler remembers encountering a "silence such as there must have been before the days of creation" (p. 188). His memoir is a response to that silence, making it into an eloquent silence of plenitude, and not the gaping silence of the void. The movement from the latter to the former is the memoir's movement from the anti-world that the Nazis created to the world of human kindness and care.

SELECTED WORKS BY THE AUTHOR

The Healing Echo. London: Souvenir Press, 1985; *A Link in the Chain*. London: Bodley Head, 1962; *Night of the Mist*. Trans. André Ungar. New York: Vanguard, 1959; *The Storm (The Tragedy of Sinai)*. London: Menard Press, 1976; *Survival in Society*. New York: Wiley, 1975.

David Patterson

Herzberg, Abel Jacob (1893–1989)

By the time Holocaust diarist Abel J. Herzberg was deported to Bergen-Belsen in mid-January 1944, he was already known in his native Amsterdam as a Jewish community leader; from 1934 to 1939, in fact, he served as chairman of the Dutch Zionist Association. Herzberg was equally well known as a man of letters: he was the editor of *De Joodse Wachter*, and he wrote numerous stories, novels, and dramas. He is also the author of a study of Dutch Jewry under Nazi occupation called *Kroniek der Jodenvervolging*, 1956 (Chronicle of the persecution of the Jews), and he covered the Eichmann trial as a reporter for a Dutch daily.

By the time Herzberg wrote his diary in Bergen-Belsen, he was a mature, cultivated, and accomplished man. Originally published in the May 6, 1950, edition of *De Groene Amsterdammer* under the title *Tweestroomen-land*, the diary appeared in English translation under the title *Between Two Streams: A Diary from Bergen-Belsen* in 1997. For his accomplishments as a citizen of Holland, Herzberg was made Knight of the Order of Orange-Nassau; for his achievements as an author he was awarded the Dutch prize for literature in 1974. He remained a prominent literary figure in Holland until his death in 1989.

Herzberg's father, a diamond dealer, left Lithuania for Amsterdam around 1880 to flee the pogroms; Abel Herzberg was born in 1893 and brought up in a religious but non-Orthodox home. After serving in the Dutch army during World War I, he earned a law degree. Soon after the Nazi occupation of Holland in May 1940, he, his wife, Thea, and their three children went into hiding. In March 1943 they were arrested and sent to the camp at Barneveld; before they were sent on to Westerbork in September 1943, however, they managed to smuggle the children out to a nearby farm, where they remained safe. After being transported to Bergen-Belsen in January 1944, they were among 172 prisoners selected for exchange for Germans abroad and placed in the Bergen-Belsen camp known as the Sternlager (after the yellow star Jews had to wear) or the Vorzugslager (camp for "privileged" people). Herzberg and other prisoners of the Sternlager enjoyed privileges that inmates in the rest of the camp were denied: he was allowed to see his wife each day and to keep his clothes and a little luggage. More importantly for the body of Holocaust literature, he was able to keep a diary.

Herzberg called his diary *Between Two Streams* because, he explains, throughout the concentrationary universe "two irreconcilable principles of life fought invisibly in the visible battle": National Socialism and Judaism (p. 4).

It is one of only a few diaries that were written in concentration camps and not in ghettos or in hiding. With entries running from August 11, 1944, to April 26, 1945, Herzberg's diary is a highly literary, highly literate testimony to the invisible, spiritual battle that, as he saw it, characterized the Holocaust. Herzberg had a keen eye for the little things that go into the making of civilization and for the ways in which they came unraveled in the anti-world of the camp. "Do you know what I would like to see?" he asks, for instance. "An ordinary person—just a person, walking in the street" (p. 31). Living in a realm devoid of bodily warmth, Eros, and a human touch, he comments on the excitement of inmates who return from a work detail with the tale of some vision of normalcy.

Herzberg also undertook a daily exploration of one of the issues most fundamental to the Holocaust kingdom: the relation between hunger and morality. Gazing upon the starved and tortured body of humanity around him, however, he is able to offer two very important words in response to the cliché "First food, then morality": *and yet.* Contrary to the Nazi dictum that power is the only reality, Herzberg demonstrated that the good has a reality of its own, despite the powerlessness of its adherents. Nevertheless, looking at the other "stream," Herzberg had a very dark vision of modern humanity, which he saw emulated in the SS man, who "transports corpses" of women and children as if he is "transporting manure." Beholding such cruel indifference, he asserted, "One knows: this is man. *Ecce homo!*" (p. 141). The twentieth century, as Herzberg saw it, has replaced the face of humanity with the death's head that the SS bear as their insignia.

One of the most striking—and most controversial—ideas in Herzberg's diary is his partial explanation for Christendom's persecution of the Jews and the reason why a Christendom become heathen ultimately attempts to exterminate the Jews. It is not because the Jews killed Christ—it is because they gave birth to him. "Christ's death," he maintains, "is a wishful thought of the heathen living among the Christians which he has shifted onto the Jews. The guilt that the Christian feels because his hea-then soul rebels against Christ seeks to avenge itself on the one who placed him in the torment of ambivalence. That person is the Jew" (p. 68). The otherness of the Jew is not a mere otherness: it is the absolute otherness of a transcendent, absolute Law—a Torah—to which a rebellious humanity does not want to be accountable. For the Christians, Christ is an uncomfortable reminder that the self and world are not all there is; and the Jews are the source of the Christ.

Thus Herzberg sees a certain connection between Christ and Torah. And it is the fundamental teaching of the Torah that he opposes to National Socialism in the heart of the anti-world that the Nazis introduced to the world. That fundamental teaching is simply this: God is One—the deepest meaning of which, according to Herzberg, lies in "creating and justifying a moral standard, *justice* for the individual and for the community." And the community is humanity. For the oneness of God implies the unity of a humanity everywhere created in the same holy image, and not a humanity divided by the accidents of race or the struggle for power. More than a daily chronicle—even more than a voice for the dead—Herzberg's diary is an affirmation of a faith and a truth that the Nazis set out to destroy.

SELECTED WORKS BY THE AUTHOR

Aartsvaters: Het Verhaal van Jakob en Jozef. Amsterdam: Querido, 1992; *Amor Fati: Zeven Opstellen over Bergen-Belsen.* Amsterdam: Moussault, 1946; *Between Two Streams: A Diary from Bergen-Belsen.* Trans. Jack Santcross. London: I. B. Tauris, 1997; *Brieven aan Mijn Kleinzoon.* The Hague: Bert Bakker, 1967; *De Schaduw van Mijn Bomen.* The Hague: Bert Bakker, 1969; *Drie Rode Rosen.* Amsterdam: Querido, 1975; *Eichmann in Jerisalem.* The Hague: Bert Bakker, 1962; *Het Joodse Erfgoed.* Amsterdam: Querido, 1991; *Pro Deo: Herinneringen aan een Vooroordeel.* The Hague: Bert Bakker, 1969; *Sauls Dood.* Amsterdam: De Arbeiderspers, 1958; *Zonder Israel Is Elke Jood een Ongedekte Cheque.* Amsterdam: Querido, 1992.

FOR FURTHER READING

Kristel, Conny, *Geschiedschrijving als Opdracht: Abel Herzberg, Jacques Presser en Loe de Jong Over de Jodenvervolging.* Amsterdam: Meulenhoff, 1998; Kuiper, Arie, *Een Wijze Ging Voorbij: Het Leven van*

Abel J. Herzberg. Amsterdam: Querido, 1998; Visser, Willem M., *Abel J. Herzberg.* Nijmegen, Netherlands: B. Gottmer, 1979.

David Patterson

Hillesum, Etty (Esther) (1914–1943)

Etty Hillesum's diary *An Interrupted Life* captures the last two years of her life from the ages of twenty-seven to twenty-nine. Her diary, often compared to Anne Frank's*, is a grown-up version since Etty was more than fifteen years older than Anne. Hillesum's writing also depicts a sensitive young woman with an unusually optimistic spirit. She is Dutch and when writing her diary was living in Amsterdam. Hillesum's diary has been published in fourteen countries and translated into twelve languages. Published along with her diary entries are Hillesum's letters from Westerbork (Dutch detention camp) where she went first as a volunteer in 1942 until her deportation to Auschwitz in September 1943.

Etty Hillesum was born January 15, 1914, in Middelburg, Netherlands, to parents Louis and Rebecca. She had two brothers, Mischa and Jaap. Not very much is known about Etty's life before she began writing her diary in Amsterdam. She had a degree in law from the University of Amsterdam, she also studied in the Faculty of Slavonic languages, and at the time she wrote her diary she was predominantly interested in the study of psychology though tutoring individuals in Russian. On July 22, 1942, Etty got a job on the Jewish Council as a typist. This council was formed by the Nazis to force Dutch Jews to implement their decrees. Etty next volunteered to go to Westerbork and work in the hospital there. At first she was able to leave the camp and did so a dozen times to visit her friends in Amsterdam and carry letters and return with medicines and gifts. Her mother, father, and brother Mischa eventually arrived at the camp, and ultimately they were all deported to Auschwitz in September 1943 where all went to the gas chambers. Jaap was able to stay out of the camp a bit longer because he was a doctor, but he did not survive the war either.

Etty's diary is less a description of her everyday life and more a description of her interior journey. She often wrote about her relationships and their struggles. Someone Etty was particularly preoccupied by was Julius Spier, a psychochirologist. He had a reputation for an unusual gift of reading palms and having an almost magical personality. She saw him professionally, but this was a time of experimentation in psychoanalysis and her relationship with him moved well outside of the professional sphere by today's standards. For example, Spier and Etty literally wrestled on the floor as part of her therapy, and she constantly struggled against her intense physical desire for him. To love him without needing to possess him physically is a goal Etty set for herself. Her soul-searching throughout has to do with learning how to love and live passionately yet not superficially.

Another main feature of Etty's diary is her relationship with God. Thus her diary has been viewed as a spiritual biography. It is in this area that the reader witnesses the most growth or change in Etty as her awareness of the evil around her grew. She was affected by the Nazi actions and, as she witnessed the devastation of seeing 30,000 people held in a camp originally made for 1,500, her resistance to despair and depression strengthened. Her faith in God seemed to grow as the conditions worsened. She often transformed ugly realities into a reflective process in her writing. She wrote of the suffering she witnessed and yet concluded it must ultimately strengthen her. Not only did Etty constantly appeal to God for assistance to endure what she feels and sees but also to deepen her faith. She was in continuous dialogue with God and praised the divinity throughout. On her final postcard, written on the train on the way to Auschwitz, she wrote to a friend, "The Lord is my high tower." Loving God, loving family and friends especially, and comforting others are all ways in which Etty kept her spirits high while at Westerbork. Many readers find Etty remarkable in her ability to resist the Nazis spiritually by not surrendering the loves she knew they could not take away.

SELECTED WORK BY THE AUTHOR
An Interrupted Life and Letters from Westerbork. Trans. Arnold J. Pomerans. New York: Henry Holt, 1996.

Sarita Cargas

Hochhuth, Rolf (1931–)

Rolf Hochhuth's *Der Stellvertreter*, 1963 (*The Deputy*, 1964) is one of the most important plays of the twentieth century. In it he uses archival material, historical evidence, and elements of documentary theater to indict the Vatican of Pope Pius XII for its failure to act decisively on behalf of European Jews during the Holocaust. The five-act play is 260 pages long. The author's 60-page "Sidelights to History" follows the text of this unusual and controversial drama. It is widely believed that Hochhuth single-handedly started the debate over the Catholic Church's role in Adolf Hitler's genocidal war against the Jews. Along with another German historical drama about the Shoah—Peter Weiss's* equally controversial *Die Ermittlung*, 1965 (*The Investigation*)—*The Deputy* serves as a yardstick by which many of today's Holocaust plays are being judged.

Rolf Hochhuth was born in Germany in 1931, attended the Munich and Heidelberg universities, and worked as a bookseller and editor. After the publication of *The Deputy* Hochhuth moved to Basel, Switzerland, where he lives today. He has written other plays, most notably *Soldaten*, 1968 (*Soldiers*) and *Guerillas* (1970). He is the author of a film script about an affair between a German soldier's wife and a Polish laborer during World War II, *Eine Liebe in Deutschland*, 1978 (A love story in Germany). In addition to drama, Hochhuth has written fiction, poetry, essays, and film scripts.

In Hochhuth's scheme as laid out in *The Deputy*, the Pontiff is a man who put pragmatism above morality, self-interest before justice. The Holy Father's reluctance to condemn the Nazis publicly for their treatment of the Jews is politically motivated: as he sees it, anything critical of Germany only helps Joseph Stalin and communism—and Hitler is the lesser of the two evils. The Pope—a man who holds deep admiration for Germany and German culture—is not eager to criticize the leadership in Berlin. Pius XII is not a spiritual leader but a shrewd politician, a man obsessed with Vatican finances and the realignment of forces in postwar Europe. The Holy Father is more worried about the effects of the war on Vatican properties and investments, than the Jews. To his credit, he does not stand in the way of monasteries sheltering Jews, but he is steadfast against any public condemnation of Germany. He argues that such measures would only incite Hitler to commit worse crimes, as well as undermine existing aid operations on behalf of the war victims. When all else fails, Pius XII invokes the 1933 Concordat, a pact between his predecessor and Hitler, a document that explicitly prevents him from "interfering" in Germany's "internal affairs." At the insistence of a very persistent Father Riccardo Fontana, a priest modeled after two martyred clerics to whom the play is dedicated—Provost Bernhard Lichtenberg of Berlin and Poland's Father Maximilian Kolbe—the Pope agrees to issue a general statement condemning violence regardless of nationality or religion.

Father Fontana's heroics and eventual martyrdom at Auschwitz are matched by those of Kurt Gerstein (a historical figure), a Protestant youth leader who joins the ranks of the SS to fight the monster from within. An officer and technical consultant to the Nazi architects of mass destruction, including the use of Zyklon B, Gerstein is privy to a great deal of information, some of which, at great peril to himself and his family, he manages to share with the underground forces in Germany and Poland. Like Father Fontana, Gerstein is an extraordinary Christian who opposes Nazism, one of the few who is not "Hitler's Willing Executioners." Through the figures of Fontana, Gerstein, and the Pope, Hochhuth re-creates a cataclysmic historical moment, emphasizing the moral and spiritual dimensions of history.

The Deputy shows more than the tragedy of moral failure in high places. Through the figure of the "Doctor," Dr. Josef Mengele, Auschwitz's "Angel of Death," Hochhuth offers a unique glimpse into the world of amorality, a world where there is no right or wrong, only duty. In this case, it is the task of killing as many as possible, as quickly as possible, and with as little effort (physical and emotional) as possible. By stripping Mengele of his name and referring to him simply as the "Doctor," Hochhuth underscores the irony of the situation: the medical profession, which works to heal and prolong life, is engaged in promoting mass death and suffering. The breakdown in morality extends to Germany's business leaders as well: industrial giants like Krupp, Siemens, and I.G. Farben, are enthusiastically cooperating with the SS, and are a major reason why Mengele, Adolf Eichmann, and Rudolf Hoess were so successful in carrying out their murderous acts.

As theater, *The Deputy* is an extremely ambitious play. Among others, the action takes the viewer into the mysterious inner chambers of the Vatican, the Jagerkeller near Berlin where Eichmann hosts a group of Nazi high officials, and Auschwitz where Jewish prisoners are seen marching to the gas chambers. Hochhuth employs a mix of realism and surrealism to evoke the atmosphere of the moment. He uses documents, including memoirs and letters, to recreate the exact manner of a character's speech, demeanor, and gestures. Unfortunately, his drama is too long to be produced successfully. For students of the Shoah, however, *The Deputy* offers an extraordinary stage for exploring a host of moral and religious issues. The play is an excellent model for debating the issue of collective versus individual responsibility. Finally, one cannot resist comparisons of Pope Pius XII with the present Pope, John Paul II, who also lived through the war, in Poland. Unlike his predecessor, this pope is trying very hard to heal 2,000 years of Church anti-Semitism.

SELECTED WORK BY THE AUTHOR:
The Deputy. Trans. by Richard Winston and Clara Winston. New York: Grove Press, 1964.

FOR FURTHER READING
Bentley, Eric, ed., *The Storm over the Deputy*. New York: Grove Press, 1964; Cornwell, John, *The Secret Life of Pius XII*. New York: Viking Press, 1999; Glenn, Jerry, "Faith, Love, and the Tragic Conflict in Hochhuth's *Der Stellvertreter*," *German Studies Review* 7 (1984); Murdaugh, Elaine, "The Apostate Ethic: The Alternative to Faith in Hochhuth's *Der Stellvertreter*," *Seminar: A Journal of Germanic Studies* 15 (1979); Schumacher, Claude, and Derek Fogg, eds., *Hochhuth's* The Representative at the Glasgow Citizens. Glasgow: Glasgow Theater Studies, 1986.

Michael Taub

Huberband, Shimon (1909–1942)

The historian Rabbi Shimon Huberband was a member of the executive of the underground *Oneg Shabbat* archive in the Warsaw ghetto and the most prolific writer among its contributors. When Emmanuel Ringelblum* wrote of his difficulties in establishing the archive project, he recognized Huberband as "one of its best co-workers" and added that the archival work only became successful after the rabbi joined the staff (Kermisch, p. 4). In the archive, Huberband's chief responsibility was the documentation of religious life, but his collected essays, written in Yiddish, document a wide spectrum of Jewish history and ghetto life. Many of his historical findings survived in no other sources. Ringelblum called the report on the Kampinos Labor Camp, apparently based on Huberband's own experience, "one of the most important documents on Hitlerite brutality committed on working Jews" (Kermisch, p. 13).

Huberband's writings were discovered in the archive, in 1946, under the ruins of the ghetto, and first published as a collection, in Hebrew, as *Kiddush ha-Shem: Ketavim mi-yeme ha-Sho'ah* (1969). *Kiddush Hashem: Jewish Religious and Cultural Life in Poland During the Holocaust* (1987) followed. The title of the collection, meaning "to sanctify the name of the Lord," was taken from the title of one of the essays which catalogued, with gripping intensity, reports of Jews who had sacrificed their lives to save other Jews or to rescue synagogues and Torah scrolls in locations across Poland.

His research for the archive followed the scholarly and scientific guidelines for dealing with source materials established by *Oneg Shabbat* archivists and the YIVO Institute. With a concise and unemotional style of inquiry, he gathered much of the information firsthand from witnesses, from refugees in the ghetto or from his personal experiences. Most are short, unpretentious reports without literary embellishment;

a few are outlines of scholarly monographs. Many seem fragmentary and hurried, which gives them immediacy and credibility. He worked under constant fear and a sense of the approaching end. In fear of discovery, he signed most of his writings as "Brand" or "Zamenhof," the street where he lived, or with his initials. Cautiously, he sometimes referred to the Germans, using veiled terms such as "they" or "the evil ones."

Born in Checiny, near Kielce, Poland, on April 19, 1919, Huberband, whose mother was the daughter of the Checiny Rebbe, grew up in his grandfather's Hasidic court. He established himself as a writer of Jewish intellectual articles, poetry, and short fiction, in Otwock, and had published the first of a series of journal articles on the lives of Jewish physicians in Piotrków from the seventeenth century before the war. He was serving as vice president of the Kehilah in Piotrków Trybunalski when the Germans invaded.

When news that war had been declared reached Piotrków, he wondered, with foreboding: "Lord Almighty, will such a good and beautiful world actually be destroyed?" (p. 7). Seeking safety, he fled with his family to neighboring Silev (Sulejow) where his wife, Rivka, young son, Kalman, and his father-in-law, "the crown of our family" (p. 32), perished in a German bombing raid. Huberband returned to Piotrków, in tormented grief, and apparently worked briefly at the *Judenrat* (Jewish Council). In early 1940, he moved to Warsaw, perhaps to be near his brother in Otwock. There he directed the religious department of the Jewish Social Self-Help Organization.

In Warsaw, Huberband married the daughter of Yitzak Zilbershteyn, the rabbi of Prague. When the rabbi passed away, he was named to the Warsaw rabbinate. In spite of bouts with typhus, hunger, forced labor—where he endured the name "Moses Dung the boot-shiner" (p. 67)—and constant fear, he worked with great fury to preserve a record of the Jewish heritage in Poland. In July 1942, he and his wife sought shelter in the brushmaker's workshop during the first major deportation. On September 18, they were caught in an *Aktion*, as the Germans re-ferred to their raids upon the ghetto, and taken to the *Umschlagplatz*. They perished at Treblinka. Menachem Kon*, a fellow archive worker, eulogized him passionately as, "a great scholar . . . he was a fiery Hasid with a burning heart, but he nonetheless wished to comprehend things with his own common sense" (p. 108).

Huberband's writings fall generally into three types: autobiographical pieces, descriptions of life in the ghetto, and reports on the destruction of Jewish communities, their cultural treasures, and their way of life. Unfortunately, not all of these works were saved. Several were damaged by dampness and left illegible, and he had other materials at home or with him when he was deported. Also, when he first started to work, he cautiously made notes in the margins of books and these, too, were lost. Not all of the hidden archive was recovered after the war; however the first part of his historical investigation of rabbinical *Responsa,* undertaken at Ringelblum's suggestion, survived and was published in Warsaw in 1951.

At the start of one essay, he clarified that what he was writing about "was not, regrettably, an empty dream, nor a mad fantasy, or an evil tale, but naked and bitter reality" (p. 334). He wrote about efforts to maintain religious practices, giving a suspenseful account of his going in secrecy to the ritual baths before Yom Kippur, of the dangers encountered by ritual slaughterers, and about the Love of Torah and Fear of Heaven study group. He described the changes in Jewish clothing, the humiliations endured by men who wore beards, weddings, questions of Jewish law, and the fate of sacred books and religious artifacts.

He was critical of the loss of morality in the ghetto. With sadness, he described the bribes accepted by the Jewish police and their brutality, adding; "This was one of the most horrible misfortunes of the war—the footsteps of the Jewish policeman and one Jew's fear of another Jew" (p. 103). He also passed harsh judgment on women. In his essay "The Moral Decline of the Jewish Women During the War," he lamented that "only very rarely did a Jewish woman open her purse to give a groschen to a starving Jew" (p. 240), even as they were still going to nightclubs. The story of his father-in-law's death after being swindled appears in his essay "The Extortion of Money from Jews by Jews."

He also reported on the effect of the ghetto on Hasidic youth. He recorded seeing three drunken Yeshiva students who "were dead drunk. They swayed their bodies in all directions" (p. 131) in the summer of 1942. He described the lifestyle of a group of Gerer Hasidim as the "harsh ones." They were educated "in the spirit of harshness" (pp. 176–77) and did not devote time to the study of Torah. But, surprisingly, he wrote a study of "Wartime Humor," including jokes, puns, and legends from the ghetto and a piece about a photo gallery which brought brief enjoyment to the ghetto.

One of the women laborers he interviewed explained, "We literally 'lost the image of God'" (p. 438). This seems to be his chief motivation in the archive work. He wrote to restore the image of the divine to the victims tortured by German atrocities and to destroyed communities. Thus, he took great effort to record the names of those who "sanctified his name" and of the condemned and the persecuted. He wrote, in despair, that "the heavens did not spurt out any fire to burn those who had caused the conflagration" (p. 288) when many Jews died in the burning of the Bedzin synagogue, and he hoped "that on the day of the reckoning, every fact will cry out: I accuse! I demand revenge!" (p. 260), but this "pious rabbi" continued his record as a legacy for the future.

SELECTED WORKS BY THE AUTHOR
Kiddush Hashem: Jewish Religious and Cultural Life in Poland During the Holocaust. Trans. David E. Fishman, and ed. Jeffrey S. Gurock and Robert S. Hirt. New York: Ktav and Yeshiva University, 1987; *Kidush ha-Shem: Ketavim mi-yeme ha-Sho'ah (mitokh arkhiyon Ringelblum be-geto Varshah).* Ed. Nachman Blumenthal and Joseph Kermish. Tel Aviv: Zakhor, 1969.

FOR FURTHER READING
Kermish, Joseph, ed. *To Live with Honor and Die with Honor.* Jerusalem: Yad Vashem, 1986; Lewin, Abraham, *A Cup of Tears: A Diary of the Warsaw Ghetto.* Ed. Antony Polonsky. Oxford: Basil Blackwell, 1988; Ringelblum, Emmanuel, *Notes from the Warsaw Ghetto: The Journal of Emmanuel Ringelblum.* Ed. and trans. Jacob Sloan. New York: Schocken, 1958.

Susan Lee Pentlin

K

Kahane, David (1903–1998)

Rabbi David Kahane's *Yoman Geto Levov*, 1978 (*Lvov Ghetto Diary*, 1990) is one of the few Holocaust diaries to come out of the Lvov ghetto. The work of a learned man of forty, the diary contains profound meditations on the religious and philosophical implications of the plight of Polish Jewry. In addition to conveying Rabbi Kahane's daily reflections, the diary is a valuable chronicle of the events that transpired in Poland and the Ukraine from the time of the Nazi invasion in the summer of 1941.

Born in 1903, Rabbi Kahane had a religious upbringing and was a young man when he became a spokesman for the Jews of Lvov and the surrounding area. Shortly after the Nazi invasion, for example, Rabbi Kahane went to Metropolitan Andrei Sheptytsky to protest the Nazis' enlistment of Ukrainians into the service of the SS. Sheptytsky protested to Heinrich Himmler, but to little avail.

Rabbi Kahane saw his parents for the last time on Yom Kippur 1941, when they were taken from the Lvov ghetto to be murdered in Belzec. After securing a hiding place for his three-year-old daughter in August 1942, Rabbi Kahane was sent to the labor camp in Janowska the following November; however, he managed to escape the death that awaited him there. In September 1943, two months after the liquidation of the Lvov ghetto, Rabbi Kahane and fifteen other Jews went into hiding in Sheptytsky's home in Lvov. When he went into hiding he began to write his diary. When the war ended, Rabbi Kahane became the chief rabbi of Poland. As the situation of Polish Jews deteriorated, however, he moved to Israel, where he became chief rabbi of the Israeli Air Force. He died in 1998.

A major literary distinction of Rabbi Kahane's diary is the way in which he drew the classic religious texts of the Jewish tradition into his own text; in doing so, he joined his words to the words of the tradition and brought to light a variety of metaphysical implications of the event. He contrasted the Jewish policemen of the Lvov ghetto with the Israelite taskmasters of ancient Egypt, for example, and he noted the midrashic text claiming that in Egypt the Jewish taskmasters risked their lives to protect the Jews; in Lvov, stated Kahane, they merely tried to save their own lives (p. 17). When he observed Jewish women trying in vain to work as maids for the Germans, he wrote, "The words of the prophet were thus fulfilled: 'And you will sell yourselves to your enemy as servants and housemaids and they will want you not'" (p. 31). As he watched the Germans loading Torah scrolls into a truck to be burned, he recalled a passage from the Talmud: "As it is written: 'The scrolls are consumed in flames and the letters fly up in the air'" (p. 40).

Rabbi Kahane pointed out that in such associations with religious texts and traditions many Jews found courage, despite their despair. When his friend Rabbi Anshel Schreiber was martyred, for example, the memory of Rabbi Akiba's martyrdom under the Romans gave him comfort: "Is there a more beautiful moment in the life of a Jew," said Rabbi Schreiber, "than the moment he is told he will die for the Sanctification of the Name?" (p. 46). When Rabbi Kahane was in the Janowska camp, he was convinced that he would come out alive because the digits of his number, 2250, added up to nine, a number which, in Jewish mysticism, signifies life and truth. "To me," he said of his number, "it seemed a sign from heaven" (p. 97).

These words, however, should not be taken too lightly. Along with his faith there is a strain of rebellion in Rabbi Kahane's diary, as when he recalled Yom Kippur 1942 and cried out, "Master of the world, why? . . . . Are the Ukrainians, the Poles, the Germans better than we are? Are other nations' moral standards higher than ours?" (p. 76). Indeed, the strain of rebellion in Rabbi Kahane's diary may be its most religious element. For here he joined his words to the words of Job, a man known for his righteousness—not because he acquiesced but because he cried out.

SELECTED WORKS BY THE AUTHOR

Achare Ha-mabul. Jerusalem: Yad Vashem, 1981; *Lvov Ghetto Diary.* Trans. Jerzy Michalowicz. Amherst: University of Massachusetts Press, 1990; *Perakim B'toldot Ha-Yehudim B'Polin.* Jerusalem: Mosad ha-Rav Kook, 1983.

David Patterson

Kalmanovitch, Zelig (1885–1944)

First appearing in Volume 25 of the annual journal *YIVO Bleter* (1951), the Vilna ghetto diary of Zelig Kalmanovitch was among the earliest Holocaust diaries to appear in print. Two years later Kalmanovitch's original Hebrew text was translated into English and published in the *YIVO Annual of Jewish Social Sciences* under the title "A Diary of the Nazi Ghetto in Vilna." The diary is the work of a mature man of letters who brought to bear all his literary talent to articulate the scope of the horror unfolding before his eyes. Herman Kruk*, who also wrote a diary in the Vilna ghetto, discovered

Kalmanovitch's notebook in the ruins of the liquidated ghetto. He entrusted the diary to Abraham Sutzkever*, a well-known Yiddish poet and partisan. Thanks to Sutzkever, Kalmanovitch's diary ultimately found its way into the Yiddish Scientific Institute (YIVO).

Born in Goldingen, Courland (Latvia), on October 30, 1885, Zelig Kalmanovitch settled in Vilna in 1929, where he became a founding member of the YIVO Institute. He served as head of the institute and editor of its journal, *YIVO Bleter,* from 1939 to 1940. Before reaching the age of thirty, Kalmanovitch had published studies on the influence of Hebrew on Yiddish and various Yiddish dialects. He translated works by Jewish historians Josephus and Simon Dubnow, as well as by English novelist and historian H.G. Wells into Yiddish. During the Nazis' occupation of Vilna, Kalmanovitch was forced to select rare books from local libraries for shipment to Germany, a task which, in fact, enabled him to salvage many irreplaceable texts. When the ghetto was liquidated in September 1943, he and his wife were sent to a camp in Estonia, where the two of them were murdered the following winter.

Kalmanovitch's diary exhibits a profound understanding of the human being, both as victim and as executioner. Commenting on the loss of the human image in the executioner, he said of the notorious SS officer Martin Weiss, "His face, the face of a murderer, becomes him. He drinks blood and is not sated. I am stupefied. How does a man live like this?" (p. 38). And yet in the Nazi Kalmanovitch beholds the face of a modern humanity that is indifferent toward the fate of European Jewry. The murderers, he declared on December 27, 1942, "will stand in the pillory forever and ever. Humanity will look at them in horror and be afraid of itself" (p. 44). Kalmanovitch added, however, that humanity will then "endeavor to refrain from sin" (p. 44), for the world will realize that, in their attempt to annihilate the Jews, the Nazis set out to eliminate more than humanity: their assault was on the basis of human sanctity.

In the entry dated May 25, 1943, Kalmanovitch maintained that the Nazis' war against the Jew "is not merely directed against one link in the triad [of Israel, Torah, and God]

but against the entire one: against the Torah and God, against the moral law and Creator of the universe" (p. 52). Kalmanovitch accentuated this metaphysical dimension of the Holocaust by incorporating various biblical texts into the text of his diary; writing in the holy tongue, he saw a history of the holy at work in the history of the Holocaust. In a play on verses from Psalms 37, for example, he wrote of the Nazis, "Their sword shall enter into their own heart, and all their bones shall be broken . . . . The waters come even unto the soul!" (p. 58). Later in the same entry (dated July 9, 1943), however, Kalmanovitch cried out, "Awake, why sleepest Thou, O Lord?" (p. 59); it is as though he feared he was witnessing the elimination of the holy from history.

The diary of Zelig Kalmanovitch—his testimony to the fragile life of the holy within the human—was not eliminated from history. By becoming part of human history, this diary calls forth what is most dear in the human image, lest that image be lost—or murdered.

SELECTED WORKS BY THE AUTHOR
"A Diary of the Nazi Ghetto in Vilna." *YIVO Annual of Jewish Social Sciences* 8 (1953): 9–81; *Yoman B'gito Vilna.* Tel Aviv: Sfrit Poalim, 1977.

David Patterson

Kaniuk, Yoram (1930–)

One of Israel's premier novelists, Yoram Kaniuk writes in a style that is expressionistic and surrealistic, exaggerating scenes and moods from everyday life and synthesizing them into metaphors of unforgettable agony and desperation. As a critic of the Israeli scene, and specifically of its war ethic, he is notable for the forceful portraits of the horror of extreme situations. And these situations are not rare, but rather the commonplace experience of the average Israeli, confronted with absurdity and constant pain. The authorial voice pours scorn on the absurdities of everyday life, but also on the country which practices violent warfare whilst exalting peace, and which makes fundamental and, to his mind, unfounded and disastrous distinctions between Jews and Arabs.

Born in Tel Aviv in 1930, Yoram Kaniuk fought in the 1948 War of Independence. He then lived in New York for ten years, working as a painter and a journalist; in 1961 he returned to Israel. His books have been translated into twenty languages, and he is the recipient of numerous literary awards.

Kaniuk's first novel, *Hayored lemaalah* (The acrophile) came out in 1962. It places the first-person narrator in New York, which is not only strange (i.e., foreign to the narrator), but is the ultimate in effecting estrangement. He complains that he feels dissociated not only from his surroundings, but even from his own body, which he describes as apparently acting independently of his will. The city seems to be indifferent to him. Unlike his Israeli home, New York makes no demands of him, and, as befits his inclination, it allows him to be alone, and to flourish in his isolation. But this isolation ultimately only comes to compound his sense of self-disgust. The detachment experienced is that of separation from the rest of humanity.

This sense of separation and disgust constitutes the theme of many of Kaniuk's successive novels, which dig away at the fringes of human experience and degradation. It is well known that survivors of the Holocaust often suffer from guilt feelings precisely because they managed to survive when the vast majority did not. They must have been complicit in some way. *Adam ben kelev*, 1968 (*Adam Resurrected*, 1971) takes as its central figure a survivor who escaped from the gas chambers by acting the clown in the camp and by playing the dog to the commandant. Now, he acts out his new part in a sanatorium in the Israeli Negev, donated by a somewhat unbalanced lady philanthropist. Frantic situations are matched by frantic writing. Betrayal seems to be the sustaining factor in our lives, and it is these apparently marginal episodes that are our characteristic markers.

To illustrate some of the absurdities inherent in rigid notions of identity, the author plays with the idea of someone who is both Jew and Arab, and who suffers on both counts, in the novel *Aravi tov*, 1984 (*Confessions of a Good Arab*, 1987). This is a fiction written in the form of a confessional statement made in the name of Yosef Sherara. Since the narrator turns out to be an Arab on his father's side, his application to join the Israeli army is turned down. Critical decisions turn on factors which should be cut and dried, but which are in fact marginal. In Israel, it is absolutely crucial whether you are a Jew or an Arab; it is life or death, and, in any case, it determines your life's course. But in real life, these things are often not very clear, and so is the case in the novel, where the narrator is of an ambiguous status. This is not the sort of status which the narrator enjoys, and his ultimate desire has always been to belong fully to the central Israeli kernel, to be in fact like his model, Rami, the typical Israeli whom everyone there adores. He says of himself, "I simply wanted to belong, to get into the seam between the levels of loneliness, between the estrangements" (12). Since he could never do that, and since the source of that estrangement had never lain within his power, he feels a deep anger, which must then express itself in political action.

Kaniuk's novels are novels of extreme situations, where the characters are driven to the limits of pain, frustration, and fury, clutching at the apparent offers of salvation, and usually failing ingloriously. Possibly his most ambitious work hitherto, *Ha-yehudi ha-acharon*, 1982 (The last Jew), a massive and gutsy work, explores, as the title suggests, the ultimate issues of being a Jew in the postwar, post-Holocaust, postmodern situation. The most characteristic posture is intense anger, fury at the torture, the hatred, the physical disfigurement, and the human separation, which becomes savage revenge, misdirected and undirected, flailing, in fact, in all directions. Now, the fate of the Jew, the "last Jew," is in the hands of the aging teacher Avadiah Henkin, who is going to tell his story, the story of the teacher who is bereaved of his son in Israel's wars, and who now sees the end of the people. We can understand this metaphorically, as Jewish life has been so transformed by the Holocaust on the one hand, removing the Jewish population, and by the creation of Israel on the other, putting the Jews into another realm, that of an aggressive, military power. But perhaps it can also be seen, through Kaniuk's eyes, as a literal representation.

Selected Works by the Author
Adam Resurrected. Trans. Seymour Simckes. New York: Atheneum, 1971; *Commander of the Exodus.* Trans. Seymour Simckes. New York: Grove, 1999; *Ha-yehudi ha-acharon*. Tel Aviv: Sifriat Poalim, 1982.

Leon I. Yudkin

Kaplan, Chaim (1880–1942 or early 1943)

An established Hebrew educator and linguist in Warsaw, Chaim Aron Kaplan began writing his diary in 1933, as European events darkened the horizon. While his early entries are extant, his published diary *Scroll of Agony* (1965) [*Megilat yisurin: yoman Geto Varshah*, 1966] and its revised edition *The Warsaw Diary of Chaim A. Kaplan* (1972; page numbers from the revised edition of the diary) contain only entries made after the German invasion of Poland. It is a unique document, not only because it is the most extensive testimony to survive from the Warsaw ghetto in Hebrew, but also for the power of its literary text, the honesty of its emotions, and the completeness of its account.

Kaplan chronicled the establishment of the ghetto, the responses of the Jewish community to German cruelty, and the deportations in the summer of 1942. Emmanuel Ringelblum* considered his diary to be of inestimable worth as a historical document: "Kaplan's outlook was not particularly broad, but he knew what the average Warsaw Jew was experiencing at the time: his feelings and sufferings, his thirst for vengeance and so on." He regretted that "time and again I begged Kaplan to deposit his diary with the O.S *(Oneg Shabbat),*" but he only would agree to parts being copied (Kermish, p. 18).

Born in 1880 in Horodyszcze in the Russian empire, Kaplan received a Talmudic education at the renowned Yeshiva of Mir and continued his studies at the government Pedagogical Institute in Vilna. In about 1902, he moved to Warsaw and established a private elementary school, known as the Sixth Grade Grammar Elementary School of Ch. A. Kaplan. The daily lessons were given in Hebrew. To learn Hebrew, he advocated the direct method of teaching, and he was a pioneer in the use of the Sephardic dialect. In 1921 he visited the United States and in 1936, Palestine where his two children had settled.

In Warsaw he was active in the Society of Writers and Hebrew Journalists. By 1939 he was an established Hebraist and author, having published his first book on teaching at progressive *heders* or religious schools, in 1907 and one for Hebrew schools in 1914. In 1917 he published a Hebrew language reader and in 1926 a Hebrew grammar. In 1922 he authored a book of games, and in 1926 he coauthored a *Hagadah* for children. He published *Pezuria,* a collection of articles on Hebrew language and education which he had authored in 1937. He also published frequently in Hebrew-language periodicals.

Under the barrages of the German *blitzkrieg,* in his diary he questioned, "Why is the world silent?" (p. 54). By November 1939 the impact of the occupation on him was already evident, as he admitted: "we have begun to look upon ourselves as 'inferior beings,' lacking God's image" (p. 74). After a bomb killed a religious man's family, he questioned, with anguish; "Is this the way the Almighty looks after His dear ones?" (p. 76), but it is difficult to know how the events affected his Judaism. While he clearly took heart from Zionism, there is little discussion of religious observances or beliefs in the diary, although he lamented, "Nazism has maimed the soul even more than the body!" (p. 290).

Referring to his diary as "our scroll of agony," his sense of purpose grew stronger after war broke out. He explained, "This idea is like a flame imprisoned in my bones, burning within me, screaming: To record!" (p. 144). He sought to leave a record so others could seek vengeance after the war and to provide testimony for historians. "The cage surrounds us completely. A stroll inside the ghetto wall fills one with a sense of helpless fury, a burning rage at the humiliation to which we are subjected" (p. 312). Although the diary is, in many senses, deeply personal, it includes little detail about himself or his family and never mentioned his name. Whenever he become too emotional or concerned about himself, he apologized.

He often despaired and since he was not in good physical condition, the diary kept him company and was an emotional outlet for a man who had devoted his career to language. He believed he might be the only person keeping a diary. He knew that "anyone who keeps such a record endangers his life, but this does not frighten me" (p. 104). When he thought of how to save his record, he confessed, "This journal is my life, my friend and ally . . . in keeping this diary I find spiritual rest" (p. 278). He characterized his writing style, explaining, "My words are not rewritten: momentary reflexes shape them" (p. 104). He feared his ability was limited and he did not know all the facts.

He supported himself and his wife by running a secret Hebrew school, with two of his teachers, in his apartment at Nowolipki Street. He struggled with *Judenrat* (Jewish Council) officials for support of private schools and, in 1940, he was elected to chair a group of educators and represent them at the *Judenrat.* He frequented gatherings at the former *Hatechiyah* center at 13 Zamenhof Street, where a Zionist soup kitchen and refugee center were located. This kitchen, a center of Hebrew-Zionist social activity, was under the patronage of historian Isaac Schiper and Menachem Kirszenbaum, leader of the General Zionists. There he found relief in "the atmosphere and the warmth of Zionism" (p. 256).

Unlike such diarists as Emmanuel Ringelblum, Adam Czerniaków,* or Janusz Korczak,* Kaplan was not a well-known figure, but he stayed in touch with colleagues, family, and friends and had a good grasp of what was going on around him, including the latest German orders and rumors. He reported, usually accurately, on the expulsion of the Jews from communities such as Lublin and Grodzisk. In the summer of 1942, he was briefly protected by a certificate from the Jewish Social Self-Help Organization, but he and his wife were deported to their deaths at Treblinka most likely in December 1942 or January 1943.

Kaplan's diary contains his commentary on the social chaos created by the ghetto. He realized that the Germans had created a situation that threatened the sense of community and ethical behavior. He despaired that "we [Jews] have turned into animals: some of us into domestic animals and some of us into carnivorous animals" (p. 44); furthermore, "We are left neither a nation nor a community, but rather a herd" (p. 52). With cynicism he wrote about the self-important, perhaps fictitious, "Menachem-Mendl," a Zionist leader who shared responsibility for conditions with the Germans. He was critical of the *Judenrat* and the Jewish police, referring to Adam Czerniaków, the chair of the *Judenrat*, as a "nincompoop among nincompoops" (p. 215), but he also realized they would share the same fate.

In his grief, his style often grew tense and bombastic. Sometimes in fury and desperation, he seemed to choke on the inexpressible, but usually he maintained an objective, scholarly style and described life in the ghetto with remarkable, simple images. He conveyed that his diary was, in essence, a "chronicle of famine" (p. 267) with a short sketch on "potatoes" and what they meant to the ghetto. Occasionally he expressed himself with quiet humor. To explain how hungry the ghetto was and how tightly the walls were constructed against smuggling, he commented, "Every crevice has been sealed and even an Aryan mouse would find all access blocked" (p. 276).

In spite of the conditions, he fought to remain hopeful and not to despair. To continue his record with honesty, he invented the literary device "Hirsch." "Hirsch" was apparently his alter ego. As an outsider, Hirsch could admit that the increasing executions were without cause. He also observed the painful reality that "all of you are condemned to die, only the date of execution has not yet to be set" (p. 347). By June 1942, Kaplan prepared for the approaching end, confessing, "The candle of our souls is still flickering but we sense that in a moment it will be extinguished" (p. 362).

He continued writing, although he knew Hirsch's pessimism was correct and his own life was "suspended over nothingness" (p. 398). He made his last entries on August 4, 1942, when the streets near his apartment were being cordoned off and people were being rounded up for deportation. As he and his wife prepared to leave their apartment, the last line he recorded was the question, "And what will become of my diary?" (p. 400). Shortly thereafter, he had his journal smuggled out of the city. Abraham Katsch purchased parts of the diary and published them in 1965. In 1973, he located missing entries from 1941 and 1942 and included them in a revised edition. This made Kaplan's fervent hope that fate would someday see his record become historical source material a reality.

SELECTED WORKS BY THE AUTHOR
Megilat yisurin: Yoman Geto Varshah. Jerusalem: Yad Vashem, 1966; *Pezuria; mehkarim, reshimot u-felyetonim, 1900–1936.* Warsaw: Va'ad ha-yovel, 1937; *Scroll of Agony, the Warsaw Diary of Chaim A. Kaplan.* Trans. and ed. Abraham L. Katsch. New York: Macmillan, 1965; *Warsaw Diary of Chaim A. Kaplan.* Rev. ed., trans. and ed. Abraham L. Katsch. New York: Collier, 1973.

FOR FURTHER READING
Gutman, Yisrael, *The Jews of Warsaw, 1939–1943, Ghetto, Undergrouund, Revolt.* Bloomington: Indiana University Press, 1982; *To Live with Honor and Die with Honor.* Kermish, Joseph, ed., Jerusalem: Yad Vashem, 1986; Ringelblum, Emmanuel, *Notes from the Warsaw Ghetto: The Journal of Emmanuel Ringelblum.* Trans. and ed. Jacob Sloan. New York: Schocken, 1958; Ringelblum, Emmanuel, "The 'Oneg Shabbath' Archives—Its Establishment and Activities." In *To Live with Honor and Die with Honor.* Ed. Joseph Kermish. Jerusalem: Yad Vashem, 1986; Rosenthal, David, "The Unvanquished Sector of the Warsaw Ghetto: Its School System." *Jewish Frontier* 46, no. 4 (4 April 1979): 18–21; Wdowinski, David, *And We Are Not Saved.* New York: Philosophical Library, 1985.

Susan Lee Pentlin

Karmel, Ilona (1925–)

Based on her experience in the Krakow ghetto, as well as in Płaszow and Skarzysko labor camps, Ilona Karmel's two novels *Stephania* (1953) and *An Estate of Memory* (1969) are among the earliest women's artistic responses to the Holocaust. *Stephania* explores ghettoization and survivor memory, and *An Estate of Memory* confronts the universe of labor and concentration camps. Both are important contributions to women's literary testimonies to the event.

Ilona Karmel, who was born in Krakow in 1925, comes from a large Jewish family which lived in Krakow from the seventeenth century until the Holocaust. When the family entered the ghetto, Karmel and her sister depended solely upon their mother, for their father was already dead. Karmel credits her mother with saving her life when she spirited her out of the hospital upon learning that patients were being killed and again when she saved both daughters by hiding them under a mattress during a selection, an incident Karmel incorporated in her fiction.

Set almost entirely in a Swedish hospital, where the protagonist undergoes surgical and therapeutic treatments for a war-induced back injury mirroring Karmel's three years of surgical rehabilitation for leg injuries, *Stephania* employs memory and metaphor to engage the Shoah. The Krakow ghetto emerges organically through survivor recollections and conversation with hospital roommates. The protagonist's mental agony arises from her need to bear witness coupled with her recognition of the difficulty of conveying the reality of the Holocaust to innocent auditors.

By contrast, through integration and individuation of the narrative strands of four women, *An Estate of Memory* charts ghetto and labor camp ordeals. Karmel's powerful descriptions of dreadful camp conditions and her poignant representation of their physical and psychological impact on inmates are among the best in Holocaust literature. Illustrative is the attention to the details of camp routine and the terror of internment: the agony of hunger, illness, routine roll calls transformed from mere bureaucratic attendance checks to a twice daily ritual calculated to demoralize the victims, and special punishment roll calls subjecting the women to rigorous calisthenics, beatings, lengthy periods of kneeling on gravel, and death by shooting or hanging.

Karmel's distinctive accomplishment is her delineation of female-gendered suffering and coping strategies. Friendship and bonding in makeshift camp families, as a strategy for coping with Holocaust atrocity, pervade the novel.

Karmel's fictional group demonstrates how solidarity enhances the individual's chances for survival. The women beg and peddle their belongings to feed one another; warm each other; nurse each other in childbirth and illness; commiserate in hunger and pain; bolster the depressed and terrorized; comfort the bereaved who have lost friends and relatives in the punishment roll calls and selections; and share memories of and plans for a better life in the future.

Through careful delineation of resistance efforts, Karmel joins other writers in exploding the myth of Jews going passively to their slaughter. Lacking access to weapons and substantive assistance from non-Jewish resistance forces, Jewish opposition to the Germans in the ghettos and camps, of necessity, takes primarily a nonmilitary form. Spiritual and psychological resistance, far more evident than militant resistance in the camps, is a powerful force for survival and a critical element of Karmel's universe. The novel's bonding and resistance themes merge most complexly in Karmel's depiction of the women's shared determination to bring a pregnancy to successful term and to smuggle the infant to safety. Although militant resistance is impossible, subversion of Nazi goals in the form of sabotage is constant as the prisoners stage work stoppages and damage goods destined for the German war effort. Foiling selections is a cooperative effort of the women and an O.D. man, the inmate barrack and work supervisor.

Nazis play only peripheral roles in *An Estate of Memory*, often appearing as one-dimensional figures from the perspective of their victims, yet their appearance enhances Karmel's nuanced exploration of radical evil. Typically, she describes the SS metonymically in military images of helmets and glistening boots, fists, or "the arm with the swastika band" (204) designating victims for work assignments, punishment, or death. The only historic figure Karmel presents is SS Strumbannführer Amon Goeth, who is shown denying inmates even the meager rations they were allotted by German law and striding through the camp accompanied by an attack dog trained to strike in response to the word *Jude*.

Karmel's Germans evidence no moral or ethical dilemmas about their Holocaust behavior. Only the Jews contend with these issues: whether to save themselves or to resist escape knowing collective retaliation will follow; whether to protect themselves during a "selection" or allow another to use one's hiding place; how much food to eat when everyone is starving; how to decide whose suffering should be alleviated and whose should be ignored; and how to cope with one's own moral transformation.

An Estate of Memory is clearly Karmel's masterpiece, heralded by Sidra Ezrahi as "a monumental story of the struggle for survival" (p. 70), by Sara Horowitz as "a powerful psychological portrayal of life in a concentration camp" (p. 155), and by S. Lillian Kremer for "historic truthfulness, psychological complexity, moral integrity, and literary artistry" (p. 65).

SELECTED WORKS BY THE AUTHOR
An Estate of Memory. New York: Feminist Press, 1986; *Stephania.* Boston: Houghton Mifflin, 1953.

FOR FURTHER READING
Angress, Ruth K., "Afterword." *An Estate of Memory.* New York: Feminist Press, 1986, 445–57; Ezrahi, Sidra DeKoven, *By Words Alone: The Holocaust in Literature.* Chicago: University of Chicago Press, 1980; 67–95; Horowitz, Sara R., "Ilona Karmel." In *Jewish American Women Writers: A Bio-Bibliographical and Critical Sourcebook,* ed. Ann R. Shapiro. Westport, Conn.: Greenwood Press, 1994, 146–57; Kremer, S. Lillian, "Ilona Karmel." In *Women's Holocaust Writing: Memory and Imagination.* Lincoln: University of Nebraska Press, 1999.

S. Lillian Kremer

Katz, Josef (1918–)

Although it is written like a diary, with dated entries, *One Who Came Back: The Diary of a Jewish Survivor* (1973) by Josef Katz is not, strictly speaking, a diary; he wrote it immediately upon his liberation from a camp near Neustadt on March 8, 1945. A few entries pertain to the early years of the Third Reich and convey the author's recollections of life under the Nazis in his native Germany. But the book

actually begins its tale of agony with December 1941, when Katz was deported from his hometown of Lübeck to Latvia. He spent the next three years in the ghettos of Riga and Liepaja, as well as in slave labor at various camps, including the infamous Stutthof.

Joseph Katz was born in 1918. When, at the age of two, Katz lost his father, his widowed mother worked hard to give Katz and his four siblings an orthodox Jewish upbringing. That upbringing shows in his response to the horror he endured. He conscientiously recorded the death of a Jew who, for example, died as a result of refusing to eat even the meager bits of leavened bread that they had during the first Passover he spent in a camp (p. 45). He related his spiritual pain when the sheer numbers of the dead made saying Kaddish (the Prayer for the Dead) and the El Molei Rachamim (God, Full of Compassion) for each one impossible (p. 47). On his last Rosh Hashanah in captivity, in 1944, Katz offered an unusual account of a worship service held on a Nazi ship taking a group of Jews to Danzig. The praying Jews carried his thoughts back home, to a realm that still had a place for the sacred; but he soon realized, "I am not at home" (p. 201).

Another striking feature of Katz's account is his treatment of death and what might be called "the death of death," that is, the removal of death from anything resembling life in the world of humanity. When his mother passed, for example, she died with the words of the Shema (the "Hear, O Israel" prayer) on her lips, which is as it should be for a Jew. As the tide of death became more and more overwhelming, however, all the prayers, rites, and rituals of mourning and bereavement—everything that affirmed the dearness of the life that had faded away—disappeared. When the living no longer mourn the dead, one realizes, they are as though dead. Thus, stated Katz while working on a mass burial detail, "It is as if the dead were carrying the dead" (p. 48). And the dead cannot die, so that those who are still alive do not die—they are devoured, processed, and otherwise exterminated.

If situating death within the contexts of life is a sign of humanity, then when death loses its significance people lose their humanity: men who are as though dead are not men. Katz noted some revealing consequences of such a condition. He recalled, for example, the time in Kaiserwald, in February 1944, when he reported to a Nazi guard that he had brought thirty men for washing, as ordered. "What do you mean?" the Nazi asked, unable to understand what Katz meant—until Katz corrected himself, saying, "Thirty Jews" (p. 153).

Of course, the man who cannot recognize Jews as men has lost his own humanity. Near the end of his tale, Katz lamented the Nazis' success in dehumanizing the Jews by refashioning them after the Nazis' own image. In January 1945, after surviving a death March from Danzig to Germany, he looked upon what is left of his party and declared that they are human "only in outward appearance. They have lost all civilization or humanity" (p. 245), living, as they do, like Nazis, feeding on other lives. A month later he confessed, "I have known for a long time that only the worst and most brutal kind of person can survive here. Everyone else is fated for the mass grave" (p. 249).

Here Katz is able to drive home the true horror of how complete was the Nazis' assault upon the Jews. Those whom they did not murder they made into creatures who, like the Nazis, lived by devouring their neighbor, so that even the Jews who still lived did not live as Jews.

SELECTED WORKS BY THE AUTHOR
One Who Came Back: The Diary of a Jewish Survivor. Trans. Hilda Reach. New York: Herzl Press, 1973.

David Patterson

Ka-tzetnik 135633 (1909–2001)

A descendant of the famous Hasidic master Rabbi Nachman of Breslov, Yehiel De-Nur became famous as a Holocaust novelist under the pen name Ka-tzetnik 135633. Indeed, his novel *Salmanderah*, 1946 (*Sunrise over Hell*, 1977) was the first Holocaust novel to be written and published. The story of how he acquired the pen name of Ka-tzetnik 135633 and the story of how he came to write the novel are two tales woven into the single story of his life as he knew it before and during the Holocaust.

Yehiel De-Nur was born in Poland in 1909. After losing his entire family to the Nazis— mother, father, wife, sister, and brother—he spent two years in Auschwitz. Several days before the evacuation of the camp, De-Nur found himself among a group of men whom the Nazis were taking outside the camp to be shot. Suddenly he bolted and ran for the forest. Thus he escaped from Auschwitz and eventually made his way to Italy, where he ended up in a hospital just as the war was coming to a close. When the doctors told him he was about to die, he asked for pencil and paper, so that he could repay a debt to the dead. Two weeks later he had completed the novel.

Having accomplished his task he entrusted the manuscript to a Jewish soldier. The soldier looked at the manuscript and said, "There is no author's name here. Who shall I say wrote it?"

"Who wrote it?" De-Nur answered. "*They* wrote it. Put *their* name on it: Ka-tzetnik."

Thus the great author of Holocaust literature was anonymously born, taking the name Ka-tzetnik, which means "camp inmate." By having had the dead speak through him, Ka-tzetnik made what was described as a miraculous recovery; soon he was on his way to Israel. He settled in Tel Aviv, where he died in 2001. His book preceded him; before Israel became a state, every household in the land had a copy of Ka-tzetnik's book. But no one, including the publisher, knew who the author was. At that time, as he himself puts it, he was living on one park bench during the day and on another during the night. Nina De-Nur (later known as Eliyah De-Nur), the woman who was to become his wife and the translator of his books from Hebrew into English, spent a year tracking him down; ultimately she saved his life.

When asked to testify at the trial of Adolf Eichmann, Ka-tzetnik replied that, although he spent two years in Auschwitz, he could not say what Auschwitz was (subsequently he did testify). And yet, through the sum of his literary response to Auschwitz, he says as well as anyone what Auschwitz was. His novels deal with his life and the lives of his family, whom he portrays as the Preleshniks. "All I've ever written," he explains in his memoir *Shivitti* (1989), "is in essence a personal journal, a testimonial on paper of I, I, I: I who witnessed . . . I who experienced . . . I who lived through. . . I, I, I, till half through a piece, I suddenly had to transform *I* to *he*" (p. 71). The main character in his first work, *Salmanderah*, is a violinist, Harry Preleshnik. The tale, which opens in Metropoli in the summer of 1939, traces Harry's path through the ghetto life that was soon forced upon him and his wife, Sanya, and ends with his escape from Auschwitz as the camp was being evacuated.

Already in this first work Ka-tzetnik displays his genius for examining the implications of the Holocaust for our understanding of the nature of God, the world, and humanity. In a moment that sums up the novel, Harry holds the body of his friend Marcel in his arms: "Prone before his eyes, he saw the values of all humanity's teachings, ethics and beliefs, from the dawn of mankind to this day. Marcel's carcass-face revealed to him the true face of man in the image of God. He bent, stretched out his hand and caressed the head of the Twentieth Century" (p. 111). Which image, for Ka-tzetnik, is most emblematic of the twentieth century? It is the *Muselmann*, the camp term used to refer to one who looks dead but is not dead. In the end, therefore, his escape is not a movement into life, for he escapes as a corpse to enter a world bereft of its humanity.

Based on the actual diary of Ka-tzetnik's sister, the novel that follows *Salmanderah* is *Bet Ha-Bubot*, 1953 (*House of Dolls*, 1955). Although Harry Preleshnik is an important character in the book, it is primarily the tale of his sister Daniella. The fourteen-year-old girl left home one day in 1939 to go on a school trip with her classmates, but she never returned. She was picked up by the Nazis and selected to work as a prostitute for German soldiers. Harry discovers the terrible fate that befell his sister when he sees her with the SS while working as a physician at Niederwalden. In the novel Ka-tzetnik brilliantly outlines the tearing of meaning from words and sense from reality that characterizes the Holocaust. One sees two children, for ex-

ample, pushing an old man in a baby carriage through the ghetto: children were old, and old men were as helpless as children. Commenting on the camp itself, he wrote, "Anything goes here, anything is possible, the way anything goes and is possible in insanity. Death and life dwell together here. Blood and wine are drunk from the same flasks. The Carrion Shed and the SS rooms are one. Borders erased. Boundaries lost" (p. 212).

Ka-tzetnik's third major novel is *Kareu lo Pipl*, 1961 (*Atrocity*, 1963; reprinted under the title *Moni*, 1963). It is the story of Harry Preleshnik's brother Moni, who was sent to Auschwitz at the age of eleven and selected to be a *pipel*, that is, a boy whom the block chiefs of Auschwitz would use for their sexual orgies. Opening with Moni's arrival in the camp, the novel explores the many dimensions of the camp from beginning to end, as seen both in its murderers and in its victims. Above all, the novel is about the distinctive nature of the Holocaust as an assault on the child, understood not just as a little person or even merely as one who is innocent: understood, rather, as the messianic bearer of a future and a meaning, of truth and redemption. In the Holocaust that is precisely what is rendered unrecognizable: "Nobody recognizes him. Nobody knows who he is. And Moni doesn't recognize anybody either. He dissolves among thousands of *Mussulmen*. He is a drop in a skeleton river flowing to a sea of ash" (pp. 228–29).

Moni reappears in Ka-tzetnik's tale of deportation, dehumanization, and death titled *Kokhav Ha-Efer*, 1966 (*Star of Ashes,* 1967; reprinted in English as *Star Eternal*, 1971). Based on an earlier work titled *Ha-sha'on Asher Me-'al La-rosh*, 1960 (The clock overhead), the book contains very few names; Auschwitz itself—or the word-devouring silence that is Auschwitz—is its main character. Indeed, silence stands out more prominently in this series of vignettes from the anti-world than in Ka-tzetnik's other novels. The children's scream, for example, silently "howls out of the mother's eyes" (p. 55). Left to the shadow of Auschwitz, the world itself is made of silence: "Silent are the heavens, silent the yellowed fields; silent the readied rifles, silent the ghetto hovels" (p. 53). It is this silence that ultimately leads an inmate named Ferber to declare to a rabbi, "Admit now, Rabbi of Shilev, God of the Diaspora Himself flounders here in this snarl of bones—a Mussulman!" (p. 179). Because *Star of Ashes* is precisely about silence, it addresses precisely the task facing the author/survivor: "I vow on your ash embraced in my arms, to be a voice unto you, and unto the Ka-Tzet now voiceless and consumed" (p. 191). In contrast to those works that precede this one, Ka-tzetnik does not go back in this case and change "I, I, I" to he. He retains the first person, but often in the form of a you addressed simultaneously to himself and to his reader: "You are outside. On top of the earth. You weren't buried in the pit" (p. 35).

Ke-Hol Me-Efer, 1966 (*Phoenix over the Galilee*, 1969), the next novel, takes up the life of Harry Preleshnik and his wife, Galilea, in postwar Israel. Daniella and Moni, however, are still silently and persistently there, for Harry understands that his "life had been spared to voice the strangled scream of these two children" (p. 123). In the novel Ka-tzetnik compares the lives of those turned into ash to words that have been burned with the paper they are printed on. "This is how they had been burned at Auschwitz," he says, "those whose bodies had turned to ash, whose lives had been unlived. Where did their souls go?" (p. 170). Perhaps their souls go into this story about the profound love between Harry and his wife and their efforts to seek a humane, if not a loving, relationship between the Arabs and the Israelis. For these two, making that effort appears to be the one way in which they might transform a world gone mad with hatred into a world of sense and sensibility.

Ka-tzetnik published very little during the 1970s, but began to struggle more than ever with the nightmares that had haunted him ever since Auschwitz. For thirty years he did not sleep at night but would nap as best he could during the day. In 1976 his devoted wife finally persuaded him to seek the help of Professor Jan C. Bastiaans in the Department of Psychiatry at the State University in Leiden, Holland. Using methods of LSD therapy, Professor Bastiaans specialized in treating Holocaust survivors suf-

fering from nightmares. Ka-tzetnik went to Bastiaans and subjected himself to four LSD therapy sessions which, he says, provided him with the key to Auschwitz, a key that finally freed him from his nightmares. He was determined to write about the "key," but ten years passed before he could come to the first line, out of which the rest of the book flowed. The result was *Tsofen: E.D.'M.A.*, 1987 (*Shivitti: A Vision*, 1989).

E.D.'M.A., Ka-tzetnik explains, is an unvoiced combination of letters that would come to his lips each time he was near death while in Auschwitz; the letters can be found at the beginning of his books, and they appear at the beginning of his LSD therapy in *Tsofen*. If the letters have any meaning beyond that, Ka-tzetnik will not say what it is. It is likely, however, that they stand for *Eloha deMeir aneni* (God of Meir answer me). An ancient invocation of the talmudic sage Rabbi Meir, Jews in the mystical tradition use this code to summon help in times of need. The English title *Shivitti* is taken from the inscription that appears in the artwork that adorns many synagogues and that is frequently part of the visions recorded in the book. The inscription is *Shivitti adoshem le-negedi tamid*, or "I have set the Lord before me always" (Psalms 16:8). *Tsofen*, in fact, has many biblical verses interwoven with the visions of the anti-world with which Ka-tzetnik collided during his LSD therapy sessions. The visions consist of remembrances and reenactments of his time in Auschwitz, where each moment "revolved around the cogwheels of a different timesphere." The "key" is made of those visions.

One piece of the key arises, for example, in his memory of the time he was being loaded into a truck to be taken to the gas chambers. Gazing at the SS man whose job was to send him to his death, Ka-tzetnik cries out to God, saying, "You know that at this moment the two of us, dispatcher and dispatched, are equal sons of man, both created by you, in your image" (p. 11). Hence, he realizes, each of them could be standing in the place of the other. The most powerful vision, however—the vision that ended his therapy, despite Professor Bastiaans's recommendation that he undergo one more session—is the fourth and last vision. While bits and pieces of his other visions and memories appear in his novels, this one unearths something that does not appear in any of his previously written pages. It is a vision of his mother: "My mother, naked. Going to be gassed. I behold my mother's skull and in my mother's skull I see me. And I chase after me inside my mother's skull. And my mother is naked. Going to be gassed" (p. 101). His mother holds up her murdered children to God. But who is this God? It is Nucleus, the Destroyer of worlds. What strikes Ka-tzetnik here is that precisely while death was being "manufactured" in the Nazi death factories, the atomic bomb was being built in Los Alamos.

On February 14, 1992, Eliyah De-Nur, the one whom Ka-tzetnik called "the light of my world," passed away. It would seem, then, that the title of his collection of writings, *Kaddish* (English and Hebrew, 1998), may have been selected with her, as well as the 6,000,000, in mind (the Kaddish is the Prayer for the Dead). His mother shows up here too, but this time in a poetic portrait with his sister. The volume contains a variety of poetry, heartrending renditions of the fate of the children, and harrowing descriptions of the physical and spiritual violence of the concentrationary universe—written at times realistically, at times surrealistically, and always with a rhythm of ritual, akin to prayer. While Ka-tzetnik 135633 is one of the most insightful, artistic, and profound voices to emerge from Planet Auschwitz, he is also one of the most invisible. He never sought to publish anything he wrote—his wife attended to that business. He never made a public appearance and never promoted a word he wrote, mainly because the words are not his. "*They* wrote it," he insists. While he is invariably included in scholarly works on Holocaust literature in general, there are no book-length studies of this remarkable body of work which demands a book-length treatment.

SELECTED WORKS BY THE AUTHOR
Atrocity. Trans. Nina De-Nur. New York: Kensington, 1977; *Ha-sha'on Asher Me-'al La-rosh*. Jerusalem: Mosad Bialik, 1960; *House of Dolls*. Trans. Moshe M. Kohn. New York: Pyramid, 1958; *Kaddish*. New York: Algemeiner Associates, 1998; *Phoenix over the Galilee*. Trans. Nina De-Nur. New York: Harper and Row, 1969; Shivitti: *A Vision*. Trans. Eliyah N. De-Nur and Lisa Herman. New York: Harper and Row, 1989; *Star of Ashes*. Trans. Nina De-Nur. Tel-Aviv: Hamenora, 1971; *Sunrise over Hell*. Trans. Nina De-Nur. London: W.H. Allen, 1977.

David Patterson

Katznelson, Yitzhak (1886–1944)

One of the twentieth century's major authors in Hebrew and Yiddish literature, Yitzhak Katznelson is also one of the most prominent of Holocaust literature. His *Dos Lid fun oysgehartgetn Yidishn folk*, 1948 (*The Song of the Murdered Jewish People*, 1980) is the most significant epic poem written during the time of the murder of European Jewry. And his *Pinkas Vitel*, 1988 (*Vittel Diary*, 1972) is one of the most powerful diaries to be retrieved from the ashes of the Holocaust. The manuscripts of both works are extant thanks to the efforts of a member of the French underground named Miriam Novitch, who was a prisoner in Vittel at the time when Katznelson was there in 1943. Katznelson placed the manuscripts of the poem and the diary into three bottles; he and Novitch then buried them in a park. Later, with the help of a laundress named Marcelle Rabichon, Novitch managed to get the manuscripts out of the camp. Rabichon placed them in tins and hid them in her mother's house, where they remained until the end of the war.

The child of a long line of rabbis and Hebrew scholars, Katznelson was born in 1886 in the town of Karelitz in the Minsk district of White Russia. Having written his first play at the age of twelve, he followed in his father's footsteps and became a teacher. He founded a school in Łódź and fled to Warsaw in November 1939 when Łódź was overrun by the Nazis. His wife, Chanah, and three sons—Ben Zion, Binyamin, and Zvi—soon joined him, and he became an active member of the Jewish underground. The most prolific writer in the Warsaw ghetto, Katznelson wrote thirty literary works between June 1940 and early 1942. On August 14, 1942, his wife and their two younger sons, Ben Zion and Binyamin, were deported to Treblinka. Yitzhak and his son Zvi escaped from the ghetto before its destruction in May 1943 but did not escape from the Nazis: they found themselves on a transport to the camp at Vittel in eastern France. There he began writing his *Vittel Diary*, which he kept until September 16, 1943. On October 3, he set his pen to *The Song of the Murdered Jewish People*, which he completed in January 1944. On April 18, 1944, Katznelson and Zvi were transported to Drancy; on April 29, they were sent to the gas chambers of Auschwitz.

The Song of the Murdered Jewish People contains fifteen cantos; each canto consists of fifteen four-line stanzas. The poem recounts the aftermath of the German invasion of Poland, the liquidation of Warsaw Jewry, the agony of the children in the orphanages, the Warsaw ghetto uprising, and other key events in the annihilation of the body of Israel. Darker than the vision of Ezekiel, in which the bones of the dead were returned to life (Ezekiel 37:5–6), Katznelson's vision is biblical in its depth but not in its hope, for he sees no prospect that the dry bones of the Holocaust dead will rise. Indeed, they have been reduced to ashes. Beholding the eyes of his wife and children among the murdered, Katznelson situates himself among the dead as part of the body of Israel. One of the greatest torments he expresses in the poem, moreover, is the involvement of the Jewish police in the deportation of the Jews to the murder camps.

Greater than the poet's shame over the complicity of the police, however, is his agony over the plight of the children. Here, as throughout the poem, Katznelson makes his point regarding the slaughter of the people of Israel by focusing his gaze upon a single individual, a child grown old and robbed of her childhood. For this "tiny Jewish girl, a hundred years old in her seriousness and grief" (p. 38), has seen far more than her grandmother ever feared to see. And in each child, he beholds a messiah, sanctified by pain and punishment (p. 40). Perhaps more than all the other suffering explored in the poem, the suffering of the little ones leads Katznelson to compare the tale of the Holocaust to a biblical tale in which the cruelty of the Germans far exceeds that of Amalek (p. 85).

Many of the themes of *The Song of the Murdered Jewish People* appear also in Katznelson's *Vittel Diary*. There he sees the children as "the messiahs of the world even while still in their mothers' wombs" (p. 128)—and that is precisely where the Nazis took their assault: "These Jewish mothers with babes in their wombs! This murderous German nation! That was their chief joy! To destroy women with child" (p. 109). Perceiving the messianic significance of the child, Katznelson regarded the metaphysical significance of the Holocaust as an assault on the very basis of holiness in the world. "The Bible of Israel and its moral laws are at the root of all that is good in the nations," he asserted. "Without the people of Israel, the Bible is void of content and has no meaning" (p. 81). Katznelson pursued the implication of this singular feature of the Holocaust for the Christians, declaring that the Christians fail to realize that "the God of Israel and the people of Israel are one. They fail to appreciate that Jesus is not an isolated phenomenon but something that is continued in Israel" (pp. 122–23). Thus, he maintained, the world looked on while "a great and vast nation of Jesuses . . . has been murdered" (p. 204). By murdering the Jews, the Christian world murdered its redeemer.

One of the most striking features of this professional writer's diary is his consciousness of the act of writing and of his relation to the reader. Far more than a chronicle of events, Katznelson's diary is an essential feature of his tenuous existence. "This pen of mine," he says, "has become a living part of me. This pen, too, is broken, like myself, like my soul, like everything within me" (p. 187). Why broken? Because his soul cannot endure the weight of the dead for whom it has become a cemetery: "As I write these words, I want to weep. And if perchance I shed a tear, then Chanah, Ben Zion, and Binyamin are there within it . . . . Do not seek them out in Treblinka, nor in the mounds of the earth, for you will find no trace of them. You must look for them in my tiny tear" (pp. 232–33). Of course, readers must do more than look for them—they must heed them.

Readers who encounter the silent voices of the dead in the pages of this diary not only acquire information and insight—they are implicated as witnesses to the slaughter. To be sure, Katznelson works at transforming his readers into witnesses: "On and on, up to seven million . . . . Count! Count!—you must not stop!—this is a memorial service for the departed souls. Count on, count on, until your lips and tongue dry up in your mouth" (p. 194). Regarding the encounter between his readers and his text as a memorial service, Katznelson elevates his outcry to the level of prayer and summons his readers to add their voices to his own. For Katznelson, a reader is a participant.

SELECTED WORKS BY THE AUTHOR

Al naharot Bavel. Trans. Shalom Lurya, ed. Mosheh Kupferman. Tel Aviv: Hakibbutz Hameuchad, 1995; *Elegy.* Trans. Rose Freeman-Ishill. Berkeley Heights, N.J.: Oriole Press, 1948; *HaShir al haRabi m'Radzin.* Trans. M.Z. Volfovsky. Tel Aviv: Hakibbutz Hameuchad, 1971; *Ketavim.* Tel Aviv: Hakibbutz Hameuchad, 1981; *Ketavim acharonim: b'Geto Varshah.* Tel Aviv: Hakibbutz Hameuchad, 1988; *Mahazot.* Tel Aviv: Hakibbutz Hameuchad, 1982; *Mahazot tanakhiyim.* Tel Aviv: Hakibbutz Hameuchad, 1984; *Mayanot.* Tel Aviv: Hakibbutz Hameuchad, 1984; *Sipurim umasot.* Tel Aviv: Hakibbutz Hameuchad, 1982; *The Song of the Murdered Jewish People.* Trans. Noah H. Rosenbloom. Tel Aviv: Hakibbutz Hameuchad and Ghetto Fighters' House, 1980; *Vittel Diary.* Trans. Myer Cohen. Tel Aviv: Hakibbutz Hameuchad and Ghetto Fighters' House, 1972.

FOR FURTHER READING

Szeintuch, Yechiel, *Yitzhak Katznelson: Ketavim sh'nitslu.* Jerusalem: Magnes Press, 1995.

David Patterson

Kessel, Sim (1919–)

"In December 1944, I was hanged at Auschwitz," Sim Kessel begins his remarkable memoir *Pendu à Auschwitz,* 1970 (*Hanged at Auschwitz,* 1972). From the outset, then, this memoir is a man's memory of his own death and his testimony to the deaths of millions.

Born in Paris on July 26, 1919, Kessel was not quite twenty-three when the Gestapo arrested him in Dijon on July 14, 1942; he had been a member of the French Resistance since December 20, 1940, and was charged with the crime of "terrorism." After his interrogation and deportation to Drancy, he spent twenty-three months in the concentration camp universe: two months at Birkenau, three months at Jaworzno (an Auschwitz annex and coal mine), fourteen months in the main camp at Auschwitz, and four months in Mauthausen and Gusen II.

Containing very few details about growing up in his native Paris—except to note that he had been a boxer—Kessel's memoir is unusual not only for the tale of his miraculous survival but for its capacity to convey a multitude of dimensions in the Nazis' assault on humanity. Kessel understands, for example, the ramifications of having no law or justice to appeal to; he recalls the "pure terror" that would overwhelm him between torture sessions and remembers the terror of the children "clutching at their mothers' skirts" in Drancy (p. 46). Indeed, much of Kessel's memoir is a memory of the children. Tracing the path of his descent from Drancy to the sealed train to Auschwitz, Kessel clearly delineates the process of transforming human beings into something other than human. Once in the camp, "it only took a few days for us to realize once and for all that we were no longer men" (p. 59)—a realization not so much arrived at as imposed upon the consciousness. "A serial number dispenses you from having had a name, having had a soul, or having had a life" (p. 169).

Kessel also brings out other implications of what it means to no longer be a human being. He describes, for instance, how it leads to a loathing for oneself, to a deadly solitude, and to an indifference toward the suffering of others. The one thing that enabled him to maintain a trace of his humanity was the thought of escape—a feat that he managed to accomplish in December 1944, only to be quickly recaptured and sentenced to be hanged. And so he was. But the rope around his neck broke, making him perhaps the only survivor to record the memory of ascending the gallows with the eyes of his fellow prisoners upon him. Kessel was then sentenced to be shot, but the *kapo,* or foreman, assigned to do the job let him go; he too had been a boxer, and that created a certain bond between them. Thus Kessel was left to wander the camp and blend in with prisoners as best he could—like a dead man among the dead—until they were evacuated in January 1945.

There is one remarkable feature about Kessel's tale: within weeks of his liberation from Gusen II on May 7, 1945, he was able to return home to his parents, both of whom survived the war. Although at the time of his liberation he "became shatteringly aware that we meant exactly nothing to anyone" (p. 185), he soon found a way to escape from his new quarantine camp and contact a former comrade from the Resistance. He discovered that the Resistance had protected his parents with false documents, so that, unlike most other survivors, Kessel had a mother and a father to return home to. Indeed, he insists that without a family to return to, he could never have returned to life: the family is the very origin of the *meaning* in life that the Nazis set out to annihilate.

SELECTED WORK BY THE AUTHOR:
Hanged at Auschwitz. Trans. Melville Wallace and Delight Wallace. New York: Stein and Day, 1972.

David Patterson

Kielar, Wieslaw (1921–)

Regarded as a definitive work on Planet Auschwitz, the memoir *Anus Mundi: Wspomnienia Oświęcimskie*, 1972 (*Anus Mundi: 1,500 Days in Auschwitz/Birkenau*, 1980) written by Polish film director Wieslaw Kielar won two national literature prizes when it was first published in Poland. The book went on to become a best-seller in its German edition in 1979. Hörst von Glasenapp, a German judge who presided over the war crimes trials, described Kielar's memoir as one of the most important intellectual works to emerge in postwar Germany. Other than letting the reader know that Kielar was a Polish Catholic, the memoir provides very little information on his life before June 1940 or after the end of the war.

Born in 1921, Kielar was only nineteen years old when he and three of his comrades were arrested in June 1940 for their activities in the Polish underground and were sent immedi-

ately to Auschwitz; that is where the memoir begins. What follows is a day-by-day person-by-person account of life in the anti-world. The power of Kielar's memoir lies not only in his understanding of conceptual ramifications of the concentrationary universe but also in his insight into the broad range of humanity he encounters there. With brief but expressive portraits of people, their sufferings, and their crimes, Kielar imparts a face to a realm calculated to breed faceless anonymity.

One of the very few to survive such a long stint in the camp, Kielar traces the evolution of Auschwitz from a concentration camp into the Auschwitz/Birkenau murder camp. His story, moreover, is not the tale of an annihilated Jewish family or community but primarily of the Nazis' persecution of the Poles. Because, as a Pole, Kielar had a freer access to a wider range of camp existence than most Jews, he is able to transmit to his reader a broader range of experience than most memoir writers. Indeed, as one of the workers on the corpse detail—those who collected bodies in the camp and delivered them to the crematoria—Kielar saw nearly every inch of the ash-covered grounds: from "Canada," or the warehouse where the belongings of the dead were stored, to the crematoria, from the punishment block to the transit site, from the women's camp to the Gypsy camp.

Although he is not a Jew, Kielar attests to the brutal, systematic slaughter for which the Jews were singled out. Recalling transport after transport of Jews—now the Greek, now the Slovak, now the Hungarian Jews—he relates the fate of these victims not with sweeping generalizations but by recalling specific individuals, whose humanity he brings to life. He also provides his reader with unusual glimpses of the fate of other prisoners, including the Russian prisoners of war and the Gypsies; he frequently recalls the *Muselmänner*, the walking dead who were in a category of their own. In contrast to the holy image that links each human being to every other, the *Muselmänner* exemplified the Nazis' undoing of that image and a leveling of all humanity into a meaningless and indifferent sameness.

Kielar even provides the reader with a glimpse of the inner world of the crematoria and an insightful commentary on the psychological issues faced by members of the *Sonderkommando*, the Jews who were forced to work in the crematoria. In addition, he presents a portrait of Josef Mengele, the infamous head physician of Auschwitz, and relates some of the famous tales from Auschwitz. One incident, for example, concerns a young woman who took a gun from a Nazi officer at the entrance to the gas chamber and shot him. Another account deals with his close friend Edek Galinski, with whom he had planned an escape with Edek's lover, Mala. Indeed, as one reads the many memoirs of Auschwitz, one discovers that the lovers Edek and Mala were all but legendary in the camp. They represented a trace of life and hope in a realm devoid of both, not only in their devotion to one another but also in their determination to escape. They did indeed escape but were caught and brought back to be hanged; the two of them went defiantly to their deaths.

In early November 1944 Kielar was on a transport from Auschwitz to Oranienburg in Germany; from Oranienburg he was sent to Porta Westfalica, a satellite camp of Neuengamme, for forced labor. As the Allies advanced, he and his fellow prisoners were moved to the labor camp at Schandelach, then from Schandelach to Webeling, where he was liberated by the Americans.

SELECTED WORKS BY THE AUTHOR

Anus Mundi: 1,500 Days in Auschwitz/Birkenau. Trans. Susanne Flatauer. New York: Times Books, 1980; *I Nasze Młode Lata: Wspomnienia.* Wrocław: Wydawn, 1987.

David Patterson

Klein, Gerda Weissmann (1924–)

With the publication of her memoir *All but My Life* in 1957, Gerda Weissmann Klein became one of the first women to offer her memories of the Holocaust to the world. Although her book did not receive widespread acclaim at the time, its testimony became known throughout the world in 1996 when *One Survivor Remembers*, a film based on Klein's Holocaust experience, won the Academy Award for Best Documentary. Her memoir is particularly striking for its insight into the Nazi assault on the family and on the human ties that create a family. It reveals that the Nazis set out to annihilate not only mothers and fathers but also the very relationships and values that constitute a mother and a father, a family, and a home.

Born in Bielitz, Poland, on May 8, 1924, Klein and her brother, Arthur, lived peacefully with their mother and father until the German invasion in September 1939. Older and more independent, Arthur left for the East two months after the Germans' arrival; the fifteen-year-old Klein remained with her parents in Bielitz until May 1942. Shortly after her eighteenth birthday she was separated from her parents and deported to the camp at Sosnowitz; she never saw her family again. She was sent from camp to camp until January 1945, when she set out on a forced march of nearly 1,000 miles from Silesia to Czechoslovakia. Klein was among the few to make it as far as Volary, Czechoslovakia, where she was liberated on May 6, 1945. Among her liberators was Lieutenant Kurt Klein, the man she would marry. In 1946 she and her American husband settled in Buffalo, New York.

Writing with a deep sense of paying a debt to the dead, Gerda Klein wrote with a sense of the spiritual catastrophe that came with the murder of the body of Israel. Near the end of her memoir, for instance, she recalled the time of her liberation and cried out to her lost mother and father: "'Papa, Mama'—I murmured the words, to hear their sound again—'help me! Help me find my way!'" (p. 242). Having lost her most fundamental reference point for finding her way in the world—her family and home—Klein endeavored to reconstitute that point in a movement of memory. Thus, in an effort to find her way, she recorded this memory of the very ones to whom she cries out. For Gerda Klein, remembering their loss is a way of finding her way back to a place where life has sanctity. It is a way of remembering what a mother and father represent. By remembering how they were murdered, she remembers why they matter.

She related, for example, how her father deteriorated by degrees; he was not killed outright but was drained of his soul before the Nazis murdered his body. Just days after the Nazis took over, for example, she stated, "Papa seemed so old, so gray. He had changed so much" (p. 8). And when her brother left for the East, she remembered seeing her father cry for the first time, rendered as helpless as she was. "I embraced Papa," she wrote, illustrating the reversal of the roles of parent and child. "A suppressed and terrible sobbing cry rose from his throat, a cry which I will never forget, which had no resemblance to the human voice . . . . I was to hear that cry later, many times, when people were being killed" (p. 20). This image conveys the death not only of the father but also of the word, the teaching, and the tradition signified by the father. It is a death that repeats itself in a pattern of the extermination of the human image itself.

Similarly, Klein opened up a deeper understanding of the Nazi assault on the home as an extension of the assault on the love and compassion associated with the mother. When the Nazis came to Bielitz, she wrote, "The sanctity of our home was gone, the chain of tradition broken, the shrine built by love and affection desecrated" (p. 31). As it goes with parents and dwelling place, so it goes with children: "I had learned to associate children with death. Children were not permitted to live, to laugh" (p. 227). With the breakdown in the meaning of family and home, Klein is rendered homeless. To be sure, her memoir makes it clear that one aim of the Nazis, who had determined that the Jews have no place in the world, is to render the Jews homeless before they slaughter them. After she arrived in the camp—the realm of ultimate homelessness—she often called out to her mother and father in her dreams, but "there was no comfort—only pain and loneliness" (p. 109). Thus she is left to the homelessness of an orphan in an orphaned world.

Klein's memoir demonstrates, moreover, that the homeless condition of the Jew follows her into the world even after she is liberated; indeed, liberation itself becomes problematic for one who has no home to return to. With "freedom" in sight, Klein reflected, "Perhaps we will survive, but what then? I will go home, of course . . . . [But] the thought of going home did not ring right" (p. 210). It did not ring right because,

with the murder of her family and the assault on the idea of a family, home was no longer on her spiritual map. That is why she called out to her mother and father to help her find the way. For Klein, as a Holocaust survivor, authoring the memoir is one means of reconstituting a home through the avenue of memory, even when all other avenues have been obliterated.

SELECTED WORKS BY THE AUTHOR
All but My Life. New York: Hill and Wang, 1957; *The Hours After*, with Kurt Klein. New York: St. Martin's Press, 2000.

David Patterson

Klonicki-Klonymus, Aryeh (1906–1943)

One striking aspect of Aryeh Klonicki-Klonymus's Holocaust diary *Yoman Avi Adam*, 1969 (*The Diary of Adam's Father*, 1973) lies in the conditions under which it was written: "It is not indoors that I am writing these lines," he himself explained in the opening entry (July 5, 1943), "but outside in a field of wheat where I am hiding with my wife" (p. 21). The field where he and his wife hid in the summer of 1943—and where they were soon captured— was located in the vicinity of Kovel in the Ukraine where he was born in 1906. Klonicki-Klonymus kept the diary for the sake of his infant son, Adam, who was hidden with a Christian family in Kovel, and "to leave some remembrance at least to those of my brothers fortunate enough to be living in lands untouched by the hand of Hitler" (p. 21). A local peasant recovered the diary after Klonicki-Klonymus and his wife were captured and sent to their deaths in August 1943.

Klonicki-Klonymus not only wrote the diary for his son, but his son is often the focus of his entries. "My son's name is Adam." He explained early on why he so named his son: "I wanted to emphasize by this that the Germans, worse than all beasts of prey, will finally be conquered by human beings. Therefore I called him Adam (human being)" (p. 21). The terrible question he faces, however, is whether anything will remain of the human being after the Nazis have done their work. "How many times would I look at my little child," he wrote on July 5, 1943, "and it would seem to me that it is not a child I am looking at but a box of ashes" (p. 24). So pervasive is the Nazi assault on the Jews that it invades a father's vision of his child.

And yet Klonicki-Klonymus clung to his child and protected him, until he could find a safe haven for him. He related, for example, a tragically familiar incident which occurred when he and his family were hiding in a cellar with other Jewish families. Some of the mothers in the group had already been forced to suffocate their babies, so that the cries of the little ones would not give them all away. When they tried to get Klonicki-Klonymus to do the same to his three-month-old son, he refused, "As long as I was alive such a thing would not come to pass" (p. 31). He is a witness to the fate of other children as well, noting that "they are burying children alive" in the mass graves where adults were lined up and shot (p. 32). With this assault on pure innocence, on the most holy of human beings created in the image of the Holy One, Klonicki-Klonymus perceives a terrible metaphysical question: "Is there a God in this world or is lawlessness at the very core of the universe?" (p. 32). He fears that what the Nazis do *in* the world may reveal some dark truth *of* the world.

The metaphysical issue, however, soon gives way to the issue of survival. On July 11, 1943, for instance, Klonicki-Klonymus asserted that it would be better for the Jews to be the People of the Sword than the People of the Book (p. 55). In his last entry, dated July 18, 1943, he lamented the fact that his father did not train him in a trade but taught him only Torah and Talmud; for a trade might have saved him, but the teachings of the sages would not (pp. 74–75). And yet he named his son Adam to affirm the vision of humanity handed down through generations of Jewish teachers of Torah and Talmud.

SELECTED WORK BY THE AUTHOR:
The Diary of Adam's Father. Trans. Avner Romaschiff. Tel-Aviv: Ghetto Fighters' House and Hakibbutz Hameuchad, 1973.

David Patterson

Kon, Menachem (1882–1942)

The diary of Polish-born Menachem Kon was among those recovered from the *Oneg Shabbat* archives. The *Oneg Shabbat* circle consisted of a group of people from a variety of backgrounds organized by the historian Emmanuel Ringelblum* to chronicle the events that transpired in the Warsaw ghetto. Titled "Fragments of a Diary (August 6, 1942–October 1, 1942)," Kon's diary is included in *To Live with Honor, To Die with Honor: Selected Documents from the Warsaw Ghetto Underground Archives,* a collection compiled by Joseph Kermish and published by Yad Vashem in 1986.

Menachem Kon was born in 1882. Just as Kon's diary was recovered in fragments, however, so is the information on his life fragmentary. His diary covers the period of the *Aktions* of 1942, when the Nazis undertook massive deportations of the Jews from the Warsaw ghetto to the murder camp at Treblinka. The diary ends on October 1, because Kon himself fell prey to the murderers. In his last entry he cried out, "Know ye, Jews of the wide world, the extent of their crimes" (p. 86). A mature man of sixty, Kon appears to have had the wisdom to indeed know both the extent and the ramifications of the Nazi atrocities. "History does not know anything like [this slaughter]," he wrote on September 7, sensing a uniqueness about what had already transpired (p. 83).

One distinctive feature of the Holocaust that can be seen in Kon's diary is how the Nazis made the very old and the very young their first targets, as if they were setting out to obliterate both the memory and the hope harbored by the Jewish community. In his first entry, dated August 6, he observed that "the Hitlerite beast uses any means. They shoot, murder the older and sick on the spot in the gory square" (p. 80). In the same entry he attested to the assault against the children: "The children are being hidden since they are the most sought after by the murderers. I made up my mind not to go into the cellar, I shall not take up room where some more children could be hidden. The children have preference to be saved" (p. 80).

In this last remark we see a distinctive feature of the Holocaust diary: unlike many diaries that recount the day or engage in an exploration of the soul, the Holocaust diaries are written as testimonies to and for the sake of a larger community. Kon's concern is not for himself but for other human beings, for the children, and for the community. That is why he is so sensitive both to the impossibility and to the necessity of bearing witness to events that defy description. "No pen can write down what the eye saw," he asserted on September 13, "no phantasy can picture it. Still in a nightmare, we find it very hard to write at all . . . . But I shall try . . . . It should be for the world to read" (p. 84). And yet, written in a spirit of profound urgency and devotion, Kon's assertion concerning the impossibility of assertion conveys the horror that transcends utterance.

SELECTED WORK BY THE AUTHOR:
"Fragments of a Diary (August 6, 1942–October 1, 1942)." Trans. M. Z. Proves. In *To Live with Honor, To Die with Honor: Selected Documents from the Warsaw Ghetto Underground Archives.* Ed. Joseph Kermish. Jerusalem: Yad Vashem, 1986, pp. 80–86.

David Patterson

Korczak, Janusz (1878–1942)

Janusz Korczak's *Pamiętnik z getta*, 1984 (*Ghetto Diary*, 1978) is the work not only of a courageous man who undertook a testimony to the atrocities perpetrated by Germans upon the Jews in the Warsaw ghetto; it is also the work of a renowned physician, author, and educator. His diary is particularly powerful for its eloquence, as well as for its advocacy for the children of the ghetto. In reading Korczak's diary, one realizes that the Nazis' assault on the children was a definitive feature of the Holocaust. As Korczak himself once implied, the orphaned condition of the children in the Warsaw ghetto underscored the orphaned condition of the human spirit (p. 27). And the Nazis were the chief architects of that condition.

Janusz Korczak was born Henryk Goldszmidt in 1878 to a wealthy, assimilated family of Warsaw Jews. From his early adulthood, when he became a physician, Korczak devoted his time and energy to alleviating the plight of homeless orphans and other underprivileged children. After authoring several provocative works on the horrific state of poverty-stricken children—including *Children of the Street* (1901) and *A Child of the Salon* (1906)—Korczak was appointed head of a Jewish orphanage in Warsaw in 1911. Over the next thirty years, Korczak became an internationally known advocate for children, based on his success at the orphanage in Warsaw and on his numerous writings. With the exception of his service as a medical officer in World War I, Korczak retained his position as the head of the Warsaw orphanage for the rest of his life.

In the 1930s, with the rise of Nazism in Germany and anti-Semitism in Poland, Korczak assumed greater and greater depth in his identity as a Jew. In 1934 and 1936 he traveled to Palestine, where he met with many of his former pupils. Impressed by the kibbutz movement, Korczak wished to settle in Israel; but, faithful to the children in his orphanage, he remained in Warsaw. When the Nazis forced the orphanage to move into the Warsaw ghetto in 1940, Korczak worked to save as many children as possible from the deadly ghetto streets. The Nazis ordered him to have the children of the orphanage report for deportation on August 5, 1942. To allay the children's fears as long as possible, Korczak told them that they were going on a picnic in the country. On that day he led their orderly procession to the deportation site. Due to the doctor's fame, the Nazis offered Korczak a last-minute opportunity to escape death. Korczak, however, refused: he chose to go with his children to Treblinka, so that he could comfort them to the end.

Korczak's devotion to children shows itself in a number of ways in his *Ghetto Diary*. "Don't refuse a child," he wrote on May 15, 1942, "if he asks you to tell the same story over and over again" (p. 106). And yet the story he tells in the diary, over and over again, is the story of how death encompasses the child. Indeed, the sight of dead children is so pervasive in the ghetto that it becomes mundane. He recalls, for instance, a group of youngsters playing in the ghetto streets; nearby the body of a dead boy was lying in the gutter. "At one point," he wrote, "they note the body, move a few steps to the side, go on playing" (p. 121). The dead boy lying in the street added to Korczak's vision of dead children, until his nights were haunted by a nightmare: "Bodies of dead children. One dead child in a bucket. Another skinned, lying on the boards in the mortuary, clearly still breathing" (p. 146). When dead children become part of the landscape of the commonplace, children become something other than children. Korczak underscored this overturning of existence when he commented that his orphanage had turned into a home for the elderly (p. 166). This insight reveals a definitive dimension of the Nazis' extermination project: they set out to annihilate not only children but also the very image and essence of the child.

Another unique feature of Korczak's diary is the way he incorporates texts from the children's diaries into his own text. Joining the voices of the children to his own voice, Korczak often recorded lines from the children's diaries. In keeping with his lifelong commitment to make the children heard, Korczak demonstrated the profundity of the children's outcry by including lines from their notebooks; for example, "A widow sits at home and weeps. Perhaps her older son will bring something from smuggling. She does not know that a gendarme has shot her son dead" (p. 158). In another example, "That siddur [prayer book] which I want to have bound is a souvenir since it belonged to my brother, who died, and it was sent to him for the day of his bar mitzvah by his brother in Palestine" (p. 159). In these passages Korczak showed that during the Holocaust the tearing of the essence from the child is a tearing of the child from mothers, from brothers, from prayers, and from memory. Restoring the outcry of the child by adding it to his own outcry, Korczak attempted to restore at least the testimony to that tearing.

As he indicates in the entry for July 15, 1942, Korczak shared his diary with the children: "The children moon about. Only the outer appearances are normal. Underneath lurks weariness, discouragement, anger, mutiny, mistrust, resentment, longing. The seriousness of their diaries hurts. In response to their confidence, I share mine with them as an equal" (p. 166). By sharing his diary with the children, Korczak shares both the responsibility and the helplessness overwhelming them all in the face of the death that surrounds them. In an entry from July 1942, for example, he wrote, "There are prob-lems that lie, like bloodstained rags, right across the sidewalk. People cross to the other side of the street or turn their eyes away to avoid seeing. I do the same" (p. 164). As Korczak's diary assumes a confessional tone, his humanity and his humility unfold even as his personal sense of shame deepens. His greatest shame is that he remains alive in the face of so much death, as he sees the finest human beings among the first to fall (p. 149). Indeed, he knows that when children die before their elders, the world has been turned on end. Perhaps this is where the Nazis attain their most devastating victory: deeming the very life of the Jew to be criminal, they lead the Jew to feel guilty for being alive.

And yet this assault on life's substance makes his daily testimony to life's dearness a matter of even greater urgency. Hearing shots fired, for example, as he writes on the night of July 21, 1942, he wonders whether his windows are sufficiently blacked out to hide his "crime" of writing. "But I do not stop writing," he asserted. "On the contrary: it [the shooting] sharpens (a single thought) the thought" (p. 175). For Janusz Korczak, the diary is not so much a commentary on his life as his life was a commentary on his diary. Lamenting what the Nazis have made of life, he remains determined to attest to the dearness of life. In the world created by the Nazis, however, the person who persists in being a witness to life was often condemned to death for his persistence. So it happened with Janusz Korczak. Although in one of his last entries he struggled in vain to bless the world (p. 185), he did not act in vain when he joined the children in the sealed train to Treblinka. The man who was a spokesman for the children of the ghetto lived by his words by remaining with them, even unto death.

SELECTED WORKS BY THE AUTHOR
Ghetto Diary. Trans. Jerzy Bachrach and Barbara Krzywicka. New York: Holocaust Library, 1978; *The Ghetto Years, 1939–1942*. Tel Aviv: Hakibbutz Hemeuchad and Ghetto Fighters' House, 1980; *Pamiętnik z getta*. Ed. Alicja Szlązakowa. Poznan, Poland: Wydawnictwo Poznańskie, 1984.

FOR FURTHER READING
Cohen, Adir, *The Gate of Light: Janusz Korczak, the Educator and Writer Who Overcame the Holocaust*. Rutherford, N.J.: Fairleigh Dickinson University

Press, 1994; Jaworski, Marek, *Janusz Korczak*. Trans. Karol Jakubowicz. Warsaw: Interpress, 1978; Laird, Chrisa, *Shadow of the Wall*. New York: Greenwillow, 1990 [a novel about Korczak]; Lifton, Betty Jean, *The King of Children: A Biography of Janusz Korczak*. New York: St. Martin's Press, 1997.

David Patterson

Kosinski, Jerzy (1933–1991)

Jerzy Kosinski is best known for his novel *The Painted Bird* (1965), which itself is known for the controversy it caused. It is the story for which he was attacked and labeled a liar first by angry Poles wishing to defend Poland's name and honor against the novel's depiction of the country's peasants as anti-Semitic, primitive, and violent. The attacks had, as Kosinski claimed, the approval of the Polish Communist government and were carried out on two levels at once: in the form of harassment of Kosinski's mother in Poland and in the form of constant physical and psychological intimidation of the writer himself (*Passing By*, pp. 201–2). It was almost fifteen years before the "Polish campaign" came to a halt, only to give room to the writings of a mixed group of journalists and commentators scrutinizing Kosinski's life. Some maintained that the story of the *Painted Bird* had no basis in reality, but they never proved their claims. The years since World War II had built a forty-year-old wall around the tale of the child Kosinski repeatedly recounted. As more years passed, what remained important was that Kosinski himself insisted on the reality of the story and that being a Jewish child in Poland during the German occupation was an experience capable of registering images, story lines, and characters more frightening and devastating than anyone could imagine in an "ordinary" chamber of horrors.

Born in Łódź, Poland, on June 14, 1933, Kosinski lived through the Holocaust in his German-occupied country and experienced traumas of enormous proportions. At the outbreak of World War II, the boy's parents placed him in the care of a peasant woman who was living in the Polish-Soviet borderland. While the parents themselves were in hiding, the woman died. The child remained alone, roaming by himself in the Polish countryside, trying to survive in a hostile environment. The Polish villagers did not want to compete with outsiders for the scarce resources they had at their disposal; nor were they willing to tolerate anyone different from those living in their towns and farms. With his dark complexion and urban accent, the child appeared to them as a stranger, even a Jew or perhaps a Gypsy. Chased from place to place, the boy witnessed their rampages of rape and murder and fell victim to their sadism, beatings, and torture. When he was driven into a cesspool, the nine-year-old was so frightened that he lost his speech. But he emerged from the pit and continued his wanderings until the end of the war. After his parents found him in an orphanage in 1945, he had to re-learn the ways of living in civilized society. Kosinski regained his speech in 1947, after a nearly catastrophic skiing accident.

As for his life in Poland after the Holocaust, Kosinski eventually graduated from high school and studied history and political science at the University of Łódź. After obtaining a master's degree in each of these fields, he registered at the Lomonosov University in the USSR. The excesses he observed there sealed his decision to escape from the Communist system. When he arrived in New York in December 1957, Kosinski had $2.80 in his pocket. A year later he became a doctoral candidate at Columbia University.

In 1982 another campaign was launched against him; it involved two critics of the *Village Voice*. They accused Kosinski of being a CIA stooge and a cheat who employed others to write his fiction. The statements drove Kosinski into despair, although, just like the first set of accusations, they could not be substantiated. He tried to disprove and run away from them, but he suffered from the damage for many years. By the late 1980s, after years of turbulence, his private life appeared to become more satisfactory. He seemed to be happy in his marriage and did not appear to be depressed. Of course, now as before, he acted eccentrically. He liked to mislead his critics and supporters by telling them contradictory tales about himself, and when the occasion arose, he enjoyed hiding from everyone, including friends and relatives. His pranks shortly before his death, then, seemed to be typical rather than extraordinary. Then came the sudden explosion: Kosinski was found dead on May 3, 1991, in the bathtub of his New York apartment with a plastic bag wrapped around his head. His tragic death revealed once more that the shattering impact of the Shoah is still with the world and will remain for quite some time.

Kosinski's first two books were nonfiction: *The Future Is Ours, Comrade* (1960) and *No Third Path* (1962). Both came out under the pseudonym, Joseph Novak, and both revolve around the collectivization of life in the Soviet Union. But it was with his third publication, *The Painted Bird*, that Kosinski's talent as a fiction writer became manifest. In subsequent years, he penned eight more novels: *Steps* (1968)*, Being There* (1971), which was also made into a film, *The Devil Tree* (1973), *Cockpit* (1975), *Blind Date,* (1977)*, Passion Play* (1979), *Pinball* (1982), and *The Hermit of 69th Street* (1988). He also wrote a number of essays and two award-winning screenplays (one of them was *Being There*), and he played the role of Zinoviev in Warren Beatty's film *Reds*. A visiting professor at a number of major academic institutions, Kosinski won several national awards and was elected president of the American Center of P.E.N.

As for the impact of his Holocaust novel, *The Painted Bird* influenced deeply both late twentieth-century American and international literature. One year after its American publication, *The Painted Bird* won the Best Foreign Book Award in France (1966), and it has retained its status as one of the major works of Holocaust literature in our age. Emerging in a wide variety of languages, it has been scrutinized by some of the world's most renowned literati. For Elie Wiesel,* *The Painted Bird* is nothing less than a quintessential Auschwitz novel: "If we ever needed proof that Auschwitz was more a concept than a name, it is given to us here with shattering eloquence in *The Painted Bird*, a moving but frightening tale in which man is indicted and proven guilty, with no extenuating circumstances" (Tepa-Lupack, p. 49).

Often characterized as a picaresque novel, *The Painted Bird* has also been described as a fairy tale dominated by demons, witches, giants, and magic. Absorbed by its dark and grotesque domain, the boy who is the main character lives his life in fear of evil and pain. As he is thrown amid creatures of unspeakable brutality, he asserts his own struggle for domination and survival. But whether he contends against beasts or humans, the creatures surrounding him carry no manifest differentiation. Emblematic of this world is the central symbol of the novel, the "painted bird," whose wings, head, and breast are painted with bright colors by the frustrated bird-catcher, Lekh, who lets his victim loose just when a great number of birds of the same species gather in the sky. Angry at the "outsider," the birds attack and kill their painted "fellow bird." The universe of the boy is not different from that of the beasts: besides legendary spells and mythological evil weaving their texture into the story, he is plunged into a merciless existence, with no hope for redemption.

While it is evident that allegory and fantasy express the events of *The Painted Bird*, close scrutiny reveals that these literary devices also create a correlative to the *tremendum,* or profound mystery, of the murder of the Jews. Amid the novel's mythological events and magical characters, rattling trains constantly cut across the Polish countryside. Carrying their human cargo, the boxcars transport Jews to the newly created concentration camps. At times, some of them escape from these trains, only to suffer violence, rape, torture, and death. No one survives among them. No one. And although most of the atrocities depicted in the book appear as forms of mythological or archetypal evil, one must not forget the context of the novel, with the little boy left behind by his parents as they try to escape the Holocaust, or the realistic scenes directly implicating the Germans and the locals in their treatment of the Jews. Of course, one must also note that after the Germans disappear from the scene, the world is not redeemed—perhaps because the world has become irredeemable after the Holocaust. But the revenge the Kalmuks mete out by raping, torturing, and killing the people of the countryside and, in turn, the cruelties of the Russian Army, along with the boy's own derailing of the train and causing the deaths of dozens of people, demonstrate the cosmic dominion of evil.

SELECTED WORKS BY THE AUTHOR
The Painted Bird. New York: Pocket Books, 1965; *Passing By.* New York: Random House, 1992.

FOR FURTHER READING
Cronin, Gloria L., and Blaine H. Hall, *Jerzy Kosinski: An Annotated Bibliography.* Bibliographies and Indexes in American Literature, no. 15. New York: Greenwood Press, 1991; Lilly, Jr., Paul R., *Words in Search of Victims: The Achievement of Jerzy Kosinski.* Kent, Ohio: Kent State University Press, 1988; Stokes, Geoffrey, and Eliot Fremont-Smith, "Jerzy Kosinski's Tainted Words," *Village Voice,* June 22, 1982; pp. 41–43; Teicholz, Tom, ed. *Conversations with Jerzy Kosinski.* Jackson: University Press of Mississippi, 1993; Tepa-Lupack, Barbara, ed., *Critical Essays on Jerzy Kosinski.* New York: G.K. Hall, 1998.

Zsuzsanna Ozsváth

Kotlowitz, Robert (1924–)

The work of Robert Kotlowitz, an American-born novelist, makes a significant contribution to Holocaust literature inasmuch as it assesses the relationship of the fate of European Judaism to the Jews in America. He deftly juxtaposes the impending doom of Europe's Jews on the eve of the Shoah and the historical innocence and assimilationist impulse of the American Jewish community. Kotlowitz's work reveals the dissolution of tradition on American shores while simultaneously recognizing that the Jews of Europe bear the burden of history. The struggle for the soul of American Judaism is waged between those who wish to ignore events in Europe, and those who see themselves reflected in the precarious situation of their European brothers and sisters. The readers, unlike Kotlowitz's characters, understand that the destruction of European Judaism will have enormous and far-reaching implications on the fate of the Jewish community in America.

The author was born in Baltimore in 1924, but both of his parents were from Poland. His father was a cantor, and the son was raised in a traditional household. The parents were in regular correspondence with Polish relatives and friends, and from time to time entertained visitors from Warsaw. Kotlowitz recalls that his home was permeated with four themes: "Judaism, Zionism, culture, and his sister's future" (David, p. 239). Kotlowitz observes of American Judaism on the eve of the Holocaust that "all the time history crept up on us, not quietly but with constant reverberations, echoes, signals, subtle warnings, and the sight and sound of noisy, sad events unrolling in grimy black-and-white on the newsreel screen" (David, p. 247).

Among Kotlowitz's novels, four deal with the upheavals and historic transformations of Judaism and Jewish life during the 1930s and 1940s. Taking place on the eve of World War I, *Somewhere Else* (1972) tells of the journey of a rabbi's son from a Polish *shtetl* to London; it won the Edward Lewis Wallant Award in 1972 and, one year later, the National Jewish Book Award. *The Boardwalk,* discussed below, the author's most direct engagement with the implications of the soon-to-be-unleashed Holocaust, appeared in 1976. He published *Sea Changes,* a novel about adjusting to life in a new country, in 1986 and *His Master's Voice,* dealing with the faith crisis of a Baltimore cantor, in 1992. Kotlowitz also served as an associate editor at Harper's and as a public television executive in New York City.

The Boardwalk is an exquisitely wrought novel that treats a two-week period late in the summer of 1939. Fourteen-year-old Teddy Lewin (né Levin) travels from Baltimore to vacation in an Atlantic City hotel. During this time two events occur that shock the youth and create great anxiety. He discovers that his parents have an unfaithful marriage. Furthermore, the youth grows increasingly uneasy about the news from Europe. What, he wonders, will become of his Warsaw relatives? Mirroring the paralysis of the allies in the face of Nazism, Teddy's father believes there will be no war, and his mother does not even discuss the situation. Kotlowitz's skillful use of dialogue underscores the difference between those Jews who ally themselves with the destiny of the global community of Israel, and those whose concern is to acculturate: to cast off what they perceive as the disabling yoke of Judaism. The assimilationists view anti-Semitism as a surmountable obstacle.

Kotlowitz's novel underscores both the impact of the impending cataclysm and the naïve belief in assimilation by stressing several issues. First, the lives of Teddy's Warsaw cousins very much resemble his own. They think themselves safe. Second, the author places a young Jewish boy from Germany, Teddy's age, as a guest in the hotel. The youth's mother is stranded, without a visa, in Germany. To make matters worse, the boy's father is proud to be a German citizen. He admits that there are no Jews left in the Frankfort am Main orchestra, but nevertheless he remains a staunch nationalist, believing the German army invincible. Additionally, the boy's Polish relatives, thinking themselves immune because of their assimilation, ignore pleas to leave. "They were all new Jews, Western liberals and assimilated Europeans, [who] had absolute faith in their world" (p. 205).

Authentic Jewish identity, argues Kotlowitz, cannot be imparted by assimilated American Jews. Consequently, he introduces the figure of Gustav Levi, a veteran of World War I; he had been a pioneer in Palestine, speaks Hebrew, and knows Jewish history. Gus becomes Teddy's teacher. In the face of the breakdown of all moral authority in the West, Levi views his task as twofold. He needs to help Teddy think historically: "being able to think about the world—with the authentic conviction that it didn't just begin the day you were born" (p. 32). Moreover, he deepens Teddy's understanding of the importance of his Jewish kinship ties. The study of Hebrew, he tells the youth, "comes to a way of connecting." "It adds up," he continues, "to a way of learning how to link your life with others, now and then" (p. 129).

For Kotlowitz, the Holocaust is a terrible reminder of the failure of the self-delusion of assimilation. Further, the catastrophe underscores the unbridgeable gap between Judaism and Christianity. Jews, by their very persistence, prove a stumbling block to Christians. Moreover, Jewish historical existence is itself a summons to further study of, and commitment to, authentic Jewish identity.

SELECTED WORKS BY THE AUTHOR
Before Their Time. New York: Alfred A. Knopf, 1997; *The Boardwalk.* New York: Alfred A. Knopf, 1976; *His Master's Voice.* New York: Alfred A. Knopf, 1992; *Sea Changes.* San Francisco: North Point Press, 1986; *Somewhere Else.* New York: Charterhouse, 1972.

FOR FURTHER READING
Berger, Alan L., *Crisis and Covenant: The Holocaust in American Jewish Fiction.* Albany: SUNY Press, 1985; David, Jay, ed., *Growing Up Jewish.* New York: William Morrow, 1969.

Alan L. Berger

Kovner, Abba (1918–1987)

While on tour in the United States in 1972, Holocaust survivor Abba Kovner once told an audience that when he writes he is like a man praying; he went on to say that the one place in the world where there are no cemeteries is poetry (*Canopy*, p. xiii). A poet whose soul burns with the flames of the Holocaust, Abba Kovner brings to his poetry all the struggles he endured as a leader in the United Partisan Organization of the Vilna ghetto. Perhaps more than any other single figure, the image of a certain young girl haunts Kovner's writing. She crawled out of the mass grave at Ponary to return to the Vilna ghetto and warn the Jews of what the Nazis had in store for them. Kovner was among the few who believed her: after hearing her story, he wrote the first call to arms in the Vilna ghetto.

Abba Kovner was born in 1918 in the Crimean city of Sevastopol. After the end of World War I his family moved to Vilna, where he attended Hebrew school and joined the Zionist Socialist youth movement Hashomer Hatsair. In 1947 Kovner set out for Palestine as an illegal immigrant. Captured and imprisoned by the British, he was rescued by the Haganah and served as the cultural officer of the Givati Brigade on the southern front during the War of Independence. After the war Kovner returned to his home in Kibbutz Ein Hachoresh, where he dedicated most of his time to his writing. The author of a novel about the War of Independence and numerous volumes of poetry, Kovner was awarded the Israel Prize for Literature in 1970 and the International Remembrance Award for Literature in 1971. He died in Israel in 1987.

Sensitive to the voices of the Jewish people, both living and dead, Kovner often shifts from one voice to another in his poetry, speaking as I, we, you, he, she, and they. His verses are filled with echoes not only from the Holocaust but also from the biblical traditions that shape Hebrew language and literature. An excellent example of his biblical and liturgical style is *Achoti Ktana*, 1967 (*My Little Sister*, 1986; also included in *A Canopy in the Desert*, 1973). The tale of a child hidden in a convent with the Catholic sisters during the Holocaust, this poem is indeed a prayer in the form of a poem; it draws heavily not only on Hebrew scriptures but also from the Midrash and Talmud. Early in the poem the nuns look upon the little sister and see "ashes that speak" (*Canopy*, p. 21); Kovner enables us to hear those ashes.

Kovner realizes that the Germans may have lost the war, but the Jews enjoyed no victory; the same is true of every struggle the Jews have faced, a point that Kovner makes in *Pridah Mehadarom*, 1949 (included in *A Canopy in the Desert*, 1973). It is a piece about the death of the soldier Dambam, whose sacrifice harbors the shadows of the martyrs of the Holocaust and all of Jewish history. Near the end of the poem, as the soldiers march on to create a Jewish homeland, the poet has a sense of multitudes who follow the soldiers, as if they were somehow resurrected through the devotion of the soldiers to the new land (*Canopy*, p. 92).

Among Kovner's most powerful works—certainly from works translated into English—is *Chupah Bamidbar*, 1970 (*A Canopy in the Desert*, 1973). The canopy here is a wedding canopy, but it is for a wedding that does not happen; regarding the desert, the poems in this volume call to mind the desert the Israelites entered when they came out of Egypt. The aim of the Exodus was to receive the Revelation of the Torah at Mount Sinai, an event that the sages compare to a wedding between God and Israel. It is also the desert where the Israelis fought three wars for the very existence of the Jewish state. Embodying the dead from the Vilna ghetto fighters, the partisans, and the Israeli soldiers, the narrator of the poems wanders through a desert of ghosts and memories in search of a new revelation.

A Canopy in the Desert is divided into twelve "gates," where the Hebrew word for "gate," *sha'ar*, is also used to designate an entry into a book or a walled city. The gates here also call to mind the gates of prayer, which are associated with the gates of the Temple in the heavenly Jerusalem. Kovner tries to penetrate those gates, not only by crying out to the canopy of the sky but also by digging into the earth, until he can hear the voices of those buried in the earth (*Canopy*, p. 128). The marriage that the poet seeks is the marriage of what was torn asunder in the Holocaust: the marriage of word and meaning, so that he compares the word to a bridegroom approaching his bride (*Canopy*, p. 184). Near the end of the volume, when the poet asks the birds, which are symbols of the prophetic, what they see, they answer, "Abyss within abyss" (*Canopy*, p. 204); and so the voice of the poet is the voice of deep crying unto deep, to the "sea of silence" (*Canopy*, p. 205) both above and within. That is the sea that has flooded the world since the time of the Holocaust; that is the sea that Abba Kovner struggled to part through his poetry.

Selected Works by the Author

Achoti Ktana. Tel Aviv: Sifriyat Poalim, 1967; *A Canopy in the Desert: Selected Poems*. Trans. Shirley Kaufman. Pittsburgh: University of Pittsburgh Press, 1973; *Chupah Bamidbar*. Tel Aviv: Sifriyat Poalim, 1970; *El*. Tel Aviv: Hakibbutz Hameuchad, 1980; *Kol Shire Aba Kovner*. 3 vols. Ed. Dan Miron. Jerusalem: Mosad Bialik, 1997; *Megilot Haedat*. Ed. Shalom Lurya. Jerusalem: Mosad Bialik, 1993; *Mikol Haahavot*. Tel Aviv: Sifriyat Poalim, 1965; *My Little Sister and Selected Poems, 1965–1985*. Trans. Shirley Kaufman. Oberlin, OH: Oberlin College Press, 1986; *Pridah Mehadarom*. Tel Aviv: Sifriyat Poalim, 1949; *Scrolls of Testimony*. Trans. Eddie Levenston. Philadelphia: Jewish Publication Society, 2001; *Slon Ketering: Poemah*. Tel Aviv: Hakibbutz Hameuchad, 1987; *Tatspiyot*. Tel Aviv: Sifriyat Poalim, 1977.

For Further Reading

Ben-Yosef Ginor, Tseviyah, *Ad Kets Habedayah: Iyun B'Shirat Aba Kovner*. Tel Aviv: Hakibbutz Hameuchad, 1995; Lurya, Shalom, *Aba Kovner: Mivhar Maamre Bikoret al Yetsirato*. Tel Aviv: Hakibbutz Hameuchad, 1988; Shoham, Reuven, *Hamareh V'Hakolot: Keriah Keshuvah bi "Feridah Mehadarom" l'Aba Kovner*. Tel Aviv: Sifriyat Poalim, 1994.

David Patterson

Kruk, Herman (1897–1944)

After serving for several years as the director of the Grosser Library in Warsaw, Herman Kruk fled to Vilna during the second week of September 1939 in the wake of the Nazi invasion of Poland. On June 26, 1941, however, the Germans occupied Vilna; after a series of mass murders, the Jews who were left were crowded into the Vilna ghetto. Kruk was one of them. His Yiddish *Togbukh fon Vilner Geto*, 1961 (*Diary of the Vilna Ghetto*, 1965) records the terrors that swept through the city and the ghetto from September 4, 1941, to June 12, 1943.

Born in Plock (then in Russian territory) in 1897, Herman Kruk studied photography in his teenage years and went on to become an active participant in Hatsomir and other Jewish socialist groups. After serving in the Polish army from 1918 to 1920, he joined the Bund; while serving the political aims of the Bund, Kruk became deeply involved in library and archival work. In the 1930s he was a chief administrator in the Warsaw library; when the war broke out in 1939, he and his family fled to Vilna. Once installed in the Vilna ghetto, Kruk diligently undertook the task of rebuilding the library—an achievement both remarkable and rare in the ghettos. On September 10, 1941, the library was once again lending books; in an entry dated December 13, 1942, Kruk noted that the 100,000th book was borrowed from the library. When the ghetto was liquidated in September 1943, Kruk was one of the Jews sent to Estonia. He was murdered there on September 18, 1944, at the age of forty-seven.

Because Vilna was a center of Jewish religious and cultural life, the Vilna ghetto was unusual not only for its library but also for its celebration of Jewish history, philosophy, and literature. Kruk noted several evenings in the ghetto devoted to the celebration of Jewish authors from Judah Halevi to I.L. Peretz. It is also possible to follow Nazi actions and Jewish observances corresponding to the Jewish holy calendar in Kruk's diary (the Nazis used the holy calendar to plan their atrocities). On September 12, 1942, for example, he commented on the festive mood in which the Jews of the ghetto greeted the New Year, despite measures being taken against them. On September 29 of the same year, with the advent of Sukkoth, he observes that there were three sukkahs in the ghetto. Hanukkah was ushered in with the same enthusiasm, but by Passover, a darkness had descended over the entire ghetto: "All are convinced that our end is approaching," he wrote on April 19, 1943 (p. 63).

In addition, one can find several rare accounts from survivors of the infamous killing site at Ponary in Kruk's diary. Indeed, Ponary is a recurring theme in the diary. "In my room," he noted on September 4, 1941, after a reference to the mass graves at Ponary, "there is a silence as if in the presence of a dead person. In reality, there are many dead here" (p. 16). On July 25, he observed, "The word [Ponary] is in the mouths of all. It 'sustains' many a home. Ponary means the mention of a father, a mother, a sister, a fiancée, and so on" (p. 36). And on Yom Kippur 1942, when the notorious chief of the Jewish police Jacob Gens announced new actions to be taken by the Germans, Kruk related, "A loud weeping breaks out as soon as he [Gens] begins. A gust of Ponary bursts into the hall, breath of death, memories of men, women, and children snatched away" (p. 41).

In Kruk's diary one discovers, moreover, a very important entry made on February 5, 1942: "Today the Gestapo summoned the members of the Judenrat and notified them: No more Jewish children to be born" (p. 20). These lines provide evidence of the ontological scope of the Nazis' annihilation of the Jews, whereby their very being constituted a crime. Never before has a government identified birth with crime. Never before has a literary text dealt with such a subject.

SELECTED WORK BY THE AUTHOR:
"Diary of the Vilna Ghetto," *YIVO Annual of Jewish Social Sciences* 13 (1965): 9–78.

David Patterson

Kuznetsov, Anatoli. *See* Anatoli, A.

L

Langfus, Anna (1920–1966)

Novelist, playwright, and short story writer, Anna Langfus is the author of one of the earliest French Holocaust novels, *Le Sel et le soufre*, 1960 (*The Whole Land Brimstone*, 1962). She belongs to the generation of Eastern European survivor-writers who came to France after the war, adopted French as their literary language, and opted to transpose their Holocaust experience into fiction. These writers include Piotr Rawicz,* Manès Sperber, and Elie Wiesel*.

While *Le Sel et le soufre* is fiction, the narrative closely follows the author's life. Born in Lublin in 1920, Anna Langfus, like her protagonist, Maria, was an only child of upper middle-class assimilated Polish Jewish parents. At the age of seventeen, she married a boy of eighteen. In 1938 they went to Belgium to study at the Ecole Polytechnique de Verviers with the intention of becoming textile engineers and eventually managing the factory of Anna's parents.

Langfus and her husband came back to Poland for a vacation in 1939 and soon found themselves in Occupied Poland. Along with their parents, they were relocated to the Lublin ghetto and then the Warsaw ghetto. She and her husband escaped from the ghetto, lived under false identity papers, joined the Polish Resistance, and were arrested and tortured by the Gestapo. Her young husband was shot, and she was sent to various prisons and labor camps. Her parents were deported to the death camps.

In 1946 she made her way to Paris and taught math at an orphanage outside of Paris. The following year, she married Aaron Langfus whom she had known in Poland, and in 1948, they had a daughter, Maria. Anna Langfus died in 1966 in Sarcelles, a suburb of Paris where she lived with her family.

Langfus is the author of two other novels, *Les Bagages de sable*, 1962 (*The Lost Shore*, 1964), which won the prestigious French Prix Goncourt, and *Saute, Barbara*, 1965 (Jump, Barbara). Her plays include *Les Lépreux* (The lepers), staged in Paris in 1956, and *Amos ou les fausses espérances* (Amos or false hopes), staged in Brussels in 1963.

Les Lépreux is about a family in hiding in Poland in 1941. When Langfus saw members of the audience leave the theater, unable to tolerate the raw facts of history represented on the stage, she realized she had to depict the event in a way that would not be offensive to the public. In her next work, *Le Sel et le soufre*, she chose to express herself in a more sober, restrained tone. The form of a novel rather than a memoir allowed her the necessary emotional detachment and control over the subject. She discussed her ideas about writing and distance in an important text, written in 1963 and published after her death, "Un cri ne s'imprime pas" (A cry can not be written) (*Les nouveaux cahiers*, no. 115 (Winter 1993–1994).

Le Sel et le Soufre depicts the coming of age of Maria, a privileged, somewhat spoiled, immature, and egocentric young woman about nineteen years old, growing up in a closely knit, assimilated Jewish household in Lublin, Poland. Thrust into a series of grotesque wartime nightmares, Maria learns to adapt as her secure world collapses. She is depicted as cynical and selfish, when, for example, she escapes from the ghetto with her mother and husband, leaving her father behind because of his "Jewish" appearance. In the ghetto, she willfully sets herself apart from the starving "creatures" propped against the wall (pp. 28–29). When thrown into the rounded-up "monstrous body" of beings reduced to parts of the body battling to survive at the *Umschlagsplatz,* where the trains set out for the death camps, she manages to free herself, and is indifferent to the fate of the others (pp. 55–57). Eventually she too endures pain and torture in prison. Langfus depicts the imperfections of a protagonist whose hardened nature and comportment have been manifestly afflicted by Holocaust evil. The author deliberately establishes a distance between herself and her creation, thereby creating an alienated character who alienates the reader as well.

If Maria of *Le Sel et le soufre* is somewhat stoic and a fighter, the protagonists of the following novels, *The Lost Shore* and *Saute, Barbara,* are victims scarred by their Holocaust experience, obsessed by images of horror, and in constant dialogue with the dead they carry within themselves. Maria in *The Lost Shore* wanders around Paris following strangers, finally meeting an older man who has a relationship with her and tries to heal her. But she remains haunted by the ghosts of her dead parents and husband who seem more alive than the people around her. Emotional sores and memories fester beneath her skin; she has contracted *la maladie de guerre* (war sickness) (p. 53). Filled with self-pity, rage, and guilt, she feels she belongs to "a different species" (p. 10).

Michael, the protagonist of *Saute, Barbara,* is also a prisoner of his past. He seeks revenge on the Nazis who have murdered his wife and young daughter by kidnapping after the war a little German girl resembling his own child. The attempt to replace his daughter and to start a normal life fails. His memory oppresses him; words and gestures open up wounds. His life is

without meaning and he is unable to connect to others.

Anna Langfus's trilogy portrays the devastating effects of the Holocaust on the individual during the event and in its aftermath. She offers the perspective of a witness and the literary language and imagery of a novelist, a combination that is among the first in Holocaust literature.

SELECTED WORKS BY THE AUTHOR
The Whole Land Brimstone. Trans. Peter Wiles. New York: Pantheon Books, 1962; *The Lost Shore.* Trans. Peter Wiles. New York: Pantheon Books, 1964; *Saute, Barbara.* Paris: Gallimard, 1965. **Plays:** *Amos ou les fausses espérances,* 1963. Théâtre de Pôche, Brussels; *Les Lépreux,* 1956. Théâtre d'Aujourd'hui, Alliance Française, Paris. **Essays and Short Stories:** "Un cri ne s'imprime pas" (a cry cannot be written); "Un conte de là-bas" (A tale from over there); "L'éternuement" (the sneeze). In *Les nouveaux cahiers,* no. 115 (Winter 1993–1994).

FOR FURTHER READING
Fine, Ellen S., "Le témoin comme romancier: Anna Langfus et le problème de la distance." *Pardés* 17 (1993): 93–109; Friedmann, Jo, "Comique et tragique: De l'insouciance la brisure, le rire dans les romans d'Anna Langfus." *Cahier Comique Communication* 3 (1985): 93–111; Solotaroff, Theodore," Witnesses of the Holocaust: Anna Langfus and Piotr Rawicz." In *The Red Hot Vacuum.* New York: Atheneum, 1970.

Ellen S. Fine

Laqueur, Renata (1919–)

Renata Laqueur's *Dagboek uit Bergen-Belsen,* 1979 (Bergen-Belsen diary) (published in German as *Bergen-Belsen Tagebuch* in 1983) is one of the few Holocaust diaries written in a concentration camp, and not in a ghetto or in hiding. The diary, therefore, provides its readers with a rare account of "life" in a concentration camp, recorded as it unfolds.

Born in the Netherlands in 1919, Laqueur was arrested in Amsterdam on February 18, 1943. After being detained for a short time in Vught, she was sent to Westerbork. In March 1944 she was deported to Bergen-Belsen, where she undertook the courageous task of keeping a diary. Unlike most diarists, however, Laqueur went on to write a scholarly study of diaries written in concentration camps. The study was the topic of her Ph.D. dissertation, *Writing in Defiance: Concentration Camp Diaries in Dutch, French, and German*, which she completed at New York University in 1971 (her dissertation was written under the name Renata Laqueur Weiss).

One of the most prominent features of Laqueur's writing is her preoccupation with home, a concern that comes in response to the Nazis' calculated destruction of the home. Her sense of being exiled in an anti-world and her longing for home are so great, in fact, that she associates such feelings with a kind of madness, since the reality of home is so radically different from her current reality. "I am homesick," she cried on April 11, 1944, "so horribly homesick; I have such a longing for everything that 'once was'" (p. 29). Her chief longing for what "once was" is a longing for her mother and father, those two beings are at the center of the home.

While the thought of returning to their own homes possesses the other women in the camp, Laqueur is aware of a fear that haunts them as well. "Will we be able to explain to anyone who has not had a similar experience?" she wondered in an entry dated June 15, 1944. "Can we put into words what the experience of the camp has meant to us?" (p. 65). A few months later, on October 2, she sees that the fear of not being understood is tied to a fear that she will never be able to return to a normal life (p. 83). Like many Holocaust diarists, Laqueur realized that the return home requires being able to tell her story and being understood, if she is indeed to find liberation.

In her study she draws on her own experience in an attempt to understand more fully the phenomenon of the Holocaust diary. She sees the Holocaust diary—and therefore her own diary—as an attempt to "write [herself] out of the concentration camp world," not through pure escapism but by clinging to an ideal (p. 8). In her diary she lamented, "We do not know whether we have any future" (p. 22), indicating a collapse of time; clinging to an ideal, on the other hand, opens up something to live *for* and restores a future tense.

For Laqueur, then, writing the diary is not only a way of seizing the day but also a way of moving toward the *next* day. Thus she asks, "What will become of this diary?" (p. 57). And in so asking, she makes the reader of the diary part of its future.

SELECTED WORKS BY THE AUTHOR
Bergen-Belsen Tagebuch. Hannover: Fackelträger, 1983; *Schreibern im KZ: Tagebücher 1940–1945*. Hannover: Niedersachische Landeszentrale für Politische Bildung, 1991; *Writing in Defiance: Concentration Camp Diaries in Dutch, French, and German*. Ann Arbor, Mich.: University Microfilms, 1971.

David Patterson

Leitner, Isabella (1924–)

Isabella Leitner's memoir *Fragments of Isabella* (1978) is striking for its brief but powerful images of people and moments taken from the unreality of Auschwitz. Keeping her sentences simple and her chapters short, she poetically captures the depth and the horror of the Holocaust a sentence, a page, and a paragraph at a time. Seven years after her Holocaust memoir appeared, she published a sequel in 1985 about the time following her liberation and her life in New York; this sequel to her memoir was titled *Saving the Fragments: From Auschwitz to New York*. In 1993 her husband, Irving Leitner, staged a production of *Fragments of Isabella,* which premiered in Saint Petersburg, Russia. In 1994 the husband-and-wife team combined the first two works into a single volume under the title *Isabella: From Auschwitz to Freedom*. Ending with Isabella's short essay on the language of the camp, this last book reveals the fundamental assault on language that characterizes the anti-world that was the Holocaust.

Isabella Leitner was born Isabella Katz in 1924 in the Hungarian town of Kisvárda. Her father lived all his life in the anti-Semitic atmosphere of Hungary and therefore was astute enough to see the implications of the rising Nazi tide; in 1939 he went to America to obtain immigration documents for his wife and six children. After the war broke out, however, he could not get back. In May 1944 Isabella and her family were swept up in the storm of the deportation of the Hungarian Jews to Auschwitz. Her mother and youngest sister were sent to the gas chambers immediately upon their arrival; her oldest sister was murdered in Bergen-Belsen. On May 8, 1945, the day the war in Europe ended, Isabella and her two remaining sisters became the first survivors of Auschwitz to set foot on American soil. Six months later her brother, who also survived, reached the United States. Isabella Leitner currently lives in New York, where she is very active not only in the efforts to preserve the memory of the victims of the Holocaust but also in numerous community service activities.

In *Fragments of Isabella* Leitner brings out several distinguishing features of the Holocaust as only a woman can bring them out. Among the most prominent of those features is the Nazis' assault on the mother, as it unfolds on various levels. Early in the memoir, for example, she recalls the almost supernatural force of her mother's love, as her mother gazes upon her with an eerie smile during the deportation of the Jews from the Kisvárda ghetto. "She knows that for her there is nothing beyond this," wrote Leitner. "And she keeps smiling at me, and I can't stand it . . . . I gaze at her tenderly and smile back" (p. 6). Upon their arrival in the camp, she recalled, Josef Mengele selected her mother for death before they could exchange a last look of goodbye (pp. 19–20). And, once in the camp, the prisoners are engulfed by the murder of the mother: "The smoke was thick. The sun couldn't break through. The scent was the smell of burning flesh. The burning flesh was your mother" (p. 94). For Leitner, this tearing of her mother from her—this murder of the one who most deeply manifests love in the world—became emblematic of the Holocaust.

In a one-page chapter titled "The Baby," Leitner brings out the Nazis' most profound assault on the mother: deeming the existence of the Jew to be criminal, they make becoming the mother of a Jew a capital crime. Therefore the women in the camp are placed in the position of having to kill newborns to save the mothers. "Most of us are born to live," she addresses one such infant. "You, dear darling, are being born only to die . . . . Your mother has no rights. She

brought forth fodder for the gas chamber. She is not a mother" (pp. 31–32). In keeping with her concern for the assault on the mother, Leitner ultimately understands her liberation—to the extent that liberation is possible—in terms of becoming a mother. Crying out to her mother upon the birth of Peter, her first child, she declared, "Peter has started the birth of the new six million" (p. 96). Jews are liberated, she suggests, not just by emerging from the camps but by becoming mothers and fathers.

Parallel to Leitner's expression of her relation to the mother is an identity issue; where she comes from is definitively tied to who she is. And the Holocaust would obliterate both. Her collapse of self begins with her inability to recognize her sister Chicha upon their initiation into the anti-world of Auschwitz. "Within seconds," she writes, "Chicha is somebody else. Some naked-headed monster is standing next to me. Some naked-headed monster is standing next to her" (p. 26). This crisis persists until the end of her memory of the concentrationary universe, when her despair itself assumes the form of a shadow ego. Trying to rid herself of her despair as liberation draws nigh, she affirms what she feared from her shadow self: "She tells me what I was afraid she'd say: '*I will live as long as you do*'" (p. 90). Thus Leitner reveals the extent of the Nazis' violence against the soul of the Jew: Auschwitz extends beyond the barbed wire to the very end of the survivor's life.

In *Isabella: From Auschwitz to Freedom*, Leitner further brings out the scope of the Holocaust, as the reader sees its horrific impact extending beyond all boundaries in time and space. Forty-five years after the event, while attending a concert of German musicians, for instance, she relates that she suddenly felt as if she were a foreigner in land where she had lived for nearly half a century. "I felt my whole *free* American being was being altered," she wrote. "I was overcome by something I have never felt at a concert—*fear*" (p. 210). And so Isabella Leitner leaves her reader with a question: Can a person who has endured a radical assault on her origin and her identity ever regain a sense of dwelling in the world?

SELECTED WORKS BY THE AUTHOR
Fragments of Isabella. Ed. Irving Leitner. New York: Thomas Y. Crowell, 1978; *Isabella: From Auschwitz to Freedom,* with Irving Leitner. New York: Doubleday, 1994; *Saving the Fragments: From Auschwitz to New York.* New York: New American Library, 1985.

David Patterson

Lengyel, Olga (1918–)

Olga Lengyel wrote *Five Chimneys*, which describes her experiences in Auschwitz-Birkenau. First appearing in France (1946) and then in the United States (1947), this memoir was one of the earliest published by a Holocaust survivor. It has been translated into many languages, including Spanish and Japanese. Lengyel focuses on the period from May 1944 to January 1945, when she was a prisoner in the women's camp at Birkenau. Some of her historical generalizations are unreliable. She states, for example, that more than 1.3 million persons were murdered at Auschwitz-Birkenau from May through July 1944–a figure three times too large–but such errors do not diminish her memoir's significance, which comes from the narrative of her personal experiences as a woman during the Holocaust.

Lengyel lived in Cluj, a city in northern Transylvania whose 1941 population of about 110,000 included more than 16,000 Jews. Formerly part of Romania, Cluj came under Hungarian control in 1940. Its residents included the family of Miklos Lengyel, a well-known Jewish physician. They were among the 725,000 Jews–about 5 percent of the population–who lived in Hungary in 1941. (Additionally, there were in Hungary about 100,000 converts or Christians of Jewish origin who would also be subject to anti-Jewish racial laws.) Assisted by his wife Olga, who had some medical training, Miklos directed a hospital in Cluj. The Lengyels had two sons, Arvad, who was adopted, and Thomas. *Five Chimneys* testifies that they were a very happy family until the Holocaust intervened.

At first, Lengyel's appreciation for German culture and science made it hard for her to believe the frightening stories of concentration camp atrocities that could be heard in Cluj as Nazi Germany's power dominated Europe in the early years of World War II. In fact, until March 1944, the Hungarian Jews were relatively safe, but then the Germans occupied Hungary, and about 430,000 Hungarian Jews were deported to Auschwitz. When the Holocaust ended, more than 560,000 Hungarian Jews were dead. Most were murdered in the gas chambers at Auschwitz-Birkenau. Olga Lengyel was her immediate family's only survivor.

Five Chimneys—the title refers to the crematoria at Auschwitz—says little about the Lengyels' Jewish identity (they were assimilated and well off economically), but it does explain that the family was deported in May 1944. Their transport was one of six that occurred between May 25 and June 9, 1944, which took the Jews of Cluj to Auschwitz. Lengyel states that her family's journey in a stifling cattle car took seven days. Upon arrival, the usual routine followed. Several thousand women, children, and men from that Cluj transport "formed fives." Men were separated from women and children: Olga's father and Miklos were in one column; Olga, her two sons, and her mother stayed in the other. Then the "selection" started.

Lengyel's intensely personal memoir describes the especially painful way in which she lost Arvad, her older son. An important source for William Styron's controversial Holocaust novel *Sophie's Choice* (1976), that moment involved a version of what the Holocaust scholar Lawrence L. Langer calls "choiceless choices." Such choices are neither normal nor made in circumstances of one's own choosing; they are "choices" that are forced between options that are unacceptable or worse. The Nazi doctor conducting the "selection" asked Lengyel about her son's age. Unable to know exactly what was coming but hoping that she was making a life-saving choice, Lengyel truthfully told the doctor that Arvad was not more than twelve. Very well, said the doctor, and the boy was sent to the "left," the same direction that Lengyel had persuaded her mother to take so that she could look after Thomas, Lengyel's younger son. Off the three went with the other children and the elderly. Lengyel never saw them again: "left" was the way to the gas chambers.

Lengyel's agonizing memory of that Auschwitz selection never left her. Nor did the hopeless, unwarranted, but still real anguish that the selection's outcome might have been different—at least in part—if she had chosen differently. Meanwhile, Lengyel's medical knowledge led to her working in parts of Auschwitz where she witnessed the deadly consequences of Nazi Germany's racist ideology.

In Auschwitz, the Germans had thousands of prisoners—most, but not all, were Jewish—at their disposal. Nazi doctors often forcibly subjected these unfortunate people to so-called medical experiments. In particular, Lengyel witnessed sterilization experiments. She stressed that men as well as women were targeted, but in that same hell the horrors differed. Their bodies were subjected to x-ray procedures; their genitals were infused with caustic substances, their uteruses and ovaries were surgically removed—in these experiments women had fundamental aspects of their womanhood stripped away. If those brutal techniques did not kill the women, the Nazi doctors usually had no further use for them, and the victims were gassed.

Nazi policy at Auschwitz produced obscene dehumanization. Nevertheless, Lengyel emphasizes, even when the prisoners could not escape physical degradation, many successfully resisted moral debasement and retained human dignity. *Five Chimneys* ends by noting that Lengyel took hope from that awareness. It kept her, she says, from entirely losing faith in humankind. After liberation, Lengyel eventually came to New York City, where she established a foundation to support Holocaust education. In 1998 her oral history was recorded by the Survivors of the Shoah Visual History Foundation, which is located in Los Angeles, California.

SELECTED WORK BY THE AUTHOR:
Five Chimneys: A Woman Survivor's True Story of Auschwitz. Rev. ed., Chicago: Academy Chicago Publishers, 1995.

FOR FURTHER READING
Clendinnen, Inga, *Reading the Holocaust.* Cambridge, England: Cambridge University Press, 1999; Fine, Ellen, "Women Writers and the Holocaust: Strategies for Survival." In *Reflections of the Holocaust in Art and Literature*, ed. by Randolph L.

Braham. Boulder, Colo.: Social Science Monographs, 1990; Goldenberg, Myrna, "Different Horrors, Same Hell: Women Remembering the Holocaust." In *Thinking the Unthinkable: Meanings of the Holocaust*, ed. by Roger S. Gottlieb. Mahwah, N.J.: Paulist Press, 1990; Langer, Lawrence L., *Versions of Survival: The Holocaust and the Human Spirit.* Albany: State University of New York Press, 1982; Rittner, Carol, and John K. Roth, eds., *Different Voices: Women and the Holocaust.* New York: Paragon House, 1993.

John K. Roth

Levi, Primo (1919–1987)

Primo Levi's memoir *Se questo e un uomo* (first Italian publication, 1947), original English title *If This Is a Man* (1959) subsequently republished as *Survival in Auschwitz* (1961), is a canonical text of Holocaust literature. In it he examines what it means "to lie on the bottom." Levi, a chemist by training, owes his life at least in part to his scientific background. The author's tone of voice combines a scientist's precision, clarity of reasoning, and acute observation with the moral authority of the witness's testimony. As an eager heir to the tradition of Italian humanism, Levi was a thoroughly acculturated Jew prior to the Holocaust. Responding to an interviewer's question, he observed, "If it hadn't been for the racial laws and the concentration camp, I'd probably no longer be a Jew, except for my last name. Instead, this dual experience, the racial laws and the concentration camp, stamped me the way you stamp a steel plate. At this point I'm a Jew, they've sewn the star of David on me and not only on my clothes" (Camon, p. 68).

The author was born in 1919 in Turin into an assimilated Jewish household. Yet he attests that the sense of being Jewish was not entirely lost; the family observed Rosh Hashanah, Passover, and Purim, and stressed the importance of education and studying. Linguistically, Levi notes the practice common among the Jews of Turin of inserting Hebrew, frequently faulty, to conform to local phonetics. At the age of twenty-two Levi received his degree in chemistry summa cum laude. He joined the partisans and was captured by the Fascist Militia in December 1943. Levi was deported to Auschwitz in January 1944. Freed when the camp was overrun by the Russian army, he traveled through Eastern Europe and was detained in Russia before being allowed to return to Italy. He wrote about this experience in *The Reawakening* (1965). Levi's 1987 death in the same Turin apartment where he had been born has been variously ascribed to suicide or an accidental fall down a stairwell.

Levi was a prolific writer who wrote in several genres. In addition to the above-mentioned works, he authored the following which have been translated into English: *The Sixth Day and Other Tales* (1990); *The Periodic Table* (1984); *The Monkey's Wrench* (1986); *Moments of Reprieve* (1986); *If Not Now, When?* (1985); *Other People's Trades* (1989); *Dialogue by Levi and Tullio Regge* (1989); *The Drowned and the Saved* (1988); and *The Mirror Maker* (1989). Moreover, he also wrote poetry, including *Shema* which prefaces his memoir, and coauthored—with a fellow Turinese survivor—a report on the medical and sanitary conditions in Monowitz. This report appeared in *Minerva Medica,* a medical journal. The author's works have won major literary prizes both in Italy and abroad, and have been translated into several languages. This entry focuses on three of Levi's works: *Survival in Auschwitz, The Periodic Table,* and *The Drowned and the Saved.* Each of these provides a distinctive angel of vision into the reflections of a writer who combined the insights of chemistry and literature.

Survival in Auschwitz portrays the death camp world and life lived under a sentence of extermination. It is a slender yet terrifying volume. Its seventeen chapters, some of which are as brief as four pages, describe with stunning precision Auschwitz's massive countertestimony to both humanism and so-called normal life. For example, Levi recalls reaching for an icicle to quench his desperate thirst. A guard brutally takes it away. Levi, who unlike many of the Italians in Auschwitz knew some German, asks, "*Warum?*" (why). The guard shoves him inside and replies, *"Hier ist kein warum"* (there is no why here" (p. 25). Earlier, after being tattooed upon arrival, the still naïve Levi asked a veteran, French-speaking prisoner "if at least they

would give us back our toothbrushes." The prisoner responded, *Vous n'etes pas à la maison,* "You are not at home, this is not a sanatorium, the only exit is by way of the chimney." At this point the author wondered what that meant.

Levi constantly contrasts the ordinary moral world, with its "free words created and used by free men," and the world of the *Lager* (camp). In the chapter "This Side of Good and Evil," the author invites his reader "to contemplate the possible meaning in the Lager of the words 'good' and 'evil,' 'just' and 'unjust'; "let everybody judge," he wrote, "how much of our ordinary moral world could survive on this side of the barbed wire" (p. 78). Levi's memoir underscores the difference between the two worlds. "It is," he wrote, "useless to think" in Auschwitz because events largely occurred in an unforeseeable manner. Moreover, thinking is harmful because "it keeps alive a sensitivity which is a source of pain" (p. 155).

Survival in Auschwitz also relates to moments which confirmed Levi's humanistic beliefs. For example, he speaks of Lorenzo Perrone, a non-Jewish Italian bricklayer at Auschwitz who, over a six-month period of time, brought the author food. More than the physical sustenance, however, it was Lorenzo's example of human compassion that enabled Levi "not to forget that I myself was a man" (p. 111). Levi also reports teaching the Canto of Ulysses to Jean, the Pikolo (semi-privileged) prisoner in his *Kommando.* This teaching reaffirmed Levi's sense of the human even in the inferno of Auschwitz—an inferno that far surpassed Dante's invention.

As a Holocaust survivor, Primo Levi lives with the tension between the necessity of bearing witness and the realization that his testimony cannot be fully understood. For instance, he observes that, "To tell the story, to bear witness, was an end for which to save oneself. Not to live *and* to tell, but to live *in order to tell.* I was already aware at Auschwitz that I was living the fundamental experience of my life" (*Beyond Survival,* p. 13). Yet in his memoir, the author recounts a dream he had in Auschwitz: he is at home, among friends and family. As he relates his experiences, he notices that his listeners "are completely indifferent: they speak confusedly of other things among themselves, as if I were not there. My sister looks at me, gets up and goes away without a word" (p. 54).

Two chapters, "Chemical Examination" and "The Drowned and the Saved," underscore the Germans' commitment to dehumanizing and destroying the Jews. Levi reports that Doktor Pannwitz, the head of the chemical laboratory, raised his eyes to look at him. The look, wrote Levi, "was not one between two men." Rather, it "came as if across the glass window of an aquarium between two beings who live in different worlds" (p. 96). Levi mused that if he had known how to explain the nature of that look, then he could "also have explained the essence of the great insanity of the third Germany." In "The Drowned and the Saved," which years later he chose as the title of his last book, Levi speaks of two different categories of men: the saved and the drowned. The latter are those who do not know how to "organize"; they have given up the struggle to survive and have become *muselmanns*. *Muselmann* (moslem) was camp slang for a prisoner who had lost the will to live.

It is instructive to listen to Levi's description of the drowned.

> All the mussalmans who finished in the gas chambers have the same story, or more exactly, have no story; they followed the slope down to the bottom, like streams that run down to the sea . . . . Their life is short. But their number is endless; they, the *Muselmanner,* the drowned, form the backbone of the camp. An anonymous mass, continually renewed and always identical, of non-men who march and labour [*sic*] in silence, the divine spark dead within them, already too empty to really suffer. One hesitates to call them living: one hesitates to call their death death, in the face of which they have no fear, as they are too tired to understand" (p. 82). The philosopher Emil Fackenheim writes that the mussalmans were the "most original, most characteristic product of the entire Nazi Reich. (*To Mend the World.* [Bloomington: Indiana University Press, 1994], 100).

Nazism followed what Jean Améry* termed the "logic of destruction." Levi describes a selection, the process whereby prisoners were singled out for death, which exemplifies this murder-ous logic. He relates three responses to a selection held in Auschwitz in October 1944. Two of the responses were by those who were doomed, one is on the part of a prisoner who was (temporarily) spared. Zeigler, a prisoner who had been selected for extermination, was given only the normal ration. But such prisoners are entitled to a double portion. After proving to the block elder that he was doomed, Ziegler is given the extra ration and "goes quietly to his bunk to eat" (p. 119).

Kuhn, an older prisoner, is praying loudly and thanking God because he has not been chosen. For Levi this is an outrageous act. He asks rhetorically, does Kuhn not see Beppo the twenty-year-old Greek "who is going to the gas chamber thc day after tomorrow and knows it . . . . [lying in his bunk] looking fixedly at the light without saying anything and without even thinking any more? Can Kuhn fail to realize that next time it will be his turn?" Levi continues by observing that the selection process is "an abomination, which no propitiatory prayer, no pardon, no expiation by the guilty, which nothing at all in the power of man can ever clean again." He concludes by observing, "If I was [*sic*] God, I would spit at Kuhn's prayer" (p. 118).

Levi's position on belief in God is frequently contrasted with that of Elie Wiesel.* While Wiesel interrogates the deity about the Shoah and divine injustice, Levi finds it impossible to believe after Auschwitz. He told Ferdinando Camon, "There is Auschwitz, and so there cannot be God" (Camon, p. 68). Levi added a penciled note to the typescript of his interview in which he observed; "I don't find a solution to this dilemma. I keep looking, but I don't find it" (p. 68). Wiesel summarizes the difference between his position and that of his friend Primo Levi: "He had seen too much suffering not to rebel against any religion that sought to impose a meaning on it. I understood him and asked him to understand me, for I had seen too much suffering to break with the past and reject the heritage of those who had suffered" (*All Rivers* p. 83). Yet there is some ambiguity in Levi's position. For instance, in commenting on the stories of the Auschwitz prisoners he observes that these tales "are simple and incomprehensible like the stories in the Bible. "But," he wonders, "are they not themselves stories of a new Bible?" (*Survival* p. 59).

The Periodic Table is an intellectual, existential, and aesthetic tour de force in which Levi speaks of the crucial moments of his life by comparing them to the properties of the chemical elements. "The reader," he wrote, "will have realized . . . that this is not a chemical treatise . . . Nor is it an autobiography . . .; but it is in some fashion a history" (p. 224). For example, the chapters titled "Argon," "Hydrogen," "Zinc," "Iron," and "Gold" tell of the pre-Shoah rise of Italian fascism. In "Zinc" the author draws a philosophical lesson from the laboratory experiment in which zinc is prepared. "I . . . am Jewish . . . I am the impurity that makes the zinc react . . . . Impurity, certainly, since just during those months the publication of the magazine *Defense of the Race* had begun, and there was much talk about purity, and I had begun to be proud of being impure" (p. 35).

In the chapter on "Iron," Levi describes the students' entrance into the laboratory to "someone who, coming into the House of the Lord, reflects on each of his steps" (p. 38). He analogizes the laboratory announcement "*Nuntio vobis gaudium magnum. Habemus ferrum.*" "*I announce to you a great joy. We have iron.*" The announcement paralleled one of a few days earlier in the same month and year (March 1939): "*Habemus Papum,*" which elevated Cardinal Eugenio Pacelli to the papacy. About Pius XII, Levi observed, "in whom many put their hopes, since one must after all put one's hope in someone or something" (p. 39).

To his fellow student and friend Sandro, Levi asserted the majesty of studying chemistry and physics which, "besides being in themselves nourishments vital in themselves, were the antidote to fascism . . . because they were clear and distinct and verifiable at every step, and not a tissue of lies and emptiness, like the radio and newspapers" (p. 42). Sandro, an excellent mountain climber, is murdered by the fascists. Remembering his friend years later, Levi states the futility of the writer's task. "Today I know," he observed, "that it is a hopeless task to try to dress a man in words, make him live again on the printed page, especially a man like Sandro" (pp. 48-49). Interestingly, Levi, who is intensely aware of the limitations of words and language, does succeed in his mission.

Unlike his earlier works, Levi's final book *The Drowned and the Saved* is darkly pessimistic. Indeed, he prefaces the book with a quote from Simon Wiesenthal* who recalls the SS admonishing the prisoners that even if some survived, no one would believe their testimony because of the monstrous nature of the events they describe. Instead, the SS, by denying everything, will be believed. Furthermore, the Nazis will write the history of the *Lagers*. Levi, for his part, observes that "human memory is a marvelous but fallacious instrument" (p. 23). This results in a monstrous injustice which is one of the many paradoxes engendered by the Holocaust: the murderers can deny their crimes or claim not to remember them. For the victims, however, memory invades; it comes unbidden and untamed. It is the survivors who feel shame (the title of one of the book's chapters). Yet, as the author notes, the entire history of the Third Reich "can be reread as a war against memory" (p. 31).

"The Gray Zone" is the book's most provocative chapter. Against the desire to simplify history, Levi posits the complexity of things. Noting that the "young above all demand clarity; their experience of the world being meager, they do not like ambiguity"—exactly like the "newcomers to the Lagers" (p. 37). The gray zoners are those people who are neither saints nor the irredeemably evil. Rather they are placed within an evil system that supports the doing of evil. Both in and outside the *Lagers* there are "gray, ambiguous persons, ready to compromise" (p. 49). Levi examines three types of gray-zone people. First he discusses the *Kapo*, low-ranking leaders of the work squads. He then turns his attention to the *Sonderkommandos* (special squads whose job it was to remove corpses from the gas chambers and burn them in ovens and who, in turn, were themselves murdered). He then turns his attention to the actions of Mordecai Rumkowski, the "king" of the Łódź ghetto. Concerning the *Sonderkommandos*, he wrote that "conceiving and organizing the squads was National Socialism's most demonic crime" (p. 53). Levi rightly contended that "no one is authorized to judge" the special squads.

Levi's classification raises two difficulties; he appears to indict the prisoners, and he includes Nazis such as the SS man Muhsfeld who ordered the murder of a young girl who, somehow, had survived the gas chamber. After the war, Muhsfeld was tried and sentenced to death. This was the correct sentence, but even he, wrote Levi, was "not a monolith." Levi suggests that had this individual lived in a different environment and epoch, "he probably would have behaved like any other common man" (p. 57). Wiesel, among others, disagrees with Levi's gray zone: "Only the criminals are guilty . . . to compare the victims in any way to the torturers was to dilute or even deny the killers' responsibility for their actions" (*And the Sea Is Never Full* p. 347).

Levi grew increasingly pessimistic about the world's learning any lessons from the Holocaust. He articulated several reasons for this. In part, it is owing to the difficulty of speaking with the young. Also many of the witnesses have died, and those who remain "have ever more blurred and stylized memories" perhaps unconsciously influenced by stories of others. Furthermore, he believed that the premise that "every stranger is an enemy" forms the basis of the logic that eventuated in Auschwitz. In short, the "genealogy of today's violence" stems from the "violence dominant in Hitler's Germany" (p. 200). Nowhere is Levi's rage more apparent, however, than in his poem *Shema,* which serves as the epigram to *Survival in Auschwitz.* The normative *Shema* is Judaism's central creed. Based on the injunction in Deuteronomy 6:4-9, it attests to the oneness of God and enjoins the Jewish people to hear this word and to write it upon the doorposts of their homes and upon their gates. The parchment inside the mezuzah contains this prayer.

Levi's post-Auschwitz *Shema* reveals the radical break between the pre- and post-Holocaust Jewish world. The poem is addressed to those who live in the safety and comfort of their warm houses surrounded by family and food. The word of the witness now stands in place of God's word. In the poem he raises the question

he regarded most essential to an understanding of the Holocaust: What is a human being? The implication of the poem is that the Nazi assault on the Jew was an assault on humanity as such. In a play on the lines from the prayer, Levi cries out for all of Israel—indeed, for all humanity—to take the image of a man and a woman made into something less than human and carve it into the heart. And he ends the poem with a curse on those who fail to do so: "May your children turn their faces from you." For without that image of what the Nazis made of the human being, we shall lose our own humanity.

SELECTED WORKS BY THE AUTHOR
The Drowned and the Saved. Trans. Raymond Rosenthal. New York: Vintage Books, 1988; *If Not Now, When?.* Trans. William Weaver. New York: Simon and Schuster, 1985; *The Mirror Maker: Stories and Essays.* Trans. Raymond Rosenthal. New York: Schocken, 1989; *Moments of Reprieve.* Trans. Ruth Feldman. London: Michael Joseph, 1986; *Monkey's Wrench.* Trans. Ruth Feldman. New York: Penguin USA, 1995; *Other People's Trades.* Trans. Raymond Rosenthal. New York: Summit, 1989; *The Periodic Table.* Trans. Raymond Rosenthal. New York: Schocken, 1985; *The Reawakening.* Trans. Stuart Wolf. Boston: Little, Brown, 1965; *Shema: Collected Poems of Primo Levi.* Trans. Ruth Feldman and Brian Swann. London: Menard, 1976; *The Sixth Day and Other Tales.* Trans. Raymond Rosenthal. New York: Viking, 1990; *Survival in Auschwitz.* Trans. Stuart Wolf. New York: Macmillan, 1961.

FOR FURTHER READING
Anissimov, Myriam, *Primo Levi: Tragedy of an Optimist*, trans. Steve Cox. New York: Overlook Press, 1999; Baumgarten, Murray, "Primo Levi's Periodic Art: *Survival in Auschwitz* and the Meaningfulness of Everyday Life." In *Resisting the Holocaust*, ed. Ruby Rohrlich. New York: Berg, 1998; Bernstein, Michael André "A Yes or a No." *The New Republic*, September 27, 1999; Boone, Susan L., Bryan Cheyette, Robert S.C. Gordon, and Jonathan Wilson, "Primo Levi and Holocaust Witness." *Judaism* 189, no. 48, (Winter 1999): 49–57; Camon, Ferdinando, *Conversations with Primo Levi,* trans. John Shepley. Marlboro, Vt: Marlboro Press, 1989; Patterson, David, *Sun Turned to Darkness: Memory and Recovery in the Holocaust Memoir.* Syracuse, N.Y.: Syracuse University Press, 1998; Schwarz, Daniel R., *Imagining the Holocaust.* New York: St. Martin's Press, 1999; Sodi, Risa, "The Memory of Justice: Primo Levi and Auschwitz." *Holocaust and*

Genocide Studies no. 4, 1 (1989): 89–104; Wiesel, Elie, *All Rivers Run to the Sea: Memoirs*. New York: Alfred A. Knopf, 1995; Wiesel, Elie, *And the Sea Is Never Full: Memoirs*. New York: Alfred A. Knopf, 1999.

Alan L. Berger

Lewental, Salmen (d. 1944)

Only about 40 percent of Salmen Lewental's diary was intact by the time it was unearthed near Crematorium III at Birkenau on October 17, 1962. Nevertheless, one may glean from this text a profound testimony of Lewental's Holocaust experience, both before and during the time he spent in the *Sonderkommando*, those units of men who were forced to do the work of removing bodies from the gas chambers and burning them. He perished with most of the rest of his unit sometime after the uprising of October 7, 1944. Apart from what can be learned from his diary, very little is known of Lewental's life.

Written in Yiddish, Lewental's diary contains details of the horrors suffered by the Jews in the ghetto of his hometown of Ciechanów, Poland. From Ciechanów he was sent to the transit camp in Małkinia and from Małkinia to Auschwitz-Birkenau, where he arrived on December 10, 1942. Immediately after his arrival he was selected to work in the *Sonderkommando* units assigned to Bunkers 1 and 2 in Birkenau. Lewental offers penetrating insights into the psychology of the prisoners assigned to the *Sonderkommando*, particularly with regard to how they "entirely lost themselves" and "simply forgot what they were doing" (p. 139). Or did they forget? They were "ashamed of one another," Lewental related, "and we dared not look one another in the face" (p. 136). Not all of them, moreover, lost themselves, as Lewental pointed out in his descriptions of some of the *Sonderkommando*'s heroic individuals, among whom were prisoners who either escaped or helped others to escape.

One of the most valuable features of Lewental's diary is his lengthy account of the preparations for the uprising that broke out—belatedly in Lewental's view—on October 7, 1944. The reader learns, for example, of the extensive resistance network that was required to stage the uprising; an essential member of that network, Lewental related, was Róza Robota, a Jewish girl who worked in the munitions factory and who transmitted explosives to a prisoner named Wróbel. Although a few of the prisoners involved in the uprising managed to escape, Lewental's account enables us to realize the uniqueness of a revolt mounted not to live but to die like human beings and in the process save the lives of others. To die as a human being is precisely to die for the sake of another: "They gave up everything sacrificing their own selves," he wrote. "Is it not a sacrifice of their own lives laid down on the altar?" (p. 170). One realizes that central to the process of the Jews' dehumanization was their being forced into a position in which they lived "at the cost of lives of other people" (p. 147).

The most harrowing parts of Lewental's diary are those dealing with the Nazis' assault on the core of the family—on women and children. In a section titled "3,000 Naked People," for example, he recounted the gassing of 3,000 women and girls, many of whom were mothers and daughters. "Mamma!" was the last utterance of one girl who died in her mother's arms (p. 145). At the end of his diary is described one of the last killing operations in Birkenau, when 600 boys were gassed in Crematorium III on October 20, 1944. "The SS men," he wrote, "at last drove them [into the bunker]. Their joy was indescribable. Did they not [have] any children ever?" (p. 178). Like his entire testimony, this question that Lewental raised concerns not only the Nazis but the one who encounters the testimony. At stake in any understanding of Lewental's diary is an understanding of the infinite importance of children.

SELECTED WORK BY THE AUTHOR:
"Manuscript of Sonderkommando Member." Trans. Krystyna Michalik. In *Amidst a Nightmare of Crime: Manuscripts of Members of Sonderkommando*, ed. Jadwiga Bezwinska. Oświęcim (Auschwitz): State Museum, 1973, pp. 130–78.

David Patterson

Lind, Jakov (1927–)

Vienna-born writer Jakov Lind burst into literary prominence in 1962 with his first book, *Eine Seele aus Holz* (*Soul of Wood*, 1964), a collection of seven stories, the most impressive of which deals with a "forest of infinite madness." Lind has been compared to a string of writers from Sholem Aleichem to Stefan Zweig, among whom he may have stood closest, in fact, to Gogol in his often baffling inventiveness. But even today he can be best understood as a Viennese of Eastern European Jewish background, whose defining experience, between the ages of eleven and sixteen, was the Nazi campaign to wipe out the Jews and his own improbable escape from it.

Born in 1927, Lind was fifty-two when in 1969 be began writing for the first time in English, to gain distance from his theme, as he explained. Lind told his remarkable story in *Counting My Steps*, the first volume of an autobiographical trilogy. In 1938, when Adolf Hitler annexed Austria to the Third Reich, Lind, at that time still Heinz Landwirth, was sent with a children's transport to Holland. There he evaded deportation to the death camps by hiding. From 1943 to 1945, with false Dutch papers, he worked on a Rhine barge within Germany itself, and finally as a messenger boy in the Air Ministry in Berlin. After the war ended, he rejoined his parents in what was soon to become the State of Israel. In *Numbers* (1972), Lind resumed his tale after his return to Europe in 1950. There he studied acting and directing at the Max Reinhardt School in Vienna, all the while restlessly traveling between countries. Finally, after remarrying, he settled in England but regularly spent longer periods in London, Mallorca, and New York. In the third part of the autobiography, *Crossing* (1991), Lind returned to his unsettled past, recounting critical stages in his life in more intimate detail, and describing his American experiences of the last twenty-five years.

Soul of Wood remains Lind's best-known book. Its long title story can be read as an allegory (with starkly realistic detail) on the psyche of the helpless victim, whose only guilt is that he exists, and on the moral depravity of his victimizers, who try to pass themselves off as his benevolent protectors to save their skins after the Nazi defeat. In an autobiographical essay, "Jahrgang 1927," 1967 (Born in 1927), Lind said of his central figure, the Jewish boy Anton Barth: "The totally crippled Anton Barth, who becomes a roe in his forest hiding place . . . is me." As the book's likewise autobiographical concluding story, "The Resurrection," suggests, Barth's surrealistic transformation can be seen as a symbolic projection of the victim's inner state. With their capture by the Germans looming, the young Weintraub tells Goldschmied, his Amsterdam partner-in-hiding: "I want to live and breathe, and I don't care how, like a dog or a frog or a bedbug, it's all the same to me" (p. 181). In another story, "The Pious Brother," Franz, a former SS man and now a Jesuit priest, slits his throat during a seduction episode, while dressed in Orthodox garb, like the Jewish youth he had murdered in the Łódź ghetto. Far from depicting Franz's act as a sign of remorse, with anger and revulsion Lind exposes the sexually charged, lethal obsession of the Nazis with Jews, and condemns the Church that not only granted absolution to the basest of killers but also actively sheltered them from pursuit by earthly justice.

In the novel *Landschaft in Beton*, 1963 (*Landscape in Concrete*, 1965), Lind created a near mythical panorama of Nazi horror. Its main figure, Sergeant Gauthier Bachmann, a mass murderer devoid of any humane stirrings, seizes on every chance to act out his destructive impulses. At the end of Lind's fierce tale, Bachmann and his Amazon-like lover, Helga, arise amid apocalyptic ruin as the sole surviving human beings. Bachmann then brutally kills Helga by biting into her throat and once more sets off in search of his now nonexistent regiment. Clearly, it was not Lind's intent to analyze the criminal madness of the Third Reich, but to depict the psychopathic as the norm to negate any notion that Hitler's Germany had been anything but a murderous plague.

Lind's next novel, *Eine bessere Welt*, 1966 (*Ergo*, 1967), is one of his most enigmatically difficult. It takes place in postwar Vienna, in a surreal, and yet all too real, company of guilt-ridden psychopaths, who both fondly recall the "good old days" of their Nazi past and try to whitewash or even justify them. Interweaving a multitude of cryptic episodes and motifs, Lind satirically excoriates Austrian—and, by extension, German—attempts to conquer the Nazi past as halfhearted and hypocritical. Morally, he shows, nothing has changed. It must be said, however, that the story line is far too intricate to allow for a clear-cut reading.

Altogether, Jakov Lind has published fifteen books, including novels, story collections, plays, and memoirs. In each one of them, whether he treats the Nazi war against the Jews and his own experience of it or not, Lind traverses what he once called a "forest of infinite madness." As their reference point, all of his books have the destructive insanity of the Hitler years. Although he has long since established himself as an English-language author, the memories of his Austrian-Jewish childhood and harrowing wartime German years cannot be undone. In his own drastically alienated manner, through narratives of allegory, the bizarre and fantastic, he remains a writer in search of meaning amid the moral disasters of his time.

SELECTED WORKS BY THE AUTHOR
Counting my Steps: An Autobiography. New York: Macmillan, 1969; *Crossing: The Discovery of Two Islands.* London: Methuen, 1991; *Ergo.* Trans. Ralph Manheim. New York: Random House, 1967; *Landscape in Concrete.* Trans. Ralph Manheim. New York: Grove Press, 1965; *Numbers: A Further Autobiography.* New York: Harper and Row, 1972; *Soul of Wood.* Trans. Ralph Manheim. London: Jonathan Cape, 1964; *The Trip to Jerusalem.* London: Jonathan Cape, 1972.

FOR FURTHER READING
Rosenfeld, Stella P. "Jakov Lind: Writer at the Crossroads," *Modern Austrian Literature* 4 (1971): 42–47.

Stella P. Rosenfeld

Lubetkin, Zivia (1914–1978)

Thanks to Zivia Lubetkin's Holocaust memoir, *B'yomei kilyon v'marad*, 1978 (*In the Days of Destruction and Revolt*, 1981), many of the courageous Jews who resisted the Nazi onslaught are remembered, for the memoir contains a list of nearly 200 people who took part in the Warsaw ghetto uprising of 1943. Based on her brief accounts of the last days of the Warsaw ghetto, published in 1947 and 1953, Lubetkin's memoir sheds much light on the political, logistical, and psychological complexities of the ghetto's resistance movement.

Zivia Lubetkin was born in Beten, Poland, in 1914. She was a member of the Zionist youth labor movement Dror and was an active participant in the Zionist dream. As soon as she was forced into the Warsaw ghetto, she became involved in the underground resistance movement. With her husband, Yitzhak Zuckerman, a leader in the Jewish Fighting Organization, Lubetkin was in the heat of battle during the Warsaw ghetto uprising in April and May 1943. She and other fighters, including her husband, escaped the ghetto through the sewers and joined the partisans. After the war, Lubetkin and her husband moved to Israel, where they were among the founders of the Ghetto Fighters' Kibbutz. She died in Israel in 1978.

The impetus behind Zivia Lubetkin's resistance during the Holocaust, as well as her memory of the Holocaust, is that "the saving of a single Jewish life is worth the risking of one's own life" (p. 79). Next to the Nazis, the greatest threat to the resistance movement in the Warsaw ghetto, stated Lubetkin, was false hope (p. 92). Early on the members of the resistance movement realized that they were isolated from a world that had turned its back on them. Even as the ghetto burned, and "the sky glowed with a terrifying red light," she related, "the [Polish] citizens of the capital walked, played, enjoyed life as usual within full view of the smoke and flames" (pp. 199–200). Thus cut off from the human community, the Jews fought to maintain their own humanity.

Lubetkin's memoir demonstrates that the Jewish fighters in the ghetto exemplified a commitment to their fellow human beings that was just the opposite of the world's indifference. Although they were terrified at the sight of their dead, their sense of responsibility brought them "back on [their] feet" (p. 236); they endured because each person was able to rely on the other and thus knew he was not alone (p. 277). By the time the fighting was over, however, they had "lost all semblance of humanity" (p. 252); the one "covenant" left to them was "a bundle of memories strewn in the scorched ashes of a burnt soul"(p. 256). And that is the covenant conveyed in Lubetkin's memoir.

Perhaps the most important point to be realized in her memoir is that the Jewish men and women who fought against the Nazis rose up with no hope of victory. Their aim was not to overcome the enemy and live, but rather to recover their humanity and die—as human beings. There lies the tragic irony of the event: to live as human beings and thus refuse the subhuman status imposed on them by the Nazis, these Jews had to die on their feet.

SELECTED WORKS BY THE AUTHOR
B'yomei kilyon v'arad. Tel Aviv: Hakibbutz Hameuchad, 1978; *Farn koved fun unzer folk.* Toronto: Organizatsye fun Yidn fun Polyn, 1961; *In the Days of Destruction and Revolt.* Trans. Ishai Tubbin. Tel Aviv: Ghetto Fighters' House, 1981.

David Patterson

Lustig, Arnošt (1926–)

Czech-born writer Arnošt Lustig is one of the premier authors of short fiction, novels, and film to come out of the Holocaust. Working both in literature and in film, Lustig's artistic response to the Holocaust is unparalleled among survivors of the event. Although his subject is a dark one, his work is characterized by a profound love for the characters he creates and for the life he affirms.

One of his best-known works of fiction, *Tma nemá stín*, 1958 (*Darkness Casts No Shadow*, 1978), originally appeared in a collection titled *Démanty noci,* 1958 (*Diamonds of the Night*, 1978), which was published in English under a separate title and made into a film in 1964. Among other collections of Lustig's short fiction are *Noc a nadeje*, 1958 (*Night and Hope*, 1959), *Ulice ztracených bratrí*, 1959 (*The Street of Lost Brothers*, 1990), *Horká vůně mandlí*, 1968 (The bitter smell of almonds); *Neslusné sny*, 1995 (*Indecent Dreams*, 1988),

and *Ohen na vode*, 1998 (Fire on water). His film titled *Transport from Paradise*, based on *Night and Hope*, was produced in 1962. In addition, Lustig's novel *Dita Saxová*, 1962 (*Dita Saxova*, 1979) was made into a film in 1968. His other major works—some of which also formed the bases for films—include *Modlitba pro Katerinu Horovitzovou,* 1964 (*A Prayer for Katerina Horovitzova*, 1973); *Bílé brízy na podzim*, 1966 (The white birches in autumn); *Milácek*, 1969 (Darling); *Tanga: Dívka z Hamburku*, 1992 (Tanga: The girl from Hamburg); *Porgess*, 1995 (Porgess), *Propast: Román*, 1996 (The abyss: a novel); and *Z deniku sedmnactileté Perly Sch.*, 1979 (*The Unloved: From the Diary of Perla S.*, 1996).

Born to a middle-class family in Prague in 1926, Lustig is among the most talented and creative writers who directly base their work on the suffering and degradation they endured during the Holocaust. Because he was a Jew, he was expelled from the technical school he attended in 1939, when the Nazis invaded Czechoslovakia. A year later, he and his family—which included his sister, parents, and uncle—were sent to Theresienstadt. From there they were transported to Auschwitz, where his father was immediately murdered because he wore glasses. His mother and sister were separated from the family and sent to work in an aircraft factory in Freiburg; from Freiburg they were transported to Mauthausen, where they were liberated as the war was drawing to a close. In the spring of 1945 Lustig and a friend managed to escape from a trainload of prisoners that was attacked by an American dive-bomber on its way to Dachau. After hiding in the Bohemian countryside, Lustig took part in the uprising that broke out in Prague that May.

At the age of twenty, Lustig began a career in journalism. In 1948 and 1949 he was a war correspondent in Israel, where he met and married Vera Weislitz. He attended college in the early 1950s, and in 1960 he became a scriptwriter for a film studio in Prague. During the early 1960s, Lustig adapted several of his works for performance on screen and television. In 1967–1968, during a time of liberalization, Lustig was elected to the Central Committee of the Czechoslovak Writers' Union. With the coming of the Soviets in August 1968, he left for Israel. After living for a short time on Kibbutz Hachotrim in Israel and then working for a Yugoslavian film company, Lustig made his way to the United States in 1970. He worked for a year at the University of Iowa and then served as a guest lecturer at Nebraska State University. In 1973 he moved to the American University in Washington, D.C.; five years later he became a professor at that university and has been there ever since.

One of Lustig's novels that best brings out the definitive features of the Holocaust is one of his earliest: *Darkness Casts No Shadow*, a work which, like many of Lustig's novels, began as a short story in the *Diamonds of the Night* collection. Based on his personal experience of escaping from the transport to Dachau, the novel begins with the question that haunts much of Lustig's work: "*Is everything lost in the darkness?*" (p. 7). The novel's two main characters, Danny and Manny—from Daniel ("God is my judge") and Emmanuel ("God is with us")—are like two facets of a single soul. Through their conversations and their memory of the camp, they bring out such dimensions of the assault on the soul as the terrible loneliness imposed on the human being, the threat of madness in a realm gone mad, and the ways in which the Nazis "*stole the meaning words used to have*" (p. 90). The novel also opens up the problematic nature of the project of storytelling itself, as one character asserts, "*Each story has three versions. The first one you tell me. The second one I tell you, and the third no one knows*" (p. 123). Yet Lustig manages to convey a trace of the tale no one knows.

An early illustration of Lustig's ability to bring out the eternally hidden side of the Holocaust through his storytelling is the collection *Night and Hope*. Unlike mainstream Czech literature, but like much of Holocaust literature, *Night and Hope* focuses on the ways in which people with nowhere to turn—children and the elderly—were victimized by the Nazis. Set for the most part in Theresienstadt, the stories address issues of identity (the plight of Hynek Tausig in "The Return" is a good example) and innocence (the innocent Ruth in "Rose Street") in the midst of a radical assault on both. Simi-

larly, *Diamonds of the Night* contains tales of the plight of children, such as the first story "The Lemon," and stories that sound the depths of the suffering of the elderly, such as "The Old Ones and Death." Reading the tales in this collection, one realizes the radical extent of the Nazis' overturning of the world to create a realm in which children were old and old people were as helpless as children. In a scene from "The Old Ones and Death," for instance, the old man Aaron Shapiro hears in the voice of his wife the voice of someone "from another world . . . like the voice of an aged, frightened child" (pp. 79–80). The other world, of course, is the anti-world imposed on the world by the Nazis.

In *The Street of Lost Brothers,* one story particularly stands out for its ability to articulate the scope of the Nazis' assault on all their victims: "My Friend Vili Feld." The title character appears in a number of Lustig's other works, including his recent collection of tales called *Ohen na vode* (Fire on water). This story is about a Holocaust survivor who can no longer find a place to dwell in the world. Another work in which Lustig explores a victim's postwar struggle to return to some semblance of life in the world is his novel *Dita Saxova*. Through his title character, Lustig expresses his own conviction both as a survivor and as a writer of Holocaust literature: "I cannot agree when people who weren't there say it's impossible to put it into words, to give it meaning." (p. 129). And yet Dita Saxova can never find a place in the world, least of all in the Western world, after the Shoah.

Lustig's next novel, *A Prayer for Katerina Horovitzova,* brilliantly demonstrates that Auschwitz casts it shadow over the entire world, with the ashes of the dead now graphically and literally part of every human being. "These ashes would be contained in the milk that will be drunk by babies yet unborn. . . . These ashes will be contained in the breath and expression of every one of us. . . . They will be contained in books which haven't yet been written and will be found in the remotest regions of the earth" (pp. 50–51). The novel's title character, a Jewish girl, tries to escape the gas chambers, along with a group of American Jews captured in Italy. Ultimately, however, the only way she can avoid becoming a victim of Auschwitz is to die while resisting its murderers.

With the publication of *Bílé brízy na podzim* (The white birches in autumn), in 1966, Lustig turned to contemporary themes and settings. It is the story of a love affair set against the background of the dehumanizing punitive units in the Czech army; the novel also represents Lustig's first critical look at socialist society and at the dubious aesthetics of socialist realism. With the Soviet invasion of 1968, Lustig's career as a Czech writer living in his native land took a downward turn. Such was the situation when Lustig published his ninth book, *Horká vůně mandlí* (The bitter smell of almonds), in 1968. The centerpiece for his collection of stories is a tale called "Dům vrácené ozveny" (The house of echoes), which Lustig reworked into a novel more than twenty years later. In this story Lustig draws on his own life to explore the plight of a Jewish family in Prague left to the mercy of the Nazis. While the Nazi evil had an impact on the world from the very beginning, this tale shows that only a few people were initially attuned to the ramifications of that evil. The bitter smell of almonds is the smell given off by the deadly gas Zyklon B, which the Nazis used to murder their victims in the annihilation camps. When Lustig later adapted this tale into a novel, he transformed this short story into a memorial to his father.

Although the shadow of invading Soviet troops—with all the attendant restrictions on artistic expression—cast itself over Lustig's homeland when *Horká vůně mandlí* was released in 1968, in 1969 he published his most wide-ranging novel to date: *Milácek* (Darling). Based on his experiences as a correspondent in Israel, the novel takes place during the Arab-Israeli conflict at the end of the 1940s. Its fundamental message is that war destroys love by destroying the soul and fiber of the human being; to be sure, the novel shows that love *is* the soul and fiber of the human being. The Communist regime of his homeland confiscated the book and demolished the typeset material, a measure that led to Lustig's decision to leave Czechoslovakia.

After he moved to America, Lustig began to do some philosophical rethinking of his views on politics, society, and literature; as a result, he went back to some of his earlier works and rewrote them. One example is a story called "Dívka u oleandrového kere" (The girl beside the oleander tree). The piece was first published in the 1959 Czech edition of *The Street of Lost Brothers;* the revised version appears in the 1990 English edition of the book. The revision makes the story into a powerful indictment of a world in which people are manipulated and basic human relationships are suppressed.

While Lustig often addresses the problematic nature of the Western world, he cannot leave behind the world of the Holocaust. In his preoccupation with that realm he is as much concerned with the suffering of women as with the hardships of men; many of his main characters, in fact, are women. One of his most recent novels to be translated into English, *The Unloved: From the Diary of Perla S.*, is a good example. It is the story of a seventeen-year-old girl who becomes a prostitute while living in the Theresienstadt concentration camp. Probing Perla's soul by using the diary as his literary form, Lustig brings out the integrity and hope that abide in a girl who is surrounded by a world of lies and horror.

With the fall of communism in 1989 Lustig once again enjoyed the renown he deserved in his native country, and he has been able to return there to receive numerous awards for his work. Working from his home in Washington, D.C., Lustig continues to be a witness to a joy in life, even as his life is overshadowed by the ashes of Auschwitz.

SELECTED WORKS BY THE AUTHOR
Children of the Holocaust. Trans. George Theiner and Jeanne Němcová. Evanston, Ill: Northwestern University Press, 1995; *Darkness Casts No Shadow.* Trans. Jeanne Němcová. New York: Avon, 1978; *Diamonds of the Night.* Trans. Jeanne Němcová. Washington, D.C.: Inscape, 1978; *Dita Saxova.* Trans. Jeanne Němcová. New York: Harper and Row, 1979; *Indecent Dreams.* Trans. Paul Wilson. Evanston, Ill: Northwestern University Press, 1988; *Night and Hope.* Trans. George Theiner. New York: Avon, 1976; *A Prayer for Katerina Horovitzova.* Trans. Jeanne Němcová. New York: Harper and Row, 1973; *The Street of Lost Brothers.* Trans. Jeanne Němcová. Evanston, Ill: Northwestern University

Press, 1990; *The Unloved: From the Diary of Perla S.* Trans. Vera Kalina-Levine. Evanston, Ill.: Northwestern University Press, 1996.

FOR FURTHER READING
Haman, Aleš. *Arnošt Lustig.* Prague: H and H, 1995.

David Patterson

M

Malamud, Bernard (1914–1986)

Bernard Malamud was moved to write by the advent of World War II and the Holocaust. In an interview with Michiko Kakutani on July 15, 1980, he told the *New York Times* book reviewer that "the suffering of the Jews is a distinct thing for me. I for one believe that not enough has been made of the tragedy of the destruction of six million Jews. Somebody has to cry—even if it's a writer, 20 years later." Malamud's literary engagement with the Holocaust, although indirect—he speaks of survivors and refugees—portrays these witnesses as exemplars of Jewish fidelity. Yet the novelist contends that he is interested in Judaism's ethicality, rather than its religious or cultural tradition. His work has also been criticized for falsely universalizing the lessons of the Shoah.

Born in 1914, the author was the older of two sons of Russian immigrants. Malamud grew up in Brooklyn. When he was fourteen his mother died. His father owned a small grocery store and worked sixteen-hour days. Malamud recalls that, as a child, his home was bereft of cultural nurture; the one exception occurred on Sundays when he listened to someone playing the piano through the living room window (interview with Kakutani). Malamud's novels include *The Assistant* (1957); *The Natural* (1963); *The Fixer* (1966), which won the Pulitzer Prize and the National Book Award for Fiction; and *God's Grace* (1982). His short story collections include *The Magic Barrel* (1958), which was awarded the National Book Award for Fiction, and *Idiots First* (1963). He also served as president of P.E.N., which during his tenure protested the treatment of writers in the Soviet Union and South Africa.

Malamud's literary attention to the Holocaust can be divided into two groups of writings: those which allude to the Shoah and those which focus more directly on the legacy of the tragedy, or portray a harbinger of the destruction. Among the former are the short stories in which refugees appear; for example, "The First Seven Years," "Take Pity," "The Last Mohican," and "The Loan." For example, Sobel, the shoemaker's helper in "The First Seven Years," (*Complete Stories*, p. 23) is a Polish refugee "who had by the skin of his teeth escaped Hitler's incinerators." Like Jacob of antiquity, this refugee must work seven years for the hand of his employer's daughter. Eva, the widowed heroine of "Take Pity" observes to her would-be benefactor that "My relatives Hitler took away from me" (p. 85). Eva's bitterness precludes the possibility of her either trusting or relying on anyone.

In "The Last Mohican," Fidelman, a failed artist from America who goes to Italy to study the Christian painter Giotto, is beset by the mysterious and intrusive Shimon Susskind, a "Jewish refugee/survivor from Israel" and from "Germany, Hungary, Poland, Where not?" (p. 143) Susskind, who appears in the guise of a schnorrer (or beggar), takes Fidelman's brief-case containing the first chapter of his proposed study of Giotto. Consequently, the author is unable to continue working because "he was lost without a beginning" (p. 156). While pursuing the thief over a period of months, Fidelman gradually discovers his own Jewish roots through three events: listening to the beadle of a synagogue whose son had been murdered by Nazis in the Ardeatine Caves, visiting the Jewish ghetto in Rome, and making a pilgrimage to the ghetto's Jewish cemetery. Embracing his Jewish identity in light of Auschwitz is Fidelman's true beginning.

In "The Loan," a friend of Leib the baker seeks to borrow money. Leib explains that "One day," after thirty difficult years, "out of misery, he had wept into the dough. Thereafter his bread was such it brought customers in from every-where" (p. 172). Leib's wife, Bessie, embodies twentieth-century Jewish suffering. Bolsheviks murdered her father and she was left destitute after her husband's death. She found refuge in the home of her older brother in Germany. Sacrificing his own chances, he sent her to America before the war, but he and his family "ended . . . in one of Hitler's incinerators." Suddenly, Bessie smells smoke. Pulling open the oven door she discovers loaves of bread "blackened bricks—charred corpses" (p. 173). Malamud's evocation of Jews burning in ovens reminds readers of the eternal anguish engendered by the death camps.

The writer's most detailed treatment of the Holocaust's impact on Jewish identity is found in two short stories—"The Lady of the Lake" and "The German Refugee,"—and his novel *The Fixer*, a fictional account of the Mendel Beiliss blood libel trial held in czarist Russia (1903). By focusing on an antecedent event, Malamud emphasizes the two most infectious forms of anti-Semitism: a religious hatred, based on the accusation that Jews used the blood of Christian children to bake matzoh, and a secular hatred of Jews. The secular hatred engendered belief in an international Jewish conspiracy aimed at world dominance, based on *The Protocols of the Elders of Zion*, a notorious forgery composed by the czarist secret police. The novel shows the increasingly precarious situation of the Jewish people in the early twentieth century and provides a "crude preview" of what lay ahead.

"The Lady of the Lake" contrasts survivors and non-witnesses while exposing what Edward Alexander terms the "universalist-humanist delusion among American Jews even in the wake of the Holocaust" (p. 125). Henry Levin, an American Jew, comes into a small inheritance and travels to Europe seeking romance. Arriving in Paris, Levin, "tired of the [limitations] of the past," (*Complete Stories,* p. 105) symbolically identifies with the French Revolution by calling himself Freeman thus denying his Jewish identity. He next travels to Italy around the time of Tisha b'Av (the fast day on which, according to traditional Judaism, both the first and second Temples were destroyed). He falls in love with a beautiful Italian woman named Isabella del Dongo whose face held "the mark of history, the beauty of a people and civilization" (p. 117). Freeman denies his Jewish identity when queried by Isabella. He muses that being Jewish had meant only "headaches, inferiorities, unhappy memories" (p. 117).

The tale's denouement occurs when "Freeman" is on the verge of proposing to Isabella. Isabella exposes her breasts revealing "on the soft and tender flesh" the tattooed numbers she had received at Buchenwald. "I can't marry you," she tells him. "We are Jews. My past is meaningful to me. I treasure what I suffered for" (p. 123). As Levin/Freeman struggles to reply, Isabella disappears into the night. Freeman, like Fidelman and many other lapsed American Jews, is both infatuated by, and ignorant of, European history. After the Holocaust, it is inexcusable that any Jew should either deny his or her Jewishness or engage in the futile attempt to escape the shadow of Auschwitz.

"The German Refugee" (*Complete Stories*) tells the story of Oskar Gassner, a critic and literary figure, who escaped from Germany shortly after *Kristallnacht,* or the night of broken glass. He had to leave his gentile wife and her anti-Semitic mother behind. Gassner, who is depressed and alone in New York, is one of several German intelligentsia being tutored in English by Martin Goldberg who narrates the story. Oskar was a writer who could now neither speak nor write; "to many of these people, articulate as they were, the great loss was language—that they could not say what was in them to say" (p. 203). Gassner was to give a series of public lectures in English on the literature of the Weimar Republic.

Gassner grows increasingly despondent. He curses the Nazis and the German nation: "they are pigs mazquerading as peacogs" (p. 206). At one point, Oskar attempts suicide. After recovering, he confesses that he has lost faith. "In my life," he attests, "there has been too much illusion." He is taken by the notion of Walt Whitman's Brudermensch (humanity), but observes—in reference to the idealism of Wiemar—that it "does not grow long on German earth" (p. 212). After successfully delivering his lecture, in which he quotes Whitman, Gassner commits suicide by sticking his head in the oven and turning on the gas. Among the possessions he bequeathed to Goldberg was a letter from his mother-in-law. Against her fervent pleas and anguish, her daughter is converted to Judaism "by a vengeful rabbi" and, despite the mother's protest that they were good Christians, she was subsequently deported to her death.

Malamud's Holocaust writing is based on his determination to interpret its legacy in terms of ethics. Consequently, his interest is with what Jews had to do to continue living. Like Whitman, the author believes in the concept of *Brudermensch* and in the notion that suffering is ennobling. Yet, as Lawrence Langer observes, "Malamud's indirect, tentative, circumscribed inroads on Holocaust reality leave untouched vast areas of harsh and unbearable experience that require fresh explorations of the conventional bond linking the word and the spirit" (p. 155).

SELECTED WORKS BY THE AUTHOR
The Assistant. New York: Farrar, Straus and Giroux, 1957; *The Complete Stories.* New York: Farrar, Straus and Giroux, 1997; *Dubin's Lives.* New York: Farrar, Straus and Giroux, 1979; *The Fixer.* New York: Penguin USA, 1994; *God's Grace.* New York: Farrar, Straus and Giroux, 1982; *Idiots First.* New York: Farrar, Straus and Giroux, 1963; *The Magic Barrel.* New York: Random House, 1958.

FOR FURTHER READING
Alexander, Edward, *The Resonance of Dust: Essays on Holocaust Literature and Jewish Fate.* Columbus: Ohio State University Press, 1979; Berger, Alan L., *Crisis and Covenant: The Holocaust in American Jewish Fiction.* Albany: SUNY Press, 1985; Kremer, S. Lillian, *Witness Through the Imagination: Jewish-American Holocaust Literature.* Detroit: Wayne State University Press, 1989; Langer, Lawrence L., *Admitting the Holocaust: Collected Essays.* New York: Oxford University Press, 1996.

Alan L. Berger

Mechanicus, Philip (1889–1944)

With entries from May 28, 1943, to February 28, 1944, the diary of Philip Mechanicus is one of the most extensive accounts of a man's life in Holland's most infamous concentration camp: Westerbork. The original Dutch edition of the diary did not appear in print until 1964, when it was published in Amsterdam under the title *In Dépôt: Dagboek uit Westerbork*; the English edition, *Year of Fear: A Jewish Prisoner Waits for Auschwitz,* came out that same year in a slightly abridged version (later appearing under the title *Waiting for Death: A Diary*, 1968). By the time Mechanicus was arrested on September 27, 1942, for failing to wear the yellow star, he was a mature man of fifty-three, and his diary reflects the experience and insight of a man of his years. It is also written with the craft of a man who made his living as a writer.

Philip Mechanicus was born in the Netherlands in 1889. A self-educated youth, Mechanicus was working as a journalist by the time he was seventeen. He traveled over much of the world and worked on such foreign newspapers as the *Sumatra Post* in Medan, Indonesia, and *De Locomotief* in Semarang, Java; in 1920 he became part of the overseas editorial staff of Holland's *Algemeen Handelsblad.* His articles on the Zionist movement in Palestine were published in a volume titled *Een Volk Bouwt Zijn Huis* (A people building itself a home) in 1933. A year later he published a volume of travel articles based on the time he spent in the Soviet Union from 1929 to 1934.

Immediately after the Germans invaded Holland in May 1940 Mechanicus was dismissed from his position on the newspaper. About a month after his arrest, on October 25, 1942, he was sent to the camp at Amersfoort; on November 7, while seriously ill, he was transported to Westerbork, where he stayed in the camp hospital until July 29, 1943. On March 8, 1944, he was sent to Bergen-Belsen, and from there he went to Auschwitz on October 9. Based on the accounts of various survivors, it appears that Mechanicus was shot with a group of 120 other prisoners three days after his arrival in Auschwitz.

Although he was in the midst of a world of meaningless suffering and slaughter, Mechanicus had a very deep sense of meaning and mission about the witness he bore through his writing. "I feel as if I am an official reporter giving an account of a shipwreck," he wrote on May 29, 1943. "We are all together in a cyclone and feel the whole ship slowly sinking" (p. 16). On October 30, 1943, he expressed the importance of continuing to write "or those who in a time to come will want to get an idea of what went on here" (pp. 181–82). The source of his sense of meaning is his sense of the history of the Jewish people, from the time of their expulsion from Egypt to the Holocaust; indeed, he seems to view the history of the Jews as a history of meaning itself. At the heart of the history of the Jewish people he sees the fate of Jewish children.

He noted on June 7, 1943, for example, that in Westerbork a day does not go by without the death of a Jewish child, as if time in that realm were measured by the undoing of a future curled up inside every child (p. 37). Whenever more Jews entered the camp, he recorded the plight of the children among them. On January 22, 1944, he wondered what would become of them; on February 9 he found out. On that day—the day of the children's transport—Mehanicus was a devoted witness to the little ones, who were "carried weeping to the long snaking train . . . . Perhaps the most abominable transport that has ever gone" (p. 248).

A voice for many who could not speak, Mechanicus reminds his reader that the Nazis murdered not only children and other individuals but also families and the idea of family. Each prisoner, he related on July 1, 1943, "points out how his family have [sic] been torn asunder" (p. 71), demonstrating the calculation with which the Nazis often destroyed the family before destroying the family member. "It is heartrending," he wrote on July 21, 1943, "to see mothers and fathers, or mothers alone with their offspring . . . or bent elderly folk . . . setting out on the journey ordained by a hater of mankind" (p. 97). Thus mothers try to smile at babies "who will not grow or thrive"; they "suckle their children not with the joy of the mother whose child is going on to a secure future, but with a feeling of anxiety" (p. 132). What would be a moment of joy in the world of humanity is a moment of dread in the anti-world.

This dread becomes reality each time one group of Jews must say farewell to another which has been selected for deportation to Auschwitz and other grim destinations. "Every good-bye is like another splash in the sea of misery," stated Mechanicus in an entry dated February 1, 1944 (it was a Tuesday, the weekly day of deportations). "Where are you, you thousands and tens of thousands who have been carried away. . . ? You are silent because they will not let you speak" (p. 240). That is why Mechanicus speaks.

Conscious of his responsibility not only as a witness but as a Jewish witness, Mechanicus is conscious of a metaphysical implication to these events unfolding in the physical realm. Although he does not take sides in the debates that he reports between the religious and the nonreligious Jews of Westerbork, he does relate the joy that Sabbath candles and Sabbath songs can bring. He also records some remarks of Chief Rabbi De Vries, who, like Mechanicus, made comparisons between the current plight of the Jews and their enslavement in Egypt. "God and Israel are inseparable," said the rabbi. "Jews may perish, but Israel is eternal" (p. 94). Mechanicus, however, is painfully aware that this time the angel of death did not pass over the Jews but laid claim to them; surely the eternity of Israel is threatened when so many of its children are slaughtered.

Although an air of hopelessness and despair pervades the diary of Philip Mechanicus, the very existence of the diary—the fact that he wrote it—bears an affirming implication. Man may be "good for nothing," as he says on the last page of the diary (p. 266), but the diarist must offer his testimony if he is to remain a man. And so he writes when he has lost all reason to write. He writes for the sake of people reduced to the silence of ashes and people yet abiding in the silence of the future.

SELECTED WORKS BY THE AUTHOR
Een Volk Bouwt Zijn Huis: Palestijnsche Reisschetsen. Amsterdam: Algemeen Handelsblad, 1933; *Year of Fear: A Jewish Prisoner Waits for Auschwitz.* Trans. Irene S. Gibbons. New York: Hawthorne Books, 1964.

David Patterson

Meed, Vladka (1922–)

In the introduction to the English edition of Vladka Meed's memoir *Fun beyde zaytn getomoyer,* 1948 (*On Both Sides of the Wall,* 1973) Elie Wiesel* wrote, "In the ruin of her childhood lies the memory of humanity, and possibly its salvation" (p. 7). If the memory of humanity lies hidden in this memoir, it is because here Vladka Meed offers a deeply stirring account of the Nazis' assault not only against human beings but also against the very idea of a human being. She transmits memories of how humanity turned its back on the human beings who were slated for annihilation. And she recalls how those who were dehumanized struggled to retain a trace of their human image.

Vladka Meed was born Feigele Peltel in Warsaw in 1922. As soon as the Nazis entered Poland in September 1939, she became part of an underground resistance organization in Warsaw. Since her "non-Jewish" features and fluency in Polish enabled her to pass for an Aryan, Feigele Peltel changed her name to Vladka Kowalska and operated outside the Warsaw ghetto under a false identity. She worked on both sides of the wall surrounding the ghetto to smuggle weapons to the Jewish Fighting Organization, and she went on humanitarian missions to labor camps. Having lost her entire immedi-

ate family, she and her husband, Benjamin Meed, settled in New York after the war. Both became very much involved in Holocaust education and remembrance projects.

Meed's memoir focuses on the period from July 22, 1942, when the mass deportations from Warsaw to Treblinka began, to early 1945. One motif that runs throughout the memoir is a profound sense of responsibility. Remembering the eyes of people as they marched to the trains for deportation, she wrote, "What grief was reflected in their eyes! What mute reproach! We stood there silent, stupefied and conscience-stricken. . . . Why did no one help them? Why didn't someone—why didn't I—plead for them?" (pp. 39–40). Later, when she was risking her life working outside the ghetto walls, she again experienced guilt feelings. "We on the Aryan side were conscious," she recalled, "of a sense of guilt at being outside the ghetto at so crucial a time" (pp. 184–85). Such a sense of obligation underlies Meed's devotion to others.

Because she is devoted to her fellow human beings, she is appalled at the Poles who either aid the Nazis or turn their backs on the Jews. She remembers how some Poles harassed Jews; others looked on and then "resumed their Sunday stroll. Why did the Poles remain silent?" (p. 113). When the Jews in the ghetto mounted their revolt, "there was no response from the rest of the city. And the rest of the world, why was it keeping so silent?" (p. 185). In Meed's memoir, the world's silence stands in sharp contrast to the silence of the victims, especially the children whom she smuggled to temporary safety and the women to whom she brought aid in the labor camps.

Perhaps the most overwhelming silence was the silence that hung over the ruins of Jewish Warsaw when the war finally came to an end. A witness robbed of her words, Meed found enough words to say, "Perhaps it is better only to gaze in silence upon this dead and desolate wilderness, where each stone, each grain of sand is soaked in Jewish blood and tears. Silence." (pp. 333–34). Then there is the double silence of the dead who had been attacked in their very graves—"Yes, Jews were persecuted even in their graves" (p. 335)—in the desecration of the Jewish cemetery. And yet the stones among the ruins and the dry bones of the cemetery find a voice in the cry of memory that rises up from survivors like Vladka Meed.

SELECTED WORKS BY THE AUTHOR
Fun beyde zaytn geto-moyer. New York: Workman's Circle, 1948; *On Both Sides of the Wall.* Trans. Benjamin Meed. Tel-Aviv: Hakibbutz Hameuchad, 1973.

David Patterson

Michelson, Frida (1905–)

Frida Michelson was one of only two women who survived the Nazis' slaughter of approximately 30,000 women and children near the pits of the Rumbuli Forest in Latvia in December 1941. In a series of *Aktionen* or actions they were taken from the Riga ghetto into the forest, where they were murdered in large groups. In keeping with the procedure, the women in Frida's group were forced to undress alongside the pit that would become their mass grave; before she was noticed, however, Frida hid under the pile of clothing and stayed there until the killing was over. After that her story consists of moving from one hiding place to another, from the kindness of one stranger after another—including some Jehovah's Witnesses—in and around Riga.

Frida Michelson was born Frida Frid in 1905 in the Latvian capital of Riga. Her father died when she was a very small child in Riga, and the Nazis murdered her mother, her stepfather, and three of her brothers and sisters. Two of her sisters, Sarah and Neha, survived. She married Mordekhai Michelson shortly after her liberation in 1944. Like many Jews in the Soviet bloc, however, she and her husband came under the suspicion of the KGB, and he was arrested in 1951. He was released a broken man in 1956, but he lived long enough to help his wife compile the notes that became her deeply moving Holocaust memoir *Ya perezhila Rumbulu* (*I Survived Rumbuli,* 1979). Although the book was completed in 1967, it was not published until after 1971, when Frida and her husband left the Soviet Union for Israel. The original Russian edition was published in Israel in 1973; it was followed by the publication of the English edition in 1979 in the United States.

Few memoirs are written with such a powerful sense of mission to the living and indebtedness to the dead. "*I swear to you,*" she declared to the ones who cannot speak, "I will tell them, the living, everything. . . . Your blood flows in my veins, and your ashes throb in my heart. I swear to tell the *Truth*" (p. 11).

In contrast to many memoir writers who can find no trace of God in their memories and even harbor a rebellion toward Him, Michelson sees Him at work everywhere. And to see Him is to be commanded by Him—that is what impels her to survive. "The idea," she asserted early on, "that God had chosen me to be His witness sustained me throughout the whole ordeal" (p. 42). Later she reiterated the idea that "God has chosen me to be His witness. This thought had come to me over and over again" (p. 92). As she survived more and more close encounters with death, she became convinced that "someone is looking out for me. I must help Him. . . . I have a mission, a duty to perform. I must stay alive—I am Thy witness" (p. 113). Not only does Frida see her survival as a summons from beyond; several of her rescuers see it in the same terms. "This is a miracle, God's miracle," one righteous gentile tells her (p. 133).

The question underlying these remarks from the memoir does not concern the matter of why God does not help her, even though she endured terrible ordeals. For Michelson, rather, it is a question of whether she will help God with regard to speaking the truth and sustaining life. It is true that Michelson brings forth a serious indictment not only of the Nazis but also of the Latvians who aided them; it is true that she outlines the methodical means by which one group of human beings isolates another from all humanity. And yet she discovers the truth of divine presence and divine duty in the caress of an old woman who saved her life. Therefore the Truth that she swears to tell is more than the truth of the atrocities committed; it is the Truth of lives committed to serving and saving life.

SELECTED WORK BY THE AUTHOR
I Survived Rumbuli. Trans. Wolf Goodman. New York: Holocaust Library, 1979.

David Patterson

Miller, Arthur (1915–)

Arthur Miller, arguably the greatest American playwright and the greatest dramatist of the twentieth century, has written some of the most enthralling and thought-provoking Holocaust dramas, plays such as *Incident at Vichy*, *Playing for Time*, and *Broken Glass*. Although Miller is known primarily for his dramas, he also published a novel, *Focus* (1945), which concerns anti-Semitism and, to some extent, the Holocaust. The novel, written as the Holocaust was coming to an end, concerns an anti-Semite who, upon donning glasses, is perceived as a Jew by those who encounter him. The novel concerns untenable antipathy and prejudice expressed toward those who are considered different, the attempt to ostracize "the other," in this instance, Jews.

What distinguishes Miller among Holocaust dramatists is his focus on the themes of conscience and moral responsibility; those who failed to help Jews and looked the other way during the Holocaust are, Miller implies, accomplices because of their inaction. Miller's concentration on the aforementioned themes is especially apparent in *Incident at Vichy* (1964) and in *Broken Glass* (1994). The playwright portrays von Berg (*Incident at Vichy*) and Sylvia Gellburg (*Broken Glass*) as bystanders who feel the desire to aid Jews during the plight but who nonetheless have been living as bystanders (and thus accomplices) because of their fears. It is noteworthy that in these two plays with a similar theme, the former hero is a Christian prince while the latter is a Jewish housewife; thus, Miller manifests that everyone, regardless of their religion, background, and gender, could have helped the Jews in Europe, that social and moral responsibility knows no boundaries. The dramatist suggests that this common bond in helping to protect the innocent and to fight injustice should bring people together and involve the interrelationships of human beings. Von Berg's altruism dramatizes the importance of moral responsibility yet also manifests that it sometimes comes at a high price.

Born on October 17, 1915, in Manhattan, Miller worked in the clothing and in the auto parts businesses upon his graduation from Abraham Lincoln High School in 1932. He eventually was accepted by the University of Michigan, who had rejected his application previously because of poor math grades. While in college, he met Mary Grace Slattery and was married to her from 1940 until 1956—the year that he married Marilyn Monroe. Miller involved himself in Communist activities throughout the 1940s and in 1956 was cited by the House on Un-American Activities Committee for contempt of Congress and convicted of contempt the following year. The U.S. Court of Appeals overturned the conviction in 1958. The playwright worked in 1964 as a commentator for the *New York Herald-Tribune* at the Holocaust trials held in Frankfurt, which probably influenced his play *Incident at Vichy*. Miller married photographer Inge Morath in 1962.

Incident at Vichy concerns the plight of eight men and a boy who are prisoners in a Nazi office in occupied Vichy and who are led, one by one, into a room for interrogation; after the questioning, they are never heard from again. The Jewish psychiatrist Leduc bitterly tells von Berg, the only prisoner, aside from the Gypsy, who is not Jewish (von Berg, a prince, is captured by mistake and is expected to be released), that he (von Berg), being an Aryan, has no right to claim that he is sympathetic and feels terrible about what happens to the Jews. Leduc argues that Aryans who feel pathos for the plight of Jews cannot comprehend what the Jews endure and, despite their pity, nonetheless benefit from the Holocaust. The psychiatrist argues that although von Berg is well meaning, he, like all Aryans sympathetic to Jewish suffering, experiences an unconscious relief in knowing that he is not a victim. Leduc also suggests that even those Aryans who empathize with Jews have an unconscious hatred of them. He wants moral responsibility, not guilt, from the prince. Leduc also asserts that all who fail to help Jews are partly to blame for the atrocities committed during this tragedy because they, as bystanders, are Nazi accomplices. When the prince protests that he empathizes with Jewish suffering, so much that he has even contemplated suicide, the psychiatrist points out that von Berg remains friendly with his cousin, Baron Kessler, even though Kessler has been instrumental in removing all Jews from the medical school—a point the prince has suppressed because of his fondness for his Nazi cousin. Then the Nazi anthropology professor, who conducts the interviews with the prisoners, calls von Berg into his office and quickly determines that the prince is indeed an Aryan and thus provides him with a pass that permits him to leave the building and to return home. However, touched and shamed by the psychiatrist's observations, von Berg gives his pass to Leduc, allowing the Jew to escape. The play concludes with Leduc's escape and von Berg's arrest for enabling a Jew to flee. Leduc has placed a burden on von Berg to act in a morally responsible way, and the prince endangers his life to save that of a Jew. As the play concludes, the challenge lies with the psychiatrist who, given another chance, must also act to save lives; if not, Leduc, himself, is an accomplice, for the prince has passed the burden onto him. Miller distinguishes between two Aryans: von Berg and the Nazi major. Both men express sympathy for Jews, but the major refuses to act (in fact, he contributes to the Final Solution) because he argues that he if did not perform his job, someone else would; von Berg, contrariwise, manifests that during the Holocaust some people did, in fact, comport themselves in a morally responsible fashion—even at the expense of their own lives.

The Crucible (1953) generally has been accepted as a work in which Miller, by using the Salem witch trials as a metaphor, voices his displeasure about McCarthyism, the scapegoating and destruction of innocent people. Critics, unfortunately, have failed to make the connection between *The Crucible* and the Holocaust. Miller discerns a correlation between the Salem witch trials, McCarthyism, and the Holocaust, for scapegoating and destruction obviously occurred in all three cases. Both the Salem witch trials and the Holocaust were caused, in part, by economic opportunism (Salem farmers denounced their neighbors as witches and then seized their lands, and Nazis took advantage of the destruction of Jews by confiscating their valuables and homes). For those who might doubt this connection between *The Crucible* and the Holocaust, Miller's play

After the Fall (1963) makes this correlation unmistakable.

After the Fall deals with both the Holocaust and McCarthyism; Miller, in fact, interweaves the two throughout his play. In both cases, people suffer because they are scapegoated and because bystanders refuse to help and to demonstrate their moral responsibility. Quentin visits an unnamed concentration camp with his lover, Holga. He admires her when she discusses her moral responsibility, her work as a courier for those officers plotting to murder Hitler, and her admission that although she tells him that she had no idea that there were concentration camps (and atrocities committed within them), she wonders, with a self-accusatory tone, how she could not have known. In other words, by refusing to realize what horrors were occurring near her, Holga admits that she is an accomplice. Miller links bystanders and accomplices during the Holocaust with those during McCarthyism.

Broken Glass, like *Incident at Vichy*, manifests Arthur Miller's preoccupation with moral responsibility and altruism. Sylvia Gellburg, a Jew living in Brooklyn, New York, becomes obsessed with photographs that she views in the newspaper in late November 1938. The photographs, taken only weeks after *Kristallnacht* (November 9, 1938, a night of pogroms against the Jews throughout Germany), portray Nazi officers committing atrocities against Jews, including a photo of an elderly Hasidic Jew cleaning a street with a toothbrush while Nazis observe with delight and mock him.

Sylvia, unlike her family members, identifies with the hapless Jew, noting a correlation between him and her grandfather, and between herself and Jews everywhere. Outraged by her family's indifference (they are not bothered because they note that the problems are in Germany and consequently do not affect them in New York) and guilt-ridden because of her inability to aid the German Jews, she symbolically joins them by becoming paralyzed. As her doctor notes, there is no physical reason for Sylvia's paralysis. She simply wants to suffer, just like the Jews in Germany. *Broken Glass* dramatizes the indifference of people in the

United States, even of American Jews, toward Jews in Germany and demonstrates, through the character of Sylvia Gellburg, the need to be morally responsible. Regrettably, her paralysis, though noble because it symbolizes her empathy for, and identification with, the suffering of others, is nonetheless an impotent gesture.

Miller's *Playing for Time* (1981) is a television drama the playwright adapted from the autobiography of Fania Fénelon*, a French singer who survived Auschwitz by participating in the death camp's all-female orchestra. Miller's play dramatizes the concentration camp inmate's strong desire to survive—to endure and serve as a witness to the atrocities. In addition to Fénelon's endurance, other significant themes in the work include her moral responsibility (she aids and protects other prisoners, even those who do not act benevolently toward her) and her attempt to make sense out of the irrationality of the atrocities and the anti-Semitism that she endures.

Selected Works by the Author
After the Fall. New York: Penguin, 1980 (rpt.); *Broken Glass.* New York: Penguin, 1994; *The Crucible.* New York: Penguin, 1976; *Incident at Vichy.* New York: Penguin, 1985 (rpt.); *Playing for Time.* New York: Bantam, 1981.

For Further Reading
Balakian, Janet N., "The Holocaust, the Depression, and McCarthyism: Miller in the Sixties." In *The Cambridge Companion to Arthur Miller*, ed. Christopher Bigsby. Cambridge, England: Cambridge University Press, 1997; pp. 115–38; Cook, Kimberly K., "Self-Preservation in Arthur Miller's Holocaust Dramas." *Journal of Evolutionary Psychology* 14 (1993): 99–108; Isser, Edward, "Arthur Miller and the Holocaust." *Essays in Theater* 10 (1992): 155–64; Meyer, Kinereth, "A Jew Can Have a Jewish Face." *Prooftexts: A Journal of Jewish Literary History.* 18 (1998): 239–58; Schlueter, June, and James K. Flanagan, *Arthur Miller.* New York: Ungar Publishing, 1987; Sterling, Eric, "Fear of Being" "'The Other': Racial Purity in Arthur Miller's *Incident at Vichy*." *Publications of the Arkansas Philological Association* 20 (1994): 67–75.

Eric Sterling

Modiano, Patrick (1945–)

Owing to the problems that they tackle, Patrick Modiano's works are significant to Holocaust literature, inasmuch as they are representative of literature by assimilated young Jewish authors who discover at the same time anti-Semitism, the Shoah, and a sense of belonging to the Jewish people. For Modiano the discovery of anti-Semitism, particularly among key figures of French literature, brings about the breaking off of harmony with the world and with the word, as well as the revelation of his originality and of his need to write.

To escape the void, after being "excluded" from the only culture he knows, all that remains to the assimilated writer is the language of others, a beloved language, a treacherous and betrayed language. Modiano takes a certain vengeance by imitating the transparent and sustained style of the great masters and having French turn upon itself from the inside. Accordingly, Modiano retains skeletal structures, a form which gives his novels a "pseudo-classical" side, an appearance hiding a message that tears it down.

Born in Boulogne-Billancourt in 1945, Patrick Modiano considers himself Jewish like his father. He feels a strong bond with this elusive man, who, involved in shady dealings, was arrested during the Occupation and managed to survive with a set of forged documents. To Modiano, he symbolizes the condition in which European Jews were forced to live. He is also the embodiment of the anguish, the passiveness, and the Jewish pusillanimity about which Franz Kafka writes. Modiano loves this "eternal traveler" and wants to protect him. He transposes those feelings in his novels and in the main character of *Les Boulevards de ceinture* (1972).

Writing for Modiano is an instrument of revenge, but it is also, first and foremost, an act of faithfulness to his father, who was rendered mute when confronting the anti-Semites. It expresses the feeling of total strangeness of the uprooted one and acts as a memory for his time quite prone to oblivion. No identity is possible without memory. Modiano experiences the tragic years of Nazism only through an obsessive feeling. Relying on the memory of the others, he tries to imagine this past and re-creates it in novels that deal with the Occupation, the persecution, and the extermination.

Modiano, however, is neither a historical nor a realistic novelist. He does not tell the reader how it was, but by using allusions and suggestions he makes the reader imagine and feel what those events were like and what are their consequences on today's life. The great originality of his writing is a remarkable fusion of invention and memory (see, for example, *Livret de famille*, 1977 [Family booklet]). His novels require a sensitive reader attentive to the slightest details. For instance, a song, a catchy German tune, a fashionable aperitif, a misty light, names of places evoking sad memories, an unusual term, an address, a name in a phonebook, or official papers are enough to re-create the atmosphere of the Nazi Occupation. Symbols with cultural values mark the gap between the Jew and the others. Modiano sketches his characters with the help of a few suggestive details sufficient to locate them. Without any discernible identity, criminals and heroes cross the path of a seeking narrator who is possessed by memory. He describes those who were hunted down and tries to understand their choices, the strategies for survival during those "venomous" years when a minor mistake could prove fatal.

In Modiano's novels the plot generally stretches on two time lines: the present of the narrator, who guides the story; and the past, his own or another character's, which is the object of the investigation. This investigation is often both a quest for a Jewish identity, suggested by the father's presence, or a detail such as a name (e.g., Stern), a yellow light, or the name of a street (see *Rue des boutiques obscures*, 1978 [The street of dark shops]). With the exception of *La Place de l'Etoile*, 1968 (The place of the star) and *Dora Bruder*, 1997 (*Dora Bruder*, 1999), the Shoah is rarely mentioned in Modiano's works. The novels always effectively convey its presence by the themes they treat: memory and forgetfulness, fear, the disappearance of people who leave no trace.

The title of the novel *La Place de l'Etoile* suggests a civilization that is both prestigious and abject; like the antithesis formed by the first

and last names of the novel's hero, it announces the ambiguity of the situation of the Jew torn between forgetfulness and memory. In search of an identity and of a writing style, the narrator finds himself traveling within the hallucinating confines of his own memory. Every step of this spiritual journey constitutes an attempt to conform to a set of values, to put down roots in a geographical, historical, and cultural landscape. The memory of anti-Semitism and the Shoah causes those attempts ultimately to fail. Assimilation offers no solution. It becomes synonymous with forgetting and hence betrayal. This betrayal is apparent in the caricature-like "double" for the protagonist, Le Vicomte Charles Lévy-Vendôme. The State of Israel itself, which is accused of having abandoned Jewish values, can hardly be used as a refuge. Pastiches, parodies, and ironic references in the novel satirize anti-Semitic literature, the literature of the assimilated Jews and of the "*bien-pensants*," the writers between the two world wars. As to the existentialists who after the war renounce their origins, the narrator judges them to be insincere.

The titles of Modiano's first three novels—*La Place de l'Etoile* (subtitled "a pamphlet by an exasperated Jew"), *La Ronde de nuit*, 1969 (*Night Rounds*, 1971), and *Les Boulevards de ceinture*, 1972 (Boulevards of enclosure)—symbolize the situation of the narrator caught in the trap of history and a prisoner of a haunted past. Swinging back and forth between a group of police killers to one of resistant fighters, the hero of *La Ronde de nuit* discovers that he shares nothing in common with either. He becomes a martyr neither by choice nor out of love for heroics, but rather because he was propelled by a kind of inner necessity of faithfulness to himself.

In *Villa triste*, 1975 (*Villa Triste*, 1977), the narrator begins to distance himself in time and space. Although he tries to forget, his memory always succeeds in resuscitating an unpleasant past. In this work the background and the character, which are familiar in Modiano's novels, become more precise. The life he describes resembles still waters in which are reflected the lean silhouettes of characters, of the persecuted, anguishing, and anguished, who are about to sink in the murky depths of memory. The plot is more substantial, and the writing takes on the pseudo-classical appearance sought by the author.

In *Rue des boutiques obscures*, as in a "remembrance of times past," Modiano frees himself from the temptation of oblivion by imagining an amnesic narrator. He is a detective, and re-creating his past becomes the object of his investigation. Questioning witnesses whose defective and egocentric memory regurgitates a fragmented and uncertain past and referring to dubious administrative documents, he identifies himself at first as Freddie, and then as Pedro, whose real name was probably Jimmy Stern who was born on La Rue des Boutiques obscures, located in Rome. This identification triggers off an imaginative regrouping and formation of all the collected information. What results is the pieced-together life of Jimmy Stern and his wife, Denise Coudreuse, who disappears during her escape across the Swiss border. This reconstitution is a mélange of reality and invention, as is every life re-created by memory. The secondary plot lines and the various witness accounts tell the story of those who were uprooted and displaced in France in the twentieth century.

Furthermore, in this very elaborate novel, the author pursues a dialogue with Marcel Proust on time and on memory. He rejects the Proustian theory of the unconscious and the romantic conception of childhood. There is nothing in common between the marvelous Proustian childhood and that of the uprooted son of expulsion and persecution for whom Paradise is lost forever. We also recognize in the same novel humorous allusions to Georges Perec's *W, ou le souvenir d'enfance*, 1975 (W, or the memory of childhood). Modiano does not refrain from criticizing certain elements of surrealism as well as techniques employed in the "nouveau roman." He prefers novels that draw on life experience.

In *Dora Bruder* Modiano starts from a missing person's notice to reconstruct the last few months of a young Jewish girl's life in Paris. Dora Bruder was deported in September 1942. The work is not a fiction but an extraordinary process whereby the author identifies himself with Dora, who was exterminated. Modiano's writing is a testimony to the girl's existence and preserves her memory. But there remain things about her last days we shall never know. Modiano is very much aware of the limits of testimony by those who did not experience those events themselves. And yet he becomes a messenger for people like Dora Bruder, as he turns to the word and struggles to fathom what they knew too well.

SELECTED WORKS BY THE AUTHOR
Les Boulevards de ceinture. Paris: Gallimard, 1972; *Dora Bruder*. Trans. Joanna Kilmartin. Berkeley: University of California Press, 1999; *Livret de famille*. Paris: Gallimard, 1977; *Night Rounds*. Trans. Patricia Wolf. New York: Alfred Knopf, 1971; *Out of the Dark*. Trans. Jordan Stump. Lincoln: University of Nebraska Press, 1998; *La Place de l'Etoile*. Paris: Gallimard, 1968; *Rue des boutiques obscures*. Paris: Gallimard, 1978; *Villa Triste*. Trans. Caroline Hillier. London: V. Gollancz, 1977.

FOR FURTHER READING
Guyat-Bender, Martine, and William Vanderwolk, eds., *Paradigms of Memory: The Occupation and Other Hi/stories in the Novels of Patrick Modiano*. New York: Peter Lang, 1998; Morris, Alan, *Patrick Modiano*. Oxford: Berg, 1996; Roux, Baptiste, *Figures de l'Occupation dans l'oeuvre de Patrick Modiano*. Paris: Harmattan, 1999; Wardi, Charlotte, "Memory and Writing." *Dappim: Research in Literature*, Supplement no.1 (1985).

Charlotte Wardi

Müller, Filip (dates unknown)

Filip Müller's memoir *Auschwitz Inferno: The Testimony of a Sonderkommando*, 1979 (also published under the title *Eyewitness Auschwitz: Three Years in the Gas Chambers*, 1999) is the work of the only member of the Auschwitz *Sonderkommando* to survive to tell his tale. Selected for forced labor in the gas chambers and crematoria, prisoners in the *Sonderkommando* were typically sent to the gas chambers within three months of being given their grisly detail. Müller arrived in Auschwitz with the first transport of the Slovak Jews on April 20, 1942. In May he was sent to the gas chambers—not to be murdered but to drag the bodies of the murdered from the gas chambers to the ovens. He left Auschwitz on January 18, 1945, when the Germans were evacuating the camp; after going from one camp to another, he was finally liberated in a small camp in the forest near the German town of Wels.

Müller made his first attempt to record his experiences in 1945 or 1946, when he assisted two survivors who were compiling an archive of information on the camps. Twenty years later, this early draft of his memoir was translated from Czech and appeared in an English edition under the title *The Death Factory: Document on Auschwitz*. During the Auschwitz trial of 1964, held in Frankfurt, Müller went back to his memoir to produce the current version.

Telling tales of murderers and martyrs from the depths of the death camp, Müller explores the question perhaps most fundamental to the Holocaust: What is a human being? His response to that question is both complex and disturbing. And at the core of the question is an indictment as powerful as it is obvious: "Hitler and his henchmen had never made a secret of their attitude to the Jews nor of their avowed intention to exterminate them like vermin. The whole world knew it, and knowing it remained silent" (*Auschwitz Inferno* p. 36). Müller points out that, in fostering an Aryan notion of the human being, the Nazis refashioned the men in the *Sonderkommando* after their own image: ironically, to "look more like human beings," the prisoners "imitated their torturers by aping their way of dressing" (p. 62). Here the "human being" was not the one who harbored the image of the divine but the one who wielded the power.

Addressing such an issue, Müller's memoir is an excellent example of the efforts on the part of the author to recover his humanity through the act of remembrance. In Müller's case the memory of his family—even of the loss of his family—is central to the recovery of his identity. As long as the loss of family and identity are not forgotten, it is not irrevocable. "What could I have said to my father," he asks, for example, when reflecting on his wretched condition, "this good and honest Jew who still put his trust in the truthfulness of his fellow men? . . . Your son Filip, the promising grammar-school boy, ... is a stoker in the crematorium!" (*Auschwitz Inferno* pp. 47–48) And who is the father in the Jewish tradition? He is the teacher of Torah, the one who bequeaths to his children a view of humanity steeped in a relation to divinity.

Hence, even though he "sought in vain to comprehend [God] in Auschwitz" (*Auschwitz Inferno* p. 35), Müller recalls with deep affection numerous examples of Jews who struggled to maintain their relation to the Holy One. The prisoner Fischl, for instance, wrapped invisible tefillin around his head and arm as he began to pray; he would cry out to his fellow prisoners that "it's prayer which makes you a human being" (p. 28). And Müller and others would follow his example in spite of themselves: "we felt strengthened by his faith" (p. 29). As part of their assault on the strength and humanity of these Jews, the Nazis forced the prisoners from the *Sonderkommando* to burn not only bodies but also prayer books and religious texts, which were the words of their fathers.

As a Jew, however, Müller knows that the key to maintaining one's humanity in the midst of its undoing is to maintain a relation to another human being. His memoir is very revealing in this regard. For, contrary to what might seem to be the case at first glance, the importance of seeking out and sustaining human contact in the camp was not to get help from someone but to have someone to help. "The main motives for seeking the relationships with women," he explains one example, was "simply the need to have someone to care for; all family ties had been forcibly and abruptly severed, and it was this feeling of desolation, of being utterly alone in the world, which awoke in almost everyone the longing for somebody to care for" (*Auschwitz Inferno* p. 63). Müller's memoir is itself written from this profound sense of care—for the dead whose bodies he burned and for the living whose souls he sets on fire.

SELECTED WORKS BY THE AUTHOR
Auschwitz Inferno: The Testimony of a Sonderkommando. Trans. and ed. Susanne Flatauer. London: Routledge and Kegan Paul, 1979; *The Death Factory: Document on Auschwitz*. Trans. Stephen Jolly. London: Pergamon Press, 1966.

David Patterson

N

Nir, Yehuda (1930–)

Yehuda Nir's memoir *The Lost Childhood* recounts the author's harrowing experiences as a hidden child during the Holocaust. Nir, who was nine years old when the Germans attacked his native Poland, tells the story of how he, his mother, and sister—his father was murdered in 1941—survived in a hostile and murderous environment. The author, who is a professor of psychiatry at Cornell University Medical School, was denied the psychological luxury of childhood. Instead, his life depended upon his developing the resources to outwit Nazis, their Polish sympathizers, and hostile Soviet troops—all of whom wished him dead. In ten concise chapters, Nir describes his fourfold transformation from a member of a prosperous Jewish family, to a hidden child, to a battle-tested veteran of the resistance, to a homeless refugee at war's end. En route he paints a vivid and horrific account of the psychological impact of having to change one's identity, while telling of unremitting Polish anti-Semitism, and the ingenuity which allowed the three family members to survive.

Nir was born in Stanislavov, Poland. His father, Samuel, was a successful carpet manufacturer in Lvov. Samuel and his wife, Sidia, had a nanny for Yehuda and his sister Lala, and a German maid who also did the cooking. Following Samuel's murder by the Nazis, the family decided that their only hope lay in trying to pass as Christians. The three fled first to Kraków, and then to Warsaw. In Warsaw the author and his sister became assistants to German dentists. Their mother was a domestic for a wealthy German philanderer. Yehuda Nir joined the Polish resistance army in Warsaw. He and his sister and mother all survived. Following the war, Nir came to the United States in 1959 and became a naturalized citizen nine years later. The author teaches psychiatry at both New York University and Cornell University.

Like Nechama Tec,* Nir experienced the trauma of having to assume a Christian identity—acquiring a new name, a new family history, and, above all, learning a new religion and accompanying rituals. Passing as a Christian required total familiarity with Christian rituals, prayer, and liturgy. Even the Christian calendar could prove fatal. For example, at one point the thirteen-year-old boy asks his nineteen-year-old female colleague on what date Christmas fell. This accidental query caused his colleague to accuse him of being a Jew, and could have cost him his life. Taught by circumstance the necessity of inventiveness, however, Nir in turn accused the young woman of sleeping with their employer's boyfriend. The two teenagers agreed not to tell on each other.

Owing to the fact of circumcision, hiding was even more difficult for Jewish males; if there was the slightest suspicion, the suspect was told to drop his pants. If this occurred, not even forged identity documents and baptismal certificates would save one's life. The author shares his experience of having to bathe with the son of his hiding family. Faced with the prospect of discovery, Nir "accidentally" knocked over the one kerosene lamp in the home, thereby plunging the room into lifesaving darkness as he and his companion bathed. There are also frequent references to operations performed to conceal the fact of circumcision.

The Lost Childhood is distinctive, however, in describing two types of hiding which were engendered under Nazism. One could be in hiding and hidden; the best known example of this is the story of Anne Frank.* One could also, however, be in hiding and visible. That is to say, one could "pass" as a Christian. Nechama Tec's *Dry Tears* is the classic presentation of this phenomenon. Nir experienced both types of hiding. He was in hiding and hidden when taken in by the Zagajska family. After leaving their home, he volunteered in a Polish resistance unit where he was taken for a Pole. Here he was in hiding and visible. During the six years of the war, the author had to act as a Christian while remembering his authentic Jewish identity.

Nir's memoir is at its best in describing the anguish of being a hidden Jew in Warsaw. At one point his sister Lala, whose resourcefulness saved all their lives, his mother, and the author were all hiding in different places in Warsaw, "fearing the cumulative effects of our Jewish looks." Owing to the dark roots of his dyed blond hair, "even getting a hair cut could be a life-threatening experience." The youth learns an ugly political lesson: the enemy of my enemy is not my friend. For many Poles, hating the Germans did not preclude fighting the Jews. ("Resistance, Polish style," Nir wrote, "helps the enemy you fight)." But the author's most profound anguish comes when he is "passing" as a Pole and witnesses a cargo train full of Jews being deported. He and Lala see several "panic-stricken faces" through the barred windows. The prisoners wondered where they were going. Neither he nor Lala looked at each other "for fear that one of us might burst out crying." By then they knew about Auschwitz, Majdanek, and Treblinka. The author observed that it was no longer possible for him to believe in a God who helped.

SELECTED WORK BY THE AUTHOR
The Lost Childhood: A Memoir. New York: Harcourt Brace Jovanovich, 1989.

Alan L. Berger

Nissenson, Hugh (1933–)

Hugh Nissenson's literary response to the Shoah is marked by the unbearable tension between evil and holiness. His theological quandary is how to account for the existence of both the deity and the death camps. Biographically, the author recalls two childhood events that inaugurated a lifelong wrestling with the issue of theodicy. Shortly after his birth, Adolf Hitler came to power. The author remembers seeing newsreels and photographs of the tyrant. Furthermore, the boy and his parents once listened to one of Hitler's tirades on shortwave radio. Nissenson attests that Hitler "dogged my childhood" ("A Sense of the Holy," p. 135). The second event was the death, from breast cancer, of his mother's thirty-one-year-old friend. He writes that "My love for [God], which was mixed with fear, became hate. I gave up my faith. I hate the idea that a just and loving God allows cells to metastasize and men to make gas chambers" ("A Sense of the Holy," p. 137).

Born in New York in 1933, Nissenson graduated from Swarthmore College. Shortly afterward, he became a Wallace Stegner Literary Fellow at Stanford University. The author has contributed short stories to a variety of magazines and periodicals including *The New Yorker*, *Harper's*, *Esquire*, *Playboy*, and *Midstream*. In addition, a *Pile of Stones* (1965), his first collection of short stories, received the Edward Lewis Wallant Award. His 1985 novel *The Tree of Life* was a finalist for both the National Book Award and the PEN Faulkner Award, and it won the Ohio Honor Award for the best book about Ohio history. Nissenson's report on the Adolf Eichmann trial was published in *Commentary*. The author and his wife live in New York City.

Nissenson creatively employs Jewish mythic paradigms in writing about the struggle against evil. Writing in a variety of genres—journals, short stories, and novels which include his own art—the author situates his characters in America, Europe, and Israel. In terms of time, Nissenson's work ranges from pre-Holocaust to the twenty-first century. His literary protagonists embrace one of two positions in relationship to God. The first position is that of contending with the deity. Thus, in short stories such as "The Blessing," "Lamentations," "Going Up," "The Law," and "The Prisoner," the protagonists protest against a God who permits the existence of evil; yet they are struck by a sense of holiness.

Nissenson's three novels reveal the second stage of the author's theological position: the death of God and the impossibility of belief. *My Own Ground* (1987), a novel, treats Jewish life in early twentieth-century New York City and its rich array of responses to modernity: socialism, mysticism, atheism, and secularism. The novel is a memoir of the protagonist, Jacob Brody, who is recounting his experiences as a youth. Illustrating the contemporary meaning of Jacob's wrestling Esau, Nissenson portrays Brody literally wrestling with Schlifka the pimp who seduces and eventually destroys Hannele Isaacs, the daughter of a rabbi who embodies the heretical mysticism of the sixteenth-century Sabbatai Zvi. The author prefigures the Holocaust in two ways: Rabbi Isaacs predicts that the Jewish people will be buried alive, and by the use of violent and degrading sex as metaphors of Jewish fate under Nazism.

Nissenson's second novel, *The Tree of Life*, universalizes the impact of theodicy. The author tells the story in journal form, of Thomas Keene. Keene is a widower whose wife's death has left him bereft of faith. Looming in the background is the increasing tension between Native Americans and white settlers on the nineteenth-century Ohio frontier. Genocidal acts in the form of sadism, torture, and murder are committed by both sides. Fanny, the widow whom Keene eventually marries, had initially refused his proposal because he was an infidel. After witnessing the torture murder of her best friend, Fanny admits to having lost her own faith. She asks Tom Keene to "help [her] live without Jesus." Nissenson wisely employs the tree of life as the book's central metaphor. This tree grew in the Garden of Eden, from which Adam and Eve were expelled. This tree also is an *axis mundi* connecting earth and heaven. Furthermore, Judaism portrays the Torah as a tree of life, and the Christian cross may equally be seen as such a tree. But Nissenson views holiness as coming from within, rather than having a divine referent. Consequently, he portrays the tree of life as growing from the head of John Chapman, a fictional Johnny Appleseed and adherent of Swedenbourg mysticism.

The Song of the Earth, Nissenson's most recent novel, is set in the twenty-first century. The protagonist, John Firth Baker, is the world's first genetically engineered artist. Essentially a meditation on history, the author introduces the Holocaust through Baker's concern with the life and work of Charlotte Solomon in honor of whose memory Baker does a drawing. Nissenson's novel juxtaposes the continuing presence of Jews—and anti-Semitism—in the future. As in his earlier novels, Nissenson continues to focus on the theme of creation and destruction as part of the same process. Holiness, for the author, is something that comes from within and signifies neither God nor transcendence. The Holocaust cost Nissenson his faith in a Lord of History. After Auschwitz the novelist must entertain yet also be responsive to the religious impulse. Human compassion, for Nissenson, may be the meaning of holiness in the post-Auschwitz universe.

SELECTED WORKS BY THE AUTHOR
The Elephant and My Jewish Problem: Selected Stories and Journals. New York: Harper and Row, 1988; *In the Reign of Peace.* London: Secker and Warburg, 1972; *My Own Ground.* New York: Perennial Library, 1987; *Notes from the Frontier.* New York: Dial, 1968; *Pile of Stones: Short Stories.* New York: Scribner, 1965; "A Sense of the Holy." In *Spiritual Quests: The Art and Craft of Religious Writing,* ed. William Zinsser. Boston: Houghton Mifflin, 1988; *The Tree of Life: A Novel.* Philadelphia: Paul Dry Books, 2000.

FOR FURTHER READING
Berger, Alan L., "Holiness and Holocaust: The Jewish Writing of Hugh Nissenson." *Jewish Book Annual* 48 (1990–1991: 6–25); Furman, Andrew, *Israel Through the Jewish-American Imagination: A Survey of Jewish-American Literature on Israel, 1928–*

1995. New York: SUNY Press, 1997; Kurzweil, Arthur, "An Atheist and His Demonic God." *Response* 36 (Winter 1978–1979).

Alan L. Berger

Nomberg-Przytyk, Sara (1915–1996)

Translated from an unpublished Polish manuscript written in 1966, the appearance of Sara Nomberg-Przytyk's memoir *Auschwitz: True Tales from a Grotesque Land* in 1985 marked the emergence of one of the most penetrating expressions of women's ordeal in the concentrationary universe to date. By exploring specific individuals and incidents from that realm in a series of brief vignettes, Nomberg-Przytyk captured the horrific essence of the death factory. A skilled storyteller, she conveys the unbearable nature of her experience in a manner accessible to her reader, bringing out the depths of a will to live even within the confines of the kingdom of death.

Born in 1915 in Lublin, Poland, Nomberg-Przytyk grew up in a Hasidic family. Her grandfather was a renowned Talmudist who served as the headmaster of a yeshiva in Warsaw; many of Nomberg-Przytyk's relatives, in fact, were rabbis. Living in the Jewish area of Lublin, she came to know the meaning of poverty at an early age. She attended gymnasium in Lublin and enrolled at the University of Warsaw. As a result of her social activism, she was incarcerated for five years as a political prisoner. When Germany invaded Poland in 1939, she fled to Białystok in the east, where she had taught school before the war. From 1941 to 1943, she was confined to the Białystok ghetto; when the ghetto was liquidated, she was sent to the concentration camp in Stutthof. From Stutthof she was transported to Auschwitz. After her liberation in 1945, she lived in Lublin until 1968, when she was forced to leave Poland. From Poland she went to Israel, and in 1975 she left Israel to settle in Canada with her two sons. Sara Nomberg-Przytyk died in 1996.

One especially powerful motif that runs through the tales in Nomberg-Przytyk's memoir is the assault on the mother as the origin of life and of love in the world. She recalls, for instance, songs about the loss of the mother which were sung in the camp at Stutthof (pp. 7–8) and in Auschwitz (p. 18). She often refers to the phenomenon of the "camp mother" or "camp daughter," where one woman would take another under her protection. And she presents a beautiful, tragic portrayal of a mother and daughter in the tale of Marie and Odette. Perhaps the most devastating example of the assault on the mother comes in the story of "Esther's First Born." It is the tale of a young woman who gave birth to a beautiful child in the camp, only to be told by her fellow inmates that newborns in the camp must be killed to spare the mothers. Esther refuses to allow them to take her infant, and she goes to her death with her baby in her arms.

As harrowing as the tale of Esther is, the story of "A Living Torch" is even more so. Here the women in the camp are inundated with the sound of children crying out, "Mama!" as if "a single scream had been torn out of hundreds of mouths" (p. 81). As the children were sent to be burned alive in pits of flames, a scream broke out from the women in the block. She ends the tale with a question that continues to haunt the world: "Is there any punishment adequate to repay to criminals who perpetrated these crimes?" (p. 82).

Not all of Nomberg-Przytyk's portraits of women in the camp are about bonding and nurturing. Images of something monstrous can be found in her memory of women like Orli Reichert and the infamous Cyla, who was in charge of Block 25, the block where women were sent to await their turn for the gas chambers. Cyla explains herself by saying, "I put my mother in the car and took her to the gas. You should understand that there remains for me nothing so terrible that I could not do it. The world is a terrible place. This is how I take my revenge on it" (p. 57). Cyla is one of Josef Mengele's favorites in the camp, and Nomberg-Przytyk's memoir contains several accounts of Mengele's words and deeds, including his explanation of why he sends mothers to their deaths with their children. "It would not be humanitarian," said Mengele, "to send a child to the ovens without permitting the mother to be there to witness the child's death" (p. 69). Such is the Nazi notion of kindness.

A question that recurs in Nomberg-Przytyk's memoir is the issue of whether new arrivals should be informed of the fate that awaits them. While the matter of whether people should be given a short time to prepare themselves for their deaths is left unresolved, Nomberg-Przytyk presents a heroic example of such a preparation in her tale called "The Dance of the Rabbis." There the Nazis order a transport of Hasidic rabbis to dance and sing before they are murdered, but the rabbis transform the Nazis' order into their own affirmation of the holiness that imparts meaning to life—even as they are going to their deaths. This they accomplished by refusing to allow the Nazis to determine the meaning of the words that came from their lips.

Nomberg-Przytyk, indeed, is especially attuned to the Nazis' assault on words and their meaning and how that assault most profoundly defines the Holocaust. Realizing that the violence done to the word parallels the violence launched against the meaning of the human being, she wrote, "The new set of meanings [imposed on words] provided the best evidence of the devastation that Auschwitz created in the psyche of every human being" (p. 72). Skillfully making use of words to remember this assault on words, Nomberg-Przytyk returns meaning to words in a way that not only attests to the kingdom of death but also bears witness to the dearness of life.

SELECTED WORKS BY THE AUTHOR
Auschwitz: True Tale from a Grotesque Land. Trans. Roslyn Hirsch, ed. Eli Pfefferkorn and David H. Hirsch. Chapel Hill: University of North Carolina Press, 1985; *Kolumny Samsona.* Lublin: Wydawn, 1966.

David Patterson

Nyiszli, Miklós (1901–1956)

Within a year of the end of World War II, a Hungarian physician, Doctor Miklós Nyiszli, had written his memoir of Auschwitz titled *Dr. Mengele boncol—orvosa voltam az Auschwitz-I Kremat—riuman*, 1947 (*Auschwitz: A Doctor's Eyewitness Account*, 1960). The memoir is remarkable for its intimate exploration of an area of the camp that few saw and lived to describe: the gas chambers and crematoria. It also presents a rare and detailed portrait of Dr. Josef Mengele, the death camp's chief physician, known for the hundreds of selections and grisly medical "experiments" that he conducted at Auschwitz-Birkenau. In fact, many of the details that the world has about those experiments come from Nyiszli's memoir.

Born in 1901, Nyiszli was deported to Auschwitz with his wife and fifteen-year-old daughter by cattle car in May 1944. He was separated from them upon his arrival. Mengele asked a group of physicians in the transport if any of them had forensic experience. Nyiszli stepped forward. From that moment onward, until the forced march out of the camp, Nyiszli worked as Mengele's assistant in the crematoria area, where he witnessed unspeakable atrocities. He did, however, manage to have his family transferred out of the camp just before the order came to exterminate all the women in their block. After his liberation in Melk, Austria, Nyiszli returned home, where his wife and daughter soon joined him after surviving their own horrific experiences from Auschwitz to Bergen-Belsen.

Realizing that Auschwitz is "a cemetery without a single grave" (p. 151), Nyiszli has a deep sense of being summoned as a voice for the ashes that cannot speak, as a kind of marker for the dead who have no graves. "I had no reason to be here," he recalled of his descent into the world of the crematoria, "and yet I had come down among the dead. I felt it my duty to my people and to the entire world to be able to give an accurate account of what I had seen" (p. 46). Nyiszli realized that memory is threatened not only by the absence of memorial stones for the dead but also by the perversion of language which characterized the concentrationary universe. He noted, for example, that in "SS medical language" the murder of tens of thousands of people was called "the intensive battle against the spread of infection." The results of that struggle, he added, "were always one or two truckloads of ashes" (p. 75). In his memoir Nyiszli also alerted the world to the existence of two zinc containers—two vessels of memory—holding eyewitness accounts written by members of the *Sonderkommando* (the forced labor detail assigned to the crematoria); some fifteen years later, those containers were discovered.

In Nyiszli's account of his return home, moreover, one sees the moral and metaphysical difficulties inherent to any liberation from the camps, particularly from the crematoria, the innermost circle of that anti-world. "I dreaded the truth," he recalled of his trek homeward, "fearing to return to an empty, plundered home" (p. 159)—fearing, in other words, that he could find no liberation. He describes his entry into his house—which, remarkably, had not been taken over by others—saying, "Now, home again, nothing. I wandered aimlessly through the silent rooms. Free, but not from my bloody past, nor from the deep-rooted grief that filled my mind and gnawed at my sanity" (p. 160). Only when his wife and daughter found their way back to him did Nyiszli begin to find his way back into a life liberated from the horrors of the camps—only then is he free: a point that reveals the problematic nature of liberation and return for the thousands who were left with no home or family.

Perhaps the restoration of his family instilled in Nyiszli an even deeper sense of urgency to put his memory to paper, as a voice not only for those who could not speak but also for those who survived but lost their families.

SELECTED WORK BY THE AUTHOR
Auschwitz: A Doctor's Eyewitness Account. Trans. Tibere Kremer and Richard Seaver. New York: Fawcett Crest, 1960.

David Patterson

O

Oberski, Jona (1938–)

Jona Oberski's memoir *Childhood* (1983), translated from the Dutch *Kinderjaren* (1978) by Ralph Manheim, is a chilling account of a childhood warped by the Holocaust. By turns astounding and full of pathos, the author conveys the confusion, innocence, and rage of a young child whose sense of security and safety is overwhelmed by the chaos of death and suffering. Told from a child's point of view, and dedicated to his foster parents who, writes the author, "had quite a time with me," the story raises questions about justice and happiness which remain with the reader long after finishing the book. *Childhood* has been critically acclaimed and translated into sixteen languages including German, Finnish, Italian, Hebrew, and French. In 1993 the book was made into a prize-winning film, *Jona who Lived in the Whale*.

The author, an only child, was born in Amsterdam. His German-born parents had fled to the Netherlands with Jona shortly after Jona's birth. The Oberski family was deported to Bergen-Belsen, via Westerbork, when Jona was a toddler. Both of his parents perished in Bergen-Belsen. The seven-year-old Jona returned to Amsterdam after the war and was adopted by foster parents under whose guidance he began the slow and difficult process of working through his losses. Oberski still lives in Amsterdam where, until his early retirement in 1997, he worked in particle physics research.

Oberski's memoir is a slim volume which, in 119 pages, describes the destruction of a childhood. The memoir begins with the comforting words of his mother, "Don't be afraid. Everything's all right. I'm here." From this reassuring gesture, so necessary and natural for children, the author's world collapses. This collapse assumes even more poignancy because of the fact that he is unable to comprehend what is happening. Instead, his innocence both protects him and shatters the reader. His initial experience of Jew hatred comes in the form of taunting by a somewhat older child who buries the youngster's pail and shovel in the sand and mocks his "crazy Jewish coat." The worst is, however, yet to come.

His early childhood is spent in Bergen-Belsen. While there, his father falls fatally ill in the infirmary. Jona is sent to summon his mother before it is too late. Not realizing what is at stake, he dawdles on his way, playing in the wet grass. He becomes lost, finally finds his way back to his mother, and then forgets to give her the message. Returning to the infirmary, the boy witnesses his father's death and kisses the corpse's hand. That evening, the mother asks if he is crying because his father is dead. Jona says yes, but also he is afraid of dying himself because he had kissed his father and recalls that his mother had told him not to kiss anyone in the camp because it was dangerous. Comforting him, the mother distinguishes between kissing family members and strangers. Uttering a warning which will haunt the youngster after the war, his mother says, "You must never kiss anyone on the lips, because that's really dangerous" (p. 71).

Children play games and have rites of initiation. Even in concentration camps. Oberski writes of having to pass a test imposed by the older children. He is taken to a darkened shack which the children call the dreadhouse. Dared to go in, the youngster agrees only if one of the older boys accompanies him. Led inside, Jona finds himself in a room with "white things lying on the floor and in a pile next to the dark wall" (p. 74). Other children came inside, most of them holding their hands over their noses. He realizes that he is surrounded by dead people, "bundles of bodies," mutilated torsos, "separate arms and legs" (p. 75). Desperately, the young boy searches for his father's corpse. That evening his mother, a remarkably caring and resourceful woman, asks him what he had done during the day. She tells him that the building is not a dreadhouse but a deadhouse. Learning what he has done, the boy's mother washes him all over with disinfectant. The youngster remembers that "it stank."

Adopted after the war, Jona has understandable psychological difficulties. He barely touches his food and has crying spells. "Aunt Lisa," his foster mother, is greatly concerned about the child's welfare. She tells her ward that he will die unless he eats. Attempting to comfort him, she kisses the youth on his lips. The boy, remembering his mother's admonition, screams, "You kissed me on the lips. Now I'll die. My mother told me so herself" (p. 119). He vomits and is told to clean up the mess because he is no longer a baby. *Childhood* is a stunning memoir. The author's ability to retain the literal point of view of a child renders his experience profoundly chilling.

SELECTED WORKS BY THE AUTHOR
Childhood (Kinderjaren). Trans. Ralph Manheim. New York: Doubleday, 1983; *De eigenaar van Niemandsland* (The proprietor of no man's land). Amsterdam: BZZToH, 1998.

FOR FURTHER READING
Lezzi, Eva, "KZ-Haft in fruher Kindheit und ihre literarische Evozierung. Zu Jona Oberskis

'Kinderjahre'." In *Für ein Kind war das anders: Traumatische Erfahrungen judischer Kinder und Jugendlicher im nationalsozialistischen Deutschland*. Berlin: Metropol Verlag, 1999; Lezzi, Eva, *Verfolgte Kindheit: Literarische Autobiographien zur Shoah*. Vienna: Bohlau Verlag, 2001.

Alan L. Berger

Oz, Amos (1939–)

Amos Oz has been internationally acknowledged as a leading modernistic writer. In 1991 he was elected a full member of the Academy of the Hebrew Language. In 1992 he was awarded the Frankfurt Peace Prize. Furthermore, in 1997, French President Jacques Chirac awarded him the French Légion d'Honneur. Most recently, in 1998, he was awarded the Israel Prize for Literature.

Amos Oz was born in Jerusalem in 1939. At the age of fifteen he left the city to live in Kibbutz Hulda but returned to the city of his birth to study philosophy and literature at Hebrew University. In 1986 he left Hulda and moved to Arad, a town in the south of Israel. Currently he teaches literature at Ben Gurion University of the Negev. Oz is at once a writer of short stories, novellas, and novels as well as an active essayist with a high political profile. Since the 1967 Six-Day War, his voice has consistently been heard on Israeli issues, principally as the most prominent member of the "Peace Now" movement.

How political is Oz's fiction? Certainly not political in the narrow sense of ideology and indoctrination. Rather, it is concerned with a far-reaching malaise in Israeli society, a malaise shaped by many factors. Yet there is a dichotomy between Oz's strongly held political views and his highly individualistic and subjective fiction which reaches great psychological depths. Indeed, it has been said that Oz exorcises his psychological and political ghosts in his fiction.

For Oz, and for other writers, Jerusalem is filled with messianic dreamers, of all faiths. Oz's fiction is rooted in the here and now. However, his aim is not to reproduce the surrounding world in realistic terms. His fiction can instead be read on a materialistic and mythic level.

In his novel *Laga'at Ba-Mayim Laga'at Ba-Ruah*, 1973 (*Touch the Water, Touch the Wind*, 1974), Oz is fascinated with the demonic and fantastic as viable elements in the human psyche. In touching on the Shoah, experience melds to the fantastic. Oz's fantastic story has its roots in Hasidic lore and the mysticism of the Kabbala. This extraordinary story is about a Polish Jew, Elisha Pomeranz, a teacher and a mathematician who survives the Holocaust through the exercise of superhuman power. "He rose and floated on the dark air . . . borne high and silent over woods and meadows, over churches, huts and fields (p. 8). Elsewhere we read that "Pomeranz had suddenly had enough . . . so he played his mouth organ at them with all his might and main, until the Russians heard and burst across . . . and the war ended" (p. 27).

Oz points in a mock-heroic tone to the secret of Jewish survival: spirituality, tenacity, a belief in miracles, and an unquenchable quest for meaning. The protagonist proves his superhuman power by combining pure mathematics with Hasidic miracles. He moves to Israel and settles as a watchmaker in Tiberias on the shore of the Sea of Galilee, one of the lowest geographical points in Israel. From there he moves to a kibbutz in the upper Galilee, one of the highest points, and there he lives as a shepherd and watchmaker. While there—in typical Oz fashion—he succeeds in solving one of the most baffling puzzles about the mathematical concept of infinity.

Pomeranz, his wife, and Professor Zaicek, all survivors of the Shoah, move in an inexorable cycle of ascent and descent. They must come down to touch reality, to be defiled and humiliated by it, before they can ascend and gain pure vistas. The last appearance of the protagonist and his wife finds them on the evening when the kibbutz is shelled. Oz describes the earth opening, as if a mouth, gently allowing the two characters to descend.

Oz introduces the fantastic in a highly stylized way. It allows him to venerate the spiritual as well as its victory over the base. Reality is pitted against actuality, with true reality often performing miracles. Oz presents us with a modern neo-Hasidic miracle tale employing fantasy and magic. The Hasidic fantastic tale of miracles has two recurring themes: the magical power of the *tzadik* (the holy man) to soar and fly over distances and the revelation of the holy man to his student. Pomeranz is the pupil, and Professor Zaicek is his mystical teacher. When the two meet in surrealistic, unreal places the mathematician and the philosopher exchange melodies. The holy man is torn between the desire to leave the world of futile vanities and the desire to stay since he has redemptive qualities. Magic and fantasy in this tale are essentially hagiographic: Oz transformed its structure into a myth of survival. Spiritual characters defy boundaries and earthly limitations. They can command the elements with music as well as with pure intellect. Oz uses irony and paradox in this interesting and challenging novel. Only through paradox and the affirmation of the fantastic can humans fathom the dimension of potential reality.

Oz is a critic and a lover of the unfolding reality in Israel since its inception. His modernistic approach, whether in novels such as *Michael Sheli*, 1968 (*My Michael*, 1972) or *Al Tagidi Layla*, 1994 (*Don't Call It Night*, 1996) coexists with his fascination with varying aspects of Israeli life. He is a master of language and its nuance, and he captures mood and tone. This applies to his fiction, to his essays, and to his world's view.

SELECTED WORKS BY THE AUTHOR
Don't Call It Night: Trans. Nicholas de Lange. San Diego: Harcourt Brace, 1996; *My Michael*. Trans. Nicholas de Lange. New York: Alfred Knopf, 1972; *Touch the Water, Touch the Wind*. Trans. Nicholas de Lange. New York: Harcourt Brace Jovanovich, 1974.

FOR FURTHER READING
Balaban, Abraham. *Between God and Beast: An Examination of Amos Oz's Prose*. University Park: Pennsylvania State University Press, 1993.

Gila Ramras-Rauch

Ozick, Cynthia (1928–)

Cynthia Ozick is a dazzling essayist as well as a novelist. Perhaps the most cerebral of Jewish-American writers, her work is suffused with traditional ritual and history. Specifically concerning the Shoah, she contends, "To be a Jew means to be a carrier of that kind of history (Holocaust remembrance); there is no way out of it" (Debate p. 77). For Ozick, the Holocaust is a watershed event in Jewish and world history. Yet she is concerned that aesthetics will first blur and eventually obliterate the specificity of the Shoah. Warning against this, Ozick asserted: "The task . . . is to retrieve the Holocaust freight car by freight car, town by town, road by road, document by document. The task is to save it from becoming literature" ("The Uses of Legend," 6).

Ozick's European-born parents owned a drugstore in the Bronx where she and her brother were raised. She recalls that as a youngster she delivered prescriptions, but always "refuse—out of conscience—the nickel tip" ("A Drugstore in Winter," in *Art & Ardor*, p. 300). One of the few Jewish children in her public school, the author, an avid reader, wrote that "in P.S. 71 I am publicly shamed in Assembly because I am caught not singing Christmas carols; in P.S. 71 I am repeatedly accused of deicide" ("Drugstore," 302). Her mother's brother was the Hebrew poet Abraham Regelson. Ozick received a bachelor's degree from New York University and a master's degree from Ohio State University.

Among the important Jewish influences in her life was Leo Baeck's essay on romantic religion which she read at age twenty-five, which "impassioned me in terms of distinction-making, [his] distinction between romantic and classical religion" (Haberman, p. 159). Consequently, Ozick's writing is infused with rationalism as opposed to mystical or emotional currents. Among her awards are the National Endowment for the Arts fellowship, American Academy of Arts and Letters, Mildred and Harry Strauss Living Award, Guggenheim Fellowship, four O. Henry First Prizes, and the Rea Award for the Short Story. Her books have also been finalists for the National Book Award and the National Book Critics Circle Award. She and her husband live in Westchester, New York.

Ozick's literary engagement with the Shoah is expressed in a variety of genres: essays, novels, a play, poems, and short stories. Additionally, the author translates Yiddish poetry. Her best-known Holocaust stories are "Rosa," "The Shawl" (later combined in a novel entitled *The Shawl*); "Levitation," and "Bloodshed"; novels include *Trust* (1966), *The Cannibal Galaxy* (1983), and *The Messiah of Stockholm* (1987). The author, a non-witness herself, faces an inherent tension in attempting to represent the Shoah. For example, after the appearance of "The Shawl," a survivor chastised Ozick for writing about what she had not personally experienced. Ozick responded by making an analogy to the Passover Haggadah. If I am supposed personally to experience an event which occurred 4,000 years ago, "how much more strongly am I obliged to belong to an event that occurred only 40 years ago" (cited by Cohen, 148).

Ozick's Holocaust fictions contend with a contradiction. On the one hand, she insists that literature has a moral center and an obligation to history. Yet, on the other hand, she remains uneasy with the very concept of literature fearing that it too easily lends itself to idolatry. Consequently, like Elie Wiesel,* she believes that after Auschwitz "art for art's sake" is immoral. After Auschwitz, everything needs to be reevaluated, including and especially the role of literature. For Ozick, true literature is "liturgical," it has "the configuration of the ram's horn: you give your strength to the inch-hole and the splendor spreads wide" (Toward in *Art & Ardor*, pp. 174–75). Such literature has a choral (communal) voice and carries the echo of the Lord of History.

The author's numerous Holocaust fictions are rigorously specific and address several major post-Auschwitz issues. From *Trust*, her first novel which she describes as having "begun for the Christians and finished for the Jews," to the more recent *The Shawl* (1990), Ozick's writing illuminates the inherent tensions and distinctions between the Jewish covenantal way and modernity, between Christianity and Judaism, and between allegiance to history and the distortions of art. Although clearly the work of a writer of Ozick's talent addresses a variety of issues, several major Holocaust concerns are illuminated in her writings: the salvific role of survivor testimony ("Levitation"); the trauma of survival ("Rosa"); the mother-daughter relationship (*The Shawl*); interrogating the tradition by both survivors and non-witnesses ("Bloodshed"); the obligation to remain a Jew after Auschwitz (*Trust, The Pagan Rabbi*); distinguishing between types of survivors and lessons learned from the Shoah (*The Cannibal Galaxy*); and messianic delusions (*The Messiah of Stockholm*).

This entry focuses on two short stories, "Levitation" and "Bloodshed," and two novels, *The Cannibal Galaxy* and *The Shawl*. "Levitation" links the deterioration of Judaism in America with the inability to be moved by the Holocaust. Feingold and Lucy, his Christian wife, are third-rate novelists; Ozick refers to them as "anonymous mediocrities." She combines elements of the Hasidic tale and the Holocaust in revealing distinctions between Feingold and Lucy, as well as between Jews who respond to survivor testimony and those disconnected from Judaism and indifferent to the Shoah. The story is set in the context of a party hosted by the Feingolds, which is attended only by mediocre writers like themselves. Here Feingold becomes aware of the self-deceits of his existence.

Feingold lights a fire in the fireplace, in spite of Lucy's objections, when he notices his seminary friend who has brought with him a survivor. Lucy is uneasy around her husband's "theological" associates, preferring Christian or, better, pagan illuminations to Jewish particularity. The witness begins to tell his story. Ozick describes the speaker in a manner which evokes Elie Wiesel*; the survivor employs his voice as an artist uses a brush, his whisper "carved" the Jewish victims "like sculptures." While listening to the testimony, the Jews become transfixed. The room "rose like an ark on waters" (p. 15). Lucy, for her part, feels that she has given up true religion—the glorification of Nature—"on account of the God of the Jews"—the God of History. Even as the living room ascends, Lucy wonders how long can the Jews go on about the Holocaust.

"Bloodshed" deals with both psychological and theological dimensions of American post-Holocaust Judaism. Unlike "Levitation," the story is concerned with the intra-Jewish response to Auschwitz. Ozick begins her tale with the journey of Jules Bleilip, an attorney and skeptic, to visit his cousin Toby who lives in a Hasidic community in upstate New York. Toby had left college, married Yussel, a Hasid, and become the mother of four ultra-religious boys. Yussel is a survivor, as are the majority of the enclave's inhabitants. Bleilip is invited to *mincha* (evening service), where he hears the rebbe (Hasidic mystic), whose workman's cap and ordinary appearance mask his true identity, speak about the contemporary meaning of the ancient rite of Azazel, the sacrifice of a scapegoat laden with the sins of Israel. Azazel, commonly understood as wilderness, can, the rebbe suggests, be seen as randomness or "instead of." The mystic equates the sacrifice of the goat to the Holocaust, and survival itself dependent on randomness.

The rebbe, a Buchenwald survivor, interrupts his own discourse and accuses Bleilip of believing that "instead of" applies to survivors. He orders the visitor to empty his pockets; he has two guns, one toy and one real. Reflecting on his experience with Nazi euphemism and deception—"soap" stones and "showers"—the holy man contends, "It is the toy we have to fear" (p. 71). After dismissing his followers, the rebbe admits the dialectical nature of post-Auschwitz belief: "it is characteristic of believers sometimes not to believe. And it is characteristic of unbelievers sometimes to believe" (p. 72). The mystic descends, as it were, to elevate the skeptic. Classical Hasidism termed this act *yeridah le-zorekh aliyah*, the descent on behalf of the ascent. It is, however, the rebbe who maintains a true skepticism: "Firm believers in monotheism are the real skeptics and realists because their belief excludes magic" (Klingenstein, p. 55).

The Cannibal Galaxy is simultaneously a reflection on the impossibility of combining Hebraic and Western culture, and the importance of the midrashic method in the post-Auschwitz world. Ozick employs a host of Jewish historical figures who lived after historical upheavals, including Rabbi Akiba, Edmond Fleg, and André Neher, as paradigms of authentic Jewish response to catastrophe. Joseph Brill, hidden in a convent cellar during the Holocaust, has just two texts to study: the Tractate Ta'anit, dealing with fasts, and the work of Edmund Fleg, a fellow

Jew who found his way back to the tradition following the Dreyfus affair. After the war, Brill immigrates to America and founds the Edmund Fleg Hebrew Day School based on a dual curriculum of Western and Jewish culture. The school is a failure. Brill himself appears not to have followed the school's Latin motto *per aspera ad astra* (through hardship to the stars). But Brill, who had studied astronomy prior to the war, "stops too soon."

Hester Lilt, a mysterious intellectual of European origin, is an "imagistic linguistic logician" (p. 63) who serves as Brill's theological interlocutor. She also plays the gadfly in exposing the multiple weaknesses of Brill's pedagogical enterprise. Lilt's daughter, Beulah, is a mediocre student at Brill's school. Lilt, whose name may derive from the Hebrew *leyl* (night) or from the demoness Lilith, delivers a lecture dealing with the "unsurprise of surprise." The lecture exposes the many weaknesses of Brill's pedagogy. First, it critiques the folly of predicting the future based on the present. For example, by the novel's end, Beulah Lilt becomes a highly successful abstract painter. Next, Ozick retells the midrash "There Ran the Little Fox" which tells of Rabbi Akiba's laughter when informed of the destruction of the Temple (*Makkot* 24b). Lilt also speaks of the relationship between bees and flowers, and, finally, cannibal galaxies which "devour smaller brother galaxies." This also refers to history (e.g., Europe's cannibalizing of the Jews).

Lilt's position resembles that of Rabbi Akiva, which is itself a manifestation of the midrashic method. His laughter symbolizes that destruction is not the final word. Based on the biblical verse Isaiah 8:2, which joins Uriah the priest and Zechariah, Uriah foretells the destruction of Zion and Jerusalem. Zechariah prophesied the rebuilding of Jerusalem; "to stop at Uriah without the expectation of Zechariah is to stop too soon" (p. 68). Midrash itself derives from the word meaning to search or to seek. But Brill has ceased to seek. Yet his answer to the question of post-Auschwitz Jewish identity is the failed dual curriculum. His own son, Naphtali, cares nothing for Judaism and aspires not to the stars, but to become secretary of transportation to facilitate cross-country road travel.

By novel's end, Brill has retired to Florida, and Hester Lilt has returned to Europe. Up till this point, Ozick has refrained from directly engaging the Holocaust experience.

The Shawl is Ozick's single attempt to recreate the Holocaust experience of a survivor. Divided into two unequal parts, and told from the perspective of an omniscient narrator, the tale tells of the pre-war, the Holocaust, and the post-Shoah life of Rosa Lublin, the daughter of a cultured and assimilated Jewish family in Poland. The opening of the tale is jarring and unexpected: "Stella, Rosa's teenaged niece, is cold, cold, the coldness of hell." In the brief space of ten pages, Ozick focuses on Rosa's failed attempt to protect her infant daughter, Magda, and her suspicion of her niece, Stella, whom she imagines as having cannibalistic intentions toward Magda. Ozick brilliantly renders the "choiceless choice" of Jewish mothers both in the deportation experience and in the death camps. Amidst the frozen landscape, Rosa is unable to suckle Magda, the mother's dried-up nipple is a "dead volcano . . . a chill hole" (p. 4). She wraps the young child in a "magic" shawl, a corner of which Magda sucks and "milked it instead" (p. 4); the smell of "cinnamon and almonds" (p. 5) emanated from Magda's tiny mouth.

Although the nurturing shawl helped sustain Magda, Rosa knows that when her daughter begins to walk, the little girl is "going to die very soon" (p. 6). Rosa, who "slept with the weight of her thigh on Magda's body," was afraid that she would smother the child. Owing to the deprivations of the camp, Rosa was growing thinner. "Rosa and Stella," writes Ozick, "were slowly turning into air." The shawl, which "was Magda's own baby" (p. 15), kept her alive. It has been interpreted as a symbolic tallis (prayer shawl) which protects both Magda and Rosa (Berger, p. 53). Separated from the shawl, Magda dies. The child is lifted into the air by a German guard and hurled against the electrified fence. Magda "looked like a butterfly touching a silver vine" (p. 9). The fence's electric voices began to chatter wildly, "Maamaa, maaamaaa," in mimesis of Magda's only words uttered in the "ash-stippled wind."

Seeing her child thrown against the fence, Rosa stuffs the shawl in her own mouth "until she was swallowing up the wolf's screech [ascending now through the ladder of her skeleton] and tasting the cinnamon and almond depth of Magda's saliva" (p. 10). Had she reacted to her child's murder, she herself would have been executed as Nazism decreed that having a child in the camps was a capital offense. Rosa physically survives, but she blames Stella for Magda's death and veritably worships the shawl.

Thirty-five years later, the reader discovers that Rosa lives in Brooklyn with her niece Stella, whom she calls "the Angel of Death" because the niece insists on facing the truth that Magda is dead, and owns an antique/junk shop. Rosa protests her customers' indifference to the Holocaust by destroying her store with a hammer. Protesting indifference has both biblical and Holocaust roots. From Jeremiah to Shmuel Zygelbaum, a Jewish member of the Polish government in exile in London, Jews have protested either by smashing flasks or committing suicide.

Rosa is spared legal action when Stella convinces the authorities to permit her aunt to go to Florida where she can recover from her "nervous breakdown." Miami's heat contrasts with the Shoah's coldness. In Miami Rosa meets Shimon Persky, a refugee and a commoner, also from Warsaw. Distinguishing between them, Rosa tells him, "My Warsaw is not your Warsaw" (p. 19). Persky, seeking to penetrate Rosa's aristocratic and somewhat anti-Semitic attitude, retorts that it does not matter as long as "your Miami, Florida, is my Miami, Florida" (p. 19). Florida is not much better than Brooklyn. Rosa sees what she deems sexual perversion in the form of a homosexual beach surrounded by barbed wire. Certain that "only Nazi's catch innocent people behind barbed wire," she accuses the Jewish manager of being a Nazi and an SS man. Ozick also critiques those who would reduce the enormity of Holocaust survivors' suffering by introducing the figure of Dr. Tree who believed that certain camp inmates emulated the Buddhist ideal of non-craving and non-attachment. In reality, Tree's book, *Repressed Animation*, had totally misunderstood the *Muselmänner*, camp inmates who had lost the will to live.

Rosa tells Persky that her life was divided into three parts—the life before, our real life; the life after, which is a joke; and the life during—only this life stays. Both Stella and Persky insist Rosa cannot live in the past. She must abandon her fantasies, such as imagining different career paths for the long dead Magda, who was conceived when a German raped Rosa. At the end of the novel, Rosa permits Persky to see Magda's shawl. She then wraps the shawl around the telephone and begins "speaking" to Magda. Finally, Rosa unwraps the shawl causing Magda's voice to disappear: "Shy, she ran from Persky. Magda was away" (p. 70).

Ozick's literary response to the Holocaust is both a striving to protect history from the incursions of literature, and a recognition that Jews are summoned to respond to the Shoah. The author's own method in writing about the Holocaust is ably summarized in the following: "Ozick's response to the Holocaust combines fragmentation and completion into an experimental narrative shape" (Gottfried, p. 40). Ozick's work challenges the reader to confront the fact that literature has a moral purpose especially after Auschwitz.

SELECTED WORKS BY THE AUTHOR

Art & Ardor. New York: E.P. Dutton, 1984; *The Cannibal Galaxy.* New York: Alfred Knopf, 1983; "Debate: Ozick vs. Schulweis," *Moment*, May/June 1976, 77; *Fame & Folly.* New York: Vintage, 1997; *Levitation: Five Fictions.* Alfred A. Knopf, 1982; *The Messiah of Stockholm.* New York: Alfred A. Knopf, 1987; *Metaphor & Memory.* New York: Alfred A. Knopf, 1989; *The Pagan Rabbi and Other Stories.* New York: Schocken Books, 1976; *Quarrel & Quandary.* New York: Alfred A. Knopf, 2000; *The Shawl.* New York: Vintage, 1990; *Trust.* New York: E.P. Dutton, 1966; "The Use of Legend: Elie Wiesel as Tsaddik," *Congress Bi-Weekly*, June 9, 1969: 6.

FOR FURTHER READING

Berger, Alan L., *Crisis and Covenant: The Holocaust in American Jewish Fiction.* New York: SUNY Press, 1985; Cohen, Sarah Blacher, *Cynthia Ozick's Comic Art: From Levity to Liturgy.* Bloomington: Indiana University Press, 1994; Gottfried, Amy, "Fragmented Art and the Liturgical Community of the Dead in Cynthia Ozick's *The Shawl.*" In *New Voices in an Old Tradition, 1994 Annual, Studies in American Jewish Literature*, vol. 13, 39–51; Haberman, Joshua

O., *The God I Believe In*. New York: Free Press, 1994; Klingenstein, Susanne, "Hard for a Goy to Make Out"? Thoughts About Cynthia Ozick's "Bloodshed." In *Modern Jewish Studies Annual* 10 (Yiddish 10.4), 1997; Kauvar, Elaine M., *A Cynthia Ozick Reader*. Bloomington: Indiana University Press, 1996; Kremer, S. Lillian, *Witness Through the Imagination*. Detroit: Wayne State University Press, 1989.

Alan L. Berger

P

Pagis, Dan (1930–1986)

Dan Pagis is one of the most prominent Holocaust poets whoever wrote in the Hebrew language. The Shoah emerges in Pagis's third collection of poems titled *Gilgul*, 1970 (Transformation). His lucid, non-melodramatic tone reflects his attempts to transcend horror through a clarity of imagery. A purity engulfs his poetry, largely as a result of its ultimate attempt not to obfuscate language. Pagis is not a "confessional" poet. Often he resorts to archetypes and places them in a contemporary situation: (e.g., Eve and her son Abel in a sealed freight car on their way to extermination). Through allusions to early texts he combined past and present into a moving poetic fabric. Time is a major element in Pagis's poetry and he related to it as a constant in a variety of modes. He referred to life pulsating between his temples—the brain and cranium as a black hole in space, the locus of mystery and the inscrutable.

Pagis was born in Bukovina, Romania, in 1930. His childhood was abruptly terminated by the outbreak of World War II, during which he was interned for several years in Auschwitz. He arrived in Israel in 1946 and became a teacher in a kibbutz. He later earned his Ph.D. from the Hebrew University in Jerusalem, where he ultimately became one of the most prominent professors of Hebrew medieval literature. His publications include poetry, major studies on the aesthetics of medieval poetry, and a critical edition of David Vogel's collected verse. Vogel, an important modernist Hebrew poet, was deported to a death camp and was never heard from again. Pagis died in Jerusalem in 1986.

Pagis's poetry is tight and pure, almost antithetical to his chaotic childhood. His poetry may ultimately be regarded as a combination of memory, myth, history, and culture, tinged by a very ironic, wry tone.

Pagis's verse reflects one of the persistent fears of humanity, namely, that of being forgotten, of being eradicated from life and memory. Philosophical themes reminiscent of Jean-Paul Sartre appear throughout Pagis's work. The negation of being is presented in an ironic, almost whimsical way. Occasionally the world appears as a skull, the ultimate site of human consciousness, and the eyes are the two wounds through which a man peers at the world. Those images in their existential modernity are reminiscent of images in the poetry of the medieval Hebrew poet Shlomo Ibn Gabirol.

Pagis's richness as a poet and versatility allowed him to bring forth classical Hebrew motifs and myths, like the Akeda (the Binding of Isaac), as well as various physiological images. His poetry is not purely descriptive; indeed, irony and whimsicality (it may be argued, in the tradition of some Central European poets) exists in his poems. Indeed an affinity exists between his poetry and the poetry of another

Bukovina-born poet, Paul Celan.* Pagis returns to Shoah themes in his collection *Milim Nirdafot,* 1982) (Persecuted words).

For Pagis language is an object of fascination. On his deathbed he completed a book about the riddle in medieval and Renaissance Hebrew poetry. A keen surveyor of the maps of words, his last book of poems reverts to poetry in the form of prose.

Time and death are conjoined in Pagis's poetry. How does a poet grapple with the theme of the Shoah? This open question takes a variety of forms of expression. Conceptualization and representation lie at the heart of every aesthetic endeavor, Pagis finds poetry as a vehicle for his role as a witness—a witness that paradoxically avoids the confessional mode.

In his poetry we all are transformations of Adam. We are one and not many. Pagis's speaker in his poem "Autobiography" in *Selected Poems* identifies ironically with Abel, the one who invented silence, the first human victim. In this poem the forces of Cain are gathering strength on the face of the earth, while numerically, the numbers of Abel's forces underneath the face of the earth multiply. The story of the first family in the book of Genesis has an almost prescriptive tone in Pagis's poetry, exploring human experience from the archetype, through the genealogy of the primordial family.

Pagis, a great scholar, applied images from canonic literature; the Bible, the Talmud, and medieval Hebrew poetry are deftly incorporated in profound and important work. "Written in Pencil in the Sealed Railway-Car" in *Selected Poems* captures at once the sense of modernity and the canonical which are at the heart of Pagis's work. It is written in the persona of Eve, who is trapped in a train car with her son Abel. The poem ends with a gaping hole in the soul. Eve addresses the reader and says that, if the reader should see her other son, Cain, "tell him that I . . . " (*Points of Departure,* translated by Stephen Mitchell, p. 23).

SELECTED WORKS BY THE AUTHOR
Gilgul. Ramat Gan: Masadah, 1970; *Milim Nirdafot.* Tel Aviv: Hakibbutz Hameuchad, 1982; *Points of Departure.* Trans. Stephen Mitchell. Philadelphia: Jewish Publication Society, 1981; *Selected Poems.* Trans. Stephen Mitchell. Oxford, England: Carcanet, 1972; *The Selected Poems of Dan Pagis.* Trans. Stephen Mitchell. Berkeley: University of California Press, 1996; *Variable Directions: The Selected Poetry of Dan Pagis.* Trans. Stephen Mitchell. San Francisco: North Point, 1989.

Gila Ramras-Rauch

Piercy, Marge (1936–)

Gone to Soldiers (1987) by American-born Marge Piercy is one of the most striking novels written about the Holocaust. The novel treats the Holocaust in the context of the world at war, integrating documentary evidence within a fictional context. Through juxtaposition of varied narrative modes, including refugee interview, diary, journalistic report, dramatic conflict, and dream fantasy, Piercy dissolved the boundaries between discourses to create an epic novel of monumental scope and vision encompassing the European and the Pacific theaters of war, as well as the American home front.

Born in 1936, Piercy was deeply affected during her childhood by her grandmother's and mother's response to Holocaust coverage in the Jewish press, by their realization "that Jews were being rounded up, put in camps, and that many were being killed" (Dark Thread, p. 173). Her marriage to a French Jew, whose family experienced the war in France and as refugees in Switzerland, reinforced Piercy's connection to the Holocaust and created an opportunity for her to talk intimately with people possessing direct knowledge.

Composed as a choral work of many voices, *Gone to Soldiers* links the stories of two generations of a multibranched single family, the Lévy-Monots, with the stories of professional associates directly engaged in war-related work and the Holocaust. The strongest, most fully realized character in the Holocaust chapters is the daughter, Jacqueline, who transforms herself from arrogant, adolescent, Franco-Jewish, assimilationist to a chastened Jewish resistance fighter. One of the younger twin sisters, Naomi, is sent to safe haven in the United States, and the other, Rivka, disappears with their mother into the clutches of pro-Nazi French, followed by incarceration in Drancy and then in Dora Nordhausen. The father serves in the French army. After the army's defeat and his escape as a prisoner of war, he enters the Jewish resistance.

Although Piercy dramatized most of the events in the novel, she conveys the early stages of the Nazi rise to power in Germany through a social scientist's interviews with refugees and reports Aryanization and the collaboration of France primarily through Jacqueline's diary accounts. This effective fusion of narrative methods informs readers of occupation abominations ranging from the decree compelling the Jews of France to wear the yellow star embossed with the black lettered word *JUIF* to the roundup and imprisonment of indexed Parisian Jews. Woven between the extended passages recording Jacqueline's responses to specific edicts are brief third person accounts of diminishing Jewish presence in society. The finale is the July 1942 roundup and arrest in Drancy, prior to deportation to Auschwitz, of almost half the Parisian Jews who acquiesced to police registration. Paralleling authentic representation of historic French collaborationist initiatives is Piercy's correction of the myth of passive Jewish acquiescence to slaughter. She pays homage to those who fought fascism in the cafés of Paris, in the countryside hideouts, in Montaigne Noire, in the Pyrenees, and in the torture chambers of the Milice and Gestapo by modeling her characters after members of the Jewish and French Resistance units. The fictional treatment of the Jewish Resistance, derived from extensive historic research and knowledge Piercy gained from her husband's family and their friends, is centered in the Lévy-Monot patriarch's multiple duties as a leader and in Jacqueline's and her friends' work as couriers and saboteurs.

Despite circumscribing her fictional treatment of the concentration camps, Piercy evokes the full range of camp themes incorporating the physical and psychological struggles of prisoners. The concentrationary period is presented dramatically, through Jacqueline's incarceration, impressionistically from the distanced imagination of Jacqueline's younger sister, Naomi, and objectively through the perspective of postwar investigative journalism. While readers gain an impressionistic overview of camp adversity from Naomi's reveries, it is through the dramatic presentation of Jacqueline's and Daniela's experiences that the daily ignominy of being under the Nazi boot is realized. Prisoners are beaten, stripped, tattooed, shaved of head and body hair—each action is calculated to depersonalize and debase the victims. Within sight of the crematoria smoke and falling ash of the Auschwitz-Birkenau of 1944, the women labor as SS leased workers to German industrialists who manufacture armaments or in jobs designed simply to exhaust them.

More so than most authors, Piercy employs the dramatic context of the novel to expose the myriad social and political manifestations of anti-Semitism. Her fiction corroborates the view of historians who attribute the success of Germany's war against European Jewry to the continent's enduring Christian anti Semitism manifested in centuries of edicts, expulsions, pogroms, and mass murders. Chapters devoted to nine of the novel's major and minor characters direct attention to the traditional forms of anti-Semitism that offered a critical foundation and recurring support for Nazi efforts to annihilate world Jewry. Illustrative is Jacqueline's postwar bill of accusation against her countrymen. Estrangement from her compatriots is the result of her Holocaust-wrought understanding that Jews are hated, not for what they have done, but simply for being; that anti-Semites make Jews "stand for an evil they invent and then they want to kill it in us" (p. 255). She now counts herself among the Jewish "we," and the gentile French have become "they" or the "others." The Holocaust and her understanding of its direct link to historic European anti-Semitism has transformed Jacqueline from being a self-denying, nominal Jew to a self-affirming Jew reclaiming her Judaic cultural and religious heritage and to a communal-affirming Zionist dedicated to building a Jewish nation and a secure homeland.

There is broad agreement among literary critics that a major significance of the Piercy canon springs from its union of the personal and the political. Characteristic is Susan Mernit's observation that Piercy "sees human beings as interconnected in a social network, having both duties and responsibilities to one another; and it is this conviction, more than anything, that makes her fiction political." *Gone to Soldiers* extends Piercy's narrative pattern of relating the personal to the political by compellingly addressing radical evil in a private sphere and in the public realm, thereby sustaining Holocaust memory.

SELECTED WORKS BY THE AUTHOR

"The Dark Thread in the Weave." In *Testimony: Contemporary Writers Make the Holocaust Personal*, ed. David Rosenberg. New York: Random House, 1989; *Gone to Soldiers*. New York: Summit Books, 1987; **Interviews**: With Sue Walker and Eugenie Hammer. *Ways of Knowing: Essays on Marge Piercy*, ed. Sue Walker and Eugenie Hammer. Mobile, Ala.: Negative Capability Press, 1991. "A Woman Writer Treads on Male Turf," with Alvin Sanoff. *US News and World Report*, May 8, 1987; p. 74.

FOR FURTHER READING

Kremer, S. Lillian, "Marge Piercy." In *Women's Holocaust Writing: Memory and Imagination*. Lincoln: University of Nebraska Press, 1999; Mernit, Susan, "Suburban Housewife Makes Good." *Women's Review of Books* 1, no. 11 (August 1984): 18; Shands, Kerstin W, *The Repair of the World: The Novels of Marge Piercy*. Westport, Conn.: Greenwood Press, 1994.

S. Lillian Kremer

Pinter, Harold (1930–)

Although not famous for writing about the Holocaust, British playwright Harold Pinter treats the Holocaust in three screenplays, *Langrishe, Go Down* (1978), *The Heat of the Day* (1989) and *Reunion* (1989) and in two plays, *The Hothouse* (1980) and *Ashes to Ashes* (1997). Pinter is a very political writer, as demonstrated by his essays, poems, and some of his plays, and his dramas often focus on characters who are scapegoated and thus mistreated because they are considered alien and different. According to Harold Bloom, Pinter's drama "has some undefined but palpable relation to the Holocaust, inevitable for a sensitive dramatist, a third of whose people were murdered before he was fifteen. A horror of violence, with an obsessive sense of the open wound, is Pinter's unspoken

first principle" (p. 1). Although it is difficult to classify the plays of someone as prolific as Harold Pinter, it has often been written that his plays belong in the category of the theater of the absurd. His plays are rich in metaphor and can at times be esoteric. Pinter does not address the Holocaust directly or literally in his plays. As a playwright intrigued by politics, he dramatizes, through the use of metaphor of the Shoah, his disdain for violence, for prejudice against those who are perceived as different, and for political oppression.

Harold Pinter was born in Hackney, East London, in 1930. His father was a Jewish tailor. In 1939 he was evacuated from London because of the war. The playwright refused to satisfy his military duty in 1948 by declaring himself a conscientious objector. He was awarded the Commander of the Order of the British Empire in 1966 because of his writing achievements. Although Pinter is generally acknowledged a great writer, people are often unaware of his achievements as an actor and director. Pinter married actress Vivien Merchant in 1956; after their messy divorce (she sued on the grounds of adultery) in 1980, he married biographer Lady Antonia Fraser.

Langrishe, Go Down tells the story of a German student who has a sexual relationship with an Irishwoman at the outbreak of the German invasion of Austria. Because he espouses Nazi ideals, he wishes to return home to study in a place where fascist theories are taught. *Heat of the Day* tells the story of Stella, whose boyfriend (Robert) is employed by the British War Office and who is using his position there to send war secrets to the Nazis. Although Robert is English, he finds the answers to his emotional troubles (he has a dysfunctional relationship with his mother) in Nazism and thus embraces fascist ideology while betraying his country. He craves structure and mistakenly believes that he finds it in fascism. *Reunion* tells the story of two German friends—a Jew named Hans and an Aryan classmate, Konradin—in Pinter's effort to dramatize the emergence of Nazism in Germany. Hans believes that Konradin is a Nazi sympathizer but finds out later that the friend took part in the plot to murder Hitler.

Neither *The Hothouse* nor *Ashes to Ashes* focuses literally or directly on the Holocaust. Rosette C. Lamont, in her article entitled "Harold Pinter's *The Hothouse*: A Parable of the Holocaust," argues convincingly that this drama concerning workers in a mental institution actually is about the Shoah; the mental institution is a metaphor for a concentration camp. It must be pointed out, however, that Lamont's persuasive and logical argument that this play is about the Holocaust is, nonetheless, her interpretation, not a universally held assumption made by Pinter scholars. The patients (inmates) of the institution are classified merely by number and are thus reduced to numbers; they are faceless beings who have been stripped of their identities—even of their names. This dehumanization resembles, of course, a similar evil that took place during the Holocaust; the numbers assigned to the mental institution inmates should remind the audience of the numbers tattooed on the arms of concentration camp prisoners, which served as their identities during their imprisonment. The manager of the mental institution, Roote, complains about the heat, saying that the institution resembles a crematorium, an obvious reference to a concentration camp. A patient gives birth to a baby, and Roote demands that they must get rid of the baby and the mother, which should remind audiences of what occurred in the camps. Roote mentions with great reverence a predecessor named Mike, who created a semblance of order and who became a hero and idol whom the people blindly worshiped. Mike can be likened to Hitler, who, like Roote's predecessor, took charge and was followed blindly by the people. The mental institution also serves as a trope in *The Hothouse* because it resembles the Nazi bureaucracy, complete with its bureaucratic jargon, and there exists medical experimentation and torture (the electrodes placed on the head of the scapegoated Lamb). Pinter never shows the audience the mental patients; it is, ironically, the institution's staff that is mindless, like the Nazi officers in the death camps who blindly followed orders, without questioning the inhumanity and immorality of their acts.

Pinter has admitted that he would like to write about the Holocaust but has yet to find the voice that would allow him to address it directly in his plays; nonetheless, the dramatist, influenced by his reading of Gitta Sereny's book entitled *Albert Speer: His Battle with Truth*, penned *Ashes to Ashes*. D. Keith Peacock observes that, in this play, Rebecca's suave former boyfriend, who runs a factory as if he were a dictator, resembles Albert Speer in his refined behavior and in his employment of slave labor (p. 159) in the factory he supervises. Peacock notes that, as with other Pinter dramas, the playwright's references are indirect and that Rebecca might have been modeled after the unnamed woman with whom Speer had an affair in the 1980s (see Sereny's book) and that the references to children being stripped from their mothers' arms might derive from Pinter's viewing of Holocaust films such as *Schindler's List* (p. 159). Pinter confesses that he has "always been haunted by the image of the Nazis picking up babies on bayonet-spikes and throwing them out windows" (Billington, p. 375), and upon reading Sereny's book, he felt the need to write *Ashes to Ashes*. Peacock observes that *Ashes to Ashes* dramatizes "that men like Speer, who are cultured, charming, and adoring lovers, can, nevertheless, sanction the most hideous crimes against humanity" (p. 160). Pinter acknowledges in an interview entitled "Writing, Politics, and *Ashes to Ashes*," that he, like Rebecca, has been haunted by images of Holocaust atrocities and that, although the character has not experienced the atrocities directly, she is, nonetheless, affected by them (Pinter, *Various Voices*, p. 64).

SELECTED WORKS BY THE AUTHOR
Ashes to Ashes. New York: Grove Press, 1997; *The Hothouse*. New York: Grove Press, 1980; *Various Voices: Prose, Poetry, Politics 1948–1998*. London: Faber and Faber, 1998.

FOR FURTHER READING
Billington, Michael, *The Life and Work of Harold Pinter*. London: Faber and Faber, 1996; Bloom, Harold, "Introduction." In *Modern Critical Views: Harold Pinter*. New York: Chelsea House Publishers, 1987, 1–5; Burkman, Katherine H., "Harold Pinter's *Ashes to Ashes*: Rebecca and Devlin as Albert Speer." In *The Pinter Review; Collected Essays 1997 and 1998*, ed. Francis Gillen and Stephen H. Gale. Tampa, Fla.: University of Tampa Press, 1999, 86–96; Lamont, Rosette C., "Harold Pinter's *The Hot-*

house: A Parable of the Holocaust." In *Pinter at Sixty*, eds. Katherine H. Burkman and John L. Kundert-Gibbs. Bloomington: Indiana University Press, 1993, 37–48; Peacock, D. Keith, *Harold Pinter and the New British Theater*. Westport, Conn.: Greenwood Press, 1997; Sereny, Gitta, *Albert Speer: His Battle with Truth*. New York: Knopf, 1995, 91–97; Zarhy-Levo, Yael, "The Riddling Map of Harold Pinter's *Ashes to Ashes*." *Journal of Theater and Drama* 4 (1998): 133–46.

Eric Sterling

Pisar, Samuel (1929–)

Samuel Pisar's memoir *Le sang de l'espoir*, 1979 (*Of Blood and Hope*, 1980) is more than a recollection of the collisions he suffered in Majdanek, Blizin, Auschwitz, Sachsenhausen, and Kaufering; it is a reflection on the future that follows in the wake of the Holocaust. Unlike many other survivors who have recorded their memories, Pisar writes from the perspective of one who has acquired a very broad view of the world. A leading international attorney who works in London, Paris, and New York, he holds doctorate degrees from Harvard and the Sorbonne. Pisar also served as an adviser for the Kennedy administration and the U.S. Senate. Working in the areas of international politics and law, he situates his memoir within those contexts.

Pisar was born in Białystok, Poland, in 1929, where he and his family were swept up in the German invasion of the Soviet Union launched on June 22, 1941. After losing first his father and then his mother and little sister, he was the only survivor of his immediate family. As the war was nearing an end, he and two of his friends escaped from Kaufering and were rescued by the Americans. He was sixteen years old. After living for a time with relatives in France and Australia, he immigrated to the United States in the early 1950s.

With nearly half of his volume dealing with his postwar involvement in international law and politics, Pisar's memoir has a very pronounced orientation toward the future. Indeed, he insists that he writes not about the past but about the future (p. 23). Early in the book he explains: "I feel as though in that indescribable period when

a man-made typhoon shattered my world, my existence, and my mind, and took me lower than the slaves of ancient Egypt and Babylon, I experienced what is yet to come" (pp. 22–23). Near the end of the book he reiterates, "The gratuitous retelling of the gruesome events of my youth has never appealed to me. . . . But when I . . . see mankind heading once again toward some hideous collective folly, I feel that I must either lapse into silence or broadcast to the world my urgent sense of the horrors that threaten to destroy our own and our children's future" (p. 304). Thus framing his journey through the past with a sense of urgent apprehension, Pisar cries out to his reader as a messenger from the future that awaits the world.

Pisar's memory of the concentrationary universe revolves around memories of human relationships, the very thing the Nazis set out to destroy in their assault not only against humanity but also against the idea of a human being. Chief among his own relationships were the ones he lost first, the relationships to his mother and father. Sensing a profound connection to them, he realized that his life was not his own and that he had a responsibility to them to survive (p. 62). In a realm where the "animal instinct to eat" was "the only predominant reality" (p. 59), where "every human tie" threatened to "bring on complications" that could threaten one's life (p. 67), Pisar nonetheless formed very deep friendships which enabled him to retain the traces of his humanity.

Retaining a trace of one's humanity entails maintaining a recognition of the humanity within the other person. Realizing that recognizing and being recognized by the other person is essential to life, Pisar revealed the vulnerability of the camp inmates not only before the Nazis but also before one another. "In this world without mirrors," he explained, "with nothing that could give us even a faint reflection of ourselves, we were psychologically vulnerable to others' estimation of our physical state, and in our camp there was a terrible sentence that one inmate could pronounce on another: 'You are a Mussulman'" (p. 75). In this realm of the most extreme assault on the human being, human responsibility takes its most extreme form: the inmate must be mindful of the look in his eyes as he searches the eyes of the other for the look that might condemn him.

Seeing that he writes with a sense of a doom hanging over the world, one is not surprised to find that for Pisar liberation was more problematic than elevating. "We should be ecstatic, but we feel strangely empty," he wrote. "What should I do? Who was I? I felt lost. Peace had come to Europe; I could go where I pleased. But where could I find a place called home? Where?" (pp. 97–98). In his reflection on the condition of the world after the Holocaust, moreover, Pisar made it clear that not only the "liberated" prisoner but also the world itself are turned over to a fundamental condition of homelessness. The Nazis lost the war, but the world lost its center, its soul, and its future. Pisar remembers the Holocaust to restore a piece of that future.

SELECTED WORKS BY THE AUTHOR
Of Blood and Hope. Boston: Little, Brown, 1980; *La ressource humaine*. Paris: J.C. Lattès, 1983.

David Patterson

R

Radnóti, Miklós (1909–1944)

One of Hungary's greatest poets, Miklós Radnóti was also one of the great tragic voices to speak from the depths of the Holocaust. A number of his poems, indeed, were resurrected from the mass grave in which Radnóti himself lay buried, to speak from beyond the grave. A year and a half after he was murdered, the mass grave was discovered, yielding the corpses of the men with whom he was slaughtered. After Radnóti's body was exhumed, an address book containing ten poems—its pages soaked by blood, mud, and rain—was found in the pocket of the poet's raincoat. Some of these carefully dated pieces were composed during his time in the labor camp; others were written during the death march; the last ones were penned just a few days before his murder. Their rise from the grave has marked an unparalleled moment in history. Testifying to mass murder and the pain of the victims of the Shoah, these poems have imparted new feelings, visions, and textures to the Western literary tradition. Thus Radnóti's poetry, like his life, was steeped in a darkness that wove his life and his art into a single shroud.

Born in Budapest in 1909, Radnóti's life was fraught with hardship from the very beginning. At his birth, his mother and twin brother died. When he turned twelve, his father died, and his stepmother moved with his sister to Romania. He stayed in Budapest with relatives. At the age of sixteen, he started to dabble in poetry, forging legends from his own experience and creating myths about his origins. He chose the tale of Cain and Abel to explain the drama of his birth and appropriated the role of the Hungarian poet-hero, who, in accord with tradition, resisted the forces of destruction, fought for the freedom of his country, and, if need be, sacrificed his life for its sake.

After high school, Radnóti went to Reichenberg, Czechoslovakia, where he studied textile engineering. When he returned nine months later to Budapest, he decided to dedicate his life to literature. By the end of the 1920s, he was a contributor to and editor of three avant-garde publications: *1928*, *Goodness*, and *Contemporary*. His literary activities notwithstanding, as a Jew, Radnóti was not allowed to enroll at the university in Budapest. After several attempts, he matriculated in the Department of Humanities at the Ferenc József University in Szeged, Hungary. He studied to become a high school teacher and became involved in a Left-populist artist organization called the Art College of Szeged Youth. Highly idealistic, the members believed in the humanizing potential of the artistic imagination and regarded the education of the country's poverty-stricken peasants as their highest goal.

Leaving the university with a Ph.D., Radnóti moved from Szeged back to Budapest in 1935. He hoped for opportunities that would both challenge his literary exploits and launch him into a job. As for the former, his desire materialized, at least for a while. He functioned actively in the art scene of the city until the Second Anti-Jewish Measures of 1939 put a moratorium on the publication of his poetry. His hope for a job, however, could never be realized. Because he was a Jew, Radnóti did not find a job in Hungary. He married his high school sweetheart, Fanni Gyarmati, and the couple lived on the meager income she earned as a teacher in her father's school of communication and the little money he made as a translator, editor, and occasional lecturer.

In the summer of 1940, Jewish field labor companies were established in Hungary. Radnóti was called up for three months during that year and for ten months in 1942. His health and frame of mind undermined, he foresaw the coming disaster. Yet he kept on writing lyrics and love poems and continued to work on a series of profoundly moving eclogues he had started to compose in 1939. Like most of Radnóti's poems written after 1936, this series differs significantly from his early modernist lyrics. Seeing the world threatened by barbarism, he summoned the great achievements of high civilization, appropriating the poetic structures of the Western classical tradition. Following this tradition, he produced beautiful, high-minded lyrics, which, he hoped, would counteract chaos and violence and thus bring the civilizing force of art and lyrical splendor to the world.

By the time of his move from Szeged to Budapest, Radnóti had published four volumes of poetry: *Pagan Invocation*, *Song of New-Fangled Shepherds*, *Convalescent Wind*, and *New Moon*. These collections comprise a variety of lyrics swirling around idealistic, socialist, and populist themes, in addition to a number of nature and love poems. One of them, "Like a Bull" (1933) in *Miklós Radnóti: The Complete Poetry*, captures a world, heretofore undiscovered by the Western poetic sensibility: a world in which violence dominates with no hope for redemption. A wolf pack emerges amid an idyllic landscape, while the poem's speaker envisions a bloodthirsty mob and his own death. Indeed, the piece uncannily creates an image that would later become a twentieth-century literary prototype: atrocity destroying innocence, without any indication of purpose or mercy. This

is the first of Radnóti's poetic images that anticipate murderous groups attacking the innocent. It also is the first of the young poet's vow of resistance which resounded throughout the rest of his oeuvre: "Even so will I struggle and so will I die" (p. 16). No matter what the "wolf pack" does, the poet promises, he will always bravely fight against the evil of destruction.

Indeed, earlier than most European literati, Radnóti saw the world threatened by forces other than warfare. In "War Diary" (1936), the hair-raising vista of the mass grave appears, foreshadowing the dam near Abda where, eight years thence, the poet would be buried (pp. 22-23). Indeed, in the fourth section of the poem, the speaker appears as a soothsayer auguring the destruction that would swallow up the poet himself. Projecting mass murder again and again, Radnóti started to call for resistance, as his persona does in "Guard and Protect Me" (1937). His characteristically heroic determination and belief in the redemptive power of poetry also suffuses the last stanza of the "Fourth Eclogue" (1943), in which he ultimately urges the poet in himself to "write, though all is broken on the sky" (p. 84). The last volume of poetry published during Radnóti's lifetime, *Just Walk on, Condemned to Die!*, came out in 1936. The May 1939 promulgation of the Second Anti-Jewish Measures put an end to his publications. He was allowed to publish his translations but no more original work.

He penned eight poems during the time stretching from the German occupation of Hungary until his entrainment to Yugoslavia (March-May 1944). Among them, "Oh Ancient Prisons" projects the shards of the art of the past and bemoans the end of the world as he knew it; and "The Gibbering Palm Tree" revolves around the opprobrium of the yellow star Jews had to wear in public. "The Fugitive" insists on the miracle posed by the blooming cherry tree; and "Neither Memory nor Magic" reveals both the speaker's sense of abandonment and his awareness of the end. And yet, despite his visions of imminent destruction, the poet knew that neither atrocity nor death could erase his verse from the world.

Dispatched to Bor in May 1944, Radnóti was subjected to the cruelest treatment. Yet even in the camp, despite hunger, exhaustion, and maltreatment, he composed some of the most poignant and moving verses of our century. Appearing in the measure and cadence of the classical tradition, the poems of the Bor Address Book bear out a unique achievement in the literature of the Western literary tradition. This notebook, which Radnóti received from a Yugoslavian gardener in the camp, was found by the coroners after his death in the pocket of his raincoat. Two eclogues emerge in this collection, in addition to an elegy in hexameters on poetic memory and the future now lost in the past. A beautiful love poem to Fanni is among them, as well as one on tree roots and the inevitability of his death. The last poem, written in the camp in fall of 1944, "Forced March," imbricates the Niebelungen and the Alexandrine measures and marks the beginning of the death march.

Between 3,200 and 3,600 servicemen in Radnóti's contingent started the trek northward from Bor, near the Bulgarian border. By the time they reached Hungary, the column was decimated. Yet even under these conditions, Radnóti continued to compose poetry, holding fast to the only way he knew to resist terror in the world. A series of four poems carrying the title, "Razglednicas" (Picture postcards), plays out and testifies to Radnóti's experience on the march. Despite the dark visions they project, the first two lyrics of the series still glimmer, even though only for a poetic second, in the light of another world. The third one, however, captures nothing beyond the doomed column, and the fourth one stares at the grave: "I fell beside him and his corpse turned over" (Radnóti, *The Complete Poetry*, p. 117). A few days after he composed this poem, Radnóti was placed in a horsedrawn carriage with twenty-one of his comrades and taken to a dam near the town of Abda, in the western Hungarian countryside. There he was shot in the back of the neck with the rest of the men and buried in a mass grave.

Such earthshaking events and such powerful tales, however, never stay behind the border of one culture alone. They spread from one place to another, from one language to another, making themselves known all over the world. This is what has happened with both Radnóti's poetry and his personal legend. By now, well known across five continents, they have been retold in scores of languages, inspiring new lyrics and new legends, moving international audiences to the core, and enriching our linguistic, artistic, and cultural experience.

SELECTED WORKS BY THE AUTHOR

Foamy Sky: The Major Poems of Miklós Radnóti. Trans. Zsuzsanna Ozsváth and Frederick Turner. Princeton, N.J.: Princeton University Press, 1992; *Forced March: Selected Poems.* Trans. Clive Wilmer and George Gömöri. Manchester, England: Carcanet, 1979; *Miklós Radnóti: The Complete Poetry.* Ed. and trans. Emery George. Ann Arbor, Mich.: Ardis, 1980; *Miklós Radnóti: Under Gemini, a Prose Memoir and Selected Poetry.* Trans. Kenneth McRobbie, Zita McRobbie, and Jascha Kessler. Athens: Ohio University Press, 1985; *Radnóti Miklós művei.* Budapest: Szépirodalmi Kőnyvkiadó, 1982.

FOR FURTHER READING

Birnbaum, Marianna D., *Miklós Radnóti: A Biography of His Poetry.* Munich: Veröffentlichungen des Finnisch-Ugrischen Seminars an der Universität München, 1983; George, Emery, *The Poetry of Miklós Radnóti: A Comparative Study.* New York: Karz-Cohl, 1986; Ozsváth, Zsuzsanna, *In the Footsteps of Orpheus: The Life and Times of Miklós Radnóti.* Bloomington: Indiana University Press, 2000.

Zsuzsanna Ozsváth

Rawicz, Piotr (1919–1982)

Although Piotr Rawicz is internationally known for only one Holocaust novel, when *Le sang du ciel* (*Blood from the Sky*, 1964) was published in Paris in 1961, Rawicz was compared to Albert Camus and Franz Kafka. The comparison was justified. Exhibiting a technique of his own, he interweaves realism with surrealism, the past with the present, to convey both the cosmic and the individual nature of the catastrophe called the Holocaust. As much as anyone else who has dared to write a "Holocaust novel," Rawicz conveys a profound sense of what it means to be a witness in spite of oneself, a witness by constraint, who struggles to find a medium for his testimony.

Born in the Ukraine in 1919, Rawicz studied religion, Indian philosophy, and Russian literature at various universities in Russia, Poland, and France. In 1942 he was arrested by the Gestapo and endured three years in Auschwitz-Birkenau and Leitmeritz. Upon his liberation in 1945, he became a journalist in Poland and wrote poetry. In 1947 he moved to France to study Hindi at the Ecole Nationale for Living Oriental Languages; he also earned a degree at the Sorbonne. After working as a diplomatic correspondent for various foreign newspapers from 1949 to 1953, he devoted the rest of the 1950s to writing. The main result was *Le sang du ciel*, a novel that won him a distinguished literary prize, the Prix Rivarol. Having once declared that everything after 1939 seemed totally unreal to him, Rawicz committed suicide in 1982.

Written from the first-person viewpoint of a man known at times as Boris, at times as Yuri, *Blood from the Sky* traces the step-by-step path that led to the annihilation of the Jews of Europe. Although the character survives the murder of his people, he is entrusted with the life of a little girl named Naomi for whom he must live, just as he must bear witness to and for the dead. Faced with living for a single child, he realizes that the dearness of what was lost does not lie in numbers but in the infinite dearness of a single human being. That infinity is the infinity conveyed by the many voices that summon his testimony.

Rawicz conveys this condition of one confronted with being a vessel of many voices, dead and alive, by interweaving a multitude of voices within his text. Although the first-person voice is the dominant one, he sometimes shifts to third-person and to second-person voices, drawing his reader into the novel. Indeed, Rawicz's main character reflects his own shifting of voices as an author and a witness, for the reader is told that "when speaking of himself, Boris used sometimes the first and sometimes the third person" (p. 139). Adding to the multitude of voices, Rawicz also makes use of footnotes, making the reader aware of what is happening within the author as he tells his tale. In fact, chapter 17 is subtitled "In Which the Author Speaks Again" (p. 138). In this way he explores—and calls into question—the process of writing as a vehicle of testimony, as well as the process of reading as a means of receiving that testimony.

Accentuating the urgency of testimony in the novel, Rawicz asserted, "Those who lived would *have* to remember. They would *have* to stop others from forgetting" (p. 149). One of his characters, Leo, declares, "The only thing that matters, that *will* matter, is the integrity of the witnesses" (p. 27). And yet Rawicz demonstrated that the integrity of the witness is compromised not so much by a character flaw as by the very medium of testimony, by language. "One by one," says his narrator, "words—all the words of the human language—wilt and grow too weak to bear a meaning" (p. 132). Such an idea, of course, calls literature itself into question, a problem of which Rawicz is very much aware: "Literature: anti-dignity exalted to a system, to a single code of behavior. The art, occasionally remunerative, of rummaging in vomit. And yet, it would appear, *navigare necesse est*: one *has* to write" (p. 134). Silence is not an option for the witness.

To be sure, in *Blood from the Sky* the problem of silence, with its many variations, is a recurring theme. Most notably, the tension between word and meaning parallels a tension between word and silence. "This boundless pool of silence within a single human being," wrote Rawicz, "would catch at one's throat" (p. 211). For Rawicz, that silence is not an emptiness; on the contrary, that silence does battle with the emptiness of words, but not without paying a price—not without obscuring the presence of silence, or a silent presence. Hence Boris wonders whether "our only real betrayal is the one we commit against silence" (p. 295). And what abides in the silence within? The other human being—the silenced human being, that is, the *murdered* human being—who calls the author to the witness stand, just as the author Rawicz summons the reader. Thus one cannot be a silent reader of Rawicz's novel without being implicated by silence.

SELECTED WORKS BY THE AUTHOR
Bloc-notes d'un contre-revolutionaire ou la Guele de bois. Paris: Gallimard, 1969; *Blood from the Sky*. Trans. Peter Wiles. New York: Harcourt, Brace and World, 1964.

FOR FURTHER READING
Rudolf, Anthony, *Engraved in the Flesh: Piotr Rawicz and His Novel* Blood from the Sky. London: Menard Press, 1996.

David Patterson

Reiss, Johanna de Leeuw (1932–)

Johanna de Leeuw Reiss's award-winning autobiographical novel *The Upstairs Room* (1972) is a moving account of the plight of hidden children in Holland as seen through the eyes of Annie, the novel's young protagonist who, along with her teenaged sister, Sini, spends two and one-half years in concealment. As the German noose tightened around the necks of the Dutch Jews, the family became increasingly isolated. Annie's father was not allowed to do business, and her oldest sister, Rachel, was fired from her teaching position. The-eight-year-old Annie felt the impact in a different way; her best friend refused to sit next to her in school because she was Jewish. "Why," she wonders, "was I Jewish anyway?" (p. 9). After disguising themselves to escape detection, Annie and Sini were sent into hiding. Reiss's work also reveals the fear and courage of the Oosterveld family in whose upstairs room the two young girls lived.

The author, the youngest of three sisters, was born in Winterswijk, Holland, in 1932. Their father, Ies, was a cattle dealer. Sophie, the girls' mother, died shortly after Annie and Sini left their home. Following the war, Reiss attended high school and college in Holland. After graduating, she taught elementary school for several years. Johanna Reiss then came to the United States. She has been a consulting editor for Atlas magazine. She and her family live in New York City and regularly visit the Oostervelds in Holland. Among the awards received by *The Upstairs Room* are the following: Newbery Honor Book (1973); Notable Children's Books of 1971–1975 (ALA); Outstanding Children's Books of 1972 (NYT); Jane Addams Award Honor Book (1973); and the Buxtehude Bulla Prize of 1976 (German Award for Outstanding Children's Book Promoting Peace). The author's 1976 sequel, *The Journey Back*, which describes the post-Holocaust re-

uniting of her biological family, was designated a Notable 1976 Children's Trade Book in Social Studies.

The poignancy of *The Upstairs Room* lies in the author's faithfulness to the perspective of her childhood memories of that time. For example, the Nazis posted their anti-Semitic policies and decrees on a tree in the town square. The author wrote, "The tree had asked for Jewish volunteers. They were the people on the trains" (p. 19). Later, in hiding, the young girl has a "conversation" with a window about the trees whose leaves were turning green with the advent of spring (p. 150). Being hidden meant stifling the spontaneity of childhood. For example, when concealed in a barn, Annie is overjoyed when a playful dog runs in, but when she follows the dog outside, she is quickly reminded to return to the barn before someone sees her. Holland has many German sympathizers [NSBers] "who think like Hitler" (p. 6).

Reiss has painted a vivid portrait of her foster family. Johan Oosteveld, his wife, Dientje, and his mother, Opoe, were uneducated people, but they risked their lives to hide Annie and Sini. Although Johan continuously refers to himself as a "dumb farmer," he is resourceful and ingenious, fashioning a hidden closet in the upstairs room where the girls stay. His wife, however, is very upset because of the danger. Sini senses this and tells Annie, "Dientje is frightened. She can't wait till we go back" (p. 58). Opoe, for her part, is supportive. Despite the tensions caused by hiding, and the difference in culture— initially the girls do not eat the pork that is served—there are also moments of humor centered primarily on the psychodynamics of the relationship between Johan and Opoe. Reiss emphasizes a further difficulty faced by both hidden children and their foster parents in noting that after the war ended, Annie and Sini are reluctant to leave the Oostervelds. When they do leave, Opoe exclaims, "You're closer to me than my own family. What am I going to do now?" (p. 164).

The Upstairs Room raises important questions about the meaning of courage and the importance of compassion. Readers are implicitly invited to compare their own childhoods with that of the author. Annie and Sini were denied the luxury of personal freedom yet had the resiliency to survive. Moreover, Reiss's portrayal of her hiding family reveals them to be ordinary people who acted in an extraordinary manner during a time when Jewish life itself was a death sentence. The author herself observed that she tried to "write a simple, human book," and in this she succeeded admirably.

SELECTED WORKS BY THE AUTHOR

The Journey Back. New York: Thomas Y. Crowell, 1976; *The Upstairs Room.* New York: Thomas Y. Crowell, 1972.

Alan L. Berger

Ringelblum, Emmanuel (1900–1944)

When World War II broke out, Emmanuel Ringelblum was a young scholar and a teacher of social history—and he rapidly became a part of history. Realizing the import of the events unfolding around him, he organized a group of people devoted to recording everything that transpired in the Nazis' assault upon the Jews. Known as the *Oneg Shabbat* circle, the group produced many diaries and documents, one of the chief among which is Ringelblum's *Notitsn fun Vaeshever geto*, 1952 (*Notes from the Warsaw Ghetto*, 1958). To safeguard his notes for posterity, Ringelblum divided them into two parts and hid each part in the ghetto. The first set of his daily entries was found in September 1946; the second set, in December 1950.

Born in 1900 in the Polish town of Nowy Soncsz, Ringelblum worked his way through gymnasium and enrolled at the University of Warsaw in 1919. After completing his doctoral degree in 1927, he taught at a gymnasium in Warsaw until 1939. Ringelblum was an active member of the Labor Zionist Young Workers Federation and was a delegate to the World Zionist Congress in Geneva in August 1939. As Germany was mobilizing, he was faced with the decision of whether to flee from Geneva to Palestine, Britain, or the United States, or to return to Poland. He decided to return to Poland. He began recording his diary on the Nazi slaughter of the Jews in January 1940; for two years, he dedicated himself to the task.

A participant in the Warsaw ghetto uprising, Ringelblum was captured in May 1943 and sent to the slave labor camp at Poniatow. He escaped from Poniatow two days before an uprising broke out in the camp and found a hiding place in Warsaw for himself, his wife, and their son. There he continued his work on a volume which was later published under the title *Polish-Jewish Relations During the Second World War,* 1992. In March 1944 Ringelblum and his family were discovered by the Gestapo; the three of them were executed, along with thirty-five other Jews, in the midst of the ruins of the Warsaw ghetto.

To minimize the risk to himself and his family in the event that his diary should be discovered, Ringelblum often disguised his entries as letters to his father or to a friend. In the diary he refers to the Nazis as "They," to the Poles as "Others," to Hitler as "That One" or "Horowitz," to himself as "Muni," and to the world outside the ghetto as the "Other Side." Although he wrote most of the diary in Yiddish, he often used Hebrew whenever he was writing about something that might be particularly sensitive. Taking up his pen, Ringelblum not only recorded a history of atrocity, he offered a testimony to the dearness of humanity. Evidence of his commitment not only to his work but also to his community can be seen in a number of themes that run through his notebooks.

Children, for example, play a prominent role in Ringelblum's diary. In September 1940, to cite one instance, Ringelblum attests to the devotion of the children to the children, "At the funeral for the small children from the Wolska Street orphanage, the children from the home placed a wreath at the monument with the inscription: 'To the Children Who Have Died from Hunger—From the Children Who Are Hungry'" (p. 52). On April 26, 1941, he pointed out that "three-year-old children are out begging in the streets" (p. 158), and on August 31, 1941, he related the tale of a six-year-old boy who lay on the street "gasping all night, too weak to roll over to the piece of bread that had been thrown to him" from someone's balcony (p. 205). The reader realizes that this assault on the child is a defining feature of the ghetto when, from November 14, 1941, "Frozen children are becoming a general phenomenon . . . children's bodies and crying serve as a persistent background for the Ghetto" (p. 233). Ringelblum makes us hear that persistent crying and the question that it harbors for the world: Where are you?

In addition to bearing witness to the systematic extermination of Jewish children, Ringelblum was deeply aware of its implications. "In the past," he wrote on June 10, 1942, "whatever was done with the grownups, the children were always permitted to live—so that they might be converted to the Christian faith. . . . But the Hitlerian beast is quite different. It would devour the dearest of us, those who arouse the greatest compassion—our innocent children" (pp. 293–94). Ringelblum helps his reader to see that the holiness that manifests itself through the child is precisely what the Nazis would exterminate from the world. In Jewish life and tradition, the human image that most closely resembles the divine is the child; hence, the bodies of dead children were sometimes covered with posters that read, "Our Children, Our Children Must Live—A Child Is the Holiest Thing" (p. 233). Under the Nazis, the thing most threatened is precisely the holiest thing.

Indeed, although he was not religious, Ringelblum was careful to take note of the explicit attack on the holy dimensions of Jewish being. He reported, for instance, the desecration of Torah scrolls (p. 80) and observed that, when the ghetto was established, the Nazis tore the mezuzahs—small containers of scripture which remind a Jew of God's sovereignty—from the doorposts of Jewish apartments and shops (p. 152). As the High Holy Days of 1940 were approaching, he noted that "in one city They assembled all the rabbis *and they were killed*" (p. 48). Early in 1942, he related, "a group of Jews were locked up in the synagogue until they hacked the holy ark to bits. Heard this explanation: The only purpose is to see to it that no vestige of the Jewish past survives in Poland" (p. 127). And, reporting on the events of Yom Kippur 1942, he simply wrote, "The practice of torturing Jews in the cities on Yom Kippur" (p. 314). The sign of Jewish tradition and teaching—the sign of a Jewish presence in the world—is the sign of the presence of the Holy One in the world. And that is precisely what the Nazis try to erase from the world, so that one could see a relation between the Nazis' assault on the child and their assault on the holy.

Even for one who is not religious—even for Ringelblum—the sense of meaning and mission that derives from a relation to the holy is essential to the labor of testimony. Here one discovers another remarkable dimension of Ringelblum's diary: his insight into the importance of meaning in life and the threat of madness in the assault on meaning. Early in his notes he observes a "noticeable increase in the number of madmen" in the ghetto (p. 21), and the remainder of the diary is punctuated with references to madness and madmen, as well as mad children. Yes, children: "In a refugee center an eight-year-old child went mad. Screamed, 'I want to steal, I want to rob. I want to eat, I want to be a German'" (p. 39). Perhaps here lies the ultimate victory of the Nazi: to re-create the Jew in his own demented, bestial image.

In his effort to dehumanize the Jew, however, the Nazi loses his own humanity, a point that Ringelblum illustrated very well when he related a revealing incident: "A police chief came to the apartment of a Jewish family, wanted to take some things away. The woman cried that she was a widow with a child. The chief said he'd take nothing if she could guess which of his eyes was the artificial one. She guessed the left eye. She was asked how she knew. 'Because that one,' she answered, 'has a human look'" (p. 84). The other eye, the human eye, resembled a dead eye, just as, in the camps, the Nazis manufactured a Jew who looked like a dead person with dead eyes, in the form of the *Muselmann.* Here lies one of the most earthshaking revelations from Ringelblum's diary: in their effort to exterminate the Jews from the world, the Nazis overturned the world to create a total confusion between life and death, leaving no place in the world for either. In the concentrationary universe, the living are as though dead, and the dead are as though they had never lived.

SELECTED WORKS BY THE AUTHOR
Notes from the Warsaw Ghetto: The Journal of Emmanuel Ringelblum. Ed. and trans. Jacob Sloan. New York: Schocken Books, 1974; *Polish-Jewish Relations During the Second World War.* Ed. Joseph

Kermish and Shmuel Krakowskio, trans. Dafna Allon, Danuta Dabrowska, and Dana Keren. Evanston, Ill.: Northwestern University Press, 1992.

David Patterson

Rivosh, Elik (d. 1942)

Although little is known about the Latvian sculptor from Riga named Elik Rivosh or about his diary, he wrote one of the most eloquent and moving accounts of the suffering of Riga's Jews to be recorded during the Nazi occupation of Latvia. The diary was among the documents gathered by Ilya Ehrenburg and Vasily Grossman for inclusion in their *Chernaya Kniga*, 1944 (*The Black Book*, 1981), which is a collection of diaries, letters, affidavits, and other firsthand accounts of Nazi activities in the east. The Germans entered Riga on July 1, 1941; on October 24, the last of the Jews of Riga were herded into the ghetto. Among them were Rivosh, his wife, Alya, his five-year-old son, Dima, his toddler daughter, Lida, and his mother. The sculptor's entire family was sent to their deaths in December 1941 when the last of the Jews, except able-bodied men, were deported from the ghetto. Left alone, Rivosh continued to work until sometime in 1942, when, it seems, he too, was murdered.

With an eye for profound meaning in small details and a talent for understated eloquence, Rivosh wrote his diary in a subtle, literary style. He is able to place the reader in the midst of the events by drawing the reader into his thoughts and emotions. For example, children are slain as children before they are taken away: "One never sees even one child playing; all of them, like beasts at bay, cling timidly close to their mothers or sit in the gateways" (p. 324). He brings out the amazingly common humanity that was lost in the children and their families when he talks about wanting to build a snowman with his little boy or read stories from Pushkin to his children (p. 335). Such images of normalcy, however, are thin veils that fail to conceal something as deadly as it is monstrous.

By degrees that "something" sets in. "The word 'action' was heard," wrote Rivosh. "It somehow passed by us, we did not understand it" (p. 335). Then: "The children instinctively sense their own destruction—they are quiet and dejected, and they display neither caprices, nor tears, nor nervousness" (p. 336). Finally: "In one day puddles of blood have become an ordinary sight" (p. 340). The reader, moreover, peers deeply into the soul of this man when he describes his last night with his family, before being separated into a group of workers: "The alarm clock ticks peacefully, the arrow mercilessly goes its way, the hours pass. Alya's head is on my shoulder. . . . What is going on in her soul, in the souls of the thousands of women like her? No one can know because this cannot be expressed in words. . . . The alarm clock keeps ticking" (p. 336). In the end Rivosh is left alone, one of the walking dead whose assignment is to bury the dead. Relating how he stood with other men in the burial detail and said Kaddish, the Prayer for the Dead, he noted, "I do not understand the words of the prayer, and the meaning is not comprehensible to me. I only know that this picture has been burned into my memory as if with a red-hot iron" (pp. 345–46). Of course, his difficulty in understanding the prayer is not a linguistic one—it is the difficulty of understanding anything when the basis of everything has been destroyed. Thus by taking the reader into his memory throughout his diary, Rivosh brands the reader's memory with his own, so that the words of his diary become part of a testimony the reader is summoned to assume.

SELECTED WORK BY THE AUTHOR
"From the Diary of the Sculptor Rivosh (Riga)." In *The Black Book*, ed. Ilya Ehrenburg and Vasily Grossman, trans. John Glad and James S. Levine. New York: Holocaust Library, 1981, pp. 324–46.

David Patterson

Rosen, Norma (1925–)

Convinced that the Holocaust is "the central occurrence of the twentieth century. . . the central human occurrence," Norma Rosen describes herself as a "witness-through-the-imagination," a role she considers appropriate for the American novelist (*Accidents,* p. 9). Removed in time and space from the Holocaust landscape, but powerfully impacted by its enduring resonance, Rosen's American women of her major Holocaust work, *Touching Evil* (1969), absorb the testimony of eyewitnesses and take that history to heart. The novel is distinctive in its deliberation on American Holocaust reaction and a feminine perspective.

Born in New York City in 1925, Norma Rosen attended Mount Holyoke College and Columbia University, where she graduated with a master's degree in 1953. After working for Harper and Row Publishers in the 1950s, she took a position as a creative writing instructor at the New School for Social Research in the 1960s. She has also held teaching positions at Harvard University, the City University of New York, and the College of New Rochelle. Most recently she taught at the Tisch School of the Arts at New York University. Rosen's interest in the Shoah stems from her 1960 marriage to Viennese-born Robert Rosen, who escaped from Austria in a children's transport in 1938, her witness of the televised Eichmann trial, and her reading of Emmanuel Ringelblum's* diary of the Warsaw ghetto and *The Black Book of Polish Jewry*.

Rosen worked on *Touching Evil* while she was teaching at the New School for Social Research. Set in New York City in 1961, the novel is haunted by the shadows of murdered European Jewry. Jews appear only as imagined Holocaust victims and televised court witnesses. Past and present collide and merge as the novel alternates between diary recollections of 1944—the year the protagonist, Jean Lamb, learned of the Shoah through newspaper photographs of concentration camps—and the Jerusalem trial of Adolf Eichmann, the vehicle for a younger woman's initial Holocaust discovery. Setting the fiction during the 1960s trial rather than in the wartime era is Rosen's declaration that the Shoah ought not be conveniently put to rest; that it continues to influence our thinking.

That pre-Holocaust normality can never be regained is evidenced in the fictive women's obsession with Holocaust thought and imagery. In an act of political solidarity with her European sisters, Jean forswears marriage and motherhood. She takes a lover, primarily because he was a camp liberator, and befriends Hattie in Shoah solidarity. Hattie's response to the television coverage of the trial echoes Jean's earlier reaction to the newspaper photographs of the camps. The pregnant Hattie, like the author who watched the trial during her own pregnancy, takes it thoroughly into her consciousness, senses it in her body. The two gentile women become witnesses for the murdered Jewish women; they empathize powerfully and repeatedly with the women of the camps, Jean with the woman who "was shot but did not die and dug her way from under a mountain of corpses that spouted blood" (p. 221) and Hattie with a pregnant woman on a forced march and another giving birth in lice-infested straw. For these women, the Holocaust becomes the categorical imperative. Holocaust imagery and associations inform their thinking and speech.

The subject of Holocaust transmission attains both thematic and structural significance culminating in a narrative design of manuscript within manuscript within manuscript for subjective responses, complementing the newspaper accounts and trial testimony to convey historic evidence. Jean's letters and Hattie's diary entries reveal the connection between receiving the news and making it one's own. The distance between listening and telling is traversed as Jean's revelatory memory is sparked by trial testimony. Acting both as Jean's foil and as her double, Hattie embraces the responsibility for transmitting Holocaust history to the next generation through her diary, a form that evokes victim and survivor diaries and testimonies and simultaneously suggests how personal the Holocaust has become for this "witness through the imagination." The pattern of transmission is established for another generation: as history has been passed from Jean to Hattie, so it will be passed from Hattie to her daughter. Each woman bears witness directly, Jean in her diary-letters and Hattie in multiple manuscripts for a play, a memoir, a novel. Thus voices of the indirect witnesses merge with testimonial voices at the Eichmann trial.

Rosen's short stories generally turn from the non-Jewish perspective to the Holocaust concerns and impressions of Jewish Americans and Holocaust survivors. She continues to maintain her distance, never setting the fiction directly in the Holocaust arena, yet her Holocaust-haunted characters grow ever more complex as they live with the knowledge of the Shoah. "What Must I Say to You?" in *Green*, "The Cheek of the Trout" (1989), and "Fences" (1986) incorporate a husband-survivor and an American wife, who grapple with Holocaust remembrance and response. In these works themes emerge exploring the impact on Holocaust-era contemporaries and second-generation figures as well as problems inherent in Holocaust transmission. An autobiographical story, "The Cheek of the Trout," entertains the theme of Jewish-German confrontation, as does "The Inner Light and the Fire." In the first instance the narrative is set in postwar Vienna, the city of the survivor's birth and brief residence, where his enjoyment of the city is marred by his memories of lost family and speculation of the Austrians' usurpation of his family's property. The city's history is revealed in its cemetery: grandly carved stones celebrate prewar honored citizens, and modest stones testify to the Holocaust slaughter of Vienna's betrayed Jews. In "The Inner Light and the Fire," the survivor speaks freely about the Holocaust crimes he witnessed both to educate innocent Americans and in a trial, futilely designed to bring an aged Nazi to justice. Here, too, Rosen gives voice to Holocaust-era Germans and second-generation Germans—the elder still harboring anti-Semitic prejudice; the younger, confessing that his family knew what was happening and revealing his own childhood witness of a hundred ghostlike women herded to work. The title of the symbolic and multilayered short story, "Fences," alludes to concentration camp fences as well as to the psychological barriers survivors erect and dismantle between themselves and non-witnesses. Here, Rosen develops the delicate psychological balance of survivors in dialogue and dramatic presentation more thoroughly than she had earlier, and she introduces the theme of Holocaust impact on the second generation.

Rosen's careful meditation about the radical impact of the Holocaust in these works and *At the Center* (1982), a novel about childbirth and abortion told from the narrative perspective of a daughter of Holocaust survivors, has earned her well-deserved critical acclaim by scholars of Holocaust literature, including Sidra DeKoven Ezrahi, Alan Berger, and S. Lillian Kremer, who value Rosen's rendering of Holocaust metamorphosed lives, lives transformed by a malevolence so absolute that it overpowers earlier concepts of good and evil.

Selected Works by the Author
Accidents of Influence: Writing as a Woman and a Jew in America. Albany: State University of New York Press, 1992; *At the Center.* Boston: Houghton Mifflin, 1982; "The Cheek of the Trout." In *Testimony: Contemporary Writers Make the Holocaust Personal*, ed. David Rosenberg. New York: Times Books, Random House, 1989, 398–411; "Fences." *Orim* (1986): 75–83; *Green.* New York: Harcourt, Brace, and World, 1967; "The Inner Light and the Fire." *Forthcoming: Jewish Imaginative Writing* 1, nos. 3/4(Fall 1983): 4–9; *Touching Evil.* New York: Harcourt, Brace, and World, 1969

For Further Reading
Klingenstein, Susanne, "Destructive Intimacy: The Shoah Between Mother and Daughter in Fictions by Cynthia Ozick, Norma Rosen, and Rebecca Goldstein." *Studies in American Jewish Literature* 11, no. 2 (1992): 162–73; Kremer, S. Lillian, "Norma Rosen." In *Women's Holocaust Writing: Memory and Imagination.* Lincoln: University of Nebraska Press, 1999; Kremer, S. Lillian, "The Holocaust in Our Time: Norma Rosen's *Touching Evil.*" *Studies in American Jewish Literature* 3(1983): 212–22.

S. Lillian Kremer

Roth, Philip (1933–)

One of the most celebrated American writers, Philip Roth is known for his brilliant artistic insights into the traumas that have swept through American Jewry in the wake of the Holocaust. While the Holocaust is not often in the foreground of his work, its presence can almost always be felt in the souls of his characters.

Philip Roth was born in Newark, New Jersey, on March 13, 1933. The year of his birth coincided with the beginning of one of the darkest periods in history: Adolf Hitler's rise to power, which culminated in the Holocaust. While growing up in the Jewish household of Herman and Bess Roth, the future writer was fully aware of the threat posed by the Nazis to the Jews of Europe. In the postwar years, as survivors started to settle in the predominantly Jewish Newark where he attended the Weequahic High School, he became privy to many eyewitness accounts of the Nazi genocide.

According to Roth's own admission, the Holocaust helped shape both his Jewish and artistic sensibilities. "For most reflective American Jews," Roth maintains, the Holocaust "is simply there, hidden, submerged, emerging, disappearing, unforgotten. You don't make use of it—it makes use of you" (*Reading Myself and Others*, p. 136). In his novel *The Anatomy Lesson* (1983), the second part of his trilogy *Zuckerman Bound* (1985), the mother of his protagonist Nathan Zuckerman leaves her son a deathbed testament, a piece of paper that contains a single word, "Holocaust." Asked to comment on the meaning of the note, Roth makes it clear that "without this word there would be no Nathan Zuckerman. . . . There would of course be no Amy Bellette, the young woman in *The Ghost Writer* who he likes to think could have been Anne Frank. . . . If you take away that word—and with it the fact—none of these Zuckerman books would exist" (*Reading*, p. 136). It is not surprising, then, that a number of Roth's works reflect upon the Shoah's lessons and legacies, often questioning the nature of the artist's role in shaping a new post-Holocaust Jewish identity, in redefining aesthetic and moral responsibilities, and in finding new ways to commemorate the dead and the brutally destroyed world of his forefathers.

In 1959 Roth published "Eli, the Fanatic," a short story that raises a number of Holocaust-related issues. It concerns the hostile reaction displayed by a group of unaffiliated Jewish suburbanites toward the establishment of a yeshiva comprising eighteen children, a dean, and a teacher, all Holocaust survivors, in Woodenton, Long Island. In their attempt to blend into the non-Jewish milieu of Woodenton and leave their identities behind, the young Jews are apprehensive that the presence of the yeshiva would cause anti-Semitic feelings to surface among the town's gentile community. Eli, a local lawyer and himself an assimilated Jew, is dispatched to rid the town of the problem. Contrary to everyone's expectations, and as a result of com-

ing in close touch with the survivors, he is horrified by the ordeal and the losses they sustained. In an act of solidarity, Eli assumes the identity of the Hasidic teacher, provoking both horror and revulsion in his fellow Jews. Through the seemingly illogical actions of his protagonist, Roth asserts that the American Jewish community commits a crime if it remains indifferent to its surviving European brethren. By denying the survivors the opportunity to practice Judaism and by obliterating their Jewish identity, the Woodenton Jews inadvertently ally themselves with the Nazi intention to rid the world of Jews. If anything, Roth asserts, it is a moral obligation to remember the Holocaust as a way of creating a new identity for the post-Holocaust American Jew. Roth thus rejects assimilation as a viable means of combating anti-Semitism and xenophobia.

Pitting Eli's defiance of his co-religionists' fears of provoking another Jewish catastrophe if they adhere to their identity as Jews against their demand that he do their bidding, Roth foreshadows yet another confrontation invoked in many of his works—that of the Jewish artist and the community of fellow Jews. His often biting portrayal of human shortcomings in his Jewish characters leads to accusations of self-hatred and anti-Semitism. *The Ghost Writer* (1979), his first novel in the *Zuckerman Bound* trilogy, is the writer's answer to his accusers. Nathan Zuckerman, an aspiring artist, rejects his parents' plea to refrain from publishing an autobiographical story because it depicts the family in an unfavorable way. He is also deeply insulted by Judge Wapter's suggestion that only by identifying with Holocaust victims could he use his art not only as a means of commemorating the Holocaust but also as a way to neutralize potential victimizers. To defend the autonomy of his art, Nathan is ready to distance himself from his parents and community.

Distancing does not translate into total severance from Jewish roots, insists Zuckerman; it is, rather, a necessary precondition to write in an imaginative and assertive manner. Furthermore, by writing about the joys and sorrows of everyday Jewish life in prewar Europe, he underscores the tragic enormity of the Holocaust which brought about the loss of an entire civilization. Roth accentuates this sense of loss by having Nathan imagine Amy Bellette, a young Holocaust survivor and Lonoff protégé he meets at the master's house, to be, in fact, Anne Frank. Metamorphosing Anne Frank from a cultural icon into an aspiring writer, Roth endows her with a humanity the loss of which becomes even more horrendous by a heightened understanding of what Anne could have become had she not been victimized by a fascist totalitarian order. The horror of the Holocaust is that a talented girl like Anne Frank had to perish for one sin only—she was born a Jew. Roth, through his risky artistic feat, accomplishes a great deal: he removes the banality and sentimentality, and therefore the distortion, with which the Holocaust has often been treated in popular culture.

Roth's concern with how the Holocaust is commemorated and treated goes beyond the American scene. Roth has often visited the Communist countries in Eastern Europe and has observed how the Holocaust, because of continuous postwar anti-Semitism, was denied its particularity and was folded into the general fabric of World War II. As a result, the Jews were robbed of their identity and the right to their own history. In *The Prague Orgy* (1985), both a self-contained novel and the epilogue to the *Zuckerman Bound* trilogy, Roth has Nathan Zuckerman travel to Prague with the sole purpose of retrieving the unpublished manuscripts of a Yiddish writer, a victim of the Holocaust murdered by a Nazi officer. Upon arrival he is told that the Yiddish writer is not a victim of the Holocaust but of a simple bus accident. The artist, thus, is victimized twice—while snuffed out by the Nazis, his life now serves as an aid to a totalitarian state's criminal intent to deny the Jews the right to their history and identity. In addition, by denying Zuckerman the opportunity to retrieve the manuscripts and have them published in the West, the party officials deny the artist's desire and obligation to commemorate the Holocaust. However, by re-creating the life of a martyred artist, Roth commemorates the memory of the victims.

The assault on Jewish memory and remembrance in Europe reenforces Roth's conviction of the importance of Israel, a state born out of the ashes of the Holocaust, as both a monument to the victims and as a guarantor of Jewish survival. In his novel *The Counterlife* (1987), he presents as ludicrous the idea advanced by one of the characters, Jimmy Lustig, that the constant remembrance of the Holocaust generates anti-Semitism, and that the Jews would be better off by returning to the Diaspora. Although Nathan Zuckerman is skeptical of the nationalist Greater Israel concept promoted by Mordechai Lippman, a Jewish settler, he is convinced nevertheless that only a strong Israel, informed by the memory of the Holocaust, can ensure Jewish survival.

How crucial the Holocaust is to Roth's artistic sensibility is manifested in *Operation Shylock* (1993), in which Roth explores an artist's ability to imagine the Holocaust, as he ponders the consequences of historical revisionism upon the fate of both state and individual when he attends the trial of Demjanuk, the alleged Ivan the Terrible of Treblinka and considers the Palestinian-Israeli conflict through the moral prism of Jewish suffering and exile. He visits Aharon Appelfeld who reiterates his belief that the Holocaust reality is beyond human imagination. For Roth, however, not to have at least tried to re-imagine the Shoah would have amounted to an artistic defeat.

SELECTED WORKS BY THE AUTHOR

The Anatomy Lesson. New York: Farrar, Straus and Giroux, 1983; *The Counterlife*. New York: Farrar, Straus and Giroux, 1987; "Eli, the Fanatic." In *Goodbye, Columbus*. Boston: Houghton Mifflin, 1959; *The Ghost Writer*. New York: Farrar, Straus and Giroux, 1979; *Operation Shylock: A Confession*. New York: Simon and Schuster, 1993; *The Prague Orgy*. London: Cape, 1985; *Reading Myself and Others*. New York: Farrar, Straus and Giroux, 1975.

FOR FURTHER READING

Baumgarten, Murray, and Barbara Gottfried. *Understanding Philip Roth*. Columbia: University of South Carolina Press, 1990; Berger, Alan L. *Crisis and Covenant: The Holocaust in American Jewish Fiction*. Albany, N.Y.: SUNY Press, 1985; Bloom, Harold, ed., *Philip Roth*. New York: Chelsea House, 1986; Halio, Jay, *Philip Roth Revisited*. New York: Twayne, 1992; Milbauer, Asher Z., and Donald G. Watson, eds., *Reading Philip Roth*. New York: St. Martin's Press, 1988; Pinsker, Stanford, ed., *Critical Essays on Philip Roth*. Boston: G. K. Hall, 1982.

Asher Z. Milbauer

Rubinowicz, Dawid (1927–1942)

The *Pamiętnik Dawida Rubinowicza*, 1960 (*The Diary of Dawid Rubinowicz*, 1982) was first published a year after Maria Jarochowska discovered it in 1959 while she was researching war crimes in Bodzentyn, Poland. It is the thoughtful reflection of a teenager whose testimony was literally retrieved from the ruins of his slaughtered community.

Born on July 27, 1927, in the Polish village of Krajno, near Bodzentyn, Dawid Rubinowicz was twelve years old when he began keeping his diary on March 21, 1940. He continued to make regular entries describing the Nazis' gradual destruction of the Jews of his community until June 1, 1942; in September 1942, he and his family were taken from the Bodzentyn ghetto to Suchedni, where, it seems, they met their end.

Despite his young age, Rubinowicz had a deep sense of what it meant to live in a realm that is beyond the protection of the law. He knew that such a realm was not a world but an anti-world, or the end of the world. "I can scarcely believe it," he commented, for example, on the random killing of a girl on April 10, 1942, "but everything is possible. A girl pretty as a picture—if *she* could be shot, then the end of the world will soon be here" (p. 56). For the word *possible* one may substitute the word *permissible*. With penetrating insight Rubinowicz realized that when all things are permitted, the human being has no value: the status of the law and the status of the person are interconnected.

This realization parallels Rubinowicz's recurring concern for his father; he realized that the Nazis' perversion of the law expressed itself in their assault on the father. Dawid spent most of his days in the ghetto keeping a vigil to see when and whether his father would return from various work details. His constant worry was that his father would somehow be deemed "illegitimate" because he could not get his pass signed: "How on earth will he come if the pass isn't signed?" he worried (p. 50). Dawid was devastated, then, when his father was taken to the forced labor camp at Skarżysko on May 6, 1942: "I cried out: 'Papa!—Papa, where are you? If only I could see you once more'... and

then I saw him on the last lorry; his eyes were red with weeping" (pp. 69–70).

For Rubinowicz, the absence of his father signified more than the absence of a person; it was the absence of truth, meaning, and direction, comparable to the absence of God. In an entry dated May 8, 1942, for example, he indicated his efforts to sense the presence of his father in his Sabbath prayers (p. 72); by May 22, however, the longing for his father all but eclipsed his prayers, despite the association between his father and his prayers. "While praying I felt a deep yearning for Father. I saw other children standing with their fathers, and the parts of their prayers that they didn't know were told them by their fathers, and who is there to tell me? ... only God alone" (p. 82). The last entry of Rubinowicz's diary, dated June 1, 1942, opens with the words, "A happy day," because it was the day his father was finally returned to the family. Perhaps with the return of the father he felt no need to write further. And yet the diary ends in mid-sentence, leaving behind an open-ended question in the midst of its assertions.

SELECTED WORKS BY THE AUTHOR
The Diary of Dawid Rubinowicz. Trans. Derek Bowman. Edmonds, Wash.: Creative Options, 1982.

David Patterson

Rubinstein, Erna F. (1922–2000)

Holocaust writer Erna F. Rubenstein's works stress the importance of love rather than hate, and the imperative of tolerance. Her books, *The Survivor in Us All: Four Young Sisters in the Holocaust* (1982) and *After the Holocaust: The Long Road to Freedom*, (1995) are accounts of her survival and its aftermath. The first book recalls in harrowing detail her survival—from the Kraków ghetto, to the Plazow concentration camp, and from there to Auschwitz. Each stage along the road of horror is seen through the eyes of a seventeen-year-old girl who, through determination, resourcefulness, and luck, was able to help her three sisters live through the Shoah. The author's story sheds light on gender issues, and its accessible styyle makes her memoir readable. Rubinstein's life after the war, in which she worked aiding displaced persons, confirmed her commitment to helping others.

Rubinstein was born in Jelesnia, Poland. Her parents, Joseph and Tonia Ferber, owned a dry goods and food store. The Ferbers were one of only three Jewish families in the village. Erna was the eldest of five children. Following the German invasion, her family fled east in a horse-drawn wagon. The fleeing refugees were attacked by Nazi airplanes, prompting one Red Cross worker to exclaim, "This is a civilian massacre like the world has never seen before." The author began writing about her experience while imprisoned in Plaszow. Although the Nazis had criminalized writing, and Rubinstein had to hide her notes, she stated in an interview that writing "gave me physical and emotional strength" (interview with author). Her mother and eleven-year-old brother, Moshe, were gassed in Auschwitz. Her father died of starvation in Matthausen, shortly before the end of the war.

Following the war, the author and her three sisters found themselves in Czechoslovakia where Erna worked as a translator for the U.S. Army. They went to Germany where she worked for the United Nations Relief and Rehabilitation Administration (UNRRA) assisting displaced persons. The author received many commendations for her work. In 1949 Rubinstein and her husband, Henry, whom she had married in 1946, and their infant daughter came to New York, where three years later the youngster died of leukemia. Two other children, born in America, survive. After settling in Syracuse, the author began lecturing and writing about the Holocaust. She spoke about her experiences at the inaugural session of an upstate conference for educators held in 1978. In 1998 Erna Rubinstein received the Elie Wiesel Holocaust remembrance award.

The Survivor in Us All raises important psychological, sociological, and theological issues. For example, how could the Germans so callously murder Jewish children? The author reports seeing such children shot and having their heads smashed against stone walls. Why was there such widespread indifference on the part of so many Christians? And why did some Christians help the Jewish people? What is God's re-lationship to the Holocaust? These issues, overwhelming for anyone, caused great consternation in the mind of the recent high school graduate. Early on in her book, Rubinstein tells of being recognized as a Jew by a young Christian woman. Responding to Erna's query, the young woman says she knew Erna was Jewish because "your eyes looked so sad" (p. 38). Rubinstein reports on the many horrors in the Kraków ghetto including her own narrow escape from being gang raped by German soldiers. Her family was, however, able to sustain each other through their mutual support and love.

On the brink of deportation, the author's father gives advice to his daughters that will prove life saving: "Try to stay together, girls, if you can" (p. 76). Deported to Plaszow in 1943, Erna worked in the uniform factory of Jules Madritch, who was an associate of Oskar Schindler. While in Plaszow, the young girl was "adopted" by the older women at the sewing table. They helped her meet the daily quota of fifty uniforms. The Ferber sisters also shared their meager rations, thereby sustaining each other physically as well as emotionally. Erna met a prisoner whom she refers to as "Mrs. B" who did two things that made an enormous difference in the author's life. She shared recipes for pierogi, and she treated the author as a daughter-in-law, saying to her, "you are going to marry my son, aren't you?" (p. 88). Mrs. B maintained this position even after she received a box of ashes from Auschwitz purporting to be those of her son. Mrs. B, herself, was later sent to Auschwitz-Birkenau where she was gassed.

Throughout their experience, the four sisters, obeying their father's admonition, stayed together. When they were about to be tattooed at Auschwitz, Erna told them that they must each give a different family name so that the Nazis would not know they were a family unit. Moreover, she persuaded friends to stand between the sisters in the tattoo line so that the Ferber girls would not be recognized as a family. Reflecting on her new identity as a number, the author observed, "stripped of clothing, feelings, moral obligations, and human qualities, one was better off being a number" (p. 130). The author reported that, owing to conditions in the camp, women stopped menstruating. This, she recalled, "was a blessing under those circumstances."

In *After the Holocaust: The Long Road to Freedom*, Rubinstein reports on her postwar life. She muses on the difference between the treatment of Jewish and non-Jewish displaced persons. Repatriation trains left Germany daily taking former prisoners to their former homelands. The Jews, however, were unwanted. Like many survivors, Rubinstein reflects on how she survived, enumerating four factors: faith in God, being with her sisters, luck, and some "wonderful people around us."

Unable to respond to her sisters' theological skepticism, Rubinstein reported, "For me there was God and always will be. My own faith was never shaken, even though I couldn't find the answers to my sisters' questions" (p. 36). While working for UNRRA in Germany, Erna met a group of young Polish doctors who were survivors. She married one of them, Henry Rubinstein, the son of Mrs. B.

SELECTED WORKS BY THE AUTHOR
After the Holocaust: The Long Road to Freedom. North Haven, Conn.: Archon, 1995; *The Survivor in Us All: Four Young Sisters in the Holocaust*. North Haven, Conn.: Archon, 1982.

Alan L. Berger

Rudashevski, Yitskhok (1927–1943)

When the Red Army liberated Vilna in July 1944, a young woman named Sore Voloshin went to the apartment in Vilna where her family had hidden their relatives, the Rudashevski family, upon the liquidation of the Vilna ghetto. There she discovered what would become known as one of the most penetrating, most literary adolescent accounts of the Nazi horrors in the east: the Vilna ghetto diary of her cousin, Yitskhok Rudashevski. She showed the diary to poet Abraham Sutzkever, with whom she had served in a partisan unit. Sutzkever turned over the original Yiddish manuscript of the diary to the YIVO Institute in New York and delivered a microfilm copy to Yad Vashem. Excerpts from the diary were first published in volume 15 of the Yiddish journal *Di Goldene Keyt* (The golden chain) in 1953. A Hebrew translation of the diary was published in 1968, and the complete English edition appeared in 1973 under the title *The Diary of the Vilna Ghetto: June 1941–April 1943*.

Born in Vilna on December 10, 1927, Yitskhok Rudashevski was just thirteen when the Germans invaded Lithuania on June 22, 1941. Sensing the gravity of the historical moment, he began keeping a diary when the Germans brought the war to his native city; the last entry of the diary is dated April 7, 1943. Rudashevski's family was forced into the Vilna ghetto on September 6, 1941, where they remained until the ghetto was liquidated on September 23, 1943. From there they went into hiding with his Uncle Voloshin, who had a residence on Disne Street. On October 5 or 7, the Rudashevskis were discovered and sent to the killing field at Ponary.

A major center of the world's Jewish learning, Vilna continued to be a place where Jews engaged in the study of letters as long as they were alive. Even at his young age, Yitskhok Rudashevski was heavily involved in that activity. He belonged to a circle of Yiddish writers, for example, and declared that to the members of his group, "Ghetto folklore which is amazingly cultivated in blood, and which is scattered over the little streets, must be collected and cherished as a treasure for the future" (p. 81). He recorded the establishment of a Jewish historical society in the ghetto on November 10, 1942, "We resolved to learn, to study Jewish history, and to deal with the problems in Jewish history that interest us and can have current application" (p. 91). He was careful to note the literary celebration on December 13, 1942, that was held in honor of the circulation of the 100,000th book from the ghetto library: "The book unites us with the future, the book unites us with the world" (p. 106).

As he wrote his own book, Rudashevski has a deep understanding of the significance of the book for history and for humanity. To be sure, he saw a definitive connection between the status of the book and the status of the human being. Therefore, his book attests to the undoing of the human being. "Into what kind of helpless, broken creature can man be transformed?"

he asked (p. 38). Of course, in Vilna, the Jews were not just broken—they were murdered, primarily at Ponary, and Rudashevski's diary bears witness to the meaning of Ponary from beginning to end. In the fall of 1941, he wrote, "Ponar[y]—the word with a wound written in blood. . . . Ponar[y] is the same as a nightmare, a nightmare which accompanies the gray strand of our ghetto-days" (p. 41). And in one of the diary's last entries, dated April 5, 1943, he noted, "Round 5,000 persons were not taken to Kovno as promised but transported by train to Ponar[y] where they were shot" (p. 138).

Like many Holocaust diaries, Rudashevski's diary chronicles the assault on the holy within the human as it unfolds on the holy days. On Yom Kippur 1941, for example, he recorded the uprooting of several thousand people from the ghetto and added, "These people never came back" (p. 36). The Yom Kippur roundup was followed by one of many pogroms, whereupon Rudashevski wrote, "The old synagogue courtyard is pogromized. Phylacteries, religious books, rags are scattered under one's feet" (p. 46). On Yom Kippur 1942, he affirmed that, even though he was not religious, "This holiday drenched in blood and sorrow which is solemnized in the ghetto, now penetrates my heart" (pp. 56–57). The holiday penetrates his heart because the holiness of the holiday manifests itself through the human beings who embrace it—and those human beings have been murdered.

Rudashevski's youth found eloquent expression in his longing for a place and a sense of belonging in the world; indeed, that was one reason why books were so dear to him. The more intense the destruction of the world—the destruction of the *idea* of a world—the more intense the longing. He saw how ruined lives parallel ruined families, homes, and buildings and cried out, "How much tragedy and anguish is mirrored in every shattered brick, in every dark crack, in every bit of plaster with a piece of wallpaper" (p. 63). As a natural longing for a sense of place, his longing was also a longing for nature. He joined a nature group and declared, "We are not cut off from nature in spirit" (p. 78). In the spring of 1943, the year of his death, he wrote, "I revel in the spring breeze, catch the spring rays and my heart is full of strange yearning" (p. 136). Those who have been young know that yearning. In reading Rudashevski's diary, one realizes that even that yearning was subject to annihilation.

Hauntingly and with terrible prescience, Rudashevski's diary ends with the words, "We may be fated for the worst" (p. 140). The question confronting the reader who comes to the end of Rudashevski's testimony is: What will be the fate of his diary?

SELECTED WORKS BY THE AUTHOR
The Diary of the Vilna Ghetto: June 1941–April 1943. Trans. Percy Matenko. Tel-Aviv: Ghetto Fighters' House and Hakibbutz Hameuchad, 1973.

David Patterson

S

Sachs, Nelly (1891-1970)

The recipient of numerous awards for her literary achievement, Nelly Sachs achieved the highest possible honor when, on October 20, 1966, she was awarded the Nobel Prize in literature, which she shared with Shmuel Y. Agnon. Her recognition notwithstanding, Nelly Sachs could never forget the years of terror during the reign of the Third Reich. Like so many of her fellow survivors, she felt burdened by the weight of the past. Having lived with constant death threats during the 1930s, she still felt the raw impact of those attacks. Yet, like Paul Celan* and other exiles, she wrote in German. This had good reasons, of course. The most important among them was expressed by the German philosopher Theodor Adorno, another refugee of the period, who maintained, that for a person who has lost his country, writing becomes a place to live. Thus Sachs re-created her homeland in her exile in Sweden and felt no particular need for the country of her birth, from which she fled for her life. As a matter of fact, she felt uncomfortable in Germany, crossing its border only when she had to go there. Even then, she stayed for only a short while.

Nelly Sachs was born in Berlin on December 10, 1891. She grew up in a wealthy, highly assimilated Jewish family which showed no particular interest in its ancient roots. The young girl learned languages in school and took private lessons in dance and music. She read books, wrote puppet plays, and composed poetry. Her first published volume was a collection of short stories, *Legenden und Erzählungen*, 1921 (Legends and tales). Neither this volume nor her lyrics earned much acclaim. Nothing showed through in this early work that would presage her stature in the contemporary world as one of the greatest poets of the Holocaust.

Following World War I, Nelly Sachs lived quietly, dedicating her life to the pursuit of literature. Her world changed drastically, however, when Adolf Hitler took power in 1933. Within the next few years, the infamous anti-Jewish measures eliminated her freedom, restricted her work to Jewish publications, erased her family income, and turned the poet and her widowed mother into exiles in their own country. During these years of intensifying attacks on Jewish life and being, Nelly Sachs withdrew from the outside world and studied texts from Hasidic literature and the Kabbalah. These mystical texts, in turn, affected her writing, providing it with religious themes and religious significance. Still, not even her spiritual, artistic discoveries could suppress her awareness of the threats to her life in Germany during the late 1930s or the rumors of the ongoing destruction of the Jews in Europe. Nelly Sachs knew that, unless she escaped with her mother, they would be murdered. But to leave Germany, mother and daughter first had to get visas, which by the end of the 1930s was an almost impossible task.

That they succeeded was the direct result of the work of Sachs's friend in Sweden, Selma Lagerlöf, the world-renowned novelist, with whom Sachs had corresponded for decades. With Swedish visas in their hands, the Sachses secured permission to leave Germany; by the time they arrived in Stockholm in May 1940, however, Lagerlöf had died. Shaken by this tragedy and the strain of their flight, Sachs never forgot their escape to their adopted country. Within the next twelve to eighteen months, most of their friends, relatives, and acquaintances were rounded up, entrained, and murdered in the death camps. Saved from the slaughter, the Saches remained in Stockholm throughout the war. After her mother's death, Nelly stayed alone, immersed in the poetry she composed about the fate of the Jews.

Indeed, as they underwent a change during the war years, Sachs's lyrics revolved around the theme of Jewish destruction. Using concrete images of the Shoah, they appropriated scenes and symbols of the Bible and drew openly from writings of the Jewish mystical tradition. Suffused by both the ancient world of the covenant and the new one of death and darkness, these poems move freely across the present, past, and future, finding cosmic connections among these entities, projecting the murder of the Jews as an ancient element of Jewish martyrdom and possible redemption. Several pieces of her first volume of poetry, *In the Habitations of Death* (1946), summon the horror of the camps, but they also draw on Biblical figures, whose pain and suffering they evoke. Emblematic of this approach is her poem "O the Chimneys," which projects images of powerless and defenseless Jews turned into dust in the crematoria. But the piece also calls on Jeremiah and Job, interconnecting their anguish with that of the martyred Jews. In another poem, "To You That Build the New House," the voice of the poem reminds the reader of the everlasting presence of the murdered Jews haunting even those who would curl up in their warm beds, for their dreams will mingle "with the sweat of the dead" (*Habitations*, p. 5). And in "O the Night of the Weeping Children!," a disconsolate speaker mourns for the slain children of Israel (Sachs, p. 7).

Yet at times, in the world of her work, even in its darkest corners of brutality, images of a mysterious transformation appear. The poem "Even the Old Men's Last Breath" ends with a hint of possible reconciliation, as the poet invokes the image of the last breath of the dead rising "into its Lord's hands!" (*Habitations*, p. 11). When the poem "But Who Emptied Your Shoes of Sand" recalls the ancient pain of the Jews by connecting the present with the past, at the end, the voice projects both the death of the murderers of the Jews and the Jews' return through a mystical divine cycle.

Her next collection of poems, *Eclipse of Stars*, came out in 1949. But as with *O the Chimneys*, *Eclipse of Stars* found no connections to the German-reading public. Most poems appearing in the collection summon a disconsolate, dark realm of anguished myths which chronicle the lives of the Jews beyond time and space. In "Why the Black Answer of Hate" the voice trembles in pain when recalling Jewish suffering and loss over history. And yet again, as in Sachs's earlier poems, remote rays of reconciliation emerge. This is, in fact, what the speaker in "World, Do Not Ask Those Snatched from Death" indicates; for in exile, she says, a friend has been found in "the evening sun" (*Eclipse*, p. 75).

Unknown by the German-speaking public during the late 1940s, Nelly Sachs's work arrived suddenly in the country of her birth. Shortly after the play *Eli: A Miracle Play of the Sufferings of Israel* was brought out by a private publisher in Stockholm in 1950, it appeared in Germany. And it was noticed. Turned into a radio play, the piece became known all over the country. Her new volume of poetry, *And No One Knows How to Go On* came out in 1957, followed by another volume *Flight and Metamorphosis* in 1959. Both collections not only were recognized by the educated German public but also highly celebrated by such leading contemporary writers and poets of the time as Günther Grass, Ingeborg Bachmann, and Paul Celan.

Her next collection of poetry, *Journey into a Dustless Realm*, was published in 1961. Furthermore, she composed plays, altogether fourteen of them, which she described as "poems in acts." With their mystical world and vision of redemption, these pieces have often been compared to medieval miracle plays. Along with her last three lyrical collections—*Glowing Enigmas* (1964), *The Seeker* (1966), and *Share Yourself Night* (Posthumous, 1971)—they show further intensification of her experience of anguish in the face of the Shoah and her spiritual awareness of the ancient tradition of exile, loneliness, and death. Although the language of her plays appears at times more enigmatic than that of her poems, close reading reveals deep-seated similarities. As a matter of fact, the voices in both genres are confessional, stirring, and powerful, conveying visionary nightmares and grief. The lyrics of the collection *Glowing Enigmas* show the world as a dark place, where the exiled and dispossessed live.

Yet despite her vision of destruction, loss, and abandonment—despite her sense of an imminent apocalypse—Nelly Sachs's poetic canvas does not present the universe as absurd, grotesque, or bereft of meaning. Not only does she point toward God's immense presence in the cosmos, beyond his people's suffering and tears, but she recognizes the existence of otherworldly forces, making themselves felt amid the darkness and confusion of this world. Wherever these forces may arise, Sachs's poetry gestures toward an indestructible spiritual reality.

Appreciated, admired, and celebrated by writers and scholars everywhere, Sachs carried the memory of that "darkness" within herself into her last years in Stockholm. Her physical and psychological resistance fading day after day, she became increasingly frightened of the ghosts of the past. She had two heart attacks before falling ill for the last time, only to succumb to death after a short illness. The day she died was the day Paul Celan's body was laid to rest in Paris: May 12, 1970.

SELECTED WORKS BY THE AUTHOR
Briefe der Nelly Sachs (Letters of Nelly Sachs). Ed. Ruth Dinesen and Helmut Müssener. Frankfurt: Suhrkamp, 1984; *Sternverdunkelung* (Eclipse of Stars). Amsterdam: Bermann-Fischer, 1949; *Fahrt ins Staublose: Gedichte* (Journey into the dustless realm). Frankfurt: Suhrkamp, 1991; *Gedichte* (Poems). Frankfurt: Suhrkamp, 1977; *Son Habitations: In den Wohnungen des Todes* (In the Habitations of Death). Berlin: Aufbau, 1946; *O the Chimneys: Selected Poems, Including the Verse Play, Eli.* Trans. Michael Hamburger, Christopher Home, Ruth Mead, Matthew Mead, and Michael Roloff. New York: Farrar, Straus and Giroux, 1967; *The Seeker and Other Poems*, Trans. Ruth Mead, Matthew Mead, and Michael Hamburger. New York: Farrar, Straus and Giroux, 1970; *Suche nach Lebenden: Die Gedichte der Nelly Sachs* (Search for the living: Poetry of Nelly Sachs). 2 vols. Frankfurt: Suhrkamp, 1971; *Zeichen im Sand: Die szenischen Dichtungen der Nelly Sachs* (Sketches in sand: The plays of Nelly Sachs). Frankfurt: Suhrkamp, 1962.

FOR FURTHER READING
Stanley, Deborah A., ed., "Nelly Sachs: 1891–1970." *Contemporary Literary Criticism,* vol. 98. Detroit: Gale, 1997, 320–68.

Zsuzsanna Ozsváth

Samuels, Diane (1960–)

English playwright Diane Samuels is known primarily for her touching Holocaust drama *Kindertransport* (1995), which earned her the 1995 Meyer-Whitworth Award and the Verity Bargate Award for New British Plays. This poignant Holocaust drama is, along with Liliane Atlan's *Mister Fugue*, Lea Goldberg's *Lady of the Castle*, and Albert Hackett and Frances Goodrich's *Diary of Anne Frank*, unique in that it is one of the few dramas that focuses on the plight of children during the Shoah.

Samuels effectively and powerfully captures the predicament of Jewish children during the Holocaust, in particular the painful familial separation and the sense of loss that derived from the *kindertransports*. The drama also is significant because of its insightful psychological treatment of Jewish identity: Eva feels that she must choose between her German-Jewish background (which makes her unpopular and an object of scorn in England during the war) and reinventing herself as an English-Christian woman to escape the anti-Semitism that has destroyed her family and has made her hate herself. Eva's transformation is indicative of Jewish self-hatred, a concept that Sander Gilman has addressed in *Jewish Self-Hatred*.

Born in 1960, Samuels lives in London and writes children's drama. She worked as a teacher in London for five years before devoting herself full-time to playwriting. Samuels also works for Playwrite, an organization that teaches people to write drama. Although her other plays are children's dramas, *Kindertransport* is for adults. She has written other dramas, such as *100 Million Footsteps* (1997), a work about a shepherd who joins the army of children and attempts to save the Ash Mountain from the Great Liars. Other dramas by Samuels include *Frankie's Monster* (1991) and *Chalk Circle* (1991), both winners of the Time Out award for children's drama. Samuels's fame as a playwright, however, rests on the success of *Kindertransport*.

Samuels's play focuses on the *kindertransports* which rescued almost 10,000 Jewish children from Nazi Germany in 1938 and 1939 (the onset of World War II brought an end to the trains that rescued young Jews), bringing them to safety primarily in England, but also the United States. Parents were not allowed to travel with their children on the train journey. During the course of her research, Samuels interviewed many survivors of the *kindertransports*. Her protagonist, Eva, is not based on a specific historical figure but is, rather, a composite of several Jewish children interviewed by the playwright.

Eva, a young Jewish girl living in Nazi Germany, is sent by her parents to England on a *kindertransport*; although they will miss their daughter, they want to ensure that she will survive. Eva travels to England and initially tries assiduously to bring her parents over as well. Although her parents eventually acquire visas, the war begins before they can travel to England and reclaim their daughter. Over time, Eva becomes disillusioned because she discerns that some Englishmen, such as the mailman and the guard at the train station, do not like Germans or Jews. Consequently, she transforms herself, changing her name from Eva Schlesinger to Evelyn Miller (to be considered an Englishwoman) and ridding herself of her family heirlooms, such as the gold chain with the Star of David. When she turns eighteen, she arranges to be baptized. Hating herself because others despise her, Eva becomes a new person and sheds her former self. Samuels thus manifests how some

of the Jews on the *kindertransports*, because they left Germany without their parents, lost their identities and became like the surrogate parents who took them in.

Many of the children who took these trains to freedom never saw their parents again because the parents could not escape from Nazi Germany and perished in the concentration camps. Many children who did reunite with their parents found that the relationships never were the same. In some cases, as in Samuels's play, the children never forgave their parents for sending them away. Although the parents believed that they sacrificed by sending their children away, the children felt abandoned and hurt. In *Kindertransport*, Eva's father dies in Auschwitz, but her mother, Helga, survives and attempts to reunite with her beloved daughter; her hope to see her daughter again one day enabled her to endure the death camp. Helga is amazed to find that Eva, now Evelyn, is afraid of her. Helga chastises her daughter for not moving to New York with her and for shedding her Jewish culture. Eva/Evelyn responds, "Why did you send me away when you were in danger? . . . Didn't it ever occur to you that I might have wanted to die with you? Because I did. I never wanted to live without you and you made me! What is more cruel than that? Except for coming back from the dead and punishing me for surviving on my own?" (p. 96). Helga finds, to her dismay, that although she miraculously finds her daughter again, the girl is now a different person—a young woman who does not want to be Jewish or to be reunited with her. Samuels's moving play dramatizes that although the *kindertransports* helped saved thousands of Jewish lives, the inevitable separation between parents and children often proved traumatic and psychologically damaging.

SELECTED WORKS BY THE AUTHOR
Kindertransport. Middlesex, England: Plume, 1995.

FOR FURTHER READING
Baumel, Judith Tydor, *Unfulfilled Promise: Rescue & Resettlement of Jewish Refugee Children in the United States 1934–1945*. Juneau, Alaska: Denali Press, 1990; Drucker, Olga Levy, *Kindertransport*. New York: Henry Holt, 1992; Gilman, Sander L.,

Jewish Self-Hatred. Baltimore;: Johns Hopkins University Press, 1986; *We Came as Children: A Collective Autobiography*, ed. Karen Gershon. London: Papermac, 1989.

Eric Sterling

Sandberg, Moshe (1926–)

Moshe Sandberg's memoir *Shanah l'ayn kaits*, 1966 (*My Longest Year*, 1968) opens with the arrival of the German army in Hungary on March 19, 1944, and ends on the day of his release from the concentration camp at Mühldorf-Waldlager on April 29, 1945. The memoir is distinguished by the fact that it does not recount an experience of the death camps or any other camps in Poland; rather, it covers three main topics: life in Sandberg's hometown of Kecskemét when the Germans came, his experiences in a labor battalion run by the Hungarian military, and his stint in concentration camps at Dachau and Mühldorf-Waldlager. Sandberg first wrote his memoir in 1955, but he could not find anyone who was interested in reading it until its publication in Israel in 1966. "You spoke," he says in the preface to the memoir, "but it was as if you were talking to yourself, and you lived through it all again . . . so that even after his defeat the enemy continued to do his evil" (p. 2).

Born in Hungary in 1926, Sandberg was a gymnasium student of eighteen when the Nazis began their evil reign in his native Hungary. His father was immediately arrested and sent to a camp in Germany, from which he never returned; his mother was deported to Auschwitz, where she was murdered in the gas chambers. Sandberg himself was mobilized into a labor unit in the service of the Hungarian army; he worked in the unit until November 1944, when he was turned over to the Germans. When the war ended, he returned to Hungary and entered the University of Budapest. From there he joined the Haganah in the fight for Israel's independence and in 1949 resumed his studies at the Hebrew University of Jerusalem. He graduated in 1953 with a degree in economics.

In his remembrance of the work in the Hungarian labor unit, Sandberg emphasizes the ef-

fort on the part of the men to maintain their human integrity at a time when they had more and more reasons to give it up. "Some of the men began to stand out," he recalled, "not because of their speaking abilities or their persuasive powers but because of their honesty and their readiness to help. To give personal example was looked on as of great importance" (p. 37). While giving "personal example" was very difficult in the labor service, it was all but impossible in Dachau. Outlining this contrast, Sandberg brings into focus the essence of the Nazi evil. Whereas the Hungarians degraded human beings, the Nazis degraded the *idea* of a human being.

Upon their arrival at Dachau, for example, the men in Sandberg's group gave up everything they had, "receiving in exchange a number, which was to serve as our identity instead of our name. From that moment we ceased to be human beings" (p. 55). Once they cease to be human beings, they cease to have any human connection to one another; the problem of constantly reestablishing that connection becomes a motif in Sandberg's memoir. At one point, for instance, he saw a man from his hometown and ran to ask for news of his father. The man, however, could not speak—he could only weep. "This weeping, so characteristic of the broken and half-broken camp inmates," said Sandberg, "inhibited any real talk" (p. 66)—and therefore any real relation. All he could get from his hometown friend was a question: "Can you recognize me as I am now?" (p. 66).

Central to the status of the human being and of human relations is the status of food. Indeed, Sandberg insisted, "The problem of food was the principal one in our lives, the central theme in all our conversations, with decisive influence in the relations between one man and another" (p. 88). One might suppose that such a statement would pertain to life in general, and not just to life in the camps; it takes on a different sense, however, in the concentrationary universe, a point that becomes devastatingly clear when Sandberg recalls, "Life became topsy-turvy. It was not the pig and the dog that ate man's leavings, but the reverse" (p. 87). Sandberg's testimony to this reversal which characterizes the Holocaust is a way of reversing the reversal. For he remembers not as camp inmate number 124753 but as one human being addressing other human beings.

SELECTED WORKS BY THE AUTHOR
My Longest Year: In the Hungarian Labor Service and in the Nazi Camps. Trans. S.C. Hyman, ed. Livia Rothkirchen. Jerusalem: Yad Vashem, 1968.

David Patterson

Sassoon, Agnes (1933–)

Agnes Sassoon wrote her memoir *Agnes: How My Spirit Survived* (1983) because "I want people to know that we were not mindless bodies. We may have looked like corpses, but we still had emotions with which to feel and brains with which to reason" (p. 10). The emphasis of her memoir, then, is not so much the suffering she endured as the effort she undertook to keep from being crushed by it.

Agnes Sassoon was born in Bratislava, Czechoslovakia, in 1933. Before she was six years old, Sassoon had her first taste of the Nazis, when Adolf Hitler himself visited her hometown in 1938. His first act was to insist that any Jewish children left in the German schools be removed at once. Soon after her removal from school she, her older brother, and her parents left Slovakia for the safety of Budapest; there they enjoyed a meager but secure existence until March 1944, when the Germans entered Hungary. One day in October 1944 the henchmen of the Hungarian Arrow Cross fascists seized her and numerous other children as they were coming out of their school; many adults who were standing by were also herded into the waiting trucks. Although she was only eleven, she managed to pass for a young lady of fourteen and thereby avoided death. Those who were not sent to their deaths were sent to Dachau.

When the Allies were approaching Dachau, Sassoon and others were marched to Bergen-Belsen. When the British arrived in Bergen-Belsen, they found her lying atop a pile of bodies waiting to be burned; she had been assumed dead. With the help of the British, she was re-united with her mother and father, who had managed to survive in Budapest. After spend-ing some time with her parents, she returned to Czechoslovakia to attend school. There she met some members of the Brichah (the Zionist underground), who helped her to find her way to Israel.

Although Sassoon's memoir was first published in 1983, the manuscript that served as its basis had been written more than thirty years earlier, while Sassoon was still a teenager. The book, characterized by a refusal to succumb to despair, contains the resiliency, optimism, and passion of youth. It also bears the mark of a maturity imparted to her by her experiences; indeed, in Dachau, she wrote, she "felt more like an old woman than a girl on the threshold of her teenage years" (p. 23). Her recognition of the unreality of the camp world, moreover, led her to comment that her memory seems to be someone else's memory, or a memory of someone else—"almost as if it had been an episode enacted by people on another planet. It seems like an eternity ago; another time, another place, another me" (p. 34).

Another sign of her maturity includes her recollection of the Hungarian Catholic priest who gave her group of Jews his blessing and his prayers as they were being taken away but offered "no words of protest in the name of humanity" (p. 19). The unjust incongruity of the priest's robes and his feigned concern for the Jews parallels the incongruity of the massive slaughter of the Jews and where it took place: in the heart of Christendom. Not distracted by bitterness, however, Sassoon remains focused on her affirmation of the spirit's ability to survive.

SELECTED WORK BY THE AUTHOR
Agnes: How My Spirit Survived. Trans. Sylvia Hebden. Edgware, England: Lawrence Cohen, 1983.

David Patterson

Schaeffer, Susan Fromberg (1941–)

Susan Fromberg Schaeffer, a third-generation American, was born into a Russian Jewish family. As a child she knew nothing of the cataclysm that engulfed European Jewry; it was only much later that she became aware of the events that had transpired. She wrote in a letter that her interest in the Shoah arose from her meetings with survivors (Bilik, p. 101)— encounters which became the genesis of *Anya* (1974). Schaeffer, a university professor, has written several novels and short stories. She is also a published poet. Her novels are distinguished by their passion for history and their attention to precise societal details. She uses the genre of historical romance to weave together survivor testimony and the imagination of a non-witness.

Anya, winner of the Edward Lewis Wallant and Friends of Literature Award (1974), is the only one of the author's novels that deals with the Holocaust. It tells the story of Anya Savikin, daughter of a cultured and assimilated Jewish family from Vilna. Anya, the narrator of her tale, speaks with an unmistakably gendered voice. Apart from the 40 pages constituting the prologue and epilogue, which occur in America, the novel's 616 pages are set in Europe. The novel is divided into three main sections—"In History," "Biblical Times," and "The Lion's Den"—which describe the prewar, Holocaust, and postwar experiences of the heroine. Prior to the war, Anya studies medicine, marries, and has a daughter, Ninka, whom she deeply loves. With the advent of the Holocaust, Anya is on the eve of deportation. She gives Ninka to a Christian family to save the child's life. Throughout her many subsequent deprivations and tortures, Anya finds the strength to endure from her determination to be reunited with Ninka.

The novel underscores the devastation wrought by the Holocaust in many ways. For example, Anya's own mother tells her daughter that the time is coming when the living will envy the dead. A psychiatrist at the medical school where Anya studies is thrown into an enormous pot of boiling soup by mental patients. Christian students at the university attack Jewish female students, defacing them with nails and killing some of them. Anya is not a theologian, but she wonders why the Jews have been chosen for such torment. She believes even that the endless persecution of the Jewish people is a form of being chosen.

Schaeffer's novel is powerfully written and underscores two themes: the Holocaust was lit-erally beyond belief, and the loss inflicted by the Shoah was enormous. For instance, after the war, Ninka told her mother that she heard a "fairy tale about cooking people in ovens" (p. 567). History is so overwhelming that the little girl can deal with the Holocaust only by understanding it in terms of a fairy tale. Anya, for her part, has lost her own parents and her husband. She finds her daughter, but is never able to resume her medical studies. Schaeffer underscores the inability of American-born people to comprehend the Holocaust by having Anya tell an acquaintance about her murdered husband. Afterward, the woman asks her how her husband is.

Schaeffer's novel raises crucial questions concerning the nature of evil, the murder of Jewish children, and the presence of a precious few helpers. Anya Savikin's life illustrates Elie Wiesel's* contention that "for the survivors Holocaust continued after the Holocaust" (*A Jew Today*, trans. Marion Wiesel. New York: Random House, 1978, p. 246).

SELECTED WORKS BY THE AUTHOR
Anya. New York: Macmillan, 1974; *Falling*. New York: Macmillan, 1973; *First Nights*. New York: Alfred A. Knopf, 1993; *The Golden Rope*. New York: Alfred A. Knopf, 1996; *Love*. New York: Dutton, 1980.

FOR FURTHER READING
Berger, Alan L., *Crisis and Covenant: The Holocaust in American Jewish Fiction*. Albany, N.Y.: SUNY Press, 1985; Bilik, Dorothy Seidman, *Immigrant-Survivors: Post-Holocaust Consciousness in Recent Jewish American Fiction*. Middletown, Conn: Wesleyan University Press, 1981.

Alan L. Berger

Schwarz-Bart, André (1924–)

André Schwarz-Bart's novel *The Last of the Just* (1961) is a classic of Holocaust literature. Translated into sixteen languages, the novel won the Prix Goncourt, France's most distinguished literary prize. The author's work is a mythopoetic interpretation of the Shoah which combines history, legend, myth, and mysticism, and the role of Christianity in sowing the seedbed of the Holocaust as the novel chronicles the fate of the

Jewish people in Europe. Reworking the tale of the Lamed-Vov Zaddikim, the thirty-six hidden Just Men whose presence ensures the existence of the word, Schwarz-Bart tells the story of Ernie Levy, the last of the Just, who perishes in Auschwitz. The author reveals the futility of seeking to place the Holocaust within traditional communal archetypes of divine justice, as well as the impossibility of finding meaning in the suffering of the Jewish people during the Shoah.

Schwarz-Bart, a French Jew of Polish origin, was born in Metz in 1924. Some fifteen years later, his parents were arrested and sent to a death camp where they perished. The author himself fought in the Resistance, was arrested, escaped, and rejoined the Resistance. Following the war, Schwarz-Bart, who had no formal education, wrote *The Last of the Just*, which first appeared in 1959 in French as *Le Dernier des Justes*. The novel subsequently sold over one million copies. The author and his wife live on the island of Guadeloupe.

At the heart of Schwarz-Bart's novel is the inescapable tension between the divine promise of redemption to the Jewish people and the inexorable doom awaiting them in the Holocaust. In fact, Schwarz-Bart indicts both man and God for their roles in the Shoah. For example, after Ernie's family is deported to Auschwitz, his subsequent prayer to God is simultaneously a condemnation of divine injustice and apparent powerlessness. "If it be the will of the Eternal, our God," he prays, "I damn his name and beg him to gather me up close enough to spit in his face" (p. 321). As for the murderers, the novel's narrator observes, "The Germans reached such perfection in *Vernichtungswissenschaft*—the science of massacre, the art of Extermination—that for a majority of the condemned the ultimate revelation came only in the gas chambers" (p. 395).

The Last of the Just chronicles the history of the Levy family, one of whose members in each generation is a Lamed-Vov Zaddik, a Just Man. The legend of the Just Man, which derives from rabbinic teaching (Babylonian Talmud, *Sanhedrin* 97b and *Sukkot* 45b), was incorporated into the teachings of the Kabbalah and Jewish folklore. According to the core legend, the world contains thirty-six righteous men who behold the Divine Presence. Although the Just are humble, the world exists only because of their presence. They are especially sensitive to human suffering which they take upon themselves. In Schwarz-Bart's retelling, when an anonymous Just rises to heaven, he is so frozen by his earthly contact with human evil that God must warm him for a thousand years between His fingers before he can enter Paradise. Some of the Just cannot be revived. For every one of the Just whom God Himself cannot warm, He sets the doomsday clock ahead by one minute.

Beginning in 1185, Schwarz-Bart retells the story of the massacre of the Jews of York under the auspices of Christian preaching. Twenty-six of the town's Jews take refuge in a tower where they decide to die a martyr's death, *al kiddush haShem* (for the sake of God's name), rather than be forcibly converted to Christianity. "In the eyes of the Jews," wrote the author, "the holocaust of the watchtower is only a minor episode in a history overstocked with martyrs" (p. 4). Thus, early in the novel, Schwarz-Bart establishes the connection between Christian preachment and anti-Semitic action. Furthermore, by taking refuge in the legend of the Just, Jewish history became the story of Jewish continuity in the face of various assaults on the physical presence of Jews and Judaism.

The novel's eight chapters paint an unending portrait of what Father Edward Flannery termed the Anguish of the Jews. Yet the novel is a subtle undermining of traditional Jewish martyrology. Moreover, the author knows well the intramural divisions among European Jewry; he contrasts the piety of Polish Jews and the assimilationist tendency of much of German Jewry. Ernie's father moved from Zemyock, Poland, to Berlin. Born in Germany, Ernie, as a schoolboy, is betrayed by his German girlfriend Ilse who leads him to a trap set by his schoolmates. The German youths attack and humiliate Ernie, pulling down his underpants. In response, Ernie becomes a dog, howling and sinking his teeth into the flesh of the calf of one of his attackers. Ernie "[growled] in his throat like a dog . . ." (p. 263). Ernie's transformation into an animal results in his feeling hate for the first time. Finding himself in a meadow, he crawls on his belly, like a giant insect, and begins to crush a variety of butterflies and insects in his fingers. At this point in the story Ernie thinks, "I was not as Just Man, I was nothing" (p. 272).

Overwhelmed by the world's evil, Ernie attempts suicide. Placing this attempt in historical context, Schwarz-Bart wrote, "In 1934, hundreds and hundreds of little German-Jewish schoolboys came up for their examinations in suicide, and hundreds of them passed" (p. 287). After Ernie's "recovery," his family experiences a pogrom. Jews were not wanted anywhere. The author emphasizes the hapless situation of the Jewish people, calling the *St. Louis*, the ship loaded with Jewish passengers no country wanted, "an ark in the modern deluge." Ernie goes to France and joins the army. In the meantime, his family awaits deportation while imprisoned at Gurs. Benjamin, Ernie's father, writes a farewell letter from the French detention center in which he observes, "To be a Jew is impossible" (p. 315). Ernie leaves the army and enters on a life of profligacy in which he appears, and acts, as a dog.

The novel's penultimate chapter describes the marriage of Ernie Levy to Golda Engelbaum. While fleeing from a pogrom, Golda had injured her leg and still walked with a limp. The couple, facing increasing hardships, including wearing the yellow star, have long philosophical discussions, one of which deals with millennial Christian anti-Semitism. In response to Golda's query why the Christians hate Jews the way they do, Ernie initially responds, "It's very mysterious." He describes Jesus as a "simple Jew like [Golda's] father. A kind of Hasid." Christians, continues Ernie, "say they love [Jesus], but I think they hate him without knowing it. So they take the cross by the other end and make a sword out of it and strike us with it!" (p. 364). Comparing Jesus to one of the Just, Ernie tells Golda that Jesus would explain the Jewish plight to her father by contending that "the Jewish heart must break a thousand times for the greater good of all peoples. That is why we were chosen, didn't you know?" (p. 365).

In the final chapter, Ernie and Golda are deported to Auschwitz. In the sealed freight car he attempts to soothe one of the young children by telling him they were traveling to the King-

dom of Israel. Ernie observes to a physician who asked him how he could lie to the children, "Madame . . . there is no room for truth here" (p. 412). At Auschwitz, the inversion of human and animal again emerges. Seeing a woman prisoner stumble over a suitcase, a German shouts to his dog, "Man, destroy that dog!" (p. 414). Ernie weeps tears of blood, "the death of the Jewish people . . . written clearly . . . in the flesh of his face" (p. 414). As Ernie and Golda approach the gas chamber, he thinks, "O Lord, we went forth like this thousands of years ago. We walked across arid deserts and the blood-red Red Sea in a flood of salt-bitter tears. We are very old. We are still walking. Oh, let us arrive, finally" (p. 419).

Schwarz-Bart evocatively portrays the quandary of post-Auschwitz Jewish religious thought. The past is, on the one hand, evoked as an eternal symbol of faith and consolation. For instance, inside the gas chamber the Jews recited "the old love poem that they have traced in letters of blood on the earth's hard crust unfurled in the gas chamber: SHEMA YISRAEL ADONAI ELOHENU ADONAI EH'OTH" (Hear, O Israel, the Lord our God, the Lord is One) (p. 421). Furthermore, in the instant before his own death, Ernie "remembered happily" the ancient martyrdom of Rabbi Chanina ben Teradion. Wrapped in a Torah scroll the rabbi was burned alive by the Romans. Asked by his disciples what he saw, Rabbi ben Teradion replied, "The parchment is burning but the letters are taking wing; they are returning to their heavenly source" (Talmud, *Avodah Zarah* 18a).

After the Holocaust, is it still possible to believe in a Lord of History? The *Kaddish*, the prayer recited for the deceased, extols not the dead but God: "May his Name be magnified and sanctified." Yet by intertwining the names of the death camps with the praise of God, Schwarz-Bart portrays the feebleness of such praise in light of the Shoah. Thus, the *Kaddish* in the novel's penultimate paragraph:

> And praised. Auschwitz. Be. Maidanek. The Lord. Treblinka. And praised. Buchenwald. Be. Mauthausen. The Lord. Belzec. And praised. Sobibor. Be. Chelmno. The Lord. Ponary. And praised. Theresienstadt. Be. Warsaw. The Lord. Vilna. And praised. Skarzysko. Be. Bergen

Belsen. The Lord. Janow. And praised. Dora. Be. Neuengamme. The Lord. Pustkow. And praised. (p. 422)

The book closes with the narrator's meditation that, even though it is not possible, he cannot help thinking that Ernie Levy, "dead six million times," is still alive somewhere—perhaps as a presence, or as the "drop of pity" that fell from above on the narrator's face. Is the author challenging his readers to keep telling the legend of the Just as a way of continuing the Jewish tradition? Or does he wish to show the enormity of the Shoah through the destruction of that tradition? The author's exquisitely wrought language engraves the dilemmas and questions raised by *The Last of the Just* on the minds and hearts of his readers.

SELECTED WORKS BY THE AUTHOR
The Last of the Just. Trans. Stephen Becker. New York: Bantam, 1961.

FOR FURTHER READING
Alexander, Edward, *The Resonance of Dust*. Columbus: Ohio State University Press, 1979; Fridman, Lea Wernick, *Words and Witness*. Albany, N.Y.: SUNY Press, 2000, pp. 72–77; Horowitz, Sara R., *Voicing the Void*. Albany, N.Y.: SUNY Press, 1997, pp. 168–71; Langer, Lawrence L., *The Holocaust and the Literary Imagination*. New Haven, Conn.: Yale University Press, 1975, pp. 252–65.

Alan L. Berger

Segal, Lore Grozsmann (1928–)

Lore G. Segal's autobiographical memoir *Other People's Houses* (1964) is one of the few literary works that deals with the *kindertransport*, the trains and ships which carried 10,000 terrified Jewish children to England. The author's work is vitally important in revealing the trauma and dislocation experienced by such Jewish child refugees. While these children were not sent to the camps or gassed, their freedom was purchased at a steep price. They were torn from their families and friends, often with little or no understanding of their Jewish identity, and sent out of Europe. From France and Holland, these children went to England. Segal was ten years old when the *Anschluss*, Adolf Hitler's annexation of Austria, occurred.

The author's lifesaving odyssey brought her first to England where her father—unable to adjust to a new language and his own refugee status—died. Before it ended, she had lived in England for eight years (until the age of eighteen) in five different homes. After joining her remaining family in the Dominican Republic, she arrived in America at the age of twenty-three. Segal has been a visiting professor of creative writing and English at a variety of universities. She currently is a professor of English at the University of Illinois at Chicago Circle. Among her awards are a Guggenheim fellowship in creative writing, a National Council of the Arts and Humanities grant, and an American Library Association Notable Book Award. She is a frequent contributor of short stories, reviews, and translations to various periodicals.

The Holocaust unequivocally imposed their Jewish identity on the Grozsmann family. For the first ten years of her life, the author remembers that culture was the "religion" of her family. Her mother, Franzi, had studied at the Vienna Music Academy and Lore was a voracious reader. While the family did observe certain Jewish holidays, such as Passover, their observance frequently trivialized ritual Judaism. For instance, she recalls that her Uncle Paul "wore his parsley dipped in salt water . . . jauntily in his lapel." In England the adolescent girl overheard two patrician Christian women discuss how best to convert Lore. In response, the author became Jewish out of spite. Segal's memoir also reveals the deep rifts in the Jewish community between orthodoxy and the nonorthodox. Prior to arriving in England, the young girl had no knowledge of Orthodox Judaism and describes her discomfort at boarding with an orthodox family.

The author poses important issues for her readers. For example, there is the phenomenon of survivor guilt. Segal was only permitted on the *kindertransport* because her mother's girlfriend was a clerk at the Jewish agency that was empowered to grant emigration visas. "Yes," wrote Segal, "I wonder, once in a while, whose life I have usurped" (p. 239). In her discussion of *Other People's Houses*, Cynthia Ozick* wrote about this type of guilt. She observed that Segal is "saying something extremely complex and unresolved about the nature of guilt and the grief that follows the knowledge that it cannot ever be expiated" (Ozick, p. 90). Segal's novel also underscores the unmasterable nature of the Holocaust trauma. At the end of the novel she noted that she was roughly the same age as her mother had been when Hitler came to power. Although the author lives in New York City, is happily married to a Jewish husband, and is herself a mother, she knows that "this island of my comforts is surrounded on all sides by calamity" (p. 309).

Other People's Houses also underscores gender differences in responding to the upheaval caused by the Shoah. Franzi, a strong and resourceful woman, is the psychic glue that keeps the family together. She cares for her husband who suffers a series of strokes, holds multiple jobs, and still manages to plan family picnics. Furthermore, Franzi treats her young daughter as an equal; sharing her feelings and plans. Lore learns dignity and steadfastness from her mother's example. Yet Segal's novel gives voice to the perpetual quandary of the *kindertransport* children. Her message is that for these young people, having lost the warmth and security of their homes in their youth, they never get over the trauma.

SELECTED WORKS BY THE AUTHOR
Her First American. New York: Alfred A. Knopf, 1985; *Lucinella.* New York: Farrar, Straus and Giroux, 1976; *Other People's Houses.* New York: Harcourt, Brace and World, 1964; *Tell Me a Mitzi.* New York: Farrar, Straus and Giroux, 1970.

FOR FURTHER READING
Berger, Alan L., "Jewish Identity and Jewish Destiny, the Holocaust in Refugee Writing: Lore Segal and Karen Gershon." *Studies in American Jewish Literature* 11 (Spring 1992); Ozick, Cynthia, "A Contraband Life." *Commentary* 39 (March 1965).

Alan L. Berger

Semprun, Jorge (1923–)

Jorge Semprun is one of the major writers, as well as one of the major thinkers, to emerge from the Holocaust. He has made his mark not only in literature but also in film and in politics, having been appointed as Spain's minister of culture in 1988. Unlike most Holocaust authors, moreover, Semprun writes in two languages: Spanish and French.

Born in Spain in 1923, Jorge Semprun's work also appears under the names of Gérard Sorel and Federico Sánchez, although these pen names are easily recognized as pseudonyms. He has not seriously disguised his "Semprun" identity. His biography matches the most dramatic episodes of his eventful times; he lived in the heart of the storm and fully participated in its most violent moments. He fought on the side of the anti-Franco forces in the Spanish Civil War. Following the victory of the fascists, he fled to France with his family in 1939, where he took up residence. He again became involved in the struggle against terror, this time against the Nazi occupiers. He was captured by the Gestapo in 1943 and incarcerated in Buchenwald. It was this part of his life that became the subject of so much of his later writing. His life, and more particularly the external events that mark it, in fact, are the work.

From his teens onward, Semprun has written in French, and, throughout his career, he has oscillated between Spanish and French as a bilingual author. He has written novels and plays in both languages. To some extent, he has been principally known worldwide as a screenwriter, although also as a memoirist. His screenplays include *La Guerre est finie* (1967) and *L'Aveu* (1969). His Spanish memoir, *Autobiografía de Federico Sánchez* (1977), a best-seller, describes in some detail the inner workings of the Communist Party, with which he had considerable experience. From 1943 to 1945 he had been a member of the Politburo of the outlawed Spanish Communist Party. From 1952 to 1962 he became the secretary of the French Communist Party, but he was expelled in 1964 for deviating from what was the conformist Stalinist line. This evidently prepared the way for his admission into the realms of the Spanish establishment following the fall of Francisco Franco, so that he could be appointed minister of culture from 1988 to 1991.

His novels include *Grand voyage*, 1964 (*The Long Voyage*, 1964), which details the journey to Buchenwald in a cattle truck in 1943; *L'Évanouissement*, 1967 (The swoon); *La Deuxième mort de Ramón Mercader*, 1968 (*The Second Death of Ramón Mercader*, 1973), a complicated tale presented through a series of hybrid techniques; and *Quel beau dimanche*, 1980 (*What a Beautiful Sunday*, 1982), which is a novel set in Buchenwald itself. The "Sunday" of the title occurs in December 1944, and the novel deals with the banality of the bureaucracy and the accustomed acceptance of horror. A more recent work, *L'Écriture ou la vie*, 1994 (*Literature or Life*, 1997), is a notable example of literature of the Holocaust. The writer here experiments ambitiously with breaking down the barriers of time and genre. There is a lack of linear chronology, a feature for which the author has been criticized as well as lauded. He mixes his media and does not allow for an easy distinction to be made between fiction and memoir.

It is for this reason that it has been difficult to pigeonhole Semprun. The borderlines between fact and fiction are in any case notoriously hard to determine. It is even more problematic in a case where the borders are recognized as important, but are constantly being shifted. Semprun is both memoirist and fiction writer, but here he carries out this shift within the selfsame works.

Sometimes however, as in his films, a process of objectification takes place. *La Guerre est finie*, the scenario for which was written by Semprun for a film by Alain Resnais, was originally published in 1966. It concerns the activities of a revolutionary working for the overthrow of the Franco regime, and it proclaims as its motto words taken from a text by Jean-Paul Sartre (quoted on the frontispiece of *La Guerre est finie*): "The militant does not ask that his action justify him; he is, and needs no further justification." The plot then seems to run close to the life of the author, but it is also removed from it. The viewer is on the border of France and Spain, moving from one country to the other,

observing a cell of activists, under the control of the party, attempting to stir a general strike in Spain, believing that the time is ripe for the overthrow of the dictatorship there. But there are also many antitheses; for example, France/Spain, where Spain is both a tourist fantasy and a fascist reality. But Spain is also the site where the struggle between Right and Left was played out in its starkest form. The assertion is made that "Spain's become the lyrical rallying point of the entire Left, a myth for veterans of past wars." One is confused by the merging of myth and reality, and it is hard to disentangle them. The love element is also confusing, as it can serve as a distraction from the revolutionary imperative. All must submit to the dictates of the leaders of the struggle, and so other elements, including human passions, are subservient to that. As the hero of the film says, "Falling in love is not provided for in the life of a professional revolutionary." The detachment of the narrator from the presentation allows an exciting plot to unfold in one of the most characteristic productions of revolutionary art.

SELECTED WORKS BY THE AUTHOR

La Guerre est finie. Paris: Gallimard, 1966. *L'Évanouissement*. Paris: Gallimard, 1967; *Literature or Life*. Trans. Linda Coverdale. New York: Viking, 1997; *The Long Voyage*. Trans. Richard Seaver. New York: Grove Press, 1964; *The Second Death of Ramón Mercader*. Trans. Len Ortzen. New York: Grove, 1973; *What a Beautiful Sunday*. Trans. Alan Sheridan. San Diego: Harcourt Brace Jovanovich, 1982.

Leon I. Yudkin

Sendyk, Helen (1928–)

Helen Sendyk, who describes herself as a survivor who was "informed on, betrayed, and psychologically blocked" (letter to Berger), is the sole remaining member of the Stapler family from Chrzanow, Poland. Her memoir *The End of Days* (2000), written both as a homage to her slain family and as an attempt to "brand [the Shoah] in the memory of a forgetful world" (p. ix) in which Holocaust deniers are active, traces the tightening of the noose around the necks of Chrzanow's Jewish population. She also describes the hostile post-Auschwitz "reception" which awaited the town's few surviving Jews. Bearing witness to the memory of her family and, through them, to the millions of other murdered European Jews, Sendyk describes herself as a "survivor of survivors." Hers is an act of sharing in which she invites her readers to be her survivors, and to pass on her story to their own children.

Born in 1928, the author married another survivor after the war, and they remained in Europe until 1946, when they went to Israel where their two children were born. While in Israel Sendyk completed her studies—the Holocaust had interrupted her education at the sixth grade—and worked for the Joint Distribution Committee. The family came to America in 1962. Helen, a resident of Florida, is a life member of Hadassah, Amit, and Emunah, all of which are activist Jewish organizations. In addition, she is a member of the Chrzanow Association. The author also writes poetry and essays which she contributes to *Unhoib* (The beginning), a Yiddish-language journal, and she does translations from Hebrew for the Jewish Genealogical Society.

Sendyk's memoir is a microcosm of what befell the entire Jewish people. For example, she relates the various fates of her family members: one brother died in Siberia, another one— a member of the Polish army—was killed in battle, her parents and oldest sister were gassed, another sister and brother were killed by the Nazis, another brother managed to join the Mizrachi organization and he escaped to Palestine in 1944. The author's taut prose portrays the anxiety, fear, love, and hope felt by the teenager in 1943 as the last of Chrzanow's Jewish population was deported. While imprisoned in the grim anti-world of the death camps, Sendyk keenly observed the psychological and sociological components of camp existence. In writing about behavior in such extreme circumstances, she cast unblinking eyes on the prisoners' responses, which ranged from "ugly words, vicious name calling, and curses pronounced" (p. 198) to "devoted friends, loving sisters, and cherished relatives who cared and sacrificed for each other" (p. 198).

Devoid of sentimentality, Sendyk's memoir is nevertheless especially poignant in describing her relationship to her sister Nachcia, to whom she attributes her own survival. In countless ways, including giving Helcia, as she was then called, the bottom cot to shield her during selections, Nachcia literally saved her sister's life. When Nachcia worked in the kitchen, she clandestinely—with Helcia's assistance—provided extra soup portions to different prisoners. Nachcia's behavior exemplified the zenith of altruism. Sendyk wrote of her sister's action: "the feeling of alleviating the gnawing hunger of her friends helped Nachcia bear her own hunger and torment" (p. 203). Still other prisoners, although not biologically related, "adopted" one another as sisters and in so doing helped each other endure.

The complexity of relationships is a primary theme of *The End of Days*. For instance, Sendyk reports the brutal behavior of the women's labor camp Lagerfuherin. Fraulein Knauer's "punishments were as ingeniously barbaric as the culture that had nurtured her" (p. 207). Mysteriously, one January morning, the woman appeared in sunglasses, which unsuccessfully concealed black blotches on her face. "Puckel" (hunchback) Knauer, the woman's brother, who was a civilian worker at the factory, told Chanale, a Jewish woman prisoner with whom he was in love, that he had beaten his sister. As a Communist, he believed that all humans are equal. Moreover, as a handicapped individual, he wanted his physically healthy sister to understand the suffering of others. Ironically, however, his beating of Fraulein Knauer served only to increase her hostility to the Jewish women, to the extent that Chanale begged him to cease his "counterproductive lessons in mercy" (p. 208).

Theologically, Sendyk's memoir paints a vivid portrait of the tension between pre-war faith and the apparent divine abandonment of the Jewish people. For example, at one point, she and Nachcia were sent to a German labor camp at Langenbielau. Although thinking constantly of their parents and siblings, the girls had heard nothing from the family. One day they received a package containing underwear and other clothing items. No note was enclosed. Sendyk wrote that "it was a sign from the Almighty . . . that someone was alive in our family" (p. 196). In yet another labor camp (Faulbruck), where the conditions were wretched, the author recalled hearing her father telling the family at the Seder table to try to imagine themselves slaves in Egypt. Juxtaposing ancient and contemporary Jewish history, she mused, "Where are you, Papa and Mama? Where are you, Moses and Aaron? When will children solemnly sit around a table remembering what it was like to be Hebrew slaves in Europe?" (p. 178). The author's memoir itself can be seen as part of a Haggadah for post-Auschwitz humanity.

SELECTED WORKS BY THE AUTHOR
The End of Days. Syracuse, N.Y.: Syracuse University Press, 2000; "New Dawn" (unpublished manuscript, 1999).

Alan L. Berger

Senesh, Hannah (1921–1944)

One of the most courageous tales to come out of the Holocaust is related in *Hanah Senesh: Yomanim, Shirim, Eduyot*, 1966 (*Hannah Senesh: Her Life and Diary*, 1972). In addition to the diary of this young Hungarian woman, the volume contains letters she wrote to her family from Palestine, many of her poems, and testimonies of people who knew her, including her mother. Beginning in 1934 and continuing until the end of 1943, the diary of Hannah Senesh reveals how a young Jewish girl came of age at a time when young Jewish girls were being systematically murdered. For Hannah, it was a process that meant realizing her role in life as a Jew, from the standpoint of a tension between the nightmare of anti-Semitism and the dream of Zionism. Revealing a sense of responsibility for people and a devotion to family, the diary is characterized by a profound sense of destiny. "In my life's chain of events," wrote Hannah Senesh in one of her last entries, "nothing was accidental. Everything happened according to an inner need" (p. 131). These words become

especially powerful in the light of the fate that befell their author.

Hannah Senesh was born in Budapest in 1921. Her father was the well-known Hungarian playwright Bela Senesh; he died in 1927, leaving behind the six-year-old Hannah, her older brother George, and her mother. Although she did not have a religious upbringing, Hannah became painfully aware of being Jewish in 1937, at the age of sixteen, when she was not allowed to hold an office in her school's literary society because she was a Jew. By the time she was seventeen, she was immersed in Zionism; she was learning Hebrew and making plans to immigrate to Palestine.

In September 1939, as the High Holy Days were approaching, Hannah set out to make her home in Palestine. She worked on the land and joined the Sedot Yam kibbutz, where she wrote some of her most famous poetry. She felt a growing urgency, however, to do more for her fellow Jews as their plight in Europe became more and more desperate. In 1943 she volunteered to join an elite corps of Jewish paratroopers formed by the British and the Haganah. She was among a group that dropped behind enemy lines in Yugoslavia to rescue Allied prisoners; when she crossed into Hungary on June 7, 1944, she was arrested. After enduring months of torture, she was executed on November 7, 1944.

While reading the diary of Hannah Senesh, one is struck by the parallels between the historical developments of the period and the development of a remarkable young woman. In an entry dated May 15, 1937, she considers whether anti-Semitism has not made the Jews stronger, since it forces them to take on the strength to overcome more obstacles (p. 32). With the passage of more and more anti-Semitic legislation in Hungary in 1938, however, Hannah believes that whatever strength the Jews may have acquired should be devoted to the Zionist movement rather than to trying to live in an anti-Semitic Christian Europe. On October 17, 1938, for example, she wrote, "One needs to feel that one's life has meaning, that one is needed in this world. Zionism fulfills all this for me" (p. 63). After she moved to Israel in 1939, her sense of mission grew even deeper;

indeed, in Israel, she believed, "almost every life is the fulfillment of a mission" (p. 81).

Like many teens growing to adulthood, Hannah endured an identity crisis and experienced doubts about herself in the process of cultivating a deeper sense of meaning in her life. "I would like to know who and what I really am but I can only ask the questions," she wrote on May 18, 1940 (p. 88). Nearly a year later, in an entry dated April 12, 1941, she was still struggling, "I'm filled with discontent, hesitancy, insecurity, anxiety, lack of confidence. Sometimes I feel I am an emissary who has been entrusted with a mission" (p. 102). As Hannah's sense of mission grew, so did her sense of responsibility for the lives of others. In the entry dated July 9, 1941—just as the Nazi killing units were advancing on the Eastern Front—she asserted that she must do something "exerting, demanding, to justify" her existence (p. 105). Therefore she rejected the temptation "to seek personal happiness" and chose to find ways to join "the difficult and devastating war" for what is good for humanity (p. 113).

Indeed, Hannah believed that "the world was created for good" (p. 113), but she understood this to mean not that the world is already good or that people are basically good but that human beings must *do* good. This realization eventually took the focus of her thinking back to her home in Hungary, where the situation of the Jews was growing more and more precarious. "I feel I must be there," she noted on January 8, 1943, "to help organize youth emigration, and also to get my mother out" (p. 125). Within a month of recording this entry, she was training to join a military mission to the Balkans. "I see the hand of destiny in this," she declared about her military assignment, "just as I did at the time of my Aliyah" (p. 127). Hannah's destiny was to die as a Jew—as a Jew because she died in an effort to save the lives of Jews at a time when the world had generally turned its back on the Jews. It was a time when, for all too many, the only way to be a Jew and thus refuse to be dehumanized was to die fighting, as Hannah Senesh did.

Just before she went into Nazi territory in Hungary, Hannah said farewell to her friend Reuven Dafne and gave him a slip of paper. "If I do not come back," she told him, "give this to our people." It was her most famous poem, "Blessed Is the Match," written on May 2, 1944, just after she and her comrades had landed in Yugoslavia. The poem ends with a line that best describes the life of Hannah Senesh: "Blessed is the match consumed in kindling flame."

SELECTED WORK BY THE AUTHOR
Hannah Senesh: Her Life and Diary. Trans. Marta Cohn. New York: Schocken, 1972.

FOR FURTHER READING
Atkinson, Linda, *In Kindling Flame: The Story of Hannah Senesh.* New York: Lothrop, Lee and Shepard, 1985; Hay, Peter, *Ordinary Heroes: The Life and Death of Chana Szenes.* New York: Paragon, 1989; Masters, Anthony, *The Summer That Bled: The Biography of Hannah Senesh.* New York: St. Martin's Press, 1972; Schur, Maxine, *Hannah Szenes: A Song of Light.* Philadelphia: Jewish Publication Society, 1986; Whitman, Ruth, *The Testing of Hanna Senesh.* Detroit: Wayne State University Press, 1986.

David Patterson

Shapell, Nathan (1922–)

Recalling the aftermath of the liquidation of the ghetto in his hometown of Sosnowiec, Poland, Nathan Shapell wrote, "I went alone, into a silence of empty rooms, deathly silence, screaming silence, where thousands had passed through into oblivion only a few hours before. . . . Their screams were stilled, except in my head, where, sometimes, they still go on and on" (pp. 81–82). While the renowned Vladimir Nabokov would have memory speak, for the Holocaust survivor memory screams. Shapell's memoir *Witness to the Truth* (1974) is a skillfully written work intended to transmit the screaming silence that haunts his memory. Sensitive to the relation between the perversion of words and the degradation of people, Shapell is careful with his words. His care enables him to draw words out of the silence with which he collided in the Sosnowiec ghetto and situate them within a life recovered through his act of remembrance.

Nathan Shapell was born in 1922. Not long after the Nazis' invasion of Poland in 1939, Nathan Shapell's father and two brothers made the painful decision to flee, leaving the teen-aged Nathan to care for his mother and two sisters. Drawing upon his considerable resourcefulness, the young Shapell—or Schapelski, as he was known then—found work in the city's sanitation department. He soon won the favor of the Germans by supplying them with scarce commodities such as textiles and meat. His good standing with the Germans enabled him to protect not only his own family but other Jews as well. No Jew, however, remained in good standing with the Nazis for long. In the summer of 1942, Shapell's mother and hundreds of other Jews were forced into the ghetto established in a section of the city known as Targowa.

Shapell's status as a sanitation worker, however, enabled him to move in and out of the ghetto and to help a number of Jews disguised as sanitation workers escape from the ghetto. He smuggled small children out of the ghetto in the empty soup cauldrons. Even these rescue efforts were not enough to save the children. Commenting on one child he set free, for example, he recalled, "In the moment I looked down at her tiny, pinched face and heard my voice telling her, an infant still, that she was on her own, the insanity and depravity of the monsters who had made this moment happen engraved her small face indelibly on my heart" (pp. 75–76). The face of that child is a face that speaks in Shapell's memoir.

Shapell's rescue efforts came to a halt when the Germans began to deport the Jews from Sosnowiec in May 1942. Although he was able to save his mother for a short time, by the summer of 1943 she was in a concentration camp, and he was in Auschwitz. After surviving the death march out of Auschwitz, Shapell ended up in the camp at Waldenburg. On May 8, 1945, the Germans fled from the camp, leaving Shapell and the other prisoners free to wander the countryside looking for food. After the war he established a displaced persons community in Münchberg, where he worked with survivors for six years. In 1951 Shapell and his new wife, along with his surviving brother and sister, moved to the United States, where he became a highly successful businessman. The Germans murdered the rest of his family.

With an ear for the imposed silence that characterizes the Holocaust and an eye for the assault on the child, Shapell understands that a central feature of the Germans' assault on the soul of the Jews was an assault on the family. Not only were children torn from parents but also husbands from wives and brothers from sisters. "The Germans obviously understood only too well the family structure of the European Jew," he observed. "Our family devotion became a deadly weapon in their sadistic hands" (pp. 18–19). Beginning with the family, the Germans tore one person from another, until they eradicated the humanity that lives only in human relations. "People we had known all our life," Shapell lamented early on, "became sullen strangers and enemies who turned away from us in hatred and fear" (p. 50). During the evacuation march from Auschwitz, he recalled, Poles lined the road, their faces distorted not with horror or sympathy but with smiles and laughter (p. 111).

By reading Shapell's memoir, one also realizes that there is a connection between the problem of human relations and the problem of liberation. A key to being released from imprisonment and thus liberated is a return home; only where a person has a home can he be free. For Shapell, however, the return home was impossible—even when he went back—because he could find no greeting, no welcome, that would constitute a *home*coming and announce his freedom. "The impact of my homecoming was shattering," he wrote. "I turned the corner onto Schklarnastrasse and approached the entrance to the building I had once called home, walking more slowly, waiting to be greeted by someone, anyone. No one, not a voice I knew" (p. 167). Noting the significance of the greeting for the survivor seeking liberation and homecoming, the reader of Shapell's memoir realizes that the memoir itself summons not only a response but also a *greeting*. That summons situates Shapell's memoir firmly within Holocaust literature.

SELECTED WORK BY THE AUTHOR
Witness to the Truth. New York: David McKay, 1974.

David Patterson

Sierakowiak, Dawid (1924–1943)

On February 8, 1940, the Germans published an ordinance outlining the area in Łódź, Poland, that was to be designated as a ghetto for the Jews. Among the Polish gentiles forced to leave that area to make room for the Jews was Wacław Szkudlarek. When Szkudlarek returned to his apartment five years later, he discovered five notebooks that contained the remarkable account of a teenager who lived through the horror of the ghetto, until the lad finally succumbed to a slow death from tuberculosis and starvation on August 8, 1943. Thus the diary of Dawid Sierakowiak emerged from the darkness that consumed him. The first two notebooks of Sierakowiak's diary were published in their original Polish, in 1960. All five notebooks first appeared in an English edition in 1996. It has been determined that at least two of Sierakowiak's notebooks have been lost forever; a significant portion of what was lost covers the period from January 1, 1940, to April 5, 1941.

Born in 1924, Dawid Sierakowiak was only fifteen years old when the Nazis took over his hometown of Łódź, yet he comments on the catastrophe with great insight and maturity. He, his parents, and his younger sister were among the 160,000 Jews who were sealed into the Łódź ghetto on May 1, 1940. In the ghetto he overcame his constant fear and despair to record and comment carefully on the annihilation of a people and a world which unfolded all around him. In addition to witnessing Sierakowiak's struggle against the torment in his soul, the reader follows his battle against the deterioration of his body. He served as the president of his gymnasium student council and took the lead in the school's efforts to obtain more food from the ghetto's Jewish Administration or *Judenrat*. He was also very active in the political activity undertaken by the youth of the ghetto. His deeply rooted sense of responsibility shows itself in his constant struggle for life even as he chronicles the stages of his illness and approaching death.

The diary begins on June 28, 1939, in a time of health and happiness for him and his family, and ends on April 15, 1943, as he is plunging rapidly toward his death and his family is becoming more and more disintegrated. "We were examined by a doctor," the irony pours out from the opening page. "I'm fine" (p. 21). What the reader encounters as embedded irony, however, is soon transformed to foreboding, anxiety, and a sense of doom. On April 28, 1941, for example, he wrote, "The Devil has taken too much of a hold over us, and nothing good can happen very soon in the world. We will certainly suffer much more here" (p. 84). The Devil in this case is the Nazi: like the Devil, the Nazi robs the soul of meaning by robbing the soul of a future. "There's no help," lamented Sierakowiak. "Our grave will apparently be here" (p. 94). Here one sees a defining feature of the concentrationary universe: living in the ghetto, the Jew lives in his own grave.

The deeper he sinks into the grave, the greater his foreboding. "Everyone is ready to tyrannize me," he stated, "for my relentless pessimism. Too bad they always have to admit I am right. That's what's killing me." (p. 96). As a dark apprehension eats away at Sierakowiak's soul, moreover, hunger wracks his body: "I have been examined by a doctor at school. She was terrified at how thin I am" (p. 91). Less than two months later, on July 14, 1941, he wrote, "Everything's running out here already; most of all my health. I have a feeling that next winter the ghetto won't see me" (p. 111). He did, however, survive the winter to write on April 13, 1942, "Hunger becomes more and more routine. There is no other news" (p. 153). The entry dated May 6, 1942, demonstrates that in this realm no news is bad news: "There is no news. The silence of death" (p. 163). Death is the norm: it is not newsworthy.

What is heard profoundly and repeatedly in Sierakowiak's diary is precisely the silence of death—of his own death as it creeps into him and onto the pages of his diary. "I'm so weakened that I lie all day long as though I were dead," he observed on July 5, 1942. "Slow death has begun" (p. 194). The teenager lingered in various stages of dying for more than a year; in one of the diary's last entries, dated April 4, 1943, he reported, "My state of mind is worsening every day. The fever persists, and I look like a complete 'death notice'" (p. 265). Through the pages of his diary that look is transmitted into the soul of the reader.

Selected Work by the Author
The Diary of Dawid Sierakowiak. Trans. Kamil Turowski, ed. Alan Adelson. Oxford, England: Oxford University Press, 1996.

David Patterson

Singer, Isaac Bashevis (1904–1991)

Isaac Bashevis Singer, the 1978 winner of the Nobel Prize for literature, is a major figure not only in Jewish literature but also in world literature. Although he escaped from Poland before the outbreak of the Holocaust, his literary response to the event reflects both his artistic genius and his proximity to the catastrophe that befell his people.

Singer was born into an Orthodox Jewish family on July 14, 1904, in a small village near Warsaw. His father and both his grandfathers were rabbis, and Singer received his early education in traditional religious schools. At the outbreak of World War I, his mother returned with her children to the small town of Bilgoray. Singer continued his education in Bilgoray, studying Talmud and modern Hebrew. In 1921 Singer became a student in Warsaw's Takhkemoni rabbinical seminary, but after a year he returned to live and teach in Bilgoray. Singer spent the first thirty years of his life confronting the devastating effects on traditional Jewish identity of the intellectual, political, and social upheavals of the twentieth century. In his writings he weighs what the Jewish people gained from the emancipation against what they lost by surrendering their traditions.

When the Germans occupied Poland during World War I, Singer was only fourteen, but he felt the impact of these experiences for the rest of his life. Greater still was the trauma he underwent twenty years later when he fled Warsaw for America. Profoundly shaken by the Holocaust, he dedicated his writing career to memorializing the lost world of Polish Jewry. All his major works are concerned with the Holocaust and its effect on the people who survived it. Though he never directly deals with the Holocaust itself, it is a background to his most significant fiction.

Typical of Singer's Holocaust novels is *The Family Moskat* (1950), which traces the changing fortunes of the wealthy Moskat family through four generations. Through all its transmutations, this family is a metaphor for the condition of the Jewish people in the first forty years of the twentieth century. As Singer depicts them, the crises faced by individuals delineate shifts in the nature of Jewish identity in a changing world and question the possibility of Jewish survival in the face of genocide itself. The novel ends with the Nazi bombardment of Warsaw and the despairing cry of one of its assimilated Jews, who shouts out above the sound of bombs, "I think Death is the only Messiah!" This cry is a negation of the hopes of redemption which sustained the Jewish people for two millennia of exile.

In *The Slave* (1962), Jacob, the pious Jew who is the "slave" of this novel's title, finds himself doubly in exile. He is a Polish Jew, exiled with his people from Jerusalem, and he is a slave to a Polish peasant, into whose hands he has fallen in the aftermath of the Chmielnicki pogroms. Jacob, a paradigm of his biblical namesake, reenacts the age-old struggle of the Jewish people for identity and survival in a hostile environment. This paradigm is extended both forward and backward across history by the fact that Jacob is also the survivor of a holocaust. The Chmielnicki massacres—like those of Adolf Hitler—demand of Jews an effort to go on believing that being a Jew has some meaning. Jacob loves Wanda, the semipagan daughter of his master, and for love of Jacob, Wanda converts to Judaism and dies in bringing to birth Jacob's son.

Although Singer refused to speak openly about the Holocaust, at the height of his fame he presented his readers with English versions of two novels and three volumes of fictionalized autobiography: *Enemies: A Love Story* (1972) and *Shosha* (1978), the novels; and *A Little Boy in Search of God* (1976), *A Young Man in Search of Love* (1978), and *Lost in America* (1981), the ostensible "autobiographies." All these books view the destruction of Eastern European Jewry through the eyes of a Yiddish writer. Since Singer escaped the Holocaust and wrote in Yiddish all his life, it might seem that his work preserved both the Yiddish language and its culture. But as the number of Yiddish readers and their commitment to Yiddish culture attenuated, Singer increasingly found himself in the desolate position of writing not only of, but also for, the dead. By re-creating their murdered world with its blend of secularism and piety, Singer recognizes that Yiddish alone can define them.

The repetitive and lengthy fictions Singer produced in his maturity suggest that these longer works should chiefly be read as self-exculpatory acts of confessional atonement. These works and others that deal with the Holocaust rely on a high degree of intertextuality. In narrative technique, the autobiographical novel *Shosha* is characterized by two devices designed to give it the effect of a *yizker-bukh*, a Holocaust memorial volume: an itinerary of the streets of Warsaw; and an insistence that, as Aaron's mother says, "The comfort is that there is no death" (p. 179). Other characters in the novel assert that those physically dead in this world are spiritually alive in another, offering consolation to assuage survivor guilt. Further, the minute detail in which the narrative's delineation of the topography of Jewish Warsaw calls attention to itself is highly significant: "After breakfast I went to Shosha's and stayed there for lunch. Then I left for my room on Leszno Street. Although it would have been quicker to go down Iron Street, I walked on Gnoyna, Zimna, and Orla. On Iron Street you were vulnerable to a blow from a Polish Fascist. I had laid out my own ghetto" (p. 223). The last sentence of this passage shocks with post facto recognition, because this route can be traced out on any map of the Warsaw ghetto. Singer's topography reinforces the novel's awareness that the Jews of Warsaw "had nothing to expect on earth when the Nazis arrived except starvation and concentration camps" (p. 114).

While *Enemies: A Love Story* presents itself as fiction, it becomes possible in the light of the autobiographical books which followed it to trace within it lineaments of Singer's survivor guilt. In his exploitation of others and his moral and spiritual cowardice, Herman Broder, its chief character, bears a striking resemblance to the narrators of both *Lost in America* and *Shosha*. Dreaming about "an eclipse of the sun and funeral processions," Herman Broder is troubled by the question, "Can a condemned tribe lead itself to its own burial?" All the survivors in this novel are alienated from the materialistic American present because they are deeply rooted in a destroyed spiritual European past. Those who have survived are at once the buried and the buriers, "the dead and the mourners." The narrative continually weighs the claims of this present on that past, and vice-versa.

As *Enemies: A Love Story* presents it, the survivors are the living dead, not only because their past has been destroyed, but because America can neither sustain an inner Jewish life nor compensate for its absence. Inevitably the American way of life represents "a suicidal civilization" (p. 56), of which the subway becomes the chief metaphor for "the helter-skelter epoch" where people "even die in haste." As this narrative presents it, Jewish identity in America is proclaimed by outer tokens which have become merely club badges. Forgetfulness, which America encourages, is synonymous with assimilation and hence with spiritual death. Its comfortable materialism constantly exacerbates guilt in those like Herman who have "smuggled through" to life.

What gives *Enemies* moral strength is the fact that Herman is not the novel's sole voice. Where Herman deliberately tries to "deaden [his] consciousness, choke [his] memory, extinguish the last vestige of hope" (p. 29), his first wife, Tamara, keeps all these functions alive by carrying in her left hip one of the two bullets with which the Nazis intended to murder her (p. 59). Transformed from an agent of destruction into a symbol of survival, this physical signifier converts past sickness into present health and future life (pp. 151–52). Tamara has grown through suffering into an acknowledgement that life makes demands on the living, a recognition which leads her to insist on distinguishing between self-indulgence in a godless universe and the duty of the living to exercise the power of choice. Significantly, the pregnancy of Herman's second wife, Yadwiga, recalls Tamara to purposeful existence as defender and provider of an abandoned mother and child. Through her, the past affirms life over death.

After Singer's death in 1991, his publishers issued posthumous English translations of novels serialized in Yiddish in *Forverts*, the Yiddish daily to which Singer contributed regularly for over sixty years. To date four such posthumous novels have appeared. The first two, *Scum* (1991) and *The Certificate* (1992), rework old Singer themes. *Scum* foregrounds the world-weariness of a rich, assimilated Jew who returns to Poland in search of some meaningful connection to a lost past. *The Certificate* rehashes his autobiography which had appeared in other forms. Neither of these novels enlarges an appreciation of Singer's range or ability. Equally disappointing is *Meshugah* (1994), which attempts to chart the life of Singer's literary double, Aaron Greidinger, in his post-Holocaust life in America and his success as a writer.

Shadows on the Hudson (1998), the last of the hitherto unpublished works to be translated, displays Singer's writing at its best. This novel mounts Singer's most outspoken attack on American materialism and worldliness. Its reconstruction of the period between December 1947 and mid-November 1948 identifies the shadows Singer casts on the Hudson, his metaphor for affluent New York Jewry, as those of Hitler's Holocaust. Omnipresent and ever dark, they are thrown by monstrous beings that are still potently active. The living Stalin, for instance, is as ubiquitously present as the dead Hitler, yet many Jews embrace the mendacious salvation offered in his "socialist fatherland." Hitler's example remains the model for other nations: in Poland there is another pogrom against the Jews; in Mandate Palestine, the English still begrudge the Jew a place to lay his head. Jews determined to secure their own homeland have themselves become "throwers of bombs." The world is threatened by the intensification of the Cold War and the menace of atomic warfare.

Jewish refugees lucky enough to gain new life in America find themselves estranged and helpless, their emotional and spiritual dislocation emblematized in their self-perception as stunted outsiders. Moreover, America demands that those who want the freedom it offers should subordinate their own values to the hegemony of American economic, social, and cultural norms. Determined to cling to the old values of traditional Jewishness, Boris Makaver collects rare Jewish antiques and calls the rooms of his apartment by European names: to his salon and his cabinet, he adds his own personal prayer-room. His daughter Anna, by contrast, furnishes her home in the latest fashion.

Playacting, both real and metaphorical, dominates this novel's action and defines its theme. The capitalist system is shown to rest entirely on role playing. Grein is lifted from the poverty of teaching in a Talmud Torah through a chance encounter with a stockbroker who finds his integrity refreshingly unusual. In a culture which appears to glorify gangsterism and cherish murder and fornication, the depraved Kotik easily rockets to stardom on Broadway and in Hollywood. The world America offers is, as Grein repeatedly grieves, a moral "underworld," one that draws toward it all those who accept it as seductively as it ruthlessly spits out those who reject it.

The language available or denied to the novel's characters is another determiner of the identities they possess or lack. Margolin and Anna, who speak many languages, seem easily able to adapt to every society they inhabit; yet ultimately they do not know who or what they are. While Boris is linked to a Jewish past through his inability properly to speak any language but Yiddish, Justina Kohn loathes Yiddish because it recalls an impoverished childhood from which she sought escape on the Polish stage. Both Boris's nephew, Herman, and Anna's husband, Stanislaw Luria, speak Polish because they are both in flight from Jewish roots toward cosmopolitan rootlessness. Though they go in opposite political directions, they actually take different routes to the same destination: self-effacement and meaningless death.

Inevitably this novel's dominating image is cancer, an extended metaphor for the destructive effect of American materialism. But the indiscriminate way it cuts down its victims makes it, on a deeper level, a metonym for the spiritual condition of post-Holocaust Jewry and the arbitrariness of human existence. Hertz Grein's daughter-in-law, Patricia, may assert that Hitler is dead and the Jews are alive. The novel demands to know, however, what kind of Jews have been left alive, and what their children will become. American Jews are presented as indistinguishable from secular gentiles. Orthodox rabbis from Eastern Europe are described as old-fashioned and alien, while their clean-shaven American Reform write plays, offer drinks and cigarettes to congregants seeking spiritual guidance, and visit theaters on Friday evenings and Saturday afternoons, reshaping the Covenant in terms defined by American worldliness.

Patricia's determination to bring up her unborn child as a Jew seems to suggest that the renewal of Jewry in America will be revitalized through the new blood of converts. This prospect is balanced against the novel's darkest shadow. Boris's passionately desired son, the issue of his union with the devout and learned Frieda, is a Down's syndrome baby. Why, Frieda asks, did Boris deserve this? The lack of any answer lies at the spiritual heart of this novel. How satisfying is Grein's decision to immure himself in Talmud and Torah? What validity can the ethical imperatives of Judaism have if they can survive only behind ghetto walls, from which they have no possibility of influencing the morality of the secular world?

Isaac Bashevis Singer remains among the most disturbing Jewish writers on the Holocaust in English. His enormous popularity has enabled him to bring to international attention and acclaim the destroyed world of the shtetl. His work made formerly indifferent, even hostile, non-Jewish readers aware of the spiritual depths of the Jewish faith, and of the range and variety of Jewish life. For Jewish readers, his signal importance lies in his ability to reawaken in them a consciousness of the abiding problem of seeking a meaningful identity as Jews in a post-Holocaust, secular world far removed from traditional Orthodox observance.

SELECTED WORKS BY THE AUTHOR
The Certificate. Trans. Leonard Wolf. New York: Farrar, Straus and Giroux, 1992; *Enemies: A Love Story*. Greenwich, Conn.: Fawcett, 1972; *The Family Moskat*. Trans. A.H. Gross. New York: Alfred A. Knopf, 1950; *A Little Boy in Search of God*. Garden City, N.Y.: Doubleday, 1976; *Lost in America*. Garden City, N.Y.: Doubleday, 1981; *Meshugah*. Trans. Isaac Bashevis Singer and Nili Wachtel. New York: Farrar, Straus and Giroux, 1994; *Scum*. Trans. Rosaline Dukalsky Schwartz. New York: Farrar, Straus and Giroux, 1991; *Shadows on the Hudson*. Trans. Joseph Sherman. New York: Farrar, Straus and Giroux, 1998; *Shosha*. Trans. Joseph Singer and I.B. Singer. New York: Farrar, Straus and Giroux, 1978; *The Slave*. Trans. Cecil Hemley and I.B. Singer. New York: Farrar, Straus and Cuddahy, 1962; *A Young Man in Search of Love*. Garden City, N.Y.: Doubleday, 1978.

FOR FURTHER READING
Alexander, Edward, *Isaac Bashevis Singer*. Boston: Twayne, 1980; Biletzky, I. Ch., *God, Jew, Satan in the Works of Isaac Bashevis Singer*. Lanham, Md: University Press of America, 1995; Farrell, Grace, *From Exile to Redemption: The Fiction of Isaac Bashevis Singer*. Carbondale: Southern Illinois University Press, 1987; Friedman, Lawrence, *Understanding Isaac Bashevis Singer*. Columbia: University of South Carolina Press, 1988; Gibbons, Frances Vargas, *Transgression and Self-Punishment in Isaac Bashevis Singer's Searches*. New York: Peter Lang, 1995.

Joseph Sherman

Sobol, Joshua (1939–)

Joshua Sobol, one of Israel's leading contemporary playwrights, has composed three important Holocaust plays: *Ghetto* (1983), *Adam* (1989), and *Underground* (1990). Sobol's triptych is significant in Holocaust literature because of his effective use of history in drama and because of the complex portrayal of people who played major roles in the Vilna ghetto, a thriving ghetto with a rich cultural life. The triptych concerns significant events and the actions of important personages in the Vilna ghetto in Lithuania from the ghetto's inception (September 3, 1941) to its liquidation (September 24, 1943).

Sobol became interested in the Vilna ghetto after reading the slogan "No theatre in a graveyard"—a slogan attributed to Herman Kruk* during his protest of ghetto leader Jacob Gens's decision to implement a theater in the Vilna ghetto; Kruk, the ghetto librarian, became upset when Gens created the theater shortly after Nazi soldiers had murdered approximately

50,000 Jews in Ponary during the summer of 1941. Sobol also discovered that the Vilna artistic director (Israel Segal)—characterized as Srulik in *Ghetto*—had managed to survive the ghetto liquidation and lived near him in Tel Aviv. Sobol interviewed Segal extensively and began to conduct exhaustive research on this ghetto.

Sobol has always been fascinated by documents, and thus it is not surprising that history permeates his drama. Sobol attributes his love of documents in part to the influence of American director Nola Chilton, who showed Sobol the need for meaningful theater, more meaningful than was being produced in Israel at the time. Sobol started traveling across Israel, taping people, recording their thoughts. The playwright and Chilton collaborated on a drama entitled *Days to Come* (1971), which focused on old people living in Israel. While researching the play, Sobol interviewed elderly people and observed that "the country was living on a suppressed ocean of tears. All these old people were living with an imposed or self-imposed silence of shame and humiliation which had been suppressed and which Israel society could not allow to come out. It was the horrible experience of the Holocaust and of having survived "shamefully" (*Ghetto*, "Author's Notes"). Previously, Sobol, like many Jews, had carefully avoided investigating and thinking about the Holocaust because of the painful thoughts that would arise. Although Sobol attributes his interest in the Holocaust to the slogan that he encountered, it is conceivable that the interviews he conducted with the elderly survivors played a part in his decision to create drama about the Shoah.

Born in Tel Mond, Palestine, in 1939, Sobol lived on a kibbutz for eight years and later studied philosophy at the Sorbonne; he is especially interested in the philosophy of Baruch Spinoza. He wrote plays for the Haifa Municipal Theater, where he worked as the artistic director from 1985 to 1988. He has taught at Tel Aviv University. *Ghetto* earned Sobol the German Critics Award for Best Foreign Play in 1985 and the London Critics Award in 1989. Although Sobol currently lives in Tel Aviv, he spends approximately half of every year in other countries, sometimes directing his own plays.

Ghetto concerns the creation of the theater in Vilna during the Holocaust. The theater allows some Jews in the ghetto to work; thus they are able to receive food rations so that they can survive, preserve their Jewish culture through the performing arts, and entertain the ghetto inhabitants while temporarily allowing them to forget their sufferings. A clothing factory allows many other Jews to work, even though the factory mends Nazi uniforms and consequently contributes to the war effort. One controversy is, of course, whether the Jews should help the Nazis survive. *Adam* is Sobol's dramatization of the tragic story of Yitzhak Wittenberg, the ghetto resistance leader. Wittenberg organized a group to save the Vilna Jews, yet the ghetto inhabitants turned him over to the Nazis, sacrificing him so that they could survive (Nazi officer Kittel declares that he will liquidate the ghetto if the Jews do not find Wittenberg and turn him in). *Underground* dramatizes the true story of Dr. Abrasha Weinrib and the secret typhus ward in the Vilna hospital. The doctors are able to deceive the Nazis, who greatly feared epidemics, so that they would not burn the hospital or even liquidate the ghetto.

Basing his plays on historical documents, Sobol brings to life people who played major roles in the Vilna ghetto—people such as Jacob Gens, Herman Kruk, United Partisan Organization leader Yitzhak Wittenberg, Weiskopf (the director of the ghetto clothing factory), and Kittel, who, according to Sobol, specialized in liquidating ghettos. Sobol's dramas represent part of a new and controversial trend in Holocaust theater. Michael Taub observes that, while earlier plays dramatized the psychological suffering of Holocaust survivors, Sobol's dramas also confronted controversial issues such as Jewish complicity, the performance of theater in the ghetto, and the role of the *Judenrat* and the Jewish police. Whereas previous plays portrayed collaborators as sinister villains, Sobol dramatized the complex nature of these personages, creating three-dimensional and ambivalent characters. For instance, Harold and Edith Lieberman's play *Throne of Straw* (1973) portrays Łódź ghetto leader Mordechai Chaim Rumkowski as an egotistical tyrant who disregards the welfare of the Jewish people and who sacrifices them during selections. In Sobol's Holocaust dramas, Jacob Gens is portrayed as a complex figure who sacrifices his people during selections and turns in the Jewish resistance (the United Partisan Organization), but who, contrariwise, genuinely cares for his people and risks—and ultimately sacrifices—his life for them.

Thus, in Joshua Sobol's Holocaust drama, there exists a movement away from melodramatic theater toward a sympathetic understanding of the motives of those, such as Gens, who betrayed some Jews to save others. In *Adam*, Gens turns in ghetto resistance leader Wittenberg (named Adam Rolenick in Sobol's play) to Nazi officer Kittel, which can be perceived by an audience as a terrible act, for Wittenberg (Rolenick) plans to help Jews escape the ghetto in an armed revolt. But Gens considers an armed revolt hopeless and instead wants the Jews to remain peaceful and obedient in the ghetto, thinking that if the Jews do not attract the attention of the Nazis, they can survive in the ghetto until the Russian army rescues them. Turning in a Jewish leader might seem heinous, but Gens hopes to save many Jewish lives by doing so.

In *Ghetto*, furthermore, Sobol portrays Weiskopf, an entrepreneurial tailor who becomes wealthy and powerful in the ghetto even though he does so at the expense of other Jews and by helping the Nazis (Weiskopf opens a tailoring factory that repairs the uniforms of Nazi soldiers). Nonetheless, Weiskopf's tailoring business, which aids the Nazis, makes the Jews useful to them and provides jobs to many Jews, which helps them and their families stay alive for as long as the factory functions. When Kittel asks Weiskopf what the difference is between partial and total liquidation of the ghetto, the tailor responds that if all the Jews in the ghetto but him are killed, that is partial liquidation, but full liquidation would occur if the Nazis kill him. Weiskopf's joke—an actual joke told often in the Vilna ghetto—suggests the strong desire for self-preservation that the Jews had during the Holocaust. Although the joke connotes selfishness, one must remember that, during the Holocaust, moral norms were not the same as in other times and that one cannot judge those who acted egoistically in such an unusual and tragic time. Sobol's dramatizations of the aforementioned moral issues and the struggle to survive, as well as the vibrancy of life and the humor in the ghettos that the playwright manifests, have led to the creation of these three superb dramas which have achieved prominence on the stage and have become some of the most significant Holocaust dramas.

The complexity and sophistication, however, cause Sobol's plays to be controversial. Although Sobol's Holocaust plays concerning the Vilna ghetto have been well received and are usually considered some of the most significant contributions to Holocaust drama, he has also received some criticism. Elie Wiesel* strongly objected to *Ghetto* because Sobol deemphasizes the role of God and suggests that, during the Nazi regime's power, Jews in the ghetto are forced to choose between two evils, not between good and evil; this choice results inevitably in the isolation of those people and hinders any possibility for redemption (Langworthy, pp. 14–15). Wiesel also was bothered by the dramatization of some Jews in the ghetto as collaborators and self-centered persons. Sobol defends his work, saying that the negative portrayals are based on documented evidence and that he does not judge the characters: if, for instance, Gens or Weiskopf does something morally wrong, the audience must consider that, historically, ethical values did not apply when people were forced to choose not between good and evil, but between two evils. Although all three works in Sobol's triptych have been well received, *Ghetto* is unquestionably the most popular.

SELECTED WORKS BY THE AUTHOR
Adam. Trans. Ron Jenkins. In *Israeli Holocaust Drama,* ed. Michael Taub. Syracuse: Syracuse University Press, 1996, pp. 268–330; *Ghetto*. Trans. Jack Viertel. In *Plays of the Holocaust: An International Anthology,* ed. Elinor Fuchs. New York: Theatre Communications Group, 1987, pp. 153–225; "*Ghetto*: Author's Notes." http://freepages.pavilion.net/jmshaw/ghetto_author.html; *Postscript*. In *Plays of the Holocaust: An International Anthology,*. ed. Elinor Fuchs. New York: Theatre Communications Group, 1987, pp. 227–30; *Underground*. In *Theater* 22, no. 3 (1991): 18–43.

FOR FURTHER READING

Langworthy, Douglas, "When Choosing Good Is Not an Option: An Interview with Joshua Sobol." *Theater* 22, no. 3 (1991): 10–17; Shteir, Rachel, "In Search of Sobol." *Theater* 21, no. 3 (1990): 39–42; Sterling, Eric, "The Ultimate Sacrifice: The Death of Resistance Hero Yitzhak Wittenberg and the Decline of the United Partisan Organization." In *Resisting the Holocaust,* ed. Ruby Rohrlich. Oxford, England: Berg Publishers, 1998, pp. 59–76.

Eric Sterling

Spiegel, Isaiah (1906–1991)

One of the most important and prolific writers in Yiddish in the Łódź ghetto, Isaiah Spiegel has left the world a moving record of Jewish life under Nazi rule. His work is particularly important to Holocaust literature because much of it was written during the Holocaust.

Spiegel was born in Łódź, Poland, in 1906 of poor parents who worked as hand weavers. As a youngster, he attended a traditional Hebrew school (*cheder*), a Yiddish folk school, and a secular high school. A period of study at a teacher training college prepared him for work as a teacher. Until the Nazi invasion of Poland in 1939, he taught Yiddish and Yiddish literature in a number of Bund-sponsored schools. After the Łódź ghetto was established in May 1940, he was employed in the *Judenrat* (Jewish Council) in various departments. He was deported to Auschwitz-Birkenau in August 1944 and worked in several labor camps following the evacuation of Auschwitz in January 1945. His parents and relatives all perished during the war. A few years after the war, Spiegel immigrated to Israel, where he died in 1991.

In 1922 Spiegel began to publish his Yiddish poems in various Łódź newspapers and periodicals in Łódź. In 1930 his first book of poetry appeared, *Mitn Punim tsu der Zun* (Facing the sun). On the eve of the Nazi invasion of Poland, another book of his poetry, as well as a collection of short stories about the Jewish weavers of Łódź, was ready for publication, but these and other manuscripts were lost during the Holocaust. Despite the dreadful conditions of ghetto life, Speigel wrote a great deal of fiction and poetry. When the Łódź ghetto was liqui-

dated in August 1944, he hid some of his writing in a cellar and took other writings with him to Auschwitz where they were taken from him. After liberation, he returned to Łódź and recovered the manuscripts of sixteen of the stories he had hidden there. He modified them and also reconstructed the missing works from memory. These stories he published in Łódź in 1947 in a volume called *Malchis Ghetto* (*The Ghetto Kingdom*, 1998). The changes he made in the original manuscripts reflected a desire to stress the redemptive aspects of his material. He omitted mention of the Jewish ghetto police and the controversial *Judenrat* chairman, Mordechai Chaim Rumkowski, and he said little about the Germans who ruled the ghetto. In their modified form, his stories present simple people struggling under the unbearable conditions of ghetto life and revealing, often, their human decency and quiet heroism. His simple, understated style stands in contrast to the suffering he depicts. Seldom is he sentimental or melodramatic.

Spiegel wrote poems as well as stories in the ghetto. He is the author of two poignant ghetto songs, the lullabies "Makh Tsu die Eygelekh" (Close your precious eyes) and "Nit Keyn Rozhinkes un Nit Keyn Mandlen" (Neither raisins nor almonds). Both songs were set to original music by David Beigelman. Spiegel wrote the first after the death of his daughter, Eva, in the Łódź ghetto and after the deportations of thousands of children to the death camps. Both pieces symbolize the mass destruction of children during the Holocaust and the anguish of their parents. *Judenrat* chairman Rumkowski banned the public performance of these songs because they cast the Nazi terror in such a clear light, but Jews sang these songs nevertheless.

After the war, Spiegel returned to teaching, first in Łódź (1945–1948) and then in Warsaw, where he was also secretary of the Polish Yiddish Writers' Association. He settled in Israel in 1951 and continued to write fiction and poetry, often on Israeli themes. In Israel, he received numerous awards, including the Itsik Manger Award, the Yakov Fichman Award, and the Yaakov Glatstein Award. Spiegel has been anthologized in French, German, and English volumes. He is known to English-speaking readers mainly through the translations of two of his stories: "A Ghetto Dog," translated by Bernard Guilbert Guerney, and "Bread," translated by David H. and Roslyn Hirsch. Spiegel is considered today one of the prose masters of Yiddish literature. He will be long remembered for his artfully muted stories of Jewish suffering under Nazi domination.

SELECTED WORKS BY THE AUTHOR

Flamen fun der erd. Tel Aviv: Israel-Buch, 1966; *Geshtalten un profilen.* 2 vols. Tel Aviv: Israel-Buch, 1971–1980; *Un Gevoren is licht.* Warsaw: Yiddish-Buch, 1949; *The Ghetto Kingdom: Tales of the Łódź Ghetto.* Trans. David H. Hirsch and Roslyn Hirsch. Evanston, Ill.: Northwestern University Press, 1998; *Himlen nachen sturm: Novelen, essayin, lieder.* Tel Aviv: World Council for Yiddish, 1984; *Mitn Punim Tzu Der Zun.* Łódź, Poland: Alpha, 1930; *Shtern Laykhtn in* Tom. 2 vols. Tel Aviv: Israel Book, 1976.

Milton Teichman

Sutzkever, Abraham (1913–)

Abraham Sutzkever is one of the major poets of the twentieth century. He writes and thinks in the modernist strain and is very much given to using such modernist techniques as novel word coinages (in Yiddish, of course), convoluted syntax, and bold metaphors. However, Sutzkever differs from the Anglo-American modernist poets in his use of powerful, regular metrical and rhyme schemes. Though Sutzkever has tried his hand at narrative poetry, his true gift is that of a lyric poet.

Born in a small town near Vilna, Lithuania, in 1913, Sutzkever and his family were forced to move to Siberia in 1915; his father died soon after. With his mother and sister, the young Abraham moved back to the Vilna area in 1920; at the age of thirteen, he began writing poetry, first in Hebrew then in Yiddish, but he subsequently burned his juvenile efforts. In the ghetto, Sutzkever joined the Jewish Resistance movement, and, along with other Jewish poets and scholars, such as Abba Kovner* and Schmerke Katcherginsky, helped rescue many of Vilna's Yiddish cultural treasures from destruction. Af-

ter escaping from the ghetto, Sutzkever lived for some months in the Narocz forest and reached Moscow in March 1944. He made his way to Palestine and in 1947 entered as an illegal immigrant. In 1948 he founded *Di goldene keyt* (The golden chain), a Yiddish literary quarterly, which ceased publication in 1995. In 1985 Sutzkever was awarded the Israel Prize for Yiddish Literature.

Sutzkever has been a prolific poet (twenty-three volumes of Yiddish poetry as of 1991), but the concern here is mainly with poems he wrote in the ghetto and immediately after, many of which, unfortunately, are still not translated into English (including *Kol Nidre*, an epic narrative of a father who murders his own son to keep him from falling into the hands of the Nazi torturers). A collection of the ghetto poems was published in New York in 1945, with the title *Di Festung* (The fortress) and another in 1946, titled *Lieder fun getto* (Songs of the ghetto).

Like the earliest poems of his fellow Vilna poet, Chaim Grade, Sutzkever's pre-Holocaust poems celebrate nature. But what Sutzkever experienced and saw during the years of the Nazi occupation cast an indelible shadow on his poetic genius, converting him from a Romantic nature poet into a poet of witnessing and memory. Sutzkever was interned in the Vilna ghetto, from June 1941 till September 1943, an experience that forced him to dedicate his poetic talent to the sacred task of recording the heinous crimes committed against his dearest kin, his closest friends, and the whole of the Jewish people. After the ghetto years, Sutzkever's poems commemorated the victims and grieved for the lost souls who had fallen victim to the Nazi death machine.

Given the harsh conditions of life under Nazi occupation, it is quite remarkable that Sutzkever never stopped writing poems, even during the most harrowing moments of the ghetto ordeal. In one of the haunting prose poems in *The Green Aquarium* (1953-1954), he recalls a vision of the Angel of Poetry, who promised to protect the poet "with a flaming sword" if his song should inspire the angel. Just as other ghetto inmates kept prose diaries, so Sutzkever maintained an almost daily record of ghetto events set down in poems.

No subject was too mean or trivial to be transformed into a poem: a heap of manure ("Near a Warm Hill"), burning cherished love letters to heat water for tea ("Leaves of Ash"), the aerial circling of a colorful butterfly ("A Butterfly Flies In"), the urge to pray ("I Have an Urge to Say a Prayer"). The ghetto poems also included portraits of private and public grief: "To My Child," on the poisoning of his infant son by the Gestapo; "To My Wife"; "Teacher Mira," a tribute to a dedicated teacher who put the safety of her pupils above her own; "Itzik Wittenberg," a lament for the leader of the Jewish Resistance in Vilna, who yielded to pressure from the ghetto masses by giving himself up in response to the Gestapo's threat to liquidate the entire Vilna ghetto immediately if he did not. As he wrote these poems of the ghetto experience, Sutzkever underwent a gradual transformation from a Romantic nature poet to an ironic modernist. Like other modernist poets, he discovered that it was possible to express in powerful and beautiful metaphors the most brutal acts and the most depressing feelings of revulsion and terror. Even in the darkest ghetto days and in some of his darkest ghetto poems, he still managed to find beauty in nature (as in the poems "A Butterfly Flies In" and "A Little Flower").

What is perhaps Sutzkever's darkest Holocaust poem, "Tchias h'mesim" (Resurrection), was written in Moscow in 1945. In this poem, Sutzkever alludes, parodically, to the tradition of the coming of the Messiah and the raising of the dead from their graves. When the shofar blows, summoning the dead back to life, they refuse to be resurrected, telling the poet/Messiah who wishes to bring them back into the world of the living that they "have been liberated from . . . the punishment of living."

In 1956, during the Sinai campaign, Sutzkever accompanied the Israeli troops into the Sinai, a momentous event that resulted in one of his greatest poems, "In Midbar Sinai" (In the Sinai Desert), a poem in which the poet starts to turn aside from the bitterness he expressed in "Tchias h'mesim" and reaffirms his faith in the destiny of the Jewish people. The poem consists of ten stanzas of twelve lines each (presumably reflecting the Ten Commandments and the twelve tribes of Israel). In this sublime poem filled with images of haunting beauty, the poet seeks to reconcile three levels of time: the ancient past of the revelation on Sinai; the suffering of the Jewish people through the centuries of exile, especially the years of the Holocaust; and the redemptive rebirth of the Jewish state. Standing at the foot of the mountain, the astonished poet, witness to and survivor of the slaughter, asks how he could be worthy of approaching Mount Sinai. As he climbs the mountain, however, the poet is granted another revelation, so that the dead of Treblinka now carved the commandments on tablets that have become a record of G-d's memory.

The Hidden God, who had been absent during the tragic years of the Holocaust, now reveals Himself again, as a God of justice and retribution who in His holy mount is now confronted with a mountain of bones. Thus the poet invokes Ezekiel's valley of the dry bones, an image of resurrection, but at the same time the ghetto poet has not forgotten that he must bear witness to the memory of the innocents who were slaughtered for no other reason than their parents having obeyed the Commandments of the God of Sinai. In the last stanza, a mysterious transaction takes place between a trooper with a flag and some mysterious force that takes the flag and blesses the hero.

The poem "In Midbar Sinai" represents a turning point in Sutzkever's sensibility. He does not quite return to being the innocent nature poet he was before the Holocaust, but neither does he remain the bitter accuser of the ghetto poems. Dweller in the reborn State of Israel, standing at the foot of Mount Sinai, the great Vilna poet experiences a renewal of his mystical vision. In that moment of revelation the poet is inspired to reaffirm the spirit of biblical prophecy. But Sutzkever's affirmation is certainly not facile, nor is it an affirmation that overlooks the ravages of the past.

It has been noted that Sutzkever is a secular poet. But in his Sinai poem, the poet's youthful mystical consciousness reemerges, and it emerges as a mystical consciousness rooted in, though not necessarily limited to, biblical and Talmudic texts. Though he certainly deserves it, Sutzkever has not been given the kind of serious attention that has been accorded such poets as Nelly Sachs* and Paul Celan.*

SELECTED WORKS BY THE AUTHOR
Burnt Pearls, with introduction by Ruth Wisse. Trans. Seymour Mayne. Oakville, Ontario, Canada: Mosaic Press/Valley Editions, 1981; "Meditations on Mt. Sinai." Trans. David H. Hirsch and Roslyn Hirsch. *Midstream* 29 (October 1983): 6, 18; *Selected Poetry and Prose*. Trans. Barbara Harshav and Benjamin Harshav, with an introduction by Benjamin Harshav. Berkeley: University of California Press, 1991.

FOR FURTHER READING
Hirsch, David H., "Abraham Sutzkever's Vilna Poetry." *Modern Language Studies* 16 (Winter 1986); Roskies, David, "The Burden of Memory." In *Against Apocalypse*. Cambridge, Mass: Harvard University Press, 1984; Wisse, Ruth, "The Last Great Yiddish Poet?" *Commentary*, November 1983, 41–48.

David H. Hirsch

T

Tec, Nechama (1931–)

Nechama Tec survived the Holocaust as a hidden child in her native Poland. A distinguished sociologist, Tec has made significant contributions to the study of the Shoah, both in terms of her own memoir, *Dry Tears: The Story of a Lost Childhood* (1984), and in numerous scholarly studies. Among the latter is a landmark work on altruism, *When Light Pierced the Darkness: Christian Rescue of Jews in Nazi-Occupied Poland* (1986). Tec is the author of numerous books, chapters, and articles on various dimensions of the Holocaust. Some of her work has been translated into Dutch, German, and Hebrew. Her studies combine the moral authority of the witness and the academic discipline of the scholar.

Tec was born in 1931 in Lublin, the second daughter of Roman and Estera Bawnik [née Hachamoff]. Prior to the war, her mother kept a kosher home and was an observant Jew. Her father, disillusioned with religion, was a self-taught chemist and owned a chemical factory which was seized by the Nazis. Tec and her sister, owing to their "Aryan" looks, (blond hair and blue eyes), survived by "passing" as Christians. This experience had a profound effect on Tec's sense of Jewish identity. The parents, who "looked Jewish," were forced to remain hidden. The four family members all survived. Tec is a professor of sociology at the University of Connecticut at Stamford. She has also served as a senior research fellow at the Miles Lehrman Center for the Study of Jewish Resistance at the United States Holocaust Memorial Museum, and she has been a scholar in residence at the International Institute for Holocaust Research at Yad Vashem in Jerusalem.

She has written several award-winning books. For example, *Defiance: The Bielski Partisans* (1993) received the 1994 International Anne Frank Special Recognition Prize in Switzerland. A German edition was published in 1996 and a Hebrew translation appeared in 1997. Her study of the Jewish priest Oswald Rufeisen, *In the Lion's Den* (1990), received the 1991 Christopher Award. Two other books, *When Light Pierced the Darkness* and *Dry Tears,* each received the Merit of Distinction Award from the Anti-Defamation League of B'nai B'rith.

Dry Tears recounts Tec's harrowing experiences in occupied Poland. She exemplifies a type of hidden child that the historian Deborah Dwork terms "hiding and visible," as opposed to children such as Anne Frank who were in hiding and hidden. In both cases, Jewish identity was a death sentence. Further, Tec's memoir reveals the complexity of hiding for young Jewish children. For example, by the time the war ended, she had changed names on more than one occasion; Nechama Bawnik became Pelagia Pawlowska and Christina (Krysia) Bloch. The new names meant adopting a new history, replete with birth places and dates, different parents, family story, and extended relatives.

Moreover, there were two types of identifica-tion papers: real, those issued in the name of a living person who had moved far away; and counterfeit, documents issued in the name of a fictitious person.

Tec's memoir emphasizes the crucial role of religion in being able to survive in hiding. For example, one had to be thoroughly conver-sant with the rituals of Catholicism. This meant knowing such basic fundamentals as how and when to cross oneself and how to say the ro-sary. "To remain a stranger to Catholicism," wrote Tec, "was dangerous" (p. 71). She and her sister heard stories "about Jews who lost their lives because of religious ignorance" (p. 71). Tec wrote about how she and her sister memorized prayers and repeatedly tested each other. Moreover, there was also a crucial gen-der difference involved in hiding. Only Jews cir-cumcised their male children. Therefore, hiding—while fraught with peril for both fe-males and males—was more precarious for males.

Tec was an eight-year-old child at the out-break of World War II. She and her sister at-tended a Jewish private school which deemphasized religion. Following the Nazi de-cree banning Jews from attending school, her parents hired a tutor for the eight-year-old girl and her twelve-year-old sister. Forced from their apartment, the family was cramped into one room. Tec captures the precariousness of being a Jew in Nazi-occupied Poland by observing that the simple act of studying could eventuate in death. She wrote that, "anyone of us could be shot simply because I was trying to memorize a poem" (p. 4). Nevertheless, her parents insisted from the beginning that there would be an "af-ter the war." This belief that they would survive deeply impressed the young girl. In fact, it sup-planted any formal adherence to Jewish religion. Tec's mother, who had been observant prior to the war, abandoned the faith contending that "there is no God. If there were a God he could not tolerate all the murdering and torturing of innocent people" (p. 7).

Tec's memoir portrays the increasingly per-ilous situation of Jews in Poland. After fleeing from Lublin, the family went first to Warsaw, next to Otwock, and finally to Kielce. Each of these dangerous journeys required elaborate preparation. For example, the family could not travel together. Nechama and her older sister not only looked Christian, they spoke flawless Pol-ish. Their parents, however, were different. Mr. Bawnik, while not looking Jewish, spoke a flawed Polish marred by a Yiddish inflection. His wife not only suffered a similar linguistic difficulty, she also looked Jewish. Consequently, to travel on trains, she dressed as a Polish woman in mourning with her face covered by a veil. When the family was finally reunited in Kielce, Nechama and her sister—by now called Krysia and Danka—were able to move about, while the parents remained hidden. Tec wrote "My par-ents did not officially exist"(p. 117).

Tec has written movingly about three main issues in her experience: her "lost childhood," her Jewish identity, and Polish anti-Semitism, even among the people who helped her family. For instance, readers of her memoir will men-tally compare their own childhood to Tec's ex-perience. Childhood is a time of spontaneity, unguarded exuberance, and freedom of expres-sion. Tec, however, observes, "All my life re-volved around hiding; hiding thoughts, hiding feelings, hiding my activities, hiding informa-tion" (p. 109). Listening to the "happy clamor" of children at play in Kielce, Nechama wrote, "I knew that I could never be as carefree as they were. I had to be on guard, always on guard" (p. 141). At another point in her story, Tec recalled skipping home with her sister after work; the two sisters "briefly recaptured childhood, a luxury Jewish children could no longer afford" (p. 159). Yet, she learned resourcefulness, te-nacity, and other coping skills from her parents which enabled her to survive. For example, she worked in the black market selling baked goods made by her mother. Nechama also escaped sev-eral murderous Nazi raids on the market.

Dry Tears sheds light on the issue of Jew-ish identity, which was so perplexing for many hidden children. Tec wrote movingly about her dual Christian and Jewish identities. Living in the Catholic Polish world, Nechama always re-membered her father's warning, "Never, never, admit to anyone that you are Jewish" (p. 93). The young girl recalled becoming a "double person." In public, she not only grew "oddly accustomed to hearing antisemitic remarks," but was able to "laugh heartily with everyone else about some Jewish misfortune" (pp. 144–45). Yet this dichotomous self was profoundly wrenching on the psychological level. For example, the author wrote about seeing a group of Jewish workers from a local factory walking in the middle of the road being guarded by heavily armed German soldiers. She recalled thinking, "If dead people could walk, I would expect them to walk that way" (p. 143). Her Polish friend ridiculed the Jews but Nechama did not respond. That night, in the privacy of her home, she "cried tears of helplessness" (p. 143).

As a professor, Nechama Tec writes about the widespread existence in Poland of what she terms "diffuse cultural antisemitism." Passing in the Christian world, the young Nechama had many encounters with this phenomenon. For instance, her Polish friend, Janka, to whom the author felt especially close and who was two years older, once told the young girl a story about Jews murdering Christian children and using their blood to bake matzoh. Stunned by this assertion, Nechama/Krysia asked Janka if she had ever seen this happen. This question could have cost Krysia her life. Instead, Janka responded by saying that the Jews "do it secretly." The potentially fatal conversation ended with Janka telling Krysia, "You're still a baby, young and dumb, that is what you are!" (p. 144).

The complexity of Polish attitudes toward Jews was revealed by the Homar family who agreed—for a price—to hide Nechama and her parents. The Homars openly expressed anti-Semitic opinions and attitudes. The youngster sought guidance from her father on this matter. He told his daughter that the Homars, like most Poles, "took anti-Semitism for granted" (p. 121). Nechama was quite confused by the contradiction between negative attitudes toward the Jewish people and helping individual Jews. Furthermore, she was unsure as to the meaning of the Homars's repeated references to "real" Jews. The young girl pressed her father for more information. For Poles, he observed, "The 'real' Jew, is not real at all." "The Homars," he continued, "hated an abstraction, the stereotype of the Jew, but not actual people like us who happened to be Jewish" (pp. 121–22). Her father's

explanation may, however, have been overly benign. At the end of the war, the Homars did not want their neighbors to know that they had hidden a Jewish family. Consequently, they requested that Nechama and her family leave Kielce as Poles, without telling anyone that they were Jewish.

Dry Tears is an important book for anyone wishing to begin to understand how extremely difficult it was for Jews, and especially Jewish children, to survive not only the Nazi onslaught, but also the hostile Polish environment. Tec observed that her family was upset because the Homars "failed to reassure us that they were glad we were alive and felt gratified by the part they played in our rescue" (p. 214). The Jewish mortality rate during the Holocaust is staggering. For instance, Tec reports that the prewar Jewish population of her native Lublin was 40,000. Of this number, 150 returned, among them only three Jewish families were still intact. Tec's memoir, however, provides insight into how Jewish self-help in terms of resourcefulness and determination played an important role in her family's survival.

SELECTED WORKS BY THE AUTHOR
Defiance: The Bielski Partisans. New York: Oxford University Press, 1993; *Dry Tears: The Story of a Lost Childhood*. New York: Oxford University Press, 1984; *In The Lion's Den: The Life of Oswald Rufeisen*. New York: Oxford University Press, 1990; *When Light Pierced the Darkness: Christian Rescue of Jews in Nazi-Occupied Poland*. New York: Oxford University Press, 1986.

FOR FURTHER READING
Baumgarten, Murray, "Expectations and Endings: Observations on Holocaust Literature." Working Papers in Holocaust Studies III, Yeshiva University, September 1989.

Alan L. Berger

Topas, George (1924–)

When George Topas was summoned to Kiel, Germany, to testify at the trial of three SS guards in 1967, the memory of his torturous journey through several concentration camps was reawakened. The stirring of that memory led him to compile a penetrating memoir called *The Iron Furnace: A Holocaust Survivor's Story* (1990).

Born in Warsaw in 1924, Topas was not quite fifteen when the Nazis invaded Poland on September 1, 1939. He and his family entered the Warsaw ghetto on November 15, 1940, and remained there until he was sent to Bychawa in June 1941. From July to November 1942, he worked in the Luftwaffe camp at Bielany; he spent another four months at slave labor in the Okecie Luftwaffe camp. Then came a series of concentration camps: Budzyn, May 1943–March 1944; Majdanek, March 1944–April 1944; Plaszow, April 1944–October 1944; and Flossenburg, October 1944–April 1945. He was liberated by American troops while in transit to yet another camp, one mile from Nuremburg, on April 23, 1945. After the war Topas became a citizen of the United States, where he earned a degree in history from Rutgers University.

The Iron Furnace is remarkable for its interweaving of texts and teachings from Jewish tradition with an event that was calculated to destroy that tradition. Often recalling the pious teachings that his father had bequeathed to him, Topas struggled to cling to the belief that God looks after the righteous. Indeed, for twenty-two years he persisted in the belief that his most righteous teacher, his father, might have been spared during the war, until one day in 1967 he received evidence that his father was indeed murdered at Treblinka in 1942. Nevertheless Topas begins nearly all of his chapters with an epigram from the Bible, thus interweaving the words of Holy Writ with his own. Each text—his and the biblical text—colors the reading of the other.

Given his religious upbringing, it is perhaps not surprising that Topas frequently cast the annihilation happening all around him in religious terms. He asserted, for example, that the world "lay in ruins, like my *tefillin* [phylacteries]" (p. 84). And yet it is the memory of the tefillin that sustained him amidst the world in ruins. Similarly, Topas's memoir contains the memory of remembering; here the reader finds that life clings to life in the midst of death through memory. Topas recalled, for example, that the memory of the Sabbath as his family observed it sustained him when death drew near:

"The scene of our family sitting together around the table, enjoying the Sabbath meal, singing, hearing my father read portions of the Bible to us about our great heritage had always been a moving one: now, lost, it was more precious than ever" (p. 104). In his memoir, Topas demonstrates that what is lost is not completely lost as long as the memory of it persists.

Topas also brings out the connection between faith in God and faith in humanity. According to teachings from the Jewish tradition, the divine imitates the human; God uses human arms to offer his embrace to humanity. Thus, when Topas met a decent German named Schleswig, he began to believe that even among the Germans there are still some human beings: "Thoughts like these made life seem more bearable than it really was" (p. 136). Here Topas opens one's eyes to an important dimension of the assault that defined the Holocaust. By killing not only people but also the idea of a person, the Nazis demonstrated through their deeds that they have destroyed the humanity within themselves in their attempt to destroy the humanity of the Jews. If, however, a "decent German" remains, that destruction is not complete, just as the destruction of the Jews is not complete.

For similar reasons, Topas brought out the importance of friendship to survival and the fact that the survival of one's humanity rested not on looking out for "Number One" but on sustaining a relationship to another human being. While Topas's memoir is full of memories of other human beings, the one closest to him was a man named Mark Heering. His friendship, says Topas, "was the only good thing I had acquired in this barren captivity" (p. 218). Life, according to Topas, derives from relation, and he gives voice to this memory not for the attention called to himself but for the teaching offered to another, to his reader.

SELECTED WORK BY THE AUTHOR
The Iron Furnace: A Holocaust Survivor's Story. Lexington: University Press of Kentucky, 1990.

David Patterson

Tory, Avraham (1909–)

A young lawyer in Kovno, Avraham Tory began the first entry in his Kovno ghetto diary on the evening of June 22, 1941, in words as quiet as the day had begun: "It was a sunny Sunday morning, in the provincial capital of Lithuania" (p. 3)—which conveys to the reader the unexpectedness and the disruption of everyday life for the Jews of Kovno (Kaunus). Soon the news reached the city that German troops had crossed the Soviet border and entered Lithuania. By that evening, before the German atrocities had begun, Lithuanians attacked and murdered Jewish neighbors in the city and in the Marijampole (Slobodka) suburb of Kovno. Tory continued to keep his diary until January 1944, shortly before he escaped from the ghetto to await liberation in hiding.

Published in 1988, *Geto yom-yom: Yoman u-mismakhim mi-Geto Kovnah* (*Surviving the Holocaust: The Kovno Ghetto Diary*, 1990) is the most complete, open, and uncensored account by a member of the administrative secretariat of a *Judenrat* (Jewish Council) preserved from the Holocaust. It is also rare as a testament by a surviving member of a *Judenrat*. It is the most accurate account available of the German occupation of Kovno, the mass murders of the Jewish population at the Ninth Forth, and of Jewish life in the Kovno ghetto. After the war Tory brought his diary to court as testimony against Kazys Palciauskas, the former major of Kovno, and Helmut Rauca, the head of Jewish affairs at Gestapo headquarters in Kovno.

Tory was born Avraham Golub in the Lithuanian village of Lazdijai in 1909. His father was a graduate of the Volozhin yeshiva, and his mother's parents owned a farm. By the age of thirteen, he was active with the Maccabi Club and as a member of the General Zionist Youth Movement in Lithuania. He graduated in 1927 from the first Hebrew high school in Lithuania and began law studies in Kovno. In 1930, after a year and a half in the United States at the University of Pittsburgh, he returned to Lithuania to continue his studies in Kovno. In 1932 he visited Palestine and participated as an athlete in the first Maccabiah Games in Tel Aviv.

He graduated with a law degree in 1933. Although he was qualified to serve in the judiciary, very few Jewish lawyers in Lithuania could obtain a license to practice. Instead he worked as a clerk in the court chambers of a classmate and then as an assistant to one of the few Jewish professors at the university in Kovno. In August 1939 Tory was in Switzerland as a delegate to the twenty-first Zionist Congress, but he returned home immediately when the war broke out. Under the Soviet administration, he worked for the military construction administration before the Soviets learned of his Zionist background. In fear of the secret police, he fled and went into hiding in Vilna, shortly before the German occupation of Kovno.

The published diary is a unique compilation of various texts and documents. It contains Tory's original Yiddish diary text, including sections that he rewrote immediately after the war as a "memoir" to replace material lost, as well as original documents from the *Judenrat* and the German ghetto administration. Also included is a short memoir by Jack Braun, whose father, as a ghetto physician, hid during the typhus outbreak in 1942. Finally, the volume contains Tory's will and a revealing, emotional letter from the head of the *Judenrat*, Dr. Elkhanan Elkes, to his children abroad. As secretary of the council, Tory was a link to the resistance and, with Elkes's knowledge, he led the effort to collect and leave a hidden archive of the ghetto administration.

Tory explained the call he felt to record the German atrocities in his last will and testimony, which he laid on top of each of the five crates of archive materials he buried in the ghetto in December 1942. He wrote, "Driven by a force within me, and out of fear that no remnant of the Jewish community of Kovno will survive to tell of its final death agony under Nazi rule . . . every day, I put into writing what my eyes had seen and my ears had heard and what I had experienced personally" (pp. 167–68). As was the case with other chroniclers in the Holocaust, he wrote in full knowledge that the diary's discovery would be a death sentence. He wrote in the hope that the diary, discovered after the war, would serve as a "'corpus delicti'—accusing testimony—when the Day of Judgment comes" (pp. 168–69).

Tory attended the last meeting of the Kovno community on August 4, 1941, when Elkes reluctantly agreed to serve as head of the *Judenrat*. Tory joined the council and began to record the actions of the perpetrators unstintingly. He watched, with Elkes, on October 28, 1941, when the Gestapo arrived at Demokratu Square in the ghetto and selected 10,000 victims, recalling later, in simple words, that "it was a death procession" (p. 56). He described them, as they stood, "30,000 lonely people forgotten by God and by man" (p. 49), with openness and honesty.

The diary provides a unique insight into the mentality of the perpetrators. Tory recalled that on that horrific day in 1941 Rauca feasted on a sandwich, while "[he] . . . directed the job of selection composedly, with cynicism, and with the utmost speed . . . all those tragedies did not penetrate his heart" (p. 52). He also reported that the council and the police supported the resistance. In February 1943 he recorded, "We are dealing with wild beasts . . . mass murder is their raison d'être" (p. 238). With cunning frankness he continued to assess the perpetrators: "As they stepped over the carcasses [of cats and dogs in the synagogue], they seemed not heroes, but dwarfs or clowns in shiny uniforms" (p. 311).

On May 4, 1943, he began his entry with lyrical words, "The radiant golden rays of the spring sunshine illuminated the morning hours of the day. The air in the Ghetto was suffused with warmth, light and joy. The trees and plants basked in the sun." But he soon turned to the harsh reality of life in the ghetto, adding that "this pretty picture is sharply circumscribed, however, by the barbed-wire fence surrounding us. No painter in his artistic imagination could conjure up the combination of a fairy tale—an open landscape—and a barbed-wire fence . . . the grayness of the ghetto and all that it entails keep tugging at your heart incessantly" (p. 318).

After liberation, Tory married Pnina Sheinzon, a council secretary who had hidden the diary entries, as he wrote them. He was able to recover his diary (only three crates were located), but, in fear of the Soviet secret police, had to turn over parts of it to *Brichah* (an organization dedicated to getting Jews into Palestine) leaders in Bucharest. Together with Pnina's daughter, they arrived in Palestine in 1947. In 1950 he changed his surname to Tory which means "dove" in Hebrew (Golub has the same meaning in Lithuanian). In 1952 he began to practice law and has remained active with the Maccabi World Union. Parts of the ghetto diary and documentary material were brought to him in the 1960s from Romania; in the next ten years, further pages arrived in Israel. Tory told Elkes's son that holding the pages was like "touching fire" (Elkes, p. 13). Today, he lives in Tel Aviv and continues his testimony about the Kovno ghetto.

SELECTED WORKS BY THE AUTHOR
Geto yom-yom: Yoman u-mismakhim mi-Geto Kovnah. Ed. Dina Porat. Tel-Aviv: University of Tel-Aviv, 1988, 1992; *Surviving the Holocaust: The Kovno Ghetto.* Trans. Jerzy Michalowicz, ed. Martin Gilbert. Cambridge, Mass.: Harvard University Press, 1990.

FOR FURTHER READING
Elkes, Joel, *Dr. Elkhanan Elkes of the Kovno Ghetto: A Son's Holocaust Memoir.* Brewster, Mass.: Paraclete, 1999; Mishell, William W., *Kaddish for Kovno: Life and Death in a Lithuanian Ghetto 1941–1945.* Chicago: Chicago Review Press, 1998; United States Holocaust Memorial Museum, *Hidden History of the Kovno Ghetto.* Boston: Little, Brown, 1997.

Susan Lee Pentlin

Trepman, Paul (1916–1987)

Originally written in Yiddish, Paul Trepman's memoir, *Among Men and Beasts* was not published until its English edition appeared in 1978. It is the work of a pious, educated man who affirms the humanity of the human being through his outcry over a humanity turned bestial. The text is as remarkable and varied as Trepman's wide-ranging experiences of numerous camps and ghettos.

A graduate of the famous Tachkemoni Rabbinical Seminary in Warsaw, Paul Trepman was born Pinkhas Lazarovitch Trepman in 1916 in the Polish capital. His memoir recounts much of his life not only during the Holocaust but also before the catastrophe. Soon after his liberation, Trepman became the editor of *Unzer Shtimme*, the first Jewish periodical to be published in Germany during the postwar years. He was also a member of the Central Committee of the Liberated Jews of the British Zone. Trepman married Babey Widuchinsky, whom he met in Bergen-Belsen, and in 1948 the two of them moved to Montreal, where Trepman worked as an educator and a librarian until his death in 1987.

Trepman's memoir is divided into three parts. In Part One he recounts his experiences in the Ukraine, where he and three of his friends fled when the war broke out. They escaped the German murderers, however, only to face Ukrainian murderers, until the arrival of Hungarian troops gave them a six-week respite. Shortly after the Germans' invasion of Russia on June 22, 1941, he returned to Poland to look for his mother, only to discover that she had been murdered by the Germans.

In Part Two Trepman describes life and death in the ghettos in Warsaw and Rohatyn, his efforts to pass as a Polish Aryan, and his constant fear of betrayal by the Poles. In June 1943 he was arrested and sent to the Gestapo prison in Stanislawów; in August 1943, he was transported to Majdanek. Part Three, which makes up most of the memoir, begins with Trepman's stay in Majdanek and relates his struggle to survive in six camps: Majdanek, Gross-Rosen, Sachsenhausen, Retzow, Ellrich, and Bergen-Belsen. It contains striking portraits of the men, both good and evil, whom he met in the concentrationary universe. One of the most haunting portraits is of Dr. Ignatz Schipper, a great scholar and professor from Warsaw. In Majdanek, however, "he could be heard alternately laughing and crying, mumbling incoherent phrases. He had become the camp madman . . . . He no longer recognized me—or anyone else" (p. 88). Thus the man whose life was devoted to the learning of humanity had his humanity undone.

One of the most unforgettable characters in the memoir is Carl Jantzen, a Norwegian who helped Trepman and others maintain their human image by the example he set. Trepman met Jantzen at the Heinckel Aircraft Works near Sachsenhausen; there Jantzen urged Trepman and other prisoners to do such things as wash their bodies each day to sustain their humanity. For the act of cleaning oneself is an affirmation of one's value as a human being: one cleans what one regards as precious. More important than cleansing oneself, however, was showing kindness toward others; by being humane toward another, a man could retain his humanity. Thus, recalled Trepman, "it was not merely [Jantzen's] food from Norway that gave us new strength. It was Carl Jantzen himself, simply by being what he was. His human kindness, his words of encouragement" (p. 217). Trepman learned that to stay alive as a human being entails not stealing from another but helping another.

Like many survivors, Trepman wrote his memoir out of a profound sense of being chosen for his mission, conveying a message that transforms the reader into a messenger. On September 3, 1943, for example, all the Jews in Majdanek, Lipowa, and Camp Piasky were murdered—all except Pinkhas Lazarovitch Trepman. Commenting on that day, he wrote, "Perhaps Providence intended that I, with my false 'Aryan' identity and non-Jewish appearance, should be spared from that slaughter, so that I alone, having witnessed it, should live to record this one event which otherwise might have been omitted from mankind's testimony against Hitler" (p. 138).

A critical part of Trepman's memoir is his memory of his liberation from Bergen-Belsen—and the *problem* of liberation. "We are afraid of freedom," he recorded. "I've survived the war—but was it worth it? What kind of life will I have with my heart bleeding and my spirit broken? Now that I am free, all I feel is a terrible ache of loneliness" (p. 222). One realizes that the term *liberation* is misleading in this case. He is "liberated" but without a family or home to return to; "liberated" but unable to tell his tale, unable to find anyone to listen or who can even understand; "liberated" but unable to bury the dead and put them behind him because they have no graves; "liberated" but broken and alone. What, then, is this liberation? *Is* it liberation?

SELECTED WORKS BY THE AUTHOR
Among Men and Beasts. Trans. Shoshana Perla and Gertrude Hirschler. New York: Bergen Belsen Memorial Press, 1978; *A gesl in Varshe.* Montreal: [no publisher given], 1949.

David Patterson

V

Vrba, Rudolf (1924–)

Written with the assistance of British journalist Alan Bestic, Rudolf Vrba's *I Cannot Forgive* (1964) is the memoir of a Slovakian Jew who escaped from Auschwitz in 1944 with his friend Alfred Wetzler and provided the world with the first eyewitness account of the extermination camp. An expanded version of his original memoir was published in 1989 under the title *44070: The Conspiracy of the Twentieth Century*. Written with a much greater concern for telling the truth than for glorifying himself, *I Cannot Forgive* is more Vrba's account of Nazi atrocities than a tale of his own suffering. In addition to writing his memoir, Vrba has been involved in the production of six films on the Holocaust, including Claude Lanzmann's *Shoah*.

Born in the Slovakian town of Topolcany in 1924, Vrba was forced to leave school at the age of fifteen because he was a Jew. He was sent to Auschwitz in June 1942 for his involvement in the resistance movement against the fascist regime of Monsignor Tiso. Immediately after his escape from Auschwitz in April 1944, he and Alfred Wetzler made their way to Bratislava, where they submitted their first report on the activities in the murder camp to the Bratislava Jewish Council; the report was later delivered to Allen Dulles in Switzerland. Soon after his escape, Vrba joined the Czechoslovakian partisan movement and fought against the Nazis until the end of the war. In 1945 he en-rolled in the Czech Technical University in Prague, where he earned a doctorate degree in 1951. Known for his research in neurochemistry, Vrba worked for a variety of health institutes in Czechoslovakia, Israel, and England. In 1967 he became a professor of pharmacology at the University of British Columbia; now retired, he lives in Vancouver.

Perhaps as much as the murder of more than six million human beings, it is the Nazis' assault on the very image of the human being that Vrba cannot forgive, a point that comes out in *I Cannot Forgive* in many ways. He recalled, for example, a companion in Auschwitz who had been known for his elegant dress and now wore the "zebra stripes" of the camp. Once a talented musician, "now the music had disappeared from him" (p. 76). Gazing upon a column of women, Vrba further recalled, "It was their faces which chilled me most, faces like skulls, with eyes that were empty and unseeing" (p. 93). Thus faces that were once full of life had been made into vessels of death, as if the SS had refashioned these people after the death's head insignia on their uniforms.

To be sure, among the faces transformed by the death camp into images of death was Vrba's own face. Taking a rare opportunity to look into a mirror, for instance, he saw "the face of a Moslem" staring back at him, "the thin death's head of a man about to collapse" (p. 157). Even after his escape, the Holocaust kingdom had left its imprint on his face, so much so that when he was reunited with his mother she did not recognize him at first. "I had seen 1,760,000 people die," he wrote, "and that had left a mark on my face" (p. 251). Vrba's reader realizes that, in a sense, there is no escape from Auschwitz even for the escapee.

Other faces were refashioned after the image of the Nazis themselves. Remembering a former friend named Vrbicky, who had become a *kapo* in Majdanek, for example, Vrba wrote, "I looked in horror into the face of my old lackadaisical, lecherous, hard-drinking friend. The lazy eyes were like little stones now . . . . Vrbicky had been remodeled" (pp. 55–56). The eyes of the Nazis themselves, however, were more expressive, as Vrba demonstrated when he said of the SS that they "would burn without scruple,

indeed with patriotic fervor, one thousand children; but their eyes would grow misty when they swapped pictures of their own loved ones at home" (p. 162). Such an antithesis underlying the disparity between the worlds in which the Nazis operated is one of the best expressions of the anti-world they created. And Vrba's memoir is one of the best expressions of that radical contradiction.

SELECTED WORKS BY THE AUTHOR
44070: The Conspiracy of the Twentieth Century, with Alan Bestic. Bellingham, Wash.: Star and Cross, 1989; *I Cannot Forgive*, with Alan Bestic. New York: Bantam, 1964.

David Patterson

Wallant, Edward Lewis (1926–1962)

Edward Lewis Wallant was among the first Jewish American novelists to write about the Holocaust. Although himself a non-witness, several of his relatives survived the death camps, and he had extensive discussions with them about their experiences. His novel *The Pawnbroker* (1961) provided American readers with a glimpse of the Shoah through the eyes of Sol Nazerman, a survivor who lost his family in the conflagration. Following the war, Nazerman—who had been a university professor—remains in Europe for a brief time where he works assisting refugees. After coming to America, he lives with his sister—a prewar immigrant—and her family, and owns an East Harlem pawnshop which serves as a money-laundering front for a Mafia figure. The novel gained added cultural resonance when it was made into a motion picture.

Born in New Haven, Connecticut in 1926, Wallant worked on Madison Avenue and wrote four novels, each of which is linked by a concern for the issue of redemption from evil and suffering through rejoining the protagonist to the human community. Although *The Pawnbroker* is the only one of Wallant's novels that directly focuses on the Holocaust, the author hoped that each of his novels would sensitize people to the pain experienced by all humans. Wallant died of a cerebral hemorrhage at the age of thirty-six. An annual award for the best Jewish fiction bears his name.

Wallant wrote at a time when little cultural attention was paid to the Holocaust. Consequently, his novel was simultaneously path-breaking and traditional. His work is important because it exposes many of the fault lines of culture that were engendered by the Holocaust, including the assumption that reason will prevail over evil, that humans are innately good, and that language itself is to be trusted. Moreover, *The Pawnbroker* deals with major unresolved issues in the post-Holocaust world, such as Christian anti-Jewish teachings and feelings, the unprecedented nature of the Shoah, and the fact that the post-Auschwitz world remains unredeemed. Wallant's protagonist is a victim of a so-called medical experiment by SS doctors, and he is deeply suspicious of the social world. Along with his loss of faith, the survivor's nihilism extends to every facet of culture. He trusts nothing: "God or politics or newspapers or music or art. . . . But, most of all, I do not trust people and their talk, for they have proved that they do not deserve to exist for what they are" (p. 87).

The Pawnbroker is an ambitious novel that seeks to underscore the difference between types of suffering: Holocaust survivors, black victims of poverty, and alcoholics; those whom life has overwhelmed; the relationship of Jewish identity to the Holocaust; and continuing manifestations of anti-Semitism. Wallant brings Nazerman to America thereby juxtaposing the European Jewish experience and American culture. The protagonist supports the family of his acculturated sister, Bertha, who constantly urges her brother to forget the past. Nazerman and his nephew, Morton, an artist, are the family outcasts because they do not conform to Bertha's denial of her Jewish identity.

In his pawnshop, itself a place of failed dreams, Sol has three significant encounters. He acquires a Puerto Rican assistant, Jesus Ortiz, who will later conspire to rob him but who initially begs Nazerman to teach him the business. Mabel Wheatly, Jesus's girlfriend and a prostitute, offers herself to Sol to help Jesus. Sol rejects this suggestion although he gives Mabel the money she needs. He is stunned to learn that Murillo, his business "partner," owns the house of prostitution where Mabel works. Recalling the forced sexual enslavement of his wife in the camps, Nazerman visits Murillo to demand an end to their partnership. Instead, he is crudely assaulted with a gun and thrown out. Finally, Marilyn Birchfield, an overweight and lonely social worker attempts to befriend Sol and wonders why he is so bitter. In response, the pawnbroker contends that he is not bitter, rather," I am past that by a million years!" (p. 110).

The novel's denouement occurs when Jesus and his accomplices attempt to rob the pawnshop. Jesus steps in front of the pawnbroker as one of the robbers fires a fatal shot. Touched by this sacrificial act, Nazerman is able to experience love for the first time in many years. He prepares to rejoin the human community in two ways—by calling his nephew Morton and asking his help in running the store, and by being able to mourn his Holocaust dead. The novel ends with Sol going to the house of Tessie Rubin, who is his mistress and the widow of a friend who was murdered in Auschwitz.

Wallant makes extensive use of dream sequences to demonstrate that, for the survivors, the Holocaust continues to wound. Furthermore, the author underscores the involuntary role of memory in the lives of survivors. Every August (the ninth of Av which tradition assigns as the time of the destruction of the Temple in Jerusalem), Sol has flashbacks during which he recalls the destruction of his family. Through this device Wallant presents the chronology of his protagonist's Holocaust experience. Although

living in Westchester and working in East Harlem, Nazerman psychically inhabits the Holocaust world which he never leaves.

The Pawnbroker portrays the complexity and diversity of survivor types. Nazerman's rejection of emotional attachment contrasts with the passivity and fear of his mistress, Tessie Rubin. Mendel, Tessie's father, although bedridden and in enormous pain, retains his faith. A doctor who examines him is amazed that he is still alive and wonders if his injuries are the result of an accident. Nazerman responds, "Yes, an accident of birth," underscoring that for the Nazis Jewish birth constituted a death sentence. Goberman is a survivor who corroborated with the Germans to save his own life. In New York he preys on the guilt of survivors to collect funds for the Jewish Appeal. Nazerman refers to him as being "worse than all the Nazis."

Yet *The Pawnbroker* also reflects the cultural naiveté of the times. In this sense it is quite traditional. For example, Wallant relies on overt Christian symbolism (i.e., Jesus dies for the Jew Nazerman) and writes essentially about the universal problem of evil and suffering, issues that American audiences could understand, rather than about the Holocaust itself. Nevertheless, Wallant's novel served to begin the continuing process of educating the American people about the enormity of the Shoah.

SELECTED WORKS BY THE AUTHOR
The Children at the Gate. New York: Harcourt, Brace and World, 1964; *The Human Season*. New York: Harcourt, Brace and World, 1960; *The Pawnbroker*. New York: Harcourt, Brace and World, 1961; *The Tenants of Moonblum*. New York: Harcourt, Brace and World, 1963.

FOR FURTHER READING
Baumback, Jonathan, *The Landscape of Nightmare*. New York: New York University Press, 1965; Berger, Alan L., *Crisis and Covenant: The Holocaust in American Jewish Fiction*. Albany, N.Y.: SUNY Press, 1985; Kremer, S. Lillian, *Witness Through the Imagination: Jewish-American Holocaust Literature*. Detroit: Wayne State University Press, 1989.

Alan L. Berger

Wasser, Hersh (1912–1981)

Hersh Wasser's diary was among Emmanuel Ringelblum's *Oneg Shabbat* archives unearthed on September 18, 1946. The diary not only reflects the courage of his own efforts to attest to the Nazis' atrocities, but also affirms the courage of the entire *Oneg Shabbat* organization.

Born in Suwałki, Poland, in 1912, Wasser and his wife, Bluma, arrived in Warsaw as refugees in 1939. He survived the tribulations of the Warsaw ghetto and moved to Tel Aviv in 1950. Originally written in Yiddish, his diary covers the period from late 1939 to June 1942, shortly before the massive deportations from the Warsaw ghetto began.

There are several striking features about Wasser's diary. He is especially sensitive, for example, to the plight of the children in the Warsaw ghetto. On December 6, 1940, he wrote, "Before my eyes I saw a small boy shot down, corner of Chlodna-Zelazna. Heartrending. In the evening, on Bonifraterska, a little lad was wounded" (p. 218). Exactly one week later he attested to a spiritual dimension of the Nazis' assault on the child: "The soul of the child and youngster grows more and more tainted. The lack of schools, the gutter, absolute demoralization, leave their terrible mark. What sort of generation will grow out of all this?" (p. 233). Raising such a question, Wasser not only bears witness to his time; he puts a question to the generations of all time.

As he is attuned to the plight of the child, so is Wasser sensitive to the plight of the word that gives meaning to the child. "Here and there," he noted on December 2, 1940, "one may hear a sympathetic word, but it is drowned out in the surroundings" (p. 212); the only words that remain are words that undermine words, meaning, and compassion. As words of compassion are drowned, so is the sense of a world in which a human being may belong. Hence the ghetto appears as an "elsewhere" that is nowhere. "Everyone wants to be in 'Poland,'" says Wasser, "i.e. on the other side of the ghetto" (p. 230)— as if the ghetto were somewhere else. Thus he underlines the situation of the ghetto—and the Jew—outside the realm of existence.

Because the Jews lie outside the realm of reality, they lie outside the law; for the status of the law is definitively connected to the status of human reality—not only in the Warsaw ghetto but throughout the concentrationary universe fashioned by the Nazis. "German soldiers broke into the Łódź Ghetto," Wasser offered a case in point in an entry dated January 9, 1941, "and murdered 1,100 innocent people without any why or wherefore" (p. 242). On several occasions this undoing of meaning leads Wasser to struggle with the sense of writing. On December 3, 1940, for instance, he declared, "I've no heart for writing" (p. 212). On April 28, 1941, he lamented, "I haven't written for a long time. I've found the pen distasteful" (p. 263). And yet, even when he cannot write, he writes that he cannot write, as if a force greater than himself moves his pen across the page.

Perhaps that force manifests itself in the goodness of another diarist listed in this encyclopedia, a diarist who writes when he has every reason not to write: Menachem Kon.* A friend of Kon, Wasser attested to Kon's goodness, asserting that he is "a rare person. In every respect. Unique in our [*Oneg Shabbat*] society. His intelligent, good, human face attracts people and inspires respect, esteem, awe. How good it is to come across such a person today" (p. 232). Kon's example of goodness inspired goodness in Wasser; Kon's sense of responsibility inspired a sense of responsibility in Wasser—not only for the people in his world but for his readers, who would be born in a better world. That is why he was able to write his diary even when he could not write.

SELECTED WORK BY THE AUTHOR
"Daily Entries of Hersh Wasser." Trans. Joseph Kermish. *Yad Vashem Studies* 15 (1983): 201–82.

David Patterson

Weil, Jiří (1900–1959)

In his preface to the English edition of Jiří Weil's most renowned Holocaust novel, *Život s hvêdou*, 1946 (*Life with a Star*, 1989), Philip Roth* describes the work as "the outstanding Czech book published between 1945 and 1948" (p. vi). Written between the end of World War II and the Communist takeover—during a time of relative freedom—*Life with a Star* is based on the experiences Weil himself endured during the Nazi terror. Through the novel's narrator, Josef Roubicek, Weil explores the realities of life and death, of love and destiny, precisely at a time when those realities were rendered unreal with the onset of the Nazi evil.

Jiří Weil was born in 1900 in Praskolesy, Bohemia, a territory which became part of Czechoslovakia in 1918. He joined the Communist Party early in his life, but his writing, which portrayed Stalinism in an unfavorable light, often caused him to be at odds with party policies. He was expelled from the party in the mid-1930s for his criticisms of the living conditions in the Soviet Union. When the Nazis invaded Czechoslovakia in 1939, Weil went into hiding for a time; when he was summoned for deportation to the camps, he avoided the transport by faking suicide. After that he remained in hiding until the end of the war. His personal wartime experiences closely parallel those of Josef Roubicek in *Life with a Star*. The publication of *Life with a Star* resulted in his expulsion from the Writers' Union. Weil remained in Czechoslovakia after the war and served as director of the Jewish State Museum in Prague, until he died of cancer in 1959.

In *Life with a Star,* Josef Roubicek's efforts to escape the Nazis are interwoven with his relationship to Ruzena, the woman he loves and for whom he would give his life. Declaring to her that he did not run away because he was afraid of getting caught (p. 5), Roubicek nonetheless constantly risks being caught to be with Ruzena. Through her he realizes that his life can have meaning only if he risks his life in the pursuit of some sort of victory over the Nazis. Thus he transforms the yellow star from the sign of the subhuman outcast into a sign of humanity.

Placing his character in a graveyard detail, Weil explores the relation between language and death, just as he explores the relation between love and death. Death lies in the tearing of words from meaning; as Roubicek rakes the leaves from the graves, words are returned to meaning, for he can hear the souls of the dead form a

song in the rustling of the leaves (p. 74). Weil's examination of the word leads him to an examination of the exile of the word from meaning; here he introduces the figure of Jesus, whom the apostle John associates with the word and who is here marked for deportation (p. 118). Roubicek's close connection with Jesus can be seen in his first name, Josef, who was the father of Jesus, or the father of the word. Here the role of Jesus as the conqueror of death and fear receives greater emphasis than his role as the redeemer of sin. In the Holocaust, however, death and fear are precisely what are not conquered.

Roubicek collides with both when he discovers that Ruzena is among those who have been murdered (p. 190). The one way in which he can overcome the fear and death that rule the concentrationary universe, he concludes, is to be prepared to die rather than suffer the torture of humiliation and dehumanization. "I realized," he declares, "that the Josef Roubicek who wanted to make excuses, to evade, and to dodge, only to avoid freedom, no longer existed and would never again exist" (p. 208). Thus Roubicek overcomes the confines of his entrapment in the Nazi net.

Weil's other major work, *Na střeše je Mendelssohn* (*Mendelssohn Is on the Roof,* 1991), was first published in Czechoslovakia in 1960. Like *Life with a Star*, *Mendelssohn Is on the Roof* is set in Prague during the war; also like *Life with a Star*, its defining idea is that freedom comes with the willingness to die for freedom. While *Life with a Star* was written from the first-person point of view, *Mendelssohn* is narrated from various viewpoints, both Jewish and non-Jewish.

In the novel, Julius Schlesinger is ordered to remove a statue of the Jewish composer Mendelssohn; Schlesinger, a Nazi functionary, in turn, orders some workers to do the job. Picking the statue with the biggest nose, the workers mistakenly remove a statue of the notorious German anti-Semitic composer Richard Wagner. The core plot of the novel revolves around the question of which statue is the one of Mendelssohn. The novel, however, contains a complicated array of tangential subplots. There is the story of the Jew Rudolf Vorlitzer who contracts a disease that turns him to stone. There is the Christian Jan Krulis who tries to hide Vorlitzer's nieces, Adela and Greta. And there is the museum curator, a Jew named Doctor Rabinovich, who is beaten by the Nazis for refusing to help identify the graven image of Mendelssohn. What all these characters have in common is their refusal to bow before the Nazi oppression.

The figure who in the end embodies this position is Richard Reisinger. Coming to the aid of the partisans, Reisinger emerges as the novel's chief protagonist; he realizes that one had "to be willing to give up one's comfort, submission, and fear; one had to be willing to sacrifice one's own life, if need be, for a cause that would ultimately prevail and bring peace and freedom to other people" (p. 146). This idea that life has meaning to the extent that it is offered for the sake of others characterizes Weil's own life and work. It is the idea that he opposes to the Nazi idea of murdering others for the sake of oneself.

SELECTED WORKS BY THE AUTHOR

Dřevêna lžíce. Prague: Mladá Fronta, 1992; *Life with a Star.* Trans. Ruzena Kovarikova and Roslyn Schloss. New York: Farrar, Straus and Giroux, 1989; *Mendelssohn Is on the Roof.* Trans. Marie Winn. New York: Farrar, Straus and Giroux, 1991; *Moskva-hranice.* Prague: Mladá Fronta, 1991.

David Patterson

Weinstein, Frida Scheps (1936–)

Frida Scheps Weinstein's *A Hidden Childhood, 1942–1945* (1985) is a devastating account of a young Jewish girl whose core identity is shaken to its very roots by the experience of hiding in a convent. Told from a child's point of view, the author is six years old when the tale begins. The memoir tells the heartbreaking story of the child's shame about her refugee mother, the youngster's understanding that it is vital to conceal their Jewish identity, and her subsequent eagerness to become a faithful Christian. The author shares the plight of hidden children during the Holocaust, focusing on the issues of abandonment, silence, identity confusion, friendship, and rediscovering Jewish roots. Like Nechama Tec,* Scheps Weinstein discovers that she has a dual identity. Although she is the first to tell her Christian playmates that she does not like Jews, "Inside myself," she recalls, "I feel uneasy" (p. 8).

Frida Scheps was born in 1936 in Paris, the city to which her Russian-Jewish immigrant parents had fled. Her father, an engineer, wanted the family to move to Palestine, and he went to Jerusalem on the eve of the war to make arrangements for the move. The advent of the war trapped Mrs. Scheps and Frida in Paris, and Mr. Scheps in Jerusalem. When the Nazis began deporting Jews from France, her mother sent Frida to the convent boarding school at the Château de Beajeu. Subsequently, the mother was deported to Germany where she perished in Bergen-Belsen. At age nine the author was sent to a boarding school at Dijon where she stayed for a short time. She then spent two years in a series of "Jewish homes" in the suburbs of Paris. In 1947 she went to Jerusalem, was reunited with her father, and completed her grammar and secondary schooling. In 1954 she entered the Israeli army. From 1956 until 1961 the author lived in France, England, and Israel. She moved to the United States in 1961 and, from 1962 to 1974 worked for Agence France-Press. She married in 1970 and lives in New York.

The author shares the lessons she learned about the importance of hiding. Listening to her mother and aunt, she hears a constant refrain, "Ve gotta hide" (p. 8). Part of this concealment is the denial of feelings and emotions. For example, on the eve of her departure for the convent school, Frida does not recall if her mother hugged and kissed her, although she later learns that "all mothers cry and little girls, too, when they part." As for the young girl, she does recall a feeling of elation at parting from her mother, "I felt rid of her" (p. 11). At the boarding school, Sister Marie urges the young girls not to talk too much. The author's major act of concealment, however, concerns her Jewish identity: she takes communion, learns the catechism by heart, and analogizes the Pharisees of antiquity who were rebuked by Jesus for dealing in the market to her mother who also dealt in the [black] market in Paris (p. 27).

Lack of a baptismal certificate concretizes the fact that Frida is different. Consequently, the young girl resolves to become a good Christian. This act sets her against the Jewish people, including her own mother. For example, when Rachel, another little Jewish girl, arrives at the convent, Frida is adamantly opposed to her. Rachel simply does not fit in and no one likes her. The author hopes that Rachel will leave, and she compares Rachel to Mary Magdalene. Frida herself anxiously awaits her mother's permission to allow the young girl to be baptized. There is, however, a cruel irony. In catechism the youngsters are taught about baptism. The teachings include a negative Christian assessment of Jews and Judaism. Frida writes that the "ignorance" of some parents prevented some of the girls from receiving the sacrament at birth. Because her mother did not respond to the request to have her baptized, Frida compared it to the "betrayal by the disciples in the Gospel" (p. 50). Jews are presented as "that cursed race" (p. 98).

Frida began to experience some positive feelings about her Jewish identity with the arrival at the school of an older girl, Henriette. Henriette was thoughtful, mature, and very smart, but she kept to herself. She was also Jewish. Trying to communicate with the older girl in a secret language that no one else could understand, Frida was chagrined that she had forbidden her mother to speak to her in that language. She did, however, remember three Yiddish words which she uttered to Henriette. When the older girl asked her where she learned those words, Frida panicked and ran away. Thus although, in her childish abandon, she aspired to become a Christian saint, Frida also felt the pull of her Jewish ancestral ties. She fantasized about her home in Paris . . . "a Jewish home" (p. 127).

Scheps Weinstein's memoir provides a glimpse into the psychic travail experienced by Jewish hidden children. Frida undergoes many changes throughout the course of the novel. Beginning by hating her mother, she ends by making an icon out of a skirt her mother had sewn for her many years earlier. She learns the rites and rituals of Catholicism to become a "good Christian," including preparation of the "host" distributed at communion, but expresses her psychic distress by becoming a bedwetter. At the end of her memoir, the now nine-year-old girl cherishes her "Jewish" curly hair because her mother "used to make me beautiful curls . . . It's all that I have left of her." When she left the convent, she did not know what happened to her mother, who stopped sending her packages years ago. "Deep down inside me," wrote the author, "I'm afraid; I don't want to know" (p. 151).

SELECTED WORK BY THE AUTHOR
A Hidden Childhood, 1942–1945. Trans. Barbara Loeb Kennedy. New York: Hill and Wang, 1985.

FOR FURTHER READING
Burnley, Judith, "Memoirs of a Would-Be Catholic Girlhood." *New York Times Book Review*, September 8, 1985, Section 7: 30.

Alan L. Berger

Weiss, Peter (1916–1982)

Peter Weiss's play *Die Ermittlung* (1965) (*The Investigation*, 1966), a documentary drama concerning the Auschwitz trials held in Frankfurt, Germany from 1963 to 1965, is considered one of the greatest Holocaust dramas. Before writing the play, Weiss attended the trials and traveled to Auschwitz in 1964. He also read Bernd Naumann's trial reports, which appeared in the *Frankfurter Allgemeine Zeitung*. *The Investigation* is an important Holocaust drama because of its powerful treatment of the trial, which includes the devastating and memorable testimonies of the witnesses, and partly because it is unquestionably one of the finest Holocaust plays written in German by a German author. The only German Holocaust plays that have achieved the same status as *The Investigation* are Bertolt Brecht's *Private Life of the Master Race* and Rolf Hochhuth's* *The Deputy.*

Klaus L. Berghahn considers Weiss's play one of the finest dramatic representations of the Holocaust and claims that the play serves as a "turning point in the literary as well as political sphere of the Federal Republic of Germany" (p. 94). The fact that Weiss's play was performed on fifteen different stages in Germany at the same time and was shown on television manifests that the work reached a large segment of the German people, many of whom knew very little about the Holocaust until the appearance of this drama. Weiss concerned himself with universalizing the suffering so that it would apply not only to the past (to the Holocaust and to National Socialism), but also to current situations and to the oppression of people in general (Ellis, p. 43).

Peter Weiss, playwright, novelist, artist, and filmmaker, was born in Nowawes, near Berlin, in 1916, but he immigrated to London with his family in 1934 to escape the Nazis. Weiss and his family subsequently moved to Czechoslovakia in 1936 and to Sweden in 1939; he became a Swedish citizen in 1945. Weiss studied art in Berlin and Prague. In addition to writing, Weiss spent time as a painter (he held several art exhibitions) and as a draftsman. He married artist Helga Henschen in 1943, and their daughter, Randi, was born in 1944, the year they divorced. He married costume and set designer Gunilla Palmstierna in 1964, and they had a daughter, Nadja, in 1972.

Weiss has claimed that Auschwitz was a place that he was destined for but had managed to escape. Consequently, Weiss experienced pangs of guilt for not suffering the pain and atrocities suffered by many Jews, guilt that surfaces in his semiautobiographical novel entitled *Fluchpunkt* (*Vanishing Point*, 1962). The Frankfurt Auschwitz trials profoundly affected Weiss and his subsequent writings. His play *The Investigation* deals, of course, with what he witnessed during the trials, but the trials also affected his political thought, and thus his political writings, for the rest of his life. Weiss believed strongly in socialism, and he visited Cuba and North Vietnam. Weiss died of a heart attack in Stockholm, Sweden, on May 10, 1982.

The Investigation is a condensation, in poetry, of the Auschwitz trials in Frankfurt. The work contains eleven oratorios, beginning with "The Song of the Platform" and concluding with "The Song of the Fire Ovens"; the oratorio immediately before "The Song of the Fire Ovens" is entitled "The Song of Cyklon B." The drama, therefore, follows a chronological progression of the inmates' lives in Auschwitz, from their arrival on the platform after riding on the freight cars until their deaths and subsequent burning in the crematoria. The description by the witnesses of what occurred on the platform when a freight car of Jews arrived is vivid and shattering, reminiscent in many ways of a similar description offered by Tadeusz Borowski* in *This Way for the Gas, Ladies and Gentlemen*. But Weiss is not as concerned with the actual events that occurred in Auschwitz as he is with the testimony given during the Frankfurt trials. The playwright is also not specifically concerned with realism and even remarks in his introductory notes that no attempt should be made by the director to represent in a realistic way the courtroom in Frankfurt, just as no play could accurately portray the atrocities that were committed in Auschwitz. Weiss admits that, in his play, the hundreds of witnesses lose their identity and individuality as he condenses them into nine witnesses whom he, in his introductory note, labels "speaking tubes" (p. v). However, each of the eighteen of the accused does, in fact, represent an individual.

Weiss's personal feelings infiltrate the play, an approach disliked by Otto F. Best. Best disapproves of Weiss's use of the oratorio form, which he considers ornamental rather than substantive, and he remarks that the playwright diminishes his credibility by repeatedly correlating "the monumental event that provoked the investigation with his own biographical involvement even as he defends a system that confines its unpopular writers in mental institutions, a system as familiar with electrically charged barbed wire, murder, and dehumanization as the one symbolized by Auschwitz" (p. 91). It is indeed controversial how Weiss universalizes the events in Auschwitz and links, to some extent, National Socialism with capitalism. For some, this makes the play more powerful, while others do not appreciate the dramatist's decision to universalize the suffering of the Jews in Auschwitz. Regardless of Weiss's political statements, *The Investigation* provides a powerful and informative understanding of some of the atrocities suffered by the Auschwitz prisoners at the hands of the Nazis as well as an understanding of the feeble ex-

cuses offered by the Nazi guards in their defense at the Auschwitz trials in Frankfurt.

SELECTED WORKS BY THE AUTHOR
The Investigation. Trans. Jon Swan and Ulu
Grosbard. New York: Atheneum, 1966; *Leavetaking*
and *Vanishing Point.* Trans. Christopher Levenson.
London: Calder and Boyas, 1966.

FOR FURTHER READING
Berghahn, Klaus L., "Our Auschwitz": Peter Weiss's
The Investigation Thirty Years Later." In *Rethinking
Peter Weiss*, ed. Jost Hermand and Marc Silberman.
New York: Peter Lang, 2000; pp. 93–118; Best, Otto
F., *Peter Weiss.* Trans. Ursule Molinaro. New York:
Frederick Ungar, 1976; Cohen, Robert, *Understand-
ing Peter Weiss.* Columbia: University of South Caro-
lina Press, 1993; Eldh, Åsa, *The Mother in the Work
and Life of Peter Weiss.* New York: Peter Lang, 1990;
Ellis, Roger, *Peter Weiss in Exile: A Critical Study
of His Works.* Ann Arbor, Mich.: UMI Research Press,
1987.

Eric Sterling

Wells, Leon Weliczker (1925–)

Leon Weliczker Wells authored an unusual eyewitness account of the gruesome concentration
camp work of the death brigade, *Death Brigade*,
1978 (originally published as *Janowska Road*,
1962). It is unusual primarily because very few
men survived this work. The death brigade was
forced to exhume graves and burn the murdered
victims of the Nazis. The policy was to kill the
men who did this work every few weeks. Wells
also authored two other books concerning the
Holocaust: *Who Speaks for the Vanquished?*,
1987, and *Shattered Faith: A Holocaust Legacy*,
1995. In the former he questions the role of the
American Zionists before and during the war,
and in the latter he writes about the fate of his
own faith after the Shoah.

Wells was born on March 10, 1925, in
Stojanov near Lvov, Poland, which is now in
modern Ukraine. About 50 percent of the town's
Jews were Hasidic, and Wells was raised in this
religious atmosphere. His father, Abraham, was
a fairly affluent businessman in the lumber industry, with partial ownership of several companies which made the Wells family one of the
wealthiest among the primarily poor Jewish residents. His father and mother, Chana, had seven
children between the ages of seven and nineteen when the Germans invaded Poland. Leon
was the only member of his family to survive
the war. His first residence outside of Poland
after the war was in Munich, Germany, where
he earned his Ph.D. at the University of Munich
in mechanical engineering in 1949, the same
year he published a book in applied mathematics. In 1949 he came to the United States on a
scholarship to study physics at Lehigh University. He married and settled in the United States
with his wife and their three children. He spent
most of his career working as a mechanical engineer and became president of one company.

Death Brigade (*Brygada Smierci*, 1946)
provides an account of Wells's upbringing before the war, as well as an account of his life
during the war years and immediately after liberation. As a child he was raised in a religious
family in a religious town. Wells's parents followed the Hasidic customs of sending their son
to the local religious school and later to the yeshiva when they moved to Lvov; he was also
brought up conscientiously to offer charity to
the local poor. Wells absorbed the Hasidic beliefs and practiced them enthusiastically. He
liked to study and enjoyed the holiness with
which the holidays and Sabbath were imbued.
When he was sixteen, the Germans invaded and
he and his father were initially dragged away
during the day, or for days at a time, to perform
forced labor. Wells was the first of his family to
be placed in the Janowska concentration camp.
At one point, naked, he was lined up to be shot,
but through a series of events he escaped. During the year before he was caught again and sent
back, he lost his four sisters, mother, and father
in various German *Aktions* carried out in Lvov
and Stanjanov. When he was taken to Janowska
the second time, in June 1943, his two younger
brothers were with him. On the same day he
witnessed the shooting of his youngest brother—
"He tried to make himself quite small, hoping
the SS men would not notice him. But they did.
They shot him"—and watched his last sibling
led off to execution (p.130). Leon happens to
be the "right" age for work.

Wells became a member of the death brigade, the prisoners used to destroy all evidence of the Nazi murders. His work crew uncovered the graves and built towering infernos of bodies. Sometimes the graves and the bodies were fresh, sometimes months old. The bodies sometimes fell apart in the workers' hands. The Germans overseers yelled at them to work faster, hit them, threatened them with guns, and at the end of the day forced the prisoners to admit that they were happy. To have any complaints was yet another death sentence. Wells eventually escaped and went into hiding in Lvov until it was liberated by the Russians in May 1944. The family who hid him, who called Wells "Baby," did not know Wells's nor did they ever learn his real name.

Death Brigade is written in an almost unemotional style. The writing is sparse and factual. Wells lets the story itself speak the horror and relate the unspeakable pain. The guilty are condemned not by Wells's accusations but simply by his facts. Characteristically, in one or two sentences, he answered how the liberated survived their nightmare past when he wrote, "The affirmation of life had slowly begun to erase the feelings of hatred against everyone. How can one live despising the world?" (p. 285). And so he began to rebuild his life.

Wells's other autobiographical work, *Shattered Faith*, provides the interior story of Wells's journey from faith to atheism. Again, he seldom editorializes as he presents the memories and images. Wells walks the reader through seven of his Yom Kippurs from childhood through old age. The early ones are very holy experiences for the faith-filled child and indeed for the whole Jewish population. By Yom Kippur 1994, when Wells celebrated at a synagogue in Poland, which was not packed with local Jews but rather included tourists and many empty seats, he explained his loss of faith: "This synagogue for me was proof that 'what was was and is no more' . . . Dead is dead. It is all gone, completely eradicated" (p. 147). At an earlier service in a Reform synagogue in America he was pained by the prayer for the Holocaust victims in which the congregants thank God that they were the victims and not the murderers. There was no choice but to be a victim. When they could hide their Jewishness many, many tried. "I was astonished at what lengths we went to thank God for being the killed and not the killers" (p. 135). He forces the reader to question if it is possible to pray after the Holocaust and thus also the way in which we pray.

In *Who Speaks for the Vanquished?: American Jewish Leaders and the Holocaust,* Wells again lets history speak for itself when he questions the role of the American Zionists during the Nazi years. He presents the primary source documents of Zionist organizations and biographies of leaders of the period which show how little they attempted to rescue or help European Jews. Their first concern was often Zionism and not for the people of Zion. The last sentence of *Death Brigade* asks, "Does the world care?" Through his writings, Leon Wells asks this of each reader, and each reader cannot but feel personally challenged by the question.

SELECTED WORKS BY THE AUTHOR
The Death Brigade. New York: Holocaust Library, 1978; *Shattered Faith: A Holocaust Legacy.* Lexington: University Press of Kentucky, 1995; *Who Speaks for the Vanquished?: American Jewish Leaders and the Holocaust.* New York: Peter Lang, 1987.

Sarita Cargas

Wiesel, Elie (1928–)

One of the world's foremost figures in Holocaust literature, Elie Wiesel is an author and thinker whose work has defined the entire field of Holocaust studies. In addition to being the author of the most famous of all the Holocaust memoirs—*Night*—he is the most prolific of those who emerged from the concentrationary world to write fiction, poetry, and drama in response to the Holocaust. Unlike most other survivors who are renowned for their writing, he is also the author of numerous nonfiction works in Jewish religion, thought, history, and culture.

Wiesel was born on September 30, 1928, in the Hungarian town of Sighet. His father was a businessman and a leader in the Jewish community; his mother was brought up in the Hasidic tradition which had a profound influence on the young Eliezer. Indeed, Wiesel's love of Hasidic tales and mystical teachings is evident throughout his literary work.

The Jews of Sighet were able to maintain an illusion of security until relatively late in the war. By the time the Nazis entered the small town in the spring of 1944, nearly five of the six million Jews murdered in the Holocaust had already been reduced to ashes. When the Wiesel family emerged from the sealed train in Auschwitz-Birkenau, Eliezer and his father were separated from his mother and younger sister forever. Eliezer remained at his father's side over the next year, until his father finally died of exhaustion, starvation, dysentery, and despair.

After surviving Auschwitz, Buna, Gleiwitz, and Buchenwald, Wiesel spent the postwar years in an orphanage in France. In 1948 he entered the Sorbonne, where he studied philosophy and literature. While working as a journalist for the French newspaper *L'Arche* he met Nobel Prize laureate François Mauriac, who urged him to record his memories of the camps. The result was his 900–page memoir *Un die welt hot geshvign* (And the world remained silent), published in 1955 in Buenos Aires after ten years of self-imposed silence. The 120–page French edition was released in 1958 under the title *La Nuit;* the English edition of *Night* first appeared in 1961. Although the book did not initially sell many copies, it was to become the most widely read memoir of the Holocaust.

Written in a deceptively simple style, *Night* is full of silences and allusions which open up the metaphysical and Jewish dimensions of the Holocaust. In subtle ways, the reader sees the assault on prayer, on the holy days, on faith, and even on the Holy One. What is targeted for annihilation is the soul which derives its life from human and divine relationships. In *Night* that deadly process unfolds in detail through the relationship between Eliezer and his father, between Eliezer and God, and between Eliezer and evil. One sees that, in the concentrationary universe, there are no fathers, no sons, no brothers—only starved stomachs that are encouraged to eat each other alive before they are slaughtered. In this context, Eliezer rebels against God and gazes into a mirror, only to have a corpse stare back at him.

Wiesel's first book illustrates a statement that he would make more than ten years later in a collection of memories and portraits called *Chants des morts*, 1968 (*Legends of Our Time*, 1968): "At Auschwitz not only man died, but also the idea of man" (p. 230). Wiesel demonstrates that the Holocaust is distinguished by a collision between two views of the human being: the Nazi view, according to which human value derives from race and a will to power; and the Jewish view, which holds that every human being is created in the image of the Holy One and therefore is infinitely and inherently dear. *Night* and *Legends of Our Time*, moreover, are not the only texts that contain Wiesel's memories and reflections on his past. Others include *Entre deux soleils,* 1965 (*One Generation After,* 1970), *From the Kingdom of Memory: Reminiscences* (1990), and the first part of his autobiography *Tous les fleuves vont à la mer,* 1994 (*All Rivers Run to the Sea*, 1995).

Night was followed by two more books: *L'Aube*, 1960 (*Dawn*, 1961), a novel set in the time of the Jewish revolt against British rule in postwar Palestine, and *Le Jour*, 1961 (*The Accident*, 1962). The story for *Le Jour* is based on an accident suffered by Wiesel when he was hit by a taxicab in New York City, where he lived while working as a reporter covering the United Nations. His injuries left him confined to a wheelchair for almost a year; forced to stay in New York, he became an American citizen in 1963 and has lived there ever since. With his move to New York, Wiesel became a feature writer for the Yiddish language newspaper *Der forverts* and a frequent speaker at Jewish events.

Although all Wiesel's writings contain elements of his Holocaust experience, his fourth work *La ville de la chance*, 1962 (*The Town Beyond the Wall*, 1964) deals specifically with the problem of the bystander and the theme of madness. It is a novel about a survivor who returns to his hometown to confront the spectator who looked on as his Jewish neighbors were taken away; he, far more than the murderer, is an enigma. The confrontation and the enigma lead the main character to the edge of madness, and he ends up in a prison behind the Iron Curtain. Hence the mystery that shrouds the bystander breeds a madness that threatens the protagonist. How is madness here overcome? By enabling another to emerge from madness, as the main character, Michael, does at the end of the novel.

Madmen are frequent figures in Wiesel's literary response to the Holocaust. Indeed, as he himself has pointed out, his literary works basically contain only three characters: the old man, the madman, and the child. Each figure receives a different emphasis in his various works, but each one is there, and the themes surrounding all three recur. The old man generally confronts the loss of understanding and the problem of transmitting a tradition in the aftermath of a collapse of truth and reality. The madman struggles with a testimony to the truth and the delivery of a message in a world that is empty of truth, deaf to the message, and bereft of its humanity. As for the child, he always bears a messianic significance and is often the innocent victim of a radical assault against innocence, purity, and holiness. Each figure needs the other to be who he is, just as the future needs a past and both need a truth.

In his next novel, *Les portes de la forêt*, 1964 (*The Gates of the Forest*, 1966), then, Wiesel further develops the theme of madness by connecting it with the problem of silence and identity, as the main character undergoes a change of name and assumes the role of a mute to avoid capture by the murderers. In *Le serment de Kolvillàg*, 1973 (*The Oath*, 1973), by contrast, an oath of silence must be broken to save a life. And in *Le testament d'un poète juif assassiné*, 1980 (*The Testament*, 1981), silence turns deadly, as Soviet tyranny imposes it upon a Russian Jewish poet named Paltiel Kossover during Josef Stalin's purge of the Jewish intellectuals in the early 1950s. To protect his father, Paltiel's son imposes a silence on himself by biting off his own tongue. The problem: how is he now to become his father's messenger?

In addition to exploring the silence of God and humanity during the Holocaust—whether they are explicitly set in that time or not—these works address the silence of the survivor and the question of whether silence may mend or destroy. To speak is to diminish and therefore to betray both the dead and the living who summon the testimony; to remain silent, however, is to reduce the voices from above and below to emptiness. As the characters in these works demonstrate, when the witness speaks, he transforms his listener into a witness. The matter of recovery, which may or may not come in the aftermath of such a problem, Wiesel addresses in *Le mendiant de Jerusalem*, 1968 (*A Beggar in Jerusalem*, 1970), a tale set in Israel during the Six-Day War. In this work, Wiesel explores the relation between two events unparalleled in Jewish history: the Holocaust and the recovery of the Temple Mount. Wiesel believes there is a meaning couched in this relation, but he offers no fixed formula or ready answer. The meaning, rather, is laden with mystery. One thing, however, he makes clear: in the Jews' journey from Auschwitz to Jerusalem, God can be affirmed or denied, but He cannot be ignored. Wiesel neither affirms nor denies God—he wrestles with Him.

The problem of conveying a message to a listener leads to the problem of how the message is received, which in turn leads to implications of the Holocaust for the survivor's family and community. Here Wiesel's novels reveal the extent of the reverberations of the Nazi evil throughout generations of Jews, as he examines the child of the survivor and the difficulties he confronts upon being made into a witness. This topic had some personal significance for him after his marriage to Marion in 1969 and the birth of their son, Elisha, in 1972. In *Le cinquième fils*, 1983 (*The Fifth Son*, 1985), for example, the son of a survivor faces several problems: understanding his father's silence, establishing a relation to his murdered sibling, and bringing a perpetrator to justice. In *L'Oublié*, 1989 (*The Forgotten*, 1992), Wiesel takes the issue of conveying memory to a deeper level in this tale about a survivor who is diagnosed with Alzheimer's disease and who therefore must transmit his memory to his son before it fades. In keeping with his usual cast of characters, both of these novels deal extensively with the old man and the child; both explore a son's relation to his father's agonizing past; and both raise the question of how the second generation may find a life of its own.

The work that Wiesel produced between these two—*Le crépuscule, au loin*, 1987 (*Twilight*, 1988)—deals extensively with madness. This tale is set in a sanatorium which specializes in treating patients who have taken on the identities of biblical figures. Titled *Twilight*, the novel suggests a return to some of the themes in *Night*, *Dawn*, and *The Accident*. It also contains an important character whose voice played a highly significant role in *The Town Beyond the Wall*: Pedro. In both novels, Pedro is closely connected to the madman and the ways in which the madman challenges our truths. The Pedro of *The Town Beyond the Wall*, for example, likes the rebellious prayer—the "madman's prayer," as he calls it—asking God for the strength to sin against Him. In *Twilight*, however, he declares that what is important to a question is not the answer but the presence of someone who knows the answer. "When I seek that presence," he says, "I am seeking God" (p. 198). Through this character, whose rebellion against God becomes a seeking after God, one can see the key to the development of Wiesel's thinking and seeking in his literary endeavor.

Madness is an important motif not only in Wiesel's novels but also in two of his plays, neither of which is set in the time of the Holocaust but both of which are laden with implications for the problematic relation between God and humanity raised in the Holocaust. One is called *Zalmen, or the Madness of God* (1974) and is set in Soviet Russia; the other is *Le proces de Shamgorod*, 1979 (*The Trial of God*, 1979), which takes place in the seventeenth century. *Zalmen* contains the righteously indignant outcry of a single Jew—perhaps the only Jew left who is capable of making an outcry—to the fading humanity around him; it is based on an imagined incident that Wiesel did not see but wished he had seen when he first visited a synagogue in the Soviet Union in 1965. *The Trial of God* brings the cry of a Jewish community to the God of all humanity, with the devil acting as God's defense attorney; it is based on a similar trial that Wiesel witnessed in a concentration camp barracks.

One of the most passionate of all the literary outcries raised in the wake of the Holocaust is Wiesel's cantata *Ani maamin: un chant perdu et retrouvé*, 1973 (*Ani Maamin: A Song Lost and Found Again*, 1973). Taking up a scenario that perhaps only poetry could articulate, *Ani Maamin* is the story of the patriarchs Abraham,

Isaac, and Jacob, who go to God on behalf of their children as their children are being consumed in the flames of the Holocaust. They try desperately to reveal to God what is happening and thus stir His compassion, but in vain: He remains silent. And so the three patriarchs decide to leave heaven and return to earth, where they would remain with the victims. As they leave, God accompanies them, whispering "*Nitzhuni banai*, my children have defeated me, they deserve my gratitude" (p. 105). The outcry of the murdered and the silence of God, the word of God and the silence of the murdered, come together in the song's final refrain, which is characteristic of Wiesel's mission and message. It is the insistence on believing "whether God is silent or weeps," on crying out to Him, "I believe in you, even against your will" (p. 107).

While his work is characterized by a constant struggle with God, humanity, and meaning, Wiesel does not succumb to despair. The author of more than thirty-five books, his writings include works of nonfiction in addition to the fiction, drama, and poetry he has written in response to the Holocaust. While the influence of Fyodor Dostoyevsky, Albert Camus, and Nikos Kazantzakis is evident in his writing, the most prominent influences on his life and his work can be seen in Wiesel's studies of biblical, Talmudic, and Hasidic teachers. The importance of the sages from the Jewish tradition to Wiesel's writing can be seen in such works as *Célébration Hassidique*, 1972 (*Souls on Fire*, 1973), *Célébration biblique*, 1975 (*Messengers of God*, 1976), *Five Biblical Portraits* (1981), *Somewhere a Master* (1982), and *Sages and Dreamers* (1991).

"For most writers," Wiesel has said, "their work is a commentary on their life; for a Jewish writer it is the opposite; their lives are commentaries on their work" (*Against Silence*, vol. 2, p. 255). Such has certainly been the case for Elie Wiesel. In addition to his extraordinary accomplishments as a novelist and thinker, President Jimmy Carter appointed him chairman of the United States Holocaust Memorial Council in 1978. In 1985 he received the Congressional Medal of Freedom, and in 1986 he was awarded the Nobel Peace Prize for his work for humanitarian causes throughout the world. Since 1976 he has served as the Andrew Mellon Professor of Humanities at Boston University.

SELECTED WORKS BY THE AUTHOR

The Accident. Trans. Ann Borchardt. New York: Avon, 1962; *Against Silence: The Voice and Vision of Elie Wiesel.* 3 vols. Ed. Irving Abrahamson. New York: Holocaust Library, 1985; *All Rivers Run to the Sea: Memoirs.* New York: Alfred A. Knopf, 1995; *And the Sea is Never Full: Memoirs.* New York: Alfred A. Knopf, 1999; *Ani Maamin: A Song Lost and Found Again.* Trans. Marion Wiesel. New York: Random House, 1973; *A Beggar in Jerusalem.* Trans. Lily Edelman and Elie Wiesel. New York: Random House, 1970; *Dimensions of the Holocaust.* Evanston, Ill.: Northwestern University Press, 1977; *Evil and Exile.* Trans. Jon Rothschild. Notre Dame, Ind.: University of Notre Dame Press, 1990; *The Fifth Son.* Trans. Marion Wiesel. New York: Summit Books, 1985; *Five Biblical Portraits.* Notre Dame, Ind.: Notre Dame University Press, 1981; *The Forgotten.* Trans. Stephen Becker. New York: Summit, 1992; *From the Kingdom of Memory: Reminiscences.* New York: Summit, 1990; *The Gates of the Forest.* Trans. Frances Frenaye. New York: Holt, Rinehart and Winston, 1966; *The Golem.* New York: Summit, 1983; *A Jew Today.* Trans. Marion Wiesel. New York: Random House, 1978; *A Journey of Faith.* New York: Donald I. Fine, 1990; *Legends of Our Time.* New York: Avon, 1968; *Messengers of God: Biblical Portraits and Legends.* Trans. Marion Wiesel. New York: Random House, 1976; *Night.* Trans. Stella Rodway. New York: Bantam, 1982. *The Oath.* New York: Avon, 1973; *One Generation After.* Trans. Lily Edelman and Elie Wiesel. New York: Pocket Books, 1970; *Paroles d'étranger.* Paris: Éditions du Seuil, 1982; *A Passover Haggadah.* New York: Simon and Schuster, 1993; *Sages and Dreamers.* Trans. Marion Wiesel. New York: Summit, 1991; *The Six Days of Destruction: Meditations Towards Hope.* Trans. Cynthia Lander and Evelyn Friedlander. Oxford, England: Pergamon, 1988; *Somewhere a Master.* Trans. Marion Wiesel. New York: Summit, 1982; *Souls on Fire: Portraits and Legends of Hasidic Masters.* Trans. Marion Wiesel. New York: Vintage, 1973; *The Testament.* Trans. Marion Wiesel. New York: Summit, 1981; *The Town beyond the Wall.* Trans. Stephen Becker. New York: Avon, 1964; *The Trial of God.* Trans. Marion Wiesel. New York: Random House, 1979; *Twilight.* Trans. Marion Wiesel. New York: Summit, 1988; *Zalmen or the Madness of God.* Adapted for the stage by Marion Wiesel. New York: Random House, 1974.

FOR FURTHER READING

Berenbaum, Michael, *Elie Wiesel: God, the Holocaust, and the Children of Israel.* New York: Behrman House, 1994; Brown, Robert McAfee, *Elie Wiesel: Messenger to All Humanity.* Notre Dame, Ind.: University of Notre Dame Press, 1983; Cargas, Harry James, *Harry James Cargas in Conversation with Elie Wiesel.* New York: Paulist Press, 1976; Fine, Ellen S., *Legacy of Night: The Literary Universe of Elie Wiesel.* Albany, N.Y.: SUNY Press, 1982; Patterson, David, In *Dialogue and Dilemma with Elie Wiesel.* Wakefield, N.H.: Longwood Academic, 1991; Roth, John K., *A Consuming Fire: Encounters with Elie Wiesel and the Holocaust.* Atlanta: John Knox, 1979; Silberman, Simon P., *Silence in the Novels of Elie Wiesel.* New York: St. Martin's Press, 1995; Stern, Ellen Norman, *Elie Wiesel: A Voice for Humanity.* Philadelphia: Jewish Publication Society, 1996.

David Patterson

Wiesenthal, Simon (1908–)

Simon Wiesenthal, a survivor of Buchenwald and Mauthausen, is internationally recognized for his efforts to bring Nazi war criminals to justice. He explains his relentless pursuit of Nazi criminals by telling the following anecdote. Asked by a fellow survivor why he did not return to his work as an architect after the war, Wiesenthal said,

> I believe in the world to come. I am certain that after we die we will all go to Heaven, and there we will meet the victims of the Holocaust. The first question that they will ask us will be: . . . You received your lives as a present. What did you do with them? One will say "I was a businessman"; another will say "I was a lawyer"; a third will say "I was a teacher." I will say "I did not forget you." (Zuroff, p. 9)

His best-known book on this matter is his memoir *The Murderers Among Us* (1967). All of his books raise important questions for Holocaust literature, but two are of special interest and will be discussed in this entry: the novel *Max and Helen* (1982), which deals with the issue of justice, and the short story/symposium *The Sunflower* (1997), which treats forgiveness.

The author was born on December 31, 1908, in Buczacz, Galicia, to Asher, a businessman, and Rosa (Rapp) Wiesenthal. He graduated from the gymnasium in 1928. Refused admission to the Polytechnic Institute in Lvov because of restrictions on admitting Jewish students, the author went to the Technical University of Prague, and to the University of Lemberg, where he received a degree in architectural engineering. He married Cyla Mueller in 1939 and worked as an architect in Lemberg. Arrested in 1941, Wiesenthal was incarcerated in five Nazi concentration camps: Janowska, Lvóv, Gross-Rosen, Buchenwald, and Mauthausen. Owing to her "Aryan" looks, his wife was smuggled out of the Lvóv camp and lived in Warsaw for two years undetected. Wiesenthal and his wife lost a total of eighty-nine family members during the Holocaust.

Following the war, from 1945 to 1947, Wiesenthal worked for the War Crimes Commission and the U.S. Office of Strategic Services. In 1947 he established the Jewish Documentation Center in Linz, Austria, to trace and bring to justice Nazi war criminals. In 1961 he established the Jewish Documentation Center in Vienna. Among his awards are the Diploma of Honor of International Resistance; Freedom Medals of Netherlands and Luxembourg; Dr. honoris causa, Hebrew Union College, Hebrew Theological College, Colby College, and John Jay College; Congressional Medal of Honor; Jerusalem Medal; and the United Nations League for the Help of Refugees Award. The Simon Wiesenthal Center in California bears his name. He and his wife have two children and live in Vienna.

In focusing on the themes of justice and forgiveness, Wiesenthal raises two of the central questions engendered by the Holocaust. All pre-Shoah assertions about the nature of these themes are called radically into question by the murder of the Jewish people. What is the meaning of justice in a criminal state where no laws were broken by murdering those whom the regime designated for death? Is forgiveness an appropriate category when speaking about the Holocaust which is the paradigm of genocide? It is the author's conscious intent to involve his readers in taking a personal stand on the issues? For example, he concludes *The Sunflower* by writing, "You who have just read this sad and

tragic episode in my life, can mentally change places with me and ask yourself the crucial question, 'What would I have done?'" As we shall see later on, this question is itself not without problems.

His 1981 book *Max and Helen*, which the author terms "a remarkable true love story," raises in an intense fashion the issue of justice both for the dead and the living. Wiesenthal's story begins in 1961. The author, traveling by train to Frankfort, is told by a fellow passenger that a Nazi war criminal is now a high executive in an important German factory. To the accuser's protestations that he is not an informer, Wiesenthal replies with two maxims: "Friendship ends where crime is concerned" and "Isn't a generation that protects criminals sowing the seed for a new generation of criminals?" (p. 16). Subsequent investigation leads the author to uncover the story of Max and Helen, two survivors of the labor camp DG 4 (Durchgangsstrasse, Highway 4) in the Ukraine. The two, who had been engaged prior to the war, not only refuse to bring their persecutor, the commandant of the camp, to justice, they persuade the author not to bring the criminal to trial.

Wiesenthal's story reveals how enmeshed the lives of the survivors are in the web of Nazi evil. On the eve of the Holocaust, Max, a medical student, and Helen, the daughter of a wealthy merchant, were engaged. Deported by the Nazis, the two were sent to labor camp DG 4 run by a sadist named Schulze who appoints Max the camp "doctor" and who is fascinated by Helen. Max escapes, after promising Helen that he will return for her. Schulze makes Helen his housekeeper and sexual slave. She confides to her sister, Miriam, also a prisoner in DG4, that she wished to kill herself and Schulze. Miriam responds that the commandant has been somewhat less ferocious to the prisoners because of Helen, and that if she killed him, the SS would murder 100 Jews in reprisal.

Twenty years pass. Both Max, who spent some of those years in a Soviet prison, and Helen, who lives in Germany under an assumed name, think each other dead. Max discovers Helen and is dismayed to learn that she has borne the commandant's son. Marek, the youth, looks precisely like his sadist father, but bears his mother's compassion and gentleness. Helen has told him that his father was a Jewish freedom fighter who lost his life during the war. Max cannot bear to look at the boy. Neither he nor Helen wish to bring the Nazi to trial because it will destroy the young man who feels himself Jewish and has hopes someday of becoming a doctor. "Is the beast," asks Helen referring to Schulze, "to get another victim, Simon?" (p. 153). Wiesenthal reluctantly agrees not to pursue the Nazi, musing; "Who was I to ruin the life of this decent young man in the name of the dead?" (p. 154).

Several crucial events occur in the story's concluding pages. Simon raises the possibility of divine judgment, sharing with Helen advice he once received from a Catholic priest, "Leave these criminals to the judgment of God" (p. 155). Then, in rapid succession: Schulze dies in an automobile accident; Max still refuses to see Helen; Marek is engaged to a young woman from Canada where he intends to study medicine; and Wiesenthal urges Helen to inform Max that she is now alone. *Max and Helen* seeks to personalize the quest for justice. In doing so, however, the author pits the claims of the dead against the happiness of the living. Intended or not, the reader is possibly manipulated into agreeing with the decision of Max, Helen, and Simon Wiesenthal. What would have happened if the Nazi remained alive? Or if Marek had stayed in Germany? The story raises a larger question: Is the search for justice merely contextual?

The Sunflower is a stunning work of moral philosophy. The author's focus is revealed in the book's subtitle: *The Possibilities and Limits of Forgiveness*. Wiesenthal and his fellow prisoners are daily marched past a military cemetery; each grave has a sunflower. The author muses that the flowers appeared to absorb the sun's rays, drawing them into the ground, while butterflies appeared to carry messages from grave to grave. Simon envies the dead soldiers. He knows that he will be buried in a mass grave, "where corpses would be piled on top of me" (p. 14). One day, at the makeshift hospital which prior to the war had been a technical school where he had studied, Simon is summoned to an SS man's deathbed. Karl, the German, is swathed in bandages; unable to see, he asks forgiveness for murdering Jews in the village of Dnepropetrovsk.

The victims had been herded into a house. Cans of fuel were set ablaze by hand grenades lobbed into the building. Any Jews caught escaping were shot. Karl clearly remembered a man, his wife, and their small child jumping from the second floor. All were shot. Simon wondered "why a Jew must listen to the confession of a dying Nazi soldier. If he had really rediscovered his faith in Christianity, then a priest should have been sent for, a priest who could help him die in peace" (p. 34). Simon listened as the dying man spoke of God, and mused: "But God was absent . . . on leave . . ." (p. 50). Because their crimes went unpunished, the Nazis believed that "God was a fiction, a hateful Jewish invention" (p. 51). Several times during his confession, which sounded sincere to Simon, the dying soldier groped for the author's hand. Simon listened in silence and departed, saying nothing.

Deeply shaken, Simon reported his experience to several of his fellow inmates. Arthur, a cynic, exclaimed: "One less!" (p. 64). Adam, who shared Arthur's view, responded: "So you saw a murderer dying . . . I would like to do that ten times a day. I couldn't have enough such hospital visits" (p. 64). Josek, a deeply religious prisoner, told Simon he did the correct thing. Jewish theology attests that one can forgive, if they wish, only what has been done to them. One has no right to forgive in the name of others. Josek continued: "I believe . . . in life after death . . . where we will all meet again after we are dead. How would it seem then if you had forgiven him? Would not the dead people from Dnepropetrovsk come to you and ask: 'Who gave you the right to forgive our murderer?'" (pp. 65–66).

Near the end of the tale, Simon visited Karl's mother "inspired [by] a vague sense of duty . . . and perhaps the hope of exorcising forever one of the most unpleasant experiences of my life" (p. 85). He listened to her describe her dead son as a good person who had been an altar boy as a child. Karl was fascinated by Nazism, and alienated from his father. Karl joined the Hitler Youth. His father had been killed during the bombing of his factory. Karl's mother viewed what happened to her family as divine punishment. Simon was again silent. He told the mother neither of her son's murderous activity, nor of his confession. Rather, he told her, "The question of Germany's guilt may never be settled. But one thing is certain: no German can shrug off the responsibility. And the non-guilty must dissociate themselves publicly from the guilty" (p. 93).

The symposium portion of *The Sunflower* contains the responses of forty-six leading thinkers, including survivors, Christians, and non-Christians. While it is not possible to analyze each response, several issues emerge. For example, Lawrence Langer questions Wiesenthal's invitation to put oneself in his place. "Role playing about Holocaust reality," Langer accurately observes, "trivializes the serious issues of judgment and forgiveness that *The Sunflower* raises" (p. 177). Many responses, including those of Alan Berger, Abraham Joshua Heschel, and Deborah Lipstadt, comment on the theological and moral inappropriateness of Karl's request. One respondent views silence itself as the main protagonist of the tale (Berger, p. 118). Others, especially Cynthia Ozick*, descry the weakness of the Catholic Church's teachings, which were unable to prevent wholesale apostasy on the part of its adherents. The Dalai Lama distinguishes between forgiving and forgetting; he believes in the former but not the latter. Survivors Primo Levi* and Nechama Tec* uphold Wiesenthal's silence. Some (Harry James Cargas and John Pawlikowski) make a plea for forgiveness.

The issues raised by *The Sunflower* continue to have great resonance for both Holocaust studies and Christian-Jewish relations. The book is required reading at many Catholic seminaries. Further, following the release of the revised and expanded edition of the book in 1997, public interest was so great that an on-line discussion group was initiated. Various scholars who participated in the symposium served as hosts (Berger and Eugene Fisher, among others). They responded to queries sent by readers. As with *Max and Helen*, *The Sunflower* underscores the importance of rethinking the pre-Holocaust moral "certainties" which, in the light of Auschwitz, appear very fragile.

SELECTED WORKS BY THE AUTHOR

Grossmufti-Grossagent der Achse. Salzberg, Austria: Reid Verlag, 1947; *Ich jagte Eichman*. Gütersloh: Bartlesmann Lesering, 1961; *KZ Mauthausen*. Linz, Austria: Ibis Verlag, 1946; *Max and Helen*. Trans. Catherine Turner. New York: William Morrow, 1982; *The Murderers Among Us*. New York: McGraw Hill, 1967; *Sails of Hope: The Secret Mission of Christopher Columbus*. Trans. Richard Winston and Clara Winston. New York: Macmillan, 1973; *The Sunflower*. Rev. and ex. ed., with a symposium edited by Harry James Cargas and Bonnie V. Fetterman. New York: Schocken Books, 1997.

FOR FURTHER READING

Pick, Hella, *Simon Wiesenthal: A Life in Search of Justice*. Evanston, Ill.: Northwestern University Press, 1996; Zuroff, Efraim, *Occupation: Nazi Hunter*. Hoboken, N.J.: KTAV in association with the Simon Wiesenthal Center, 1994.

Alan L. Berger

Y

Yerushalmi, Eliezer (1900–1962)

While the diary kept by Eliezer Yerushalmi in the Shavli (Siauliai) ghetto was published in Hebrew by Yad Vashem in 1950, a substantial portion of it was originally included in the *Chernaya Kniga* (*The Black Book*, 1980), a lengthy volume in Russian consisting of hundreds of eyewitness accounts of Nazi activities in Eastern Europe. *The Black Book* was initially compiled by Ilya Ehrenburg and Vasily Grossman in 1944; portions of it were published in 1947. When the English edition appeared in 1980, however, it was based on a manuscript smuggled out of the Soviet Union to Yad Vashem, and all the materials from Lithuania, including Yerushalmi's diary, were missing. After the Soviet regime fell in 1991, Ehrenburg's daughter, Irina Ehrenburg, recovered the documents from Lithuania and included them in a complete Russian edition of *The Black Book* published in Vilnius in 1993. That edition contains the latest—albeit still incomplete—edition of Yerushalmi's diary.

Eliezer Yerushalmi was born in Lithuania in 1900. He received a university education and was known as a scholar and a teacher. When the Nazis entered Shavli on July 28, 1942, Yerushalmi was already past forty years of age and working as a history teacher in one of Shavli's middle schools. A leader in the community of more than 8,000 Jews (the second largest in Lithuania), he was selected to serve on the Shavli *Judenrat* (Jewish Council). The Shavli *Judenrat* was distinguished by its efforts to serve as an advocate for the Jews of the ghetto. When on August 31, 1943, for example, the Nazis issued a decree demanding that the *Judenrat* turn over fifty Jews from the ghetto to be executed, they unanimously refused to comply with the order and offered themselves instead. Both Yerushalmi and his diary survived the war, which for Shavli ended in July 1944, when the Germans retreated from the advancing Red Army. After the war, Yerushalmi moved to Israel, where he lived until his death in 1962.

Because of his position with the *Judenrat*, Yerushalmi had a broader view of the ghetto than most of the Jews imprisoned there; indeed, he often knew of an *Aktion* or a roundup of Jews before it took place, and he warned as many people as he could. His diary includes much information about the general events, decrees, and atrocities that transpired throughout the ghetto, as well as in the surrounding areas. Yerushalmi provided figures, for instance, on the number of Jews working at the local airfield, in the tannery, at the peat bog, and at other forced labor sites—as well as the number murdered in those places. He reported on *Judenrat* activities, ranging from their struggle to strike a balance between obedience to the Nazis and betrayal of the Jews, to their efforts to set up and maintain schools (as well as closing those schools in October 1943). He recorded the Nazi decrees as they were issued and the horrors that followed in the wake of those decrees. And he attested to the crimes committed by men such as Gebietskommissar Hans Heweke.

In reading Yerushalmi's diary in the *Chernaya Kniga*, one sees that he is as much concerned with cases of individual suffering as he is with the general misery that pervades the ghetto. In an entry dated May 6, 1943, for example, he offered a very moving account of how two Jews named Davidovich and Kerbel were forced to hang Betsalel Mazovetsky (p. 270). And on October 17, he related how Gershon Zhemaitishek was shot simply for complaining about a stomach ailment as he was boarding a transport (p. 277). The diary's testimonies on individual suffering pertain not only to people in the Shavli ghetto but also to Jews in concentration camps at Daugiliai and Pavenchia. On October 1, 1943, for instance, Yerushalmi wrote, "The situation in Daugiliai is catastrophic. The unfinished barracks was designed to hold sixty prisoners; right now there are 246 people there. Four people share plank beds seventy centimeters wide" (p. 276). One of the most dramatic and heartrending entries in the diary is dated November 5, 1943; it begins, "Today was the darkest day of our unhappy life in the ghetto: they took away the children" (p. 278). Looking at the Hebrew edition of the diary, one sees that Yerushalmi anticipated such a catastrophe six months before it happened. He cried out, "What can I do to avert a danger such as this?" (p. 189).

Other differences between the Hebrew edition of the diary and the portions included in the Russian *Chernaya Kniga* are worth noting. Missing from the Russian edition, for example, is a religious dimension found in the Hebrew diary. There, in an entry dated July 22, 1943,

Yerushalmi followed his invocation of the God "who has chosen us from all the nations" with the assertion that "the aim and the truth of the Covenant made by Moses is Israel itself" (p. 253). Further, while the pages of the diary included in the *Chernaya Kniga* contain accounts of the righteous among the Lithuanians, the Hebrew edition also describes the march of the Jews as they were forced into the Shavli ghetto: "Many Lithuanians follow these sorrow-ridden people along the sidewalks out of curiosity. Very few have anything in common with their affliction; the vast majority either look upon this migration with indifference or shout insults at them" (p. 229).

Because so much of Yerushalmi's diary is concerned with facts and figures, ghetto and camp conditions, the deeds of key Germans and Jews, measures taken by the *Judenrat*, and other matters of historical record, it may seem at first glance that his diary does not convey the soul-searching or the personal outcry that characterizes many other Holocaust diaries. Yerushalmi's soul-searching, however, shows itself precisely in this forgetfulness of himself for the sake of testifying to the suffering of others. His diary contains not a line of self-indulgence or self-pity, even though it was written under conditions of cold, exhaustion, and hunger and at the risk of his own life.

SELECTED WORKS BY THE AUTHOR
Be'ohole sifrut. Haifa: Mi-ma'amakim, 1965.
"Dnevnik E. Yerushalmi." In *Chernaya Kniga*, ed. Vasily Grossman and Ilya Ehrenburg. Vilnius: Yad, 1993, pp. 262–79; *Pinkas Shavli: Yoman mi-geto Litai*. Jerusalem: Yad Vashem, 1950.

David Patterson

Z

Zylberberg, Michael (1907–1971)

Originally serialized in the *Forverts* (the Yiddish-language newspaper published in New York), Michael Zylberberg's book *A Warsaw Diary: 1939–1945* (1969) is both a diary and a reflection on a diary. Zylberberg began keeping a diary in the winter of 1942 and continued writing it, with a hiatus from May 1943 to December 1944, until the end of the war. It contains an account of his experiences both in the Warsaw ghetto and on the Aryan side of the wall. What makes the diary more than a diary is that Zylberberg includes his reflections on the events twenty-five years after they happened. The volume is both an outstanding work of literature and an excellent resource for information on prominent personalities from the Warsaw ghetto, including Janusz Korczak,* Yitzhak Zuckermann, Mordecai Anielewicz, Adam Czerniaków,* and others.

Born in the Polish town of Plock in 1907, Michael Zylberberg received a rabbinical education and worked as a teacher of Jewish history and literature from 1931 to 1939. During the early years of the war, when schools were still permitted to the Jews, he was the headmaster of a school in the Warsaw ghetto and worked closely with the famous child-care specialist Janusz Korczak. After the short-lived uprising of January 1943, Zylberberg escaped from the ghetto and went into hiding with his wife, Henrietta. In May 1943 he had to flee from the town of Skolimow, where he was hiding, and was forced to leave behind his diary; he took up his daily record once again in December 1944. After the war, Zylberberg moved to London, where he worked with the YIVO Institute for Jewish research in England. Twenty years after the original diary had been lost, a British tourist, who was visiting Skolimow, found it. Once the document was returned to Zylberberg, he put the two parts of his record together to form the current volume.

In keeping with his religious training, Zylberberg paid particular attention to the Nazis' actions—as well as to the Jews' reactions—that took place on the holy days. He noted, for example, that the first deportation order was issued in the Warsaw ghetto on the Ninth of Av, 1942, which is the day for mourning the destruction of the Temple; as the body of Israel is consigned to the flames, it is indeed as though the Temple were being destroyed (p. 75). The diary also contains a remarkable account of the Jews' response to a roundup that took place on Rosh Hashanah, the Jewish New Year, 1942. One Jew, he related, came out of hiding and started looking for stones to throw at God in the heavens. "This scene," he wrote, "spelt the disintegration of a deep religious faith" (p. 57); that faith, as Zylberberg's diary demonstrates, is precisely what was targeted for disintegration.

Zylberberg shows, moreover, that it was targeted with the complicity of Christendom: "The worst atrocities against us [the Jews and the Poles] had been perpetrated by our common enemy in a country whose population consisted of devout Catholics" (p. 151). What is disturbing to Zylberberg is that it appeared as though one could be a devout Catholic and turn one's back on the Jews without falling into any contradiction. By Passion Week of 1944, he noted, Warsaw was officially free of Jews, and the churches were packed. "Men, women, and children," said Zylberberg of the complacent Christians, "found religion a great source of inspiration and comfort" (p. 150). Unfortunately, for most Catholic Poles, religion consisted of little more than taking communion and saying prayers.

Zylberberg reminds his reader that, from a Jewish standpoint, faith concerns not only a regard for God but also a regard for humanity. And the regard for humanity manifests itself not only in how one treats the living but also in a certain reverence for the dead. Zylberberg revealed a definitive feature of the Holocaust when he pointed out that, on Sunday afternoons, the Nazis would take their girlfriends for a stroll to the morgue, where they would laugh and take pictures of the Jewish dead (p. 31). By January 1945 it was as if the entire Warsaw ghetto had been transformed into a wasteland, with even the signs of the dead erased. Zylberberg related how he visited the site of the ghetto, which had been leveled in May 1943 after the Warsaw ghetto uprising. "There was no recognizable sign of what had once existed there," he wrote. "It was eerie and terrifying" (p. 211). Even the cemetery had been destroyed: "It seemed to break down the division between life and death" (p. 212). In reading Zylberberg's diary, one realizes that a definitive feature of the Holocaust was the erasure of such boundaries. A major task of Zylberberg's diary and his later reflections is to regain the distinction between life and death.

SELECTED WORK BY THE AUTHOR
A Warsaw Diary: 1939–1945. London: Valentine, Mitchell, 1969.

David Patterson

Appendix 1
Authors by Date of Birth

Unknown	Salmen Lewental	**1909** *(cont.)*	Miklós Radnóti
	Filip Müller		Avraham Tory
	Elik Rivosh	**1911**	Tuvia Borzykowski
		1912	Jean Améry
1878	Janusz Korczak		Hersh Wasser
1880	Adam Czerniaków	**1913**	Charlotte Delbo
	Chaim Kaplan		Abraham Sutzkever
1882	Menachem Kon	**1914**	Silvano Arieti
1885	Zelig Kalmanovitch		Romain Gary
1886	Yitzhak Katznelson		Etty (Esther) Hillesum
1889	Philip Mechanicus		Zivia Lubetkin
1891	Nelly Sachs		Bernard Malamud
1893	Emil Dorian	**1915**	Arthur Miller
	Abel Jacob Herzberg		Sara Nomberg-Przytyk
1894	Uri Zvi Greenberg	**1916**	Paul Trepman
1897	Herman Kruk		Peter Weiss
1900	Emmanuel Ringelblum	**1917**	Ka-tzetnik 135633
	Jiří Weil	**1918**	Fania Fénelon
	Eliezer Yerushalmi		Josef Katz
1901	Miklós Nyiszli		Abba Kovner
1903	David Kahane		Olga Lengyel
1904	Isaac Bashevis Singer	**1919**	Sim Kessel
1905	Alexander Donat		Renata Laqueur
	Viktor Emil Frankl		Primo Levi
	Vasily Grossman		Piotr Rawicz
	Frida Michelson	**1920**	Paul Celan
1906	Josef Bor		Anna Langfus
	Aryeh Klonicki-Klonymus	**1921**	Ilse Aichinger
	Isaiah Spiegel		Ida Fink
1907	Michael Zylberberg		Wieslaw Kielar
ca. 1908	Salmen Gradowski		Hannah Senesh
	Simon Wiesenthal	**1922**	Tadeusz Borowski
1909	Elie Aron Cohen		Eugene Heimler
	Shimon Huberband		Vladka Meed

1922 *(cont.)*	Erna F. Rubinstein	**1928** *(cont.)*	Helen Sendyk
	Nathan Shapell		Elie Wiesel
1923	Dannie Abse	**1929**	A. Anatoli
	Karen Gershon		Hanna Demetz
	Haim Gouri		Anne Frank
	Jorge Semprun		Thomas Geve
1924	Mary Berg		Samuel Pisar
	Judith Dribben	**1930**	Yoram Kaniuk
	Gerda Weissmann Klein		Yehuda Nir
	Robert Kotlowitz		Dan Pagis
	Isabella Leitner		Harold Pinter
	André Schwarz-Bart	**1931**	Livia E. Bitton-Jackson
	Dawid Sierakowiak		Rolf Hochhuth
	George Topas		Nechama Tec
	Rudolf Vrba	**1932**	Aharon Appelfeld
1925	Elżbieta Ettinger		Johanna de Leeuw Reiss
	Ilona Karmel	**1933**	Jerzy Kosinski
	Norma Rosen		Hugh Nissenson
	Leon Weliczker Wells		Marge Piercy
1926	Hanoch Bartov		Philip Roth
	Moshe Flinker		Agnes Sassoon
	Kitty Hart	**1936**	Marge Piercy
	Arnošt Lustig		Frida Scheps Weinstein
	Moshe Sandberg	**1937**	Jurek Becker
	Edward Lewis Wallant	**1938**	Jona Oberski
1927	Jakov Lind	**1939**	Amos Oz
	Dawid Rubinowicz		Joshua Sobol
	Yitskhok Rudashevski	**1941**	Susan Fromberg Schaeffer
1928	Arthur A. Cohen	**1943**	Myriam Anissimov
	Cynthia Ozick	**1945**	Patrick Modiano
	Lore Grozsmann Segal	**1960**	Diane Samuels

Appendix 2
Authors by Country of Birth

Austria (or Austro-Hungarian Empire)
Ilse Aichinger
Jean Améry
Viktor Emil Frankl
Uri Zvi Greenberg
David Kahane
Olga Lengyel
Jakov Lind
Lore Grozsmann Segal
Jiří Weil
Simon Wiesenthal

Czechoslovakia
Livia E. Bitton-Jackson
Josef Bor
Hanna Demetz
Arnošt Lustig
Agnes Sassoon
Rudolf Vrba

England
Harold Pinter
Diane Samuels

France
Charlotte Delbo
Fania Fénelon
Sim Kessel
Patrick Modiano
André Schwarz-Bart
Frida Scheps Weinstein

Germany
Anne Frank
Karen Gershon
Thomas Geve
Rolf Hochhuth
Josef Katz
Nelly Sachs
Peter Weiss

Hungary
Eugene Heimler
Isabella Leitner
Miklós Nyiszli
Miklós Radnóti
Moshe Sandberg
Hannah Senesh
Elie Wiesel

Italy
Silvano Arieti
Primo Levi

Latvia
Zelig Kalmanovitch
Frida Michelson
Elik Rivosh

Lithuania
Romain Gary
Yitskhok Rudashevski
Abraham Sutzkever
Avraham Tory
Eliezer Yerushalmi

Netherlands
Elie Aron Cohen
Moshe Flinker
Abel Jacob Herzberg

Netherlands (cont.)
Etty (Esther) Hillesum
Renata Laqueur
Philip Mechanicus
Jona Oberski
Johanna de Leeuw Reiss

Palestine
Hanoch Bartov
Haim Gouri
Yoram Kaniuk
Amos Oz
Joshua Sobol

Poland
Jurek Becker
Mary Berg
Tuvia Borzykowski
Adam Czerniaków
Alexander Donat
Elżbieta Ettinger
Ida Fink
Salmen Gradowski
Kitty Hart
Shimon Huberband
Ilona Karmel
Ka-tzetnik 135633
Wieslaw Kielar
Gerda Weissmann Klein
Menachem Kon
Janusz Korczak
Jerzy Kosinski
Anna Langfus
Salmen Levental
Zivia Lubetkin
Vladka Meed
Yehuda Nir
Sara Nomberg-Przytyk
Samuel Pisar
Emmanuel Ringelblum
Dawid Rubinowicz
Erna F. Rubinstein
Helen Sendyk
Nathan Shapell
Dawid Sierakowiak
Isaac Bashevis Singer
Isaiah Spiegel
Nechama Tec
George Topas

Paul Trepman
Hersh Wasser
Leon Weliczker Wells
Michael Zylberberg

Romania
Emil Dorian
Dan Pagis

Russia (Czarist)
Vasily Grossman
Chaim Kaplan
Yitzhak Katznelson
Aryeh Klonicki-Klonymus (Ukraine)
Abba Kovner
Herman Kruk

Spain
Jorge Semprun

Switzerland
Myriam Anissimov

Ukraine (Soviet Union)
A. Anatoli
Aharon Appelfeld
Tadeusz Borowski
Paul Celan
Judith Dribben
Piotr Rawicz

United States
Arthur A. Cohen
Robert Kotlowitz
Bernard Malamud
Arthur Miller
Hugh Nissenson
Cynthia Ozick
Marge Piercy
Norma Rosen
Philip Roth
Susan Fromberg Schaeffer
Edward Lewis Wallant

Unknown
Filip Müller

Wales
Dannie Abse

Appendix 3
Authors by Birth Name

Author	Birth Name	Author	Birth Name
Jean Améry	Hans Maier	Kitty Hart	Kitty Felix
A. Anatoli	Anatoli Kuznetsov	Eugene Heimler	Jancsi Heimler
Myriam Anissimov	Myriam Frydman	Ka-tzetnik 135633	Yehiel De-Nur
Mary Berg	Miriam Wattenberg	Janusz Korczak	Henryk Goldszmidt
Livia E. Bitton-Jackson	Livia Freedmann	Isabella Leitner	Isabella Katz
Josef Bor	Josef Bondy	Vladka Meed	Feigele Peltel
Paul Celan	Paul Antschel	Frida Michelson	Frida Frid
Alexander Donat	Michal Berg	Nathan Shapell	Nathan Schapelski
Fania Fénelon	Fania Goldstein	Avraham Tory	Avraham Golub
Karen Gershon	Kaethe Lowenthal	Paul Trepman	Pinkhas Lazarovitch Trepman

Bibliography of Primary Works of Holocaust Literature

Fiction

Abse, Dannie. *Ash on a Young Man's Sleeve*. London: Vallentine, Mitchell, 1973.

Aichinger, Ilse. *The Bound Man and Other Stories*. Trans. Eric Mosbacher. Freeport, N.Y.: Books for Libraries, 1971.

———. *Herod's Children*. Trans. Cornelia Schaeffer. New York: Atheneum, 1964.

———. *Selected Short Stories and Dialogue*. Trans. James C. Aldridge. Oxford: Pergamon, 1966.

Akavia, Miriam. *An End to Childhood*. Trans. Michael P. McLeary and Jeanette Goldman. Ilford, England: Vallentine, Mitchell, 1995.

Amichai, Yehuda. *Not of This Time, Not of This Place*. Trans. Shlomo Katz. New York: Harper and Row, 1968.

Anatoli, A. *Babi Yar*. Trans. David Floyd. New York: Pocket Books, 1971.

Appelfeld, Aharon. *The Age of Wonders*. Trans. Dalya Bilu. Boston: Godine, 1981.

———. *Badenheim 1939*. Trans. Dalya Bilu. New York: Washington Square, 1980.

———. *The Conversion: A Novel*. Trans. Jeffrey M. Green. New York: Schocken, 1998.

———. *For Every Sin*. Trans. Jeffrey M. Green. New York: Weidenfeld and Nicolson, 1989.

———. *The Healer*. Trans. Jeffrey M. Green. New York: Grove Press, 1994.

———. *The Immortal Bartfuss*. Trans. Jeffrey M. Green. New York: Weidenfeld and Nicolson, 1988.

———. *The Iron Tracks*. Trans. Jeffrey M. Green. New York: Schocken, 1998.

———. *Katerina*. Trans. Jeffrey M. Green. New York: Random House, 1992.

———. *The Retreat*. Trans. Dalya Bilu. New York: Dutton, 1984.

———. *To the Land of the Cattails*. Trans. Jeffrey M. Green. New York: Weidenfeld and Nicolson, 1986.

———. *Tzili: The Story of a Life*. Trans. Dalya Bilu. New York: E.P. Dutton, 1983.

———. *Unto the Soul*. Trans. Jeffrey M. Green. New York: Random House, 1994.

Arieti, Silvano. *The Parnas*. New York: Basic Books, 1979.

Arnold, Eliot. *A Night of Watching*. New York: Charles Scribner's Sons, 1970.

Bartov, Hanoch. *The Brigade*. Trans. David Segal. Philadelphia: Jewish Publication Society, 1967.

———. *Whose Little Boy Are You?* Trans. Hillel Halkin. Philadelphia: Jewish Publication Society, 1978.

Bassani, Giorgio. *The Garden of the Finzi-Continis*. Trans. William Weaver. New York: Harcourt Brace Jovanovich, 1977.

Becker, Jurek. *Jacob the Liar*. Trans. Leila Vennewitz. New York: Plume, 1997.

Bellow, Saul. *Mr. Sammler's Planet*. New York: Penguin, 1977.

Ben-Amotz, Dan. *To Remember, to Forget*. Trans. Eva Shapiro. Philadelphia: Jewish Publication Society, 1980.

Biber, Jacob. *Violence and Devotion: A Novel of the Holocaust*. San Bernadino, Calif.: Borgo Press, 1996.

Bor, Josef. *The Terezin Requiem*. Trans. Edith Pargeter. New York: Avon, 1963.

Borowski, Tadeusz. *This Way for the Gas, Ladies and Gentlemen*. Trans. Barbara Vedder. New York: Viking Press, 1967.

Bryks, Rachmil. *A Cat in the Ghetto*. Trans. S. Morris Engel. New York: Behrman House, 1959.

———. *Kiddush Hashem*. Trans. S. Morris Engel. New York: Behrman House, 1977.

Chaneles, Sol. *Three Children of the Holocaust*. New York: Avon, 1974.

Cohen, Arthur A. *Acts of Theft*. Chicago: University of Chicago Press, 1988.

———. *A Hero of His Time*. Chicago: University of Chicago Press, 1988.

———. *In the Days of Simon Stern: A Novel*. Chicago: University of Chicago Press, 1988.

Demetz, Hana. *The House on Prague Street*. New York: G.K. Hall, 1980.

———. *The Journey from Prague Street*. New York: St. Martin's Press, 1990.

Epstein, Leslie. *King of the Jews*. New York: Coward, McCann and Geoghegan, 1979.

Ettinger, Elżbieta. *Kindergarten*. Boston: Houghton Mifflin, 1970.

———. *Quicksand*. London: Pandora, 1989.

Fink, Ida. *The Journey*. Trans. Joanna Weschler and Francine Prose. New York: Plume, 1993.

———. *A Scrap of Time and Other Stories*. Trans. Francine Prose and Madeline Levine. Evanston, Ill.: Northwestern University Press, 1995.

———. *Traces: Stories*. Trans. Philip Boehm and Francine Prose. New York: Henry Holt, 1993.

Forman, James. *The Survivor*. New York: Farrar, Straus and Giroux, 1976.

Fuks, Ladislav. *Mr. Theodore Mundstock*. Trans. Iris Unwin. New York: Ballantine, 1969.

Gary, Romain. *The Company of Men*. Trans. Joseph Barnes. New York: Simon and Schuster, 1950.

———. *The Dance of Genghis Cohn*. Trans. Romain Gary and Camilla Sykes. New York: World Publishing, 1968.

———. *King Solomon*. Trans. Barbara Wright. New York: Harper and Row, 1983.

———. *The Life before Us*. Trans. Ralph Manheim. New York: New Directions, 1986.

———. *Promise at Dawn*. Trans. John Markham Beach. New York: Harper, 1961.

———. *The Roots of Heaven*. Trans. Jonathan Griffin. New York: Simon and Schuster, 1958.

Gascar, Pierre. *Beasts and Men and the Seed*. Trans. Jean Stewart and Merloyd Lawrence. New York: Meridian, 1960.

Gershon, Karen. *The Bread of Exile*. London: V. Gollancz, 1985.

———. *Burn Helen*. Brighton, England: Harvester Press, 1980.

———. *The Fifth Generation*. London: V. Gollancz, 1987.

Gotfryd, Bernard. *Anton the Dove Fancier and Other Tales of the Holocaust*. New York: Pocket Books, 1990.

Gouri, Haim. *The Chocolate Deal*. Trans. Deymour Simckes. Detroit: Wayne State University Press, 1999.

Green, Gerald. *Holocaust*. New York: Bantam, 1978.

Grossman, Vasily. *Forever Flowing*. Trans. Thomas P. Whitney. Evanston, Ill.: Northwestern University Press, 1997.

———. *Life and Fate*. Trans. Robert Chandler. New York: Harper and Row, 1986.

Grynberg, Henryk. *Child of the Shadows*. London: Vallentine, Mitchell, 1969.

———. *The Victory*. Evanston, Ill.: Northwestern University Press, 1993.

Habe, Hans. *The Mission: A Novel*. Trans. Michael Bullock. New York: Coward-McCann, 1966.

Hersey, John. *The Wall*. New York: Alfred A. Knopf, 1950.

Hilsenrath, Edgar. *The Nazi and the Jew*. New York: Doubleday, 1977.

———. *Night*. Trans. Michael Ruloff. New York: Doubleday, 1966.

Jabès, Edmond. *The Book of Questions*. Trans. Rosemarie Waldrop. Middletown, Conn.: Wesleyan University Press, 1976.

———. *The Book of Yukel and Return to the Book*. Trans. Rosemarie Waldrop. Middletown, Conn.: Wesleyan University Press, 1977.

Kanfer, Stefan. *The Eighth Sin*. New York: Random House, 1978.

Kaniuk, Yoram. *Adam Resurrected*. Trans. Seymour Simckes. New York: Atheneum, 1971.

———. *Commander of the Exodus*. Trans. Seymour Simckes. New York: Grove, 1999.

Karmel, Ilona. *An Estate of Memory*. Boston: Houghton Mifflin, 1969.

———. *Stephania*. Boston: Houghton Mifflin, 1953.

Ka-tzetnik 135633. *Atrocity*. Trans. Nina De-Nur. New York: Kensington, 1977.

———. *House of Dolls*. Trans. Moshe M. Kohn. New York: Pyramid, 1958.

———. *Phoenix over the Galilee*. Trans. Nina De-Nur. New York: Harper and Row, 1969.

———. *Star of Ashes*. Trans. Nina De-Nur. Tel Aviv: Hamenora, 1971.

———. *Sunrise over Hell*. Trans. Nina De-Nur. London: Allen, 1977.

Kertesz, Imre. *Fateless*. Trans. Christopher C. Wilson and Katharina M. Wilson. Evanston, Ill.: Northwestern University Press, 1992.

———. *Kaddish for a Child Not Born*. Trans. Christopher C. Wilson and Katharina M. Wilson. Evanston, Ill.: Hydra Books, 1997.

Kis, Danilo. *Hourglass*. Trans. Ralph Manheim. Evanston, Ill.: Northwestern University Press, 1997.

Kosinski, Jerzy. *The Painted Bird*. Boston: Houghton Mifflin, 1975.

———. *Passing By*. New York: Random House, 1992.

Kotlowitz, Robert. *The Boardwalk*. New York: Alfred A. Knopf, 1976.

Langfus, Anna. *Lost Shore*. Trans. Peter Wiles. New York: Pantheon, 1964.

———. *The Whole Land Brimstone*. Trans. Peter Wiles. New York: Pantheon, 1962.

Laqueur, Walter. *The Missing Years*. Boston: Little, Brown, 1980.

Levi, Carlo. *The Watch*. New York: Farrar, Straus and Yoring, 1951.

Levi, Primo. *If Not Now, When?* Trans. William Weaver. New York: Simon and Schuster, 1985.

———. *The Mirror Maker: Stories and Essays*. Trans. Raymond Rosenthal. New York: Schocken, 1989.

———. *The Monkey Wrench*. Trans. Ruth Feldman. New York: Penguin USA, 1995.

———. *Other People's Trades*. Trans. Raymond Rosenthal. New York: Summit, 1989.

———. *The Periodic Table*. Trans. Raymond Rosenthal. New York: Schocken, 1985.

———. *The Sixth Day and Other Tales*. Trans. Raymond Rosenthal. New York: Viking, 1990.

Levin, Meyer. *Eva: A Novel of the Holocaust*. New York: Simon and Schuster, 1959.

———. *The Harvest*. New York: Simon and Schuster, 1978.

———. *My Father's House*. New York: Viking, 1947.

———. *The Stronghold*. New York: Simon and Schuster, 1965.

Lind, Jakov. *Ergo*. Trans. Ralph Manheim. New York: Random House, 1967.

———. *Landscape in Concrete*. Trans. Ralph Manheim. New York: Grove Press, 1966.

———. *Soul of Wood and Other Stories*. Trans. Ralph Manheim. New York: Fawcett Crest, 1966.

Lustig, Arnošt. *Children of the Holocaust*. Trans. George Theiner and Jeanne Němcová. Evanston, Ill.: Northwestern University Press, 1995.

———. *Darkness Casts No Shadow*. Trans. Jeanne Němcová. New York: Avon, 1978.

———. *Diamonds of the Night*. Trans. Jeanna Němcová. Washington, D.C.: Inscape, 1978.

———. *Dita Saxova*. Trans. Jeanne Němcová. New York: Harper and Row, 1979.

———. *Indecent Dreams*. Trans. Paul Wilson. Evanston, Ill.: Northwestern University Press, 1990.

———. *Night and Hope*. Trans. George Theiner. New York: Avon, 1976.

———. *A Prayer for Katerina Horovitzova*. Trans. Jeanne Němcová. New York: Harper and Row, 1973.

———. *The Street of Lost Brothers*. Trans. Jeanne Němcová. Evanston, Ill.: Northwestern University Press, 1990.

———. *The Unloved: From the Diary of Perla S.* Trans. Vera Kalina-Levine. Evanston, Ill.: Northwestern University Press, 1996.

Malamud, Bernard. *The Complete Stories*. New York: Farrar, Straus and Giroux, 1997.

———. *The Fixer*. New York: Penguin USA, 1994.

———. *Idiots First*. New York: Farrar, Straus and Giroux, 1963.

———. *The Magic Barrel*. New York: Random House, 1958.

Malaparte, Curzio. *Kaputt*. Trans. Cesare Foligno. New York: E.P. Dutton, 1946.

Margolian, Abraham. *A Piece of Blue Heaven*. Fredericton, N.B., Canada: New Elizabethan, 1956.

Mazzetti, Lorenza. *The Sky Falls*. Trans. Marguerite Waldman. New York: McKay, 1963.

Modiano, Patrick. *Dora Bruder*. Trans. Joanna Kilmartin. Berkeley: University of California Press, 1999.

———. *Night Rounds*. Trans. Patricia Wolf. New York: Alfred A. Knopf, 1971.

———. *Out of the Dark*. Trans. Jordan Stump. Lincoln: University of Nebraska Press, 1998.

———. *Villa Triste*. Trans. Caroline Hillier. London: V. Gollancz, 1977.

Morante, Elsa. *History, A Novel*. Trans. William Weaver. New York: Alfred A. Knopf, 1977.

Morgenstern, Soma. *The Son of the Lost Son*. Trans. Joseph Leftwich and Peter Gross. Philadelphia: Jewish Publication Society, 1946.

———. *The Testament of the Lost Son*. Trans. Jacob Sloan and Maurice Samuel. Philadelphia: Jewish Publication Society, 1950.

———. *The Third Pillar*. Trans. Ludwig Lewisohn. New York: Farrar, Straus and Cudahy, 1955.

Nissenson, Hugh. *The Elephant and My Jewish Problem: Selected Stories and Journals*. New York: Harper and Row, 1988.

———. *In the Reign of Peace*. London: Secker and Warburg, 1972.

————. *My Own Ground*. New York: Perennial Library, 1987.

————. *Notes from the Frontier*. New York: Dial, 1968.

————. *Pile of Stones: Short Stories*. New York: Scribner, 1965.

————. *The Tree of Life: A Novel*. Philadelphia: Paul Dry Books, 2000.

Obletz, Rose Meyerson. *The Long Road Home*. New York: Exposition, 1958.

Orlev, Uri. *The Island on Bird Street*. Trans. Hillel Halkin. Boston: Houghton Mifflin, 1984.

————. *The Lead Soldier*. Trans. Hillel Halkin. New York: Taplinger, 1980.

Oz, Amos. *Touch the Water, Touch the Wind*. Trans. Nicholas de Lange. New York: Harcourt Brace Jovanovich, 1974.

Ozick, Cynthia. *Bloodshed and Three Novellas*. Syracuse, N.Y.: Syracuse University Press, 1995.

————. *The Cannibal Galaxy*. New York: Alfred A. Knopf, 1983.

————. *Levitation: Five Fictions*. New York: Alfred A. Knopf, 1982.

————. *The Messiah of Stockholm*. New York: Alfred A. Knopf, 1987.

————. *The Pagan Rabbi and Other Stories*. New York: Schocken Books, 1976.

————. *The Shawl*. New York: Vintage, 1990.

————. *Trust*. New York: E.P. Dutton, 1966.

Piercy, Marge. *Gone to Soldiers*. New York: Summit Books, 1987.

Pinkus, Oscar. *The Son of Zelman*. Cambridge, Mass.: Schenkman Publishing, 1982.

Prager, Moshe. *Sparks of Glory*. Trans. Mordecai Schreiber. New York: Shengold, 1974.

Presser, Jacob. *Breaking Point*. Trans. Barrows Mussey. New York: World, 1958.

Raczymow, Henri. *Writing the Book of Esther*. Trans. Dori Katz. New York: Holmes and Meier, 1995.

Rawicz, Piotr. *Blood from the Sky*. Trans. Peter Wiles. New York: Harcourt Brace Jovanovich, 1964.

Rebhun, Joseph. *The Embers of Michael: A Historical Epic*. Claremont, Calif.: Or Publications, 1993.

Rose, Leesha. *The Tulips Are Red*. New York: Barnes, 1978.

Rosen, Norma. *At the Center*. Boston: Houghton Mifflin, 1982.

————. *Touching Evil*. New York: Harcourt, Brace and World, 1969.

Roth, Philip. *The Anatomy Lesson*. New York: Farrar, Straus and Giroux, 1984.

————. *The Counterlife*. New York: Farrar, Straus and Giroux, 1987.

————. *The Ghost Writer*. New York: Farrar, Straus and Giroux, 1979.

————. *Goodbye, Columbus*. Boston: Houghton Mifflin, 1959.

————. *Operation Shylock: A Confession*. New York: Simon and Schuster, 1993.

————. *The Prague Orgy*. London: Cape, 1985.

Roth-Hano, Renée. *Touch Wood: A Girlhood in Occupied France*. New York: Puffin, 1989.

Rudnicki, Adolf. *Ascent to Heaven*. Trans. H.C. Stevens. New York: Roy McLeod and Dennis Dobson, 1951.

Samuels, Gertrude. *Mottele: A Partisan Odyssey*. New York: Harper and Row, 1976.

Sayre, Joel. *The House Without a Roof*. New York: Farrar, Straus, 1948.

Schaeffer, Susan Fromberg. *Anya*. New York: Macmillan, 1974.

Schwarz-Bart, André. *The Last of the Just*. Trans. Stephen Becker. New York: Bantam, 1961.

Segal, Lore. *Other People's Houses*. New York: Harcourt, Brace and World, 1964.

Seiden, Othniel J. *The Survivor of Babi Yar*. Denver, Colo.: Stonehenge, 1980.

Semprun, Jorge. *The Long Voyage*. Trans. Richard Seaver. New York: Grove Press, 1964.

————. *The Second Death of Ramón Mercader*. Trans. Len Ortzen. New York: Grove Press, 1973.

————. *What a Beautiful Sunday*. Trans. Alan Sheridan. San Diego: Harcourt Brace Jovanovich, 1982.

Silberstang, Edwin. *Nightmare of the Dark*. New York: Alfred A. Knopf, 1967.

Singer, Isaac Bashevis. *The Certificate*. Trans. Leonard Wolf. New York: Farrar, Straus and Giroux, 1992.

————. *Enemies: A Love Story*. Greenwich, Conn.: Fawcett, 1972.

————. *The Family Moskat*. Trans. A.H. Gross. New York: Alfred A. Knopf, 1950.

————. *A Little Boy in Search of God*. Garden City, N.Y.: Doubleday, 1976.

————. *Lost in America*. Garden City, N.Y.: Doubleday, 1981.

————. *Meshugah*. Trans. Isaac Bashevis Singer and Nili Wachtel. New York: Farrar, Straus and Giroux, 1994.

————. *Scum*. Trans. Rosaline Dukalsky Schwartz. New York: Farrar, Straus and Giroux, 1991.

————. *Shadows on the Hudson*. Trans. Joseph Sherman. New York: Farrar, Straus and Giroux, 1998.

————. *Shosha*. Trans. Joseph Singer and I.B. Singer. New York: Farrar, Straus and Giroux, 1978.

————. *The Slave*. Trans. Cecil Hemley and I.B. Singer. New York: Farrar, Straus and Cudahy, 1962.

————. *A Young Man in Search of Love*. Garden City, N.Y.: Doubleday, 1978.

Solomon, Michael. *The 'Struma' Incident: A Novel of the Holocaust*. Trans. Carlo Dunlop-Herbert. Toronto: McClelland and Stewart, 1979.

Sperber, Manès. *The Abyss*. Trans. Constantine Fitzgibbon. Garden City, N.Y.: Doubleday, 1952.

————. *Journey Without End*. Trans. Constantine Fitzgibbon. Garden City, N.Y.: Doubleday, 1954.

————. *. . . than a tear in the sea*. Trans. Constantine Fitzgibbon. New York: Bergen-Belsen Memorial Press, 1967.

Spiegel, Isaiah. *Ghetto Kingdom: Tales of the Łódź Ghetto*. Trans. David H. Hirsch and Roslyn Hirsch. Evanston, Ill: Northwestern University Press, 1998.

Spiraux, Alain. *Time Out*. Trans. Frances Keene. New York: Times Books, 1978.

Steiner, Jean-François. *Treblinka*. Trans. Helen Weaver. New York: Simon and Schuster, 1976.

Stern, Daniel. *Who Shall Live, Who Shall Die?* New York: Crown, 1963.

Suhl, Yuri. *On the Other Side of the Gate*. New York: Avon, 1976.

Traub, Barbara Fishman. *The Matrushka Doll*. New York: Richard Marek, 1979.

Uris, Leon. *Mila 18*. New York: Doubleday, 1961.

————. *QB VII*. New York: Doubleday, 1972.

Wallant, Edward Lewis. *The Pawnbroker*. New York: Harcourt Brace Jovanovich, 1978.

Weil Jiří, *Life with a Star*. Trans. Rita Klimova and Roslyn Schloss. Evanston, Ill.: Northwestern University Press, 1998.

————. *Mendelssohn Is on the Roof*. Trans. Marie Winn. New York: Farrar, Straus and Giroux, 1991.

Wiesel, Elie. *The Accident*. Trans. Anne Borchardt. New York: Hill and Wang, 1962.

————. *A Beggar in Jerusalem*. Trans. Lily Edelman and Elie Wiesel. New York: Random House, 1970.

————. *Dawn*. Trans. Anne Borchardt. New York: Hill and Wang, 1961.

————. *The Fifth Son*. Trans. Marion Wiesel. New York: Summit, 1985.

————. *The Forgotten*. Trans. Stephen Becker. New York: Summit, 1992.

————. *The Gates of the Forest*. Trans. Frances Frenaye. New York: Holt, Rinehart and Winston, 1966.

————. *The Oath*. Trans. Marion Wiesel. New York: Avon, 1973.

————. *The Testament*. Trans. Marion Wiesel. New York: Summit, 1981.

————. *The Town Beyond the Wall*. Trans. Stephen Becker. New York: Avon, 1964.

————. *Twilight*. Trans. Marion Wiesel. New York: Summit, 1987.

Memoirs

Adelsberger, Lucie. *Auschwitz: A Doctor's Story*. Trans. Susan Ray. Boston: Northeastern University Press, 1995.

Adler, Alice Dunn. *Boriska's Prophecy: A True Story of Survival's Renewal, Never Told Before: An Autobiography*. Reston, Va.: Acropolis Books, 1991.

Adler, Sinai. *Your Rod and Your Staff: A Young Man's Chronicle of Survival*. Trans. Tzvi Barish. New York: Feldheim, 1996.

Alland, Bronislawa. *Memoirs of a Hidden Child During the Holocaust*. Trans. George Alland. Lewiston, Idaho: Edwin Mellen, 1992.

Améry, Jean. *At the Mind's Limits: Contemplations by a Survivor on Auschwitz and Its Realities*. Trans. Sidney Rosenfeld and Stella P. Rosenfeld. Bloomington: Indiana University Press, 1980.

Apitz, Bruno. *Naked Among Wolves*. Trans. Edith Anderson. Berlin: Seven Seas, 1960.

Appleman-Jurman, Alicia. *Alicia: My Story*. New York: Bantam, 1988.

Arditti, Léon. *The Will to Live: Two Brothers in Auschwitz*. New York: Shengold, 1996.

Auerbacher, Inge. *Beyond the Yellow Star to America*. Unionville, N.Y.: Royal Fireworks, 1995.

Banet, Chana Marcus. *They Called Me Frau Anna*. New York: CIS, 1990.

Barlev, Zvi. *Would God It Weren't Night: The Ordeal of a Jewish Boy from Cracow—Through Auschwitz, Mauthausen, and Gusen*. Trans. Michael Sherbourne. New York: Vantage, 1991.

Barosin, Jacob. *A Remnant*. New York: Holocaust Library, 1988.

Bau, Yosef. *Dear God, Have You Ever Gone Hungry?* Trans. Shlomo Sam Yurman. New York: Arcade, 1998.

Bauman, Janina. *Winter in the Morning: A Young Girl's Life in the Warsaw Ghetto and Beyond, 1939–1945*. New York: Free Press, 1986.

BenGershom, Ezra. *David: The Testimony of a Holocaust Survivor*. Trans. J.A. Underwood. Oxford, England: Oswald Wolff, 1988.

Benish, Pearl. *To Vanquish the Dragon*. New York: Feldheim, 1991.

Bernstein, Sara Tuvel. *The Seamstress: A Memoir of Survival.* New York: Putnam, 1997.

Bertelsen, Aage. *October '43.* Trans. Milly Lindholm and Willy Agtby. London: Museum Press, 1955.

Biber, Jacob. *Risen from the Ashes: A Story of Jewish Displaced Persons in the Aftermath of World War II: Being a Sequel to* Survivors. San Bernadino, Calif.: Borgo Press, 1990.

———. *Survivors: A Personal Story of the Holocaust.* San Bernadino, Calif.: Borgo Press, 1986.

Bielawski, Shraga Feivel. *The Last Jew from Wegrow.* Ed. Louis W. Leibovich. New York: Praeger, 1991.

Birenbaum, Helina. *Hope Is the Last to Die.* Armonk, N.Y.: M.E. Sharpe, 1996.

Birger, Trudi. *A Daughter's Gift of Love: A Holocaust Memoir.* Philadelphia: Jewish Publication Society, 1992.

Birmbaum, Jacob. *I Kept My Promise: My Story of Holocaust Survival.* Lexington, Mass.: Jason R. Taylor, 1995.

Bitton-Jackson, Livia E. *Elli: Coming of Age in the Holocaust.* New York: Times Books, 1980.

———. *My Bridges of Hope: Searching for Life and Love after Auschwitz.* New York: Simon and Schuster, 1999.

Blatt, Thomas Toivi. *From the Ashes of Sobibor: A Story of Survival.* Evanston, Ill.: Northwestern University Press, 1999.

Bradfield, Susi. *But Some Became Stars.* Hewlett, N.Y.: Geffen, 1998.

Brand, Sandra. *Between Two Worlds.* New York: Shengold, 1982.

———. *I Dared to Live.* New York: Shengold, 1978.

Brewster, Eva. *Vanished in Darkness: An Auschwitz Memoir.* Edmonton, Alberta: NeWest Press, 1986.

Breznitz, Shlomo. *Memory Fields.* New York: Alfred A. Knopf, 1993.

Church, Gene. *80629: A Mengele Experiment.* Albuquerque, N.M.: Route 66, 1996.

Cohen, Elie. *The Abyss: A Confession.* Trans. James Brockway. New York: W.W. Norton, 1973.

Curtis, Denis. *Dead Martyrs and Living Heroes: Testimony of the Holocaust.* New York: Shengold, 1983.

Defonseca, Misha. *Misha: A Memoire of the Holocaust Years.* Boston: Mt. Ivy Press, 1997.

Delbo, Charlotte. *Auschwitz and After.* Trans. Rosette C. Lamont. New Haven, Conn.: Yale University Press, 1997.

———. *Days and Memory.* Trans. Rosette C. Lamont. Marlboro, Vt.: Marlboro, 1990.

———. *None of Us Will Return.* Trans. John Githens. Boston: Beacon Press, 1968.

Denes, Magda. *Castles Burning: A Child's Life in War.* New York: Simon and Schuster, 1998.

Deutsch, Mina. *Mina's Story: A Doctor's Memoir of the Holocaust.* Toronto: ECW Press, 1994.

Deutschkron, Inge. *Outcast: A Jewish Girl in Wartime Berlin.* Trans. Jean Steinberg. New York: Fromm, 1989.

Donat, Alexander. *The Holocaust Kingdom.* New York: Holocaust Library, 1978.

Draenger, Gusta Davidson. *Justyna's Narrative.* Trans. Roslyn Hirsch and David H. Hirsch, ed. Eli Pfefferkorn and David H. Hirsch. Amherst: University of Massachusetts Press, 1996.

Dribben, Judith. *And Some Shall Live.* Jerusalem: Keter Books, 1969.

Drix, Samuel. *Witness to Annihilation: Surviving the Holocaust: A Memoir.* Washington, D.C.: Brassey's, 1994.

Drukier, Manny. *Carved in Stone: Holocaust Years, A Boy's Tale.* Toronto: University of Toronto Press, 1996.

Durlacher, Gerhard. *Drowning: Growing Up in the Third Reich.* Trans. Susan Massotty. New York: Serpent's Tail, 1994.

———. *The Search: The Birkenau Boys.* Trans. Susan Massotty. New York: Serpent's Tail, 1994.

———. *Stripes in the Sky.* Trans. Susan Massotty. New York: Serpent's Tail, 1994.

Edvardson, Cordelia. *Burned Child Seeks the Fire: A Memoir.* Trans. Joel Agee. Boston: Beacon, 1997.

Eichengreen, Lucille. *From Ashes to Life: My Memories of the Holocaust.* San Francisco: Mercury House, 1994.

Eisner, Jack. *The Survivor.* Ed. Irving A. Leitner. New York: Morrow, 1980.

———. *Survivor of the Holocaust.* New York: Kensington, 1995.

Elias, Ruth. *Triumph of Hope: From Theresienstadt to Auschwitz to Israel.* Trans. Margot Bettauer Dembo. New York: John Wiley, 1998.

Elienberg-Eibeshitz, Anna. *Breaking My Silence.* New York: Shengold, 1985.

———. *Sisters in the Storm.* New York: CIS, 1992.

Faber, David. *Because of Romek: A Holocaust Survivor's Memoir.* El Cajon, Calif.: Granite Hills Press, 1996.

Farkas, Helen. *Remember the Holocaust: A Memoir of Survival.* Santa Barbara, Calif.: Fithian, 1995.

Feld, Marilla. *I Choose to Live.* New York: Woodhill, 1979.

Fénelon, Fania. *Playing for Time.* Trans. Judith Landry. New York: Atheneum, 1977.

Ferderber-Salz, Bertha. *And the Sun Kept Shining.* New York: Holocaust Library, 1980.

Fettman, Leo. *Shoah: Journey from the Ashes*. Chandler, Ariz.: Five Star, 1999.

Fishman, Lala. *Lala's Story: A Memoir of the Holocaust*. Evanston, Ill.: Northwestern University Press, 1997.

Frank, Jacob. *Himmler's Jewish Tailor: The Story of Holocaust Survivor Jacob Frank*. With Mark Lewis. Syracuse, N.Y.: Syracuse University Press, 2000.

Frankl, Viktor E. *Man's Search for Meaning*. Trans. Ilse Lasch. Boston: Beacon Press, 1962.

Freeman, Joseph. *Job: The Story of a Holocaust Survivor*. Westport, Conn.: Praeger, 1996.

Freilich, Samuel. *The Coldest Winter: The Holocaust Memoirs of Rabbi Samuel Freilich*. New York: Holocaust Library, 1995.

Fried, Hedi. *The Road to Auschwitz: Fragments of a Life*. Trans. and ed. Michael Meyer. Lincoln: University of Nebraska Press, 1996.

Friedländer, Saul. *When Memory Comes*. Trans. Helen R. Lane. New York: Avon, 1980.

Friedman, Henry. *I'm No Hero: The Journeys of a Holocaust Survivor*. Seattle: University of Washington Press, 1999.

Gabor, Georgia M. *My Destiny: Survivor of the Holocaust*. Arcadia, Calif.: Amen Publishers, 1981.

Garbarz, Moshe. *A Survivor*. Trans. Jean-Jacques Garbarz. Detroit: Wayne State University Press, 1992.

Garlinski, Jósef. *The Survival of Love: Memoirs of a Resistance Officer*. Cambridge, Mass.: Blackwell, 1991.

Gastfriend, Edward. *My Father's Testament: Memoir of a Jewish Teenager, 1938–1945*. Philadelphia: Temple University Press, 1999.

Gelb, Ludwig. *My Third Escape*. Dallas: Rossel, 1993.

Gelissen, Rena Kornveich. *Rena's Promise: A Story of Sisters in Auschwitz*. Boston: Beacon Press, 1995.

Gershon, Karen. *A Lesser Child: An Autobiography*. London: Dufour, 1994.

Gershon, Karen, ed. *We Came As Children: A Collective Autobiography*. London: V. Gollancz, 1966.

Geve, Thomas. *Youth in Chains*. Jerusalem: Rubin Mass, 1981.

Gilboa, Yehoshua. *Confess! Confess!* Trans. Dov Ben Aba. Boston: Little, Brown, 1968.

Gisser, Solomon. *The Cantor's Voice*. Ed. David Patterson. Memphis: Serviceberry Press, 2000.

Glas-Larsson, Margareta. *I Want to Speak: The Tragedy and Banality of Survival in Terezin and Auschwitz*. Trans. Lowell A. Bangerter, ed.

Gerhard Botz. Riverside, Calif.: Ariadne Press, 1991.

Gold, Ruth Glasberg. *Ruth's Journey: A Survivor's Memoir*. Gainesville: University Press of Florida, 1996.

Goldstein, Bernard. *The Stars Bear Witness*. Trans. Leonard Shatzkin. New York: Viking Press, 1949.

Gordon, Harold. *The Last Sunrise*. Salinas, Calif.: H and J Publishing, 1989.

Graf, Malvina. *The Kraków Ghetto and the Plaszów Camp*. Tallahassee: Florida State University Press, 1989.

Gray, Martin. *For Those I Loved*. Trans. Anthony White. Boston: Little, Brown, 1972.

Gruber, Samuel. *I Chose Life*. New York: Shengold, 1978.

Gurdus, Luba Krugman. *The Death Train*. New York: Holocaust Library, 1979.

Harshalom, Avraham. *Alive from the Ashes*. Trans. Petetz Kidron. Tel Aviv: Milo, 1990.

Hart, Kitty. *Return to Auschwitz*. New York: Atheneum, 1982.

Hartz, Ruth Kapp. *Your Name Is Renée: Ruth's Story as a Hidden Child: The Wartime Experiences of Ruth Kapp Hartz*. Brunswick, Maine: Biddle, 1994.

Heimler, Eugene. *Night of the Mist*. Trans. Andre Ungar. New York: Vanguard, 1959.

Heller, Fanya Gottesfeld. *Strange and Unexpected Love: A Teenage Girl's Holocaust Memoirs*. Hoboken, N.J.: Ktav, 1993.

Hersh, Gizelle, and Peggy Mann. *"Gizelle, Save the Children!"* New York: Everest House, 1980.

Hochman, Peretz. *Daring to Live*. Tel Aviv: Ministry of Defense, 1994.

Hoffman, Judy. *Joseph and Me: In the Days of the Holocaust*. Hoboken, N.J.: Ktav, 1979.

Hoffmann, Maurie. *Keep Yelling!: A Survivor's Testimony*. Trans. Rosanna Cairo, ed. Ari Unglik. Richmond, Australia: Spectrum, 1995.

Holczler, Moshe. *Late Shadows*. New York: CIS Publishers, 1989.

Horn, Joseph. *Mark It with a Stone*. New York: Barricade Books, 1996.

Hyatt, Felicia B. *Close Calls: The Autobiography of a Survivor*. New York: Holocaust Library, 1991.

Issacson, Clara. *Clara's Story*. Philadelphia: Jewish Publication Society, 1984.

Isaacson, Judith Magyar. *Seed of Sarah: Memoirs of a Survivor*. Urbana: University of Illinois Press, 1991.

Iwens, Sidney. *How Dark the Heavens: 1400 Days in the Grip of Nazi Terror*. New York: Shengold, 1990.

Jacobs, Benjamin. *The Dentist of Auschwitz: A Memoir*. Lexington: University Press of Kentucky, 1995.

Jagendorf, Siegfried. *Jagendorf's Foundry: A Memoir of the Romanian Holocaust, 1941–1944*. Ed. with commentary by Aron Hirt-Manheimer. New York: HarperCollins, 1991.

Joffo, Joseph. *A Bag of Marbles*. Trans. Martin Sokolinsky. New York: Bantam, 1977.

Kacel, Boris. *From Hell to Redemption: A Memoir of the Holocaust*. Niwot: University Press of Colorado, 1998.

Kagan, Jack, and Dov Cohen. *Surviving the Holocaust with the Russian Jewish Partisans*. London: Vallentine, Mitchell, 1998.

Kahn, H.G. *Luck and Chutzpah*. With Hillel Halken. New York: Gefen House, 1997.

Kalib, Goldie Szachter. *The Last Selection: A Child's Journey Through the Holocaust*. Amherst: University of Massachusetts Press, 1991.

Kantor, Alfred. *The Book of Alfred Kantor: An Artist's Journal of the Holocaust*. New York: Schocken, 1987.

Kaplan, Helene C. *I Never Left Janowska*. New York: Holocaust Library, 1989.

Ka-tzetnik 135633. *Kaddish*. New York: Algemeiner Associates, 1998.

———. *Shivitti: A Vision*. Trans. Eliyah De-Nur and Lisa Herman. New York: Harper and Row, 1989.

Kessel, Sim. *Hanged at Auschwitz*. Trans. Melville Wallace and Delight Wallace. New York: Stein and Day, 1972.

Kielar, Wieslaw. *Anus Mundi*. Trans. Susanne Flatauer. New York: Times Books, 1980.

Kimmelman, Mira Ryczke. *Echoes from the Holocaust: A Memoir*. Knoxville: University Of Tennessee Press, 1997.

Klein, Cecile. *Sentenced to Live: A Survivor's Memoir*. New York: Holocaust Library, 1988.

Klein, Gerda Weissmann. *All but My Life*. New York: Hill and Wang, 1957.

Kogon, Eugene. *The Theory and Practice of Hell*. Trans. Heinz Norden. New York: Farrar, Straus, 1950.

Kohn, Nahum, and Howard Roiter. *A Voice from the Forest: Memoirs of a Jewish Partisan*. New York: Holocaust Library, 1980.

Kor, Eva Mozes. *Echoes from Auschwitz: Dr. Mengele's Twins: The Story of Eva and Miriam Mozes*. Terre Haute, Ind.: Candles, 1995.

Korn, Abram. *Abe's Story: A Holocaust Memoir*. Ed. Joseph Korn. Atlanta: Longstreet, 1995.

Kornblit, Michael, and Kathleen Janger. *Until We Meet Again: A True Story of Love and Survival in the Holocaust*. Alexandria, Va: Charles River Press, 1995.

Kornbluth, William. *Sentenced to Remember: My Legacy of Life in Pre-1939 Poland and Sixty-Eight Months of Nazi Occupation*. Ed. Carl Calendar. Bethlehem, Pa.: Lehigh University Press, 1994.

Kotkowski, Itzhak. *The Wiles of Destiny*. El Paso, Texas: I. Kotkowski, 1991.

Krakowski, Avraham. *Counterfeit Lives*. New York: CIS Publications, 1994.

Kroh, Aleksandra. *Lucien's Story*. Trans. Austryn Wainhouse. Evanston, Ill.: Northwestern University Press, 1996.

Kshepitsky, Tirza. *On a Tightrope*. Trans. Walter Shapira and Gudette Shapira. Petach Tikva, Israel: Lilach, 1993.

Kubar, Zofia S. *Double Identity: A Memoir*. New York: Hill and Wang, 1989.

Kulka, Erich. *Escape from Auschwitz*. South Hadley, Mass.: Bergin and Garvey, 1986.

Kuper, Jack. *Child of the Holocaust*. Garden City, N.Y.: Doubleday, 1968.

Lax, Martin H. *Caraseu: A Holocaust Remembrance*. Cleveland, Ohio: Pilgrim Press, 1996.

Lebovitz, Shirley. *The Enduring Spirit*. Trans. Magda Willinger. Phoenix, Ariz.: Gildith, 1993.

Leitner, Isabella. *Fragments of Isabella*. Ed. Irving Leitner. New York: Thomas Crowell, 1978.

———. *Isabella: From Auschwitz to Freedom*. New York: Anchor, 1994.

Lengyel, Olga. *Five Chimneys*. Trans. Paul B. Weiss. London: Granada, 1972.

Lerner, Lily Gluck. *The Silence*. Secaucus, N.J.: Lyle Stuart, 1980.

Levi, Primo. *The Drowned and the Saved*. Trans. Raymond Rosenthal. New York: Vintage Books, 1988.

———. *Moments of Reprieve*. Trans. Ruth Feldman. London: Michael Joseph, 1986.

———. *The Reawakening*. Trans. Stuart Wolf. Boston: Little, Brown, 1965.

———. *Survival in Auschwitz*. Trans. Stuart Wolf. New York: Macmillan, 1961.

Lewinska, Pelagia. *Twenty Months at Auschwitz*. Trans. A. Teichner. New York: Lyle Stuart, 1968.

Lichter, Uri. *In the Eye of the Storm: A Memoir of Survival Through the Holocaust*. New York: Holocaust Library, 1987.

Lind, Jakov. *Counting My Steps*. Trans. Ralph Manheim. New York: Macmillan, 1969.

Lubetkin, Zivia. *In the Days of Destruction and Revolt*. Trans. Ishai Tubbin. Tel Aviv: Hakibbutz Hameuchad, 1981.

Mandel, Edmund. *The Right Path: The Autobiography of a Survivor.* Hoboken, N.J.: Ktav, 1993.

Maurel, Micheline. *An Ordinary Camp.* Trans. Margaret S. Summers. New York: Simon and Schuster, 1958.

Mayer, Bernard. *Entombed: My True Story: How 45 Jews Lived Underground and Survived the Holocaust.* Ojus, Fla.: Aleric, 1994.

Meed, Vladka. *On Both Sides of the Wall.* Trans. Benjamin Meed. Tel Aviv: Hakibbutz Hameuchad, 1973.

Mermelstein, Mel. *By Bread Alone: The Story of A-4685.* 2d ed. Huntington Beach, Calif.: Auschwitz Study Foundation, 1981.

Micheels, Louis J. *Doctor #117641: A Holocaust Memoir.* New Haven, Conn.: Yale University Press, 1989.

Michelson, Frida. *I Survived Rumbuli.* Trans. Wolf Goodman. New York: Holocaust Library, 1979.

Millu, Liana. *Smoke over Birkenau.* Trans. Lynne Sharon Schwartz. Philadelphia: Jewish Publication Society, 1991.

Mirchuk, Petro. *In the German Mills of Death, 1941–1945.* Washington, D.C.: Survivors of the Holocaust, 1985.

Morgens, Frank. *Years at the Edge of Existence: War Memoirs 1939–1945.* Lanham, Md.: University Press of America, 1996.

Muchman, Beatrice. *Never to Be Forgotten: A Young Girl's Holocaust Memoir.* Hoboken, N.J.: Ktav, 1997.

Müller, Filip. *Auschwitz Inferno: The Testimony of a Sonderkommando.* Trans. Susanne Flatauer. London: Routledge and Kegan Paul, 1979.

Müller-Madej, Stella. *A Girl from Schindler's List.* London: Polish Cultural Foundation, 1997.

Nelken, Halina. *And Yet I Am Here!* Trans. Alicia Nitecki. Amherst: University Of Massachusetts Press, 1999.

Nir, Yehuda. *The Lost Childhood: A Memoir.* New York: Harcourt Brace Jovanovich, 1989.

Nomberg-Przytyk, Sara. *Auschwitz: True Tales from a Grotesque Land.* Trans. Roslyn Hirsch. Chapel Hill: University of North Carolina Press, 1985.

Novac, Ana. *The Beautiful Days of My Youth: My Six Months in Auschwitz and Plaszow.* New York: Henry Holt, 1997.

Novack, Judith Mandel. *The Lilac Bush.* New York: Shengold, 1989.

Nyiszli, Miklos. *Auschwitz: A Doctor's Eyewitness Account.* Trans. Tibere Kremer and Richard Seaver. Greenwich, Conn.: Fawcett Crest, 1960.

Oberski, Jona. *Childhood: A Remembrance.* Trans. Ralph Manheim. New York: Doubleday, 1983.

Oliner, Samuel P. *Narrow Escapes: A Boy's Holocaust Memories and Their Legacy.* St. Paul, Minn.: Paragon House, 2000.

———. *Restless Memories: Recollections of the Holocaust Years.* Berkeley, Calif.: Judah L. Magnes Museum, 1986.

Orenstein, Henry. *I Shall Live: Surviving Against All Odds, 1939–1945.* New York: Simon and Schuster, 1989.

Pahor, Boris. *Pilgrim among the Shadows.* Trans. Michael Biggins. New York: Harcourt Brace, 1995.

Peck, Jean M. *At the Fire's Center: A Story of Love and Holocaust Survival.* Urbana: University of Illinois Press, 1998.

Penney, Frances. *I Was There.* Trans. Zofia Griffen. New York: Shengold, 1988.

Perechonik, Calel. *Am I a Murderer? Testament of a Jewish Ghetto Policeman.* Trans. and ed. Frank Fox. Boulder, Colo.: Westview Press, 1996.

Perl, Gisella. *I Was a Doctor in Auschwitz.* New York: International University Press, 1948.

Pinkus, Oscar. *The House of Ashes.* Schenectady, N.Y.: Union College Press, 1990.

Pisar, Samuel. *Of Blood and Hope.* Boston: Little, Brown, 1979.

Rebhun, Joseph. *Leap to Life: Triumph over Nazi Evil.* New York: Ardor Scribendi, 2000.

———. *Witness to History: God and Man in Two Worlds.* San Bernadino, Calif.: Borgo Press, 1996.

Reiss, Johanna. *The Journey Back.* New York: Thomas Y. Crowell, 1976.

———. *The Upstairs Room.* New York: Thomas Y. Crowell, 1972.

Roesler, Karl-Georg. *No Time to Die.* Montreal, Quebec: Robert Davies Multimedia, 1998.

Rose, Leesha. *The Tulips Are Red.* South Brunswick, N.J.: A.S. Barnes, 1978.

Rosen, Donia. *The Forest My Friend.* Trans. Mordecai S. Chertoff. New York: Bergen-Belsen Memorial Press, 1971.

Rosen, Sara. *My Lost World: A Survivor's Tale.* London: Vallentine, Mitchell, 1993.

Rosenberg, Blanca. *To Tell at Last: Survival Under False Identity 1941–1945.* Urbana: University of Illinois Press, 1993.

Rosenberg, Carl. *As God Is My Witness.* New York: Holocaust Library, 1990.

Rotem, Simhah. *Memoirs of a Warsaw Ghetto Fighter: The Past Within Me.* Trans. Barbara Harshav. New Haven, Conn.: Yale University Press, 1995.

Rubinstein, Donna. *I Am the Only Survivor of Krasnostav.* New York: Shengold, 1982.

Rubinstein, Erna. *After the Holocaust: The Long Road to Freedom.* North Haven, Conn.: Archon, 1995.

———. *The Survivor in Us All: Four Young Sisters in the Holocaust.* Hamden, Conn.: Archon, 1986.

Rybak, Rywka. *A Survivor of the Holocaust.* Cleveland, Ohio: Tricycle Press, 1993.

Safran, Alexandre. *Resisting the Storm: Romania 1940–1947.* Ed. Jean Ancel. Jerusalem: Yad Vashem, 1987.

Sandberg, Moshe. *My Longest Year.* Trans. S.C. Hyman. Jerusalem: Yad Vashem, 1968.

Sanik, Leibel. *Someday We'll Be Free.* New York: CIS Communication, 1994.

Sassoon, Agnes. *Agnes: How My Spirit Survived.* Edgeware, England: Lawrence Cohen, 1983.

Schloss, Eva. *Eva's Story: A Survivor's Tale.* New York: St. Martin's Press, 1989.

Schulman, Faye. *A Partisan's Memoir: Woman of the Holocaust.* With Sarah Silberstein Swartz. Toronto, Ontario: Second Story Press, 1995.

Schupack, Joseph. *The Dead Years.* Trans. Paul Kleinbart. New York: Holocaust Library, 1986.

Schwarz, Renée Fodor. *Renée.* New York: Shengold, 1991.

Semprun, Jorge. *Life or Literature.* Trans. Linda Coverdale. New York: Penguin USA, 1998.

Sender, Ruth M. *The Cage.* New York: Macmillan, 1986.

———. *To Life.* New York: Macmillan, 1988.

Sendyk, Helen. *The End of Days.* Syracuse, N.Y.: Syracuse University Press, 2000.

Sevillias, Effikos. *Athens-Auschwitz.* Trans. Nikos Stavroulakis. Athens: Lycabettus, 1983.

Shapell, Nathan. *Witness to the Truth.* New York: David McKay, 1974.

Siegal, Aranka. *Grace in the Wilderness: After the Liberation, 1945–1948.* New York: Farrar, Straus and Giroux, 1985.

———. *Upon the Head of the Goat: A Childhood in Hungary, 1939–1944.* New York: Farrar, Straus and Giroux, 1981.

Silten, R. Gabriele S. *Between Two Worlds: The Autobiography of a Child Survivor of the Holocaust.* Santa Barbara, Calif.: Fithian, 1995.

Spies, Gerty. *My Years in Theresienstadt: How One Woman Survived the Holocaust.* Trans. Jutta R. Tragnitz. Amherst, N.Y.: Prometheus Books, 1997.

Stabholz, Thasseus. *Seven Hells.* Trans. Jacques Grunblatt and Hilda R. Grunblatt. New York: Holocaust Library, 1990.

Starer, Henry. *Why?* New York: Vantage, 1991.

Starkopf, Adam. *The Will to Live: One Family's Story of Surviving the Holocaust.* Albany, N.Y.: SUNY Press, 1995.

Sternberg, Yitzhak. *Under Assumed Identity.* Trans. Ilan Steinberg. Tel Aviv: Hakibbutz Hameuchad and Ghetto Fighters' House, 1986.

Stiffel, Frank. *The Tale of the Ring: A Kaddish.* Wainscott, N.Y.: Pushcart Press, 1984.

Sutin, Jack, and Rochelle Sutin. *Jack and Rochelle: A Holocaust Story of Love and Resistance.* Ed. Lawrence Sutin. St. Paul, Minn.: Graywolf, 1995.

Szep, Erno. *The Smell of Humans: A Memoir of the Holocaust in Hungary.* Trans. John Batki. Budapest: Central European University Press, 1994.

Szereszewska, Helena. *Memoirs from Occupied Warsaw 1940–1945.* Trans. Anna Marianska. London: Vallentine, Mitchell, 1997.

Szmagelewska, Seweryna. *Smoke over Birkenau.* Trans. Jadwiga Rynas. New York: Henry Holt, 1947.

Szpilman, Wladyslaw. *The Pianist.* Trans. Anthea Bell. Thorndike, Maine: Thorndike Press, 2000.

Szwajger, Adina B. *I Remember Nothing More: The Warsaw Children's Hospital and the Jewish Resistance.* New York: Simon and Schuster, 1992.

Tarrasch, Ena. *Farewell to Fear: The Memoirs of a Holocaust Survivor.* Centreville, Va.: Denlinger's Publishers, 1997.

Tec, Nechama. *Dry Tears: The Story of a Lost Childhood.* New York: Oxford University Press, 1984.

Tedeschi, Giuliana. *There Is a Place on Earth: A Woman in Birkenau.* Trans. Tim Parks. New York: Pantheon, 1992.

Temchin, Michael. *The Witch Doctor: Memoirs of a Partisan.* New York: Holocaust Library, 1995.

Tillion, Germaine. *Ravensbrück.* Trans. Gerald Satterwhite. Garden City, N.Y.: Doubleday, 1975.

Toll, Nellie S. *Behind the Secret Window: A Memoir of a Hidden Childhood During World War Two.* New York: Dial Press, 1993.

Topas, George. *The Iron Furnace.* Lexington: University Press of Kentucky, 1990.

Toren, Rose.. *A New Beginning.* New York: Shengold, 1996.

———. *Destiny.* New York: Shengold, 1991.

Trepman, Paul. *Among Men and Beasts.* Trans. Shoshana Perla and Gertrude Hirschler. New York: Bergen-Belsen Memorial Press, 1978.

Turgel, Gina. *I Light a Candle.* London: Vallentine, Mitchell, 1995.

Urbach, Sarah Selver. *Through the Window of My Home: Recollections from the Łódź Ghetto.* Trans. Sioma Bodansky. Jerusalem: Yad Vashem, 1986.

Velmans-Van Hessen, Edith. *Edith's Book.* New York: Viking, 1998.

Vinocur, Ana. *A Book Without a Title.* Trans. Valentine Isaac and Ricardo Iglesia. New York: Vantage, 1976.

Vrba, Rudolf, and Alan Bestic. *I Cannot Forgive.* New York: Bantam, 1964.

Wainapel, David. *From Death Row to Freedom.* New York: Block, 1984.

Walshaw, Rachela, and Sam Walshaw. *From out of the Firestorm: A Memoir of the Holocaust.* New York: Shapolsky, 1991.

Waterford, Helen. *Commitment to the Dead: One Woman's Journey Toward Understanding.* Frederick, Colo.: Renaissance House, 1987.

Wdowinski, David. *And We Are Not Saved.* New York: Philosophical Library, 1985.

Weinberg, Werner. *Self-Portrait of a Holocaust Survivor.* Jefferson, N.C.: McFarland, 1985.

Weinstein, Frida Scheps. *A Hidden Childhood, 1942–1945.* Trans. Barbara Loeb Kennedy. New York: Hill and Wang, 1985.

Weiss, David W. *Reluctant Return: A Survivor's Journey to an Austrian Town.* Bloomington: Indiana University Press, 1999.

Wells, Leon W. *The Death Brigade.* New York: Holocaust Library, 1978.

———. *Shattered Faith: A Holocaust Legacy.* Lexington: University Press of Kentucky, 1995.

Wermuth, Henry. *Breathe Deeply, My Son.* London: Vallentine, Mitchell, 1993.

Werner, Harold. *Fighting Back: A Memoir of Jewish Resistance in World War Two.* Ed. Mark Werner. New York: Columbia University Press, 1992.

White, Naomi Rosh. *From Darkness to Light: Surviving the Holocaust.* Melbourne, Australia: Collins Dove, 1988.

Whiteley, Suzanna Mehler. *Appel Is Forever: A Child's Memoir.* Detroit: Wayne State University Press, 1999.

Wiesel, Elie. *From the Kingdom of Memory.* Trans. Marion Wiesel. New York: Summit, 1990.

———. *Legends of Our Time.* New York: Avon, 1968.

———. *Night.* Trans. Stella Rodway. New York: Hill and Wang, 1960.

———. *One Generation After.* Trans. Lily Edelman and Elie Wiesel. New York: Pocket Books, 1970.

Wiesenthal, Simon. *The Murderers Among Us: The Simon Wiesenthal Memoirs.* Ed. Joseph Wechsberg. New York: McGraw-Hill, 1967.

———. *The Sunflower.* Trans. H.A. Piehler. New York: Schocken, 1997.

Wijze, Louis de. *Only My Life: A Survivor's Story.* Trans. Victor de Wijze. New York: St. Martin's Press, 1997.

Willenberg, Samuel. *Surviving Treblinka.* Trans. Naftali Greenwood. ed. Wladyslaw T. Bartoszewski. Oxford, England: Basil Blackwell, 1989.

Wygoda, Hermann. *In the Shadow of the Swastika.* Ed. Mark Wygoda. Urbana: University of Illinois Press, 1998.

Zar, Rose. *In the Mouth of the Wolf.* Philadelphia: Jewish Publication Society, 1983.

Zeidman-Dziubas, Ruth. *Light in the Darkness.* Trans. Yehudit Kirstein. Jerusalem: R. Zeidman-Dziubas, 1988.

Zeller, Frederic. *When Time Ran Out: Coming of Age in the Third Reich.* Sag Harbor, N.Y.: Permanent Press, 1989.

Zelman, Léon. *After Survival: One Man's Mission in the Cause of Memory.* Trans. Meredith Schneeweiss. New York: Holmes and Meier, 1998.

Zuckerman, Abraham. *A Voice in the Chorus: Life as a Teenager in the Holocaust.* Hoboken, N.J.: Ktav, 1991.

Zuckerman, Yitzhak. *A Surplus of Memory: Chronicle of the Warsaw Ghetto Uprising.* Trans. Barbara Harshav. Berkeley: University of California Press, 1993.

Zuker-Bujanowska, Liliana. *Liliana's Journal: Warsaw, 1939–1945.* New York: Dial Press, 1980.

Zyskind, Sara. *Stolen Years.* Trans. Margarit Inbar. Minneapolis, Minn.: Lerner, 1981.

———. *Struggle.* Minneapolis, Minn.: Lerner, 1989.

Zywulska, Krystana. *I Came Back.* Trans. Krystyna Cenkalska. London: Dennis Dobson, 1951.

Diaries

Adler, Stanislaw. *The Diary of Stanislaw Adler.* Trans. Sara Chmielewska Philip. Jerusalem: Yad Vashem, 1981.

Berg, Mary. *The Warsaw Ghetto: A Diary.* Trans. Norbert Glass and Sylvia Glass. ed. S. L. Schneiderman. New York: L. B. Fischer, 1945.

Borzykowski, Tuvia. *Between Tumbling Walls.* Trans. Mendel Kohansky. 2d ed. Tel Aviv: Hakibbutz Hameuchad, 1976.

Cyprys, Ruth Altbeker. *A Jump for Life: A Survivor's Journal from Nazi-Occupied Poland.* Ed. Elaine Potter. New York: Continuum, 1997.

Czerniakow, Adam. *The Warsaw Ghetto Diary of Adam Czerniakow.* Trans. Stanislaw Staron, et al., ed. Raul Hilberg, Stanislaw Staron, and Joseph Kermisz. New York: Stein and Day, 1979.

Diment, Michael. *The Lone Survivor: A Diary of the Lukacze Ghetto and Svyniukhy*. Trans. Shmuel Yahalom. New York: Holocaust Library, 1992.

Dorembus, Helena Elbaum. "Through Helpless Eyes: A Survivor's Diary of the Warsaw Ghetto Uprising," *Moment* (April 1993): 56–61.

Dorian, Emil. *The Quality of Witness*. Trans. Mara Soceanu Vamos, ed. Marguerite Dorian. Philadelphia: Jewish Publication Society, 1982.

Flinker, Moshe. *Young Moshe's Diary*. Trans. Shaul Esh and Geoffrey Wigoder. Jerusalem: Yad Vashem and Board of Jewish Education, 1971.

Frank, Anne. *The Diary of a Young Girl*. Trans. B.M. Mooyaart-Doubleday. New York: Modern Library, 1952.

Gabel, Dina. *Behind the Ice Curtain*. New York: CIS Communication, 1992.

Gefen, Aba. *Hope in Darkness: The Abe Gefen Diaries*. New York: Holocaust Library, 1989.

Gradowski, Salmen. "Manuscript of Sonderkommando Member." Trans. Krystyna Michalik. In *Amidst a Nightmare of Crime: Manuscripts of Members of Sonderkommando*, ed. Jadwiga Bezwinska. Oświęcim, Poland: State Museum, 1973, pp. 75–108.

Herzberg, Abel Jacob. *Between Two Streams: A Diary from Bergen-Belsen*. Trans. Jack Santcross. London: I.B. Tauris, 1997.

Heyman, Éva. *The Diary of Éva Heyman*. Trans. Moshe M. Kohn. Jerusalem: Yad Vashem, 1974.

Hillesum, Etty. *An Interrupted Life*. Trans. Arno Pomerans. New York: Pantheon, 1983.

Huberband, Shimon. *Kiddush Hashem: Jewish Religious and Cultural Life in Poland During the Holocaust*. Trans. David E. Fishman, ed. Jeffrey S. Gurock and Robert S. Hirt. Hoboken, N.J.: Ktav and Yeshiva University Press, 1987.

Kahane, David. *Lvov Ghetto Diary*. Trans. Jerzy Michalowicz. Amherst: University of Massachusetts Press, 1990.

Kalmanovitch, Zelig. "A Diary of the Nazi Ghetto in Vilna." Trans. and ed. Koppel S. Pinson, *YIVO Annual of Jewish Social Sciences* 8 (1953): 9–81.

Kaplan, Chaim A. *The Warsaw Diary of Chaim A. Kaplan*. Trans. and ed. Abraham I. Katsh. New York: Collier, 1973.

Katz, Josef. *One Who Came Back: The Diary of a Jewish Survivor*. Trans. Herzl Reach. New York: Herzl Press and Bergen-Belsen Memorial Press, 1973.

Katznelson, Yitzhak. *Vittel Diary*. Trans. Myer Cohn. 2d ed. Tel Aviv: Hakibbutz Hameuchad, 1972.

Klemperer, Victor. *I Will Bear Witness: A Diary of the Nazi Years 1933–1941*. Vol. 1. Trans. Martin Chalmers. New York: Random House, 1999.

———. *I Will Bear Witness 1941–1945: A Diary of the Nazi Years*. Vol. 2. Trans. Martin Chalmers. New York: Random House, 2000.

Klonicki-Klonymus, Aryeh. *The Diary of Adam's Father*. Trans. Avner Tomaschaff. Tel Aviv: Ghetto Fighters House and Hakibbutz Hameuchad, 1973.

Kon, Menahem. "Fragments of a Diary (August 6, 1942–October 1, 1942)." Trans. M.Z. Prives. In *To Live with Honor and Die with Honor: Selected Documents from the Warsaw Ghetto Underground Archives "O.S.,"* ed. Joseph Kermish. Jerusalem: Yad Vashem, 1986, pp. 80–86.

Korczak, Janusz. *Ghetto Diary*. Trans. Jerzy Bachrach and Barbara Krzywicka. New York: Holocaust Library, 1978.

Kruk, Herman. "Diary of the Vilna Ghetto." Trans. Shlomo Noble. *YIVO Annual of Jewish Social Sciences* 13 (1965): 9–78.

Langfus, Leib. "Manuscript of Sonderkommando Member." Trans. Krystyna Michalik. In *Amidst a Nightmare of Crime: Manuscripts of Members of Sonderkommando*, ed. Jadwiga Bezwinska. Oświęcim, Poland: State Museum, 1973, pp. 112–22.

Levy-Hass, Hanna. *Inside Belsen*. Trans. Ronald L. Taylor. Totowa, N.J.: Barnes and Noble, 1982.

Lewental, Salmen. "Manuscript of Sonderkommando Member." Trans. Krystyna Michalik. In *Amidst a Nightmare of Crime: Manuscripts of Members of Sonderkommando*, ed. Jadwiga Bezwinska. Oświęcim, Poland: State Museum, 1973, pp. 130–78.

Lewin, Abraham. *A Cup of Tears: A Diary of the Warsaw Ghetto*. Trans. Christopher Hutton, ed. Antony Polonsky. Cambridge, Mass.: Blackwell, 1989.

Lissner, Abraham. "Diary of a Jewish Partisan in Paris." Trans. Yuri Suhl. In *They Fought Back*, ed. Yuri Suhl. New York: Crown, 1967, pp. 282–97.

Lozansky, Riva. *If I Forget Thee: The Destruction of the Shtetl Butrimantz*. Trans. Eva Tverskoy, ed. Olga Zabludoff and Lily Poritz Miller. Washington, D.C.: Remembrance Books, 1998.

Malz, Moshe. *Years of Horror—Glimpse of Hope: The Diary of a Family in Hiding*. New York: Shengold, 1993.

Marcuse, Günther. "The Diary of Günther Marcuse (The Last Days of the Gross-Breesen Training Centre)." Trans. and ed. Joseph Walk. *Yad Vashem Studies* 8 (1970): 159–81.

Matzner, David. *The Muselmann: The Diary of a Jewish Slave Laborer*. Hoboken, N.J.: Ktav, 1994.

Mechanicus, Philip. *Year of Fear: A Jewish Prisoner Waits for Auschwitz*. Trans. Irene S. Gibbons. New York: Hawthorne, 1964.

Opoczynski, Peretz. "Warsaw Ghetto Chronicle—September 1942." Trans. M.Z. Prives. In *To Live with Honor and Die with Honor: Selected Documents from the Warsaw Ghetto Underground Archives "O.S.,"* ed. Joseph Kermish. Jerusalem: Yad Vashem, 1986, pp. 101–11.

Redlich, Gonda. *The Terezin Diary of Gonda Redlich*. Trans. Laurence Kutler, ed. Saul S. Friedman. Lexington: University Press of Kentucky, 1999.

Ringelblum, Emmanuel. *Notes from the Warsaw Ghetto*. Trans. and ed. Jacob Sloan. New York: Schocken, 1974.

Rivosh, Elik. "From the Diary of the Sculptor Rivosh (Riga)." In *The Black Book,* ed. Ilya Ehrenburg and Vasily Grossman, trans. John Glad and James S. Levine. New York: Holocaust Library, 1981, pp. 324–46.

Roubickova, Eva. *We're Alive and Life Goes On: A Theresienstadt Diary*. Trans. Zaia Alexander. New York: Henry Holt, 1998.

Rubinowicz, David. *The Diary of David Rubinowicz*. Trans. Derek Bowman. Edmonds, Wash.: Creative Options, 1982.

Rudashevski, Yitskhok. *The Diary of the Vilna Ghetto*. Trans. Percy Matenko. Tel Aviv: Ghetto Fighters' House and Hakibbutz Hameuchad, 1973.

Seidman, Hillel. *The Warsaw Ghetto Diaries*. Trans. Yosef Israel. Southfield, Mich.: Targum, 1997.

Senesh, Hannah. *Hannah Senesh: Her Life and Diary*. Trans. Marta Cohn. New York: Schocken, 1972.

Sheinkinder, S. "The Diary of S. Sheinkinder." *Yad Vashem Studies* 5 (1963): 255–69.

Sierakowiak, David. *The Diary of David Sierakowiak*. Trans. Kamil Turowski, ed. Alan Adelson. New York: Oxford University Press, 1996.

Stanford, Julian Castle. *Reflections: The Diary of a German-Jew in Hiding*. Trans. Eva Einstein, ed. Rebecca Fromer. Oakland, Calif.: Magnes Museum, 1965.

Tory, Avraham. *Surviving the Holocaust: The Kovno Ghetto Diary*. Trans. Jerzy Michalowicz, ed. Martin Gilbert. Cambridge, Mass.: Harvard University Press, 1990.

Wasser, Hersh. "Daily Entries of Hersh Wasser." Trans. Joseph Kermish. *Yad Vashem Studies* 15 (1983): 201–82.

Wells, Leon. "The Death Brigade." Trans. Leon Wells. In *The Death Brigade (The Janowska Road)*. New York: Holocaust Library, 1978, pp. 131–224.

Werber, Jack. *Saving Children: Diary of a Buchenwald Survivor and Rescuer*. New Brunswick, N.J.: Transaction Books, 1996.

Zuckerman, Yitzhak. "From the Warsaw Ghetto." *Commentary* (December 1975): 62–69.

Zylberberg, Michael. *A Warsaw Diary*. London: Vallentine, Mitchell, 1969.

Poetry

Abse, Dannie. *Ask the Bloody Horse*. London: Hutchinson, 1986.

———. *Remembrance of Crimes Past: Poems*. New York: Persea, 1993.

———. *Small Desperation: Poems*. London: Hutchinson, 1968.

———. *White Coat, Purple Coat: Collected Poems 1948–1988*. New York: George Braziller, 1992.

Balbin, Julius. *Dwellings of Doom*. Lewiston, N.Y.: Edwin Mellen, 1999.

Bryks, Rachmil. *Ghetto Factory 76*. Trans. Theodor Primack and Eugen Kullman. New York: Bloch, 1967.

Celan, Paul. *Breathturn*. Trans. Pierre Joris. Los Angeles: Sun and Moon, 1995.

———. *Last Poems*. Trans. Katharine Washburn and Margret Guillemin. San Francisco: North Point, 1986.

———. *The Poems of Paul Celan*. Trans. Michael Hamburger. New York: Persea, 1989.

———. *Selected Poems*. Trans. Michael Hamburger and Christopher Middleton. Middlesex, England: Penguin, 1972.

———. *Selected Poems and Prose of Paul Celan*. Trans. John Felstiner. New York: W.W. Norton, 2000.

———. *65 Poems*. Trans. Brian Lynch and Peter Jankowsky. Dublin: Raven Arts, 1985.

———. *Speech-Grille and Selected Poems*. Trans. Joachim Neugroschel. New York: E.P. Dutton, 1971.

———. *Threadsuns*. Trans. Pierre Joris. Los Angeles: Sun and Moon, 1999.

Clenman, Doria Blumenfeld. *A Scroll of Remembrance*. North York, Ontario: Flowerfield and Littleman, 1995.

Gershon, Karen. *Legacies and Encounters: Poems 1966–1971*. London: V. Gollancz, 1972.

———. *Selected Poems*. New York: Harcourt, Brace and World, 1966.

Glatstein, Jacob. *Poems*. Trans. Etta Blum. Tel Aviv: I.L. Peretz, 1970.

———. *The Selected Poems of Jacob Glatstein*. Trans. Ruth Whitman. New York: October House, 1972.

Gouri. Haim. *Words in My Lovesick Blood:* Poems. Trans. Stanley F. Chyet. Detroit: Wayne State University Press, 1996.

Gurdus, Luba Krugman. *Painful Echoes: Poems of the Holocaust from the Diary of Luba Krugman Gurdus*. New York: Holocaust Library, 1985.

Hecht, Anthony. *The Hard Hours*. New York: Atheneum, 1967.

———. *Millions of Strange Shadows*. New York: Atheneum, 1978.

Herzberger, Magda. *The Waltz of the Shadows*. New York: Philosophical Library, 1983.

Katznelson, Yitzhak. *The Song of the Murdered Jewish People*. Trans. Noah H. Rosenbloom. Tel Aviv: Hakibbutz Hameuchad and Ghetto Fighters' House, 1980.

Klein, A.M. *Collected Poems*. Toronto, Ontario: McGraw-Hill Ryerson, 1974.

Klein, Magdalena. *Pearls and Lace: Poems*. Trans. and ed. Susan Simpson Geroe. Santa Barbara, Calif.: Fithian, 1996.

Kolmar, Gertrude. *Dark Soliloquy: The Selected Poems of Gertrude Kolmar*. Trans. Henry Smith. New York: Seabury, 1975.

Korwin, Yala H. *To Tell the Story: Poems of the Holocaust*. New York: Holocaust Library, 1987.

Kovner, Abba. *A Canopy in the Desert*. Trans. Shirley Kaufman. Pittsburgh: University of Pittsburgh Press, 1973.

———. *My Little Sister and Selected Poems*. Trans. Shirley Kaufman. Oberlin, Ohio: Oberlin College Press, 1986.

———. *Selected Poems of Abba Kovner and Nelly Sachs*. Trans. Shirley Kaufman and Nurit Orchan. Middlesex, England: Penguin, 1971.

Levertov, Denise. *Candles in Babylon*. New York: New Directions, 1982.

———. *Collected Earlier Poems, 1940–1960*. New York: New Directions, 1979.

———. *The Great Unknowing: Last Poems*. New York: New Directions, 1999.

———. *Light Up the Cave*. New York: New Directions, 1972.

———. *Poems, 1960–1967*. New York: New Directions, 1983.

———. *Poems, 1968–1972*. New York: New Directions, 1988.

Levi, Primo. *Shema: Collected Poems of Primo Levi*. Trans. Ruth Feldman and Brian Swann. London: Menard, 1976.

Mezei, András. *Testimony: Voices of the Holocaust*. Trans. Thomas Land. London: Alpha World Features, 1995.

Molodowsky, Kadia. *Paper Bridges: Selected Poems of Kadia Molodowsky*. Trans. and ed. Kathryn Hellerstein. Detroit: Wayne State University Press, 1999.

Pagis, Dan. *Points of Departure*. Trans. Stephen Mitchell. Philadelphia: Jewish Publication Society, 1981.

———. *Selected Poems*. Trans. Stephen Mitchell. Oxford, England: Carcanet, 1972.

———. *The Selected Poetry of Dan Pagis*. Trans. Stephen Mitchell. Berkeley: University of California Press, 1996.

———. *Various Directions: The Selected Poetry of Dan Pagis*. Trans. Stephen Mitchell. San Francisco: North Point, 1989.

Pilinszky, János. *Crater: Poems 1974–1975*. Trans. Peter Jay. London: Anvil, 1978.

———. *Selected Poems*. Trans. Ted Hughs and Janos Cskotits. New York: Persea, 1976.

Radnóti, Miklós. *Clouded Sky*. Trans. Steven Polgar, et al. New York: Harper and Row, 1972.

———. *Foamy Sky: The Major Poems of Miklós Radnóti*. Trans. Zsuzsanna Ozsváth and Frederick Turner. Princeton, N.J.: Princeton University Press, 1992.

———. *Forced March: Selected Poems*. Trans. Clive Weaver and George Gömöri. Manchester, Eng.: Carcanet, 1979.

———. *Miklós Radnóti: The Complete Poetry*. Trans. and ed. Emery George. Ann Arbor, Mich.: Ardis, 1980.

———. *Miklós Radnóti: Under Gemini, a Prose Memoir and Selected Poetry*. Trans. Kenneth McRobbie, Zita McRobbie, and Jascha Kessler. Athens: Ohio University Press, 1985.

Rezinokoff, Charles. *Holocaust*. Los Angeles: Black Sparrow, 1975.

Rosensaft, Menachem Z. *Fragments: Past and Future*. New York: Shengold, 1968.

Rózewicz, Tadeusz. *"The Survivor" and Other Poems*. Trans. Magnus J. Krynski and Robert A. Maguire. Princeton, N.J.: Princeton University Press, 1976.

Sachs, Nelly. *O the Chimneys: Selected Poems*. Trans. Michael Hamburger, et al. New York: Farrar, Straus and Giroux, 1967.

———. *The Seeker and Other Poems*. Trans. Ruth Mead and Matthew Mead, et al. New York: Farrar, Straus and Giroux, 1970.

Silten, R. Gabriele S. *Dark Shadows, Bright Life*: Poems. Santa Barbara, Calif.: Fithian, 1998.

———. *High Tower Crumbling: Poems*. Santa Barbara, Calif.: Fithian, 1991.

Sutzkever, Abraham. *Abraham Sutzkever: Selected Poetry and Prose*. Trans. Barbara Harshav and Benjamin Harshav. Berkeley: University of California Press, 1991.

———. *Burnt Pearls: Ghetto Poems of Abraham Sutzkever*. Trans. Seymour Mayne. Oakville, Ontario: Mosaic Press, 1981.

———. *The Fiddle Rose: Poems, 1970–1972*. Trans. Ruth Whitman. Detroit: Wayne State University Press, 1990.

———. *Laughter Beneath the Forest: Poems from Old and Recent Manuscripts*. Trans. Barnett Zumoff. Hoboken, N.J.: Ktav, 1996.

Taube, Herman. *A Chain of Images*. New York: Shulsinger Brothers, 1979.

Torren, Asher. *Seven Portholes in Hell: Poems of the Holocaust*. New York: Holocaust Library, 1991.

Wiesel, Elie. *Ani Maamin: A Song Lost and Found Again*. Trans. Marion Wiesel. New York: Random House, 1973.

Zychlinsky, Rajzel. *God Hid His Face*. Trans. Barnett Zumhoff, et al. Santa Rosa, Calif.: Word and Quill, 1997.

Drama

Amir, Anda. *This Kind Too*. Trans. Shoshana Perla. New York: World Zionist Organization, 1972.

Cristofer, Michael. *The Black Angel*. New York: Dramatists Play Service, 1984.

Eliach, Yaffa, and Uri Assaf. *The Last Jew*. Trans. Yaffa Eliach. Israel: Alef-Alef Theatre Publications, 1977.

Goldberg, Leah. *The Lady of the Castle*. Trans. Ted Carmi. Tel Aviv: Institute for the Translation of Hebrew Literature, 1974.

Goodrich, Frances, and Albert Hackett. *The Diary of Anne Frank*. New York: Random House, 1956.

Grumberg, Jean-Claude. *The Workroom*. Trans. Daniel A. Stein. New York: S. French, 1984.

Hochhuth, Rolf. *The Deputy*. Trans. Richard Winston and Clara Winston. New York: Grove, 1964.

Krall, Hanna. *To Steal a March on God*. Trans. Jadwiga Kosicka. Amsterdam: Harwood Academic, 1996.

Lampell, Millard. *The Wall*. New York: Alfred A. Knopf, 1961.

Lebow, Barbara. *A Shayna Maidel*. New York: New American Library, 1988.

Meged, Aharon. *The Burning Bush*. Trans. Shoshana Perla. New York: World Zionist Organization, 1972.

Miller, Arthur. *Broken Glass*. New York: Penguin USA, 1994.

———. *Incident at Vichy*. New York: Penguin USA, 1985.

———. *Playing for Time*. London: N. Hern, 1990.

Pinter, Harold. *Ashes to Ashes*. New York: Grove Press, 1997.

Samuels, Diane. *Kindertransport*. New York: Plume, 1995.

Shaw, Robert. *The Man in the Glass Booth*. Middlesex, England: Penguin, 1969.

Sobol, Joshua. *Ghetto*. Trans. Miriam Shlessinger. Tel Aviv: Institute for the Translation of Hebrew Literature, 1986.

Sylvanus, Erwin. *Leo Baeck: A Radio Play Based on Authentic Texts*. Trans. Robert Wolfgang Rhee and David Dowdy. New York: Peter Lang, 1996.

Tabori, George. *The Cannibals*. London: Davis-Poynter, 1974.

Tomer, Ben-Zion. *Children of the Shadows*. Trans. Hillel Halkin. New York: World Zionist Organization, n.d.

Watts, Irene N. *Goodbye Marianne*. Toronto, Ontario: McClelland and Stewart, 1998.

Weiss, Peter. *The Investigation*. Trans. Jon Swann and Ulu Grossbard. New York: Atheneum, 1966.

Wiesel, Elie. *The Trial of God*. Trans. Marion Wiesel. New York: Random House, 1979.

———. *Zalmen or The Madness of God*. Trans. Nathan Edelman, adapted for the stage by Marion Wiesel. New York: Random House, 1974.

Anthologies

Boas, Jacob, ed. *We Are Witnesses: Five Diaries of Teenagers Who Died in the Holocaust*. New York: Henry Holt, 1995.

Brown, Jean E., ed. *Images from the Holocaust: A Literature Anthology*. Lincolnwood, Ill.: NTC Publishing Group, 1996.

Ehrenburg, Ilya, and Vasily Grossman, eds. *The Complete Black Book of Russian Jewry*. Trans. David Patterson. Piscataway, N.J.: Transaction Publishers, 2001.

Eliach, Yaffa, ed. *Hasidic Tales of the Holocaust*. New York: Oxford University Press, 1982.

Friedlander, Albert, ed. *Out of the Whirlwind: A Reader of Holocaust Literature*. New York: Schocken, 1976.

Fuchs, Elinor, ed. *Plays of the Holocaust: An International Anthology*. New York: Theatre Communications Group, 1987.

Gillon, Adam, ed. *Poems of the Ghetto: A Testament of Lost Men*. New York: Twayne, 1969.

Glatstein, Jacob, et al. , eds. *Anthology of Holocaust Literature*. Philadelphia: Jewish Publication Society, 1968.

Greene, Joshua M., and Shiva Kumer, eds. *Witness: Voices from the Holocaust*. New York: Free Press, 2000.

Holliday, Laurel, ed. *Children in the Holocaust and World War II: Their Secret Diaries*. New York: Washington Square, 1996.

Kramer, Aaron, and Saul Lishinsky, eds. *The Lost Lullaby: Poetry from the Holocaust*. Syracuse, N.Y.: Syracuse University Press, 1998.

Landau, Elaine, ed. *We Survived the Holocaust*. New York: Franklin Watts, 1991.

Langer, Lawrence L., ed. *Art from the Ashes: A Holocaust Anthology*. New York: Oxford University Press, 1995.

Levi, Isaac Jack, ed. *And the World Stood Silent: Sephardic Poetry of the Holocaust*. Urbana: University of Illinois Press, 2000.

Ramras-Rauch, Gila, ed. *Facing the Holocaust: Selected Israeli Fiction*. Philadelphia: Jewish Publication Society, 1986.

Raphael, Linda Schermer, and Marc Lee Raphael, eds. *When Night Fell: An Anthology of Holocaust Short Stories*. New Brunswick, N.J.: Rutgers University Press, 1999.

Rittner, Carole, and John K. Roth, eds. *Different Voices: Women and the Holocaust*. New York: Paragon House, 1993.

Rochman, Hazel, and Darlene Z. McCampbell, eds. *Bearing Witness: Stories of the Holocaust*. New York: Orchard, 1995.

Rothchild, Sylvia, ed. *Voices from the Holocaust*. New York: New American Library, 1981.

Rothenberg, Joshua, ed. *And They Will Call Me: Poems from the Holocaust in Yiddish and English Translation*. Trans. Ronald Bucholz, et al. Waltham, Mass.: Brandeis University Press, 1982.

Schiff, Hilda, ed. *Holocaust Poetry*. New York: St. Martin's Press, 1995.

Silwowska, Wiktoria, ed. *The Last Eyewitnesses: Children of the Holocaust Speak*. Trans. Julian Bassgang. Evanston, Ill.: Northwestern University Press, 1998.

Skloot, Robert, ed. *The Theatre of the Holocaust, Volume I, Four Plays*. Madison: University of Wisconsin Press, 1999.

———. *The Theatre of the Holocaust, Volume II, Six Plays*. Madison: University of Wisconsin Press, 1999.

Taub, Michael, ed. *Israeli Holocaust Drama*. Syracuse, N.Y.: Syracuse University Press, 1996.

Teichman, Milton, and Sharon Leder, eds. *Truth and Lamentation: Stories and Poems on the Holocaust*. Urbana: University of Illinois Press, 1994.

Volakova, Hana, ed. *I Never Saw Another Butterfly: Children's Drawings and Poems from Terezin Concentration Camp, 1942–1944*. Trans. Jeanna Nemcova. New York: Schocken, 1994.

Zych, Adam A., ed. *The Auschwitz Poems: An Anthology*. Oświęcim, Poland: Auschwitz-Birkenau State Museum, 1999.

Bibliography of Critical Studies of Holocaust Literature

Aaron, Frieda W. *Bearing the Unbearable: Yiddish and Polish Poetry in the Ghettos and Concentration Camps*. Albany, N.Y.: SUNY Press, 1990.

Aldridge, James C. *Ilse Aichinger*. London: Wolff, 1969.

Alexander, Edward. *Isaac Bashevis Singer*. Boston: Twayne, 1980.

———. *The Resonance of Dust: Essays on Holocaust Literature and Jewish Fate*. Columbus: Ohio State University Press, 1979.

Altman, Linda Jacobs. *Simon Wiesenthal*. San Diego: Lucent Books, 2000.

Anissimov, Myriam. *Primo Levi: Tragedy of an Optimist*. Trans. Steve Cox. New York: Overlook Press, 1999.

Balaban, Abraham. *Between God and Beast: An Examination of Amos Oz's Prose*. University Park: Pennsylvania State University Press, 1993.

Banner, Gillian, and Colin Richmond. *Remembrance and Holocaust Literature: The Memory of the Offense*. London: Vallentine, Mitchell, 2000.

Baumgarten, Murray, and Barbara Gottfried. *Understanding Philip Roth*. Columbia: University of South Carolina Press, 1990.

Bentley, Eric, ed. *The Storm over the Deputy*. New York: Grove Press, 1964.

Berenbaum, Michael. *Elie Wiesel: God, the Holocaust, and the Children of Israel*. New York: Behrman House, 1994.

Berger, Alan L. *Bearing Witness to the Holocaust, 1939–1989*. Lewiston, N.Y.: Edwin Mellen, 1991.

———. *Children of Job: American Second-Generation Witnesses to the Holocaust*. Albany, N.Y.: SUNY Press, 1997.

———. *Crisis and Covenant: The Holocaust in American Jewish Fiction*. Albany, N.Y.: SUNY Press, 1985.

Best, Otto F. *Peter Weiss*. Trans. Ursule Molinaro. New York: Frederick Ungar, 1976.

Biletzky, I. Ch. *God, Jew, Satan in the Works of Isaac Bashevis Singer*. Lanham, Md.:University Press of America, 1995.

Bilik, Dorothy. *Immigrant-Survivors: Post-Holocaust Consciousness in Recent Jewish-American Fiction*. Middletown, Conn.: Wesleyan University Press, 1981.

Billington, Michael. *The Life and Work of Harold Pinter*. London: Faber and Faber, 1996.

Birnbaum, Marianna D. *Miklós Radnóti: A Biography of His Poetry*. Munich, Germany: Veröffentlichung des Finnish-Ungrischen Seminars an der Universität München, 1983.

Bloom, Harold, ed. *Cynthia Ozick*. New York: Chelsea House, 1986.

———. *Philip Roth*. New York: Chelsea House, 1986.

———. *A Scholarly Look at the Diary of Anne Frank*. Broomall, Pa.: Chelsea House, 1999.

Bosmajian, Hamida. *Metaphors of Evil: Contemporary German Literature and the Shadow of Nazism.* Iowa City: Iowa University Press, 1979.

Bower, Kathrin M. *Ethics and Remembrance in the Poetry of Nelly Sachs and Rose Auslander.* Suffolk, England: Boydell and Brewer, 2000.

Braham, Randolph L., ed. *Reflections of the Holocaust in Art and Literature.* Boulder, Colo.: Social Science Monographs, 1990.

Brenner, Rachel Feldhay. *Writing as Resistance: Four Women Confronting the Holocaust: Edith Stein, Simone Weil, Anne Frank, Etty Hillesum.* University Park: Pennsylvania State University Press, 1997.

Brown, Robert McAfee, *Elie Wiesel: Messenger to All Humanity.* Notre Dame, Ind.: Notre Dame University Press, 1983.

Camon, Ferdinando. *Conversations with Primo Levi.* Trans. John Shepley. Marlboro, Vt.: Marlboro Press, 1989.

Cargas, Harry James. *Harry James Cargas in Conversation with Elie Wiesel.* New York: Paulist Press, 1976.

Cargas, Harry James, ed. *Responses to Elie Wiesel: Critical Essays by Major Jewish and Christian Scholars.* New York: Persea Books, 1978.

———. *Telling the Tale: A Tribute to Elie Wiesel on the Occasion of His 65th Birthday: Essays, Reflections, and Poems.* St. Louis, Mo.: Time Being Books, 1993.

Cicioni, Mirna. *Primo Levi: Bridges of Knowledge.* Washington, D.C.: Berg, 1995.

Clendinnen, Inga. *Reading the Holocaust.* Cambridge, England: Cambridge University Press, 1999.

Cohen, Robert. *Understanding Peter Weiss.* Columbia: University of South Carolina Press, 1993.

Cohen, Sarah Blacher. *Cynthia Ozick's Comic Art: From Levity to Liturgy.* Bloomington: Indiana University Press, 1994.

Colin, Amy Diane. *Paul Celan: Holograms of Darkness.* Bloomington: Indiana University Press, 1991.

Delbo, Charlotte. *Days and Memory.* Trans. Rosette C. Lamont. Marlboro, Vt.: Marlboro Press, 1990.

Del Caro, Adrian. *The Early Poetry of Paul Celan: In the Beginning Was the Word.* Baton Rouge: Louisiana State University Press, 1997.

Des Pres, Terrence. *The Survivor: An Anatomy of Life in the Death Camp.* New York: Oxford University Press, 1976.

Dresden, Sem. *Persecution, Extermination, Literature.* Trans. Henry G. Schogt. Toronto, Ontario: University of Toronto Press, 1997.

Ducharme, Robert. *Art and Idea in the Novels of Bernard Malamud.* The Hague: Mouton, 1974.

Dwork, Deborah. *Children with a Star: Jewish Youth in Nazi Europe.* New Haven, Conn.: Yale University Press, 1991.

Ellis, Frank. *The Genesis and Evolution of a Russian Heretic.* Oxford, England: Berg, 1994.

Ellis, Roger. *Peter Weiss in Exile: A Critical Study of His Works.* Ann Arbor, Mich.: UMI Research Press, 1987.

Ezrahi, Sidra DeKoven. *By Words Alone: The Holocaust in Literature.* Chicago: University of Chicago Press, 1980.

Farrell, Grace. *From Exile to Redemption: The Fiction of Isaac Bashevis Singer.* Carbondale: Southern Illinois University Press, 1987.

Felstiner, John. *Paul Celan: Poet, Survivor, Jew.* New Haven, Conn.: Yale University Press, 1997.

Fine, Ellen S. *Legacy of Night: The Literary Universe of Elie Wiesel.* Albany N.Y.: SUNY Press, 1982.

Fioretos, Aris, ed. *Word Traces: Readings of Paul Celan.* Baltimore, Md.: Johns Hopkins University Press, 1994.

Flanzbaum, Hilene, ed. *The Americanization of the Holocaust.* Baltimore, Md.: The Johns Hopkins University Press, 1999.

Frassica, Pietro, ed. *Primo Levi as Witness.* Florence, Italy: Casalini, 1990.

Fridman, Lea Wernick. *Words and Witness: Narrative and Aesthetic Strategies in the Representation of the Holocaust.* Albany, N.Y.: SUNY Press, 2000.

Friedman, Lawrence. *Understanding Cynthia Ozick.* Columbia: University of South Carolina Press, 1991.

———. Understanding *Isaac Bashevis Singer.* Columbia: University of South Carolina Press, 1988.

Friedman, Saul S. *Holocaust Literature.* Westport, Conn.: Greenwood Press, 1993.

Fuchs, Esther, ed. *Women and the Holocaust: Narrative and Representation.* Lanham, Md.: University Press of America, 1999.

Gadamer, Hans Georg. *Gadamer on Celan: "Who Am I and Who Are You?" And Other Essays.* Albany, N.Y.: SUNY Press, 1997.

Galloway, David. *Edward Lewis Wallant.* Boston: Twayne, 1979.

Garrard, John, and Carol Garrard. *The Bones of Berdichev: The Life and Fate of Vasily Grossman.* New York: Free Press, 1996.

George, Emery. *The Poetry of Miklós Radnóti: A Comparative Study.* New York: Karz-Cohl, 1986.

Gibbons, Frances Vargas. *Transgression and Self-Punishment in Isaac Bashevis Singer's Searches*. New York: Peter Lang, 1995.

Gitay, Yehoshua, ed. *Literary Response to the Holocaust, 1945–1995*. Lanham, Md.: International Scholars Publications, 1997.

Gömöri, George, and Clive Wilmer, eds. *The Life and Poetry of Miklós Radnóti: Essays*. New York: Columbia University Press, 1999.

Guyot-Bender, Martine, and William Vander Wolk. *Paradigms of Memory: The Occupation and Other Histories in the Novels of Patrick Modiano*. New York: Peter Lang, 1998.

Haft, Cynthia. *The Theme of Nazi Concentration Camps in French Literature*. The Hague: Mouton, 1973.

Halio, Jay. *Philip Roth Revisited*. New York: Twayne, 1992.

Halperin, Irving. *Messengers from the Dead: Literature of the Holocaust*. Philadelphia: Westminster Press, 1970.

Heineman, Marlene. *Gender and Destiny: Women Writers and the Holocaust*. Westport, Conn.: Greenwood Press, 1986.

Helterman, Jeffrey. *Understanding Bernard Malamud*. Columbia: University of South Carolina Press, 1985.

Hermand, Jost, and Marc Silberman, eds. *Rethinking Peter Weiss*. New York: Peter Lang, 2000.

Horowitz, Sara R. *Voicing the Void: Muteness and Memory in Holocaust Fiction*. Albany, N.Y.: SUNY Press, 1997.

Immell, Myra, ed. *Readings on* The Diary of a Young Girl. San Diego: Greenhaven, 1998.

Isser, Edward R. *Stages of Annihilation: Theatrical Representations of the Holocaust*. Teaneck, N.J.: Fairleigh Dickinson University Press, 1997.

Kauvar, Elaine M. *Cynthia Ozick's Fiction: Tradition and Invention*. Bloomington: Indiana University Press, 1993.

Kielsky, Vera Emma. *Inevitable Exiles: Cynthia Ozick's View of the Precariousness of Jewish Existence in a Gentile Society*. New York: Peter Lang, 1989.

Kohn, Murray. *The Voice of My Blood Cries Out: The Holocaust as Reflected in Hebrew Poetry*. New York: Shengold, 1979.

Kopf, Hedda Rosner. *Understanding Anne Frank's* The Diary of a Young Girl. Westport, Conn.: Greenwood Press, 1997.

Kremer, S. Lillian. *Witness Through the Imagination: Jewish-American Holocaust Literature*. Detroit: Wayne State University Press, 1989.

———. *Women's Holocaust Writing: Memory and Imagination*. Lincoln: University of Nebraska Press, 1999.

Lang, Berel, ed. *Writing and the Holocaust*. New York: Holmes and Meier, 1989.

Langer, Lawrence L. *Admitting the Holocaust: Collected Essays*. New York: Oxford University Press, 1996.

———. *Art from the Ashes*. New York: Oxford University Press, 1995.

———. *The Holocaust and the Literary Imagination*. New Haven, Conn.: Yale University Press, 1975.

———. *Holocaust Testimonies: The Ruins of Memory*. New Haven, Conn.: Yale University Press, 1991.

———. *Preempting the Holocaust*. New Haven, Conn.: Yale University Press, 1998.

———. *Versions of Survival: The Holocaust and the Human Spirit*. Albany, N.Y.: SUNY Press, 1982.

Leak, Andrew, and George Paizis, eds. *The Holocaust and the Text: Speaking the Unspeakable*. New York: St. Martin's Press, 1999.

Leftwich, Joseph. *Abraham Sutzkever: Partisan Poet*. New York: T. Yoseloff, 1971.

Lilly, Jr., Paul R. *Words in Search of Victims: The Achievement of Jerzy Kosinski*. Kent, Ohio: Kent State University Press. 1988.

Marks, Jane. *The Hidden Children: The Secret Survivors of the Holocaust*. New York: Fawcett, 1993.

Mass, Wendy, ed. *Readings on Night*. San Diego: Greenhaven, 2000.

Milbauer, Asher Z., and Donald G. Watson, eds. *Reading Philip Roth*. New York: St. Martin's Press, 1988.

Mintz, Alan. *Hurban: Responses to Catastrophe in Hebrew Literature*. New York: Columbia University Press, 1984.

Morris, Alan. *Patrick Modiano*. Oxford, England: Berg, 1996.

Neher, André. *The Exile of the Word: From the Silence of the Bible to the Silence of Auschwitz*. Trans. David Maisel. Philadelphia: Jewish Publication Society, 1981.

Ozsváth, Zsuzsanna. *In the Footsteps of Orpheus: The Life and Times of Miklós Radnóti*. Bloomington: Indiana University Press, 2001.

Patraka, Vivian M. *Spectacular Suffering: Theatre, Fascism, and the Holocaust*. Bloomington: Indiana University Press, 1999.

Patruno, Nicholas. *Understanding Primo Levi*. Columbia: University of South Carolina Press, 1995.

Patterson, David. *Along the Edge of Annihilation: The Collapse and Recovery of Life in the Holocaust Diary*. Seattle: University of Washington Press, 1999.

————. *In Dialogue and Dilemma with Elie Wiesel.* Wakefield, N.H.: Longwood Academic, 1991.

————. *The Shriek of Silence: A Phenomenology of the Holocaust Novel.* Lexington: University Press of Kentucky, 1992.

————. *Sun Turned to Darkness: Memory and Recovery in the Holocaust Memoir.* Syracuse, N.Y.: Syracuse University Press, 1998.

Peacock, D. Keith. *Harold Pinter and the New British Theatre.* Westport, Conn.: Greenwood Press, 1997.

Pick, Hella. *Simon Wiesenthal: A Life in Search of Justice.* Evanston, Ill.: Northwestern University Press, 1996.

Pinsker, Stanford, ed. *Critical Essays on Philip Roth.* Boston: G.K. Hall, 1982.

Ramras-Rauch, Gila. *Aharon Appelfeld: The Holocaust and Beyond.* Bloomington: Indiana University Press, 1994.

Reiter, Andrea Ilse Maria. *Narrating the Holocaust.* New York: Continuum, 2000.

Rittner, Carol, ed. *Anne Frank in the World: Essays and Reflections.* Armonk, N.Y.: M.E. Sharpe, 1997.

Rittner, Carol, and John K. Roth, eds. *Different Voices: Women and the Holocaust.* New York: Paragon House, 1993.

Rogers, Audrey T. *Denise Levertov: The Poetry of Engagement.* Teaneck, N.J.: Fairleigh Dickinson University Press, 1993.

Rohrlich, Ruby, ed. *Resisting the Holocaust.* New York: Berg, 1998.

Rosenfeld, Alvin. *A Double Dying: Reflections on Holocaust Literature.* Bloomington: Indiana University Press, 1980.

Rosenfeld, Alvin, and Irving Greenberg. *Confronting the Holocaust: The Impact of Elie Wiesel.* Bloomington: Indiana University Press, 1978.

Rosenthal, Bianca. *Pathways to Paul Celan: A History of Critical Responses as a Chorus of Discordant Voices.* New York: Peter Lang, 1995.

Roskies, David. *Against the Apocalypse: Responses to Catastrophe in Modern Jewish Culture.* Cambridge, Mass: Harvard University Press, 1984.

Roth, John K. *A Consuming Fire: Encounters with Elie Wiesel and the Holocaust.* Atlanta: John Knox, 1979.

Rudolf, Anthony. *At an Uncertain Hour: Primo Levi's War Against Oblivion.* London: Menard Press, 1990.

————. *Engraved in the Flesh: Piotr Rawicz and His Novel* Blood from the Sky. London: Menard Press, 1996.

Salzberg, Joel, ed. *Critical Essays on Bernard Malamud.* Boston: G.K. Hall, 1987.

Schlant, Ernestine. *The Language of Silence: West German Literature and the Holocaust.* London: Routledge, 1999.

Schoenfeld, Joachim. *Holocaust Memoirs: Jews in the Lwow Ghetto, the Janowski Concentration Camp, and as Deportees in Siberia.* Hoboken, N.J.: Ktav, 1985.

Schumacher, Claude, and John Ireland, eds. *Staging the Holocaust: The Shoah in Drama and Performance.* Cambridge, England: Cambridge University Press, 1998.

Schwarz, Daniel R. *Imagining the Holocaust.* New York: St. Martin's Press, 1999.

Shapiro, Robert Moses. *Holocaust Chronicles: Individualizing the Holocaust through Diaries and Other Contemporaneous Personal Accounts.* Hoboken, N.J.: Ktav, 1999.

Sibelman, Simon P. *Silence in the Novels of Elie Wiesel.* New York: St. Martin's Press, 1995.

Sicher, Efraim, ed. *Breaking Crystal: Writing and Memory After Auschwitz.* Urbana: University of Illinois Press, 1998.

————. *Breaking Marginality: Anglo-Jewish Literature After the Holocaust.* Albany, N.Y.: SUNY Press, 1985.

Skloot, Robert. *The Darkness We Carry: The Drama of the Holocaust.* Madison: University of Wisconsin Press, 1988.

Sodi, Risa B. *A Dante of Our Time: Primo Levi and Auschwitz.* New York: Peter Lang, 1990.

Solotaroff, Robert. *Barnard Malamud: A Study of the Short Fiction.* Boston: Twayne, 1989.

Stein, André. *Hidden Children: Forgotten Survivors of the Holocaust.* New York: Penguin, 1994.

Stenberg, Peter. *Journey to Oblivion: The End of East European Yiddish and German Worlds in the Mirror of Literature.* Toronto, Ontario: University of Toronto Press, 1991.

Stern, Ellen Norman. *Elie Wiesel: A Voice for Humanity.* Philadelphia: Jewish Publication Society, 1996.

Strandberg, Victor. *Greek Mind/Jewish Soul: The Conflicted Art of Cynthia Ozick.* Madison: University of Wisconsin Press, 1994.

Taub, Michael, ed. *Israeli Holocaust Drama.* Syracuse, N.Y.: Syracuse University Press, 1997.

Teicholz, Tom, ed. *Conversations with Jerzy Kosinski.* Jackson: University Press of Mississippi, 1993.

Tepa Lupack, Barbara, ed. *Critical Essays on Jerzy Kosinski.* New York: G.K. Hall, 1998.

Van Alphen, Ernst. *Caught by History: Holocaust Effects on Contemporary Art, Literature, and Theory.* Stanford, Calif.: Stanford University Press, 1997.

Van Galen Last, D., et al., eds. *Anne Frank and After: Dutch Holocaust Literature in a Historical Perspective*. Ann Arbor: University of Michigan Press, 1997.

Vice, Sue. *Holocaust Fiction: From William Styron to Binjamin Wilkomirski*. London: Routledge, 2000.

Weiss, Renata Laqueur. *Writing in Defiance: Concentration Camp Diaries in Dutch, French and German*. Ann Arbor, Mich.: University Microfilms, 1971.

Young, James. *Writing and Rewriting the Holocaust: Narrative and the Consequences of Interpreta-tion*. Bloomington: Indiana University Press, 1988.

Yudkin, Leon I. *Hebrew Literature in the Wake of the Holocaust*. Teaneck, N.J.: Fairleigh Dickinson University Press, 1993.

Yuter, Alan J. *The Holocaust in Hebrew Literature: From Genocide to Rebirth*. Port Washington, N.Y.: Associated Faculty Press, 1983.

Zuroff, Efraim. *Occupation: Nazi Hunter*. Hoboken, N.J.: Ktav in association with the Simon Wiesenthal Center, 1994.

Index

Boldface indicates main entry.

Contributors

Alan L. Berger occupies the Raddock Eminent Scholar Chair for Holocaust Studies and is the Director of the Holocaust and Judaic Studies at Florida Atlantic University. With more than eighty articles and book chapters, Berger has lectured on the Holocaust and on Jewish literature and theology throughout America and in Europe, Australia, South Africa, and Israel. Among his books are *Crisis and Convenant: The Holocaust in American Jewish Fiction* (1985)*, Methodology in the Academic Study of the Holocaust* (coeditor, 1985), *Judaism in the Modern World* (editor, 1994), *Children of Job: American Second-Generation Witnesses to the Holocaust* (1997), and *Second-Generation Voices: Reflections by Offspring of Holocaust Survivors and Perpetrators* (coeditor, 2001). He is also editor of the Religion, Theology, and the Holocaust series for Syracuse University Press and an associate editor of *Studies in American Jewish Literature* and serves on the editorial boards of *Literature and Belief* and *Jewish Affairs*.

Sarita Cargas earned her B.A. at St. John's College, Annapolis, in 1990. She also holds an M.A. in psychology from Georgetown University (1997) and an M.A. in theology from the Aquinas Institute of Theology (1998). She is currently studying for a master's degree in theological studies at Oxford University.

Ellen S. Fine is Professor Emerita of French at Kingsborough Community College of the City University of New York. She is the author of *Legacy of Night: The Literary Universe of Elie Wiesel* (1982). She served as coeditor of the Holocaust issue of the journal *Centerpoint*

(1980) and has lectured widely in English and in French on Holocaust literature.

Myrna Goldenberg directs the Paul Peck Humanities Institute at Montgomery College, Maryland, where she is also a professor of English. Her research and teaching focus primarily on Holocaust and genocide studies (at Montgomery College and Johns Hopkins University Graduate School), but she is also active in women's studies, particularly studies on Jewish women. The recipient of several awards and fellowships for teaching, including the ACCT Award for Outstanding Teacher of the Year, she founded the Montgomery College's Women's Studies Program, the annual Holocaust Commemoration Program, and a partnership with the Smithsonian Institution and the College. She has contributed many articles and chapters to publications on women and the Holocaust and on curriculum development in the community college. She earned her doctorate from the University of Maryland, her master's from the University of Arkansas, and her bachelor's from the City College of New York.

David H. Hirsch (d. 1999) was Professor of English and American Literature at Brown University and the author of numerous and varied scholarly works. He and his wife, Roslyn Hirsch, are the translators of Sara Nomberg-Przytyk's *Auschwitz: True Tales from a Grotesque Land*, Gusta Davidson Draenger's *Justina's Narrative*, and Isaiah Spiegel's *Ghetto Kingdom: Tales of the Łódź Ghetto*. One of Hirsch's most influential books is *The Deconstruction of Literature: Criticism After Auschwitz* (1991).

S. Lillian Kremer holds the rank of Professor at Kansas State University, where she teaches American literature, Holocaust literature, and film. She is the author of *Witness Through the Imagination: Jewish-American Holocaust Literature* (1989) and *Women's Holocaust Writing: Memory and Imagination* (1999).

Asher Z. Milbauer is Associate Professor of English at Florida International University. He has taught in Israel and in the former Soviet Union. Milbauer is the author of *Transcending Exile: Conrad, Nabokov, I. B. Singer* (1988) and the coeditor of *Reading Philip Roth,* (1988).

Zsuzsanna Ozsváth is Professor of Literature and the History of Ideas and Director of the Holocaust Studies Program at the University of Texas at Dallas. She won the Milan Füst Prize of the Hungarian Academy of Sciences for her translation of Miklós Radnóti's *Foamy Sky* (1992). She is also the translator of Attila József's *The Iron-Blue Vault* (1999). In addition to having published numerous scholarly articles on Holocaust literature, Ozsváth is the author of *In the Footsteps of Orpheus: The Life and Times of Miklós Radnóti* (2001).

David Patterson holds the Bornblum Chair in Judaic Studies at the University of Memphis and is a winner of the Koret Jewish Book Award. The author of more than ninety articles and book chapters, Patterson's books include *Along the Edge of Annihilation* (1999), *Sun Turned to Darkness* (1998), *The Greatest Jewish Stories Ever Told* (1997), *When Learned Men Murder* (1996), *Exile* (1995), *Pilgrimage of a Proselyte* (1993), *The Shriek of Silence* (1992), *In Dialogue and Dilemma with Elie Wiesel* (1991), *Literature and Spirit* (1988), *The Affirming Flame* (1988), and *Faith and Philosophy* (1982). He is also the translator of the complete critical edition of *The Black Book of Russian Jewry* (2001).

Susan Lee Pentlin teaches German and Holocaust courses at Central Missouri State University. Her areas of research include the history of German teaching in the United States, radio propagandist Dr. Otto Koischwitz, and Holocaust memoirs. She is currently preparing a new edition of Mary Berg's *Warsaw Ghetto: A Diary* (forthcoming).

Gila Ramras-Rauch is Lewis H. Weinstein Professor of Hebrew and Jewish Literature at Hebrew College. She is a recipient of the Skirball Fellowship at Oxford University and is the author of *The Protagonist in Transition* (1982), *The Arab in Israeli Literature* (1989), and *Aharon Appelfeld: The Holocaust and Beyond* (1994). She is coeditor of a volume on the Holocaust in Israeli fiction titled *Facing the Holocaust* and has written a volume in Hebrew on the early twentieth-century novelist J.C. Brenner.

Sidney Rosenfeld is Professor Emeritus of German Language and Literature at Oberlin College. He is co-translator of *At the Mind's Limits: Reflections by a Survivor on Auschwitz and Its Realities* by Jean Améry (1980), *Radical Humanism: Selected Essays* by Jean Améry (1984), and *Jewish Life in Germany: Memoirs from Three Centuries*, ed. Monika Richarz (1991). He has written articles on Austrian writers Jean Améry, Joseph Roth, Karl Kraus, Alfred Polgar, and others. His book on Joseph Roth will appear in 2001.

Stella P. Rosenfeld is Professor Emeritus of German Language and Literature at Cleveland State University. She is co-translator of *At the Mind's Limits: Reflections by a Survivor on Auschwitz and Its Realities* by Jean Améry (1980), *Radical Humanism: Selected Essays* by Jean Améry (1984), and *Jewish Life in Germany: Memoirs from Three Centuries*, ed. Monika Richarz (1991). She has written articles on Jakov Lind.

John K. Roth is the Russell K. Pitzer Professor of Philosophy at Claremont McKenna College. In addition to service on the United States Holocaust Memorial Council and on the editorial board of *Holocaust and Genocide Studies*, he has published more than twenty-five books and hundreds of articles and reviews, including *A Consuming Fire: Encounters with Elie Wiesel and the Holocaust* (1979), *Approaches to Auschwitz* (1987), *The Holocaust: Religious and Philosophical Implications* (1989), and *Ethics After the Holocaust* (1999). In 1988 Roth was named U.S. National Professor of the Year by the Council for Advancement and Support of Education and the Carnegie Foundation for the Advancement of Teaching.

Joseph Sherman is currently Associate Professor in the Department of English at the University of the Witwatersrand, Johannesburg. The author of more than forty academic articles and the editor of nine books, he has lectured widely in the United States, the United Kingdom, and South Africa. He has published a volume of selected South African Yiddish stories in English translation under the title *From a Land Far Off* (1987) and has edited and introduced an annotated English translation of Leibl Feldman's Yiddish monograph *Oudtshoorn: Jerusalem of Africa* (1989). He is a specialist in the work of Isaac Bashevis Singer and the translator of Singer's *Shadows on the Hudson* (1987). He is also the translator of Dovid Bergelson's *Opgang* (*Descent*) (1999).

Eric Sterling is Associate Professor of English at Auburn University, Montgomery. He has published several articles on the Holocaust, primarily on Holocaust drama. He is currently completing two books, one on Holocaust drama and the other on ghettos during the Holocaust. His essay on Martin Sherman's *Bent* won a statewide as well as a national writing award.

Michael Taub teaches Jewish studies, film, and literature at SUNY Purchase. He has taught at Vassar College as well as Binghamton, New York, Rutgers, and Cornell universities. He is the editor of *Israeli Holocaust Drama* (1997) and *Modern Israeli Drama* (1992), as well as the coauthor of *Contemporary Jewish American Novelists* (1997) and *Contemporary Jewish American Dramatists and Poets* (1999).

Milton Teichman is Emeritus Professor of English at Marist College, where he has taught courses on Holocaust literature for more than twenty-five years. In addition to having published numerous essays on the literature of the Holocaust, he is coeditor of *Truth and Lamentation: Stories and Poems on the Holocaust* (1995) and *The Burdens of History: Post-Holocaust Generations in Dialogue* (2000).

Charlotte Wardi is Professor of French and Comparative Literature at the University of Haifa. The author of numerous scholarly articles on literary representations of the Holocaust, she has also made several translations of Hebrew poetry into French. Her books include *Le Juif dans le roman français* (1973) and *Le Génocide dans le fiction romanesque* (1986).

Leon I. Yudkin teaches Hebrew and Comparative Literature at University College in London. He has published numerous articles and lectured throughout the world. He is the author of *Isaac Lamdan: A Study in Twentieth Century Hebrew Poetry* (1971), *Escape into Siege: A Survey of Israeli Literature Today* (1974), *Jewish Writing and Identity in the Twentieth Century* (1982), *1948 and After: Aspects of Israeli Fiction* (1984), *On the Poetry of Uri Zvi Greenberg* (1987), *Else Lasker-Schüler: A Study in German Jewish Literature* (1991), *Beyond Sequence: Current Israeli Fiction and Its Context* (1992), *A Home Within: Varieties of Jewish Expression in Modern Fiction* (1996), *Modern Jewish Writing: Public Crisis and Literary Response* (2000). Yudkin is also the editor of *Modern Hebrew Literature in English Translation* (1987), *S.Y. Agnon: Texts and Contexts in English Translation* (1988), *Hebrew Literature in the Wake of the Holocaust* (1993), and *Israeli Writers Consider the "Outsider"* (1993). He is coeditor of *Meetings with the Angel: Seven Stories from Israel* (1973).